Through the Bible in 80 Days

with

David W Cooke

© 2004

www.biblein80days.co.uk
email: David@biblein80days.co.uk

*Dedicated to the memory of my father,
Don Cooke,
who originally inspired my love for the Bible
through his Bible teaching
and who encouraged me to write this book
– something he would love to have done himself –
after reading the first chapters.*

Contents

Bible Book Outlines iv
List of Figures v
List of Timecharts vi
List of Maps vii
Introduction ix
How to Use "Through the Bible in 80 Days" x
Acknowledgements xi

Day 1	Introduction to the Bible	1
Day 2	Overview of the Old Testament – Part 1	8
Day 3	Overview of the Old Testament – Part 2	18
Day 4	Overview of the New Testament	29
Day 5	Creation	38
Day 6	The Early World	45
Day 7	Noah and the Flood	51
Day 8	God Chooses a Man	57
Day 9	Abraham, God's Friend	62
Day 10	Isaac, Jacob and Sons	67
Day 11	Joseph – Dreamer to Prime Minister	72
Day 12	The Israelites move to Egypt	76
Day 13	Job – The Trouble Starts	82
Day 14	Job – The Debate and the Conclusion	87
Day 15	Life in Egypt	93
Day 16	The Plagues of Egypt	99
Day 17	Out of Egypt	102
Day 18	To Sinai and the Old Covenant	106
Day 19	The Ten Commandments	111
Day 20	Making Israel into a Nation	119
Day 21	Preparing to Enter the Land	126
Day 22	Into the Promised Land	132
Day 23	The Battle of Jericho	135
Day 24	Taking the Land	142
Day 25	The Time of the Judges	148
Day 26	Samuel	156
Day 27	The Call for a King	161
Day 28	Saul – The First King of Israel	164
Day 29	Saul and David	168
Day 30	David – Israel's Greatest King	172
Day 31	The Songs of David – Psalms	177

Day 32	David – the Man	183
Day 33	Solomon – The Wisest Man that ever Lived	189
Day 34	The Wisdom of Solomon – Proverbs	192
Day 35	Proverbs, Ecclesiastes and Song of Songs	197
Day 36	The Kingdom Divides	203
Day 37	Elijah	211
Day 38	To the Brink	217
Day 39	Israel into Exile	224
Day 40	Judah after Israel's Exile	229
Day 41	The Prophets	235
Day 42	Hosea to Zephaniah – Nine Minor Prophets	242
Day 43	Isaiah's Calling	251
Day 44	The Gospel in Isaiah	256
Day 45	Isaiah's Message of Hope	261
Day 46	Jeremiah's Message	266
Day 47	Hope for the Future	272
Day 48	The End of Judah	275
Day 49	Ezekiel, the Prophet in Exile	279
Day 50	Ezekiel's Message	283
Day 51	Daniel	286
Day 52	Return from Exile – The Temple Rebuilt	293
Day 53	Nehemiah Rebuilds the Walls of Jerusalem	299
Day 54	A Story from Exile and the Promised Messiah	303
Day 55	Between the Old and New Testaments	310
Day 56	The Four Gospels	322
Day 57	The Birth of Jesus	332
Day 58	Jesus Hits the Headlines	335
Day 59	Apostles, Parables and Miracles	338
Day 60	The Sermon on the Mount	343
Day 61	Miracles and Revelation	346
Day 62	Compassion and Confrontation	350
Day 63	The Scene is Set	353
Day 64	Jesus' Last Week on Earth	357
Day 65	Jesus' Death and Resurrection	360
Day 66	The Church is Born	365
Day 67	Early Days	371
Day 68	The Gospel for the Gentiles	377
Day 69	Paul's First Missionary Journey	381
Day 70	The Rest of Paul's Journeys	386
Day 71	Paul's Letters	393
Day 72	Correcting Wrong Ideas	402
Day 73	Romans	409
Day 74	The Fruit and Gifts of the Spirit	417

Day 75	Practical Teaching for Churches and Leaders	424
Day 76	Letters from Leaders	432
Day 77	Getting to Grips with the Bible	441
Day 78	Revelation – Letters to Churches	451
Day 79	What must take place	456
Day 80	The End of All things – and Beyond!	461

| Appendix A | Timecharts of the Bible | 468 |
| Appendix B | Reading through the Bible in a Year | 483 |

| Index of Bible Readings and Quotations | 496 |
| General Index | 504 |

Bible Book Outlines

Brief outlines of each book of the Bible are included for reference in the appropriate Day. Most are in the form of a table apart from those marked with an asterisk (*) below.

Book	Page	Book	Page
Genesis	39	Nahum *	248
Exodus	93	Habakkuk	249
Leviticus	117	Zephaniah	249
Numbers	122	Haggai *	297
Deuteronomy	129	Zechariah	307
Joshua	132	Malachi	308
Judges	148	Matthew, Mark, Luke, John	330
Ruth	156	Acts	366
1 & 2 Samuel	157	Romans	410
1 & 2 Kings	206	1 Corinthians	420
1 & 2 Chronicles	175	2 Corinthians	421
Ezra	294	Galatians	419
Nehemiah	299	Ephesians	424
Esther	304	Philippians	427
Job	83	Colossians	399
Psalms	180	1 Thessalonians	417
Proverbs	193	2 Thessalonians	417
Ecclesiastes	199	1 Timothy	429
Song of Songs	201	2 Timothy	430
Isaiah	252	Titus	430
Jeremiah	269	Philemon *	401
Lamentations *	276	Hebrews	433
Ezekiel	281	James	435
Daniel	290	1 Peter	436
Hosea	244	2 Peter	437
Joel	237	1, 2 & 3 John *	438
Amos	243	Jude *	439
Obadiah *	244	Revelation	452
Jonah	247		
Micah	248		

List of Figures

Figure 1	– The Bible Bookcase around 1000 BC	13
Figure 2	– The Bible Bookcase around 900 BC	17
Figure 3	– The Bible Bookcase before the Exile	24
Figure 4	– The Bible Bookcase – The Old Testament	27
Figure 5	– The Bible Bookcase	36
Figure 6	– The 12 Sons of Jacob and the 12 Tribes of Israel	80
Figure 7	– Approximate Dates for the Principal Characters in 1 & 2 Samuel	165
Figure 8	– The Attack on David's Line: Jehoram kills his brothers	219
Figure 9	– The Attack on David's Line: Jehu and Athalia wipe out Judah's Royal Family	221
Figure 10	– The Attack on David's Line: Joash Survives	223
Figure 11	– Members of the Family of Herod mentioned in the New Testament	319
Figure 12	– Paul's Life and Letters	396
Figure 13	– The Themes of Paul's Letters	397
Figure 14	– The Themes of Letters from Leaders	432
Figure 15	– Getting to Grips with the Bible	442

List of Timecharts

Timecharts are included in the appropriate Day but are also reproduced together in Appendix A on page 468 where general notes may be found.

Timechart 1	– Creation–1800 BC:	Events in Genesis 10
Timechart 2	– 1600–1000 BC:	Israel from Egypt to a United Nation 15
Timechart 3	– 1000–400 BC:	The Kingdoms of Judah and Israel 20
Timechart 4	– 400 BC–AD 200:	The Time around the New Testament 30
Timechart 5	– 1450–1240 BC:	The Exodus, Conquest of Canaan and early Judges 150
Timechart 6	– 1210–1000 BC:	The Time of the Judges and King Saul 151
Timechart 7	– 1000–860 BC:	David, Solomon and the Divided Kingdom 208
Timechart 8	– 860–720 BC:	Judah and Israel to the Exile of Israel .. 209
Timechart 9	– 720–580 BC:	The Exile of Judah 230
Timechart 10	– 580–440 BC:	The Exile and the Return 296
Timechart 11	– 460–180 BC:	The Time between the Testaments 312
Timechart 12	– 180 BC–AD 100:	New Testament Times 313

List of Maps

All the maps in "Through the Bible in 80 Days" come from Abingdon's Reproducible Maps, © 1994 by Abingdon Press, and are used with permission.

Map 1 – Abraham's Journey 61
Map 2 – The Exodus 107
Map 3 – The 12 Tribes of Israel Settle in Canaan 145
Map 4 – The Kingdom of David and Solomon 174
Map 5 – The Kingdoms of Israel and Judah 205
Map 6 – The Assyrian, Babylonian and Persian Empires 267
Map 7 – Israel at the Time of Jesus 317
Map 8 – Paul's First Missionary Journey 383
Map 9 – Paul's Second Missionary Journey 387
Map 10 – Paul's Third Missionary Journey 389
Map 11 – Paul's Journey to Rome 391

Introduction

In 1873, when Jules Verne first published his best selling novel, it was considered a great challenge to go "Around the World in 80 Days." Today this feat could easily be accomplished in three days. But of course, if you were to circumnavigate the globe so quickly you would come back with no impressions of the places you had travelled through at all. The advantage of taking 80 days is that you would return with a better knowledge of the world.

"Through the Bible in 80 days" takes you on a journey of exploration through the Bible. What is the Bible about? How do the different parts relate to one another? And what relevance does it have to me today? As you journey through the Bible you will discover the answers to these questions and many others too.

At the end of his journey, Phileas Fogg, the hero of "Around the World in 80 days", returned having seen the world, made a friend and fallen in love.

As you embark on your journey "Through the Bible in 80 days" you will see and experience the many landscapes in the Bible. There are gardens and battlefields, valleys of despair and mountains of delight, tight corners and open spaces – you will experience the full panorama of God's purpose for mankind.

You will get the opportunity to spend time with Joseph, David, Jeremiah, Nehemiah, Paul and many other characters from the Bible who have their stories and writings recorded in order to teach you more about God. You will get to know them better and make friends that you will want to read more about in years to come.

But above all, as you journey through the Bible you will learn more about the author of the book, God himself, whose love for people shines through on every page, from creation all the way through to life on a glorious new earth. My aim is that you will know more about him at the end of your journey "Through the Bible in 80 days" and learn to love him too.

David Cooke
August 2004

How to Use "Through the Bible in 80 Days"

This book is designed to be used alongside the Bible. Within the 80 chapters you will find highlighted instructions to read a passage from the Bible:

> **Read Genesis 1**

When you see these shaded areas stop reading my notes and read the part of the Bible indicated. My notes assume that you have read these passages so if you skip over them you will not be able to follow the plot!

Set aside 20–25 minutes a day to read the notes and Bible passages. Remember that the aim of this book is to give you an overview of the whole Bible so you will have to try and resist the temptation to spend more time in each section if you want to get to the end in 80 days! You might want to keep a notebook handy to jot down passages or characters that you would like to come back and look at in more detail later.

If you are not familiar with the way in which Bible passages are referred to then read the introduction to Appendix B – Reading through the Bible in a Year on page 483.

Above all else, enjoy this book. You do not need to complete it in 80 days and if you miss a few days it doesn't matter. I took seven years to complete a three year Bible Study course once! The important thing is to keep going so you see the whole picture from Genesis to Revelation.

Acknowledgements

First and foremost I have to thank my father, to whom this book is dedicated, for firing my initial love for the Bible and giving me a good understanding of its structure and purpose and to my mother for encouraging me to read and study the Bible daily.

I have been very privileged to hear many great Bible teachers, both in churches I have belonged to and at Bible weeks, and I want to thank all of them for the time they have spent studying and preparing to speak. In working through the book I have been particularly aware of the influence of Dick Bell, Robin Talbot, Bryn Jones, Allan Johnson, C J Mahaney, Alun Davies, Terry Virgo and David Bracewell in specific sections, although I know that there are many others who have contributed to my knowledge and thinking too, including writers.

The book started its life as a course called "Through the Bible in 50 days". Eight years later David Alliston, who was leading the Kings Church Horsham, encouraged me to run it again and in 1998 I presented a "Bird's Eye View of the Bible". It was after completing that course that it was suggested that I turn it into a book and the idea for "Through the Bible in 80 days" was born. My thanks to David for his encouragement.

Having completed the book I had a fantastic team of reviewers who read through the manuscript and gave me extensive feedback which has been very helpful. A special thanks to Mike Parry who spotted many typing and grammatical errors (though I take full responsibility for those that remain!) and to Gill Mallalieu for the fullest set of quality comments and outstanding encouragement. Thanks also to my mother, Heather Broadbent, Sally Burrows (I ignored her questions as they were far too difficult but included some of her perceptive observations!), Peter Hazael, Janet Johnson and Les Russell. My thanks to my son Sam, who also provided comments, drew the Bible Bookcase, brought my sketchy cover design to life and provided the web site. I also want to say a special thank you to John Hosier for taking the time to review the manuscript, provide some valuable feedback and encourage its publication – a big commitment of time from a busy man.

Final thanks are due to my wife and family for allowing me the time to write this book and providing encouragement along the way.

The Bible Bookcase

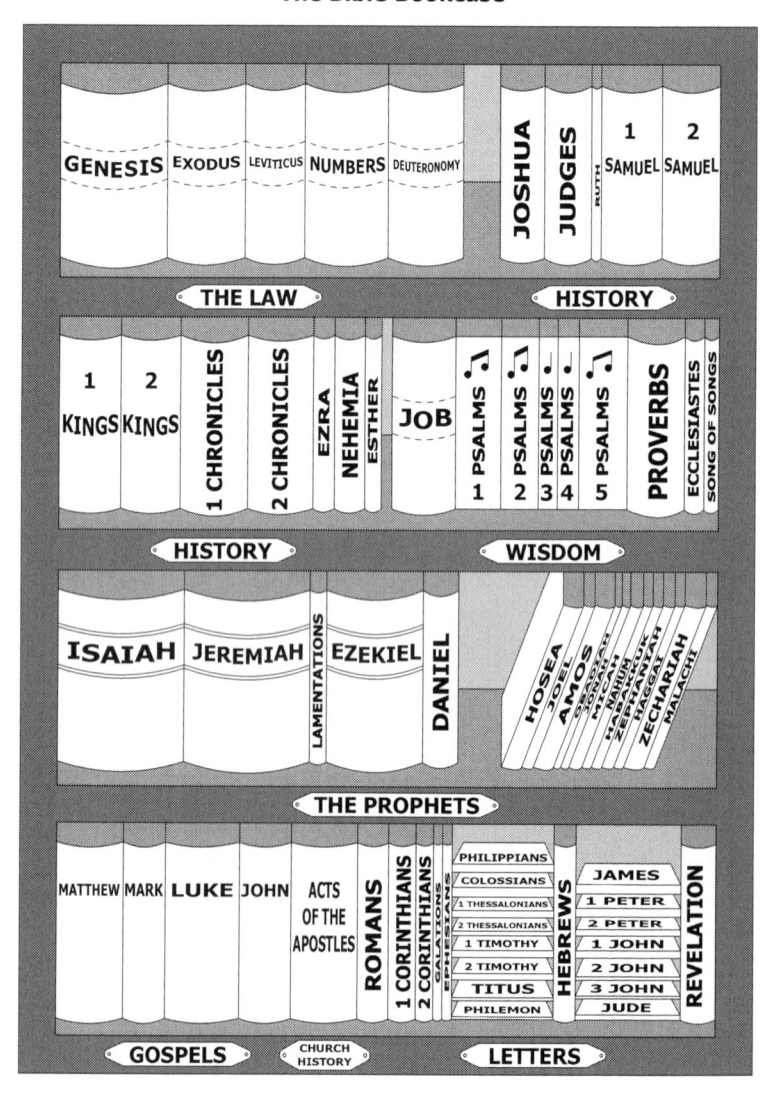

Day 1
Introduction to the Bible

Welcome to Day 1 of your exploration of the Bible. Before we start looking at it in detail we are going to start our journey by answering some basic questions about the Bible. Today we will look at what the Bible is, how it is structured, who wrote it, why it was written and how to use it.

What is the Bible?

The word "Bible" comes from the Greek word "Biblia", which means "Books" or "Library", because the Bible is actually 66 "books". The Bible Bookcase – see opposite – shows what it would be like if the books of the Bible were made to scale and put onto a bookshelf. As you can see from this picture the books vary widely in size. Leaving aside the Psalms, which is a collection of songs rather than a "book", Jeremiah is the largest in the sense that it has the most words, although Isaiah has more chapters and, because most of it is written as poetry, it takes up more pages. At the other end of the scale the little letter of 2 John has less than 300 words, hardly a book! The Bible is divided into two parts, the Old Testament and the New Testament, and you can see from the Bible Bookcase that the Old Testament is nearly three times the size of the New Testament.

As well as being different sizes the books are written in a wide range of styles. The Bible starts with five large books – Genesis, Exodus, Leviticus, Numbers, Deuteronomy – which are legal books known as the Books of the Law. As well as containing legal regulations they also contain the early history of the world and of God's people, Israel. These five books form the foundation of the rest of the Bible. Then there are twelve History books – Joshua, Judges, Ruth, 1 and 2 Samuel, 1 and 2 Kings, 1 and 2 Chronicles, Ezra, Nehemiah and Esther – which record about a thousand years of the history of the nation of Israel from around 1400 – 400 BC. The next five books are sometimes collectively known as the Wisdom books as they contain many wise sayings about life and philosophical issues in addition to songs of praise to God. Job is a drama, Psalms is the song book of the Bible, Proverbs and Ecclesiastes are full of practical advice and Song of Songs is a love poem. The rest of the Old Testament is taken up with the Prophets.

The first four are very large volumes known as the Major Prophets because of their size – Isaiah, Jeremiah along with a small book of poems called Lamentations, Ezekiel and Daniel – and the last twelve – Hosea, Joel, Amos, Obadiah, Jonah, Micah, Nahum, Habakkuk, Zephaniah, Haggai, Zechariah and Malachi – are called the Minor Prophets. The Minor Prophets are so small that in Jesus' time they were all written onto one scroll sometimes known as "The Book of the Twelve".

The New Testament opens with four books known as the Gospels, a word meaning "Good News", as Matthew, Mark, Luke and John give an account of the good news about God himself coming to earth as Jesus to die for our sins and rise again to give us new life. These are followed by a second volume by Luke called the Acts of the Apostles, or just Acts, which gives an account of the early history of the church. Then the rest of the New Testament is taken up with letters to churches and to individuals. Some are quite long and would have made quite a thud when they first came through the letter box, while some are very short, almost postcards! Thirteen were written by Paul – Romans, 1 and 2 Corinthians, Galatians, Ephesians, Philippians, Colossians, 1 and 2 Thessalonians, 1 and 2 Timothy, Titus and Philemon – while the other nine were written by five other early church leaders – Hebrews, James, 1 and 2 Peter, 1, 2 and 3 John, Jude and Revelation.

How is the Bible Structured?

As we have already seen, the Bible has two distinct halves: the Old Testament and the New Testament. On the Bible Bookshelf the Old Testament takes up the top three shelves and the New Testament is on the bottom one. The word "Testament" comes from a Latin word which was used to translate a Greek word meaning "Covenant", which is a legal term for an agreement between two people. The Old Testament is an account of God's old covenant with his chosen people, the nation of Israel. This was a two way covenant with requirements on both parties. God kept his half of the covenant but the people of Israel did not keep theirs. God was very patient with them over hundreds of years but eventually he promised to replace it with a new covenant. The New Testament is an account of God coming to earth as a man – Jesus – who fulfilled the requirements of the old covenant and then went on to pay the price required for man's disobedience to God under the old covenant – death – and to bring in the new covenant which is freely offered to all. Unlike the old covenant, all the conditions in the new

Day 1 – Introduction to the Bible

covenant have to be met by God and he has already fulfilled them. We just have to believe and accept what Jesus has done. It is also offered to everyone, both Jew and Gentile (non–Jew).

The Old and New Testament complement one another and there is a useful saying which explains how:

"The New is in the Old Concealed;
The Old is in the New Revealed."

Right in the third chapter of the Old Testament there is a passing reference to Jesus dying. It is not immediately obvious – it is concealed – but once you know about the new covenant then it is obvious what is being said. The truths of the Old Testament are revealed through the lens of the New Testament.

Who Wrote the Bible?

The books of the Bible were written over a period of about fifteen hundred years by a variety of writers, including a warrior, kings, prophets, fishermen, farmers and a theologian, but although it was written by these men, the Bible is quite clear that it was not just written by men. Peter, the leader of Jesus' twelve disciples, wrote, *"you must understand that no prophecy of Scripture[1] came about by the prophet's own interpretation. For prophecy never had its origin in the will of man, but men spoke from God as they were carried along by the Holy Spirit." (2 Peter 1:20–21)*. Although the books of the Bible were written down by men, God himself, in the person of the Holy Spirit is the author of this book. I remember hearing about this as a child and it puzzled me how this happened. How did these men hear from God? In my mind it conjured up a mental picture of a man sitting in a darkened room with a pen, a scroll and a blank mind, his face looking up to heaven as he wrote down words coming to him direct from God without them registering in his own brain! But you do not have to look very deep into the Bible to see that it was not like that.

The prophet Amos wrote: *"You oppress the righteous and take bribes and you deprive the poor of justice in the courts." (Amos 5:12)*. How did Amos know that there was injustice in the courts? In another place Amos spoke out against *"dishonest scales" (see Amos 8:5)*. How did he know that the market traders were cheating their customers? Did the words come to him in a vacuum while he was thinking about

---

[1] The word "Scripture" comes from the Latin word for writing and has come to mean sacred writings in general and the Bible in particular.

something else? No. He saw it going on in the courts and while he was doing his shopping in the marketplace and because of what he knew about God's love of justice he was so angered that he prayed about it. God responded and Amos wrote down these words of prophecy. The words came from God but the motivation and passion in his writing also came from his experience.

When Luke wrote his account of the life of Jesus he wrote that, *"since I myself have carefully investigated everything from the beginning, it seemed good also to me to write an orderly account for you ..." (Luke 1:3)*. Luke's gospel clearly did not just come to him in a trance. He talked to eyewitnesses, read other accounts that people had written and carefully checked his facts before he was prepared to send his account to his friend. The result is a gospel which contains references to events of the time, such as who was governing certain Roman provinces, and is clearly an authentic historical account of the life of Jesus. The Holy Spirit inspired him, but this did not stop Luke having to put in the effort. The Holy Spirit worked alongside Luke in searching out the truth. The work was 100% Luke's and 100% God's. So it is with the rest of the Bible.

Why was the Bible Written?

So much for the structure of the Bible and how it was written. A more important question is "Why did God write the Bible?" What is its purpose?

The Bible is God's love letter to the world. It is the full written expression of his love for you and me and for everyone who has ever lived on this planet or ever will. Love letters are very significant to us. If you are in love but living at a distance from the one you love then a letter from them is very precious. If it lands on the doormat along with letters from other friends or a load of bills then there is no question over which one gets opened first! When I was engaged to my wife we lived in different parts of the country and I remember how precious the letters I received from her were. They were read and re–read as I would take them to work with me and read them on the bus. They were part of the process of me getting to know her better. In the same way the Bible is precious to us as we live in a world where we cannot see God face to face. Through reading and re–reading his love letter to us we will get to know him better.

You may be thinking that some parts of the Bible do not sound much like a love letter. What about all those instructions on how to live? But having instructions in a love letter is not unusual. The love letters I received included instructions on which train to meet. Train timetables are not usually considered as love poetry but by following those instructions I got to meet the one I loved. It is no good feeling great about receiving the letter and then ignoring the instructions. A love letter is great, but not when it is compared to the one you love! So, God's love letter to us contains instructions on how to live because his love for us is so great that he wants us to live with him forever. The letter points to the one who loves us and is intended to draw us towards loving him. Ultimately – after heaven and earth have passed away – we will see God face to face and be with him forever. Then the Law will pass away (see Matthew 5:18). All my love letters are in a box in the loft now as I have been living with the one I love for over 20 years. It would be very sad if I came in each day and read the letters my wife sent all those years ago in preference to spending time with her in person now! So one day we will not need God's word as we will live with him forever. But until that day comes let us treasure his love letter to us and take note of his instructions.

How do we use the Bible?

Paul describes the purpose of the Bible like this: *"All Scripture is God–breathed and is useful for teaching, rebuking, correcting and training in righteousness, so that the man of God may be thoroughly equipped for every good work." (2 Timothy 3:16)*. The goal of the Bible is to enable us to live good lives, pleasing to God and challenging to other people and Paul lists four ways in which the Bible can be used to achieve this goal. There is nothing extraordinary about these four ways, we use them in everyday life.

Think about what you would do if you needed to drive from your home to a town some distance away that you have never visited before. The first step is to get directions or look in a map and *teach* yourself the journey. It all looks fine on paper so you set off. Of course when you are driving things look different and when you are on the fast lane of a motorway in heavy traffic you may not find it so easy to remember or follow the directions you learned. If you have someone with you they may suddenly say, "You've gone the wrong way!" This is a *rebuke*. It can be upsetting or annoying at the time, especially if it comes from someone close to us, but it is essential that you realise that you are going the wrong way. Having realised that you are travelling in the wrong direction, you need to take a look at the map once again and decide what to do about it. You may need to go back to the route you were on before or it may be best to find a new route to your destination. It is not always essential to retrace your steps, the important thing is that you find a *correct* route to your destination. (As we read the Bible we will see how amazing God is. There are so many accounts of people who set out in the right direction but then went astray. But when they realised they were going in the wrong direction God didn't give up on them but showed them the way back to him and set them on a right course once again.) Eventually you will arrive at your destination. If you need to do the route again you are unlikely to make the mistakes you made last time but you may make new ones. After a while you become *trained* to do the journey so that if anyone asked you the way you would not only tell them the route but would also be able to warn them about those spots where you need to take care not to go down the wrong route. That is maturity.

In order to become mature Christians, *"thoroughly equipped for every good work"*, we need to study God's word and apply it to our daily life.

Are all the bits of the Bible equally important?

As we have already seen, the Bible is a big book and a question that has intrigued me over the years is, are all the bits of the Bible equally important? Take a look at the first chapter of the history book 1 Chronicles. This has 54 verses containing lists of names! Now take a look at the letter to Titus in the New Testament. This has only 46 verses which provide a complete recipe for building a church. Which is the most important?

One way of thinking about it is to think of the Bible as being like the body. All of it is important, but some parts are more important than others. I would not want to lose any part of my body but if I had to choose I would rather lose a toe than an eye. So it is with the Bible. All of it helps us understand who God is and teaches us about his love. But if we had to choose, then the gospels, which tell us about Jesus, are the most important part, without which we would be the poorest.

The Bible as a whole is relevant to all people in all situations at all times. But some parts are particularly relevant to the young, some to the old, some relate to marriage, some to being a parent, and some to other special times in your life, like when you are going through hard times. So, the relevance of different parts of the Bible to you will change as you go through life. Another picture is to think of the parts of the Bible as being like the things you have in your house. You

Day 1 – Introduction to the Bible

probably have hundreds of objects in your house and some are used every day, while others, which are just as important, are only used occasionally. So, all of the Bible is important, but some parts are more important than others! If you get to the end of the 80 day journey you have started on today and read the Bible passages indicated then you will become familiar with most of the important sections while becoming aware of the rest. That is the aim of this book.

Having dealt with some introductory questions about the Bible we will spend the next three days going through the whole Bible from start to finish. That will prepare us for the more in–depth journey over the remaining 76 days!

Day 2
Overview of the Old Testament – Part 1

Before we start studying the Bible in more detail we are going to go through the story of the entire Bible over the next three days. Getting a good overview of the whole story will help to make sense of the individual books and characters as we go through the detail.

To help understand the flow of history we will look at two Timecharts that cover the period from Creation to the reign of King Solomon and we will see how the Bible grew by looking at "the Bible Bookcase".

Beginnings

The Bible starts with a book called Genesis which means, "beginnings" and it is a book which deals with many beginnings. It starts with the greatest of all beginnings, creation, when God created the world, the universe – everything that we know – and mankind in the form of Adam and Eve. And for the first two chapters of the Bible everything was perfect. Throughout the account of creation we read that "God saw that it was good", "God saw that it was good", "God saw that it was good" – everything in God's creation was good. Everything in the garden was lovely – literally.

Then in Genesis 3 there is an event known as "the fall" where Adam and Eve decided that they knew better than God and they disobeyed the only rule they had been given. In the Bible this is known as sin – to break God's law – and the punishment for that was death and we read about the death of animals and of mankind. God's perfect creation was spoiled by man's sin. As the next few chapters of Genesis unfold we see a rapid decline into wickedness. In the next generation after Adam and Eve there is murder, and within a few more generations we find a man boasting to his two wives about a murder he has committed.

Man's wickedness is so great that God gets to the point where he decides to do away with mankind that he has created. The story of Noah and the flood is very well known when the whole population of the world was destroyed apart from eight people: Noah, his three sons and their wives. After Noah emerges from the Ark the world's population increases again and it seems that God goes quiet for a time.

The first 11 chapters of Genesis cover an enormous amount of material and we shall spend some days looking at them as they form the foundation of so much of the Bible.

God Chooses Abraham

In Genesis 12 we are introduced to a man called Abram, who later became Abraham, who lived in a pagan culture where they worshipped the sun and moon and idols. Somehow – the Bible leaves so many questions unanswered! – God spoke to Abram and called him to leave the place where he was living and go to a land that he would give to his descendants. This "Promised Land" is the land we now call Israel.

Abraham is known as the friend of God and God makes a covenant with him – a legally binding agreement. God promises that all the world will be blessed through his descendants. God's heart of love for mankind shines through the whole of the Bible. Here we see the incredible way in which he works in that he chooses one man and puts his entire strategy for reaching the world in his promise to this one man. But just as amazing is Abraham's response in that he believed God's promise to him and carried on believing it despite the fact that he had no children.

Eventually he has a son called Isaac and the promise passes to him. Later Isaac has twins and the promise passes to the younger one, Jacob. After Jacob has had 12 sons God gives him a new name, Israel, which means, "he struggles with God". The rest of the Old Testament is about the story of the nation of the 12 tribes of Israel who were descended from the 12 sons of this man and about their struggle with God.

Although Abraham, Isaac and Jacob lived in the Promised Land the only pieces of the land they ever owned were two fields, one that Abraham bought as a place to bury his wife and one where Jacob pitched his tent.

One of Israel's sons is called Joseph and his story is well known. His brothers sold him into slavery in Egypt, an awful act on their part but one which is part of God's plan for Israel and his family. While Joseph was there he becomes Prime Minister, which puts him in the position of being able to bring all of Israel's family down to Egypt and they settle there.

Genesis covers all of this and is a key book in setting the scene for the rest of the Bible. All the major themes of the Bible have their origins in this amazing book. Timechart 1 (see next page) provides a rough

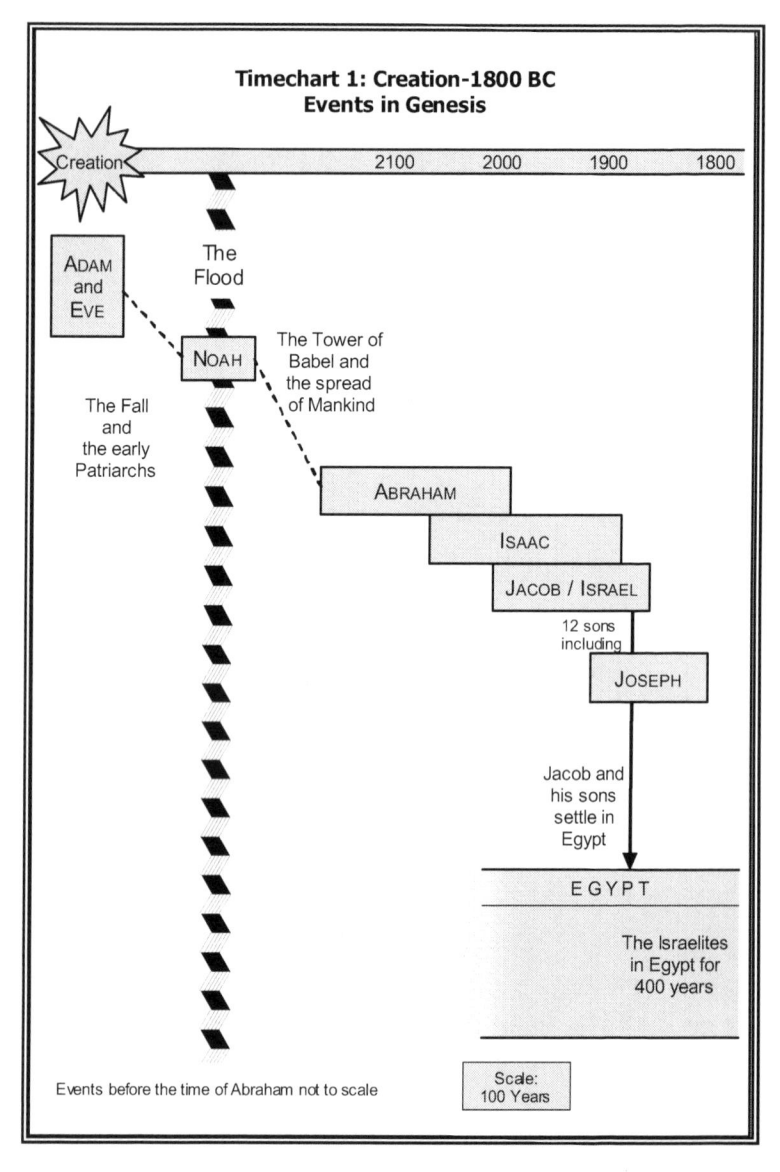

Timechart 1: Creation–1800 BC
Events in Genesis

Creation — 2100 — 2000 — 1900 — 1800

ADAM and EVE

The Flood

NOAH

The Fall and the early Patriarchs

The Tower of Babel and the spread of Mankind

ABRAHAM

ISAAC

JACOB / ISRAEL

12 sons including

JOSEPH

Jacob and his sons settle in Egypt

EGYPT

The Israelites in Egypt for 400 years

Events before the time of Abraham not to scale

Scale: 100 Years

**Timechart 1 – Creation–1800 BC:
Events in Genesis**

Day 2 – Overview of the Old Testament – Part 1   11

outline of the events in Genesis, providing probable dates from the time of Abraham onwards.

One other book tells of events which may come from this far back in history and that is Job. The book of Job tells the story of one man's suffering. It is the first "wisdom" book and it deals with the difficult issues raised by the presence of suffering in our world.

Out of Egypt – The Exodus

Exodus opens 400 years later with the story of the people of Israel, the descendants of the 12 sons of Israel. When we left Israel's sons at the end of Genesis they were living in luxury in the best part of Egypt. But when we read the first chapter of Exodus we discover that their descendants have become a large group of people who are in slavery to the Egyptians. God calls a man named Moses to go and tell Pharaoh to "let my people go" and, after a series of miraculous signs, Moses leads them out of Egypt into the desert of Sinai heading for the land promised to Abraham and his descendants.

The people of Israel had grown up as a minority ethnic group in a country where all the decisions were made by the ruling Egyptians. While they are in the desert God gave them a very distinct law – different from that of other nations at that time – and a place of worship at the centre of their camp – the tabernacle – housing the "Ark of the Covenant". This law gave them a national identity for the first time.

At the heart of the law was a covenant between God and them. This is known as the Old Covenant, or Old Testament, and God gave to the Israelites through Moses at Mount Sinai. *"Then Moses went up to God, and the LORD called to him from the mountain and said, "This is what you are to say to the house of Jacob and what you are to tell the people of Israel: 'You yourselves have seen what I did to Egypt, and how I carried you on eagles' wings and brought you to myself. Now if you obey me fully and keep my covenant, then out of all nations you will be my treasured possession. Although the whole earth is mine, you will be for me a kingdom of priests and a holy nation.' These are the words you are to speak to the Israelites.""* *(Exodus 19:3–6)*. Note that it is a conditional covenant: *"If you obey me fully ... then you will be my treasured possession."* The people are given a long list of laws to obey, which are summarised by the Ten Commandments in Exodus 20. They are the foundation of the Old Covenant and of the rest of the Old Testament.

While the Israelites were in the desert Moses wrote the five books of the Bible – Genesis, Exodus, Leviticus, Numbers and Deuteronomy – which together make up "The Law". All the rest of the Old Testament is built on the foundation of the law. In Jesus' time the Old Testament was often referred to as "The Law and the Prophets" (see for example Matthew 7:12) counting all the remaining books of the Old Testament as prophetic writings.

Into the Promised Land

Because of their disobedience to God the Israelites spent 40 years wandering in the desert before they came to the land promised to Abraham, the land of Canaan. They enter Canaan under the leadership of Joshua and settle there in territory assigned to the 12 tribes.

After the death of Joshua things go quiet again. Despite clear instructions to destroy the nations who are already living in the land they disobey God again and settle alongside them. This leads to an intermingling through trade which, in turn, leads to intermarriage which results in Israelites taking on the customs of these other nations and worshipping other gods. While they were in Egypt they maintained their distinct identity as the Egyptians would have nothing to do with them on a social basis but living among people who are prepared to mix with them is a constant danger to God's covenant people. For a period of about 280 years the people of Israel go through a series of cycles where they drift away from following God and live in evil ways following foreign gods in clear violation of God's covenant with them. In response God sends a foreign oppressor, the people cry out to God and he sends a deliverer who restores peace to the land. These deliverers are called "Judges" as part of their leading involved judging legal disputes and the book of Judges tells the stories of five men and one woman who judged the Israelites through this bleak period.

By the end of this period three books have been added to the Bible: Joshua, which tells the story of the initial conquest of Canaan, Judges, and a little love story from the time of the Judges called Ruth. Although the Bible was written over a period of about 2000 years we see that it appeared in "bursts" with periods of inactivity in between. The whole of the law was written in 40 years, Joshua followed soon after it but then Judges and Ruth appeared much later.

Before Israel became a nation the Bible Bookcase has the first eight books on it as we see in Figure 1. (We will include Job with the rest of the Wisdom section later.)

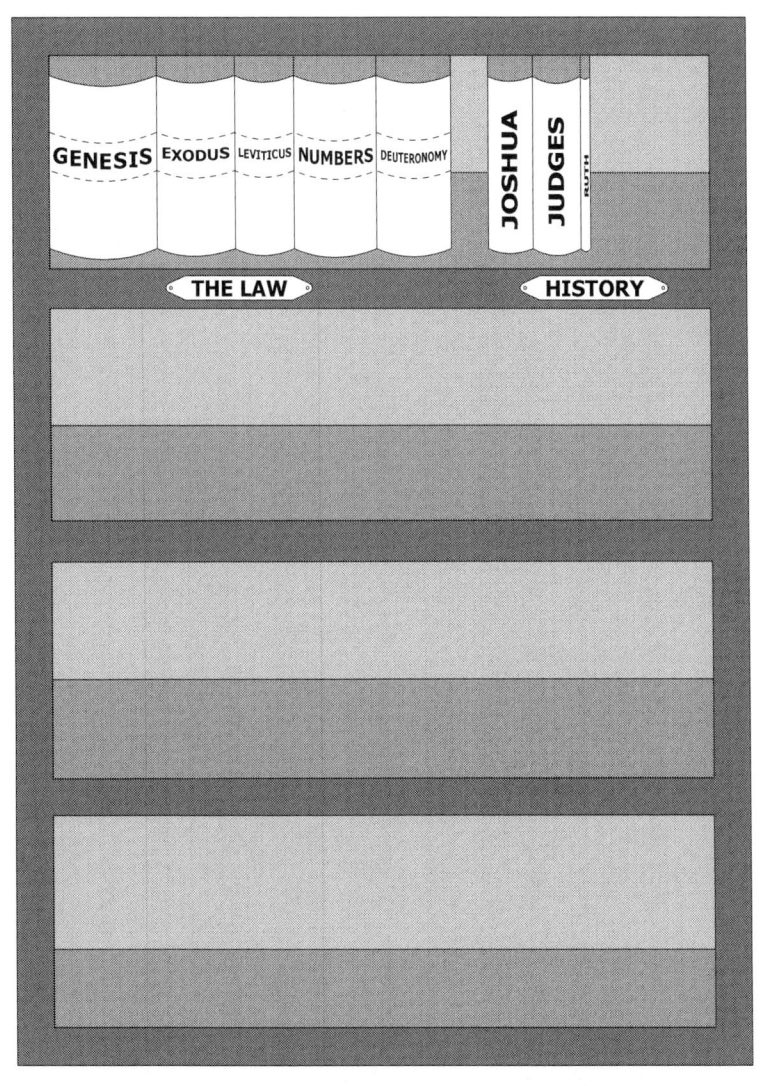

Figure 1 – The Bible Bookcase around 1000 BC

Israel the Nation

During the time of the Judges the Israelites were a fragmented group of tribes. The Judges did not lead a nation but were senior figures in their tribe with authority over one, or maybe a few, tribes. When they died their authority died with them.

The last of the Judges was a very godly man called Samuel but when he got old his sons did not follow in his ways and accepted bribes in the courts. Eventually the people were fed up with this and asked Samuel to appoint a king so they could be like the other nations. At God's command Samuel anointed Saul to be the first king over all Israel. He was tall and very impressive and the people were pleased with God's choice. But as time went on Saul, who as king of Israel was subject to the covenant law, was not careful to follow God's commands and rebelled against God. In response God sends Samuel to anoint a shepherd boy called David and he becomes the second king of all Israel.

David and his son Solomon reigned over all Israel for the next eighty years and they are very significant years in terms of the formation of the Bible.

David makes the twelve tribes of Israel into a nation for the first time – as indicated by the use of the term "United Israel" on Timechart 2 opposite. Even during the time of Saul they were more of a loose confederation of tribes but under David's leadership the nation was united. He defeated all of Israel's enemies and increased its territory to the largest it has ever been, either before or since that time. He also captured Jerusalem, a strong fortress right in the middle of Israel which was still occupied by the Jebusites, and made it both the political centre of the nation and, more importantly, the centre for worship. The Ark of the Covenant, the symbol of God's presence with his people, which Moses had made in the desert, was in someone's house and David brought it to Jerusalem, put it in a tent and got the Levites to carry out their priestly duties once again. He stamped his mark on this nation and even today Jerusalem remains at the centre of Jewish political and religious life and Israel's national flag has at its centre the Star of David.

Not only was David a warrior but he was also a songwriter and his greatest legacy to the Jews and to the church are his songs, known as Psalms. Almost half of the Psalms are attributed to David and they give us insight into God's greatness and his dealings with men. David was

Day 2 – Overview of the Old Testament – Part 1 15

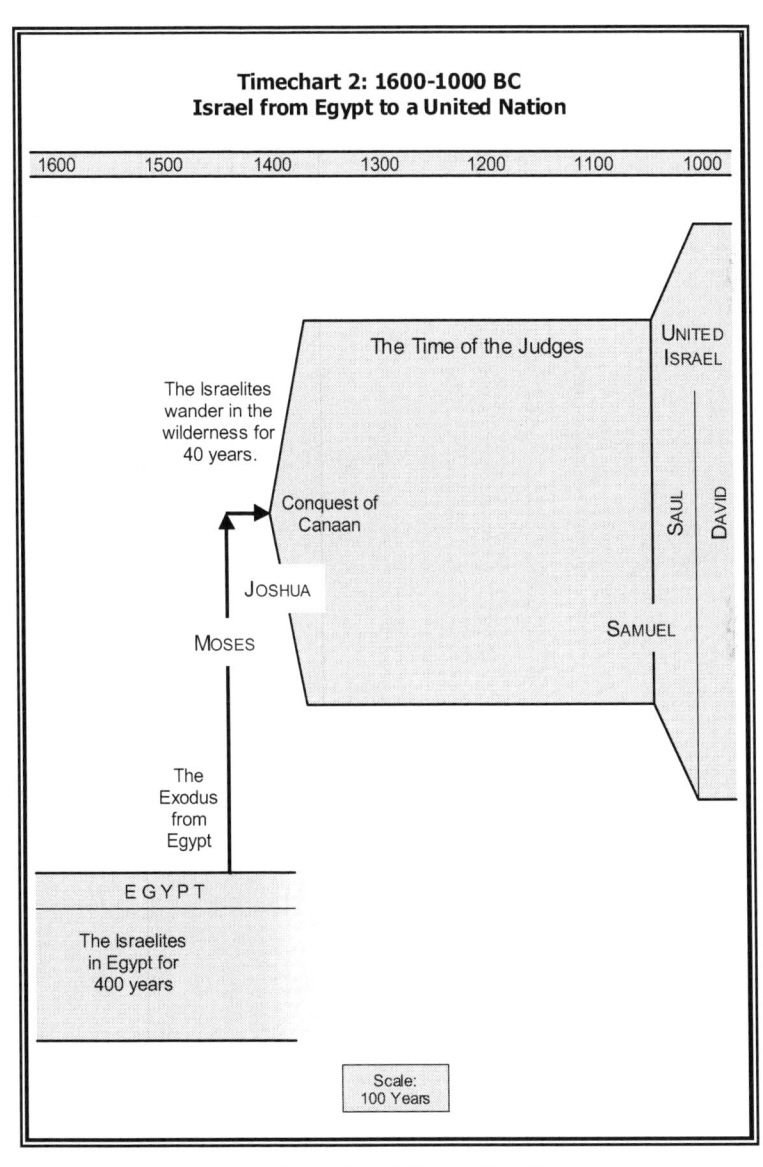

Timechart 2: 1600-1000 BC
Israel from Egypt to a United Nation

| 1600 | 1500 | 1400 | 1300 | 1200 | 1100 | 1000 |

The Time of the Judges

UNITED ISRAEL

The Israelites wander in the wilderness for 40 years.

Conquest of Canaan

SAUL

DAVID

JOSHUA

MOSES

SAMUEL

The Exodus from Egypt

EGYPT

The Israelites in Egypt for 400 years

Scale: 100 Years

Timechart 2 – 1600–1000 BC:
Israel from Egypt to a United Nation

the greatest king the nation has ever known and one of the names of his greatest descendant, Jesus, is "Son of David" signifying his right to the throne of Israel.

David's son Solomon was a complete contrast to his father. He was a peaceable man who consolidated the gains his father had made by building up a large standing army and cities throughout the land to store food for the army and house the chariot horses. He used some of the remaining Canaanites as slaves in his building projects, which included putting a wall round Jerusalem and building palaces for himself and his wives. He developed trade through a fleet of trading ships and alliances with the king of Lebanon. Under Solomon Israel became more wealthy and prosperous than ever before. Through his trade Solomon accumulated so much gold in Jerusalem that silver was considered "as common as stones".

It was also Solomon who built the first great temple in Jerusalem using huge quantities of gold to overlay the walls and furnishings. The Ark of the Covenant was moved to this magnificent new building which became the focus of worship in Israel for the next 400 years.

Early in his reign God asked Solomon what he wanted and Solomon asked for wisdom. God granted his request and made him the wisest man the world has ever known, apart from Jesus. Three books in the Bible contain Solomon's wisdom – Proverbs, which is a collection of his wise sayings (along with a few from others), Ecclesiastes which he wrote as an old man, and Song of Songs, sometimes called Solomon's Song of Songs, which is a love poem.

Reviewing the Bible Bookcase at this point these eighty years have added a lot to our Bible. 1 and 2 Samuel (and the first part of 1 Kings) tell the history of this time, and the wisdom section is now filled up, at least with started versions of Psalms and Proverbs along with Ecclesiastes and Song of Songs. The bookcase now has 15 books but these make up almost 40% of our entire Bible as we see in Figure 2.

Day 2 – Overview of the Old Testament – Part 1   17

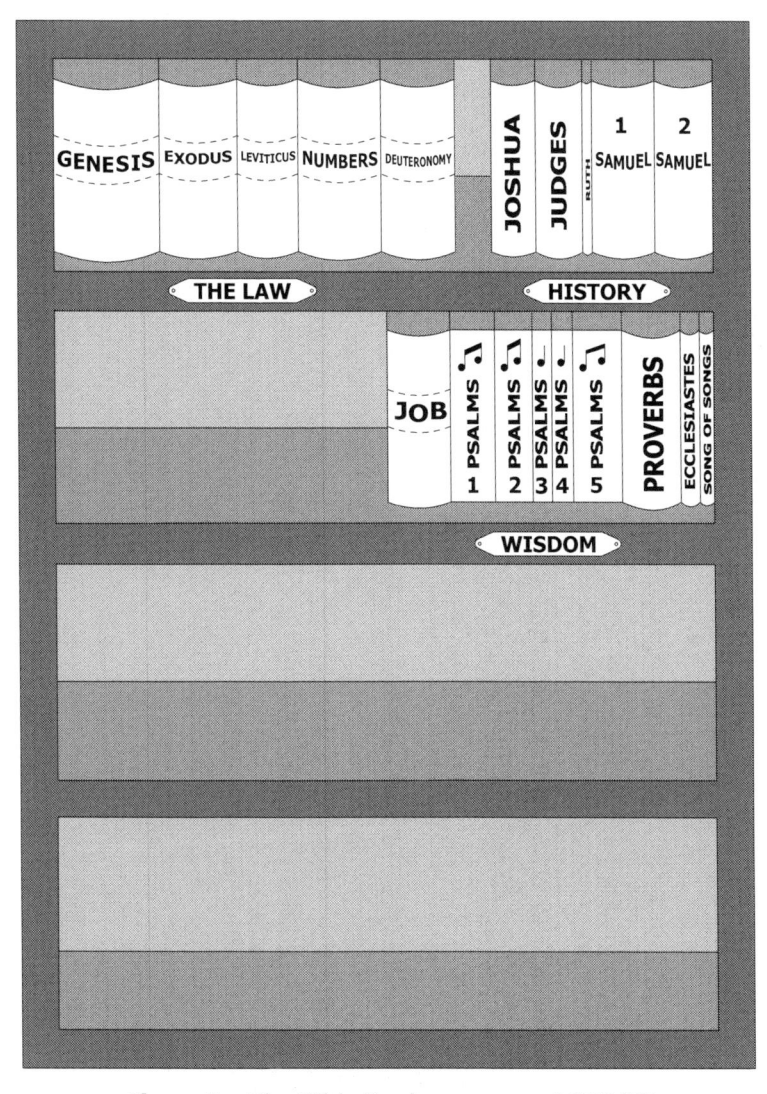

Figure 2 – The Bible Bookcase around 900 BC

Day 3
Overview of the Old Testament – Part 2

The Kingdom Divides

Solomon was very wise but also very extravagant and to pay for all his schemes he did what all extravagant governments do – he raised taxes. By the time of his death the tax burden was intolerable and the people only put up with it out of loyalty to the memory of David. When Solomon's son came to the throne, the leaders of the people told him that he would have to lower taxes to maintain their loyalty. He refused and as a result the kingdom of Israel split into two. Two tribes stayed loyal to the throne of David and became the nation of Judah; the other ten followed a man called Jeroboam and are known, rather confusingly, as Israel.

The writer of 1 Kings is clear that the split came about as a result of Solomon forsaking God. As he grew older his heart was turned away from God by his many foreign wives who worshipped other gods. God remained true to his covenant with David by having one of his descendants to reign in Judah but he punished Solomon's wickedness by taking the larger part of the kingdom away from him. The two nations almost went to war against each other – God's chosen people engaged in civil war! – and in both nations worship of other gods became commonplace. Within five years of the split Judah was overrun by the Egyptians who carried away all the treasures of the temple.

The speed of spiritual decline in the nation is alarming. This division of the kingdom came only 40 years after the death of David. Imagine how exciting it must have been to live through the time of Saul and David. An Israelite born around the middle of Saul's reign would have seen the loose confederation of tribes brought together under David, seen Jerusalem captured and made into the City of David and witnessed the joy as the Ark of the Covenant brought to Jerusalem. In his old age he would have seen the temple built and, as it was dedicated by Solomon, the glory of God fall. He would have sung worship songs written by David and read the early proverbs of Solomon.

Contrast that with his son, born thirty years later. He would have grown up as the kingdom reached its greatest power under King David, seen his children growing up with the splendour of Solomon's reign all around them and lived in peace. But during his middle age he would have noticed more and more shrines to other gods appearing on the streets of Jerusalem and in his later years he would have seen the nation disintegrate before his eyes. If he had lived into old age, then he would have seen the temple ransacked, the gold removed, and bronze shields made to replace them.

Two men, father and son, living only thirty years apart with such different lives. As the first man died he would have expected his great nation to last forever with worship of the true God at its centre. But as his son died, only thirty years later, he would be concerned about the evil influences on his children and grandchildren and worried about what the future would hold for them.

Israel and Judah – Two Nations

The years of the divided kingdoms are recorded in 1 and 2 Kings, which run straight on from the end of 1 and 2 Samuel. Timechart 3 covers this period (see next page) and it shows the two nations of Israel and Judah separating out from a United Israel in 930 BC. Below them are the world powers and superpowers of the time who came and attacked the divided kingdoms.

Judah, the southern nation, had 17 kings, all of whom were descended from David and Solomon. The royal line goes all the way through. Some of these kings were good; some were bad. Good kings like Hezekiah and Josiah led the people towards God, while others introduced idol worship and ignored their covenant relationship with God. The nation swung between periods of spiritual darkness and spiritual revival.

Israel, the northern kingdom, also had 17 kings, all of whom, according to the writer of 1 and 2 Kings were bad, apart from those who were very bad! The 17 kings were from four major dynasties. After a period of one family reigning, another man, usually an army commander, would take the throne by force.

Jeroboam, the first king of Israel, was concerned that the people would return their allegiance to the king of Judah if they went to Jerusalem to worship and so he set up two golden calves for the people to worship to stop them going to the temple. He and the subsequent kings of Israel then led the people away from the worship of God and into worship of gods that the people who lived in the land before them worshipped. These were not good days for those who followed God.

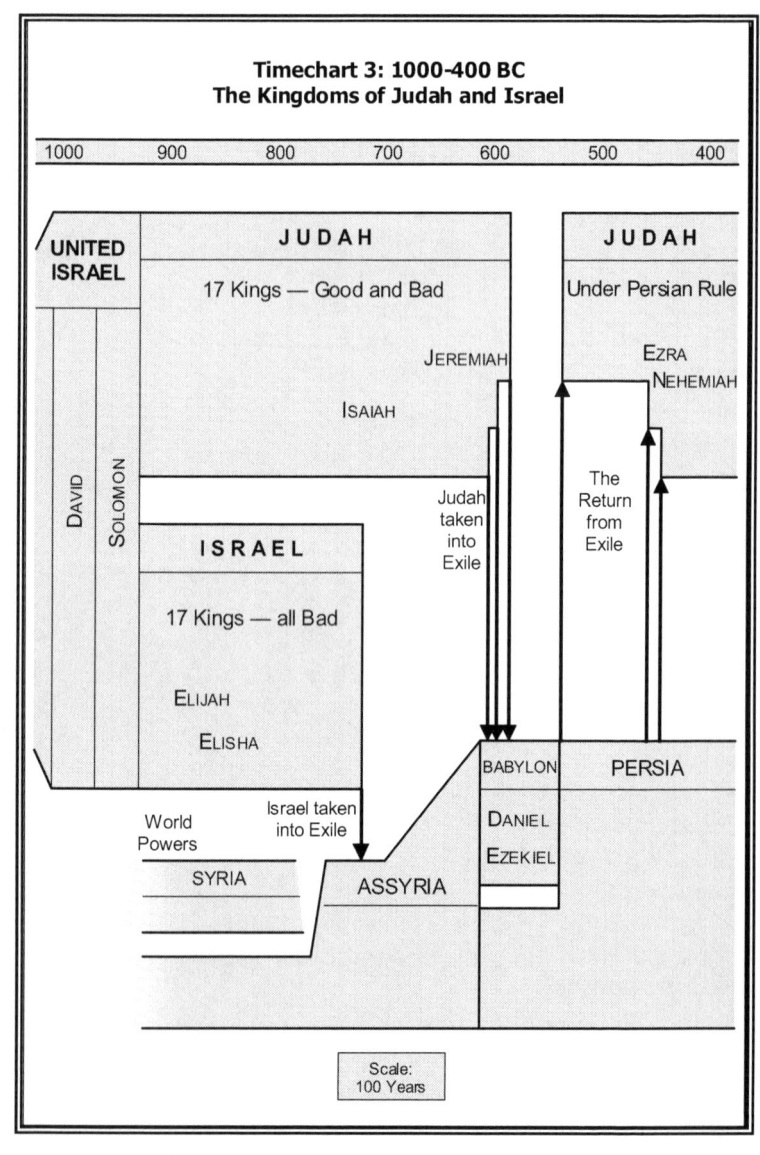

Timechart 3: 1000-400 BC
The Kingdoms of Judah and Israel

| 1000 | 900 | 800 | 700 | 600 | 500 | 400 |

UNITED ISRAEL — David, Solomon

JUDAH — 17 Kings — Good and Bad
- Isaiah
- Jeremiah
- Judah taken into Exile

ISRAEL — 17 Kings — all Bad
- Elijah
- Elisha
- Israel taken into Exile

JUDAH — Under Persian Rule
- Ezra
- Nehemiah
- The Return from Exile

World Powers: Syria, Assyria, Babylon (Daniel, Ezekiel), Persia

Scale: 100 Years

**Timechart 3 – 1000–400 BC:
The Kingdoms of Judah and Israel**

Day 3 – Overview of the Old Testament – Part 2

Prophets

When the people asked Samuel to appoint a king for them he made it clear that any king in Israel would not be like other kings. Kings of other nations had absolute power to do as they pleased but kings in Israel were, like the rest of the people, subject to God's law given them by Moses. God was the king of his people and he provided government for them through men he appointed. There are three major roles described in the law that operated in God's kingdom – king, priest and prophet – and each had its own distinct part to play.

In the time of King David we see all three roles working together in harmony. David was the king and his responsibility was to be the shepherd of the people. When he brought the Ark of the Covenant to Jerusalem he re-established worship of God and made sure that the Levites were restored to their positions as priests. Priests were there to make sacrifices on behalf of the people, bring regular worship to God through music and singing, to teach people the law and be judges for legal disputes. The third role was that of Prophet and in David's life we find that at times he sought the word of God through two prophets, Gad and Nathan. The role of the prophet was to bring God's word into a situation. They didn't contradict the law, but they made it relevant to specific situations.

King, priest and prophet worked together in the time of David and Solomon but, when things were going well, the king and the priests were most vocal. In the time of the divided kingdoms both kings and priests strayed away from God. When kings decided to worship other gods they ordered the priests to include worship of other gods in their duties and so worship of the true God became corrupted and then lost altogether. There were long periods of time when the law was ignored, not read and even became lost. In these times, when the people were not hearing the word of God from those he appointed to teach the people, the role of the Prophet became key.

In Israel the most evil kings faced two of the most formidable prophets – Elijah and Elisha. These men were called by God to go and confront kings who were ruling God's covenant people but ignoring him and his laws. Elijah, who had read God's law and knew that one of the curses on a nation that disobeyed God was drought, sought God and then went to king Ahab and told him that it would not rain in Israel without his word. At the end of three years without rain he then took on four hundred false prophets in a dramatic confrontation and demonstrated the power of God through fire.

Other prophets spoke to kings, to the peoples of Israel and Judah, and to the surrounding nations through their writings. Like Elijah they knew the law and the punishments that God would bring on his people if they disobeyed him. In Deuteronomy 28 there is a long passage setting out the blessings that the people would enjoy if they obeyed God and the curses that would come upon them if they disobeyed his covenant. Right at the end of this list, the worst possible punishment that could come upon them was this: *"You will be uprooted from the land you are entering to possess. Then the LORD will scatter you among all nations, from one end of the earth to the other." (Deuteronomy 28:63–64)* The worst of all punishments was for the people to be removed from the Promised Land and taken to a foreign land.

In Israel, Amos and Hosea warned the people that they would be taken away from the land if they did not repent. Shortly afterwards the Assyrians became the dominant world power, and they came and defeated Israel. To avoid the nations they had conquered rising up in revolt against them, the Assyrians had a policy of resettling the people of each country in other lands. So, after only 209 years as a sovereign nation, the Israelites were taken into exile in a foreign country. Israel was destroyed as a nation and never returned to the land that had been promised to them through their forefather Abraham.

God is true to his word. What he promises will come to pass. But in the exile of Israel we see God's incredible patience. Right from the time of the kingdom dividing the Israelites kept turning their backs on him but God waits for over 200 years giving them every opportunity to turn back to him. Eventually he keeps his promise but, as Moses wrote, God is *"slow to anger" (Exodus 34:6)*.

Judah

While Israel is sliding away from God under bad king after bad king, Judah has times of turning its back on God and times of revival of their faith under good kings. God raised up prophets to speak to them too. Isaiah and Micah prophesied shortly after Israel was taken into captivity warning that Judah would go the same way as her sister Israel but the people ignored their warnings. The heart of God is seen in Isaiah as he not only predicts that they will go into captivity but also looks into the future to a time when God will restore them to the land. God is not only slow to anger but his love demands that, even though

Day 3 – Overview of the Old Testament – Part 2

he must punish his people to satisfy justice, he will restore them in his love.

Judah ignores the warnings of Isaiah and their wickedness increases. God promises that the Babylonians, who have taken over as the world superpower from the Assyrians, will be the ones to destroy Judah and take her people from the land. He sends three more prophets, Zephaniah, Habakkuk and Jeremiah to tell the nation of Judah that they will be taken from the land. Jeremiah had one of the hardest assignments given to any prophet, as his message was that the nation should surrender to the Babylonians to reduce loss of life. He was imprisoned as a traitor, ignored by the kings and badly treated.

The Babylonian army came against Judah a number of times and carried the people into captivity in three campaigns, as shown on Timechart 3 by the three arrows (see page 20). Jeremiah got into more trouble by sending letters to the first exiles telling them to settle down in the lands they had been taken to as it would be seventy years before they returned. Eventually Jerusalem was captured by the Babylonians in 586BC, the walls knocked down and Solomon's temple destroyed. God had been very patient with his people Judah over almost 350 years but finally his people had to face the consequences of going against God's covenant. Jeremiah witnessed the destruction of Jerusalem and wrote a book of laments, Lamentations, which describe his response to seeing the horror of God's city in ruins.

Reviewing the Bible Bookcase

In addition to 1 and 2 Kings, 1 and 2 Chronicles also document the period from David coming to the throne through to the exile, but they concentrate only on the kingdom of Judah. These books almost complete the History section of the Old Testament.

It is during the period of the kings that a number of prophetic writings are added to the Bible. These are divided into the Major Prophets and the Minor Prophets – mainly an indication of their size. The first two Major Prophets, Isaiah and Jeremiah, are by far the largest books in our Bible (Psalms is a collection of songs rather than a single book). By the time of the exile there were also nine Minor Prophets written. This brings the total of Old Testament books to 31 before the exile – see Figure 3 overleaf.

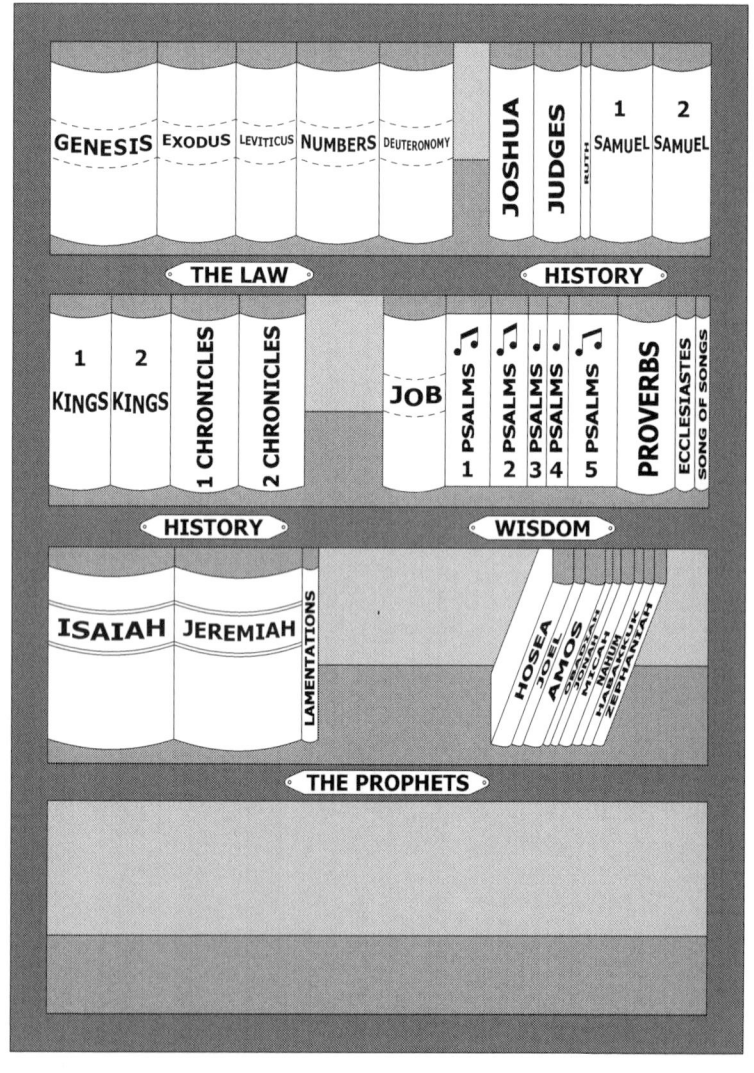

Figure 3 – The Bible Bookcase before the Exile

In Exile

While the Israelites were in exile, God continued to speak to them through his prophets. Two men, Ezekiel and Daniel, who were taken into captivity, spoke to the Jews living in exile although they worked among very different social groups. (Note that the word "Jews", which is what the other nations called the people from "Judah", is used from this time on in the Bible as an alternative word to "Israelites".) Ezekiel was a priest who lived with a group of Jews working to make bricks alongside a river in the desert. He had some amazing visions that spoke of God's sovereignty over his people. Once Jerusalem was destroyed he, like Isaiah, promised that Israel would be restored to her land

Daniel, because he was of noble birth, was selected to be part of the Babylonian civil service. He came to the attention of Nebuchadnezzar, king of Babylon, through interpreting a dream he had, and became his Prime Minister. His book contains stories of how God intervened in the lives of powerful kings, forcing these evil dictators to recognise him as the "Most High God". It also contains far reaching prophecies about what would happen to empires for hundreds of years after his lifetime and on to the end of time.

The Return from Exile

After seventy years the Babylonian Empire was overthrown by the Persians and Cyrus, king of Persia, took control of the lands previously ruled by the Assyrians and the Babylonians. By this time the people from all the different nations had all been thoroughly mixed up and he brought in a new policy of allowing people to return to their original homelands and worship their own gods. As a result of that policy the Jews were allowed to return to Judah and Jerusalem.

The books of Ezra and Nehemiah tell of three groups returning from exile, again shown on Timechart 3 by three arrows (see page 20). The first group rebuilt the temple under the direction of a governor called Zerubbabel and with encouragement from the prophets Haggai and Zechariah. The second and third rebuilt the walls of Jerusalem under the leadership of Nehemiah, the governor, and with the encouragement of Ezra, a priest.

Although some Jews returned to the land of Israel, most remained scattered around the world in the lands where they had been born and grown up. Here they kept themselves separate from other peoples, as they do to this day, and rose to positions of influence in society. A

Persian official, enraged by a Jew refusing to do him homage, arranged for all the Jews in the Persian Empire to be killed. His plan was thwarted by Esther, a Jewess, who was Queen to the King of Persia and was used by God to save the Jews from extermination.

Returning to the Bible Bookcase the books of Ezra, Nehemiah and Esther complete the History section of the Old Testament and Ezekiel and Daniel complete the Major Prophets. Haggai and Zechariah are joined by the last Old Testament prophet, Malachi, to complete the twelve Minor Prophets. See Figure 4.

The Promise of a New Covenant

The Old Testament ends with Malachi, the last prophet, writing around 430 BC and speaking to God's people who have returned from exile. It would be nice to find that they have learned their lesson from seventy years of captivity but actually we find that God's people are, once again, being unfaithful to God and are complacent about keeping his laws.

The old covenant God made with Israel did not work, as it was conditional on their obedience to him. But in Israel's darkest hour, as the Babylonians were poised to destroy Jerusalem, God gave the promise of a new covenant. In a great demonstration of his grace God announced his new covenant through the prophet who had the message with least hope. Right in the middle of Jeremiah's writings, in among the message that the people had no option but to submit to God's judgement, Jeremiah promised that God would make a new covenant with his people.

This new covenant is not conditional on the obedience of the people. All the responsibility for making it work is on God:

""The time is coming," declares the LORD,
 "when I will make a new covenant
with the house of Israel
 and with the house of Judah.
It will not be like the covenant
 I made with their forefathers
when I took them by the hand
 to lead them out of Egypt,
because they broke my covenant,

Day 3 – Overview of the Old Testament – Part 2 27

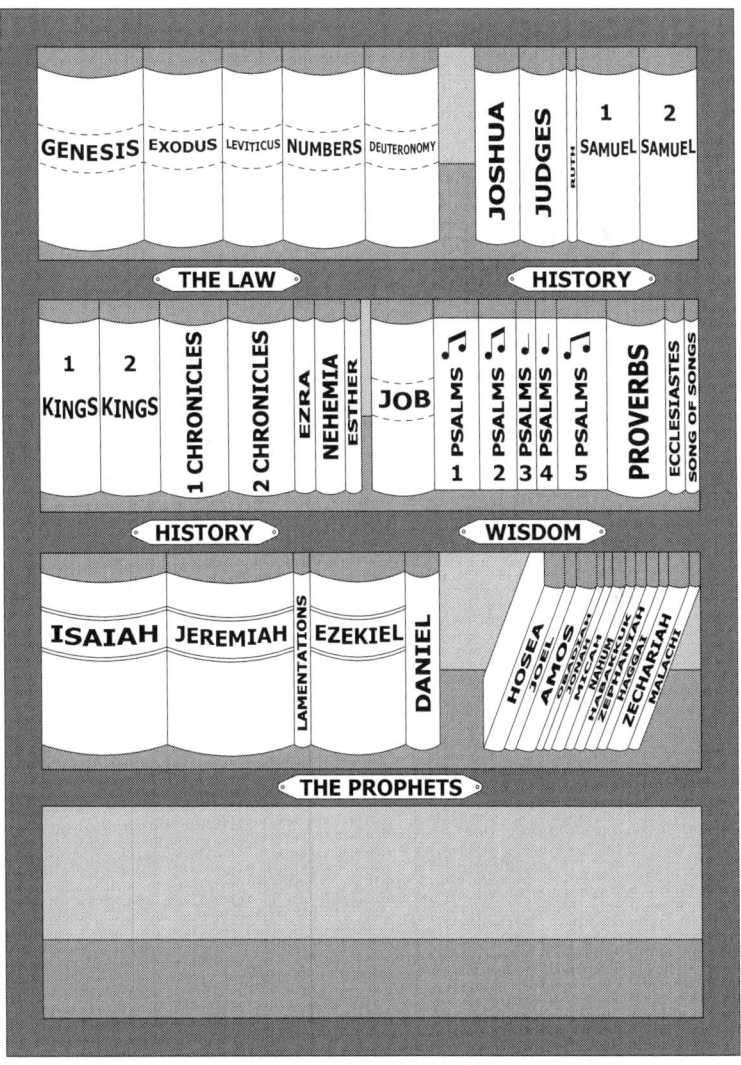

Figure 4 – The Bible Bookcase – The Old Testament

> *though I was a husband to them,"*
> *declares the LORD.*
>
> *"This is the covenant I will make with the house of Israel*
> *after that time," declares the LORD.*
> *"I will put my law in their minds*
> *and write it on their hearts.*
> *I will be their God,*
> *and they will be my people.*
> *No longer will a man teach his neighbour,*
> *or a man his brother, saying, 'Know the LORD,'*
> *because they will all know me,*
> *from the least of them to the greatest,"*
> *declares the LORD.*
> *"For I will forgive their wickedness*
> *and will remember their sins no more.""* (Jeremiah 31:31–34)

This glorious promise of a new covenant held out the prospect of being right with God without any effort on man's part. But to establish such a covenant required God himself to pay the ultimate price.

After God has spoken through Malachi he goes quiet again for over 400 years while the Jews wait for his promises to be fulfilled. Tomorrow we will look at the new covenant, or New Testament, which records how God himself came to earth to enable the new covenant to be made possible.

Day 4
Overview of the New Testament

400 Years of Silence

At the end of the Old Testament the Jews who had returned from exile were settling in the Promised Land once again. But it is not like it was before. This time they are not a sovereign nation with their own king but one of the 127 provinces of Persia ruled by a governor appointed by a foreign emperor. If we turn over the page from the last book in the Old Testament, Malachi, and start reading the New Testament we find that although the geographical setting is the same – the land of Israel – the political and social setting is radically different. In the New Testament the land of Israel is occupied by the Romans. New religious groups – the Pharisees and the Sadducees – have appeared and the main place of worship is the synagogue, rather than the temple.

What is not obvious from our Bibles is that there is a gap of over 400 years between the Old and New Testaments. In terms of God's revealed word to man, God is silent. It is not, however, a quiet time for the Jews living in the land of Israel.

Between the Old and New Testaments

Because of where Israel is, situated at the crossroads between Europe, Asia and Africa, it changed hands as different world powers emerged and set out to conquer the previous one. The world powers that were dominant in Judah at this time are shown on Timechart 4 (see next page).

Persian rule in Israel came to an end in 333 BC when Alexander the Great became king of Greece and set out to conquer the known world. He achieved this and took control of territory all the way to India before he died at the age of 33! After his death the Greek Empire broke up into four parts ruled by four Greek generals. Israel came under the control of two of them, the Ptolemies who ruled Egypt and then the Seleucids based in Syria. Up until the time of the Ptolemies the Jews were given freedom to practice their religion in peace but under Seleucid rule things changed. A Seleucid king called Antiochus Epiphanes decided to destroy the individual cultures of his subjects by imposing the Greek culture on all of them. He destroyed copies of the Old Testament throughout Israel and he set up a statue to the Greek

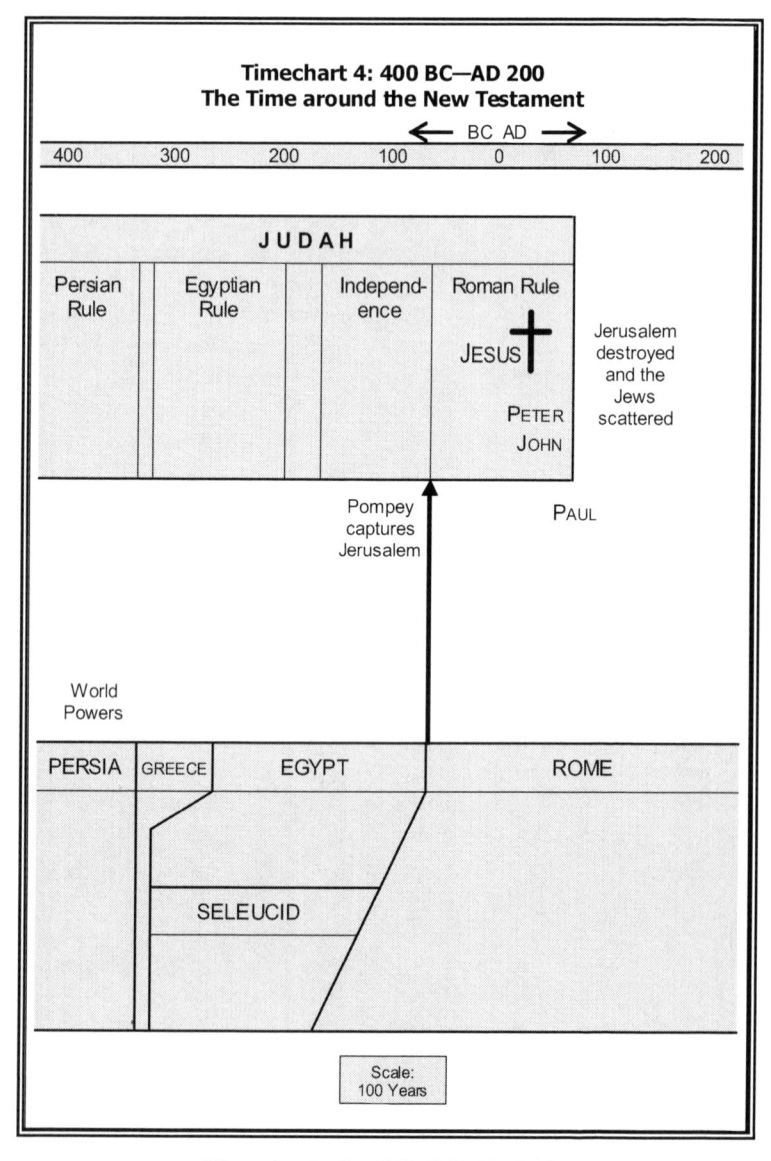

Timechart 4: 400 BC–AD 200
The Time around the New Testament

400	300	200	100	0	100	200

← BC AD →

JUDAH

Persian Rule	Egyptian Rule	Independence	Roman Rule
			JESUS †
			PETER
			JOHN

Jerusalem destroyed and the Jews scattered

Pompey captures Jerusalem

PAUL

World Powers

PERSIA	GREECE	EGYPT	ROME
		SELEUCID	

Scale: 100 Years

**Timechart 4 – 400 BC–AD 200:
The Time around the New Testament**

god Zeus at the temple in Jerusalem and sacrificed a pig on the altar. This may sound odd to us but to the Jews this was the most offensive thing he could do. The pig was an unclean animal and sacrificing it on God's altar was an affront to God and all their culture. The Jews rebelled against Seleucid rule and, after a long struggle, drove them out under the leadership of a man called Mattathias and his sons – the most famous of whom was Judas Maccabeus.

The Jews then enjoyed a period of independence for almost a hundred years before they, along with the rest of the known world, came under the rule of Rome. In 63 BC General Pompey conquered Jerusalem, killed the priests in the temple and entered the Most Holy Place. This started Roman rule in a way that the Jews neither forgave nor forgot.

Although Roman rule was not welcomed by the Jews, it actually set the scene for God to fulfil his promises and bring in the new covenant. The Roman Empire was larger than any previous one, stretching from Europe into North Africa and the Middle East. Thanks to the Romans the whole world was at peace (known in Latin as "Pax Romana") for the period during which Jesus was born and the church started. Thanks to the Romans it was possible to move around the world more quickly than ever before on excellent roads and on Roman shipping lanes. And thanks to Alexander the Great, and his vision of bringing Greek culture to the entire world, it was possible to communicate throughout the Roman Empire using a common language – Greek.

The Silence is Broken

The New Testament starts with four books called "the Gospels" from an old English word meaning "Good News". The four gospel writers – Matthew, Mark, Luke and John – tell the story of God coming to earth as a man. Jesus, conceived by the Holy Spirit and a descendant of King David through his mother came to fulfil the Old Testament prophecies concerning God's promise of a new covenant.

The 400 years of God's silence were broken by another prophet. John the Baptist appeared in the desert, as if from nowhere, and started calling people to repent and prepare themselves for the coming of the Lord. John's preaching had a huge impact. As the Jews living in Judea heard him and were baptised by him, his message spread to Jews living in all parts of the Roman Empire.

The Life of Jesus

When Jesus was about thirty, he went to John to be baptised and started a three year period of working publicly among the Jews. He went around the towns of Galilee and Judea, Roman provinces in the north and south of the land of Israel, teaching the people, healing the sick, working miracles and showing the love of God to men. Many people followed him and became his disciples and from them he chose twelve close companions to be with him, men he called "apostles". He taught his disciples how to live, how to preach and how to heal the sick and sent them out to do the things he did too.

In the gospels we have but a fraction of his teaching and miracles recorded for our instruction. One of the twelve apostles, John, says at the end of his gospel: *"Jesus did many other things as well. If every one of them were written down, I suppose that even the whole world would not have room for the books that would be written." (John 21:25)*. But in these four gospels we have enough to show us how God lived as a man, providing an example for us, and a wealth of teaching, which shows us how to live our lives.

The ordinary people loved him for his miracles and his teaching but as time went on the religious leaders became less and less impressed. They envied his popularity and feared that he might lead a revolt against the Romans, which they knew would not succeed but only lead to further bloodshed and oppression. They banded together, put aside their differences, and planned together to get rid of Jesus in order to preserve their way of life and their nation. When the opportunity came they got the people on their side and called for his death.

The New Covenant

The old covenant required the sacrifice of animals for the forgiveness of sins. The blood of a perfect animal had to be shed to meet the demands of the law. The new covenant was no different. It required the shedding of blood too, but this time it was God himself whose blood had to be shed.

All four gospel writers devote a large part of their accounts to the end of Jesus' time on earth. A third of their writings deal with the week running up to his death and his subsequent resurrection. Having lived a perfect life, Jesus was brought to trial by the Jews, unjustly sentenced to death by the Roman governor and executed by the cruellest form of execution they knew – crucifixion. God himself came to earth as Jesus, lived a perfect life to fulfil the obligations of the old covenant and then died himself to seal the new covenant in his blood so that we could receive forgiveness of sins and know the Lord ourselves. As Peter puts it so eloquently, *"Christ died for sins once for all, the righteous for the unrighteous, to bring you to God." (1 Peter 3:18)* This is the greatest news ever told!

Jesus' body was laid in a tomb but three days later he rose from the dead. Not only is there forgiveness of sins in the new covenant but Jesus also conquered death which was introduced into the world through the sin of the first man, Adam. After forty days of appearing to his disciples – on one occasion he was seen by over 500 people – Jesus returned to heaven. One day when he was with his disciples he went up into the clouds and disappeared from their sight. Angels appeared, as they did at his birth, to tell his followers that he would return the same way.

The Birth of the Church

The book of Acts, or "The Acts of the Apostles", was written by Luke. In his opening line he refers back to his gospel saying, *"I wrote about all that Jesus began to do and to teach until the day he was taken up to heaven" (Acts 1:1–2).* This makes it clear that Jesus continued his work in the world after his death through the church working in the power of the Holy Spirit. After the gospels, Acts is the only historical book in the New Testament and it provides a bridge between them and the rest of the New Testament. It follows straight on from the end of the gospels and gives us the background to the writers and recipients of the letters that make up the rest of the New Testament.

When Jesus was with his disciples he told them that he must return to his Father. But he would not leave them without help and told them that he would, *"ask the Father, and he will give you another Counsellor to be with you for ever – the Spirit of truth" (John 14:16–17).* Just before he returned to heaven, Jesus told the disciples to wait in Jerusalem until they were *"baptised with the Holy Spirit" (Acts 1:5).* This happened on the day of Pentecost when the disciples Jesus left behind were transformed. Before Pentecost they met behind locked doors in fear of the Jewish authorities. After Pentecost they spilled out onto the streets of Jerusalem in the power of the Holy Spirit, preaching the good news about Jesus to all who would listen. After Peter, the leader of the twelve apostles, preached, three thousand responded to his call for repentance, were baptised and added to their number and the church was born.

Initially the church was entirely Jewish. The gospel reached those living in Jerusalem and Judea, who were mainly Jewish and other Jews who came to worship in Jerusalem from other parts of the Roman world, like those at Pentecost. Then God led Peter to go to the house of a Gentile – a non–Jew – and tell him the good news about Jesus. This was a big hurdle for Peter who had been brought up as a devout Jew and taught not to associate with Gentiles. Although the church leadership in Jerusalem accepted that this was from God it was another church, Antioch, that became the main base for spreading the good news to the Gentiles.

The church in Antioch had been founded by Jews but from early on had included non–Jews. Later Paul, a Jew called by God to be an apostle to the Gentiles, was sent out from there on three missionary journeys and the second half of Acts describes them. Paul always travelled with a group of companions or "fellow workers" and during his second journey Luke joined his party so was able to describe what happened as an eyewitness.

Paul was not interested in just bringing people to the point of accepting Christ as Lord. In each town he visited he established a church and, after an initial period, appointed elders to oversee the affairs of the church. It is clear that Paul was not the only apostle operating in this way but the account of his way of operating provides us with a valuable insight into how the early church was founded.

Letters from Leaders

The other "books" in the New Testament that give us insight into the early church are, in fact, letters. Churches were established all around the Roman Empire and beyond by the apostles and other disciples of Jesus. Initially they travelled from church to church to teach the new congregations and ensure they did not fall into error. Having seen Jesus go into heaven and been told that he would return the same way many expected his return imminently. But as time went on and the early apostles got older, they realised that it may be after their lifetime before Jesus returned. The church continued to grow so that it became harder and harder to keep track of what was being taught and so letters were written to encourage the churches facing persecution and hardship and to correct error, either by teaching truth or by directly attacking wrong teaching.

Thirteen of Paul's letters are preserved in the New Testament and they come after Acts in our Bibles. The first nine are addressed to churches. In Romans Paul presents the gospel clearly using his extensive knowledge of the Old Testament. In 1 Corinthians he answers a

Day 4 – Overview of the New Testament

number of points raised by the Corinthian church in a letter to him. Colossians contains some amazing teaching about who Jesus is – in fact much of our understanding of what Jesus' life, death and resurrection means to us comes from Paul's letters. He also wrote four letters to individuals: three to church leaders, Timothy and Titus, give us concise but detailed instructions for building churches.

After Paul's letters there are eight from other church leaders. Hebrews is the largest, which breaks up the New Testament nicely – Paul's letters come before it, those from other writers are after it – and compares the new covenant with the old. This is followed by letters from James and Jude, brothers of Jesus, and Peter and John, two of his twelve apostles.

Completing the Bible Bookcase

Within 35 years of Jesus' death most of the New Testament was written. The first three gospels, Acts, all of Paul's letters, Hebrews, and the letters from James and Peter were probably all written between AD 50 and 70. Later, towards the end of the first century, John, the youngest of the twelve apostles, wrote his gospel, three letters and the book of Revelation, which completes our Bible, as we see in Figure 5.

The Jews Scattered Once More

In AD 66 the Jews finally revolted against the Romans and threw them out of Jerusalem and Judea. For a short while they regained their independence until the might of Rome returned to teach the Jewish nation a lesson. With all the troubles they had had with the Jews the Romans did not return just to subdue them once again. This time, after a long siege against Jerusalem when the Jews were starved into submission, they entered Jerusalem, smashed down its walls and completely dismantled Herod's temple. This fulfilled the words Jesus spoke only 40 years earlier when he was with his disciples in the temple: *"not one stone here will be left on another; every one will be thrown down" (Matthew 24:2).*

To stop the Jews ever being a problem to them again the Romans decided to do what previous empires had done and they scattered them throughout the Roman Empire. The land of Israel was no longer a hotbed for Jewish nationalism as they were scattered abroad. And so it remained with Jews living all over the world until AD 1948 when the state of Israel was born following the horrors experienced by the Jews at the hands of the Nazis.

36   *Day 4 – Overview of the New Testament*

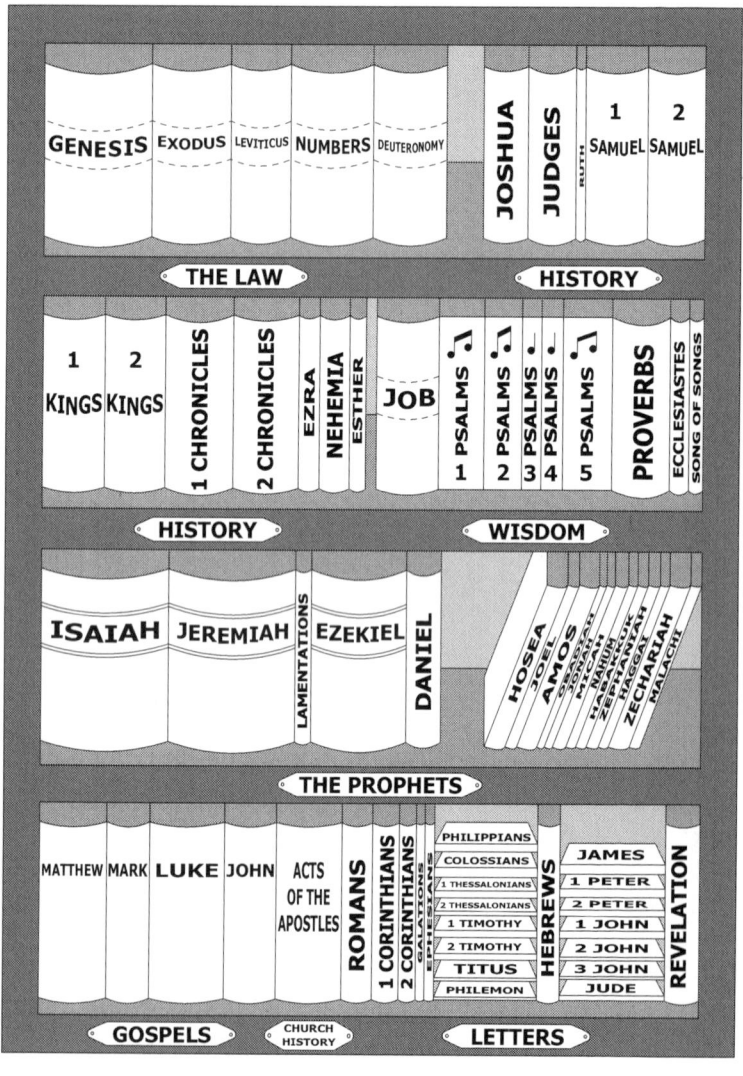

Figure 5 – The Bible Bookcase

The End of the Story

The final book of the New Testament, Revelation, is also a letter sent to seven churches in the Roman province of Asia (present day Turkey). It records a vision the apostle John had when he was in exile on the island of Patmos. Jesus appeared to him while he was worshipping and gave him warnings for the churches and an amazing revelation about what would happen in the future, from the time of John right up until the end of the world and beyond.

The church at this time was facing persecution from the Romans and Revelation urges them to overcome or endure to the end. It then goes on to record events that will take place in heaven and on earth in times to come. Many people have sought to understand the details of Revelation over the years and have come up with many different interpretations. The vision is recorded in very symbolic language which makes it very difficult to understand. In my opinion it is best to read it quickly and not dwell on the details. The important message of the book is that God is in control. Whatever is happening on the earth, even the most terrible catastrophes, God remains in control.

The last two chapters of Revelation describe God's final purpose for us as human beings. In his vision John sees a new heaven and a new earth and, coming out of the new heaven, a new Jerusalem which is not made of stones but of redeemed people. Those who overcome will be part of the bride of Christ and live with God forever in a perfect new world.

So the Bible ends with two chapters of perfection. This reminds us of the beginning of Genesis. That opens with two chapters of perfection. These are followed by 1185 chapters describing man's rebellion against God and God's love and patience in pursuing a relationship with mankind before, right at the end, there are two chapters of perfection again. In Genesis chapter 3 Satan appears and it is he who turns man against God. This is mirrored in Revelation 20, three chapters from the end, where Satan is thrown into hell, never to be released again to trouble those who have put their trust in God. In Genesis 3 Adam and Eve were driven out of the Garden of Eden to keep them away from the tree of life so that they would not live forever on earth in their sinful state. In the last chapter of Revelation the tree of life appears once more, available to those who have overcome and have eternal life.

That is the Bible: God's love letter to mankind. From tomorrow, will start going through it in much more detail!

Day 5
Creation

The book of Genesis

The first book of the Bible is called "Genesis", a name that comes from the Greek word meaning "Beginnings". The Jews referred to the books in the Old Testament by their first word or words in Hebrew so they call it "In the Beginning". Genesis is a unique book of the Bible. This is true of most of the books of the Bible but is particularly true of Genesis as it covers more than half the timespan of the whole Bible, a period of thousands of years. The rest of the Old Testament covers around 1500 years and the New Testament less than 100. Genesis is also my favourite book of the Bible. (I will only say that about a couple of other books as we go through the rest!) I have always enjoyed Genesis since I was a child. It contains some great stories and also provides an explanation of the world around us.

The Bible contains history books, prophetic books, a song book and letters and Genesis is a history book. In the Bible history is always recorded prophetically. Often we associate the word "prophet" with predictions about the future but in the Bible the word "prophet" means spokesman. So, a prophetic book is written by someone speaking on God's behalf, or from God's perspective. It does not have to be predictive.

Genesis is the first of the five books that Moses wrote which are known as "the Law of Moses" or just "the Law" (see for example Joshua 8:31 and a reference by Jesus in Luke 24:44) and it is the cornerstone of the rest of the Bible. The principles of the Law are based on actual historical events as we will see in today's passage.

It is generally accepted that Genesis, along with the other four books of the law, was written by Moses during the time he was leading the people of Israel through the wilderness around 1446 – 1406 BC. Genesis would have been compiled from earlier sources and there is some evidence of later editorial updating of place names. The book is in two distinct parts. The first 11 chapters deal with the whole world, starting with its creation and then from chapter 12 onwards the book focuses on one family: Abraham, his son Isaac, his twin sons Esau and Jacob, and finally the twelve sons of Jacob, who was renamed "Israel" and became the fathers of the tribes of Israel.

Outline of Genesis	
1–2	Creation
3–5	The fall of man. Genealogies.
6–9	The flood
10–11	The spread of the nations. The tower of Babel.
12:1–25:18	Abraham, God's friend.
25:19–26:35	Isaac, the promised son.
27–35	Jacob, the deceiver, who became Israel the one who struggled with God.
36	Esau's descendants.
37–50	Joseph, the saviour of his people.

The account of the early world before the flood is set in a civilisation we now know little about. From chapter 11 onwards the book is set in the ancient Mesopotamian and Egyptian civilisations and archaeology has unearthed historical texts from these civilisations which have close parallels with Genesis in terms of the events described, the way of life, and legal and social customs.

The book of Genesis provides a foundation for the rest of the Bible. It not only describes the beginning of the physical world – the heavens and the earth, vegetation, animals and mankind – but also the beginning of sin and redemption, of blessing and cursing, of society and civilisation, of marriage and family, of art, craft, industry, and languages. In all areas it makes very clear the sovereignty of God as creator over all created things including man. However, God is not seen as remote. His desire for relationship with men and women is seen from the beginning and, after mankind has turned his back on God, he chooses Abraham to be his friend and makes an everlasting covenant with him and his descendants to be their God (see chapters 15 and 17).

Genesis is a written as a historical account in prose. There are a few passages of poetry in it which can be spotted in most Bibles by the way they are laid out on the page. Look, for example, at the first piece of poetry in Genesis 1:27.

The expression *"This is the account of ..."* appears ten times in Genesis: e.g. *"This is the account of Noah" (Genesis 6:9)* and *"This is the account of Jacob." (Genesis 37:2)*. The number seven also crops up a number of times. The numbers seven and ten are often significant in the Bible and symbolise completeness.

The Creation of the Heavens and the Earth

Genesis 1 is an account of God creating the world. He starts with a formless, dark earth (see verse 2) and creates the world in six days: light, sky, land and sea, sun, moon and stars, plants, sea and land animals and, finally, the crowning achievement of his creation, mankind, both male and female created in the image of God. Genesis 2, from verse 4, then goes back to look at the creation of the first man and woman (as opposed to mankind) in more detail.

> **Read Genesis 1–2**

In the first two chapters of the Bible everything was perfect. "God saw that it was good" is repeated over and over throughout the creation story. After the first two chapters Satan and sin enter the world and the story from there through to the last two chapters of Revelation is the story of man's sin and of God's love drawing men back into relationship with him.

Can this be True?

Two hundred years ago this question would not have been asked about the Bible. It was accepted as true without question. But advances in science through the 1800's led people to question the Biblical account of creation and to start questioning many other aspects of the historical account in the Bible. Now at the beginning of the 21st century we "know" that science has disproved the Bible and the chapters you have just read in Genesis are just myths – stories which were made up to teach us truths but not true themselves. At least that is the accepted wisdom of today, isn't it?

If that accepted wisdom is true then we have to start our look at the Bible with serious doubts about its truth after the first two chapters! For that reason I think it is very important that we take a bit of time to consider the scientific evidence that supports current scientific thinking and see how that evidence compares to the Biblical account of the creation and the flood, which we will look at in a couple of days' time. There are two questions we can ask about this issue. Firstly, what did the writer mean when he wrote it and secondly, does it agree with science? This is a huge subject and the following is a very quick

Day 5 – Creation

overview of a topic that is worthy of more in depth study at a later date.

What did the Writer mean?

The first question to ask is, "Did the writer mean us to take his account of the creation and the flood literally when he wrote it or did he think that he was writing some stories to teach spiritual truths?" The Bible is written in a variety of styles: some of it is written as history, some is written as stories, some is poetry. How can we be sure that the creation account in Genesis is history?

Jesus told stories, or "parables", which were not true. When asked "Who is my neighbour?" he replied by saying *"A man was going down from Jerusalem to Jericho" (Luke 10:30)* and went on to tell the parable of the Good Samaritan. No such man ever existed. The story was told to illustrate a point. It is made clear in the gospels that Jesus spoke in parables to teach the people truths. In Psalm 22 David writes *"I am poured out like water, and all my bones are out of joint. My heart has turned to wax; it has melted away within me." (Psalm 22:14)*. Had David's heart really turned to wax and melted away? Obviously not! This is a poetic song and, like all poetry, the writer is using a powerful picture to convey a truth about how he was feeling. We know what he meant and the style is in keeping with the rest of the Psalms which is a book of poetry.

So what about the early chapters of Genesis? Are these written as a story or as poetry? As you read on in Genesis you will find that these chapters are written in the same style as the rest of the book and that this style is very similar to other historical writings in the Old Testament. In Genesis 1 there is an account of the seven days of creation. In Numbers 7 there is an account of twelve days of offerings. The Hebrew word for "day" is used in the same way in both chapters. So, the way in which the early chapters of Genesis are written is like other Old Testament history. The author believed he was writing historical facts. Like other Biblical history it does not give us all the facts but what we have is accurate and can be relied upon historically.

If we accept that the writer of Genesis thought he was writing a true account of events that still leaves the possibility that he was simply wrong. He obviously knew nothing of modern science so have recent discoveries disproved his account?

Does Genesis Agree with Science?

There are two main theories that are taught as fact today in education and assumed to be true across the popular media – the "Big Bang" theory and "The Theory of Evolution". A simple summary of the big bang theory is that the universe started around fifteen billion years ago from a huge explosion which created matter and space itself. As the material expanded it formed into all the galaxies, stars and planets that we can observe today, including planet earth. Evolution says that sometime around four billion years ago, some of the inorganic (non-living) chemicals on the earth came together to form a one celled living organism. Through a series of chance steps this organism reproduced itself and, over those four billion years, mutated into the many living things we see about us today: plants, fish, birds, insects, mammals and mankind.

Science deals with things that can be observed in the present. If you let go of an apple it will fall to the ground; people have known this scientific fact for thousands of years. But scientific theories are proposals that scientists make based on the facts they observe. They can only be said to be true after many people have observed that what the theory predicts does indeed happen. What made Newton a great scientist was not that he observed the apple falling but that he developed the theory of gravity. From this theory Newton made predictions about the orbits of the moon around the earth and the planets around the sun – predictions that were tested by observation.

When it comes to theories about the origin of the universe or life the scientific facts that can be observed in the world around us do not _prove_ anything. No one is proposing that big bangs are taking place today nor that life is being spontaneously created and so it cannot be observed. Whether or not you believe in evolution is not a scientific question. The answer depends on the assumptions you make about the world you observe.

Evolution

In 1859 Charles Darwin published his famous book "Origin of the Species" setting out the theory of evolution. He had observed the way in which certain animals had adapted to different environments and proposed that all living animals and plants had evolved through a series of small modifications. The principle of "survival of the fittest" meant that those that had beneficial modifications survived over those that did not and so those creatures which had the advantages of sight or hearing or sharper beaks or flight outlived those that did not.

At the time Darwin wrote he could be forgiven for thinking that the

Day 5 – Creation

building blocks of life were simple. However, over the last 150 years our knowledge of living creatures has increased beyond all recognition. The discovery of atoms and molecules, of DNA – the genetic code that tells a living organism how to grow – and of all the biochemical interactions that take place inside a cell has shown us that the complexity even of a single celled organism is mind–blowingly staggering! If you want to explore this topic further then I would recommend the book "In six days – Why 50 scientists choose to believe in creation" which has essays from 50 professors in a range of scientific disciplines giving their reasons for believing in a literal six day creation. Jerry Bergman, a biologist with two PhDs to his name, writes *"In biological organisms the smallest unit of life is the cell, and the number of parts it contains at the subatomic level is usually much larger than a trillion."*[A]. The idea that such a machine – for that is what a cell is – came together by chance is improbable to say the least. An alternative theory is that the complexity developed over time but the problem with that is that even for an individual cell to live it has to have many systems working, taking in food, disposing of the waste matter, moving oxygen around within it, generating energy and reproducing itself. How could this have developed over time given that the cell cannot live if any one of those systems is not operating?

You might expect there to be a simple "scientific" answer to this but Michael Behe, Professor of Biochemistry at Lehigh University, Bethlehem, Pennsylvania points out that *"If you search the scientific literature on evolution, and if you focus your search on the question of how molecular machines – the basis of life – developed, you find an eerie and complete silence."*[B].

But of course, cells are simple when compared to the complexity of animals and of our own bodies. How can evolution account for our eyes which contain 100 million light sensitive cells which pass information along a million nerve fibres to our brains which, through a score of processes we only vaguely understand, process it into sight? Again, despite many engaging diagrams and theories in textbooks, the evidence for such evolution is scant. What we actually see in the world around us are animals that reproduce "according to their kind" and fossils of distinct animal groups, some very similar to those alive today.

When we look at a work of art or a car or a computer, we are impressed by the handiwork of the artist or the designer. We do not think for one moment that they came about by chance (although I guess this is questionable about some modern works of art!). But any impartial consideration of the complexity of living creatures has to conclude that they are the work of a designer. This is the root of the debate between creation and evolution. It is not a scientific question – science cannot prove either, although the evidence is strongly against evolution – it is a question about belief in God. If you accept that life has a designer then you have to accept that the designer may still have designs on your life!

Paul wrote *"For since the creation of the world God's invisible qualities – his eternal power and divine nature – have been clearly seen, being understood from what has been made, so that men are without excuse." (Romans 1:20)*. Evolution gives people an excuse to carry on believing that there is no God in spite of the evidence to the contrary.

In order to give a balanced view I must say that there are many Christians who do not take the Genesis account of creation literally and who believe in both a creator God and in evolution. But for myself, having studied both the Bible and some of the scientific evidence, I believe that God created this world in six days, as set out in Genesis 1. This does not contradict the scientific evidence we see around us.

The primary reason that Genesis and the other books in the Bible were written is to teach us about God, but we can also rely on the historical accuracy of the history books in the Bible. Of course, although the history books in the Bible are historically accurate, they do not provide a complete history of everything. Similarly although they are scientifically accurate, they are not scientifically complete. There may be many details that are not included which we would like to know but what is there can be relied upon.

References

[A] *In six days, why 50 scientists choose to believe in creation,* edited by John F Ashton PhD, New Holland Publishers, 2000. p. 16. Used with permission.

[B] *Darwin's Black Box: The Biochemical Challenge to Evolution* by Michael J. Behe. Copyright © 1996 by Michael J. Behe. p. 5. Reprinted with the permission of The Free Press, a Division of Simon & Schuster Adult Publishing Group. All rights reserved.

Day 6
The Early World

Genesis as Law

Because of the theory of evolution many people are surprised that God could create the world in such a short time – six days – but once you understand the greatness of God the real question is not "How could he do it so quickly", but "Why did he take so long?!" Why didn't he just create the world in a moment? The answer is found in the Ten Commandments, the central summary of the whole of the law. The fourth commandment tells us to keep one day in seven as a day of rest. Why? *"For in six days the LORD made the heavens and the earth, the sea, and all that is in them, but he rested on the seventh day" (Exodus 20:11).* When God chose to summarise his entire law into ten statements, he devoted most words to the commandment about the day of rest, and that was because he chose to make it transparently clear that he had created the world in six days and he did it to set an example for mankind. The reason for having a seven day week can be found right there in Genesis 1.

Down through generations societies have been built out of families with the institution of marriage at the heart of them. In Genesis 2 we see that this too was not man's idea, it was God's. When Jesus was asked about the law on divorce he answered by quoting from Genesis 2:24 and added the famous words *"what God has joined together, let man not separate." (Matthew 19:6)* Only then did he refer to the later law of Moses which allowed divorce for unfaithfulness. God himself instituted marriage, creating a woman to be a helper for the man. The two started out literally as "one flesh" as the woman was taken from part of the man's side. Although polygamy – a man having more than one wife – came to be accepted in later cultures it is also clear from the creation account that this was not God's intention in the beginning.

In all this we see why Genesis is part of "The Law". The very foundations of society are based on the laws in these chapters.

Genesis as Theology

Theology is the study of God. What do we learn about God from these first chapters in creation? One of the mysteries of God is that he is both one and three. Throughout the Bible we find reference to God the

Father, God the Son and the Holy Spirit. This mystery is called the Trinity although this word is not in the Bible. When the first verse of Genesis talks about God creating the world the word used for 'God' is the Hebrew noun *"Elohim"* which is plural but the verb 'created' is singular. In verse 26 God said, *"Let us make man"*, again God talking of himself in the plural. The Holy Spirit is referred to in verse 2 and from later writers we find that Jesus is referred to as "The Word of God" so in God speaking and his word creating we find a reference to Jesus. The idea of the Trinity is established in Genesis 1.

From Genesis 1 and 2 we are left in no doubt as to the fact that God created the world. The mechanics of how he did it are not spelled out for us but the Bible never leaves us in any doubt that God is the creator of this universe we live in. The Psalmist, the prophets, Paul in his letters and Jesus himself all refer to God as the creator (see for example Psalm 148:5, Isaiah 42:5, Romans 1:20 and Mark 13:19). The fact that the world was initiated by God not that long ago links to the later teaching that God will one day step in to bring an end to this world too – and not that far in the future either.

Genesis 1 and 2 also give us some important teaching about man. Man has a special place in creation. Both men and women are made in the image of God, they are not just a highly developed animal. In this world there are millions of different types of animals. They are designed to live in this physical world. In the heavenly realms we read in the Bible about angels and other spiritual beings. Man stands alone as the only living creature that is both physical and spiritual. God created man for relationship with himself and when we are born of the Spirit we live as both physical and spiritual beings having relationship with our maker.

In Genesis 1:28 God gave mankind authority over the world to fill it, subdue it, and rule over all other living things. We have authority in this world as well as an awesome responsibility to look after it. So, despite only reading 2 chapters of the Bible, our understanding of God and the world we live in is already taking shape!

The Fall

Our understanding of the nature of man increases in Genesis 3. After two chapters of perfection we come to an event often called "The Fall of Man" or just "The Fall". Adam and Eve were only given one rule in the garden of Eden. God told them that they *"must not eat from the tree of the knowledge of good and evil, for when you eat of it you will surely*

Day 6 – The Early World

die." *(Genesis 2:17)* but in this passage they broke his rule and spoiled God's perfect world.

> **Read Genesis 3**

The chapter opens with a conversation between Eve and a serpent. This does not seem to have surprised Eve. Did all the animals talk? We don't know! But through the serpent we are introduced to Satan. Satan is a Hebrew word meaning "the adversary" or "the accuser" which is used throughout the Bible. In the New Testament he is also referred to as "The Devil" from the Greek word *diabolos* meaning "the accuser". Later we discover that Satan is a fallen angel whose pride has led him to rebel against God. He is not equal with God but a created being who has turned against his creator. Right from this introduction to Satan we see that he is determined to spoil God's creation and, in particular, destroy the relationship between man and God. He uses crafty questioning – "Did God *really* say …" – to undermine Eve's confidence in God. He misquotes God, blatantly accuses him of being a liar and tells half–truths. Eve is taken in and eats the fruit and Adam eats too.

And then the full horror of "sin", which means breaking God's law, is revealed. Was eating a piece of fruit (it doesn't say that it was an apple in the Bible) such a serious issue? It seems so minor. But they had disobeyed God and the consequences for them, for mankind, and for the entire universe are huge.

The first sign that something had happened is that Adam and Eve hide from one another. They realise that they are naked and use fig leaves to cover themselves. Then they hide from God. When God created man he wanted a relationship with him and we discover here that God came and walked with Adam and Eve in the garden in "the cool of the day". It is recorded as a normal event. Imagine that! Their relationship with God was such that they talked face to face on a daily basis, discussing the new animals they had seen and the other details of their everyday lives. That is what God wanted in the beginning and that is what he wants with us now. This image of walking with God in the cool of the day is a fantastic picture of how God wants to relate to mankind.

But after eating the fruit Adam and Eve hide. As Satan promised they have learned "good and evil" but it does not make them "like God". Rather, it makes them unable to look him in the eye. The major consequence of their sin is that man loses his special relationship with

God. He has to call them out of hiding to question them.

Adam's response to God is very quick and, like a typical man, he blames his wife and God: "It's the woman's fault – and you gave her to me!" Eve has not only sinned herself but now finds that she is being accused by Adam of being responsible for his sin before God. Adam's relationships with both God and his wife are damaged and deteriorating. Eve blames the serpent and God then works back up the line passing judgement on the serpent, then the woman and finally, Adam. As God speaks the horrifying results of Adam and Eve's disobedience become clear.

The judgement on Adam announces the arrival of death: *"... to dust you will return"*. It is clear that man was created to live as a physical being on earth forever. Without this judgement Adam and Eve would still be alive today. Death not only affects man but also the animals too. God himself kills animals to provide garments of skin to clothe Adam and Eve. In fact the impact of death on creation is even wider than that. Paul describes all of creation as being *"subjected to frustration"* and in *"bondage to decay" (Romans 8:20–21)*. In some way the whole universe was doomed to destruction as a result of man's sin.

Even after Adam and Eve sinned they had the possibility of becoming immortal by eating from another tree in the garden called "the tree of life." With the whole of creation now subject to decay man cannot be allowed to live forever in a dying universe so they are banished from the garden and cut off from the tree of life. Does this mean that God's plan for man to live forever has been thwarted? No. The last two chapters of the Bible describe the new heaven and the new earth that God will create after the old ones have passed away and the tree of life is present again in the new earth (see Revelation 22:2).

The judgement on Eve brings pain for all women in childbearing and in their relationship with men. Women will desire their husbands but find that they are ruled by them. Instead of finding love and support in a relationship women often find pain and anguish.

Plant life changes too as a result of this judgement. Not only will Adam have to work at cultivating the land now but his work will be hampered by thorns and thistles. The curses that follow man's sin provide an insight into why life on earth is as it is. God declared his creation "good" but we know that not all in the world is good today. Genesis 3 provides an explanation for the pain and death we see about us.

However, God does not leave man without hope. To the serpent God says *"I will put enmity between you and the woman, and between your offspring and hers; he will crush your head, and you will strike his heel." (Genesis 3:15)*. These words speak of far more than the hostility between mankind and snakes. This is the first prophecy about the coming of Jesus who will one day come as the offspring of a woman and crush the head of Satan. Satan will continue to bite at the heel of mankind but Jesus will defeat him.

Cain and Abel

The next chapter shows how quickly man deteriorates following the introduction of sin into the world and the breakdown of his relationship with God.

> **Read Genesis 4**

The account of Cain murdering Abel is not a story from distant descendants of Adam and Eve but it is the record of events that took place between their sons – the next generation. Adam and Eve committed one act of disobedience but their son, Cain, jealous of his brother, becomes so angry with him that he kills him! The slide into "major" sin happens very quickly.

At the end of the chapter there is a list of the descendants of Cain. Hebrew writers are very fond of "genealogies" or family trees. This one ends with Lamech who illustrates how rapidly Cain's descendants become totally godless. Five generations after Cain, Lamech not only murders a young man but is recorded as boasting about it. Cain was very sorry for what he had done. Five generations later Lamech shows no shame for his actions. Not only that, but Lamech is boasting to his *two* wives. Polygamy has become acceptable and the position of women in society downgraded.

It is interesting to note that Cain and Abel knew about bringing offerings long before the regulations for sacrifices were laid down in the law. The exact reason why Cain's gift was not acceptable is not clear to us, but God's reply to his anger makes it clear that Cain knew what was and what was not acceptable (see Genesis 4:7). Note also that Cain is able to communicate with God even though he has committed such a terrible crime.

Adam to Noah

In chapter 5 there is another genealogy, this time listing the descendants of Seth.

> **Read Genesis 5**

The same format is used to record details about each man: the age when his son was born, how long he lived after that, his total lifespan, and then the section ends with the words *"and then he died"*. The repetition of this phrase emphasises the impact of God's judgement. The only exception to this formula is Enoch. He didn't just live, he *"walked with God"* and then instead of dying *"he was no more, because God took him away"*. This is one of many mysterious little episodes found throughout the Bible which leave us with more questions than answers! (To add to the mystery Enoch is quoted in the New Testament – see Jude 14–15.) Enoch is one of only two men in the Bible who didn't die. The other was Elijah. The fact that Enoch didn't die led to a riddle that I remember my grandfather telling me: "The oldest man in the Bible died before his father". This is a reference to Enoch's son Methuselah who lived for 969 years and is the oldest recorded man in the Bible.

These early chapters of Genesis add a great deal to our understanding of our world. In the story of the flood much more will be revealed, including a possible explanation for the great ages recorded in the genealogies.

Day 7
Noah and the Flood

The Flood

Following the sin of Adam and Eve the world rapidly became very wicked and by the time of Noah things were so bad that the only righteous man God could find on earth was Noah. Among all the people that were alive – and there may have been billions –Noah and his family were the only righteous ones.

God's instruction to Noah to build an Ark required incredible faith. He spent over 100 years building a huge boat – the longest built until the Cunard liner Eturia in 1884 – miles from any water with no experience of ever seeing rain! People must have thought he was completely mad. But he was proved right when God fulfilled his promise and caused a flood to come. The language used in the story indicates that this flood was a cataclysmic event that devastated the entire world, killing all land animals including mankind. The only people and animals to come through it were those on the Ark. This story shows us God as Judge. He, as the creator of all men and the world they live in, has the right to judge mankind. If he chooses to wipe out a group of people or, as in this case, the whole world then he has the right to do so. But it also shows the heart of God the Redeemer. God does not give up his desire to have a relationship with mankind and goes to great lengths to ensure that a family survived to repopulate the world with people who can know their God.

> Read: Genesis 6–8

The Flood – Myth or Historical Fact?

Like creation, the Biblical account of the flood is also treated as a myth by most people today. At school I was taught that this story came from some local flood in the Middle East and it was not possible that the whole world was flooded. More recently I have seen the suggestion that it refers to a flood of the Black Sea area. Could this be what the Genesis account is referring to? Go back to Genesis 7 and read verses 17–23 and ask yourself if the writer could possibly be talking about a local flood. Note the use of the words "all", "entire", "every" and "only" – in all I count seven references which emphasize the world-wide nature of the flood.

In my late teens I read a book called "The Genesis Flood"[2] by John Whitcomb and Henry Morris which is a classic work setting out the arguments for the Biblical account of Creation from the evidence of science. From a careful study of the account of the flood they provide a lot of explanation for the world we see about us. More recently I also read a book called "Shattering the Myths of Darwinism" by Richard Milton. He is a science journalist who has written for the Times and leading scientific journals. He has not written the book because of any religious beliefs but because he objects to the Theory of Evolution being taught as fact when the scientific evidence does not support it. Again, much of his evidence against evolution supports the idea of a universal flood.

There is much that can be read on this subject and, once again, I would encourage you at some stage to find some of the excellent books that deal with it. For now, we will just look at the evidence in three areas of science and compare it to the scientific theories and the account in Genesis.

How Old is the Earth?

According to the Big Bang theory and evolution, the earth is said to be about 4,600 million years old. But if God made the earth in six days with man being created on the sixth day then it cannot be more than 6–10,000 years old.

The main evidence put forward to support the idea that the earth is very old comes from a number of different dating methods which are used to determine the age of rocks and fossils. All rely on the assumption that the chemical composition of the environment has been constant over time. Carbon dating, for example, assumes that the amount of radioactive Carbon in the atmosphere has remained constant over the years. Richard Milton questions the accuracy of a number of dating methods.

Carbon dating, which is probably the best known, has produced some very interesting results. A rock painting found in the South African bush was dated at 1,200 years old until a local art teacher recognised it as being produced in her art class! Some living shellfish were also tested and found to be 2,300 years old. Such incidents clearly

---

[2] The Genesis Flood is published by the Baker Publishing Group.

Day 7 – Noah and the Flood

undermine the credibility of the method but it is still held to be accurate. The underlying assumption that the amount of radioactive Carbon in the atmosphere is constant is also untrue. It is actually increasing and its rate of increase indicates that the earth's atmosphere may be only about 10,000 years old! In Hawaii, the Potassium–Argon dating method has been used on volcanic rocks and dated them at about 3 billion years old. In fact they are known to be from an eruption 190 years ago.

It is also interesting to note that if geologists are unsure of the age of a rock they refer to the palaeontologists – people who study fossils – to date the fossils contained in the rock. However, palaeontologists date many fossils from the rocks they are found in! The two disciplines feed off one another.

So, dating methods do not provide unequivocal evidence that the earth is billions of years old and it is not unreasonable to believe that the Bible is true.

What does Geology tell us?

Geological theory suggests that the layers of rock found on the earth's surface were laid down slowly and uniformly. This theory, called "Uniformitarian Geology" is a cornerstone of evolution. Over the millions of years, layers of sediment were laid down gradually – on average at the rate of about 1mm/year. Some of the animals and plants that died became fossils as they were buried in this sediment. Different types of rocks were laid down at different times and are named after the periods they were laid down in, e.g. Cambrian, Devonian, Jurassic. According to Genesis the earth was subject to a catastrophic flood. There was heavy rain for 40 days, which resulted in the whole surface of the world being covered with water. All life on land, apart from those animals in the ark, was wiped out.

These are two very different ideas, but what does the study of geology tell us? Firstly, *"some three quarters of the Earth's land mass is covered by successive layers of sedimentary rocks – that is, rocks like the chalk laid down under water and sometimes enclosing fossils."* (Richard Milton in Shattering the Myths of Darwinism[C]). This implies that the formation of such rocks is commonplace but in fact *"observations of modern geological processes show, however, that nowhere today are there rocks being formed anything like those in the geological column."*[D]. The evidence suggests that large scale flood conditions unlike anything known today were present over most of the earth in the past.

But what of the length of time we are told it takes to lay down layers of rock? From 1985 a French geologist called Guy Berthault has carried out experiments in large tanks of water to see what happens when different sediments are added. What he has shown is that with the right sediments layers of rock form almost instantaneously[3]. These results have support from the evidence of natural disasters such as the volcanic eruption at Mount St Helens in Washington State USA in 1980 which produced many layers of rock which were cut through by rivers in a matter of months. A canyon 1/40th the size of the Grand Canyon was formed demonstrating that it does not have to take millions of years for such features to develop.

So, once again, geological evidence, as opposed to theory, is not at odds with the Biblical account.

What about Fossils?

Evolution teaches that as plants and animals died they were slowly covered by mud and became fossils over long periods as they were subject to increasing pressure. But many fossils show signs of having been buried very rapidly. *"The detail and completeness with which many fossil specimens are preserved (the eyes of the trilobite, the scales of fish and even the skin of dinosaurs) is a clear indication that the creatures were rapidly buried under considerable depths of sediment. The very size of some specimens, such as the larger land–living dinosaurs, makes it absurd to suppose that they could have been preserved in a few millimeters of sediment"*[E].

'Fossil Graveyards' provide another puzzle for geologists. One is in a range of hills in northern India called the Siwalik hills: *"The hills, some 2,000 to 3,000 feet high and several hundred miles long, ... contain extraordinarily rich beds crammed with fossils: hundreds of feet of sediment, packed with the jumbled bones of scores of extinct species. Many of the creatures were remarkable; including a tortoise 20 feet long and a species of elephant with tusks 14 feet long and 3 feet in circumference. Other animals commonly found include pigs, rhinoceroses, apes and oxen. Most of the species whose fossils are found are today extinct, including some thirty species of elephant of which only one has survived in India. Beds of this sort are common in*

---

[3] Guy Berthault's experiments are described in "Shattering the Myths of Darwinism" pages 77–78.

Day 7 – Noah and the Flood

the geological record. ... These animals must have been killed by some singular event over a relatively short space of time, and an event which took place on land. And whatever the nature of the event, it resulted not only in catastrophic extinction of many species but also the formation of beds of sediment thousands of feet thick."[F]

The *facts* about geology and fossils provide the strongest evidence for a catastrophic world wide flood which supports the Biblical account of the world.

Does it Matter?

Science cannot prove either the theory of evolution or the Biblical account of creation. What I have attempted to show is that believing the Bible is not at odds with the evidence of science around us. But the way we think about where we came from has a fundamental effect on how we view ourselves, the world we live in, of God and of what the Bible teaches us about him.

Evolution teaches that man is the result of a series of accidents, a link from nothing to something which is getting better and better. If there is a God he appears disinterested in his "creation" which is developing in random steps. But according to the early chapters of Genesis man is the pinnacle of God's creation and is made in God's image. Man is so important that the decay we see in the world around us is a direct result of man's disobedience to God. But most amazing of all, God, far from being disinterested, is intimately involved with his creation and wants a close relationship with the people he has created.

Jesus had no problem with referring to Noah as a historical figure (see Matthew 24:37–38) and used the flood as a warning of the disaster that will come on those who do not believe in him when he returns to earth again, this time in judgement. Given the widespread belief now that the world begun billions of years ago it is hard for people to believe that God will one day suddenly step in and bring the world to an abrupt end. As Peter warned in the New Testament, people will come in the last days who will scoff at the idea that Jesus will come again and that the world will end saying, *"Where is this 'coming' he promised? Ever since our fathers died, everything goes on as it has since the beginning of creation." (2 Peter 3:4).* This is a perfect description of Uniformitarian Geology – evolution is mentioned in the Bible! – and of the way we are taught to think about the past and the future today. Peter's judgement of people who preach such views is that *"they deliberately forget that long ago by God's word the heavens existed* and the earth was formed out of water and by water. By these waters also the world of that time was deluged and destroyed." (2 Peter 3:5–6) and he warns that God will judge the earth and destroy it soon.

And finally, if evolution is right then what value should we put on people's lives? If people are an accident then why should it matter if I hurt someone, exploit them, or even kill them? If they are weaker than I am then surely they have no right to survive anyway! But Genesis teaches us that every human being is created by God in his image. When I look at a fellow human being I see someone of infinite value and I will be held accountable to their creator for the way I treat them. Thank God that our society still, in the main, holds to Biblical principles despite its belief in evolution.

This is a vast but important subject. At the end of the day both creation and evolution require faith to believe them. For now let us accept the message of these chapters that God is not a disinterested creator who has walked away from the world he made but remains involved to the extent that he will punish wickedness and reward righteousness.

References

[C] *Shattering the Myths of Darwinism* by Richard Milton, Park Street Press, a division of Inner Traditions International, Rochester, Vermont. © 1992, 1997 by Richard Milton. p. 68. Used with permission in the US and Canada.
British Commonwealth rights granted by 4th Estate in the UK where the book is published under the title *The Facts of Life*. © Richard Milton 1992.

[D] *Shattering the Myths of Darwinism*. p. 72.

[E] *Shattering the Myths of Darwinism*. p. 79.

[F] *Shattering the Myths of Darwinism*. p. 93.

Day 8
God Chooses a Man

After the Flood

When Noah and his family came out of the Ark God establishes a covenant with them. A covenant is a promise and in this case it is an unconditional promise from God never to flood the earth again. As a sign of that covenant God sets the rainbow in the sky, an indication that there was no rain before the flood.

> Read Genesis 9

The Tower of Babel

Genesis 10 contains lists of the descendants of Noah's sons and the nations that were descended from them. In general terms Japheth's descendants moved north–west into Europe, Ham's moved south into Canaan and Africa, and Shem's went east into Asia. The reason for the scattering of the nations is given at the start of Genesis 11 in the account of the Tower of Babel.

As mankind increased they initially stayed together and decided to build a tower, which may have been a Ziggurat or pagan temple, as a central focus for their unity. God saw that there was nothing that man planned to do that would be impossible for them. It is not clear exactly what that means but the basic message is that men have great power, for good or evil, when they are united together. God defeated man's plans by introducing languages. Up until that time all of mankind spoke the same language. At this point people began to speak a variety of languages, which meant that they could not understand one another. This is what led to people being scattered and different people groups forming. Anyone who has been to an international conference will know that language remains a major barrier to communication between people. If all the world's scientists could pool their languages then what could be achieved?

As another aside on the argument over Evolution and Creation, it should be noted that the development of language in humans presents a specific issue for evolutionists. The argument that language steadily developed from grunts and cries into the sophisticated languages we use today is not borne out by a study of languages as it is the oldest languages which are the most complex. Ancient languages such as Vedic Sanskrit, which were in use around 1500BC, demonstrate incredible complexity with hundreds of thousands of forms for their verbs. These became greatly simplified in Classical Sanskrit which was used around 500BC to 1000AD. Greek and Latin present far more complexity than modern languages such as English which have evolved from them. Most modern English verbs have less than a dozen possible forms, e.g. do, dost, does, did, didst, done, doing, and these are continuing to be simplified. The path of evolution in languages is clearly from complexity to simplicity which supports the Biblical account of what happened at the Tower of Babel.

Did Men Really Live that Long?

> **Read Genesis 11:10–32**

In Genesis 5 the genealogy from Adam to Noah records a series of men who lived around 900 years. Many people point to things like these ages for men recorded in the Bible as evidence that it is not true, it is merely made up stories. Others try and bring it in line with our current experience. I remember a Religious Studies teacher telling us that the 'years' used in Genesis 5 were shorter than our years by a factor of about 10. So, when it says that Methuselah lived 969 'years' this means that he lived to almost 97 in current years. This sounds reasonable until you read that Enoch had lived 65 'years' when he became the father of Methuselah, or about 6½ in current years! It is better to take Biblical history at face value than to try and bend it to our own understanding.

In the genealogy recording the descendants of Shem in Genesis 11 it is interesting to note that in eight generations the ages decrease from 600 to around 200. Throughout the rest of Genesis ages continue to fall to nearer the 100 mark. This indicates that something fundamental has changed about the world following the flood. In "The Genesis Flood" Whitcomb and Morris propose that the separation of water above and below the sky as described in Genesis 1:6–7 refers to the creation of a canopy of water around the earth rather like the Ozone layer there today. This would have had a greenhouse effect on the whole earth and so maintained a much warmer temperature across the whole earth, which explains why fossils around the world all come from temperate climates. It would have also reduced radiation reaching the earth's

Day 8 – God Chooses a Man

surface. They quote from research into the effects of radiation on ageing which shows that exposure to radiation has a marked affect on lifespan as well as general health. The rapid decrease in the age of men after the flood could be accounted for both by the increase in radiation and the introduction of temperature fluctuations brought about by the loss of the water canopy.

Once again we see that it is not necessary to deny the accuracy of Biblical history to fit with scientific *evidence* even if it is in conflict with some scientific *theories*.

The First 11 Chapters of Genesis

The first 11 chapters of Genesis cover a huge amount of material. They provide us with an understanding of God, ourselves and of the world around us. They contain answers to the questions about where we came from and why we are here and give us insight into why sin, pain and suffering are in the world today. However, they also leave many questions unanswered. Jewish Rabbis say that studying these chapters can send a man mad because of the questions it raises!

What is God's Plan Now?

Following the flood mankind degenerates in the same way as before. As people increase so sin multiplies. Once again it seems that God goes quiet as we read very little of his activity in the hundreds of years following the flood. Has his plan changed following the flood? During creation God blessed his creation and, in particular, mankind. To bless means to want the best for, to make happy and successful. God wanted the very best for mankind and his whole creation. After the flood God blessed Noah and his sons. His plan had not changed. He still wanted to bless the whole world. God also created mankind for relationship with him. When Adam and Eve sinned it wasn't just them who missed their evening walks with God in the garden, God missed them too! Before the flood God had special relationships with Enoch and with Noah. God works his plans out through his relationship with individuals.

After many years of silence God intervenes in history again by choosing a man. He is not looking for someone to live in awesome fear of him but someone to be his friend. All the way through the Bible God is looking for friends. Why does he want people to multiply and fill the earth? He wants lots of friends.

At the end of Genesis 11 we are introduced to a man named Abram who lived in a city called Ur. We learn from Joshua 24:2 that Abram was brought up to worship other gods but somehow God spoke to him. It would be fascinating to know how he recognised God's voice but we are not told that. In Genesis 12:1 we read that God called him to leave his country, the people he had grown up among and his family and go to a distant land. This required a step of faith as great as Noah's – the route of his journey is shown in Map 1 opposite.

What is God's purpose in calling Abram? In the next two verses God makes him an amazing promise that Abram will become a great nation and that all the peoples on earth would be blessed through him. God's purpose is to bless the whole world and he has chosen to do it through the descendants of this one man, Abram.

> **Read Genesis 12**

Abram in Canaan

When Abram reaches the land of Canaan, which we know today as Israel, God promises that he will give this land to Abram's offspring (see verse 7). But Abram himself lives the rest of his life as a nomad in Canaan. He lives in tents and moves around without ever owning land himself (apart from one field as we will see later).

Genesis 12–14 relates some incidents from Abram's early life in the land of Canaan. There is the first story about his wife Sarai who, according to Jewish tradition, was one of the three most beautiful women in the Bible along with Bathsheba and Esther. In this story her beauty is so talked about that she is taken into a king's harem which is remarkable considering that she was about 65 at the time! There are also incidents from the life of Abram's nephew Lot who accompanies Abram to Canaan but then goes to live in Sodom where he gets into various troubles.

God's purpose has not been thrown off course by the flood. He still wants to have a relationship with man and to see man blessed and he has chosen to do this through his chosen man Abram.

Day 8 – God Chooses a Man

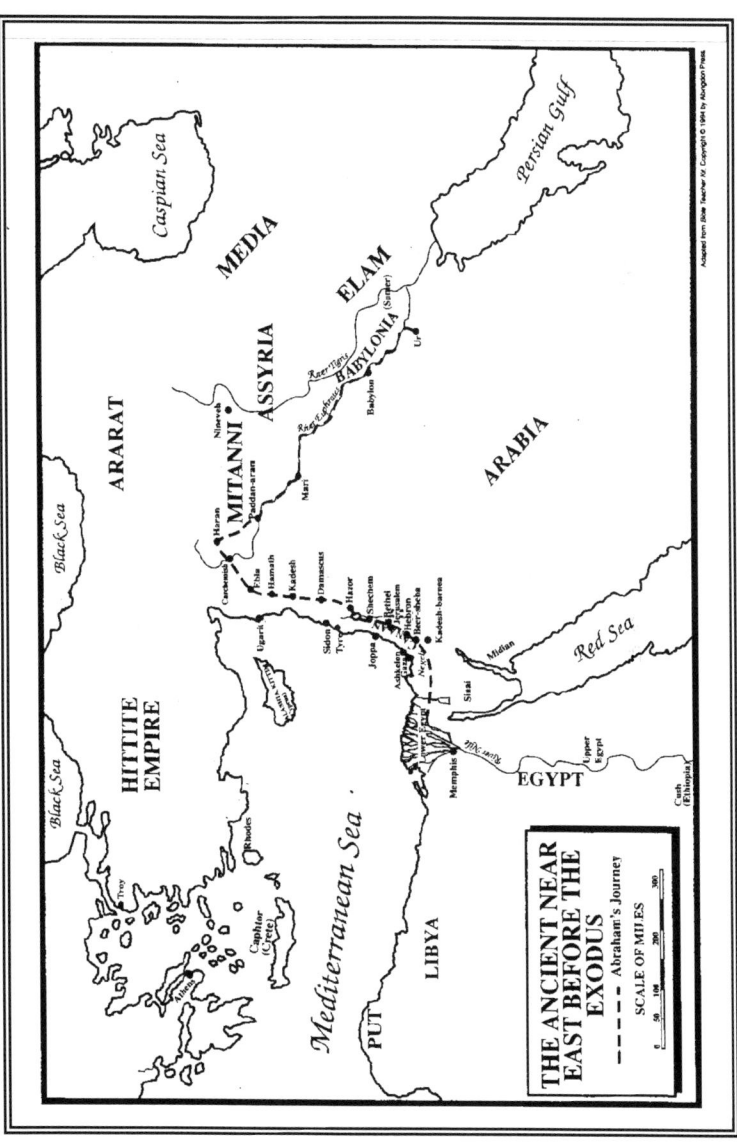

Map 1 – Abraham's Journey

Day 9
Abraham, God's Friend

As we saw yesterday, after the end of chapter 11 the focus of Genesis moves from the whole world to one man, Abram, who later became Abraham. The rest of Genesis is the story of this one man and his descendants. Timechart 1 on page 10 gives a rough outline of the events of Genesis.

> *Read Genesis 15*

God's Covenant with Abram – The Land of Canaan

After Abram has been in the land of Canaan for some time God speaks to him in a vision and makes a covenant with him to give his descendants the land of Canaan. In Genesis 15 God tells Abram to take some animals, cut them in half and put the halves in separate lines and, when Abram had fallen into a deep sleep he sees a *"smoking brazier with a smoking torch"* moving between the pieces.

This appears mysterious to us today but in Abram's time when two men wanted to make a legally binding covenant with one another they took animals, slaughtered them, and walked between the halves. The words translated *"made a covenant"* in Genesis 15:18 literally mean "cut a covenant" referring to the animals being cut in two. (In Jeremiah 34:18 the same word is translated "made" and "cut" in one sentence.) This was God's way of demonstrating to Abram his total commitment to his promise. Note that only God walked between the animals though. This covenant did not require anything from Abram. The covenant was unconditional and so cannot be broken. Abram's descendants will always own the land we now know as Israel.

Abram's Faith

From a human point of view there was a serious problem with God's commitment. The promise was that the land was given to Abram's descendants. But, although he was 75 and had been married for many years, he and Sarai had no children. At the beginning of Genesis 15 Abram questioned God as to who would inherit his estate, let alone the land, and God tells him that his own son will be his heir. God then shows him the stars and tells him that his descendants will outnumber

Day 9 – Abraham, God's Friend

them.

Not only is God's commitment amazing but Abram's response is also amazing. Genesis 15:6 tells us that *"Abram believed the LORD, and he credited it to him as righteousness."* God rewards faith. He loves it when people believe what he says. Abram's faith is held up as a shining example in the New Testament and this verse is quoted in three letters – Romans, Galatians, and James – as an illustration of how men are justified before God by their faith.

Abram's lack of Faith

Despite God renewing the promise to Abram that he would have a son, *ten years* pass without Abram having a child! In Genesis 16 Abram is 85 and Sarai, who must have felt a deep sense of failure in not producing this promised son, loses patience and gives her maidservant Hagar to Abram to be a surrogate mother. It was a traditional custom of the time that maidservants could be used to provide an heir for a wife who has not produced a son. Sarai was not suggesting an immoral act within their culture but it was a sign of unbelief in God's promise.

The result was that Hagar produced a son called Ishmael. He became the ancestor of many nations who have been hostile to Israel throughout history. Today, the Arab nations count Abraham as their father as they are descended from him through Ishmael.

After Ishmael was born there are two verses which can be read very quickly but which speak volumes about what has happened. Genesis 16:16 and 17:1 read *"Abram was eighty–six years old when Hagar bore him Ishmael. When Abram was ninety–nine years old, the LORD appeared to him and said ..."* God fell silent for *13 years* after Abram and Sarai gave up on his promise and took matters into their own hands. But he did not give up on them. When he speaks again it is to renew the covenant once again.

The lives of men and women in the Bible are recorded for our instruction and encouragement. We all make mistakes and must live with the consequences but it is very encouraging to find that, although God may fall silent for periods of time, he does not give up on those he has chosen. We are impatient and want everything to happen now but he will fulfil his promises in his own time.

Abraham – Father of Many

When God speaks in Genesis 17 it is to renew the covenant with Abram. This time, to confirm it yet again, God tells him to change his name from Abram, which means "Exalted Father", to Abraham, which means, "Father of Many"! Imagine the embarrassment Abram would have felt when talking to his friends and asking them to now call him Abraham. "Why have you changed it?" they'd ask while they would have been thinking, "This new name means father of many and you only have one son!"

God now puts a definite time on the promise and tells Abraham that he and Sarah (her name was also changed) will have a son next year. He also introduces the covenant of circumcision. This is the sign of a conditional promise God makes to Abraham and his descendants. God will play his part – see the *"As for me"* in verse 4 – as long as Abraham and his descendants play their part – see the *"As for you"* in verse 9 – to walk before him and be blameless. This covenant is passed down to the Israelites through the law.

Abraham's relationship with God is remarkable. When God tells him to circumcise his household his response is to do it *"on that very day" (Genesis 17:23)*. He is a man of great faith and obedience.

Then in Genesis 18 God himself visits Abraham with two angels and again restates that Sarah will have a child in a year's time. Initially Abraham just sees three men who he invites to stop for something to eat but as the story unfolds it becomes apparent that one is God himself. Whether this was Jesus or God the Father we are not told but the scripture is happy to refer to this person as 'the LORD' in his conversation with Abraham. This is one of a number of times in the Old Testament when God appeared to men and women in human form before the time of Jesus. Theologians call it a "Theophany" from the Greek words meaning "an appearance of God".

Genesis 19 deals with the destruction of Sodom and Gomorrah. God, the Judge of all the earth, finds the wickedness of these cities so great that he destroys them.

Abraham is Tested

In Genesis 21 Isaac, the long awaited son, is finally born. Abraham, who is now 100, and Sarah, who is 90, have the son they have been waiting for. All should now be plain sailing!

Read Genesis 22

After all this time waiting for a son Genesis 22 comes as a shock. Having got the son Abraham is now asked to sacrifice him. Again, to us, this appears a horrific thing. If God told you to sacrifice your child what would you think? Again, in the culture Abraham lived this wasn't an unusual thing. Child sacrifice was part of the religious practices of the nations he lived among. Throughout the Old Testament there are references to other nations sacrificing children to their gods. Later in the books of the law there are clear references forbidding this practice (see for example Deuteronomy 18:10).

Once again we find that Abraham obeys very quickly. He responds to God's word in verse 2 by setting off *"early the next morning"* in verse 3. Even though he is being asked to do the most costly thing possible he is quick to obey. But whereas many of us might respond impulsively to the call of God and then go back on it in the cold light of day Abraham is also a man of determination. Verse four tells us that they travelled for at least three days before Abraham had to carry out the act of killing Isaac. His obedience to God is absolute.

When they can see their destination Abraham tells the servants to wait while he and Isaac go on to "worship". One of the rules of theology is the rule of "the first mention" – the first time a word or topic is referred to has special significance. This is the first time the word "worship" is used in the Bible and it is instructive to note that Abraham is not talking about singing a few songs: he is referring to giving up the most important thing in his whole world by sacrificing his son. The next time you are in "a time of worship" or "singing a worship song" remember that the first time this word is mentioned in the Bible it refers to a man sacrificing the most precious thing he had in the world. Worship is about giving everything to God.

Another interesting connection is that the place where Abraham went to sacrifice Isaac was Mount Moriah, which later became the site of the Temple. Mount Moriah is now in present day Jerusalem and is occupied by the golden "Dome of the Rock", an impressive Mosque constructed in AD 691 which contains a large outcrop of rock which is held to be the traditional site of the intended sacrifice of Isaac.

Abraham – What a Man! What a God!!

Abraham had an incredible relationship with God. Later in the Bible he is referred to as *"the Friend of God."* (see 2 Chronicles 20:7 and Isaiah 41:8). God is not looking to find people who will live in a distant fear of him but is looking for people who he can have a relationship with. When God is about to destroy Sodom and Gomorrah God says, *"Shall I hide from Abraham what I am about to do?" (Genesis 18:17)*. In the same way as we share our secrets with our friends so God shares his thoughts with his friend Abraham.

Abraham was a man of great faith. In the New Testament Hebrews 11 is a famous chapter which lists the men and women of faith in the Old Testament and it is no surprise that gets the longest section is devoted to Abraham. Hebrews 11:8–12 and 17–19 shows that his whole life was based on faith. He was promised the land for his descendants but the only piece of Israel he ever owned was the field of Machpelah in which he buried Sarah. He believed what God had said to him without any evidence that it would come to pass.

What a man!

But what a God!!

God chose this one man, made a covenant with him and, despite all his faults and failings, God kept to his word. The Bible is not afraid to record the failings of its heroes and through these we see the grace of God who is prepared to be a friend to sinful men like us.

What has this to do with us?

The promise of God's covenant was to Abraham and his descendants. What relevance does that have to those of us who are not Jews?

In the New Testament it is made very clear that the true descendants of Abraham are those who believe. Jesus was very strong on this point with the Jews of his day. They were relying on being the descendants of Abraham for their security but Jesus made it clear that their salvation required them to do as Abraham did rather than just be his descendants (see John 8:33, 39).

Paul, a Jew, argues the same point in his letters that the true descendants of Abraham are those who believe the promises of God, not his biological descendants. Galatians 3:6–9 sums up his argument: *"Consider Abraham: "He believed God, and it was credited to him as righteousness." Understand, then, that those who believe are children of Abraham. The Scripture foresaw that God would justify the Gentiles by faith, and announced the gospel in advance to Abraham: "All nations will be blessed through you." So those who have faith are blessed along with Abraham, the man of faith."* It is the Gentiles, those not descended from Abraham biologically, who inherit the blessing that God gave to Abraham. (Paul makes the same point in Romans 4:16–17 and 9:6–8.) These promises are for us who, by faith, become children of Abraham.

Day 10
Isaac, Jacob and Sons

Isaac – The Promised Son

All the promises that God made to Abraham were passed on to Isaac, the promised son, and from him they were passed to his son Jacob. Throughout the Bible God is referred to as the God of Abraham, Isaac and Jacob and the Israelites look back to Abraham, Isaac and Jacob as their fathers. But although both Abraham and Jacob are written about in their own right Isaac is always referred to alongside the others. In Genesis his story is sandwiched in between that of Abraham and Jacob. They both get about 11 chapters each; he only gets 1 to himself plus a few bits and pieces.

This reflects the fact that Isaac's life was moulded by his parents and his children. It was 25 years from the time Abraham and Sarah received the promise of a son to when Isaac was born and, as can sometimes happen with parents who have waited a long time for a child, he was spoilt and cosseted as a result. Then somewhere in his early teens his father almost sacrificed him! This would have had a profound impact on any young life. In Genesis 24 we find that Isaac is 40 and unmarried but it is Abraham who sends his chief servant to get a wife for him.

In among all this we do see evidence that Isaac developed his own faith in God. It is first seen in Genesis 25 where his wife, Rebekah, is unable to have children. Isaac prays and, 20 years into their marriage, they have twins, Esau and Jacob. Then in Genesis 26:2–6 the Lord appears to Isaac and passes the covenant and promise on to Isaac. He responds by building an altar and *"calling on the name of the LORD" (Genesis 26:25)*.

Before the twins are born God gives Rebekah a prophecy about them (see Genesis 25:23) which indicates that it is the younger one who will be the strong one and to whom the promise will pass. Throughout the Bible it is clear that God is sovereign and he has the right to choose whoever he wants to choose. In Romans 9:10–16 Paul makes it clear that God's choice of Jacob, the younger twin, over his brother is not a sign that God is unjust but rather that he is merciful. He does not have to choose any of us. His choice of Jacob is an act of mercy – something that becomes very evident as we look at his life!

Jacob – The Deceiver

Jacob's story runs from Genesis 25–35 and the theme that runs through it is deceit! When he was born he came into the world grasping his brother Esau's heel and his name means "he grasps the heel" or, in figurative terms, "the deceiver". Throughout his life we find him deceiving others and being deceived in return.

Isaac and Rebekah's twins are a complete contrast. Esau is a "man's man". He loved the outdoor life and excelled at hunting. Isaac loved Esau's adventurous spirit – so different from his own pampered upbringing. Jacob on the other hand is described as *"a quiet man, staying among the tents"* who was doted on by his mother. It doesn't look as if the "mummy's boy" got many party invitations!

Jacob's scheming nature is seen early on when he takes advantage of Esau's tiredness to buy the birthright from him. Esau in his exhaustion agrees to hand over the double portion of their father's estate to Jacob in exchange for some bread and stew! Having tricked his brother, Jacob goes one step further in Genesis 27 and tricks his father into giving him the blessing. The birthright gave him a double portion of property; the blessing made him the senior member of the household after his father died – note the expression *"lord over your brothers"* in verse 29. These were not just nice words. In their culture they had legal significance and not even Isaac himself can undo them. All Jacob's other deceiving is put into the shade by this act of deceit and Rebekah's part in it is just as disturbing. The consequences go on throughout his life.

> **Read Genesis 27:1–40**

Jacob presents us with some difficult issues. It is clear that God chose him ahead of his brother before they were born so does that justify his actions? Clearly not. God does not need us to undertake sinful acts to help him fulfil his promises. Without any help from Jacob he could have worked things out. As it was Jacob suffered from the consequences of his actions and God used these circumstances to teach him lessons.

Esau, who has not taken his birthright seriously, is both devastated by what Jacob has done and extremely angry. We are not told how normal family life continued after this episode but Esau was prepared to wait

Day 10 – Isaac, Jacob and Sons

his time until Isaac died and he could take revenge on Jacob by killing him. Rebekah gets to hear of this and protects her favourite son by sending him to his uncle Laban for safekeeping.

Amazingly it is at this point that God reveals himself to Jacob and renews the promise given to Abraham and Isaac to give the land to Jacob's descendants (see Genesis 28:13–14). Jacob's response indicates that he has yet to know God properly. Jacob, the schemer, has the audacity to make a bargain with God – take note of his conditional offer to God at the end of this passage (Genesis 28:20–22)!

> **Read Genesis 27:41—28:22**

Jacob Meets his Match!

Genesis 29–31 tells the story of Jacob's time with his Uncle Laban. God shows his discipline (or is it his sense of humour?) in the way he uses Laban to show Jacob what it is like to be deceived. Laban is even more accomplished in the art of deception than Jacob is.

As soon as Jacob arrives at Laban's town he falls in love with his beautiful daughter Rachel and demonstrates the strength of his love by willingly working for Laban for seven years in return for her hand in marriage. The seven years flash by – *"they seemed like only a few days to him because of his love for her" (Genesis 29:20)* – and then the marriage takes place. However, after the wedding celebrations he wakes up the next morning to find out that he has married Rachel's older sister Leah whose looks are summed up in the enigmatic expression *"Leah had weak eyes"*. Laban makes no apology for his action but strikes a new deal with Jacob to work another seven years for Rachel. At least this time he gets payment in advance!

After those seven years are completed Jacob works for Laban in exchange for livestock. They agree that Jacob will get all the speckled and spotted animals. Laban tricks Jacob by removing any he finds from the flocks while Jacob tricks Laban by some interesting experiments with the breeding animals – an early attempt at genetic engineering! Through all this we learn that despite Jacob's trickery it is God who is watching over him and it is he who causes Jacob to prosper (see Genesis 31:10–13). After 20 years with Laban God then calls Jacob to return to the Promised Land.

Jacob becomes Israel

As Jacob returns to Canaan he is very fearful of meeting his brother

Esau again so he sends messengers ahead with gifts. But before he meets Esau he has a far more important encounter with God himself.

In one of those mysterious stories from the Old Testament we read that *"Jacob was left alone, and a man wrestled with him till daybreak" (Genesis 32:24)*. God appeared to Jacob in human form and wrestled with him. Jacob has spent his whole life wrestling with others, first Esau then Laban, but he now meets one he cannot beat. God wins this contest and leaves Jacob permanently wounded to remind him of the one he cannot outwit. But Jacob will not let God go until he has got his blessing. God responds by changing his name, taking away the name of Jacob, the deceiver, and replacing it with Israel, which means, "he struggles with God" (see Genesis 32:28).

When reading the Bible it is important to realise that the two names – Jacob and Israel – refer to the same man. For the rest of Genesis the writer uses the names interchangeably, sometimes switching between them from verse to verse. In the rest of the Bible the name Israel is more clearly associated with the nation that descended from him, in fact the rest of the Old Testament is the story of Israel – the nation that struggled with God – but, just to confuse us, sometimes the nation is referred to as Jacob in poetic writings, either on its own, e.g. *"You showed favour to your land, O LORD; you restored the fortunes of Jacob" (Psalm 85:1)*, or alongside Israel, e.g. *"The Lord has sent a message against Jacob; it will fall on Israel." (Isaiah 9:8)*.

In Genesis 33 Jacob meets up with Esau again and finds to his relief that he is very kind to him. This doesn't stop him immediately deceiving him again – with Jacob it is a way of life! With this hurdle out of the way Jacob builds an altar to God and, for the first time in his life, acknowledges God as *his* God by calling it "God the God of Israel". Then in chapter 35 he returns to Bethel where God had revealed himself to him all those years before and builds an altar there. Once again God passes on the promise given to Abraham and Isaac to him and once again God gives him the new name of Israel.

The Fruit of Deceit

The Bible teaches that we reap what we sow – *"those who sow trouble reap it" (Job 4:8)* – and the story of Jacob is a fine illustration of this. Having deceived others he is deceived by Laban into marrying Leah and ends up with two wives who have great rivalry. Leah is blessed by bearing him six sons but knows that she does not have the love of her husband. Rachel has his adoration but for a long time is childless.

Eventually she has two sons by her maidservant before having one of her own, Joseph. Later she dies giving birth to her second son, Benjamin. With Leah's maidservant also having two sons Jacob has 12 sons in all.

Jacob does not appear to have read the right books on bringing up children. His sons are not shining examples of godly living and are a source of grief to him. Genesis records how the oldest tries to become head of the household before his father dies by sleeping with one of his father's maidservants; the next two deceive and murder an entire Canaanite town and the fourth is involved with a prostitute.

But where Jacob reaps the worst fruit of deceit is in the loss of his favourite son Joseph. His ten oldest sons sell Joseph into slavery and deceive their father about it for 20 years! We will be looking at the story of Joseph over the next two days but from Jacob's perspective the deceit of his sons was the cruellest act that anyone could do to him. He truly reaped what he sowed.

The God of Jacob

When we looked at Abraham we saw an amazing man of faith. He had his faults but I'm sure any of us would welcome him into our church as a real asset. His son Isaac was a quiet man but one who responded to God and, again, we would not be embarrassed to have him among us. With Jacob the story is different. If Jacob, the deceiver, applied to join your church would you welcome him in the same way? What a man!

But once again we marvel at his God. When God appeared to Moses in the desert he calls himself *"the God of Abraham, the God of Isaac and the God of Jacob" (Exodus 3:15)*. God is not afraid to associate himself with this man and to be known as his God. If God is prepared to be the God of Jacob then there is hope for a sinner like me too!

"I will sing praise to the God of Jacob" (Psalm 75:9). What a God! He's a God worth knowing.

Day 11
Joseph – Dreamer to Prime Minister

God's Strategy – A Nation for Himself

When God chose Abraham he told him that he would give his descendants the land of Canaan. But when Abraham arrived he did not find a deserted landscape waiting for occupation. There were many groups living there: the Hittites, the Perizzites, the Amorites, the Girgashites and a number of other 'ites' listed at the end of Genesis 15. These people, sometimes collectively referred to as the Canaanites, were very wicked in the time that Abraham lived. They believed in many gods and their "worship" included child sacrifice, religious prostitution and occult practices.

Throughout the time of Abraham, Isaac and Jacob the Canaanites posed a threat to God's chosen people. This was not a threat to their physical safety, but rather that as God's people mixed with them they became drawn into their sinful ways. Abraham's nephew Lot went and lived in Sodom which ended in ruin (both for him and the city); Esau married Hittite women who were "a source of grief" to Isaac and Rebekah; Jacob's daughter was raped and his sons took revenge by wiping out an entire town. If God was to make them into a holy nation, a people separated from the sin of the world and ready to serve him wholeheartedly, he had to take them to a place where they had little contact with other people. The answer was for them to go to Egypt where social and religious customs restricted the locals from mixing with them.

The story that describes how the Israelites moved to Egypt is one of the best known and most moving of stories in the Bible. The central character is Joseph, the first son born to Jacob by his beloved wife Rachel. Although the youngest but one of Jacob's sons, Joseph is the only one to demonstrate an awareness of God and a moral integrity and it is he who emerges as the leader in his generation. His story starts in Genesis 37 and takes up the majority of the narrative until the end of the book and we will spend two days reading it through.

Day 11 – Joseph – Dreamer to Prime Minister 73

Joseph the Dreamer

In Genesis 37 we are introduced to Joseph as a teenager. As the oldest son of his favourite wife Rachel, who died giving birth to his younger brother Benjamin, Jacob completely spoilt Joseph. While his older brothers work hard in the fields Joseph struts around in a *"richly ornamented robe"* given to him by his father and lords it over them. But God has a special purpose for Joseph's life and Joseph has some strange dreams. As the story develops we find that God gives Joseph the gift of interpreting dreams but these first dreams are so easy that anyone could see the explanation: one day Joseph's brothers and father will bow down to him.

It would be nice to think that when God gives someone a gift he also gives them the maturity to use it wisely. But that is not always true. The Bible has many stories of people given gifting beyond their wisdom. Although this may seem dangerous it is also fortunate because if God had to wait until we were mature before he gave us gifts to bless others, we might all have to wait a long time! As Paul teaches in Romans 12, having a gifting from God is a sign of God's grace, not a sign of any merit on our part.

Joseph demonstrated great immaturity with his gift and instead of keeping the interpretation of his dream to himself he announced it over the dinner table! Needless to say, being told that they would one day bow down to Joseph did not go down well with his brothers, but he failed to notice and repeated his mistake a little while later. His brothers already had an intense dislike for their kid brother, who, unlike them, could do no wrong in the eyes of their father, but this now turned to pure hatred. An opportunity to get even came and they decided to kill him. Reuben, the oldest, just managed to save his life and instead they sold him to some passing slave traders who were on their way to Egypt.

The brothers then returned home and told their father a story about Joseph being killed by a wild animal. Jacob was distraught with grief but not one of the ten brothers told him the truth. As time went on and "normal life" resumed, all ten kept the secret about what had happened to themselves and for the next twenty years let their broken–hearted father grieve for his favourite son without saying a word!

We pick up the story in Genesis 39 when Joseph arrives in Egypt.

Read Genesis 39:1–41:40

God's Strategy – A Man for Himself

When God chose Joseph to be the ruler over his brothers anyone could see that he would need to gain a lot of maturity before he was ready to handle such responsibility. Although it only takes a short time to read Genesis 39–41 it actually covers over twenty years (compare Genesis 37:2 with 41:46 and 41:53–54). When God chooses a man he is not afraid to spend time preparing him for responsibility. The letter of James in the New Testament starts with the words *"Consider it pure joy, my brothers, whenever you face trials of many kinds, because you know that the testing of your faith develops perseverance. Perseverance must finish its work so that you may be mature and complete, not lacking anything." (James 1:2–4)*. Joseph spent twenty years developing perseverance and growing in maturity!

Perseverance is all about not giving up. The setbacks that Joseph had were enough to make anyone give up: discovering that your brothers hate you enough to kill you; being sold into slavery from a life of luxury; being wrongly imprisoned for rape; being forgotten for two years by someone who owed you a debt of gratitude. But instead of seeing a man complaining about his circumstances we find him working hard in his master's house and in the prison. He came to the attention of his master, the prison warder, and finally Pharaoh himself because of his abilities in administration and the interpreting of dreams but all three noted that "the Lord was with him" and that was what set him apart.

One of the characteristics that Joseph had was a fear of God. Proverbs 15:33 says that *"The fear of the LORD teaches a man wisdom"* and we see evidence of this in Joseph's behaviour. When Potiphar's wife approached him he responded by saying *"How then could I do such a wicked thing and sin against God?" (Genesis 39:9)*. It was his fear of God, even more than his fear of Potiphar that stopped him sinning.

His fear of God also showed when he was asked to interpret the dreams of the cupbearer and the baker. If I had to tell a man that the interpretation of his dream meant he only had three days to live then I would be seriously tempted to just tell him half of it – "In three days time you'll be out of here too…". But Joseph knew what God was saying and did not shy away from speaking all that God gave him. If he'd done any less the cupbearer would not have been able to say *"And things turned out exactly as he interpreted them" (Genesis 41:12)* two years later.

Ruler of Egypt

Joseph's gift of interpreting dreams gives him credibility in the eyes of Pharaoh, especially in the light of the cupbearer's testimony, but he also uses the opportunity to demonstrate the God given organisational abilities that he discovered in Potiphar's house and then developed in the prison. Look at the way in which his brain starts whirring as he thinks about the problems facing Egypt. Even as he has been giving the interpretation of the dream he has worked out a strategy for surviving the crisis, even down to the required tax rate – "take a fifth of the harvest". Yes. A 20% income tax should be about right! I don't think there is any doubt who Joseph had in mind when he advised Pharaoh to *"look for a discerning and wise man"* to be put in charge of Egypt!

Pharaoh has no doubts either and appoints Joseph as his Prime Minister, second only to himself in Egypt. Over the next seven years of plenty Joseph sets about storing grain – so much that his civil servants were unable to keep up with the record keeping! – and Joseph now enjoys the happiest years of his life. He is ruler of Egypt, he has two sons (a wife came with the appointment to Prime Minister!) and he has a busy and fulfilled life.

But he has not completely forgotten his family back in the land of Canaan. By the age of thirty Joseph had the gifting and character to be the ruler of Egypt, but it was still another eight years before he faced the biggest test of his life – meeting the brothers who had sold him into slavery.

Day 12
The Israelites move to Egypt

Joseph meets His Brothers

The encounters between Joseph and his brothers are described in great detail. It was over 20 years since they had sold him into slavery and the big question in our minds is "How will Joseph use the power he has over them now?" What has gone on in Joseph's mind over the years? He had clearly never forgotten his father and his family even though he called his first son Manasseh which means "forget" because he has forgotten his troubles. Life was good for him but there was still an ache in his heart for his family.

And then one day completely out of the blue ten men turned up in front of him and as they bowed down before him, in an instant, Joseph's early dreams flooded back into his memory. The dreams that had seemed like a silly childhood fancy suddenly became reality before his eyes!

Despite the power he had over them Joseph is no longer interested in revenge. What he wants to find out from them is whether their hearts have changed too over the last 20 years. Initially he deals with them harshly and locks them away for three days while he devises a plan. Then he releases them and sends them back to Canaan without Simeon, the second oldest (he has not forgotten that it is thanks to Reuben, the oldest, that he was not killed), and with a requirement that they bring Benjamin with them on their return.

The Brothers Return

The story of the brother's return to Egypt is one of the most moving in the Bible. Joseph realises that his brothers have kept their crime secret from his father for these past twenty plus years. When he first met them and quizzed them about their family they told him that of the original 12 sons *"one is no more" (Genesis 42:13)*. Joseph now tests his brothers to the limit by threatening to take Benjamin away from them and, more seriously, from their father. What will they do when faced with the prospect of seeing their father's grief once more? This is a long reading but a gripping account.

Read Genesis 43:1–45:15

Eventually it is Judah who takes the lead and speaks out in a very moving and eloquent appeal to Joseph. His speech in Genesis 44:18–34, culminating in the offer of himself as a slave in the place of Benjamin in order to save his father's grief, is deeply moving. It causes me to cry every time I read the story. His description of how Jacob's life is *"closely bound up with the boy's life"* and the pledge he made to take responsibility for Benjamin's life shows how much he loves his father and how awful the prospect would be to see his father in yet more misery. When Judah offers himself in place of Benjamin he has no idea who he is speaking to or how it will work out. In speaking those words he is saying goodbye to his life in Canaan. He has no prospect of ever seeing his family again. His only consolation will be that his father will be with Benjamin. It is a supreme sacrifice and one that lets Joseph see how deep the change in his heart has been. Joseph cannot control himself any longer and reveals himself to his brothers.

The poor brothers have an incredible emotional roller coaster in a very short space of time. They knew fear and panic when the cup was found in Benjamin's sack. But now they are terrified! Facing a stern foreign ruler was bad enough in itself: discovering that this all powerful ruler is the brother they sold into slavery twenty years earlier was horrifying! Years later Moses warned some of their descendants *"be sure that your sin will find you out" (Numbers 32:23)*. They had long since thought that they had got away with their sin but now it had to come into the open.

Jacob Goes to Egypt

We are not told how long Joseph had to wait for his brothers to return the second time. It must have been months, maybe even a year or so. All the time he was waiting for their return, wondering if they would even be able to come back or whether he would be keeping Simeon in prison for ever. But once Joseph has made himself known to them he wastes no time in getting his father and brothers to move to Egypt. The famine is severe and will get worse and so he wants to make provision for them in the best part of the land of Egypt.

The brothers return to their father to explain to him that Joseph is alive. How they went about telling him this and confessing what happened we are not told but it was the most painful event of each of their lives.

Read Genesis 45:25–46:4

Once Jacob realises that his sons are telling the truth about Joseph he sets off to join him. God reassures him in a vision at Beersheba where he offers sacrifices like his father and grandfather before him. In characteristic style the Hebrew writer breaks off before the emotional reunion between Jacob and Joseph to carefully list the descendants of Jacob who moved to Egypt. When they do finally meet, Joseph *"threw his arms around his father and wept for a long time" (Genesis 46:29)*. The twenty years of separation was over.

Once the family arrive in Egypt Joseph settles them in the best part of the land.

Jacob's Blessing on his Sons

In Genesis 48 Jacob adopts Joseph's two sons, Manasseh and Ephraim, as his own. Joseph presented them to his father with the oldest one, Manasseh, on Jacob's right so that he would receive the greater blessing but Jacob, who had tricked his father into giving him the blessing ahead of his older twin, gives the greater blessing to Ephraim. This adoption of Joseph's two sons gave him the double portion usually reserved for the firstborn.

In Genesis 49 Jacob called all his 12 sons together and gave a prophecy to each one telling them *"what will happen to you in days to come" (Genesis 49:1)*. This prophecy is not only relevant to them but to their descendants, the tribes of Israel.

There are two blessings that a father could pass to his oldest son: the blessing of leadership in the family and the blessing of a double portion – twice the inheritance of the other brothers. By adopting Joseph's sons Jacob had already assigned the double portion to Joseph but leadership among the sons was assigned to the fourth oldest, Judah (see Genesis 49:8 and compare with the blessing Jacob received from his father in Genesis 27:29). His three older brothers – Reuben, Simeon and Levi – were passed over for their sins.

Jacob's prophesy over Judah looked many years ahead: *"The sceptre will not depart from Judah, nor the ruler's staff from between his feet, until he comes to whom it belongs and the obedience of the nations is his." (Genesis 49:10)*. Many years later it was from the tribe of Judah that king David was chosen and he and his descendants ruled over Israel for hundreds of years. But it was Jesus, who was descended from Judah through his mother Mary, who ultimately fulfilled Jacob's words.

Day 12 – The Israelites move to Egypt

The 12 Tribes of Israel

The blessings of Jacob not only had significance for his sons but also had far reaching implications for their descendants. Throughout the Old Testament and on into the New the people of Israel took their identity from belonging to 12 tribes – descendants from the sons of Jacob. Given that Jacob had 12 sons it would be nice to think that the 12 sons equate to the 12 tribes but given that this is Jacob we are talking about you cannot expect it to be that simple! Jacob's adoption of Manasseh and Ephraim as his not only affected Joseph's birthright but also meant that there were 13 names from which the "12 tribes of Israel" could be chosen. Over 400 years later the children of Israel were led back into Canaan, the Promised Land, to take possession of it as their own and when they got there the land was divided into 12 territories for the "12 tribes" to settle in. So which "son" was left out?

In order to allow the tribes of Manasseh and Ephraim to each receive an allocation of land the tribe of Levi did not have one. In Jacob's blessing on his sons he prophesied over Simeon and Levi that *"I will scatter them in Jacob and disperse them in Israel." (Genesis 49:7)*. This was fulfilled in a negative way for Simeon as they became absorbed into the tribe of Judah (see Joshua 19:1 & 9). However, for the tribe of Levi this was fulfilled in a positive way. They were rewarded for carrying out the Lord's commands (see Exodus 32:28–29) and became the priests (see Numbers 1:47–54). They were not given a territory in Canaan but were given 48 towns throughout the land (see Joshua 14:4 & 21:41) from where they carried out priestly and legal duties. As time went on Judah became the strongest tribe in Israel and Ephraim the second strongest. Jacob's words had long lasting effect!

Figure 6 on the next page lists the 12 sons of Jacob along with the 12 tribes of Israel.

The Deaths of Jacob and Joseph

Soon after Jacob prophesied over his sons he died and his sons buried him with all the pomp and ceremony of an Egyptian funeral. However, he was not buried in Egypt. Before he died he asked Joseph to take his body back to Canaan so he could be buried in the cave alongside his grandfather Abraham and his father Isaac along with their wives in the field Abraham bought to bury Sarah. God had made promises to Abraham, Isaac, and Jacob that their descendants would inherit the land of Canaan and, although their descendants went to Egypt, their coffins remained in the land as a reminder of God's promise.

The 12 Sons of Jacob and the 12 Tribes of Israel			
The 12 Sons of Jacob are shown in bold: **Reuben** The 12 Tribes of Israel who received a territory in the land of Canaan are underlined: <u>Ephraim</u>			
Mother	**Sons of Jacob**	**Grandsons of Jacob**	
Leah	**<u>Reuben</u>**		
	Simeon		
	Levi		The Leader of his brothers
	<u>Judah</u>		
	<u>Issachar</u>		
	<u>Zebulun</u>		
Bilhah	**<u>Dan</u>**		
	<u>Naphtali</u>		
Zilpah	**<u>Gad</u>**		
	<u>Asher</u>		
Rachel	**Joseph**	<u>Manasseh</u>	} The double portion for Joseph
		<u>Ephraim</u>	
	<u>Benjamin</u>		

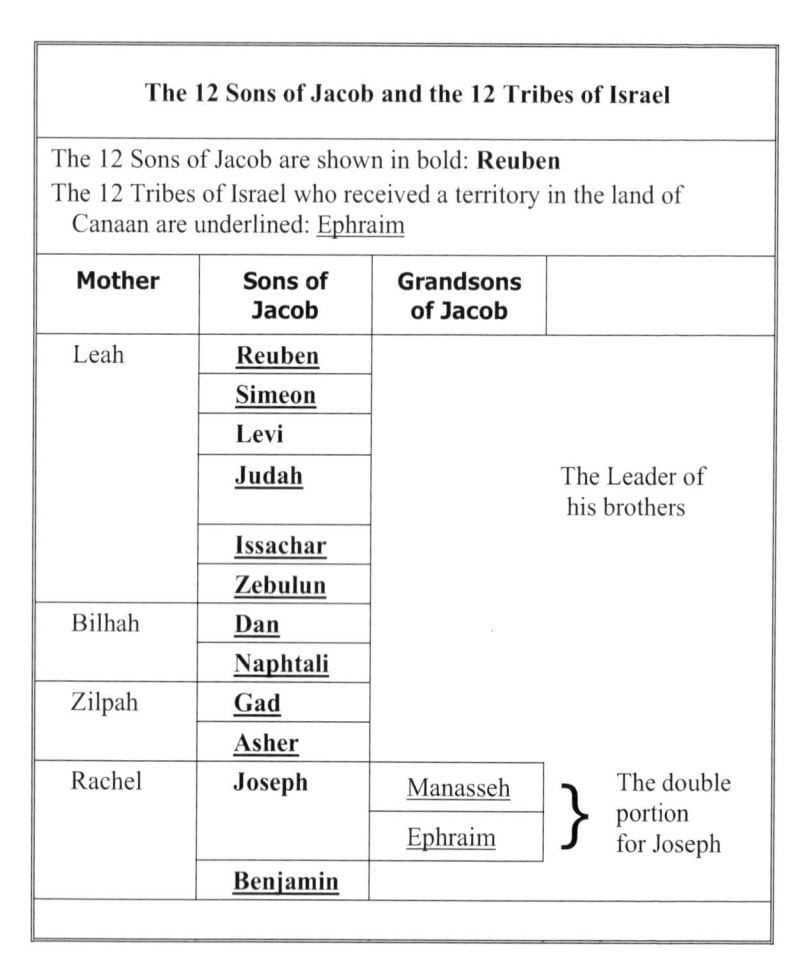

Figure 6 – The 12 Sons of Jacob and the 12 Tribes of Israel

Day 12 – The Israelites move to Egypt

After Jacob died there is a very revealing exchange between Joseph and his ten older brothers. With their father now dead the ten brothers fear reprisals from Joseph for the awful thing they did to him many years before so they concoct a message from their father asking him to forgive them. Joseph's response demonstrates the amazing way God dealt with him over the years. Through his tears he calms their fears and says *"You intended to harm me, but God intended it for good." (Genesis 50:20)*. Not only can Joseph look back over the years and forgive his brothers but he has also grasped the amazing truth that Paul spelled out 2000 years later: *"And we know that in all things God works for the good of those who love him." (Romans 8:28)*. Joseph can see the hand of God at work in his early life, even through the wicked act of his brothers. As he persevered in his love of God so God caused the sins done against him to work for his good, for the good of his family and their descendants, for the good of an entire nation and to work out the plans of God.

Joseph's final act demonstrated his confidence in God's plan. He remembered that God had promised Abraham that the people of Israel would return to the land of Canaan after 400 years. Instead of asking to be buried in Canaan immediately he asked for his body to be kept in Egypt until they returned. His unburied coffin remained as a reminder to Israel's descendants in Egypt that one day they must return to the land promised to their forefathers and possess it.

Day 13
Job – The Trouble Starts

The Book of Job

Before we return to pick up the story of Jacob's descendants in Exodus, the second book of the Bible, we will jump forward in our Bibles to take a look at the book of Job.

There are many mysteries surrounding this book. It is named after its principle character, Job, but we have no clues as to who wrote it, and no clues as to when or where it took place. All that we are told about Job is that he lived in "the land of Uz" – a territory east of the Jordan river and it seems that he lived sometime between 2000 and 1000 BC! It is possible that the events took place around the time of the end of Genesis, making him a contemporary of Abraham, Isaac or Jacob, or maybe he lived later, about the time of Moses. So, in terms of timing, this seems to be a good time to look at the book of Job.

Job is a man with a strong faith in God. However, from the words used for God in the speeches in the book it seems that neither Job nor his friends were Israelites. The author, on the other hand, is almost certainly an Israelite as he uses the Israelite covenant name for God – "*Yahweh*" – which is always written in the New International Version of the Bible as "the LORD".

The book of Job is about how God tests Job's faith to the limits. In the first two chapters Job loses his possessions, his family, and his health. The bulk of the book is then taken up with a debate between Job and his friends. They hold the traditional view that suffering results from sin and try and identify how Job has sinned. Job refuses to accept this and protests his innocence.

After many words God breaks in and ends the debate. However, God does not answer the basic questions but, instead, challenges Job's ability to question him. After Job repents he is restored to health, has a new family and becomes prosperous once again.

Job's Theme

The book of Job is a "Wisdom" book. While priests and prophets deal with spiritual matters, wisdom writers – "Sages" or "Wise men" – deal with practical and philosophical matters. The main issue that the book

Day 13 – Job – The Trouble Starts

Outline of Job	
1–2	Introduction: The Scene is Set – Job's troubles.
	The Debate:
3–27	• Job's three friends give their advice.
28	• Interlude – a wisdom poem
28–31	• Summing up for the defence.
32–37	• The speeches of Elihu.
38–42:6	God breaks in and speaks for himself.
42:7–17	The Conclusion – Job's restoration.

of Job tackles is the question, "Is suffering the result of sin?" The accepted view of Job's time is that the answer to that is "Yes". People who suffered misfortune or became sick did so because of some sin they had committed.

This view persisted into Jesus' day. In John 9 we read that Jesus was walking along with his disciples when they came across a man who had been blind from birth. His disciples asked Jesus *"Rabbi, who sinned, this man or his parents, that he was born blind?" (John 9:2)*. The fact that he was *born* blind didn't lead them to question their belief that sin had caused his blindness. The only question in their minds was whose sin was to blame. Given that he started life with a disability it seemed unlikely that it was due to his sin so they wondered whether his parents were to blame instead. In answering the question as to why the man was blind Jesus replies, *"Neither this man nor his parents sinned"* indicating that the traditional view of the Jews was flawed. Although there are times when a person's suffering results from their own sin, the Bible, and in particular Job, makes it clear that this is not the whole story.

Against the backdrop of seeing suffering as a result of sin Job also touches on another key philosophical question, or rather two questions which are two sides of the same coin – "Why do the righteous suffer?" and "Why do the wicked prosper?" These issues are also found in the other great "Wisdom" books – Psalms and Proverbs.

Interpreting Job

When we were looking at Genesis we were reading historical accounts of men and peoples. The text can be taken at face value as a true account of what happened and what was said. Occasionally in Genesis lies are recorded – as when Jacob told his father that he was Esau – but these do not present a problem of interpretation as the story makes clear that he was lying.

Interpreting other parts of the Old Testament is not quite so straightforward. Most of Job, like much of the Old Testament, is written as poetry. Poetry, by its very nature, is not intended to be taken literally. When Job says to God *"Did you not pour me out like milk and curdle me like cheese" (Job 10:10)* we know that he does not really think that God made him into food but we do get a sense of how he is feeling! So we need to take care to get the sense of what is being said rather than trying to take each line literally.

Looking in particular at the dialogue between Job and his friends as they debate Job's suffering we also need to be aware that these are men speaking from their own, limited understanding and putting forward their own ideas. They are arguing with one another and putting forward different points of view which means that not all that is said is "right", as God himself makes clear in the last chapter You cannot find the truth in Job by just looking at the surface; it requires a study of the whole book before you can interpret the individual verses. It is like looking for gold. Don't expect to find nuggets lying on the ground: you will need mining equipment to dig deep into rock before you find something of real value. This approach is true of most of the wisdom literature where contradictions are presented to make us think. Individual sentences cannot necessarily be taken at face value. As with all of scripture each part must be looked at in context and compared with other parts of the same book and with other books in order to understand what it says.

An interesting feature of Job is the insight it gives us into the understanding men had three to four thousand years ago. Elihu's description of cloud patterns in Job 37:11–12 sounds like he was looking at a satellite picture!

Job 1–2 – The Scene is Set

I have never heard of Job being performed as a play but it almost seems to have been written for the theatre. The opening chapters jump between heaven and earth as the writer gives us divine insight into the source of Job's sufferings. Then the heap of ashes provides a stark backdrop to the debate before God himself breaks in. Seeing the agony of Job's sufferings worked out on stage would leave a powerful

Day 13 – Job – The Trouble Starts

impression!

The first two chapters of Job are the first act of this play. They build up a picture of who Job is and what happens to him and set the scene for the debate that follows. They also give us insight into the reasons behind Job's suffering, reasons which Job and his friends remain unaware of throughout the book.

> **Read Job 1–2**

The background to Job's plight is given as a series of short clips. Job is introduced as a righteous man. He is very wealthy and has ten children. Then we are taken into heaven and given insight into the workings of God's court. We learn that there are times when the angels come to present themselves to God to give an account of themselves and discover that Satan is expected to do the same. Satan is not an equal power in opposition to God. He is a created being who has to give an account of himself to his maker. In the book of Job the word used for Satan is "The Accuser". In books which were written later in the Old Testament this is shortened to "Accuser", as Satan became a proper name.

This insight into heaven tells us where all Job's troubles started. We might expect trouble once Satan appears but the remarkable thing is that the whole chain of events is triggered by God himself! He initiates things by boasting to Satan about Job and his righteousness. *"Have you considered my servant Job?" (Job 1:8)* Satan's response is to accuse Job of only trusting in God because of what he gets out of it. If Job were to lose his wealth and security then he would no longer trust in God.

If you believe in a God who will protect us and our interests at all times then learn from Job that God's purposes are far higher than ours and that our comfort is not top of God's priority list. God, it seems, is not afraid to take up Satan's challenge and see where Job's security really lies. God gives Satan permission to attack Job's wealth and security – but within limits. Satan is given permission to attack *"everything he has"* but Job must not suffer physically.

After this scene in heaven we return to earth to witness the most dreadful calamities coming upon Job one after the other – culminating in the death of all ten of his children in one dreadful accident. How does Job respond to this? *"He fell to the ground in worship" (Job 1:20)*. Incredible! Job does not blame God but acknowledges the

Lord's right not only to give but also to take away. God owes us nothing.

Chapter 2 starts with a repeat of the scene in heaven from chapter 1. Once again it is God who brings up the subject of Job, this time pointing out that Job maintains his integrity despite all the troubles that Satan has brought upon him. Satan is not convinced and has a further accusation, that Job will not hold onto his integrity if his own flesh is attacked. If Job is afflicted with disease and pain he will turn against God. Once again God grants Satan permission to afflict Job, this time only with the restriction that he may not kill him. As the camera turns back to earth we find Job struck with a terrible illness, covered with painful sores all over. He is in unimaginable pain and yet still does not blame God. The only person left to comfort him is his wife and her advice is no great help!

Then at the end of chapter 2 we meet Job's three friends. They hear of his troubles and come to be with him. Overall Job's friends are not seen in a great light but when they first arrive they set a great example of how to comfort someone in great distress. We read that when they first saw him, *"they sat on the ground with him for seven days and seven nights. No one said a word to him, because they saw how great his suffering was." (Job 2:13)*. While they sat in silence with Job in his distress they were a great comfort to him. As we will see tomorrow, it is only when they started speaking that the problems began!

Day 14
Job – The Debate
and the Conclusion

Job 3–27 – The Debate – Job's Friends give their Advice

Yesterday we saw the background to Job's suffering. Hearing of his plight, his three friends come to be with him and comfort him. After they have sat with him for seven days, Job speaks. He is in the most awful distress – both physically and mentally – and wishes that he had never been born.

> Read Job 3:1–6 and 3:25–26

Once Job has broken the silence his friends start to offer their advice. A debate breaks out with each of his friends – Eliphaz, Bildad and Zophar – taking turns to offer their advice and Job responding to them.

Their understanding of the situation is entirely orthodox. Their belief is that God punishes the wicked: "you reap what you sow." As Job is being punished they are sure that he has been wicked so they urge him to confess his faults and, as the debate goes on, even make up faults for him! Their logic is faulty. You will fall over if someone pushes you hard, but this doesn't mean that everyone who is on the floor has been pushed. We also know that they were completely wrong because we have the benefit of reading the opening scenes! The truth is far more frightening than that Job has sinned. This is not an expression of God's judgement but of his confidence in Job. It is not Job's sin that has led to him being in this situation but it is his innocence that has prepared him for this ordeal!

There are three cycles of debate with his friends taking a turn to give their advice. We will get a flavour of the debate by reading short extracts from a number of speeches. In the first cycle Eliphaz starts by being complimentary about Job but quickly gets into his argument.

> Read Job 4:1–9

Eliphaz argues that Job cannot be righteous before God. But Job is not happy with this argument. His reply shows that he is happy to be

Day 14 – Job – The Debate and the Conclusion

corrected but is not yet convinced that he has done wrong. We will just read a few words from his reply.

> Read Job 6:24 and 6:28–30

When Job has finished, Bildad speaks in support of Eliphaz's argument. Note how he even uses the fate of Job's children – a very painful reminder for Job – to support his case.

> Read Job 8:1–6

After Job has replied to Bildad, Zophar takes his turn. He is angry with Job for his words and even wishes that God himself would speak against Job. His argument is simple – if Job turns from his sin he will be restored.

> Read Job 11:1–4 and 11:13–15

Job completes the first cycle of speeches with a very sarcastic reply to his three friends.

> Read Job 12:2–3

This sets the tone for the second cycle of speeches when the three friends get more angry with Job and start accusing him of wrongdoing. Eliphaz opens with a cruel attack on Job.

> Read Job 15:1–6

Job finds their onslaught crushing and pleads with them to leave him alone.

> Read Job 19:1–4

But in among his despair he also demonstrates remarkable faith. These verses are well known through being part of Handel's Messiah:

> Read Job 19:25–26

After each friend has spoken for the second time there is a shorter third cycle of speeches with one speech from Eliphaz and a short final one from Bildad. By his third speech Eliphaz, who started as the most supportive, has become very frustrated by Job's refusal to see his

Day 14 – Job – The Debate and the Conclusion   89

argument and tells Job: *"Is not your wickedness great? Are not your sins endless? You demanded security from your brothers for no reason; you stripped men of their clothing, leaving them naked."* (Job 22:5–6) and continues with a list of serious wrongdoings for which there does not appear to be any evidence at all!

By this time Job has lost all interest in defending himself against his friends. All he is interested in doing is debating his case with God who seems far away. Hear the longing of his heart for restoration of his relationship with God so that he can speak with him.

> Read Job 23:1–7

After Bildad has spoken Job dismisses all their arguments in his final speech of the debate. His attitude towards their arguments is summed up in these two verses.

> Read Job 27:5–6

Job 28–31 – Summing up for the Defence

The debate between Job and his friends has turned into an increasingly acrimonious trial with the friends trying to prove their case that Job had sinned while Job protests his innocence. After the final cycle of speeches, there is a poem about wisdom which concludes with a definition: *"The fear of the Lord – that is wisdom, and to shun evil is understanding."* (Job 28:28). This definition of wisdom also appears in the other major wisdom books – see Psalm 111:10 and Proverbs 1:7.

After the interlude there are three speeches by Job which sum up his case. In chapter 29 he looks back on his former life and talks about how righteous he was: *"How I long for the months gone by..."* (Job 29:2). In chapter 30 he bemoans his current position – *"But now they mock me, men younger than I, whose fathers I would have disdained to put with my sheep dogs."* (Job 30:1) – and then finally, in chapter 31, he protests his innocence in a series of legal oaths in the form, *"If I have done wrong ... then I accept punishment."* His concern in this is not to prove his innocence to his friends but that God would hear him and answer him: *"I sign now my defence – let the Almighty answer me; let my accuser put his indictment in writing."* (Job 31:35).

Job 32–37 – The Speeches of Elihu

After Job has finished his speech a younger man called Elihu speaks.

He is angry with Eliphaz, Bildad, and Zophar because they cannot convince Job of his sin and with Job because he is justifying himself. He has let the older men go first but now launches into four speeches. He does not have the wisdom of years on his side but believes that wisdom can come from God even to younger men: *"I am young in years, and you are old; ... But it is the spirit in a man, the breath of the Almighty, that gives him understanding."* (Job 32:6,8)

Elihu is more logical than the other three. He argues from Job's words rather than making false accusations, but is sometimes unfair in taking his words out of context. Some things Job said are due to his condition: he didn't really mean them. However, despite all this his argument is the same as the others. Note his straightforward view of how God deals with the righteous and the wicked.

> **Read Job 36:5–12**

In short, God punishes the wicked and gives prosperity to the righteous. The case is cut and dried.

Job 38–41: God Speaks for Himself!

Elihu is brought to a halt by the intervention of God himself who speaks out of a thunder storm. Job is desperate to put his case before God and get God's view of his situation so what will God say now in response to Job's suffering and questions? Read the Lord's words carefully.

> **Read Job 38:1–7**

At first reading the Lord's response is a complete surprise. Instead of answering Job's questions the Lord asks him a lot of questions that he can't answer. This is only the beginning and through these four chapters God asks questions about creation, the weather and the animal kingdom which demonstrate Job's limited understanding. God offers Job no sympathy and gives him no explanation of why he is suffering. He makes no attempt to answer Job's questions or give any reason as to why he has not spoken earlier.

In the middle the Lord stops to allow Job to answer but Job is speechless. In his earlier speeches Job has looked at his personal situation and asked questions about whether the Lord is competent, whether he is wise, and whether he is really in control. The Lord makes his competence and his wisdom in creation very clear and demonstrates that he is in control.

Job's response is total repentance.

> **Read Job 42:1–6**

All the questions that Job had before have disappeared. He was seeking to establish his righteousness but now he has seen God he knows that he cannot hope to stand before him.

Job 42 – The Conclusion

However, in the final section of the book we find that Job is not condemned but is, in fact, vindicated by God. Job's friends spoke in defence of God and God is angry with them; Job complained to God and God commends him.

> **Read Job 42:7–17**

And so Job ends with twice the number of livestock that he had before and with the same number of children – although I am sure that the memory of his first ten children never went away. Jesus promised his disciples that *"In this world you will have trouble" (John 16:33)* and so we do not have the guarantee that things will have such a neat conclusion for us in this world. However, Jesus has overcome death itself so we can be confident of our place with God beyond the grave.

Job is not a simple book to understand. Many people have struggled with it over the years. Any ideas that we have about God being "nice" are blown away by this book. In the Narnia books written by C S Lewis there is a saying about Aslan, the lion who represents God, "Aslan is not a tame lion." In Job we find that the Lord is not a tame God. He is not there to satisfy our needs or deal with our problems.

I am indebted to C J Mahaney[4] who gave an outstanding talk on Job at the Stoneleigh Bible week in 1992 for most of my insights into this book. In his conclusion he said: *"The ways of God are beyond our understanding. For us to assume that God owes us an explanation is arrogance. There is a large area of mystery about God which we will never understand. We are called to trust him because he can be utterly trusted, not question him."*

---

[4] C J Mahaney is part of the leadership team of Sovereign Grace Ministries and based in Washington, USA. He spoke at a number of the Stoneleigh Bible weeks organised by New Frontiers International.

Our knowledge of God would be poorer without the book of Job. It offers hope to any that are suffering in all places and at all times. Not a hope that our sufferings will quickly come to an end but that the Lord remains in control of our lives and our situation come what may. It also offers us advice on dealing with those who are suffering. Let us not jump to conclusions about the reasons for their misfortune. It is very easy to blame someone for their own suffering – "You haven't been healed because you have not got enough faith" – rather than learning to *"weep with those that weep" (Romans 12:15 AV)* and being mature enough to realise that we cannot understand all that happens to ourselves let alone others!

Day 15
Life in Egypt

The Book of Exodus

Today we return to the historical books of the Bible and pick up the story of Israel's descendants in the book of Exodus. Four hundred years have passed since Israel and his twelve sons moved to Egypt and his descendants are now a large group of people – probably around two million strong – and have become slaves in Egypt.

The author of the book, and its main character, is Moses, a descendant of Levi. After being educated in the Pharaoh's palace and then spending 40 years tending sheep in the desert, God calls him at the age of 80 to return to Egypt and bring the Israelites out of Egypt and take them to the land he promised to Abraham. The word Exodus means "Exit" or "Departure" as the main event in the book is the departure of the Israelites from Egypt. Moses leads them through the desert to Mount Sinai where God gives them the Ten Commandments and instructions for building a Tabernacle – a place where he can live among his people.

The book of Exodus covers the period from 1526 – 1445 BC (assuming 1446 BC for the date of the Exodus).

	Outline of Exodus
1–2	The birth and early life of Moses.
3:1–7:6	God sends Moses and his brother Aaron to ask Pharaoh to release the people of Israel.
7:7–12:51	Moses asks Pharaoh to let the Israelites leave Egypt. Pharaoh refuses and God sends ten plagues until the Egyptians plead with them to go.
13–18	The Israelites cross the Red Sea and journey to Sinai in the desert.
19–24	God gives the Ten Commandments and further laws.
25–40	God gives instructions on building the tabernacle – a focus for national worship.

The first twenty chapters of Exodus describe a very important event in the history of Israel and we will be reading most of them over the coming few days.

The Israelites' Situation

> **Read Exodus 1**

The first 14 verses of Exodus chapter 1 give us a very quick sketch of the 400 years between the events at the end of Genesis and the start of the main story in Exodus. At the end of Genesis we read how Jacob's family came to Egypt and were given a part of the land of Egypt called Goshen to settle in. Because of their social or religious customs the Egyptians would not mix with them and so the Israelites maintained a separate identity in the land of Egypt. As time went on the Israelites multiplied in numbers until they got to the point where they became a large, but still separate, group of people.

There came a point where the Egyptians became fearful of the Israelites and, to stop them turning against them, subjected them to slavery. As we know from the many monuments that survive to this day the Egyptians were great builders and the Israelites were made to work on building projects. Note that the Egyptians refer to the Israelites as "Hebrews", a name usually used to describe them by foreigners in the Old Testament. Despite being subject to hard labour the Israelites continued to multiply rapidly until, about 350 years after the time of Joseph, the king of Egypt, usually referred to by the title "Pharaoh", decided to take drastic action to reduce their numbers and issued an order to kill all newborn baby boys.

Here we see a man taking action to safeguard his country. Pharaoh was concerned that the Hebrews were a serious threat to the security of Egypt. But behind this we see the work of Satan. He knew the promise that God had made to Abraham that the Israelites would return to the land of Canaan after 400 years. Joseph's bones still lay in a coffin, unburied, as a reminder of this. So, it was Satan who incited Pharaoh to strike at this time in the hope that any potential deliverer would be killed at birth.

Moses

> **Read Exodus 2:1–10**

Day 15 – Life in Egypt

In Exodus 2 we are introduced to Moses, who was to be that deliverer. He was born a Hebrew and saved from death by the hands of a number of women. His mother hid him, his sister watched over him, and Pharaoh's daughter, the only person in the kingdom who could disobey Pharaoh's commands and get away with it, adopted him! Far from Satan's plan resulting in the death of God's chosen deliverer, it actually results in Moses being taken into Pharaoh's palace where he received the best education and training available on the planet!

Despite being brought up as an Egyptian prince, Moses does not forget that he is a Hebrew and he is disturbed by their plight. When he grows up he goes to watch them at their hard labour and God puts a desire in him to see his people released. Then he sees an Egyptian beating a Hebrew and he is so moved to anger that he killed the Egyptian. Once this becomes known he has to flee from Egypt into the desert. There he becomes a shepherd, marries and settles down.

Stephen, in the New Testament, tells us that Moses was forty when he left Egypt to go and live in Midian (see Acts 7:23) and Exodus 7:7 tells us that he was eighty when he returned to do the work God had for his life. Having had the best education did not qualify Moses to lead God's people. Even having a clear sense of God's calling on his life – to free his people from their bondage – did not qualify him. God had to take Moses into the desert to live through the frustrations of being a shepherd for forty years before he was ready to do the work that God had for him.

God Reveals His Name

Read Exodus 3

Forty long years after he left Egypt, in a way that Moses least expected, God spoke to Moses again. God now knows that Moses is ready to be used and he calls him to go and free his people from Pharaoh and lead them out of Egypt.

God introduces himself to Moses by saying *"I am the God of your father, the God of Abraham, the God of Isaac and the God of Jacob." (Exodus 3:6)*. But later on in the conversation Moses asks God what his name is and God gives him a new name for himself. God is known by many names in the Bible. God appeared to Abraham as "God Almighty" (Genesis 17:1), Moses calls him "the faithful God" in Deuteronomy 7:9, Paul starts 2 Corinthians with praise to "the Father of compassion and the God of all comfort" (2 Corinthians 1:3), and in Revelation God appears as "King of Kings and Lord of Lords" (Revelation 19:16). All these names tell us about who God is and his character but none are adequate to fully express who God is.

God's reply to Moses is very significant. *"God said to Moses, "I AM WHO I AM. This is what you are to say to the Israelites: 'I AM has sent me to you.'" God also said to Moses, "Say to the Israelites, 'The LORD, the God of your fathers – the God of Abraham, the God of Isaac and the God of Jacob – has sent me to you.' This is my name forever, the name by which I am to be remembered from generation to generation""* (Exodus 3:14–15).

God refers to himself as "I am who I am" or, the shortened version, "I am". When his people refer to him they are to say "He is who he is" or, "He is". In the Hebrew "He is" is written as "YHWH" (they did not write down the vowels) or "Yahweh" which is sometimes, incorrectly, written as "Jehovah".

In the New International Version of the Bible this special name of God "He is", is written as "the LORD" with small capitals[5]. This distinguishes it from the word "Lord" which is a title for someone with authority, which is used in the Bible for both people and God. So the passage above could be written as *"God also said to Moses, "Say to the Israelites, 'HE IS, the God of your fathers – the God of Abraham, the God of Isaac and the God of Jacob – has sent me to you'"*. God makes it clear that this is the name by which he wants to be known by his people Israel. It sums up his total character and his faithfulness.

Later in Exodus God appeared to Moses and gave him a longer explanation of his name which combines his incredible love with his righteousness: *"Then the LORD came down in the cloud and stood there with him and proclaimed his name, the LORD. And he passed in front of Moses, proclaiming, 'The LORD, the LORD, the compassionate and gracious God, slow to anger, abounding in love and faithfulness, maintaining love to thousands, and forgiving wickedness, rebellion and sin. Yet he does not leave the guilty unpunished; he punishes the children and their children for the sin of the fathers to the third and fourth generation.'"* (Exodus 34:5–7). If we just understand God as being a loving and compassionate God and ignore his righteousness,

---

[5] Note that as this special name is a Hebrew word the distinction is only made in the Old Testament. It does not appear in the New Testament which was written in Greek.

which is fiercely angry towards sin, we will get a "warm and cuddly" picture of God ready to overlook all our misdemeanours and welcome us, and everyone else, into heaven one day. On the other hand, if we just focus on God as being a judge who punishes those who do wrong, we will see him as harsh and unloving. This name of God, "I am", sums up both his righteousness and his love. God is who he is and will be who he will be. It is not for us to pick the bits we like but we must take all that the Bible says about him to get a full picture.

From this time on the Israelites knew that "He is" referred to the Lord and they treated his name with reverence. One of the ways in which Jesus made it clear that he was God was by using the expression, "I am". When he said to the Jewish leaders *"I tell you the truth, before Abraham was born, I am!" (John 8:58)* they knew that it was a claim to be God and Jesus was nearly stoned for blasphemy.

Up Against Pharaoh

In Exodus 4 Moses complained to God that the people of Israel would not listen to him so God gave him two miraculous signs to perform – turning his staff into a snake and making his hand be covered with leprosy – to convince them that his words were from God. He then protested that he was not a good speaker and so God sent his brother Aaron to meet him and accompany him back to Egypt.

They first met with the elders of the Israelites and told them what God had said to them and, initially, the Israelites were amazed and delighted by what they heard. Once they saw the miraculous signs that Moses and Aaron performed they expected to be free in a very short space of time. However, Moses and Aaron's first meeting with Pharaoh did not go as the Israelite elders expected.

> Read Exodus 5:1–6:12

To their surprise, rather than resulting in their freedom, it made life a lot worse for them. Pharaoh was not impressed at a couple of old men coming and demanding some time off for his slaves in the name of a God he'd never heard of. One of the old men was a shepherd too and the Egyptians despised shepherds!

This is the start of the relationship between Moses and the people of Israel and it is typical of what follows. They respond well to promises and miraculous signs but only for a short time. Once things go against them the people immediately blame Moses. Moses goes back to God and God gives him incredible promises for his people but they will not listen while things are so difficult for them.

But the most frightening relationship is the one between Moses and Pharaoh. Tomorrow we will see the account of a proud, powerful man who opposed God and his servant Moses.

Day 16
The Plagues of Egypt

The Plagues

As we saw yesterday, Pharaoh refused to let the Israelites leave his land, even for a few days. Moses and Aaron's request was met with a blunt refusal. God's response is to take on Pharaoh and all the might of Egypt in a head to head confrontation. The account of the plagues of Egypt is the most awesome display of God's power ever witnessed by man. (We will miss out the eighth plague to shorten the reading.)

> *Read Exodus 7:8–9:35 and 10:21–11:10*

The plagues are much more than demonstrations of God's power. They challenge everything Pharaoh stands for. His country is ruined economically, his gods are shown to be worthless, and finally his son is killed along with the next generation of Egypt. The Egyptian people suffered terribly as a result of their king's refusal to give in to God.

Can You Believe it?

Over the years many scientists have sought to come up with an explanation for the plagues. Recently two American epidemiologists (people who study where diseases come from and how they spread) undertook an investigation into the ten plagues. Dr John S Marr and Curtis Malloy started from a careful examination of the Biblical record and used the Internet to share information with scientists in the fields of animal diseases, microbiology and poisons and see if they could determine what might have caused the ten plagues. Their results were published in a medical journal in the USA and were publicised in an Equinox programme on Channel 4.

The results were amazing in that they were able to identify possible causes for all the plagues, even to the death of the firstborn, and found modern experiences of each of the plagues. I had always been taught that the Nile turning to blood was a figure of speech for it turning red with churning sand, but there is a disease which affects fish where their scales bleed into the water and in recent times rivers have literally "turned to blood" with the effect of this disease. I have never doubted that scripture was true but had never imagined that there could be a rational explanation for the death of the first born. I assumed that this had to be direct intervention by God. But after all the other devastation on the land the scientists proposed that the death of the firstborn could have resulted from mycotoxins, a toxic substance produced by a fungus or mould, growing on hastily stored crops. The oldest sons would be the most likely to be sent to get food from the stores and so the ones to die. Death from exposure to mycotoxins is very rapid and leaves no outward signs of sickness. Many died in the USSR in this way during World War II.

This explanation may or may not be what happened. Personally, I found it helpful as it underlined the accuracy of scripture. People are quick to say that accounts such as these in the Bible are stories, made up to teach a point, or legends, which have been fabricated over time. But it was the details in the account that helped these scientists to piece together an explanation. Surely a legend would have all the water in Egypt turned to blood but we read that by digging holes near the Nile the people got drinkable water, filtered by the sand. If someone were making it up then why would they let the Israelites suffer the first three plagues but not the fourth? In the scientists' explanation, the type of flies which would have affected the Egyptians and led on to the plague on livestock and boils would not have travelled far so the distance between the Egyptian and Israelites would account for why one group suffered and the other didn't. We do not need to doubt the accuracy of the Bible. It can stand the test of scientific research.

Amazing Miracles

However, providing a possible scientific explanation for the plagues does not undermine the fact that they were miraculous. Before each plague happened God spoke to Moses and Moses went and warned Pharaoh about what would happen to his land if he did not let the people of Israel go. The timing of the events was supernatural, whether or not God used natural or supernatural means to make them happen.

When the plagues started the people of Israel were in no doubt that they came from God. Pharaoh took a little longer to be convinced. He had some magicians (referred to as Jannes and Jambres in 2 Timothy 3:8) who, to start with, were able to do the same miracles that Moses did "by their secret arts". They were either clever at sleight of hand or, more likely, used demonic powers. They turned their staffs into snakes, although Aaron's swallowed theirs up! With all the Nile turned to blood they managed to find some clean water which they too turned to blood. It might have been more impressive if they'd cleaned up the Nile! They even managed to bring more frogs into Egypt when the place was completely overrun! But once the gnats came they became convinced that God was in it as they could not duplicate that plague but Pharaoh refused to believe.

During the first five plagues we read that *"Pharaoh hardened his heart" (see 8:32)* but from the sixth plague we read that *"the LORD hardened Pharaoh's heart" (9:12)*. God graciously gave him a chance to choose to obey him but there came a point where God confirmed his choice and used his disobedience to work out his purposes for his people. It is an awesome lesson. We all face choices but if we continually go against God we will, ultimately, lose the power to choose.

Moses, Man of Faith

How easy was it for Moses to go in front of Pharaoh time after time and tell him what God had said to him? It is easy to read that Moses went and stood by the Nile waiting for Pharaoh and told him that the water would turn to blood when he struck it with his staff, but it clearly took incredible faith. It may have got easier as time went on but somehow I doubt it. Each time he spoke he was putting his credibility on the line and if he got it wrong then God's credibility was at stake too.

God needed eighty years to prepare Moses for this. Moses now had the faith to be able to work incredible miracles. Even though Pharaoh refused to accept God's demands the Egyptians and Pharaoh's officials held him in the greatest respect. Moses went from obscurity to centre stage very quickly but his biggest challenge was yet to come. Tomorrow we will read how he led God's people out of Egypt and started leading the Israelites towards the Promised Land.

Day 17
Out of Egypt

The Passover

For many years to come the Egyptians would look back on the night when God brought the tenth plague on them with bitter sadness. It was the night when every household experienced death, death of the firstborn. But for the Israelites that same night was to be remembered in celebration, as a night when God delivered them from their oppressors, and the Passover has been commemorated by Jews all round the world to this day.

God gave very precise instructions to the Israelites to get them prepared for this night. They had to take a lamb, slaughter it at the set time, and then take some of its blood and put it around the front door of their houses. When the Lord came to kill the firstborn he would see the blood and "pass over" that house – note this origin of the word Passover in verse 13.

> Read Exodus 12:1–42

When God had promised to bring his people out of Egypt he said, *"I am the LORD, and I will bring you out from under the yoke of the Egyptians. I will free you from being slaves to them, and I will redeem you with an outstretched arm and with mighty acts of judgement." (Exodus 6:6)* The word "redeem" means to obtain release by means of payment. On the first Passover God required a death in every household, either of the firstborn, or of a lamb. The lamb took the place of the firstborn in the Israelite household – the firstborn was redeemed by the lamb. In Exodus 13 the Lord specifies that the Israelites are to give every firstborn male lamb to the Lord as a reminder for each generation of that redemption.

This act of redemption in the old covenant looks forward to the act of redemption in the new covenant. Under the old covenant lambs were killed year after year to redeem each generation but in the new covenant Jesus, the perfect lamb of God, died once to redeem all those who are in slavery to sin (see Hebrews 10:11–14). The last meal Jesus had before he died was the Passover meal, which he celebrated with his disciples. He took this symbol of the old covenant and made it into a remembrance of his death, which sealed the new covenant. Today Christians throughout the world remember Jesus with the bread and wine in "the Lord's Supper" (or "Communion" or "Breaking of Bread").

In the Old Testament the Passover meal was the start of a journey for God's people to a temporary, physical Promised Land. In the New Testament Jesus broke bread with his disciples before going to die on the cross which enabled us to start a journey to a permanent, eternal, spiritual Promised Land.

Leaving Egypt

As we read in Exodus 12, the tenth plague pushed Pharaoh beyond breaking point. All along he had said "No" to the Israelites going. Now he didn't just say "Yes", but he and the rest of the Egyptians *urged* the people to leave quickly.

In recording their departure from Egypt Moses reminds us that this is the fulfilment of promises made hundreds of years previously. At least some of the Israelites knew that God had said to Abraham, *"Know for certain that your descendants will be strangers in a country not their own, and they will be enslaved and mistreated four hundred years." (Genesis 15:13)* Moses notes that the children of Israel left Egypt 430 years after Israel arrived – "to the very day". Because the Egyptians were so keen to get rid of them, the Israelites took their opportunity to ask for gold, silver and clothing and so left with great wealth as payment for their years of hard labour. This too demonstrates the accuracy of God's promise to Abraham 600 years earlier as he had said, *"But I will punish the nation they serve as slaves, and afterward they will come out with great possessions" (Genesis 15:14).*

The children of Israel made another link with the faith of their forefathers by honouring Joseph's request to take his bones with them out of Egypt. In among all the haste Moses did not forget to find some strong young men to carry Joseph's coffin containing them. It would still be more than forty years before they were laid to rest back in the Promised Land (see Joshua 24:32) but they continued to serve as a reminder of the faithfulness of God.

> Read Exodus 13:17–14:31

A Shock to the System

The Israelite's departure from Egypt was a very hasty affair and a complete shock to their system. They had all grown up in slavery and, despite God's promises to their forefathers, most of them never expected any deliverance to happen in their lifetime. Now they had lived through the most remarkable demonstration of God's power ever witnessed by man and suddenly found themselves expelled from the only land they knew and walking into the desert with their families and livestock and living in tents.

The people had no difficulty knowing which way to go as God himself led them in a pillar of cloud which turned to fire by night. As slaves it is possible that most of them knew very little geography so when they were led south they just accepted it, even though the route to the Promised Land was east. Exodus 13:18 tells us that the Israelites went out of Egypt "armed for battle". Given that they had been slaves who were not trusted by their masters it is likely that the weapons they had were taken from the Egyptians and they had never been trained how to fight a serious battle. God knew that they needed time to prepare for battles ahead and so led them south rather than east towards the Promised Land. He also had yet to complete their liberation from the Egyptians although they did not know that.

Despite the fact that the Israelite God had brought devastation on the land of Egypt, and even killed every firstborn child including his own, Pharaoh had second thoughts about the Israelites leaving Egypt and set out after them to bring them back. The first indication as to the character of the Israelites is seen when they find themselves between Pharaoh's chariots and the Red Sea. We read that they were terrified, they cried out to the Lord, and they had a go at Moses! This was to be a pattern that was repeated time and time again over the coming months and years. Worst of all they said, *"It would have been better for us to serve the Egyptians than to die in the desert!" (Exodus 14:12)*. A supernatural God had just delivered them from 400 years of slavery and their response to their first difficulty is to want to go back to Egypt.

It is easy for us to judge them harshly as we know about the parting of the Red Sea but their experiences are a lesson to us. In his first letter to the Corinthian church Paul held up the experiences of the Israelite people in the Old Testament saying, *"These things happened to them as examples and were written down as warnings for us" (1 Corinthians 10:11)*. If we search our own hearts we will find that we too can forget God's wonderful grace to us very quickly and be as vulnerable as they were. It is important that we learn from their mistakes rather than judging them.

Crossing the Red Sea

God's patience with his people is incredible. Despite their complete lack of confidence in him he delivers them once again. The account of the "parting of the Red Sea" is very well known and it completed the liberation of the Israelites from the Egyptians. The impact of this miracle on them was that they *"feared the LORD and put their trust in him and in Moses his servant." (Exodus 14:31)*. The people's confidence is growing.

In Exodus 15 we read how Moses wrote a song of praise to God to celebrate his victory over the Egyptians, which made sure that they would remember the event and prepared them for the battles ahead. It is interesting to note that Moses' sister Miriam led the women in dancing even though she, like her brother, was in her eighties!

For those who have seen this depicted in the film "The Ten Commandments" it is worth noting that there were about two million Israelites plus livestock. This was a huge number of people to live in the desert for so long and tomorrow we will see how they reacted to further setbacks and how God started the process of moulding them into his nation.

Day 18
To Sinai and the Old Covenant

The Journey to Sinai

When God first appeared to Moses it was at Mount Horeb, also known as Mount Sinai, and God told him that he would lead the people of Israel out of Egypt and that they would worship him there. With such a large group of people this was a journey of three months. Map 2 on the next page shows the route they took down the eastern shore of what is today called the Gulf of Suez.

With such a large group of people it is inevitable that the key issues would be food and water. As the Israelites trudge through the Sinai desert – in Deuteronomy Moses refers to it as *"the vast and dreadful desert" (Deuteronomy 8:15)* – they went three days without water before finding a bitter spring. The people grumbled to Moses, he cried to the Lord and the Lord told him to throw a piece of wood into the water which made it sweet. Then, as they went further, food became an issue. God had just delivered them from the Egyptians and brought them through the Red Sea but these tests showed that they still did not have confidence in him to survive each day, let alone to take them all the way to the Promised Land. Again their response is to grumble and complain to Moses and against his leadership and to wish, once more, that they could return to Egypt. Their memory is fading fast and they are viewing their life in slavery in Egypt through increasingly rosy spectacles. Up against the Red Sea they thought *"it would have been better for us to serve the Egyptians rather than to die in the desert" (Exodus 14:12).* Now they are facing hunger note the references to sitting round *"pots of meat"* where they could eat *"all the food we wanted."* A few months later on Egypt is beginning to sound like a five star hotel: *"We remember the fish we ate in Egypt at no cost – also the cucumbers, melons, leeks, onions and garlic." (Numbers 11:5)* God makes it clear that he is angry with them for their lack of faith but responds with provision of meat and bread in the form of manna.

> Read Exodus 16

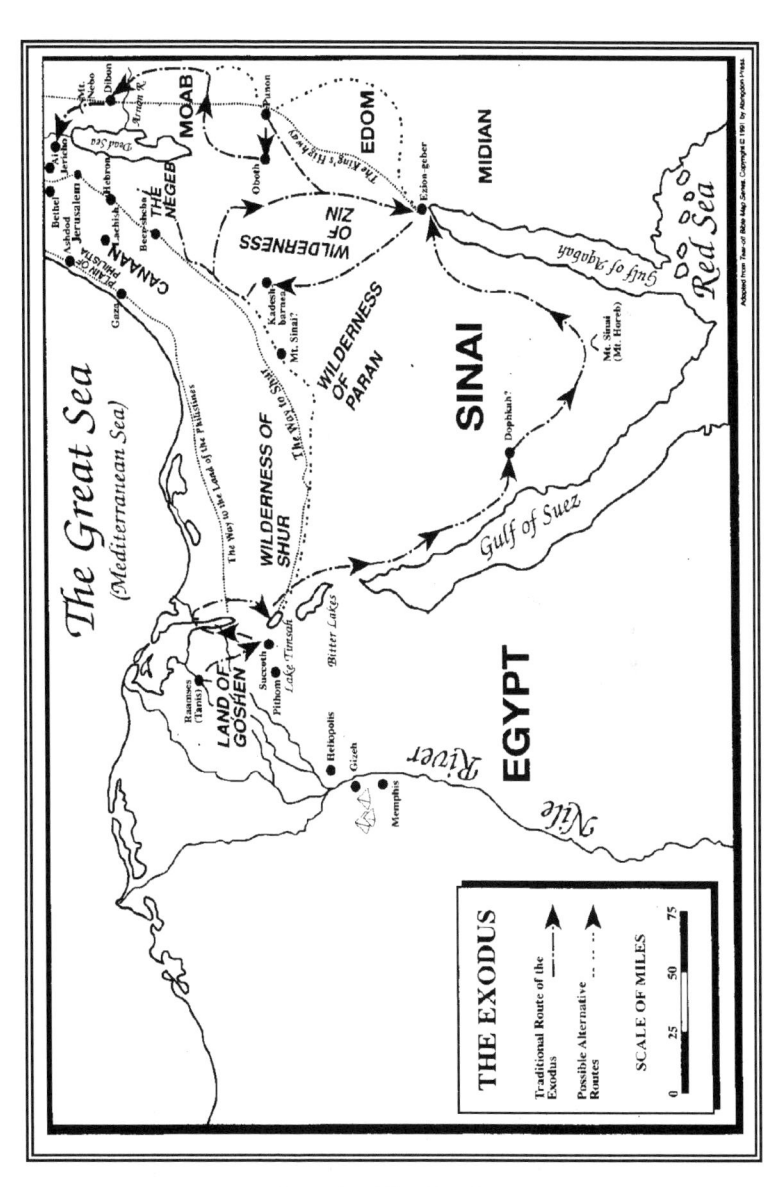

Map 2 – The Exodus

What were the People Like?

The people of Israel had been slaves in Egypt, living lives consisting of drudgery and misery, for at least 200–250 years. They lived in small mud houses and rarely had the opportunity to travel or get any education as the Egyptians had them working at manual labour as soon as they were old enough. Then suddenly, after living all their lives in this way, there was a dramatic change in their circumstances. Their journey into the wilderness was a journey into the complete unknown. All that they were familiar with was left behind and they became nomads in the desert, living in tents and looking for food and water for themselves and their livestock.

The Israelites had grown up with a sketchy knowledge of the God of Abraham, Isaac and Jacob. Moses appeared out of nowhere and introduced their God as "I am". They then lived through an extraordinary few months of miracles seeing God bring ten plagues on their oppressors and, when they thought that they were finally facing death, saw the Red Sea open up for them to cross on dry land before it returned to destroy the remains of the Egyptian army. But despite this they did not know who God was or what he was like. Growing up in Egypt they were probably involved in the worship of Egyptian gods as they showed a few months later when they built a golden calf similar to the gods of the Egyptians to worship.

They had a lot to learn about God and he shows incredible patience in teaching them. In the wilderness they were totally reliant on God for everything – even food and water – despite their lack of faith. The careful account of how some of them kept their manna to the next day, even though Moses had told them not to, and how it went bad shows how reluctant they were to rely on God's word. But despite their lack of faith they lived a supernatural existence during their forty years of wandering in the desert. God provided them with a supernatural food – Manna – and they never needed new clothes and sandals as they didn't wear out (see Deuteronomy 29:5).

As an ethnic minority, used as a slave–labour force by the dominant Egyptians, they had no national identity. They were involved in constructing great buildings which symbolised the Egyptian culture and were influenced by that culture without having any opportunity to express their own cultural identity. During the next few months God started the process of making them into a nation and giving them a distinct culture as his special people.

A Legal System

One of the first steps in making Israel into a nation doesn't come to them as a direct word from God but as words of wisdom from an older man.

> Read Exodus 18

The visit that Moses had from his father–in–law is not only of benefit to him but also to the entire Israelite nation. Jethro sees his son–in–law exhausted with the many legal disputes that come to him and suggests a systematic approach to dealing with legal matters. His advice has two parts. He advises Moses to appoint judges over the people with differing levels of responsibility. This structure has many strengths. It enables minor offences to be dealt with by people close to the situation while freeing up the time of those over thousands and Moses himself to deal with the more serious cases. It also allows leadership to be tried and tested at the small level – over tens and fifties – before people are given greater responsibility.

Alongside this advice Jethro advises Moses that he must teach the people *"decrees and laws, and show them the way to live"*. The men who were appointed as judges had to be capable, trustworthy and fear God but they also had to be taught the law. They needed guidance in dealing with all the situations they would face. The process of teaching the law started soon after this when the people arrived at Mount Sinai.

The People reach Sinai

The Israelites arrived at Mount Sinai three months after leaving Egypt and they stayed there for eleven very significant months. The second half of Exodus (chapters 19–40), all of Leviticus, and the first part of Numbers (chapters 1–10) are all set at Mount Sinai in this period. This is where Israel is transformed from an ethnic minority into a nation.

The Old Covenant

> Read Exodus 19

The first thing that happens to Israel at Sinai is that God makes a covenant with them. God had made a covenant with Abraham in Genesis 17: *"I will establish my covenant as an everlasting covenant between me and you and your descendants after you for the generations to come, to be your God and the God of your descendants after you." (Genesis 17:7)* and had renewed it with both Isaac and Jacob. The time had now come for God to renew that covenant with their descendents.

Moses is called to go up the mountain and that is where God gives him the covenant for the Israelites: *"If you obey me fully and keep my covenant, then out of all nations you will be my treasured possession. Although the whole earth is mine, you will be for me a kingdom of priests and a holy nation." (Exodus 19:5–6).* Right at the heart of the national identity of Israel is the fact that they are God's chosen people, chosen out of all the nations to be set apart for God. This is the Old Covenant or Old Testament.

But, like the covenant with Abraham, this covenant is conditional. The people have to obey God and keep his covenant – the laws and regulations that follow – in order to be God's people. Over the coming months God gave Moses many detailed laws and regulations for the Israelites. Tomorrow we will start looking at these in some more detail.

Day 19
The Ten Commandments

The Law

The first five books of the Bible – Genesis, Exodus, Leviticus, Numbers and Deuteronomy – are called "The Law". They contain the basis for personal and national life both in practical and spiritual matters. They are also sometimes known as "The Books of Moses" as, traditionally, it is thought that they were originally compiled and written by Moses. This has been challenged over the last century but there is not a strong argument for thinking that they were written by anyone else. Another name used for the five books of the Law is "The Pentateuch", which is Greek for "five books".

The Law is a mixture of history, laws and regulations for worship. The history includes stories about individuals and the Israelite nation. The laws include both civil laws and a personal moral code. The regulations for Worship set out the payment for sin, details for setting up a place of worship (the Tabernacle) and the priesthood. Many people setting out to read the Bible for the first time start at the beginning and find it a fairly easy read through to Exodus chapter 20. But after Exodus 20 the going gets tough and, if people keep reading into Leviticus, it is very hard to continue without an understanding of what it is all about. As we read through the Law we will see how some of it relates to the New Testament.

Not Just Regulations

Many of the laws and regulations are recorded in their historical setting. This is not accidental as the historical background adds to our understanding of the law. For example, marriage is introduced at the end of the account of the creation of Eve, *"For this reason a man will leave his father and mother and be united to his wife, and they will become one flesh" (Genesis 2:24)*. Later the law allowed and regulated divorce but when Jesus was asked about the grounds for divorce he refers back to the Genesis 2:24, making it clear that lifelong marriage was what God intended from the beginning (see Matthew 19:3–9). The regulations on divorce came much later, not as a command from God, but in response to the fact that men's *"hearts were hard" (Matthew 19:8)*. Jesus defends the institution of marriage from the law by taking account of the context in which the regulations were given.

Another example is the way the regulations about how to celebrate the Passover are given in great detail in Exodus 12 and 13. The story of Israel's deliverance from Egypt is just coming to a climax when the whole flow of the story is broken up by these two chapters containing regulations for celebrating the Passover in years to come and for consecrating the firstborn to the Lord. Again, this puts these ongoing ceremonies firmly in their historical settings so that future generations can understand the reasons for them.

The Ten Commandments

As we saw in Exodus 19 God made a conditional covenant with Israel. *"If you obey me fully and keep my covenant, then out of all nations you will be my treasured possession." (Exodus 19:5).* From Exodus 20 onwards the books of the law set out the detail of this covenant and what the Israelites must do to obey God fully. The balance of the writing moves from being mainly stories about people and nations with a few regulations to being mainly regulations with a few stories.

The detailed account of the covenant starts with the Ten Commandments. These are expressed in the way that royal treaties were written in those times. God makes it clear who he is – *"I am the LORD your God"* – and what he has done for his people – *"who brought you out of Egypt..."* – and then lists ten treaty obligations. The people are to obey these because of who God is and his relationship to them.

> **Read Exodus 20:1–21**

When a covenant was made between two people, two copies would be made with each party keeping one copy. This is still the practice today in law. Moses received two copies of the Ten Commandments written on tablets of stone by God himself. Both were kept before the presence of God in the centre of the nation. The Ten Commandments form the basis of the rest of the law, which in turn provides the foundation for the whole of the Old Testament. The prophets continually refer back to the law and God's covenant relationship with his people. They have also been the basis for legal systems throughout the Western world over the 4,000 years that have followed.

The individual laws and regulations that follow in Exodus, Leviticus and Numbers are based on the Ten Commandments. They provide a

Day 19 – The Ten Commandments

more detailed explanation of them and spell out the consequences of breaking them. For example, the eighth commandment is *"You shall not steal"* but the detailed regulations expand this into different punishments, depending on what is stolen, and how offenders must make restitution to their victims, etc.

Looking from twenty–first century eyes some of the laws may seem severe but when Moses brought them back to the people of Israel their response was very positive. *"When Moses went and told the people all the LORD's words and laws, they responded with one voice, 'Everything the LORD has said we will do.'" (Exodus 24:3).* The people then had no hesitation in accepting them as reasonable. The difficulty would come later when they tried to keep them!

This body of law is at a higher level than anything else that was around at that time. They demonstrate God's concern for fair justice. For example, Exodus 21:12–14 makes a clear distinction between murder and what we call manslaughter. If a man takes another man's life deliberately he is guilty of murder and punished accordingly. But if he takes the life of another unintentionally then he is not subject to the same punishment. God's laws also demonstrate his interest in the detail of our everyday lives. Exodus 21:33–34 rules that a man who leaves a pit uncovered which leads to the death of one of his neighbours' animals must compensate his neighbour for his loss. A simple ruling which accepts that accidents will happen, but ensures that they do not grow into long term resentment and feuds.

The Golden Calf

After Moses had delivered the covenant laws to the Israelites he went back up Mount Sinai for forty days receiving more detailed laws. While he was gone the people grew restless and, despite their quick response to do everything that the Lord told them, turned to Aaron and asked him to make them a god to lead them. Aaron responded by taking their gold and making an idol in the shape of a calf. The leaders of the people then said to the people *"These are your gods, O Israel, who brought you up out of Egypt" (Exodus 32:4).* Aaron arranged for burnt offerings to be made to this idol and the people set about "worshipping" it, which meant excessive eating, drinking and immoral behaviour.

It is clear that the Israelites – including their leaders – had a very poor understanding of God at this stage! Even though they had seen God work amazing miracles for them they are ready to believe that an idol

Day 19 – The Ten Commandments

made by human hands is the "god" that brought them out of Egypt. Even though they had enthusiastically embraced the covenant Moses brought to them they went completely against the first and second commandments which they had heard only a matter of weeks earlier.

God is so angry with the people that he tells Moses that he will destroy them and make Moses into a great nation instead. Moses' response to this gives us an incredible insight into his character. He starts by reminding God that he has brought them out of Egypt to fulfil his purposes and his covenant promises to Abraham, Isaac and Israel. Moses is not interested in promoting himself but shows great humility. Given how much trouble the people have been to him it is remarkable that he is prepared to plead with God on their behalf. God listens to his prayer and Exodus 32:14 records that *"the LORD relented and did not bring on his people the disaster he had threatened."* God changes his mind in response to a humble man praying in God's will and purpose. Later in the same chapter Moses goes back to God to ask him to forgive the people for their sin. In doing this he totally identifies himself with them and says to God *"But now, please forgive their sin – but if not, then blot me out of the book you have written." (Exodus 32:32).*

Moses loves the people God has put under his care and is ready to plead with God on their behalf. However, this does not mean that he overlooks their sin. He not only represents the people to God but also represents God to the people. When he comes down the mountain and returns to the people, he is so angry that he smashes the tablets of stone and punishes the people by taking the golden calf, burning it and grinding it to powder and scattering the powder on the water which the people are made to drink. He also sends the Levites to kill those involved and God also sends a plague.

In Exodus 34 Moses replaces the smashed covenant stone tablets with two new chiselled stones and returns to Mount Sinai to renew the covenant. God reveals more of his nature by proclaiming his name and its meaning to Moses: *"The LORD, the LORD, the compassionate and gracious God, slow to anger, abounding in love and faithfulness, maintaining love to thousands, and forgiving wickedness, rebellion and sin. Yet he does not leave the guilty unpunished; he punishes the children and their children for the sin of the fathers to the third and fourth generation." (Exodus 34:6–7).* This declaration of God's name is quoted many times in the Old Testament. Time after time God's people rebelled against him but we see that he is indeed "slow to anger" and so ready to forgive. This is a great comfort to those of us living under the new covenant!

The Tabernacle

In addition to receiving laws for the people while he was on Mount Sinai, the Lord also gave Moses detailed instructions for the construction of a tent to be placed right at the centre of their camp, which would be where God would live among his people. This tent was called "the Tabernacle", which means, "dwelling place", and was to be the focal point for their worship.

The whole tabernacle was surrounded by a courtyard, which was screened off by curtains, and in that there was a large bronze altar used to offer the people's sacrifices to God. The tabernacle itself was a tent split into two parts. The outer part was called "the Holy Place" and the inner part, which could only be entered through the Holy Place, was called "the Most Holy Place". This contained the most important item in the whole of Israel – the Ark of the Covenant – a wooden chest overlaid with pure gold, which represented the throne of God. Inside this ark were put the tablets ofstone with the covenant written upon them. This most sacred symbol of God's presence was to be at the heart of the Israelite camp as they journeyed through the desert and was placed in the heart of the Promised Land when they reached it.

The Tabernacle was ready about one year after the first Passover, and Moses set it up in the centre of the camp. As soon as he had finished, God put his seal of approval on the project in a dramatic way: *"Then the cloud covered the Tent of Meeting, and the glory of the LORD filled the tabernacle. Moses could not enter the Tent of Meeting because the cloud had settled upon it, and the glory of the LORD filled the tabernacle." (Exodus 40:34-35)*. From this time on the Israelites had the visible presence of the Lord, as a cloud by day and a fiery cloud by night, at the heart of their camp. This cloud acted as a guide for them throughout their stay in the wilderness. When the cloud lifted they broke camp and moved on. If it stayed then they stayed where they were. They were God's people and he lived among them.

Summary of Exodus

At the beginning of Exodus we are introduced to the Israelites as an oppressed group of slaves, in bondage to the Egyptians, with little understanding of God and no hope for the future. By the end of the book we have a group of people in covenant relationship with their

God. God has revealed himself to them, his name and his characteristics, and demonstrated his power to redeem his people. He has renewed his covenant with them, started to give them laws to live by and showed them how he is to be worshipped. Israel is becoming a nation.

Leviticus

The third book of the Bible is called Leviticus, and it is probably one of the hardest books in the Bible to read as it is almost entirely made up of laws and regulations. The name means, "relating to the Levites", as most of it refers to regulations concerning the Priests (who were also called Levites as they came from the tribe of Levi) and the detail of how worship was to be carried out at the tabernacle.

Most of the laws in Leviticus were given to Moses in the year that Israel camped at Mount Sinai in 1445BC and they build on the covenant God made with his people in Exodus. The key theme of the book is holiness – the holiness of God and of man as summed up in Leviticus 11:45: *"I am the LORD who brought you up out of Egypt to be your God; therefore be holy, because I am holy."* To say that God is holy is to say that he is morally and spiritually pure and perfect. For men to be holy they too must be perfect. Man cannot achieve this by his own efforts but must obey God's commandments and regulations in order to qualify for forgiveness of his sin. Israel was a unique nation as God had chosen them as his own people. Their response had to be to keep themselves distinct from other nations both physically separate, to avoid being polluted by their sin, and in the way they conducted their lives. The standards for this are set out in Leviticus where the word "holy" appears more often than in any other book in the Bible.

Under the new covenant we receive *"a righteousness from God" (Romans 1:17)* by accepting what Jesus has done for us in taking away our sin. We do not have to continue to carry out regulations to remain holy. For this reason it is difficult to see how to apply Leviticus to our lives under the new covenant today. Jesus has done away with the need for priests and sacrifices and special days, and we can have a direct relationship with God himself. But the principle of holiness and the detailed way in which the Israelites were to conduct their daily lives to be holy indicates to us the importance God places on holiness. We are not called to keep ourselves physically separate from those around us in the world but we are urged to keep ourselves distinct from other people in terms of the way we conduct our lives.

The book does not contain any particular structure but we will briefly look at its contents under five headings.

Outline of Leviticus	
1–7, 24:1–9	Regulations on offerings to God.
8–10, 21–22	Regulations for the Priests.
11–15, 17, 26–27	Regulations on Holiness.
18–20, 24:10–23	Moral laws.
16, 23, 25	Set days and years.

Regulations on Offerings to God

At the centre of the Israelites' worship to God was a framework of offerings. These were either livestock or, for the poor, some form of grain. The idea of making offerings to God existed from the beginning as we read that Adam and Eve's sons, Cain and Abel made offerings to the Lord. Genesis also records that both Noah and Abraham made "burnt offerings" and Isaac and Jacob made altars as part of their worship. Leviticus gives regulations for a number of different types of offerings.

The Sin Offering was required when someone had unintentionally done something wrong. When they realised that they had broken God's law they were to bring a young bull, a goat or a lamb, or, if they were poor, a dove or pigeon, or, if they were very poor, some flour. The animal was brought to the tabernacle; the man who had sinned placed his hands on the animal and killed it. God takes sin very seriously and from the beginning specified to Adam and Eve that sin led to death. Because of God's mercy man does not have to die the instant he sins but under the old covenant the animal took the place of the man and died for him. This made reconciliation between God and man or, as it is often called in Leviticus, atonement – literally "at–one–ment". God and man can be "at one" as a result of God's wrath being dealt with by the death of an animal. Other offerings dealt with unintentional sin or were used as a voluntary expression of worship.

Leviticus also formally introduced the idea of tithing, giving a tenth of all income to God. It was used to support the Levites, who in turn tithed to support the Priests, and the poor in the whole community.

These offerings represented a costly framework for the Israelites. Dealing with their sin cost them in economic terms, as animals from their herds had to be sacrificed. Special provisions were made for the poor but all had to pay a price. Clearly it also cost the animals too! Life was lost as a result of sin reminding them that *"the wages of sin is death," (Romans 6:23)* as Paul wrote hundreds of years later.

The animals that were brought for sacrifice had to be without defect. A man could not come with the weakest animal from his flock but had to present a perfect animal to the priest. In these regulations concerning offerings we see a clear pointer to the sacrifice of Jesus, God's perfect Son, who came and made the ultimate sacrifice, himself. Hebrews 7:27 says *"He sacrificed for their sins once for all when he offered himself"*. The comparison of the sacrificial system under the old covenant and the sacrifice of Jesus under the new covenant is explained more fully in Hebrews 9:13–10:18. The sacrifice of animals of itself did nothing to remove mans sin but it served as a symbol of what was to come. Fortunately for those of us living under the new covenant *"there is no longer any sacrifice for sin" (Hebrews 10:18)* thanks to what Jesus has done for us.

Although these offerings are not directly relevant to us as Christians today they teach us some important lessons: God takes sin seriously, God wants our free commitment to him demonstrated regularly, and God loves to have fellowship with us. Tomorrow we will continue to look at what Leviticus had to teach the Israelites then and us today.

Day 20
Making Israel into a Nation

Yesterday we looked at the first of five subjects covered by Leviticus. Today we will look at the other four.

Regulations for the Priests

Looking after the tabernacle and administering the offerings was the responsibility of the priests. Moses' brother Aaron and his sons were ordained as priests, which means that they were set apart from the other people for special duties. Moses was given the format for the ceremony. The priests had to be especially holy. There were stricter rules for them, both in scope and punishment. Two of Aaron's sons got the regulations wrong and God killed them (see Leviticus 10). The priests had to be holy as they represented God to man and man to God. The people could not approach God directly but had to use a priest as a mediator.

Again, this is part of the old covenant. Jesus, in the new covenant, supersedes the priesthood. Jesus was not only the sacrifice to forgive sins but was also the everlasting priest who made the sacrifice and will represent God to us and us to God forever. Hebrews 7:23–27 explains this. The fact that we can offer our worship direct to God rather than through a priestly mediator makes us all priests under the new covenant. As Peter wrote in his first letter: *"But you are a chosen people, a royal priesthood, ..." (1 Peter 2:9).* We all have direct access to God.

Holiness

The main thrust of Leviticus is for God's people to be holy. God's people were given a number of laws that set them apart from other nations in terms of behaviour. There were regulations about "cleanness" and "uncleanness", including which animals they could eat, how infectious diseases should be dealt with, and general hygiene. Once again some of the details are no longer relevant under the new covenant but the principles of holiness and being "clean", or righteous, before God are still relevant.

When Jesus came the Jewish leaders of his time were very careful to obey these laws, and others that the Jews added over the centuries whilst ignoring inner holiness. Jesus, seeing their hypocrisy, commented that *"What goes into a man's mouth does not make him 'unclean,' but what comes out of his mouth, that is what makes him 'unclean' (Matthew 15:11).*

Moral Laws

The moral laws in Leviticus are extensions of the Ten Commandments. They are summed up in a famous verse that Jesus said was the second greatest of all the commandments: *"Love your neighbour as yourself" (Leviticus 19:18).*

Set Days and Years

In addition to resting one day in seven the Israelites were also given special days and years to celebrate. In addition to the Passover they were also told that once they had settled in the Promised Land they were to spend one week a year living in tents to remind the Israelites of their life in the wilderness and God's provision. Anyone who has attended a "Bible Week" in a tent will know what that was like! The feasts of Firstfruits and Pentecost were times of thankfulness for God's provision, rather like our modern day Harvest festivals.

But the most important day of the Israelite calendar was called the Day of Atonement ("Yom Kippur" in Hebrew) when the High Priest went into the Most Holy Place to "atone" for Israel's sins. This was the only day that anyone entered the Most Holy Place and was a very solemn occasion. There was no feasting on that day: it was a national day of fasting.

The High Priest made a number of sacrifices that day. At one point two goats were brought to him. The High Priest sacrificed one and scattered its blood on the Seat of Atonement on top of the Ark of the Covenant and then confessed the sins of the people over the head of the other one before driving it into the desert symbolically taking their sins away. This second goat is called a "scapegoat."

Leviticus also sets out a pattern of years in chapter 25. Every seventh year the land was to be left fallow, which is good farming practice as it allows the land to recover its goodness. Then, after seven cycles of seven years, the fiftieth year was called the Year of Jubilee. In this year, when the land was also left fallow, all the land reverted back to being owned by the family it was originally allocated to. This meant that land could never be permanently sold, it could only be leased at a price dependant on the length of time to the next Year of Jubilee.

This provides a safety–net for the poor. There could be two men living

Day 20 – Making Israel into a Nation

alongside each other where one is hard working and the other lazy. One will die prosperous and leave a good inheritance to his sons while the other will become poor and may have to sell his land in order to make ends meet. His sons will start at a disadvantage to their wealthier neighbours through no fault of their own. But in the Year of Jubilee the slate is wiped clean and the property sold returns to the family of the man who sold it. The next generation does not go on paying the price of the previous generation's laziness or misfortune.

This is an interesting mix of Capitalism and Socialism! People can better themselves and become wealthier through their own efforts and abilities but their scope was limited by the Year of Jubilee when the playing field was levelled once again. Despite being such an excellent system there is no indication in the Bible that it was ever implemented.

Numbers

Numbers continues the story of the Israelites in the desert from Exodus and Leviticus and describes their journey from Mount Sinai to the plains of Moab on the border of Canaan. It is named after the two censuses of chapters 1 and 26. The Hebrew name is "In the Desert", which is taken from the first words of the book in Hebrew and is probably a more accurate description of the book. It was written by Moses and covers the period from 1445–1406 BC.

The history in the book falls into three sections (see next page).

Organisation of the Tribes and the Departure from Sinai

The Israelites spent a year at Sinai where they received the Ten Commandments, built the tabernacle and started to get used to being an independent nation rather than a group of slaves. But God did not lead his people out of Egypt in order for them to live in the desert. His promise to Abraham was that his descendants would inherit the land of Canaan. For the Israelites to enter into this promise they had to go and defeat the nations living there and this would mean driving them out using force. At the beginning of Numbers Moses is instructed to take a census of all the men over 20 who are able to serve in an army. There were over 600,000 men ready for military service and they were organised according to their tribes. Each tribe was assigned a place to camp around the tabernacle. The Levites were counted separately and for a different purpose. They are not to fight like the other tribes as they were set apart for God and given responsibility to care for the tabernacle and help the priests.

Outline of Numbers	
The Israelites at Mount Sinai	
1–4	The first census and other military arrangements.
5:1–10:10	Laws, Offerings, the Celebration of the second Passover
The people travel to Kadesh in the Desert of Paran	
10:11–10:36	The people leave Sinai.
11–12	Complaints about the food and about Moses.
13–14	The people refuse to enter the land through fear of its inhabitants and are condemned to spend 40 years in the desert where all the adults (except Joshua and Caleb) will die.
15–19	Various laws; Korah leads a rebellion against Moses and Aaron.
38 years later: the journey to the Plains of Moab	
20:1–20:13	Moses sins in front of the people and is not allowed to lead the people into the Promised Land.
20:14–22:1	Journey to the Plains of Moab; the defeat of Ammon and Bashan.
22:2–25:18	The King of Moab hires Balaam to curse Israel.
26–30	The second census; various instructions.
31–32	The defeat of Midian; 2½ tribes settle east of the Jordan.
33–36	Appendices: the journey; the land; inheritance for women.

After receiving further regulations the people celebrated the second Passover a year after they had left Egypt. A lot had happened in that year and the people were now ready for action. In Numbers 10 the cloud lifted from the tabernacle for the last time at Sinai and the people moved off towards the Promised Land. It is interesting to note that Moses asked his brother–in–law to accompany them to help decide where they should camp in the desert. The cloud above the tabernacle gave them general direction but wise human advice was still useful in deciding the detail.

Complaints

Having spent a year in Sinai the people got settled but once they set out on the journey to the Promised Land problems restarted. The people complained about their hardships and some of them were consumed by fire. Then they complained about the lack of variety in the food they were eating – just manna – and God sent them so many quail that some of them became sick.

Moses had got used to the people complaining but in Numbers 12 things took a turn for the worse when his brother and sister, Aaron and Miriam, also spoke against him. It seems that they were jealous of their younger brother's special relationship with God. God summoned them to the tabernacle and made it clear that Moses was indeed special in that he could speak with God face to face. Miriam was left with leprosy from this encounter and Moses cried out to God to heal her. God hears his prayer and she is healed after seven days of punishment. At the times Moses is under greatest pressure his humility shines through. A later editor of Numbers added the comment, *"Now Moses was a very humble man, more humble than anyone else on the face of the earth." (Numbers 12:3)*

At the end of Numbers 12 the people reached the Desert of Paran at the southernmost tip of the Promised Land. They were now in position to defeat the Canaanites and take possession of their inheritance.

Spying out the Land

We learn later that it was at the people's suggestion that Moses sent twelve spies into the land of Canaan to see what it is like (see Deuteronomy 1:22–23). They are impressed by the agricultural produce but are shocked by the level of fortification and size of its inhabitants. When Abraham was there four hundred years earlier Hebron was a trading place for shepherds. This was the picture of the land that had been passed down to the Israelites from generation to generation but now it is a fortified city *"with walls up to the sky" (Deuteronomy 1:28)*. Their spying mission and the reaction of the people is a pivotal moment for the Israelites.

> **Read Numbers 13–14**

The contrast between the report of the ten and the other two spies is stark. The ten bring back a report of despair while only two, Caleb and Joshua, see things from God's perspective. With God on their side they can certainly do it, but the negative report from the ten turns the people against Moses. It is him who has brought them into the desert to go to a Promised Land that is clearly beyond their ability to take. They have forgotten the miracles that God performed to bring them out of Egypt and that the land was promised to them by him. In their despair they say they will not go into the land and even talk of choosing a leader to take them back to slavery in Egypt!

God responds by telling Moses he will wipe them all out and start again with him! This is the second time he has done this and once again Moses intervenes in prayer and saves the people from instant death. However, God does not completely relent but condemns them to spend forty years wandering in the desert. This unbelieving generation will not enter the Promised Land. Their children, who they said would be taken as plunder, will be the ones to inherit it. The ten spies are killed instantly and over the next forty years all the people over twenty, except Caleb and Joshua, die in the desert.

The impact of this judgement on the people must have been devastating. All their hopes are now shattered. They respond in bitter tears, possibly more of remorse than true repentance, and decide that they should now do what God told them to do originally – to go and fight for the Promised Land. Despite Moses' warning that the Lord is not with them the people go into battle and are soundly defeated.

There are some important lessons for us from Kadesh. We see a God who is determined to work out his purposes. God has made some promises to his people and he will fulfil them. But he is not desperate to fulfil them through any generation at any cost. He remains willing to judge his people. He is prepared to wipe out an entire generation and fulfil his promises through Moses. After Moses prays he does it by patiently waiting forty years for a new generation to emerge who will obey him while the disobedient one dies out. A whole generation is passed over because of their sin.

It is also sobering to note that God's judgement comes on this people, not because of their constant complaining and looking back to Egypt, but because they refuse to take the land God has promised them. Which do we consider worse: wanting to return to the sin we have left behind or not having the faith to obey God and move forward in response to his leading? If we fail to listen to him we can find ourselves stuck in the desert. God will fulfil his promises but he may wait until a new generation has emerged to do it. He is not committed to using us at all costs.

After Kadesh

After the people have been told that they will not enter the land in Numbers 14, the first regulation recorded in Numbers 15 relates to offerings that for the Israelites *"After you enter the land"*. God has not been deflected from his purpose and continues to prepare the people even though they are now forty years from realising the promise.

Chapters 16–19 cover more rebellions and more regulations and then there is a big gap in Numbers between chapters 19 and 20. Mark it in your Bible. Thirty–eight years pass between the end of chapter 19 and the beginning of chapter 20. The wandering of this rebellious generation in *"the vast and dreadful desert"* passes without comment. Tomorrow we will pick up the story as the next generation prepare to enter the Promised Land.

Day 21
Preparing to Enter the Land

The end of a Generation

Today we pick up the story of the children of Israel in the desert, almost forty years after the spying mission to Canaan. Numbers 20 starts with the death of Miriam and ends with the death of Aaron, symbolising the death of a whole generation that has wandered in the desert as a result of their lack of faith in the Lord's promise. The generation that disobeyed God has died in the desert and it is now time for a new generation to respond to the call of God on them. Those aged forty to sixty were born in Egypt. The majority, aged under forty, were born in the desert. They have been brought up as part of an independent nation with God's laws, worshipping him and knowing his presence with them day and night in the cloud and fire over the tabernacle.

This chapter also records that Moses disobeyed the Lord in front of the people. When told to speak to a rock to provide water for the people he struck it with his staff. Although this may seem a minor offence to us, this was a serious matter. The leader of God's people demonstrated a lack of faith in God's word and as a result was told by God that he would not enter the Promised Land.

The First Battles and Balaam the False Prophet.

In Numbers 21 they start the march towards the land of Canaan. The first nations they come to are Edom, descendants of Jacob's brother Esau, and Moab, descendants of Abraham's nephew Lot. The Lord commanded Moses that the people were not to attack either of these nations as he had given that territory to them. Moses asks for permission to march through Edom and Moab but after they are refused access they go around the east of them (see Map 3 on page 145).

They then request permission to march through the land of the Amorites and Bashan but their kings, Sihon and Og, not only refuse them access but come out to attack them. They are defeated and so the Israelites take some territory to the east of the Jordan. (In recent years I have noticed a trend towards people giving their babies some of the less well known names from the Bible, but no one I know has called their baby "Og." I am still waiting for that day – it is such a great name!)

Day 21 – Preparing to Enter the Land

Numbers 22–25 records a very strange incident featuring a false prophet called Balaam. It had a serious impact on the Israelites and is held up as a warning on a number of occasions in the Bible. Despite the fact that the Israelites have gone round his country the King of Moab is afraid of them and sends for an internationally known pagan diviner called Balaam to come and curse the Israelites. Although Balaam is an occult practitioner God speaks to him on this occasion and forbids him to go, allowing him to go on the second time of asking on the condition that he only speaks the words that the Lord himself gives him. Just to make doubly sure that Balaam knows he must only speak on God's behalf about the Israelites Balaam is also met by an angel of the Lord. At first Balaam does not see him but he is allowed to see him after his donkey has spoken to him.

Balak, the King of Moab, has offered a high price to get Balaam to come and curse Israel but Balaam makes it clear that he will only speak the words that God gives him. To Balak's dismay this results in Balaam speaking words of blessing on his enemies. Undeterred Balak tries twice more to get Balaam to curse them but the result is further blessings. After the third attempt Balak sends Balaam away without pay but Balaam responds with a remarkable prophecy about the future of Israel and her future king. This is initially fulfilled by King David, but the ultimate fulfilment is by Jesus himself. It is a remarkable illustration of how God can use a wicked man to his own ends.

What is not clear from the immediate story, but which becomes apparent later, is that once he has finished his prophecies Balaam advises Balak to use the Moabite women to seduce the Israelite men into the fertility rites of their god, Baal. The worship of pagan gods involved sexual immorality. This policy is very successful and many of the Israelites are taken in. The Lord tells Moses to kill those who are involved and 24,000 are also killed in a plague. Later God tells Moses to take vengeance on Moab and 12,000 Israelites are sent into battle and totally defeat Moab without the loss of a man!

This incident with the Moabites indicates the problem that God's people will face in the land of Canaan. When they were in Egypt the Egyptians would not mix with them. In the Promised Land the people were only too ready to socialise with the result that the Israelites could get drawn into a pagan culture and worship of other gods.

The End of Numbers

Towards the end of Numbers there is a second census as, once again, they prepare for war. The total number of men is similar to the number forty years earlier – around 600,000. As Moses has been told that he will not enter the Promised Land, the Lord appoints a new leader for the people, Joshua, who is commissioned by the priest as leader of the people to succeed Moses. He has been Moses' servant for all the years in the desert and has first hand experience of seeing what is involved in the task. It is the first of many examples of leaders training younger men to take on their responsibilities.

As a result of their defeat of the Amorites and the land of Bashan, the Israelites have unexpectedly acquired territory east of the Jordan, outside the Promised Land. 2½ tribes – Reuben, Gad, and half the tribe of Manasseh – ask Moses for permission to settle in this land. This permission is granted, but only on the condition that they fight with the other tribes to conquer the land to the west of the Jordan. The Levites, who as priests were to be allocated towns among the tribes, were given towns on the east of the Jordan among these tribes.

The last chapters of Numbers contain two stories about the daughters of a man named Zelophehad that indicate the importance of the land to the Israelites and how the law evolved to cater for new circumstances. Numbers 27:1–11 records how the five daughters of Zelophehad came to Moses to ask that they be given property rights along with the men in their tribe. Their father died in the desert without leaving behind a male heir and they are concerned that his name should not be left out of the allocation of land. Moses took the case to the Lord and God told him to give the inheritance of a man who had no sons to his daughters.

Zelophehad happened to be part of the half tribe of Manasseh which was given land on the east of the Jordan and when his land was allocated to his daughters, the head men of Manasseh realised that if the daughters married outside the tribe, then the land allocated to them would go to another tribe. This could result in the tribal allocation being eaten away by other tribes. In response to this the Lord modified the law so that they had to marry within their tribe to keep the land. If they married outside the tribe then they would lose the land – it would stay with the tribe. Zelophehad's daughters married their cousins and Zelophehad's inheritance lived on and the land remained in the tribe of Manasseh (see Numbers 36:1–12).

For the Israelites the land was their inheritance from God. The importance of this cannot be underestimated and we will see how important this was both to them and to God over the next few days.

Deuteronomy

Deuteronomy means "Repetition of the Law". In Hebrew it is called "These are the words." Both are good summaries of the book which is a series of addresses from Moses restating the covenant given to the previous generation to the new generation which will take the land. It was written by Moses in 1406 BC although the introduction (chapter 1:1–5) and the report of his death (chapter 34) were added by someone else later.

There is no strong structure to the book as most of it is a record of Moses speaking to the people.

Outline of Deuteronomy	
1–4	Moses goes over their history.
5–30	Moses reiterates the covenant
31–34	Moses hands over leadership to Joshua and blesses the tribes before his death

Deuteronomy continues from the end of Numbers with the Israelites encamped on the east of the Jordan River poised to attack the land of Canaan. The addresses from Moses to the Israelites restate the law given to the previous generation forty years previously at Mount Sinai (as recorded in Exodus, Leviticus and Numbers). After going over their recent history, including the rebellion that took place before many of them were born, Moses repeats the covenant law to them starting with a reiteration of the Ten Commandments in chapter 5. Much of the material is repeated but the difference is in the style as Moses pours out his heart to the people he has looked after for forty years knowing that he will die very soon.

As the people are about to take the Promised Land some of the new material in Deuteronomy is specifically relevant for settling in the land. Moses gives them instructions to establish town judges with the back up of central law courts run by the priests for the cases too difficult for the local judges. He also sets out regulations for having a king, instructions that were not required until Samuel anointed a king some 350 years later.

The theme of the book is total commitment to the Lord and this is summed up in Deuteronomy 6:4–9 which is known as the "Shema" by devout Jews who still recite it daily.

> **Read Deuteronomy 6:4-9**

When Jesus was asked which was the most important of all the commandments in the Law he quoted the beginning of these verses (see Mark 12:30).

Moses' Final Words

Moses' main address ends with him presenting the choice the people have – whether to obey or not obey the Lord's commands – as a stark choice between life and death, blessings and curses and he urges them to *"choose life"* by following God's commands. From the end of his speech you get a sense of his passionate desire to see the people follow the Lord.

> **Read Deuteronomy 30**

After he had finished his addresses to the people Moses writes down the law and gives it to the priests who are charged with the responsibility to teach it to future generations. He is also given a terrible prophecy when the Lord tells him that the people will break the covenant and forsake him. The law, which gives them the option to choose life, will stand in judgement against them when they choose death. Finally Moses gave the Israelites a song to help them remember to choose life. His overriding concern is that they should not forget the importance of God's words: *"Take to heart all the words I have solemnly declared to you this day, so that you may command your children to obey carefully all the words of this law. They are not just idle words for you – they are your life. By them you will live long in the land you are crossing the Jordan to possess."* (Deuteronomy 32:46–47). Their whole future security as a nation depended on keeping their part of the covenant God had made with them.

The Death of Moses

Before he dies Moses blesses the tribes in Deuteronomy 33. It is interesting to compare Moses' blessing for each tribe with the blessing Jacob gave to each of his sons before he died. As we saw then, Jacob gave Simeon and Levi the same prophecy in Genesis 49 – that they would be scattered among the other tribes – but in Deuteronomy 33 Levi gets the longest blessing, as the tribe of priests, while Simeon does not even get a mention.

Moses then went up a mountain to die overlooking the Promised Land.

Day 21 – Preparing to Enter the Land

He spent forty years leading God's people towards it but is only able to see it before he dies. His faithful servant Joshua will lead the people into their inheritance.

Read Deuteronomy 34

The writer of the last chapter of Deuteronomy sums up Moses as the greatest prophet and miracle worker that ever lived. That judgement on him remains unchallenged apart from Jesus himself. Under God's power he worked great miracles and created a nation single-handed. And he started his life's work at the age of eighty! The five books of the law that he left behind are the foundation of the Bible. The Old Testament is often referred to as "The Law and the Prophets" and as we continue through the Bible we will see that time and time again the prophets refer back to the law. They are built on the foundation of God's revelation in the law. In the New Testament Jesus endorsed the Law of Moses by living it and preaching it. Half of Jesus' Old Testament quotes (27 out of 53) are taken from the law. The New Testament letters also contain many quotations from it.

When Moses died the people mourned for thirty days. But once that time was over they had to prepare themselves for battle. The Promised Land was just over the river Jordan and tomorrow we will read how they started the campaign to take their inheritance under the leadership of Joshua.

Day 22
Into the Promised Land

Joshua the Book

Today we leave the five books of the law and move on to the history section of the Bible. The book of Joshua continues straight on from the end of Deuteronomy and describes the fulfilment of God's promises to Abraham to give his descendants the land. It is not known who wrote it although some have suggested that it could have been compiled by the prophet Samuel from earlier writings around 1050 BC. It covers the period from the start of the conquest of Canaan in 1406 BC and concludes with the death of Joshua around 1370 BC (see Timechart 5 on page 150).

As with all the history in the Bible, Joshua is a prophetic book. Saying that a book is prophetic does not mean that it foretells the future, it means that it is written from God's perspective. The story is told to show God's power in keeping his promise to his people.

The book falls into four distinct parts.

Outline of Joshua	
1–5	The Israelites cross the Jordan and enter the Promised Land.
6–12	After conquering the cities of Jericho, Ai and Bethel the Israelites conquer southern and northern Canaan in two campaigns.
13–22	The land is described and its division between the tribes documented.
23–24	Joshua makes a farewell speech to the leaders of Israel and renews the covenant with them before his death.

Joshua the Man

The book of Joshua is named after its central character, Joshua the leader of the Israelites. Joshua was one of only two Israelite men over sixty to enter the Promised Land. He was born and brought up as a

Day 22 – Into the Promised Land

slave in Egypt. When he was a young man in his twenties he saw the incredible miracles God performed through Moses in Egypt and, along with all the other Israelites, he left Egypt at the first Passover and trekked into the desert.

Early into the journey Joshua's abilities came to the attention of Moses. Within months of leaving Egypt the Israelites were attacked by a group of Amalekites and Moses chose Joshua to lead the Israelite men into battle. His victory then demonstrated his military ability.

By the time the Israelites had reached Sinai, Joshua had become Moses' personal assistant. He was the only one to accompany Moses up the mountain to get the law and, when Moses set up the tent of meeting where he met with God, Joshua stayed with the tent when Moses returned to the people. Moses chose him as the representative of his tribe to be one of the twelve spies that went into the land of Canaan and he was the only one who stood with Caleb in saying that the Israelites should not be afraid to go into the land. Through his close association with Moses Joshua developed a deep trust in God and when the time came to appoint a successor to Moses the Lord told him to *"Take Joshua son of Nun, a man in whom is the Spirit" (Numbers 27:18)*. He was God's chosen man to complete Moses' work and bring Israel into the land.

Moses gave him the name Joshua, which means "The Lord Saves" in Hebrew. The Greek version of his name is "Jesus". Joshua is a "type" of Christ, a theological term which means that he foreshadowed the work of Jesus. Under the old covenant, he gave the people their inheritance – the Promised Land; under the new covenant it is Jesus who leads us into our inheritance.

Crossing the Jordan

After the death of Moses, Joshua is met by God, who commissions him for his role in leading the people. Joshua's first instruction is to work a miracle and lead the people through the River Jordan and into the Promised Land.

> **Read Joshua 1–4**

The crossing of the Jordan River is a very significant event. As we have already seen, the Israelites have taken a route that yet again leaves water between them and their destination. Just as Moses required faith to lead the people through the Red Sea so going across the flooded

Jordan required great faith too. It required great faith from Joshua who had to tell the priests what to do. He'd never worked a miracle himself before, he'd only ever watched Moses do it. Watching someone else work a miracle is easy. Performing one yourself is quite different!

It also required great faith from the priests. The water did not stop flowing until they obeyed Joshua and they then had to stand at the bottom of the river bed while two million people plus livestock crossed! It says that the people hurried across. I bet it was the priests who hurried them along! And of course it required faith from the people. They had to cross.

This miracle confirmed Joshua as leader in the eyes of the people. Moses was shown to be God's man by the miracles he performed in Egypt and at the Red Sea and now it was the same for Joshua. *"That day the LORD exalted Joshua in the sight of all Israel; and they revered him all the days of his life, just as they had revered Moses." (Joshua 4:14).*

Crossing the Jordan in a miraculous way was also significant to the inhabitants of the land of Canaan. As the spies had learned from Rahab the crossing of the Red Sea was still in their minds after forty years and now this miracle confirmed their fears about the Israelites. *"Now when all the Amorite kings west of the Jordan and all the Canaanite kings along the coast heard how the LORD had dried up the Jordan before the Israelites until we had crossed over, their hearts melted and they no longer had the courage to face the Israelites." (Joshua 5:1).* Baal, their god, was supposed to have conquered the sea god. Now Israel's God had conquered the river. They had already lost the battle in their minds, as they knew that the Lord had given the Israelites the land.

Day 23
The Battle of Jericho

Preparations for War

Crossing the Jordan marked the end of the Israelites' wanderings in the desert. There were now a few preparations to be made before they could start the assault on the land of Canaan.

Before the Israelites could enter the land they had to make sure that they were keeping God's covenant. When God promised to give the land of Canaan to Abraham and his descendants he told Abraham to circumcise all the males in his household as a sign of that covenant. For some reason while the Israelites had been in the desert they had not circumcised the new born boys but now they are about to take the land the Lord tells Joshua to circumcise the people. This is a clear sign to the people that they are about to take this land not in their own strength but as a result of a covenant keeping God. After that they celebrated the Passover, the ceremony that reminded them of their deliverance from Egypt through God's mighty power.

These events brought home to the Israelites that they were now in the Promised Land. It was not theirs yet but at this point a very significant change took place in their everyday lives which indicated to them that there was no going back. Every week–day for forty years they had got up and collected manna; it had been the staple diet for most of them since birth. But now they were in the land the manna stopped. They were now able to eat some of the produce of the land and no longer needed God's supernatural provision of food. The only way now was forward, on to take the land God had promised them.

The "Battle" of Jericho

The account of the Israelites taking Jericho (see Map 3 on page 145) is a very well known story. Even those who have not read the Biblical account know the famous Negro Spiritual, "Joshua fit de battle of Jericho". The strange part about this song is that as we read the story it becomes apparent that Joshua did not "fit de battle of Jericho"! There are a number of battles recorded in Joshua where Joshua led his army in battle but what is special about Jericho is that it was the one city taken *without* a fight!

As the Israelites prepared to fight to take the land of Canaan the Lord gave them a number of reminders that the battle to take the land was *his*, not theirs. *He* opened up the way for them to enter the land through the Jordan; *he* reminded them by circumcision of *his* covenant to give them the land; as they celebrated the Passover they remembered *his* mighty power in bringing them out of Egypt. But the way they went about capturing the first city made it completely clear to all of them who was in charge of this campaign.

We don't know how long the people were in the land before they took Jericho but Joshua obviously spent some time thinking about how they should take the city. The spies had already been there and found the people in fear of them but it was still a walled city which would not be easy to capture from a military viewpoint. In Joshua 5:13 we find Joshua surveying the city and planning his attack.

What he finds is that he is not the only one weighing up the options. The man he meets with a drawn sword is none other than the commander of the Lord's army who has come to tell Joshua the Lord's plan for taking Jericho. It is interesting to note that, when challenged, the commander of the Lord's army is not on Joshua's side. He comes to give instructions to Joshua as the commander of the Lord's earthly army. Joshua and his army are on his side. Sometimes we wonder if God is on our side in situations but actually the important issue in our lives is if we are on his side.

The instructions Joshua is given do not involve much fighting. The command to march round the city for six days was yet another test of Joshua's faith. The people followed him out of loyalty but I expect many of them had doubts about the wisdom of this strategy as they marched silently around the walls. When the trumpet blast came God worked yet another miracle to demonstrate to his people that this was his campaign which would be won in his strength. The people could not claim any credit for themselves.

> **Read Joshua 5:13–6:27**

At Jericho the people were given specific instructions to "devote" everything to God. All the people were killed along with all the livestock and the city was burned to the ground after the precious metals had been put into the Lord's treasury. The only exception to this was Rahab the prostitute who was saved, along with her family, for looking after the spies. She joined the Israelites and, although we do not read of her again in the Old Testament, we find from the New

Testament that Rahab married an Israelite called Salmon (it has been suggested that maybe he was one of the spies) and as a result became an ancestor of King David and of Jesus himself! The first book of the New Testament, Matthew's gospel, starts with a genealogy of Jesus that includes the names of only three women, one of whom is Rahab. It is fascinating to see the ancestors that Jesus had. Rahab's faith and actions in hiding the spies is also highlighted in two of the New Testament letters – Hebrews and James.

What about the Geneva Convention?

The way in which God's people Israel acted in the book of Joshua poses a number of questions to us living in the twenty-first century. Although the battle of Jericho was not a conventional battle the Israelites still went in and killed all the people – men and women, old and young. This was the first of many cities to be destroyed in the campaign to take the land of Canaan and the pattern of destroying all the people was repeated over and over again. If this were to happen today then Joshua would be indicted for war crimes under the Geneva Convention, the United Nations would pass resolutions condemning the actions of the Israelites, and the International community would be under pressure to send in troops to support the Canaanites. How do we, as Christians, defend the actions of God's people in the Bible?

Some Christians see the God of the Old Testament as very different from the God of the New Testament and seek to distance the God we know from his actions in the past. They see Jesus as coming to introduce a God of love who is very different from the vengeful God of the Old Testament. But if we accept the whole Bible as a complete revelation of God then we have to accept all aspects of God's character as revealed throughout scripture. And if we look closely at what happened at the time of Joshua we will find that it reveals aspects of God's character that are relevant in the New Testament and today.

The book of Joshua makes it clear that the Israelites carried out this military campaign at God's express instruction. As we have already seen, the Lord made it very clear that actually they were taking part in his campaign. He made a way through the Jordan for them to get into the land and he destroyed the city of Jericho – they could not carry out this campaign in their own strength. Why did God do this? Let's consider some of the reasons why God initiated this war.

God, the Judge of all the Earth

In Genesis Abraham referred to God as *"the Judge of all the earth"*. The Bible is clear that God made this world and it is his. The account of the flood shows that God has the right to destroy men as well as to create them. It is his right to exercise judgement on mankind. At the time of Joshua, the land of Canaan was occupied by people who worshipped false gods, were controlled by evil powers, were relying on their own military strength for protection, and were living in a thoroughly wicked and corrupt way. Child sacrifice and religious prostitution were just part of their "worship" of their gods. When people live in this way God will judge them. They will not go unpunished forever.

With the Canaanites, God chose to use his people, Israel, to destroy them. That was his choice. The full quote from Abraham was *"Will not the Judge of all the earth do right?" (Genesis 18:25)*. Abraham had confidence that God would make the right decision about wicked Sodom and we can have confidence that God will judge people rightly too. If nations or individuals worship other gods, seek occult knowledge, are proud of their own strength, or indulge in wicked practices God will judge them. It is his right.

The God of the New Testament is no different. God's final revelation to the apostle John talks about Jesus, the second Joshua, returning to make war on the earth and to judge the nations. *"With justice he judges and makes war. His eyes are like blazing fire, ... Out of his mouth comes a sharp sword with which to strike down the nations. "He will rule them with an iron sceptre." He treads the winepress of the fury of the wrath of God Almighty. On his robe and on his thigh he has this name written:* KING OF KINGS AND LORD OF LORDS.*" (Revelation 19:11–12, 15–16)*. This is the Jesus who came to earth as a baby and allowed himself to be put to death on a cross. He has not changed but having made the way for people to come to God does not remove his right and duty to deal with those who will not respond to his love.

God, the Compassionate and Gracious God

When God revealed himself to Moses on Mount Sinai he "proclaimed his name" to Moses: *"The LORD, the compassionate and gracious God, slow to anger, abounding in love and faithfulness, maintaining love to thousands, and forgiving wickedness, rebellion and sin. Yet he does not leave the guilty unpunished; he punishes the children and their children for the sin of the fathers to the third and fourth generation."*

(Exodus 34:6–7). In his destruction of the Canaanites God demonstrated his compassion and his grace. The Lord promised the land to Abraham about five hundred years earlier than the time of Joshua and at that time he said, *"the sin of the Amorites has not yet reached its full measure" (Genesis 15:16)*. The people in the land were wicked then but God, in his compassion, gave them time to turn to him. This is an amazing demonstration of how "slow to anger" God is.

The balance between God's love and his judgement is incredible. Isaiah prophesied about *"the year of the LORD'S favour and the day of vengeance of our God" (Isaiah 61:2)*. Jesus came to usher in the year of the Lord's favour and we are still living in that. The day of vengeance is yet to come. The balance of a year to a day demonstrates God's heart.

God, the Jealous God

Shortly after God proclaimed his name to Moses he referred to himself as *"the LORD, whose name is Jealous" (Exodus 34:14)*. At the time of Moses and Joshua nations were viewed as creations of gods and demonstrations of their power. Israel is God's nation and the way in which God gave them the land demonstrated his power over other gods. If a nation claims that its strength comes from any source other than God himself it can expect God to challenge that.

God wants the Best for His People

The Lord gave specific instructions through Moses that all the people in the land of Canaan were to be killed. This was not only judgement on them but was also vital to protect God's people from being led astray. Moses said to them *"However, in the cities of the nations the LORD your God is giving you as an inheritance, do not leave alive anything that breathes. Completely destroy them – the Hittites, Amorites, Canaanites, Perizzites, Hivites and Jebusites – as the LORD your God has commanded you. Otherwise, they will teach you to follow all the detestable things they do in worshipping their gods, and you will sin against the LORD your God." (Deuteronomy 20:16–18)*. This had already been demonstrated by their encounter with the Moabites. Balaam was quick to spot that the Israelites could be seduced by the Moabite women, which not only resulted in immorality but also the worship of other gods. As we will see in the coming days Israel's failure to carry out the command to destroy all the people did indeed result in them being led into the wicked practices of the land.

God wanted the best for his people. He wanted to give them a land "flowing with milk and honey" where they could enjoy him and his provision but this was conditional on them keeping his covenant. If the Canaanites remained in the land it would inevitably lead to the Israelites trading with them, intermarrying with them, and so being drawn into their culture and worship of false gods. Israel was given this land by God but would lose it if she failed to keep the covenant – and ultimately this is what happened.

Should Christians be at War Today?

Christians are the spiritual descendants of Israel. Many of the promises made to her apply to us. So, does the book of Joshua mean that we should be at war against evil people today?

Joshua does not provide any justification for physical warfare today, or indeed for any other time. The Israelites were given a specific brief relating to the Promised Land. In later years the nation of Israel was involved in various wars, and kings and prophets sought God about whether or not they should fight in each situation. Whether or not Christians should fight is a complex question and Joshua does not provide a simple answer. Even though one side was clearly in the right in this case the commander of the army of the Lord made it clear that he was on neither side. We have to be on God's side.

However, Christians *are* called to be at war. What Israel did in the physical realm under the old covenant is a picture of what Christians are called to do in the spiritual realm under the new covenant. In his letters Paul wrote of the Christian life as an ongoing battle: *"For though we live in the world, we do not wage war as the world does. The weapons we fight with are not the weapons of the world. On the contrary, they have divine power to demolish strongholds. We demolish arguments and every pretension that sets itself up against the knowledge of God, and we take captive every thought to make it obedient to Christ." (2 Corinthians 10:3–5).* We are to be ruthless with the powers of darkness, not with fallen people. And that includes being ruthless with the inroads evil thoughts make into our lives. In Ephesians Paul talks about how to do this by putting on the armour of God: *"For our struggle is not against flesh and blood, but against the rulers, against the authorities, against the powers of this dark world and against the spiritual forces of evil in the heavenly realms. Therefore put on the full armour of God, so that when the day of evil comes, you may be able to stand your ground, and after you have done everything, to stand." (Ephesians 6:12–13).* As Christians we are part of God's army and have to obey military orders from the commander of the Lord's army just as Joshua and the Israelites did.

Day 24
Taking the Land

Setback at Ai

Once Jericho was conquered the next town Joshua set his sights on was the town of Ai, which was fifteen miles further on. After the victory God gave them at Jericho this was going to be an easy victory for the Israelites – or so they thought.

> Read Joshua 7

As the Israelites start to take possession of their inheritance God makes it crystal clear that his promise to give them the land is dependent on their obedience. Taking note of his commands is not optional. Achan disobeyed God's command about the treasure from Jericho, and broke three of the Ten Commandments – he coveted, he stole and he lied – in order to take possession of a robe, some silver and some gold which should have been brought to the treasury of the Lord. As everyone knew about the command he gained nothing personally as he had to hide the treasure under his tent in order to avoid awkward questions. His sin was exposed before the whole nation and he and his family were treated in the same as the Canaanites. His greed meant that he ended up not getting any inheritance in the land.

More alarmingly, Achan's sin is counted as the sin of the nation of Israel. As a direct result of his sin the Israelites lose the battle against Ai and thirty–six men are killed. The whole nation is punished because of one man's sin. Israel's covenant with the Lord is corporate and this put great responsibility on each individual to obey his commands. This incident also demonstrates how important it is to get things right from the start.

Victory at Ai

Once the sin of Achan is dealt with, then the Israelites can move on and defeat the central towns of Ai and Bethel.

> Read Joshua 8:1–29

Day 24 – Taking the Land

The Importance of Covenants

Once the Israelites had captured Ai and Bethel the next major town was Gibeon. The Gibeonites decided that their chance of defeating the Israelites was slim so, instead of going into battle against them, they decided to trick them into making a pact. They sent a delegation with worn out clothes and mouldy bread who pretended that they came from a distant land to make a treaty with the Israelites. Joshua and the leaders of Israel fell for their story, failed to enquire of the Lord and made a treaty of peace with them. Three days later the Israelites discovered that they had been tricked and were now in a treaty with the next group of people they should have attacked.

It is interesting to note the importance that is placed on agreements here, both by the leaders of God's people and by God himself. Although the Israelites had been tricked into making the treaty under false pretences, the leaders are clear that the covenant they have made must be honoured. *"We have given them our oath by the LORD, the God of Israel" (Joshua 9:19)* the leaders said. This was a solemn commitment that could not be disregarded even though it was clear to everyone that it was a mistake to have made that commitment in the first place. The Israelites kept their promise to let them live but used them as labourers for the house of God.

God takes covenants very seriously, both his own, and ours. Hundreds of years later a king of Israel put some of the Gibeonites to death and God punished the country as a result of him breaking their covenant (see 2 Samuel 21:1). If we enter into an agreement with someone, such as in marriage or in business, then God expects us to fulfil our obligations. Looking back and deciding that it might not have been wise to enter into the agreement in the first place is no excuse to break the commitment we have made.

The Campaign to Take the Land

Once the Israelites captured Ai and Bethel (see Map 3 on page 145), and had a treaty with the Gibeonites, they had control of the central territory of Canaan and the land was split into two. Joshua 10 and 11 records two military campaigns, one to take the south and one to take the north.

The southern campaign started in response to the southern kings attacking the Gibeonites. The Gibeonites call for help and the Israelites honour their treaty with them and defeat the kings of five major southern cities (including Jerusalem, Lachish and Hebron which are shown on Map 3). Once again the Lord intervened: more of their enemies were killed by hail than by the sword and, at Joshua's request, God extended the day so they could complete mopping up operations. Whoever wrote Joshua is as amazed as his readers are at these events and comments, "There has never been a day like it before or since, a day when the Lord listened to a man. Surely the Lord was fighting for Israel!" (Joshua 10:14).

The northern campaign went right up to the land of Galilee. The main city in this region was Hazor (see Map 3), which was heavily fortified. The King of Hazor assembled a coalition, which fielded a large army including chariots and horses, but once again the Lord defeated the enemies of the Israelites before them. This campaign took a long time and the battles throughout the land continued for seven years or more.

Joshua's dedication to carry out God's command and the Lord's determination to destroy the wicked nations living in the land is made clear at the end of Joshua 11: *"Joshua waged war against all these kings for a long time. Except for the Hivites living in Gibeon, not one city made a treaty of peace with the Israelites, who took them all in battle. For it was the LORD himself who hardened their hearts to wage war against Israel, so that he might destroy them totally, exterminating them without mercy, as the LORD had commanded Moses." (Joshua 11:18–20).*

Dividing up the Land

From the middle of Joshua 13 through to the end of Joshua 21 there are nine chapters describing the land of Canaan and how it was to be divided up between the twelve tribes and the Levites. I am not going to ask you to read it but take a minute to look at the pages of your Bible from Joshua 13:8 through to the end of Joshua 21. It is full of lists of cities and descriptions of boundaries between tribes. In all, there are over 5000 words describing each tribe's inheritance in the Promised Land. This is five times the number in Paul's letter to Titus, which describes how to build a church! Why is so much space given over to such a detailed geography lesson in God's word?

This passage shows how important their inheritance was to them. God promised to Abraham that his descendants would inherit the land and this passage describes it in detail. Under the new covenant we inherit eternal life (see Matthew 19:29) and the Kingdom of God (see James 2:5). This, our spiritual inheritance, is described in detail in the New

Map 3 – The 12 Tribes of Israel Settle in Canaan

Testament and we must treasure it as much as the Israelites treasured their physical inheritance.

Special allocations of land are made for Caleb and Joshua, the two spies out of the twelve who encouraged the people to take the land forty years earlier. Caleb is now eighty–five, but does not appear to have lost any of his energy and zeal for inheriting what God has promised him. He asks Joshua for a hill country inhabited by the Anakites, a group known for being giants in the land, and drives them out.

Map 3 shows how the land was divided between the twelve tribes. Note that the tribes of Ephraim and Manasseh, the two sons of Joseph adopted by Jacob, are both given allocations but the Levites have no distinct territory. They are given forty–eight cities throughout the whole land where they can teach and administer the Law and carry out priestly duties for the surrounding tribes. Figure 6 on page 80 shows how the 12 sons of Jacob became the 12 tribes of Israel.

The 2½ tribes return home.

Before the Israelites crossed the Jordan the tribes of Reuben, Gad and half the tribe of Manasseh settled east of the River Jordan. Moses permitted this on the understanding that their fighting men came and assisted the other 9½ tribes in settling their inheritance. In Joshua 22 the 2½ tribes are commended by Joshua for fulfilling this pledge and are allowed to return home.

When they got to the Jordan they built a large altar as a sign of their commitment to God and to the rest of his people. This is intended to remind their descendants of the true altar, which has been built in the town of Shiloh where the tabernacle was set up containing the Ark of the Covenant, but the other 9½ tribes misinterpret their actions. They think that it is an alternative altar, which will lead the 2½ tribes away from worshipping God at Shiloh, and prepare to go to war against them! It is only thanks to a delegation led by Phinehas, the high priest, that all out civil war is averted.

Maybe there is a lesson for us today in this story. Christians are often quick to judge the actions of people in other churches or groups without taking the time to find out about their motivations. When Phinehas returned from meeting the 2½ tribes the people *"were glad to hear the report and praised God." (Joshua 22:33)*. Perhaps if we took the time to talk to other Christians we too would be able to praise God for them rather than criticising their efforts to extend God's kingdom.

Day 24 – Taking the Land

This incident demonstrates that, as the Israelites settled in the land, they had a stronger allegiance to their tribes than to a national identity. They had a central focus of worship at Shiloh but there was no political centre in Israel, and would not be for another 400 years.

Joshua Renews the Covenant

The last two chapters of Joshua record Joshua's farewell speech to the people and his plea for them to stay faithful to the Lord. The people respond by promising to serve the Lord and keep his commandments. But it is interesting to note that Joshua then has to tell them to throw away their idols showing that the people are already forsaking God's covenant with them.

The book ends with notes about the deaths of Joshua and Eleazar the priest, both of whom are buried in their inheritance. The bones of Joseph, which Moses carried out of Egypt, are also buried in the centre of the inheritance of the tribes of Ephraim and Manasseh, his sons. These burials stress that God's people are now settled in the land God promised to give them.

But what will they do now they are settled. Will they "serve the Lord" as they promised Joshua? Three verses from the end of the book there is a hint of what is to come. Joshua 24:31 says, *"Israel served the LORD throughout the lifetime of Joshua and of the elders who outlived him and who had experienced everything the LORD had done for Israel."* While there were still leaders who had seen God move miraculously to bring them into the land the people maintained their commitment to God. It doesn't say that they will not be committed after that – it is just left hanging. Tomorrow we will pick up the story of the people in the land by looking at the book of Judges.

Day 25
The Time of the Judges

Judges the Book

The book of Judges follows on from the end of Joshua and deals with the period before Israel had a king. It covers the history of Israel for a period of about 300–350 years from about 1380 – 1050 BC. This period is shown in Timecharts 5 and 6 which are shown overleaf. These are the first in a series of eight timecharts that show the history of Israel from the exodus from Egypt through to New Testament times. For general notes on the Timecharts see the introduction to Appendix A on page 468 where all the Timecharts are included together.

During this time the Israelites consistently turn away from God, reject his covenant and behave extremely wickedly. When God sends enemies to punish them, the people cry out to him for deliverance and God responds by raising up leaders called "Judges" who lead the people in defeating their enemies. They then rule over, or judge, part of Israel for their lifetime.

The book of Judges has three parts, each of which relates to the whole period.

Outline of Judges	
1:1–3:6	Introduction: Israel's failure to take the land promised to them.
	The account of six Judges:
3:7–3:11	Othniel, nephew of Caleb
3:12–3:20	Ehud
4–5	Deborah
6–9	Gideon
10–12	Jephthah
13–16	Samson
17–21	Epilogue: two stories illustrating Israel's religious and moral corruption during the period.

The author uses the expression *"In those days Israel had no king"* a

Day 25 – The Time of the Judges

number of times (e.g. Judges 18:1) which indicates that it was written after Israel had a king. The author is unknown. Traditionally it has been ascribed to Samuel although it could well have been written later, maybe during the reign of King David.

The book ends with the phrase *"In those days Israel had no king; everyone did as he saw fit" (Judges 21:25)* which sums up the age of the Judges. It was a time of great wickedness and moral relativism – everyone had their own views as to what was right and wrong – which makes it a book with great relevance for today.

Life after Joshua

The introduction to Judges describes how the tribe of Judah set about conquering the territory allocated to them after the death of Joshua, but they are unable to take possession of all of it. The other tribes are also unable to drive out their enemies and so gave up and lived among them instead. The faith in God that Joshua and his contemporaries had and their determination to take the Promised Land is not shared by the next generation. The writer provides a summary of their situation.

> **Read Judges 2:10–13**

As a result of not carrying out God's command to destroy all the people in the land, God's people were led into deserting their covenant with him and following the gods, and the practices, of the wicked nations who were in the land before them.

"Baal and the Ashtoreths"

Throughout the Old Testament the history of the Israelites contains references to the false gods Baal and the Ashtoreths. The name Baal means 'lord' and he was the god worshipped by the inhabitants of Canaan. He was believed to bring fertility both to the womb and the ground. The "Ashtoreths" is an expression that includes both Ashtoreth, the wife of Baal and a goddess of war and fertility, and Asherah the wife of El the chief Canaanite god. Throughout the Old Testament there are many references to Asherah poles, which were carved wooden poles associated with the worship of Asherah. Worship of Baal and the Ashtoreths involved sacred prostitution and other sexually immoral practices and sometimes even included child sacrifice.

From this we can see that for the Israelites to forsake their covenant with the Lord and worship these gods was a serious matter. They were

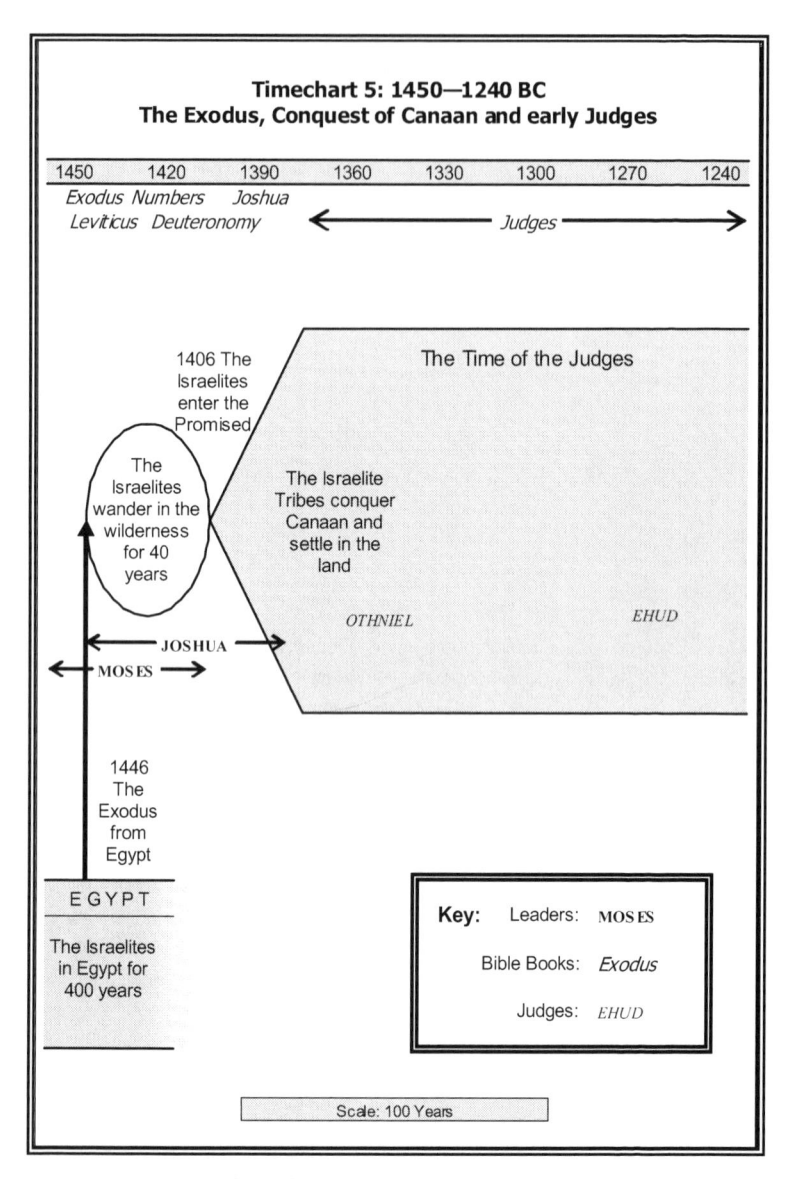

Day 25 – The Time of the Judges

Timechart 5: 1450—1240 BC
The Exodus, Conquest of Canaan and early Judges

| 1450 | 1420 | 1390 | 1360 | 1330 | 1300 | 1270 | 1240 |

Exodus   Numbers   Joshua
Leviticus   Deuteronomy   ←————— Judges —————→

1406 The Israelites enter the Promised

The Israelites wander in the wilderness for 40 years

The Time of the Judges

The Israelite Tribes conquer Canaan and settle in the land

OTHNIEL   EHUD

←— JOSHUA —→
←— MOSES —→

1446 The Exodus from Egypt

EGYPT

The Israelites in Egypt for 400 years

Key: Leaders: MOSES
        Bible Books: *Exodus*
        Judges: EHUD

Scale: 100 Years

**Timechart 5 – 1450–1240 BC:
The Exodus, Conquest of Canaan and early Judges**

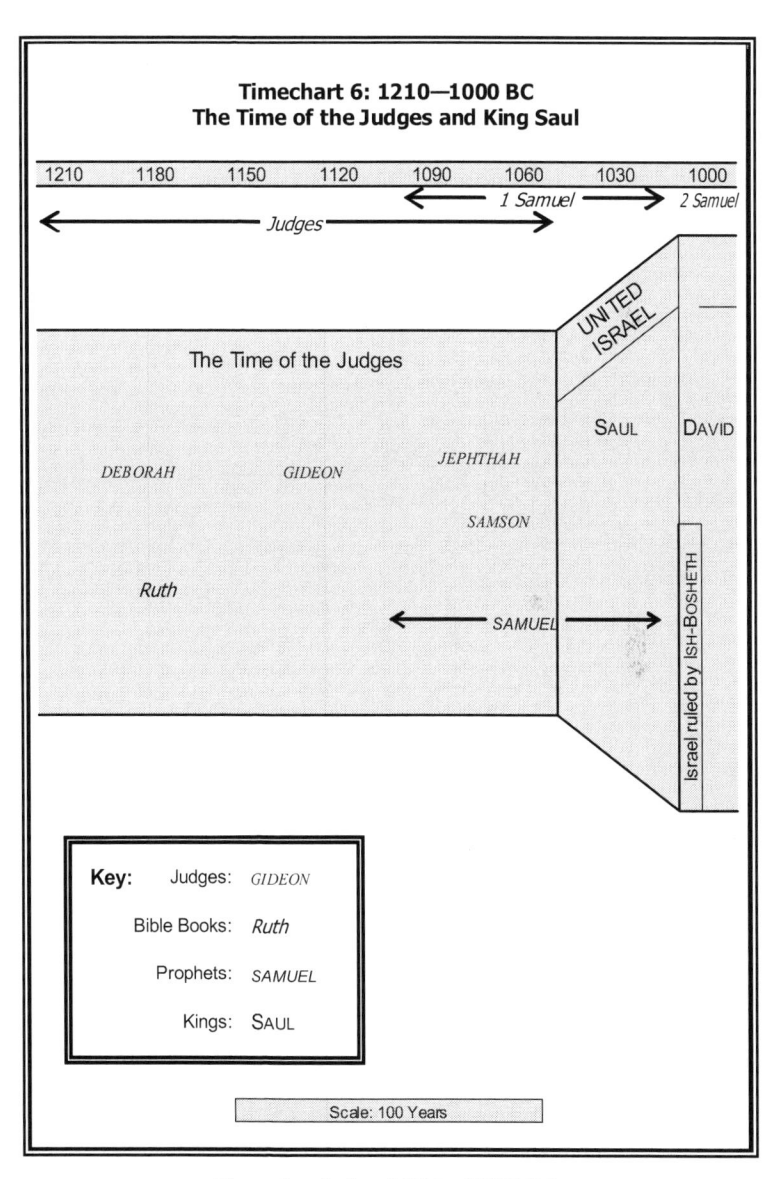

Day 25 – The Time of the Judges 151

**Timechart 6: 1210—1000 BC
The Time of the Judges and King Saul**

| 1210 | 1180 | 1150 | 1120 | 1090 | 1060 | 1030 | 1000 |

⟵——————— *Judges* ———————⟶

⟵— 1 Samuel —⟶ 2 Samuel

The Time of the Judges

UNITED ISRAEL

SAUL DAVID

DEBORAH *GIDEON* *JEPHTHAH*

SAMSON

Ruth

⟵— SAMUEL —⟶

Israel ruled by ISH-BOSHETH

Key:
Judges: GIDEON
Bible Books: *Ruth*
Prophets: SAMUEL
Kings: SAUL

Scale: 100 Years

**Timechart 6 – 1210–1000 BC:
The time of the Judges and King Saul**

trusting in false gods for their well being, they were worshipping idols and they were breaking their marriage covenants.

The Stories of the Judges

The main part of Judges describes how the Israelites behaved and how the Lord responded, a cycle of events that was repeated a number of times. Twelve Judges are mentioned in the book but we only get a detailed account of six of them (the other six only get a passing mention). We will read through the story of one of them, Gideon, and note the stages in the cycle.

> *Read Judges 6:1–6*

Stage 1: The people are wicked. Judges 6 starts after a period of peace under Deborah's leadership. We read that *"Again the Israelites did evil in the eyes of the LORD" (Judges 6:1)*.

Stage 2: The Lord oppresses the people. Despite their wickedness God does not give up on his people. He loves them too much to let them carry on going away from him. His response to their wickedness is to allow them to come under cruel oppression in order to bring them back to him: *"and for seven years he gave them into the hands of the Midianites" (Judges 6:1)*. As we saw in looking at Job, God is more interested in our relationship with him than in our comfort!

Stage 3: The people cry out to the Lord. As the people are driven to desperation we see the third stage of the cycle starting: *"Midian so impoverished the Israelites that they cried out to the LORD for help." (Judges 6:6)*. God's tactics worked!

> *Read Judges :6:11–40*

Stage 4: The Lord's response – a leader is chosen. Gideon seems a very unlikely candidate to lead the Israelites when we first meet him. He is a timid man but God himself meets him in human form, calls him "mighty warrior" and tells him to go and save Israel! However, before Gideon is sent to defeat the Midianites he is given a more serious challenge – to destroy his father's altar to Baal. The fact that there is an altar to Baal and an Asherah pole in his own home illustrates the state that the Israelites are in. God makes it clear that he is more opposed to the Israelites' false worship than to the Midianites. Gideon, true to his nature, carries out this task at night but after he has done it the Holy Spirit comes upon him for the purpose of delivering God's people.

Day 25 – The Time of the Judges

There are a number of times in Judges, and in other places in the Old Testament, where the Holy Spirit comes upon people to equip them for a specific task. In this case it is to lead the Israelites against their enemies. With Balaam, the pagan prophet, it was to prophesy from God. The fact the Holy Spirit came on people, or filled them, in this way says nothing about their level of holiness or understanding of God. Among the Judges, only Othniel and Deborah appear to have much of a relationship with God. The behaviour of the others shows little appreciation of God's covenant and his laws. The last Judge, Samson, illustrates the extraordinary way God uses a godless man who had been anointed for power. After a miraculous birth and a promising start he misused his powers and spent his time running after Philistine prostitutes. He became so indifferent to God's anointing on him that he loses the power of the Spirit. But eventually God used his weakness for a Philistine woman called Delilah to bring about the death of many Philistines.

These Old Testament experiences are different from the work of the Holy Spirit in the New Testament. Jesus prayed that the Holy Spirit would be sent to lead people into the truth and, after Pentecost, the Spirit was poured out on *all* who believed in Jesus and turned from their sins. He is a free gift, given to empower Christians for daily living, so that they may know Jesus better and have the strength to live holy lives for him.

Read Judges 7

Stage 5: God Delivers the People. Once the Lord has chosen and equipped his leader he gives the Israelites deliverance from their enemies. As we saw in the story of Gideon the deliverance comes not through a bold, well equipped, human army but through a small band of faithful men ready to listen to God's instructions. The defeat of the countless Midianites by three hundred men once again demonstrated that the Lord was the one who could save Israel, not human strength or any other, so called, gods. The victories of the other Judges make the same point.

Gideon does not get support from some Israelite towns in driving out the Midianites. Gideon came from the tribe of Manasseh and towns in Gad refused to help him, perhaps in fear of reprisals from the Midianites. The tribe of Ephraim do come to his aid but Gideon has to be very diplomatic to avoid falling out with them. Throughout Judges the tribal loyalties are stronger than any national ones. It appears that most of the Judges operated among a few tribes rather than having national significance.

> Read Judges 8:28–35

Stage 6: The People are at Peace. The defeat of Midian crippled them for a generation and enabled God's people to enjoy their inheritance once again.

Stage 7: Here we go again! *"No sooner had Gideon died than the Israelites again prostituted themselves to the Baals" (Judges 8:33)*. As soon as Gideon died the whole cycle started all over again! Wickedness is increasing and the people are heading into the same situation they were before he lived.

The end of Gideon's story is sad. He took gold from the people to make an "ephod" (a holy garment) and allowed it to become an idol which was worshipped by all Israel in his home town. He also had seventy sons by an assortment of wives and concubines (female slaves) one of whom tried to become king by killing all the rest, so causing much trouble and internal warfare.

Epilogue

The last section of Judges contains two stories illustrating Israel's spiritual and moral corruption. The first illustrates how muddled the Israelites thoughts on spiritual matters were. A man sets up an idol and a shrine in his house and appoints one of his sons to be his priest. But when a Levite is looking for somewhere to stay he jumps at the opportunity to make him his priest instead. His view is *"now I know that the LORD will be good to me, since this Levite has become my priest" (Judges 17:13)*. The Israelites see the Lord as a God to be added to their worship of many gods. They forget that the second of the Ten Commandments makes it clear that he is a jealous God who will not share man's worship with any other, so called, god.

The second story centres on the death of a woman, which demonstrates the depths of moral corruption that were present in Israel during this time. It is a harrowing account, which includes attempted homosexual gang rape, the total insensitivity of two men towards women they should have protected and a brutal sexual attack on one of them which left her dead. It has many parallels with what happened to Lot in Sodom just before the Lord destroyed it for its wickedness but the

Day 25 – The Time of the Judges

horror of this story is that this is happening in an Israelite town among God's covenant people.

The husband of the murdered woman cuts up her body into twelve parts and sends them throughout the tribes of Israel. The impact of these grisly parcels, along with the story accompanying them, shocks the whole nation – in the same way as some child murders shock nations today. The result is that four hundred thousand men assemble to hear the story first hand and decide to wipe out the city in the tribe of Benjamin where this has taken place. The tribe of Benjamin rally in support of their city and are almost wiped out as a result.

The last verse of Judges summarises the times: *"In those days Israel had no king; everyone did as he saw fit." (Judges 21:25).* It indicates the contrast between this time of anarchy and the reign of King David when godly rule was established throughout the kingdom.

Day 26
Samuel

Ruth

Judges is followed by a short book called Ruth, which is the story of a Moabite woman called Ruth who lived in the time of the Judges. It starts with a tragic account of an Israelite woman, Naomi, who goes to live in Moab with her husband and two sons during a famine. While she is there all three of the men die and she is left with her two Moabite daughters–in–law. One of these returns to her family home in Moab but the other, Ruth, returns with Naomi to her home town of Bethlehem. She demonstrates a strong loyalty both to Naomi and the Lord saying, *"Where you go I will go, and where you stay I will stay. Your people will be my people and your God my God." (Ruth 1:16).*

After Naomi and Ruth return to Israel Ruth carries out her commitment to support Naomi and in working to support her comes across a man called Boaz. The rest of the short book is the story of their love for one another and how, within the customs of their time, Boaz arranges to marry Ruth. In the wicked time of the Judges it is good to read about Boaz, who is a godly and honourable man, and the devotion that Ruth, a foreign woman, shows to Naomi and to God.

The result of Ruth's devotion is that, through her marriage to Boaz, she becomes the great–grandmother of King David and an ancestor of Jesus. Right at the start of the New Testament Matthew lists the ancestors of Jesus, and Ruth is one of four women who is mentioned, immediately after Rahab, another foreign woman who showed a similar commitment to God. Although set in a very different culture from ours, Ruth is a beautiful short story which it is well worth reading.

	Outline of Ruth
1	Naomi's time in Moab. Naomi and Ruth return to Bethlehem
2	Ruth meets Boaz
3	Ruth asks Boaz to marry her
4	Boaz marries Ruth. The birth of their son Obed, ancestor of David

Ruth not only shows us that there were godly people in Israel during the time of the Judges but also provides a link to the next period of history, which is dominated by King David.

1 & 2 Samuel

The books of 1 & 2 Samuel are named after Samuel the prophet who was the last Judge of Israel and the man who anointed Israel's first two kings. It is really one book. The division into two probably came about because it was too long to fit onto one scroll! 1 & 2 Samuel are written from a prophetic viewpoint but the actual author is unknown. It was probably written around 900 BC shortly before the death of Solomon. 1 Samuel follows on from the end of the time of the Judges, starting around 1105 BC and 2 Samuel finishes just before the death of David which took place in 970 BC. This period is covered by Timechart 6, which we saw yesterday (see page 151), and Timechart 7, which we will come to later (page 208).

Outline of 1 & 2 Samuel	
	The Life of Samuel
1 Samuel 1–3	Birth of Samuel and his early life.
1 Samuel 4–7	Israel's desperate state.
1 Samuel 8–12	The Monarchy is established and Saul made king.
	The First King of Israel – Saul
1 Samuel 13–15	Saul's failure as king.
1 Samuel 16–18	David is anointed to be king and becomes nationally famous.
1 Samuel 19–26	David on the run from Saul.
1 Samuel 27– 2 Samuel 1	David in exile. Death of Saul.
	The Second King of Israel – David
2 Samuel 2–10	David established as king. His throne established forever by God (2 Sam 7:16).
2 Samuel 11–20	David's weaknesses and failures.
2 Samuel 21–24	Appendix: Incidents from David's life.

1 & 2 Samuel is mainly the story of three men. Samuel was one of the greatest prophets who ever lived. He dragged Israel out of the time of the Judges and, under God's direction, made Israel into a kingdom with its own king. Saul was the first king of Israel. His story is a tragic one as he failed to look to God to help him lead the nation and sought to do it in his own way which ended in failure. David was the second king of Israel, and the greatest they ever had. With his heart set to follow God he established Israel as one nation with the worship of their God at the centre – the first time this had really happened since the time of Moses.

Although 1 & 2 Samuel deal with the lives of kings they are full of very ordinary, human stories. They contain detailed accounts of events from people's lives, both the good and the bad, which give us insight into the way God deals with individuals.

The Birth of Samuel

1 Samuel opens with the account of the birth and calling of Samuel.

> **Read 1 Samuel 1**

The story of Elkanah and his two wives Peninnah and Hannah is very moving. Although Elkanah loves Hannah the most, Peninnah has children but Hannah has none. (It is a very similar situation to that of Jacob and his two wives, Leah and Rachel, where Leah had children although Rachel was his favourite wife.) Once a year they go to worship the Lord in the town of Shiloh. This is where the Ark of the Covenant is kept, probably in a brick building by then, rather than in the old tabernacle (in 1 Samuel 1:it is referred to as a "temple"). Remembering that this is the time of the Judges it is good to see that some ordinary Israelites are worshipping God in the way he laid down in the Law.

This yearly ritual aggravates the rivalry between the two wives as Elkanah gives gifts to Peninnah's children but honours Hannah more than Peninnah. Peninnah is desperate for the love of her husband and takes it out on Hannah; Hannah has his love but is desperate for a child. I said earlier that 1 & 2 Samuel contain some very human stories and this account demonstrates the skill of the Hebrew writer in capturing people's feelings. The way in which Elkanah protests to his wife – *"Don't I mean more to you than ten sons?" (1 Samuel 1:8)* – is such a typical response from a man!

Anyone who has experienced infertility will know the deep heartache

Day 26 – Samuel

that goes with it, even without there being another wife with children in the home. But, as we saw in the reading, this tragic personal situation leads to desperate praying from Hannah, which God uses to bring benefit to the whole nation. She prays for a child and vows that if God gives her a son she will give him back to the Lord.

Within a year Samuel is born and Hannah devotes herself to him for the next three to four years. Clearly this little boy must have been the centre of Hannah's life but she goes ahead and keeps her vow. For a woman to make such a vow in this situation is unremarkable. For her to keep it, when she still only had one child, shows her to be a remarkable woman of God. Many people today in desperate situations pray "Lord if you help me I'll do such and such" but not so many carry out their promise once they are safe! It is much easier to say, "It would have happened anyway. My change in circumstances was nothing to do with God."

For Hannah this was the biggest sacrifice she ever made. When Samuel was just a small boy she took him to Shiloh and left him with the old priest Eli. Communication was not like it is today so there were no letters, no phone calls, just a visit once a year! Hannah's sacrifice was to bring about a complete change in the nation of Israel. Her little boy became the most remarkable prophet since Moses, but only thanks to the sacrifice of his mother.

Hannah's song of praise at the beginning of chapter 2 is very similar to the one that Mary the mother of Jesus sang when she discovered that she was pregnant with a child who was to become even more remarkable than Samuel.

Samuel's Early Life

If Hannah's sacrifice was difficult for her, it must also have been traumatic for the little boy Samuel. This next reading opens with him waving goodbye to his mother and father and starting a new life in the care of Eli and goes on to contrast Samuel's growing knowledge of the Lord with the godlessness of Eli's sons.

> **Read 1 Samuel 2:11–26**

Samuel is in a strange place being brought up by the old priest Eli and the writer's account of the way Eli and his sons work as priests is far from encouraging. Eli's two grown up sons flagrantly abuse their position as priests, taking the part of the sacrifices they wanted from the worshippers by force and sleeping with the women who served at the tent of meeting. Eli knows what is going on, but when he challenges his sons they take no notice of him and he does nothing about it. It does not sound like an ideal situation for a little boy to be brought up in!

God confronts Eli through a prophet (a notable event as prophets were rare in these times) and tells him that his family line will be wiped out as priests and that all his descendants will die in the prime of life including his two sons who will die on the same day. It is clear that although Eli has challenged his sons he is still happy to share in the meat they take from the worshippers and the Lord warns him that *"Those who honour me I will honour, but those who despise me will be disdained." (1 Samuel 2:30).*

Samuel's Calling

Samuel works in the temple under Eli's direction and even sleeps there. The story of how God called to him is a very well known Sunday School story but that does not diminish its significance in Samuel's life.

> Read 1 Samuel 3

The prophecy that the Lord gives Samuel for Eli is very similar to the one he has already received but Samuel does not know this. Samuel is young and he has to give a harsh word to the man who is a father to him. It is a hard test but he passes it and repeats the words to Eli in full. It would have been very easy for him to water it down or say something different but, like Joseph having to tell the baker that he would be hanged in three days, Samuel learned that the job of a prophet is to speak out the words that the Lord gave to him. It is only after this test that we see Samuel emerge as an infallible prophet: *"The LORD ... let none of his words fall to the ground. And all Israel from Dan to Beersheba recognised that Samuel was attested as a prophet of the LORD." (1 Samuel 3:19–20)* (The expression "from Dan to Beersheba" in this passage is like the expression "from Land's End to John o'Groats" in Great Britain. It refers to the whole extent of the land of Israel from the town of Dan in the north to Beersheba in the southern wilderness – see Map 3 on page 145.) There are many who would like to be famous prophets. This shows the price that has to be paid for such an honour.

Day 27
The Call for a King

The State of the Nation

Even though people throughout Israel recognised Samuel as a prophet of the Lord Samuel is growing up in a nation that has, in the main, turned away from God. As a result God has allowed them to come under attack from their enemies. It is some years since Samson dealt the Philistines a crushing blow and, at the beginning of 1 Samuel 4, we find that the Israelites are, once again, under attack from the Philistines and lose four thousand men in battle. The elders of Israel see this as a sign that the Lord is not on their side but instead of seeking his voice in prayer they decide to take the Ark of the Covenant into battle with them the next day *"so that it may go with us and save them from the hand of our enemies." (1 Samuel 4:3)*.

This shows how weak their understanding of their covenant God was. They are treating the Ark as God and using it in the way other nations use their gods, as a lucky charm to be manipulated by men. The Lord does not go along with their scheme and the result is that the ark is captured by the Philistines. Eli's two sons, who accompanied it, are killed along with thirty thousand Israelite soldiers. When Eli hears the news that his sons have died and that the ark has been captured he falls off his seat and dies. He is the last of the old style Judges, incapable of stopping Israel, or even his own sons, from being wicked, weakened and blinded by old age and fat from his own sin. His death prepares the way for new things.

Chapters 5 and 6 describe what happened to the ark and contain what I think is one of the most humorous stories in the Old Testament. Although God allows the ark to leave Israel he does not let the Philistines enjoy their victory. The Philistines take the ark, which they view as Israel's god, and place it in the temple of their god Dagon as a sign of his superiority. But although the ark is not God, it is a symbol of his presence and he does not allow them to treat it this lightly. The next morning the people find that their god Dagon has fallen face down in front of the Ark of the Covenant. They replace Dagon, only to find the next day that he has not only fallen down but is broken in pieces. I would love to have seen the look on their faces!

Things go from bad to worse for the Philistines as the Lord inflicts plagues and tumours on them for seven months before they decide to return the ark on a cart to Israel to avoid further trouble. The Israelites show the same contempt for the ark as the Philistines and God kills seventy of them for looking inside it. In fear, the people put it in a house for safekeeping in a town called Kireath Jearim where it stays for twenty years while the people mourn and seek the Lord. Samuel then calls the people together to repent and, after Samuel cries out to the Lord on Israel's behalf, they defeat the Philistines.

Samuel then becomes a "circuit Judge" in a similar way to the other Judges who had gone before him. (Note that Samuel left Shiloh after the death of Eli and returned to live in his parents' home town, something that must have pleased his mother Hannah.)

Read 1 Samuel 7:15–17

The Call for a King

When Samuel is old, maybe around sixty–five, his sons become Judges but they are wicked and open to bribes. The people are now fed up with Judges and decide that they need a king and ask Samuel to appoint one. This is a crucial turning point in Israel's history but it is rather confusing in the way it is described in this passage. It is made very clear that the people's request is wicked because they are rejecting God's leadership because they want to be like other nations, but on the other hand God responds to their request and gives them a king and it seems that he wants to use a king ruling under his authority to make them a godly nation.

Read 1 Samuel 8

Samuel gives them a king in response to God's command, not in response to their request, but only after he warns them of the demands a king will place on them in terms of conscription into the army and other government support services and the burden of taxation. Mind you, this will only be at the rate of 10%. Thank goodness they didn't ask for a democracy!

Introduction to Saul

Then we are introduced to Saul, a man from the tribe of Benjamin, whose father has lost some donkeys!

Day 27 – The Call for a King

> **Read 1 Samuel 9–10**

The way in which God brings Samuel and Saul together shows how God can work in the detail of our lives and in unexpected ways. I love the way Samuel casually tells Saul that the donkeys are safe during their first conversation! Saul is thoroughly bemused by this and the events that follow! He comes over as being very reticent about being king. He certainly does not start out as someone wanting to grab power for himself. First he returns home and keeps quiet about Samuel anointing him and then, when Samuel calls the whole nation together, he is found hiding in the baggage when he is publicly chosen!

Although the whole nation is excited at having a king at last, once again Saul returns home after his public anointing and in the next chapter we find him ploughing! He has not started to operate as a king at this stage. It is only once the Israelites are attacked by the Ammonites that the Holy Spirit comes upon Saul in power and he is able to lead Israel as their king. His leadership is then confirmed before all Israel.

> **Read 1 Samuel 11**

Samuel's Farewell Speech

After Saul is confirmed as king Samuel makes his final speech to all Israel as their leader. Saul is now clearly in charge and Samuel takes his leave. He once again condemns the people for asking for a king. Their reason for asking was a lack of trust in God who had always raised up Judges to help them when they turned to him before. Samuel's message to them is clear: having a king makes no difference to their covenant with God. Their king will not protect them against their enemies. It will continue to be the same as it was in the time of the Judges.

> **Read 1 Samuel 12:14–15**

From this time on the well being of the nation was bound up with the attitude of their king to the Lord and his covenant. Tomorrow we will see how Saul, the first of Israel's kings, handled this responsibility.

Day 28
Saul – The First King of Israel

Saul's Failure to Follow God's Ways

Saul, the first king of Israel, ruled over the whole nation of Israel for 40 years and very early on he turns out to be a failure as he does not put his trust in God. Immediately after his victory over the Ammonites and Samuel's rousing speech to the nation the next chapter deals with his first failure. There are hints that he is not a spiritual man early on in the story of Saul. When he lost his donkeys it is his servant who suggests that they go and find the prophet. Saul does not seem to know who Samuel is. And when he is caught up by the Holy Spirit and prophesies the people are surprised. Then in 1 Samuel 13, early on in his reign, he fails to follow Samuel's instructions. The king of Israel is subject to God's law and must listen to the prophet and respect the role that priests play. He is not to be like the kings of other nations who are above the law and can do as they please. As a result of his disobedience Samuel tells him that the kingdom will be taken away from him. The Lord will replace him with *"a man after his own heart." (1 Samuel 13:14)*. This man is David who we will read about later today.

Samuel, Saul and David are the three main characters in 1 & 2 Samuel. The figure opposite shows the dates for the main events in their lives.

Saul's Rejection as King

After his rebuke from Samuel, Saul continues to disregard the Lord's ways. We will pick up the story in 1 Samuel 15, which took place almost 25 years into his reign when Saul is about 55 and Samuel around 80.

Read 1 Samuel 15

This chapter not only shows that Saul fails to follow the Lord's instructions through Samuel but also gives us some insight into his character. Note how he builds a monument to himself in verse 12, how he lies to Samuel in verse 13 and then in verse 15, when he is caught out, how he blames the soldiers. Samuel announces his complete rejection as king. His words in verses 22 and 23 are well known and quoted throughout the Bible. Saul is full of remorse but not repentant.

Approximate Dates for Samuel, Saul and David		
1105 BC	Birth of Samuel.	1 Samuel 1
1080 BC	Birth of Saul	
1050 BC	Saul becomes King	1 Samuel 10
1040 BC	Birth of David	
1025 BC	David anointed to be Saul's successor	1 Samuel 16
1015 BC	Death of Samuel	1 Samuel 25
1010 BC	Death of Saul. Start of David's reign over Judah	1 Samuel 31 2 Samuel 2
991 BC	Birth of Solomon	2 Samuel 12
970 BC	Death of David	1 Kings 2

**Figure 7 –
Approximate Dates for Samuel, Saul and David**

Samuel leaves him and they never meet again.

The life of Saul is a warning to us. He was anointed by God's prophet and empowered by the Holy Spirit to be king of the Lord's people. But his heart is not set on following God and as a result of his disobedience he loses his kingdom. A good start does not ensure a good end. We have to persevere. As the writer to the Hebrews wrote over a thousand years after Saul: *"Therefore, since we are surrounded by such a great cloud of witnesses, let us throw off everything that hinders and the sin that so easily entangles, and let us run with perseverance the race marked out for us. Let us fix our eyes on Jesus, the author and perfecter of our faith, who for the joy set before him endured the cross, scorning its shame, and sat down at the right hand of the throne of God. Consider him who endured such opposition from sinful men, so that you will not grow weary and lose heart."* (Hebrews 12:1–3). Saul started the race well but took his eyes off the Lord and gave up following him when things got tough.

Introduction to David

With Saul rejected as king the Lord sends Samuel to anoint a replacement who will lead the nation in godly ways. He anoints David who became the greatest king Israel would ever have other than Christ himself. His influence on the Jews and Christians throughout the three millennia that have elapsed has been huge. Even today his symbol, the Star of David, is at the centre of the Israeli flag which regularly appears on our television screens in news items. But when we first meet him at the age of about 15 he is the outcast of his family!

> **Read 1 Samuel 16**

The story of David being anointed by Samuel is another famous Sunday School story. I remember being taught the lesson that Samuel learned that day: *"Man looks at the outward appearance, but the LORD looks at the heart."* (1 Samuel 16:7). It is yet another example of how the Bible contains important truths embedded in historical stories. It is also another example of concise Hebrew story telling. So much is left unsaid. Can you imagine the horror on Jesse's face as Samuel said *"we will not sit down until David arrives"* and his embarrassment as the whole hungry village had to wait because he had failed to bring his youngest son? And there would be Samuel, who was used to making small talk with the folk from Israel's towns, trying to put them at their

Day 28 – Saul – The First King of Israel

ease by talking about the harvest and the state of their livestock as they all waited!

Following David's anointing he comes to Saul's attention through two different routes. Which order they happened in is not clear but David's skill as a musician and his bravery in taking on Goliath both bring him face to face with Saul. In their meeting on the battle field we see two very different attitudes to the Lord. Saul is leading the Lord's army but he and his men have their eyes on one man and are immobilised by him. David sees things from God's perspective – *"The LORD will deliver me"* – and has a profound understanding of the Lord's covenant relationship with Israel. The Israelites are circumcised as a sign of the Lord's covenant to give the land to Abraham's descendants so when he refers to Goliath as *"this uncircumcised Philistine"* he is not being rude, he is simply pointing out that he has no right to the land. Saul is disarmed by hearing such simple faith in the Lord and lets him go to fight.

Read 1 Samuel 17

David's tactics are far from amateur in his encounter with Goliath. His faith in the Lord does not mean that he doesn't have to use his God given skills. He carefully prepares by taking five stones and then goads Goliath, who must have been getting very bored with his daily ritual by now, into a charge which positioned him for David's deadly shot. David finishes Goliath off with his own sword (and then returns to Saul *"still holding the Philistine's head"!).*

David's victory over Goliath brought him instant national fame. Tomorrow we will see how that affected him and his relationship with King Saul.

Day 29
Saul and David

David's Rise to Fame

Saul's continual disobedience to the Lord has a parallel with Pharaoh in the time of Moses. Pharaoh started out by hardening his heart against God, a process that the Lord allowed to run for some time by his grace, but after his refusal to respond to God, the Lord began to harden his heart for him in preparation for his judgement. With Saul we see a similar process. He was consistently disobedient to the Lord for a long time to the point where, even when challenged by Samuel, he is unrepentant. Following that we read the chilling words that *"an evil spirit from the LORD tormented him"* (1 Samuel 16:14). The Lord is now ready to work towards Saul's overthrow. Evil spirits remain under God's control and can even be used by him to work out his purposes.

As a result, Saul becomes increasingly moody and irritable. As a king he is ineffective – he allowed the entire Israelite army to be bogged down by one man – and so the country lacks leadership and is looking for a hero. David's sudden appearance on the national stage lifts the whole mood of the nation and changes David's life dramatically.

> **Read 1 Samuel 18**

After David's victory over Goliath, David gains a number of prizes. Firstly, he wins the heart of Saul's son Jonathan who starts a very close friendship with him. Jonathan is the crown prince and has already demonstrated a faith in God himself on a previous occasion. But living in the royal circle he has few who share his enthusiasm for the Lord and maybe this is what drew him to David when he saw his transparent faith. Jonathan makes a covenant with David and maintains a close friendship with him which continues even after Jonathan realises that David will become the next king instead of him. Later he says to David, *"You will be king over Israel, and I will be second to you"* (1 Samuel 23:17) showing that he is ready to put the Lord's will ahead of his own interests.

Secondly, David also wins the heart of Saul's people. Saul gives him a leading position in the army and he has a string of victories. This pleases all the people but Saul is far from impressed when he discovers that the new song *"Saul has slain his thousands, and David his tens of thousands"* has gone straight in at number one in the charts! This is the first time he begins to worry about David as a threat to his throne and he tries to kill him the next time David is playing the harp. The Lord saves David and Saul begins to fear because, although he is far from the Lord, he recognises that the Lord was with David.

And finally, David wins the love of Saul's daughter Michal. Saul had offered his daughter in marriage as part of the offer to entice someone to fight Goliath and, as David spends more and more time in Saul's house Michal falls in love with him. Saul uses this as another opportunity to kill David, but this fails and so they are married. David, the shepherd boy from Bethlehem is now son–in–law to the king!

Cat and Mouse

As we have already seen David's rise to fame is too much for Saul to cope with. He has lost the popular support of the nation and even his own children to David and becomes increasingly determined to kill him. David is forced to flee for his life and becomes an outlaw in the Judean countryside.

> *Read 1 Samuel 22:1–5*

David is not alone in hiding. During his time in hiding in Judah David has with him both a prophet and a priest. Despite his skills David relies on God and his men for his guidance and safety. His popularity means that he also gathers a guerrilla army of about 600 men who, although small in number, are very effective. This is able to move quickly to defend the towns of Judah against the Philistines and also to avoid a confrontation with the Israelite army which pursues it!

The second half of 1 Samuel is the story of how Saul pursues David, playing an increasingly desperate game of cat and mouse in the mountains. Saul goes to great lengths to kill David but all in vain. David's men would happily kill Saul but when David has the opportunity presented to him he surprises them all.

> *Read 1 Samuel 23–24*

David's reason for not killing Saul is simple. *"The LORD forbid that I should do such a thing to my master, the LORD'S anointed, or lift my hand against him; for he is the anointed of the LORD." (1 Samuel 24:6).* This is not a human power struggle to David. Saul is King of Israel because the Lord chose him and the Lord's prophet anointed him for the role. David is also the Lord's anointed one, chosen by the Lord and anointed by his prophet. If he is the Lord's choice then it is up to the Lord to make it happen. It is not for him to override God's will by killing his anointed one.

Saul's response is pitiful. Weeping, he tells David that he too knows that David will be the next king and pleads for David to be kind to his family when the time comes, but he is not able to bring David back into his government and they remain apart for the rest of his life. Later he sets out again with the army to find David and, once again, David spares his life.

Endings – The Deaths of Samuel and Saul

During the time that Saul and David are playing cat and mouse Samuel, the last Judge and great prophet, dies. The little boy that Hannah left with Eli over eighty years earlier had an incredible influence on the whole nation of Israel although he did not live to see the full impact of his actions. He anointed the first two kings but dies mourning the way Saul has turned out and didn't live to see David bringing about a godly rule in the land. Samuel also stirred up other prophets in the nation as there are a few references to groups of prophets (e.g. 1 Samuel 10:10) who were almost certainly taught by Samuel and these groups prepared the nation for the worship that David introduced during his reign.

Eventually David loses his confidence and, fearing that Saul will one day kill him, he goes and lives among the Philistines. It is a remarkable thing to attempt to do given how many of them he has slaughtered over the years but he gets away with it and it finally puts him beyond the reach of Saul's army. This desperate move by David almost results in the terrible prospect of him fighting against Saul and the Israelites on the side of the Philistines. In 1 Samuel 29 he and his men are saved from this by the Philistine commanders who, not surprisingly, don't trust his loyalty.

But if David's situation is bad Saul's is far worse by the end of the book. Saul, who is now about 70, is once again facing the Philistines in battle and, perhaps sensing disaster, is terrified. He is unable to hear from the Lord, Samuel is dead and so he turns to witchcraft for comfort. It is very clear throughout the Bible that the practice of witchcraft is wrong and Saul himself had expelled mediums from the land earlier on, but he finds a medium and, to her surprise, God allows Samuel to appear to him and tell him that he and his sons will die the

Day 29 – Saul and David

next day when the Philistines defeat the Israelites. Samuel's words come true and Israel is defeated and occupied. Saul commits suicide in battle and David's great friend Jonathan, along with Saul's other sons, dies in loyal support of his father.

One of the Bible's greatest teaching methods is through character studies and Saul's life is an awesome example. His story shows what can happen to a man who starts by ignoring God. He doesn't start out against God, he is just rather indifferent. But as time goes on he doesn't *fully* obey him and this starts him on a slippery slope ending in him being involved in things which are very wrong such as witchcraft. His end provides a stark warning for us.

Day 30
David – Israel's Greatest King

David Established as King

When David heard that Saul and Jonathan have been killed in battle he was devastated. He and his men mourned for them and David wrote a lament. The theme has become famous as an expression for all those who fall from high position: *"How the mighty have fallen!" (2 Samuel 1:19)*.

After a period of time David sought the Lord and then returned to live in Judah, his home tribe. The chief men of Judah recognised him as their leading man and came to Hebron to anoint him as their king. By this time the tribe of Judah had absorbed the tribe of Simeon so David had become king over two of the twelve tribes.

Meanwhile, the other ten tribes – the majority of Israel – were led by Abner, the commander of the army, who put one of Saul's sons called Ish–Bosheth on the throne as a puppet king. This results in the nation splitting into two parts, Israel (meaning the northern ten tribes) and Judah, which go to war against one another. A bloody civil war follows with Israelite fighting against Israelite for seven years before it is ended by both Saul's son and his army commander being murdered in power struggles. Following the collapse of political power in Israel, which is weak anyway because of domination by the Philistines, the ten tribes come and submit to David and make him their king by treaty. David is then anointed for the third time, this time as king of all Israel.

The two nations, Judah and Israel, have a different relationship with David. He was made king of Judah as their tribe's leading man but Israel made a covenant with him which was renewable with his sons. This difference does not appear to be a big issue during the reigns of David and his son but it re–emerges seventy years later when Israel rejects David's grandson as their king.

> Read 2 Samuel 5

Jerusalem – The City of David

Taking Jerusalem and making it his city is a masterstroke by David. It is situated right in the heart of the Promised Land and, crucially, between the two nations of Judah and Israel so neither has to submit to a king based in the other country. David builds himself a palace and Jerusalem becomes the political focus of the nation, which it remains to this day. David also established a civil service, advisors and a standing army which transformed Israel into a 'modern nation'. This is in stark contrast to Saul who had an informal court more like that of the Judges. His meetings with his officials took place under trees! (see 1 Samuel 14:6 and 22:6).

David's defeat of the Philistines, who have ruled Israel since the death of Saul, tells us a lot about him. Note how careful he is to follow God's instructions. On two separate occasions he seeks the Lord who gives him two different strategies. Despite his many victories in battle David still knows that his success comes from the Lord. Later in 2 Samuel we read how David and his army go on to defeat the other nations surrounding Israel. By the end of his reign he had pushed back the borders of Israel to their greatest extent ever – see Map 4 on the next page. At this time it occupied all of present day Israel and Jordan and much of Syria and Lebanon. Israel has never occupied more territory either before or after the time of David. Only a small strip of land around Gaza remained in Philistine control.

The Ark of the Covenant comes to Jerusalem

Once David has established Jerusalem as the capital of Israel it seems only right to him that the Ark of the Covenant – the symbol of the presence of the Lord with his covenant people – should be brought there, right into the heart of the nation. Since the death of Eli some sixty or seventy years earlier it has been in someone's house.

Read 2 Samuel 6–7

At the beginning of 2 Samuel 7 we see how David wants to build a permanent structure to house the Ark – a temple. Note how when David consults the prophet, that first Nathan gives him his opinion and then gets a word from God. Being a prophet does not mean that you get an open line to God all the time. You still need to take time to hear from him. The prophecy he gets for David is incredible: David is not to build a house for the Lord – his son will do that – but instead, God will build David a house, an everlasting throne! Once again, God makes an unconditional promise to a man, a covenant, like he did to Abraham, this time that there will always be a descendant of David on the throne. What an incredible promise!

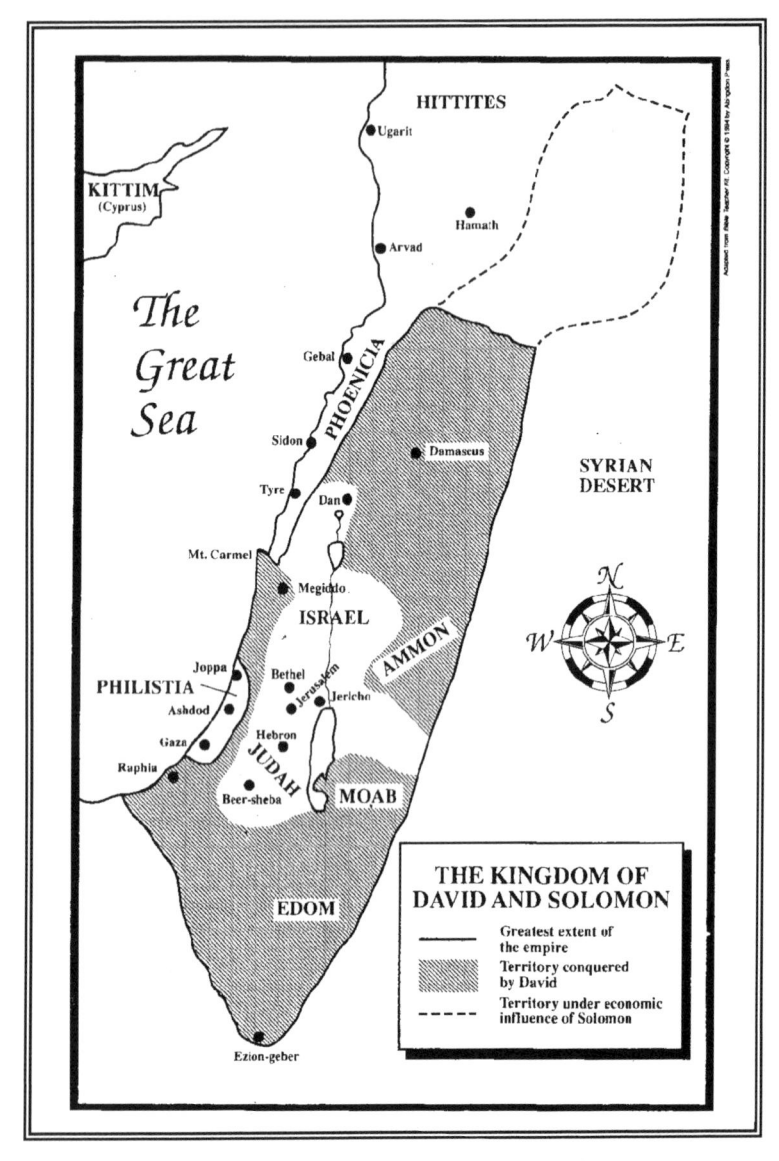

Map 4 – The Kingdom of David and Solomon

It was fulfilled over the next four hundred years in the nation of Judah as their kings descended from David. But how could the 'everlasting' bit be fulfilled? The answer is in the New Testament which opens with the words, *"A record of the genealogy of Jesus Christ the son of David" (Matthew 1:1)* and goes on to list the line of David down to his most famous descendant, Jesus. The ultimate fulfilment of this promise to David comes through the reign of Jesus himself who is reigning over this world now and will continue to reign forever.

1 & 2 Chronicles

The books of 1 & 2 Samuel are followed by 1 & 2 Kings. Between them these four books provide an unbroken history of the people of Israel from the time of King Saul through to when the kingdom of Judah went into exile. They are followed by 1 & 2 Chronicles, which are also history books that deal with the same time period.

Chronicles means "a record of events" and the book (like 1 & 2 Samuel the division into two books is artificial) was probably written after the exile, possibly by Ezra given the similarity in style to his book. Where 1 & 2 Samuel and 1 & 2 Kings are written from a prophetic viewpoint, 1 & 2 Chronicles are written from a priestly viewpoint, going into detail about things of interest to the priests, such as worship, the temple and offerings.

Given the exciting period being covered by the writer of 1 & 2 Chronicles you might expect an exciting opening. How wrong could you be! Take a look at the first nine chapters of 1 Chronicles now.

As you see it starts with a list of names! This family tree of Israel from Adam to the time of the exile was documented for the returning exiles to demonstrate their link with the past and with God's promises. While it seems very tedious to us it told the first readers that they continued to be part of the God's covenant people, linked to his covenants with Abraham, Moses and David. The story picks up in 1 Chronicles 10 with the death of Saul and the start of David's reign over all Israel.

Outline of 1 & 2 Chronicles	
1 Chronicles 1–9	Israel's Family Tree
1 Chronicles 10–29	The reign of David
2 Chronicles 1–9	The reign of Solomon
2 Chronicles 10–36	The kings of Judah

David's Temple Musicians

Despite being told that he would not build a house for the Lord, we know from 1 Chronicles that David does make detailed preparations for the temple which he passed on to his son to complete. He also establishes regular patterns of worship at the tent that housed the Ark and appoints some of the priests as musicians offering praise and worship to God daily.

> **Read 1 Chronicles 16:4–6, 37–38**

We have already seen that David was a musician and that his heart was full of worship for his God. When he was in the fields keeping sheep he had a harp with him so he could sing songs to the Lord. Now he was king in his city – Jerusalem, the City of David – he wanted the people who lived there to have worship at the centre of their lives. In David's day, over the everyday sounds of life in Jerusalem, you could always hear the sound of worship to God going on at the tent of meeting. Israelites coming to make their offerings or foreign envoys coming to do business with his government would all hear the trumpets playing and the Levites singing and praising God.

David's legacy to the Israelites is incredible. He left them as a strong nation with peaceful borders and he left the worship of God established at the heart of the nation. But his most enduring legacy to the Jews and Christians who have lived over the three thousand years since he died are the songs that he wrote himself and those written by others who ministered at the tent of meeting. Tomorrow we will look at the book of Psalms, the songbook of the Bible.

Day 31
The Songs of David – Psalms

Psalms the Book

The book of Psalms is the songbook of Israel. It is the largest book in the Bible and its value throughout history is incalculable. Nothing can compare with it for expressing such a wide range of emotions towards God. There is great joy, deep despair, humility and confusion. Throughout the book people are being very honest with God whatever emotional state they are in. However, while emotions may fluctuate, the writers maintain an unshakeable conviction that God is there and remains central to all aspects of life.

This honest expression of emotion to God combined with a solid faith reflects the heart of its main writer, David. Of the 150 songs in the book David wrote 73 himself and a further 24 were either written by men he appointed to minister to the Lord or their descendants. A further two were written by his son Solomon and one by Moses. We are not told who wrote the remaining 50. The Hebrew name for the book is "Praises" and David's Psalms are full of praise to his God. The expression "Praise the Lord" – which is "Hallelujah" in Hebrew – rings out time and again throughout the book. The English name, "Psalms" comes from a Greek word meaning "song sung to a harp" which again takes us back to David, the shepherd boy who came to the attention of Saul through his harp playing.

The book of Psalms is a collection of 150 songs, like a modern day hymn or song book, and so it cannot be analysed in the same way as the rest of the books we have looked at so far where the historical account moves on from chapter to chapter. The best way to understand the Psalms is by meditating on them, praying them and singing them. The Psalms have been set to music down through the years and many old hymns and newer choruses are taken from the Psalms.

The book of Psalms is very easy to find as it is so big and lies in the middle of your Bible. Just open your Bible in the middle and it should fall open in the Psalms!

The Structure of Hebrew Poetry

The Psalms are Hebrew poetry. You can tell this in your Bible as the words do not go right to the end of the line! If, like me, you grew up thinking that poetry had to rhyme and have a regular rhythm then you may be puzzled by this statement. Fortunately Hebrew poetry is not like that as those features would not survive translation into other languages!

The main feature of Hebrew poetry is "parallelism". This means that each line is made up of two parts where the second half complements the first half in different ways.

In Psalm 1 each sentence or thought is split into two parts with the second part of each line *completing* the thought in the first part:

"Blessed is the man
– who does not walk in the counsel of the wicked
or stand in the way of sinners
– or sit in the seat of mockers.
But his delight is in the law of the LORD,
– and on his law he meditates day and night." (Psalm 1:1–2)

Try to get the feel of this as you read the whole Psalm.

> **Read Psalm 1**

In Psalm 29 the second part *echoes* the idea in the first part:

"Ascribe to the LORD, *O mighty ones,*
(echo) – ascribe to the LORD *glory and strength.*
Ascribe to the LORD *the glory due to his name;*
(echo) – worship the LORD *in the splendour of his holiness.*
The voice of the LORD *is over the waters;*
(echo) – the God of glory thunders,
(echo) – the LORD *thunders over the mighty waters.*
The voice of the LORD *is powerful,*
(echo) – the voice of the LORD *is majestic."(Psalm 29:1–4)*

The second half is not a pure repetition but the "echo" contains the same thought but in different words. Note that the writer got carried away by the thought of the voice of the Lord in the third line and put in two echoes!

Try reading this Psalm out loud emphasising the first lines and saying the echoes quietly.

> **Read Psalm 29**

Sometimes, although this is rarer, the second part *contrasts* the first. Psalm 119:143 is an example where two contrasting thoughts are put

Day 31 – The Songs of David – Psalms

together:

> "Trouble and distress have come upon me,
> – but your commands are my delight."

In other Psalms the line is split into three parts. Psalm 100 is like that with a "headline" followed by two follow–up lines:

> (Headline) – "Shout for joy to the LORD, all the earth.
> – Worship the LORD with gladness;
> – come before him with joyful songs."
> (Psalm 100:1–2)

Read the whole of this well known Psalm and see how many reasons to worship the Lord are contained in its few verses.

Read Psalm 100

Another feature of Psalms is that some of them are "alphabetic acrostics". What this means is that each line starts with a different letter of the Hebrew alphabet. Psalm 25, which has 22 lines, is an example of this. The Hebrew alphabet has 22 letters and if you could read Psalm 25 in Hebrew you would find that each line starts with a different letter of the alphabet. So, *"To you, O LORD, I lift up my soul; in you I trust, O my God."* starts with the first Hebrew letter (aleph) and the next line, *"Do not let me be put to shame ..."* starts with the second letter (beth) and so on.

Read Psalm 25

Psalm 34, with 22 verses, is another example of an alphabetic acrostic. Psalm 37 has two verses for each letter (with slight variations which accounts for there only being 40 verses). The most amazing acrostic is Psalm 119 which has 8 lines for each letter (some Bibles have the Hebrew letter above each section.) The structure of this Psalm is very intricate as each verse is about the law of God with the writer employing eight different words for the law.

The structure displayed in the Psalms indicates that the writers were not only men who had a deep relationship with God but they were also skilled writers in the style of their time. These were not quick jottings but carefully constructed to reflect their thoughts and feelings. Having a good grasp of literature is not at odds with expressing truth about God.

Another feature of Psalms is that many of them have titles. They tell us who wrote them, some indicate the situation they were written in, and some contain musical directions. These were obviously useful at the time the songs were written but unfortunately the meaning of the Hebrew words has been lost. So, if you look at the titles to Psalms 7 and 8 you will see words which no–one knows how to translate into English.

There are also some musical directions that appear in the middle of Psalms, usually at the end of phrases, which cannot be translated. At the end of Psalm 9:16 is the expression *"Higgaion. Selah."* The word "Selah" appears frequently (see it again in Psalm 9:20) and some people think it means "stop and think about that", or "wow!", maybe while the music continued to play.

The Five Books

Outline of Psalms	
Book 1 Psalms 1–41	Probably all written by David, certainly all those that have titles indicate that they are "of David."
Book 2 Psalms 42–72	Mainly by David but include a series by "the Sons of Korah." David chose the sons of Korah from among the Levites and appointed them to sing before the Lord. These Psalms could well have been written in David's time or in later centuries. They are similar in style to David's.
Book 3 Psalms 73–89	Mainly the Psalms "Of Asaph", another man appointed to sing by David. They appear to have been written centuries after David's time by the descendants of Asaph as some refer to Israel being rejected, see for example Psalm 74 which is a prayer for deliverance that may have been written in the time of the exile.
Books 4 Psalms 90–106	Psalm 90 is a prayer of Moses. Most of the rest have no titles.
Books 5 Psalms 107–150	Mainly without titles although 15 more are ascribed to David and 1 to Solomon. It includes the "Songs of Ascents" (120–134) which were used by worshippers going up to the temple.

Day 31 – The Songs of David – Psalms

You may have seen that at the head of Psalm 1 it says "Book 1". This is because Psalms is divided into 5 books (as shown on the Bible Bookcase (see page 36). It may be that this was an attempt by those who compiled the books to mimic the 5 books of the Law. Whatever the reason this breakdown does provide a loose structure to the book.

The whole book was probably put together in its present form about two centuries before Christ, possibly for use in the temple built by Zerubbabel.

To get a feel for the "Songs of Ascents" imagine being part of that procession as you read this example.

Read Psalm 122

Being Honest with God

One of the many lessons of the Psalms is that we can be totally open and honest with God. In particular, David's Psalms are very direct in their approach to God. In this one he feels abandoned by God but rather than running away he confronts God with his feelings and his situation. The opening appears almost disrespectful to God but the underlying trust that David has in the Lord is revealed at the end of the Psalm.

Read Psalm 13

As a complete contrast see how David approaches the Lord in complete humility in this short Psalm.

Read Psalm 131

David has no fear of taking all his emotions to God and telling him whatever he is feeling and thinking. We would do well to follow his example.

An Important Book

The Psalms has been a source of great comfort to Jews and Christians throughout the centuries and contains many verses which have become well known through being part of hymns or songs, such as, *"God is our refuge and strength, an ever–present help in trouble" (Psalm 46:1)*, *"Great is the LORD, and most worthy of praise, in the city of our God, his holy mountain" (Psalm 48:1)* and *"Bless the LORD, O my soul: and all that is within me, bless his holy name." (Psalm 103:1 AV)*.

You can read and learn from other parts of the Bible and then leave them for a while but the Psalms need to be read regularly. I have heard it said that the famous evangelist Billy Graham reads 5 Psalms and 1 chapter of Proverbs a day. As there are 150 Psalms and 31 chapters in Proverbs this means he reads both books through every month.

Although the book was compiled many years after David lived it was he who wrote nearly half of the Psalms and left this amazing legacy to future generations. They bear his mark, the mark of a shepherd king who knew his God. His Psalms are simple but very profound in their understanding of God as best demonstrated in his most famous one where he compares his role as a shepherd with God's care for him.

Read Psalm 23

Day 32
David – the Man

Life in a Theocracy

What is the best way to govern a country? This is an issue that has concerned those who rule and those who have been ruled for centuries. The Greek philosophers of around 500–400 BC were particularly interested in this and have given us a whole series of words to describe styles of government. One of the words they used around that time was *"democratia"* which means government by the people and refers to a nation being ruled by a group of people appointed on behalf of its citizens. Today it is generally accepted that democracy is the best form of government.

But democracy is a fairly recent idea. Other forms of government existed before that and still do in some parts of the world. Some nations are ruled by a dictator: this is called an "autocracy", which means government by an individual with unrestricted authority. Other nations have a ruling elite, which can be called an "aristocracy" which means government by the best citizens although it is a matter of opinion as to who the "best" citizens might be. A military junta might consider itself to be the best, while others might disagree!

So how did God intend that his people should be governed?

God made it clear from the start that his nation was to be a "theocracy" meaning government by God. Hundreds of years before Israel had a king, the Lord gave Moses regulations about appointing one. This made it clear that he would not be an autocrat, one with unrestricted power, but there would be two other roles which would operate in a theocracy alongside that of the king which will limit his power and stop him becoming a dictator.

First there were the priests. One of their key roles was to be the guardians of the law. As Moses made clear, the king, like all of God's people, was to be subject to the law, not above it. *"When he (the king) takes the throne of his kingdom, he is to write for himself on a scroll a copy of this law, taken from that of the priests, who are Levites. It is to be with him, and he is to read it all the days of his life so that he may learn to revere the* LORD *his God and follow carefully all the words of this law and these decrees and not consider himself better than his* brothers and turn from the law to the right or to the left. Then he and his descendants will reign a long time over his kingdom in Israel. *(Deuteronomy 17:18–20)*. This principle of "the rule of law" does not seem surprising to us as it is fundamental to today's democracies. Although kings, queens, presidents and politicians can make laws they are not above them and must face the consequences of breaking the law. But for the Israelites this rule of law set them apart from other nations. The kings of other nations were dictators with unrestricted authority. If they said "off with his head" then someone lost his head. If they wanted some land to buy favour with a foreign power or a powerful man in their own country, or even for their own use, then they would take that land.

The second role which operates in a theocracy is that of the prophet. Again in Deuteronomy the Lord told Moses: *"I will raise up for them a prophet like you from among their brothers; I will put my words in his mouth, and he will tell them everything I command him. If anyone does not listen to my words that the prophet speaks in my name, I myself will call him to account." (Deuteronomy 18:18–19)*. When the people wanted a king they turned to Samuel, a prophet with an unquestionable track record, to appoint one for them. He sought God and the people got God's choice as king. In Israel the "divine right of kings" came from the fact that the king was appointed by God, through his prophets.

During the reign of David we clearly see all three roles working together in a theocracy. David, the king, was the shepherd of the people. He was the focal point for the identity and security of the nation. But David was not above the law. He respected the priests and sought the word of God through his prophets. Later kings ignored both the law and the word of God through his prophets and this led to their destruction and caused great distress to God's people.

It is interesting to note that the principles operating here in the old covenant – that leaders are to work together with other leaders who have different roles and that God speaks through both his written word and by his Spirit – are carried through into the new covenant. They are as relevant today as they were in Israel. In the New Testament Paul speaks of the church being *"built on the foundation of the apostles and prophets, with Christ Jesus himself as the chief cornerstone" (Ephesians 2:20)*. The church, like Israel in the Old Testament, is a theocracy: Jesus is its king. But just as Israel had a human king so Jesus has also given leaders to local churches – called pastors, overseers or elders in the New Testament – to rule his people.

Day 32 – David – the Man

However, like Israel's theocracy, they are not to rule alone. God has given apostles and prophets to work alongside them to ensure that they take heed of God's written word and hear what his Holy Spirit is saying. Any church leader who ignores either God's word or the word of the Lord to them through God's prophet is heading for trouble.

In the early part of David's reign we saw the central role of the priests in bringing the Ark to Jerusalem and establishing regular worship. They had to do things right by the law or face serious consequences as Uzzah discovered when he touched the Ark. Today we will see how the role of the prophet also requires a fear of God.

David and Bathsheba

The account of David's reign up to 2 Samuel 10 shows him to be a man who goes after God with all his heart. But the Bible is not afraid to tell us the whole truth about a person. While we can clearly learn from people who get things right it is refreshing to read of real human weaknesses and have the opportunity to learn from the mistakes of others too. The next ten chapters, 2 Samuel 11–20, deal with the human side of David, his weaknesses and his failures. (1 Chronicles, which was written to supplement the material in Samuel and Kings, does not cover this material as it assumes the reader is already familiar with it.)

> **Read 2 Samuel 1:11–12:25**

The account of "the Bathsheba affair" is an appalling blot on David's record as king. It all starts from David not being where he should have been, which was leading his army, and having time on his hands. His attention is caught by a woman, he allows his mind to follow a train of thought and he then goes down a slippery slope which leads him to break three of the Ten Commandments. He starts by coveting his neighbour's wife. He then commits adultery and, in order to cover up his sin, he commits murder, murder of a man who had shown such bravery in his loyalty to David that he was listed as one of his thirty mighty men at the end of 2 Samuel 23.

Although many people around the court must have realised what was going on it is Nathan, God's prophet, who gets the job of challenging him to his face. In any other country Nathan would have been risking his life talking to a king in this way. In God's nation he goes with the authority of God's word and his law, but it still took real guts to say *"You are the man"* when David was already angry! Once he had uttered those words I think he would have rushed through the word from the Lord detailing his punishment and then got up quickly to leave. Those who would be God's prophets have to bring the word that the Lord gives them whatever consequences it might have for them.

After more than nine months of living with his sin (the child has already been born) David's response is immediate repentance: *"I have sinned against the LORD"*. David knew what it was like to live with unconfessed sin. It breaks your relationship with God and saps you of energy. *"When I kept silent, my bones wasted away through my groaning all day long. For day and night your hand was heavy upon me; my strength was sapped as in the heat of summer. Then I acknowledged my sin to you and did not cover up my iniquity. I said, "I will confess my transgressions to the LORD" – and you forgave the guilt of my sin." (Psalm 32:3–5)*. Unlike the kings of other nations who would have had Nathan's head removed immediately David was relieved to get his sin into the open and to be, once again, in right relationship with God. His full response is recorded in Psalm 51 where David gives us an insight into repentance which is worthy of serious study and meditation.

| Read Psalm 51 |

The Consequences

The story of David and Bathsheba has many lessons to teach us but one of the most sobering is that although sin can be forgiven it cannot be undone. The Lord does forgive David but that cannot undo the consequences of David's sin. Life can never be the same.

For David, the repercussions in his family are terrible. Some years later one of David's sons rapes his half sister (one of David's daughters by a different mother) and her brother, Absalom, murders him in revenge. David's love for Absalom is mixed with an inability to control or discipline him (how can David discipline him, given what he has done himself?) and Absalom then leads an uprising against David who has to flee the country for a while. The whole country is thrown into civil war once again, which is only brought to an end by Absalom being killed. David, the man who ruled the country and the nations around it with an iron rod is shown to be totally ineffective in ruling his own household and his own sin played a big part in that.

Throughout the books of 1 & 2 Kings the author writes a summary of how well the kings followed the Lord and his covenant and David is often used as the benchmark. Hezekiah lived up to his standard: *"He did what was right in the eyes of the LORD, just as his father David had done."* *(2 Kings 18:3)*; Ahaz completely failed: *"Unlike David his father, he did not do what was right in the eyes of the LORD his God" (2 Kings 16:2)*; and Amaziah fell somewhere in between: *"He did what was right in the eyes of the LORD, but not as his father David had done." (2 Kings 14:3)*. (Note: the word "father" is used to indicate that these kings were descended from David.)

David's devotion to the Lord is held up as an example for all to follow, but with the exception of this one incident. In his judgement on the king Abijah the writer of Kings wrote: *"He committed all the sins his father had done before him; his heart was not fully devoted to the LORD his God, as the heart of David his forefather had been. ... For David had done what was right in the eyes of the LORD and had not failed to keep any of the LORD's commands all the days of his life – except in the case of Uriah the Hittite." (1 Kings 15:3,5)*. Those words *"except in the case of Uriah the Hittite"* indicate that this event cannot be forgotten. It remains a blot on an otherwise exceptional life.

The Impact of David

When David came as a shepherd boy to Saul's army facing the Philistines Israel was a ragged, dispirited group of tribes facing enemies on all sides. At the end of his reign Israel was at peace with the world, a strong nation with her enemies subdued and a strong capital in Jerusalem. When David declared that Goliath was challenging the Lord when he challenged Israel he was a lone voice in a country which had no concept of reliance on God. The priesthood was in tatters, the Ark of the Covenant was in someone's house, Samuel the prophet was old and the new king was completely disregarding God. At the end of David's reign the ark was established in Jerusalem, there was regular worship of God organised by priests, and the king was leading the people in praise of God and consulting Him on affairs of state.

David, the shepherd, the warrior, and the songwriter became Israel itself. When he was older David became exhausted in battle and was in danger of being killed. After one of his mighty men rescued him his men said, *"Never again will you go out with us to battle, so that the lamp of Israel will not be extinguished." (2 Samuel 21:17)*. David was the nation – the lamp of Israel. The only equivalent I can think of is the way in which Churchill symbolised the British nation during the Second World War. Imagine the impact that his death would have had on Britain during the war.

David is a remarkable demonstration of what God can achieve through one man whose heart is open to him. In the New Testament Paul's comment is *"David served God's purpose in his own generation" (Acts 13:36)*. What better words could be written over someone's life?

Day 33
Solomon – The Wisest Man that ever Lived

Solomon comes to the Throne

1 & 2 Samuel cover David's reign apart from its end which is the first story in 1 Kings which continues the history of Israel. We will look at the overall contents of 1 & 2 Kings in three days' time.

The end of David's life is as dramatic as the rest of it. When he is old, his oldest surviving son, Adonijah, gets some of David's key men to back him in announcing himself as king. David has already decided that Solomon will be the next king so when Nathan the prophet tells David about Adonijah's plans he immediately responds by getting Zadok the priest to anoint Solomon as king in a decisive move (an event made famous over the last few centuries by Handel's anthem, "Zadok the Priest", written in 1727 for the coronation of King George II and played at every coronation since).

Solomon was about twenty when he came to the throne and he displayed David's love and devotion to God. Soon after becoming king we are told about a very significant moment in his life when he went to worship God and the Lord offered him anything he wanted. Solomon's answer set the scene for his reign and his writings.

> *Read 1 Kings 3*

Solomon went on to become the wisest man in the world and his wisdom is described at the end of 1 Kings 4: *"God gave Solomon wisdom and very great insight, and a breadth of understanding as measureless as the sand on the seashore. Solomon's wisdom was greater than the wisdom of all the men of the East, and greater than all the wisdom of Egypt."* At this point I know what you are thinking: "What about Ethan the Ezrahite? Surely Solomon can't be as wise as him!" Don't worry, the writer has read your mind! *"He was wiser than any other man, including Ethan the Ezrahite—wiser than Heman, Calcol and Darda, the sons of Mahol. And his fame spread to all the surrounding nations. He spoke three thousand proverbs and his songs numbered a thousand and five. He described plant life, from the cedar* of Lebanon to the hyssop that grows out of walls. He also taught about animals and birds, reptiles and fish. Men of all nations came to listen to Solomon's wisdom, sent by all the kings of the world, who had heard of his wisdom." (1 Kings 4:29–34). About a third of his proverbs are preserved for us in the book of Proverbs which we will look at tomorrow.

Solomon's Temple

Solomon continued the spiritual revival started by Samuel and David. Samuel, the last Judge, established a king under God and started a prophetic revival. David, the man after God's own heart, brought the ark to Jerusalem and set up a lively system of worship in a tent. Solomon, the wise young man, then did what David had wanted to do for God; he built him a house, or temple, in Jerusalem.

Solomon's building works in Jerusalem were on a grand scale. He made a trade agreement with Hiram, the king of Lebanon, to provide timber and conscripted foreign labour to do the backbreaking work of moving the wood and stone. In seven years he built a magnificent temple, overlaid with gold, and the formal worship of God is re-established in the temple. It had a similar design to the Tabernacle with a Most Holy Place to house the Ark of the Covenant and an outer Holy Place for the tables of bread, lampstands and altar of incense.

The opening ceremony, which was on a grand scale, is described in detail in both 1 Kings and 2 Chronicles.

> **Read 2 Chronicles 5**

This is the first time God's presence had been made evident to people in the form of a cloud since the Israelites were in the wilderness. In a real sense God's people have now come home and God himself is living in the centre of their nation. Solomon prays a prayer of dedication in the next chapter and then, after more celebration of God's goodness God appears to Solomon again and puts his seal of blessing on his temple.

> **Read 2 Chronicles 7**

Note how the Lord's word contains both incredible promises to respond positively to the prayers of his people and terrible warnings of what will happen if they turn away from his commands and worship other gods.

Day 33 – Solomon – The Wisest Man that ever Lived

Solomon's Reign

Politically Solomon's reign is a complete contrast to David's. Israel is at peace throughout his reign while it was always at war during David's. David, the skilful warrior, had a small group of very loyal and skilled fighting men; Solomon establishes a large standing army with 1,400 chariots and 12,000 horses. David had a light but effective administration while Solomon creates a large civil service and conscripts a huge labour force.

David was a shepherd at heart and even as king was never very rich. Solomon is blessed by God with great riches and under him the nation becomes a rich and powerful trading force. As we saw earlier many people came to hear Solomon's wisdom and one of those was the Queen of Sheba. The record of her visit gives us insight into the healthy state of the nation during the reign of Solomon.

> **Read 1 Kings 10**

The idea of silver being *"considered of little value"* – not to mention the flourishing trade in such exotic items as ivory and baboons! – paints an incredible picture which would have been looked back on by future generations with fond nostalgia. Israel under Solomon was at its zenith and was never to be so great again. But although his wealth faded fast he left his wisdom for future generations. Before we look at the end of Solomon's reign we will take a couple of days out to look at the record we have of his wisdom in his writings.

Day 34
The Wisdom of Solomon – Proverbs

Wisdom Books

After the history books in the Old Testament and before the prophetic writings there are five books known as "The Wisdom Books" or "The Writings". We have already looked at two of these – Job and Psalms – and today we will start looking at the other three which were written by Solomon: Proverbs, Ecclesiastes and Song of Songs.

Wisdom literature was written by wise men or "sages". While prophets and priests dealt with the spiritual and religious side of life, wise men dealt with practical and philosophical matters. The Biblical wisdom books are not the only wisdom literature; similar styles of writing can be found in Egyptian and Mesopotamian literature from the same period. In the Bible, Job and Ecclesiastes deal with some difficult philosophical problems in life: Why do the wicked prosper, while the good suffer? What is life all about? Proverbs, which we will look at today, is a more optimistic book and teaches the young how to behave so that they live happy and prosperous lives.

Proverbs

We saw yesterday that Solomon asked God for wisdom and God gave him *"wisdom and very great insight, and a breadth of understanding as measureless as the sand on the seashore" (1 Kings 4:29)*. The book of Proverbs is a compilation of his wise advice and sayings along with a few writings from other wise men of the time. They were mainly written during Solomon's reign as King of Israel from 970 – 930 BC, although there is evidence of later editing into its current form during the reign of Hezekiah around 700 BC (see Proverbs 25:1).

In English today a proverb is defined as *"a short pithy saying in general use, held to embody a general truth"*[G] *(The Concise Oxford Dictionary)*. This is an interesting definition, as the truth of a proverb does not necessarily lie in the actual statement but rather what lies behind it. When we say, "a bird in the hand is worth two in the bush" we are not making a point about the price of birds, as clearly two are worth more than one! In the literal sense the saying is untrue. The point of the proverb is that there is a distinct difference between already having something and the possibility of having it. Other proverbs make

Day 34 – The Wisdom of Solomon – Proverbs

the same point using different pictures, for example: "Don't count your chickens before they are hatched" and "Many a slip 'twixt cup and lip." It is important to understand this when approaching the wisdom literature in the Bible. Like other sayings of this kind the proverbs in the Bible are not necessarily *literally* true, but like other proverbs they *contain* truth. Some contain truth at both levels.

Another point to note is that the Hebrew word translated "proverb" in the Bible has a wider meaning than our present day English word. The same word is translated "oracle", meaning a revelation, and "parable", a story with a meaning, elsewhere in the Old Testament. The first nine chapters of Proverbs are a series of essays, or oracles, on wisdom and warnings against foolish behaviour. These fall into the Hebrew definition of "proverb". Of course the best known examples of "proverbs" in the Bible by this definition are the parables told by Jesus. These stories, like the "short pithy sayings", are also not literally true but were told to convey a truth at a deeper level.

After the first nine chapters most of the rest of the book contains short sayings in no particular order.

Outline of Proverbs	
1:1–7	Introduction: Purpose and Theme
1:8–9:18	The benefits of Wisdom
10:1–22:16	The proverbs of Solomon
22:17–24:34	Sayings of the wise
25–29	More proverbs of Solomon
30	The sayings of Agur
31:1–9	The sayings of King Lemuel
31:10–31	A wife of noble character

The Purpose of Proverbs

Read Proverbs 1–2

The purpose of the book of Proverbs is spelled out in the first seven verses. It is for young people to attain wisdom and insight and live a good life; it is to help parents and teachers pass on knowledge and discretion to children; and even the wise and discerning can add to their wisdom from this book. Proverbs 1:4 mentions "the simple." Today we call people simple if they are not very clever but in Proverbs the writer is talking about people who lack judgement, particularly when it comes to making moral decisions. *"A simple man believes anything, but a prudent man gives thought to his steps" (Proverbs 14:15).* There is no benefit in being simple. The simple are encouraged to gain an understanding of the consequences of their actions.

The key to becoming wise is summed up in Proverbs 1:7: *"The fear of the LORD is the beginning of knowledge."* The same thought is expressed in Job 28:28 and Psalm 111:10 – wisdom comes from having a right attitude towards God. Everything that we do or say is seen by God and one day we will have to stand before him and give an account for it. This is an awesome thought, but if we truly grasped it then we would develop a healthy fear of the Lord – not a fear of immediate or irrational punishment, but the fear of having to look him, the one who loves so deeply, right in the eye as we discuss our embarrassing actions and idle conversations.

In contrast to the wise, we are told that *"fools despise wisdom and discipline."* Psalm 14:1 says *"The fool says in his heart 'There is no God'"* and this is the sense behind the word "fool" when it is used in Proverbs. Those who do not accept God's rules and His right to discipline them are truly foolish. Note that this is talking about people acknowledging God in their heart, not in their mind. When we talk about the heart in this way we are talking about the centre of our beings. There are many who accept that God exists in their mind but pay him no regard in their hearts. They continue to set their own direction and make their own decisions with no reference to him – behaviour that is foolish according to Proverbs.

Practical Wisdom

The first nine chapters of Proverbs are a series of essays on the benefits of wisdom and the dangers of folly. It is expressed as advice from a father to a son. At times wisdom is depicted as a woman – sometimes calling out in the street to bring the simple to their senses, sometimes preparing rich food and wine inviting them to eat and gain understanding. The way in which she is rejected in chapter 1 reminds us of the way in which Jesus was rejected and the description of the value of wisdom also reminds us of him: *"she is more profitable than silver and yields better return than gold. She is more precious than rubies; nothing you desire can compare with her." (Proverbs 3:14–*

15).

Proverbs 3 and 4 are packed full of wise sayings which set out the key priorities for our lives. I remember learning some of these verses in my teens and they have lived with me ever since. How do we make sure that we are going in the right direction? *"Trust in the* LORD *with all your heart and lean not on your own understanding; in all your ways acknowledge him, and he will make your paths straight." (Proverbs 3:5–6)*. How do we make sure that we will have what we need? *"Honour the* LORD *with your wealth, with the firstfruits of all your crops; then your barns will be filled to overflowing, and your vats will brim over with new wine. (Proverbs 3:9–10)*. How do we keep ourselves pure? *"Above all else, guard your heart, for it is the wellspring of life. Put away perversity from your mouth; keep corrupt talk far from your lips. Let your eyes look straight ahead, fix your gaze directly before you. Make level paths for your feet and take only ways that are firm. Do not swerve to the right or the left; keep your foot from evil. (Proverbs 4:23–27)*.

Warnings against Adultery

There are two dangers that young men are particularly warned to avoid. In chapter 1 the writer warns "my son" to avoid being drawn into groups who will injure or even murder for their own gain. The promise of getting rich quick is an illusion. Such men are heading towards their own destruction. The second danger is being drawn into illicit sexual pleasures by an adulteress or a prostitute. Most of three chapters are devoted to this and it is useful to read two of these to see the approach wisdom writers take.

> **Read Proverbs 5–6**

The way Proverbs tackles this subject illustrates the contrast between the Law and Wisdom. They both say the same thing but they approach it from completely different angles. The Law is from above; wisdom comes from the experience of men who have walked in the world with God.

The Law says *"You shall not commit adultery" (Exodus 20:14)* and specifies punishment. No reason is given for adultery being wrong: God just says it is, and many people today look at laws like this and think that God wants to stop people enjoying themselves. Wisdom approaches adultery from a different perspective. It also says that it is wrong but it gives reasons from man's observation and experience. It starts by recognising that sin has its pleasures: *"For the lips of an adulteress drip honey, and her speech is smoother than oil" (Proverbs 5:3)*. Does this mean that God is trying to stop us enjoying ourselves? No, because this is only half of the picture. Sin can be fun (if it wasn't then we wouldn't be tempted!) but it has its consequences: *"but in the end she is bitter as gall, sharp as a double–edged sword." (Proverbs 5:4)*. Sin is not to be avoided just because God says so but because it has a seriously damaging effect on your life! There is no law against scooping fire into your lap but it is clearly a stupid thing to do as it will have nasty consequences! Similarly, even if there was no law against committing adultery, it is a stupid thing to do as *"whoever does so destroys himself" (Proverbs 6:32)* – his wealth, his safety, his judgement and his reputation. Even with our society's liberal attitude to moral issues we regularly see public figures having their reputation destroyed and can see the financial and emotional cost to families of marriage breakdown. Adultery may be fun for a while but it is not a wise choice. Proverbs gives us a mature approach to life based on a fear of God and an understanding of life itself.

References

[G] Definition of "proverb" from "Concise Oxford Dictionary, 8th edition" (1990). By permission of Oxford University Press.

Day 35
Proverbs, Ecclesiastes and Song of Songs

Proverbs

After the essays on wisdom in Proverbs 1–9 most of the rest of the book is taken up with two line proverbs. We are told that Solomon wrote about 3,000 and about 500 of them are recorded for us. In the same way as the Psalms, Proverbs is not designed for systematic study. There does not appear to be any significance in the sequence of the proverbs, they are more for meditation. Reading a couple of chapters will give you a flavour of the book.

> **Read Proverbs 10, 20**

Some of the proverbs have an obvious meaning, others require thought and meditation. Each one has much to offer. There are many contrasts, particularly in chapters 10–15. The wise and the foolish: *"A wise son brings joy to his father, but a foolish son grief to his mother."* (10:1). The righteous and the wicked: *"The tongue of the righteous is choice silver, but the heart of the wicked is of little value."* (10:20). The lazy, who are sometimes referred to using the very descriptive word "sluggard", and the hard working: *"Lazy hands make a man poor, but diligent hands bring wealth."* (10:4). Note that these sayings contain a general truth without being a foolproof guide to what will happen in all situations. We all know those who work very hard but remain poor, but the general point that laziness will lead to poverty is true.

Some proverbs are just observations about life. For example, *"The first to present his case seems right, till another comes forward and questions him."* (18:17). We will all have seen or read about court cases, particularly in detective fiction, where a convincing argument is put forward only to be demolished by clever questioning. We need to be aware in life in general that it is easy to be taken in by someone's point of view and remember that there may be another side to a story. A similar observation warns us against being taken in when selling something: *""It's no good, it's no good!" says the buyer; then off he goes and boasts about his purchase."* (20:14). We need to be on our guard in financial negotiations!

At times Proverbs gives us instructions. Again on the subject of avoiding poverty, *"Do not love sleep or you will grow poor; stay awake and you will have food to spare." (20:13)*. On the other hand if we want to avoid having all our secrets passed round then remember *"A gossip betrays a confidence; so avoid a man who talks too much." (20:19)*.

At times Proverbs uses very pictorial language. Sometimes the pictures are amusing, *"Like a gold ring in a pig's snout is a beautiful woman who shows no discretion." (11:22)*; at other times they are more beautiful: *"A word aptly spoken is like apples of gold in settings of silver." (25:11)*. Some have immediate impact: *"Like one who seizes a dog by the ears is a passer–by who meddles in a quarrel not his own." (26:17)* – neither is a wise move! Others ring true for those unfortunate enough to have experienced or observed them: *"A quarrelsome wife is like a constant dripping on a rainy day"(27:15)* – I hasten to say that I have only observed this one from a distance! A good way of getting children and young people interested in Proverbs is to give them proverbs like these to act out while the others try and guess what they are. I still remember a young woman very noisily acting out *"If a man loudly blesses his neighbour early in the morning, it will be taken as a curse." (27:14)*. It certainly made the point!

Solomon's proverbs are supplemented by some "sayings of the wise" which are slightly longer sayings than the two line proverbs. They contain a good description of drunkenness and its effects. At the end of the book are the sayings of Agur and King Lemuel who were probably not Israelites. Agur's sayings contain some interesting observations that require wisdom to understand. Lemuel's advice is to avoid women and drink.

Throughout Proverbs there are references to a good wife being from the Lord and the book ends with a poem describing "a wife of noble character." The woman described is hard working, a business woman who buys a field and manages her own finances, generous to those in need, good at making provision for her family and a wise counsellor. Above all else she fears the Lord. No wonder that her children and husband praise her publicly and her husband is well respected!

The book of Proverbs contains a huge wealth of wisdom contained in little packets. To understand it requires meditation – mulling it over thoughtfully. It should be read regularly and in small doses as a little goes a long way. Remember Billy Graham's practice of reading one chapter a day each month.

Ecclesiastes

Proverbs is followed by the book of Ecclesiastes, which is another wisdom book written in a very similar style to Proverbs. The book is introduced as *"The words of the Teacher, son of David, king of Jerusalem." (Ecclesiastes 1:1)*. Later in the first chapter we find that the author was also a king of Israel and wiser than any of the previous kings (see 1:12,16) which are strong indications that it was written by Solomon. However, the fact that his name is never mentioned means that it may have been written by someone else. The word Ecclesiastes is the Greek word for "Teacher".

The book was written by an old man who is reflecting on his life. Although he has had a good life with many opportunities his overall belief about life is summarised in that it is meaningless. He is writing to express the meaninglessness of many pursuits – pleasure, wisdom, toil, riches – and to advise the young to enjoy what God has given them while they can.

	Outline of Ecclesiastes
1:1–11	Introduction: Author and Theme – "Everything is Meaningless".
1:12 – 2:26	The Meaninglessness of Pleasures, Wisdom and Toil
3:1–4:16	A Time for Everything. Observations.
5:1–7	Be careful in God's presence
5:8–6:12	The Meaninglessness of Riches
7:1–8:1	Proverbs on Wisdom
8:2–17	Obey the King. Observations.
9:1–10	All die
9:11–11:6	Proverbs
11:7–12:7	Advice to Youth
12:8–14	Conclusion

Day 35 – Proverbs, Ecclesiastes and Song of Songs

The first chapter gives a flavour of the book.

> **Read Ecclesiastes 1**

It is hard to find a more gloomy assessment of life than that in verse 2 – *"'Meaningless! Meaningless!" says the Teacher. "Utterly meaningless! Everything is meaningless"' (Ecclesiastes 1:2)* – and the book as a whole comes across as very pessimistic in its outlook. As we will see tomorrow, the end of Solomon's life was different from the beginning. At the beginning he asked God for wisdom and built the magnificent temple where he saw the glory of the Lord come down as a cloud but as time went on his heart turned away from the Lord. The writings in Ecclesiastes are those of a man who has known God but has wandered away from him. He is still able to point people back to God but more as an intellectual exercise rather than from his heart. It acts as a warning to all but, because of its background, we need to be careful how to interpret it. Like some of Job, it cannot be taken at face value.

Like Proverbs, Ecclesiastes is fairly unstructured and, despite its pessimistic outlook, it contains some real gems. The beginning of chapter 3 is a well known passage about there being *"a time for everything."* The fact that we learn much more in difficult times than in good times is described at the start of chapter 7. There is a section which is often used in marriage services as it describes why *"two are better than one"* and ends with the great statement *"A cord of three strands is not quickly broken" (Ecclesiastes 4:9,12)* which is a great way to view a Christian marriage with Jesus holding the couple together and taking the strain if one should become frayed round the edges!

Like Proverbs it contains some good advice. Those who are stuck in the past should move on: *"Do not say, "Why were the old days better than these?" For it is not wise to ask such questions." (Ecclesiastes 7:10)*. Those who are married should take time to enjoy it: *"Enjoy life with your wife, whom you love, all the days of this meaningless life that God has given you under the sun – all your meaningless days." (Ecclesiastes 9:9)*. We should learn to be content in bad times as well as good: *"When times are good, be happy; but when times are bad, consider: God has made the one as well as the other." (Ecclesiastes 7:14)*. The message of Ecclesiastes is that life, although it has many unanswered questions, is to be enjoyed.

After all his thoughts the Teacher rounds off the book with a conclusion which puts everything back into perspective: *"Now all has been heard; here is the conclusion of the matter: Fear God and keep his commandments, for this is the whole duty of man. For God will bring every deed into judgement, including every hidden thing, whether it is good or evil. (Ecclesiastes 12:13–14).* As at the beginning of Proverbs the fear of God is the beginning of wisdom.

Song of Songs

Song of Songs is the last of the wisdom books. It is also called "Song of Solomon" or, as the opening verse suggests, "Solomon's Song of Songs". We know from 1 Kings 4:32 that Solomon wrote 1005 songs so it is fairly safe to assume that he wrote it as a young man around 960 BC.

There are various ways of interpreting Song of Songs. At face value it is a celebration of love between two lovers which describes their growing, intimate relationship. It records the thoughts and feelings of two young people – the lover and the beloved – and poetically records incidents in their courtship and early marriage. It is not clear who is speaking when. The New International Version of the Bible identifies three speakers: the Beloved (a Young Girl), the Lover (Solomon) and Friends – a chorus of friends of the Beloved. However, this is only a suggestion.

It is not always clear when the scene changes from one meeting to another but this is a suggested outline.

Outline of Song of Songs	
1:1	Title
1:2–2:7	The First Meeting
2:8–3:5	The Second Meeting
3:6–5:1	The Third Meeting – Marriage
5:2–6:3	The Fourth Meeting
6:4–8:4	The Fifth Meeting
8:5–7	The Literary Climax
8:8–14	The Conclusion

Over the centuries some have taken the view that Song of Songs is an allegory – a symbolic story like a fable – of love between God and

Israel or Christ and the Church. Many of the Old Testament prophets liken Israel to a maiden or, later as she falls away from God, to a prostitute and in the New Testament both John the Baptist and Paul made reference to the church as a bride of Christ. It is likely that you have sung parts of Song of Songs as many songs have been taken from it. Perhaps the most famous line which has been set to music many times is *"He has taken me to the banquet hall, and his banner over me is love" (Song of Songs 2:4)* which is sung as a celebration of what Christ has given to us through his death and resurrection.

The first approach sees Song of Songs as a love poem, the second spiritualises it. Which is right? The simple answer is both as it has much to teach us about both human love and God's love for us. Given that man is made in the image of God it should come as no surprise to us that the greatest expression of human love, the commitment of a man and a woman in marriage, reflects the love of God for mankind, even if only in part.

If we look at the song in the context of it being a wisdom book it can be seen as wisdom's view of love and this makes it very relevant for us today. Among the words of the Beloved and the Lover are wise words about love. There is a recurring theme – *"Do not arouse or awaken love until it so desires" (Song of Songs 2:7)* – which speaks of waiting for intimacy, a contrast with today's view of sex. The lovers describe one another in a language which, although it may seem strange to us today, is subtle and sensuous but never crude.

Near the end of the song there is a series of statements about love which sum up wisdom's view of love.

> **Read Song of Songs 8:6–7**

What a magnificent summary of the power of love!

Very different poetry and wisdom literature flowed from the turbulent reign of David and the peaceful reign of Solomon. But in eighty years they left an enduring legacy for Israel and the Church. Tomorrow we return to the story of the kings that followed David and Solomon and the prophets that God sent to them and his people.

Day 36
The Kingdom Divides

Solomon's Folly

Solomon made an excellent start to his reign as king of Israel as we saw in the early chapters of 1 Kings. As a young man, the Lord appeared to him and granted him great wisdom so he could rule the people wisely. Then, after he had built the temple, the Lord appeared to him again and renewed the promise he made to his father David and told Solomon that his throne would be established forever if he walked uprightly before him. However, the Lord also warned him that if he turned away from him then the people of Israel would be cut off from the land. Despite that, Solomon did turn away from God in the latter part of his reign. In the Law, Moses had written a warning for the kings of Israel that *"He must not take many wives, or his heart will be led astray" (Deuteronomy 17:17)* but Solomon married an extraordinary number of wives and through them he became actively involved in the worship of foreign gods.

> *Read 1 Kings 11:1–13*

Solomon's actions had serious consequences for the whole nation as the Lord raised up enemies from the surrounding nations during his reign. He also punished Solomon by taking the kingdom away from him. Yet, for the sake of David, this punishment took place in the reign of his son and even then he was left with two of the ten tribes.

God sends a prophet to anoint Jeroboam to be king over the ten breakaway tribes and makes him a promise that he too can have one of his descendants to rule as king forever. However, this is a conditional promise – note the word "if" at the beginning of verse 38 – unlike the promise the Lord made to David which was not dependent on what David did (see 2 Samuel 7:5–16). Jeroboam can have a lasting dynasty *if* he keeps God's laws.

This puts Solomon in the same situation that Saul was in with David as he now has one of his officials anointed by the Lord's prophet to be the next king. Solomon tried to kill Jeroboam, in the same way as Saul tried to kill David, but Jeroboam fled to Egypt to wait for Solomon's death.

Day 36 – The Kingdom Divides

> Read 1 Kings 11:26–40

Rehoboam's Folly

After Solomon dies his son Rehoboam is made king and the Lord uses Rehoboam's lack of wisdom to bring about his promise to give ten of the tribes to Jeroboam. Solomon had increased the taxation burden on the people to intolerable levels – "a heavy yoke" – in order to pay for his building projects and the build up of a large army and civil service. The people have put up with it for the sake of David but now they ask for tax cuts. Rehoboam foolishly ignores the wise counsel from his elders and refuses. As a result the ten northern tribes, who had made David their king by renewable treaty just over seventy years earlier, reject Rehoboam's rule and make Jeroboam their king instead. Rehoboam gets ready to go to war against the rebels but civil war is averted by a word from God through the prophet Shemaiah.

> Read 1 Kings 12:1–24

If only all wars could be averted as simply as that!

The Divided Kingdom

As a result of Rehoboam's actions Israel splits into two separate nations. The tribe of Judah forms a nation in the south with Jerusalem as its capital. (The tribe of Simeon was allocated towns within the area allotted to Judah in Joshua 19 and has lost its tribal identity so the nation of Judah is sometimes called two tribes.) The other ten tribes form the northern kingdom which retains the name Israel. About fifty years later Samaria became the capital of Israel and "Samaria" is often used as an alternative name for the northern nation of Israel in the Bible. Map 5 on the next page shows the new political situation.

Given that the twelve tribes are split into ten and two we might expect Israel to be five times larger than Judah but in actual fact Judah was already over half the size of Israel during David's reign and grew to almost the same size as Israel in later times. There are various reasons for this. Judah was the largest tribe at the time of the conquest and the people of Judah were the most successful at taking their land. The other tribes had much more difficulty so it is likely that some people would have settled in Judah rather than in the areas their tribes were allocated. Later, David made Jerusalem the political and religious focus of the nation, which attracted people to the area of Judah where it was

Day 36 – The Kingdom Divides

Map 5 – The Kingdoms of Israel and Judah

situated. Then when the kingdom divided we learn from 2 Chronicles 11:16 that many of the Levites and others who *"set their hearts on seeking the LORD"* moved to the southern kingdom and that Rehoboam had some control over the tribe of Benjamin.

1 & 2 Kings – The History of the Kings of Israel & Judah

1 & 2 Kings, which like 1 & 2 Samuel were originally one book, record the history of the kings of Israel and Judah from David's death in 970 BC to the exile of Judah to Babylon in 586 BC. The author is unknown but it is written from a prophetic viewpoint, probably during the exile around 550 BC. After the division of the kingdom 1 & 2 Kings records the history of both kingdoms, covering the reign of a few kings in one kingdom before moving back to the other. The parallel account in 2 Chronicles only records the history of Judah after the split.

Outline of 1 & 2 Kings	
1 Kings 1–11	Solomon, the last king of all Israel
1 Kings 12:1–24	The kingdom divides into two separate nations – Israel and Judah
1 Kings 12:25–16:34	The history of the kings of: Israel from Jeroboam I to Ahab Judah from Rehoboam to Asa
1 Kings 17– 2 Kings 8:15	The ministries of the prophets Elijah and Elisha
2 Kings 8:16–16:20	The history of the kings of: Israel from Joram to Pekah Judah from Jehoram to Ahaz
2 Kings 17	Israel is exiled to Assyria.
2 Kings 18–25	The history of the kings of Judah from Hezekiah to Zedekiah and the exile of Judah to Babylon.

As 1 & 2 Kings jump backwards and forwards between the two kingdoms each new king is introduced with a set formula: when they started to reign relative to the king in the other kingdom, the length of their reign, their mother's name and whether they did right or did evil. 1 & 2 Kings is a prophetic book – meaning that it is written from the

Day 36 – The Kingdom Divides

Lord's perspective – so it gives us his assessment of their actions. The introductions to the second and third kings of Judah provide contrasting assessments.

> **Read 1 Kings 15:1–3 and 9–11**

The time covered by 1 & 2 Kings is shown on Timecharts 7 to 9. Timecharts 7 and 8 are shown overleaf for reference over the next few days. On these, the split into the two kingdoms is represented by two lines going across the page, the top one showing the kings of Judah and the bottom one the kings of Israel. There are problems with dating the reigns of the kings accurately because sometimes there were overlaps between the reigns of one king and the next as shown by slanting lines on the timechart.

Israel was ruled by a succession of kings who were either bad or very bad. There were three major "houses" or "dynasties" – those starting with Jeroboam I, Omri and Jehu – and a number of minor ones. The dashed lines between the kings on the timecharts indicate that they were from the same family while the solid lines indicate the breaks between the dynasties. Led by their godless kings, the people of Israel mostly worshipped false gods apart from a period of revival during the ministries of Elijah and Elisha. As a result of the people's sin God fulfilled his promise to take the people out of the land after about two hundred years when Israel was defeated by the Assyrians and the people were taken away from the Promised Land and into captivity.

Judah remained loyal to the house of David and was ruled by his descendants, apart from a brief time when the evil Queen Athalia ruled. Some of the kings were good – notably Jehoshaphat, Hezekiah and Josiah – but many were bad and lead the people into worship of false gods. The people of Judah remained in the land after Israel were deported but, due to the great wickedness during the long reign of the evil King Manasseh, Judah too was also judged by God and the nation was defeated by the Babylonians and the people taken into exile.

God sent many prophets to bring his word to his people in both nations. The key ones came into the wickedest times: Elijah, Elisha and Hosea to Israel and Isaiah and Jeremiah to Judah. Most of the key prophets are known through their writings so they are shown as "Bible Books" on the timecharts; Elijah and Elisha are shown separately.

Day 36 – The Kingdom Divides

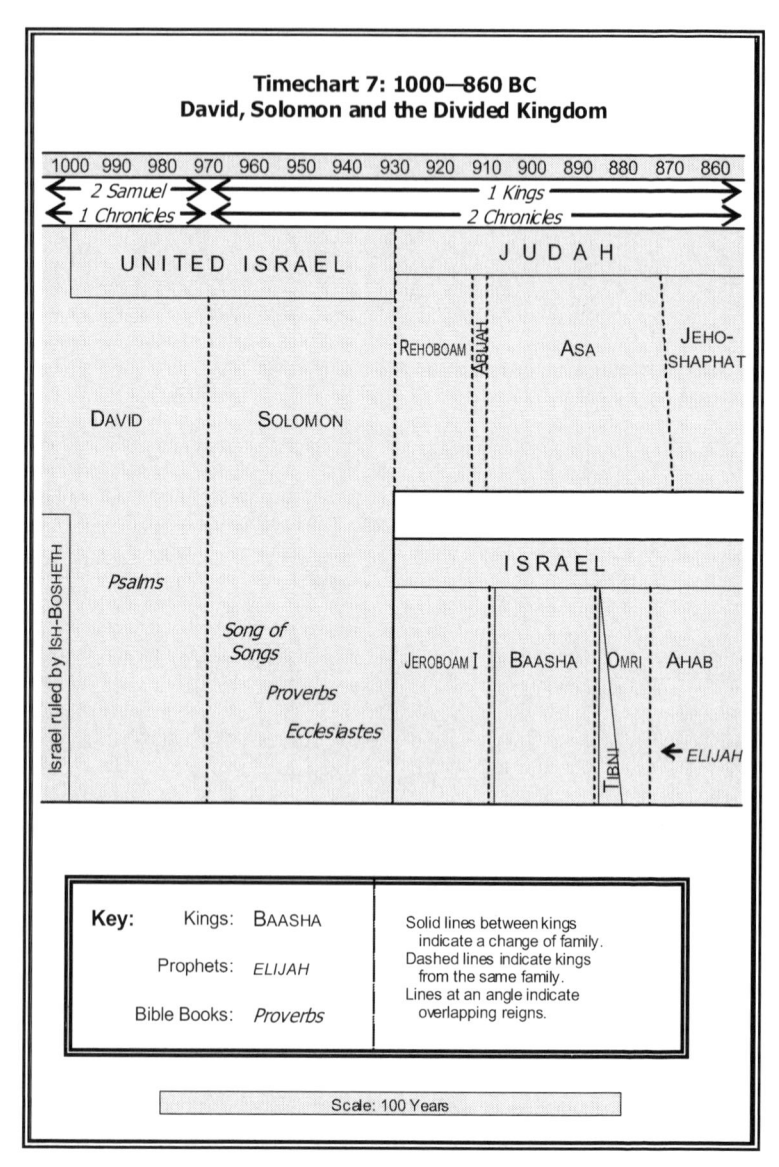

Timechart 7: 1000–860 BC
David, Solomon and the Divided Kingdom

| 1000 | 990 | 980 | 970 | 960 | 950 | 940 | 930 | 920 | 910 | 900 | 890 | 880 | 870 | 860 |

← 2 Samuel → ← 1 Kings →
← 1 Chronicles → ← 2 Chronicles →

UNITED ISRAEL | **JUDAH**

REHOBOAM | ABIJAH | ASA | JEHOSHAPHAT

DAVID | SOLOMON

Israel ruled by ISH-BOSHETH

Psalms

Song of Songs

Proverbs

Ecclesiastes

ISRAEL

JEROBOAM I | BAASHA | OMRI | AHAB

TIBNI

← ELIJAH

Key:
- Kings: BAASHA
- Prophets: ELIJAH
- Bible Books: Proverbs

Solid lines between kings indicate a change of family.
Dashed lines indicate kings from the same family.
Lines at an angle indicate overlapping reigns.

Scale: 100 Years

**Timechart 7 – 1000–860 BC:
David, Solomon and the Divided Kingdom**

Day 36 – The Kingdom Divides

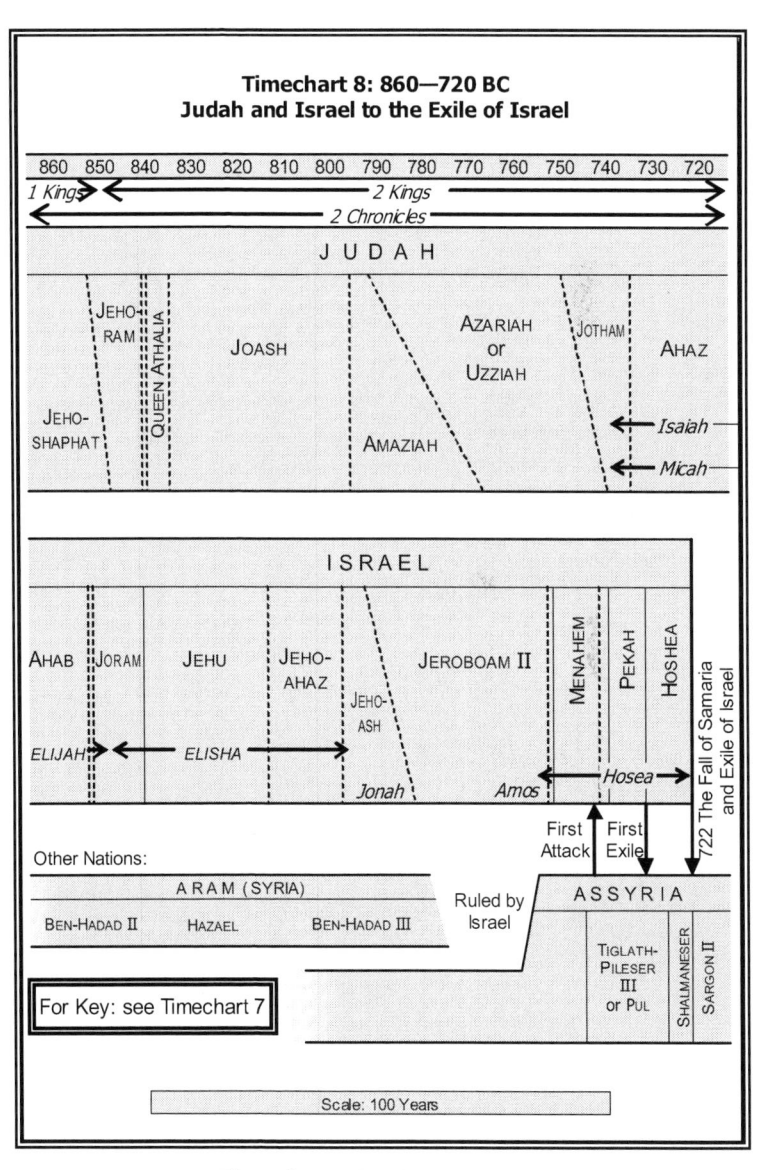

Timechart 8: 860—720 BC
Judah and Israel to the Exile of Israel

| 860 | 850 | 840 | 830 | 820 | 810 | 800 | 790 | 780 | 770 | 760 | 750 | 740 | 730 | 720 |

1 Kings ⟶ ⟵ 2 Kings ⟶
⟵ 2 Chronicles ⟶

JUDAH

JEHO-SHAPHAT | JEHORAM | QUEEN ATHALIA | JOASH | AMAZIAH | AZARIAH or UZZIAH | JOTHAM | AHAZ

⟵ Isaiah
⟵ Micah

ISRAEL

AHAB | JORAM | JEHU | JEHOAHAZ | JEHOASH | JEROBOAM II | MENAHEM | PEKAH | HOSHEA

ELIJAH ⟵ ELISHA ⟶
Jonah   Amos   ⟵ Hosea ⟶

722 The Fall of Samaria and Exile of Israel

First Attack | First Exile

Other Nations:

ARAM (SYRIA) — BEN-HADAD II | HAZAEL | BEN-HADAD III

Ruled by Israel

ASSYRIA — TIGLATH-PILESER III or PUL | SHALMANESER | SARGON II

For Key: see Timechart 7

Scale: 100 Years

**Timechart 8 – 860–720 BC:
Judah and Israel to the Exile of Israel**

The Early Years of Israel

After the kingdoms divide 1 Kings takes up the story of Israel first.

> Read 1 Kings 12:25–13:6

After the split with Judah, Jeroboam is afraid that the people will return to Jerusalem to worship God and, as a result, will continue to have an allegiance to Rehoboam. To avoid this he made two golden calves and set them up in Bethel and Dan (see Map 5 on page 205) so the people could worship there instead. He also appointed non–Levites as priests at these centres of worship, which meant that not only were the people cut off from true worship of the Lord but they were also cut off from his laws which the Levites taught the people and used to judge them. This introduction of idolatry into the heart of God's nation brings the Lord's judgement on Jeroboam. His son Nadab only rules for two years before he and all Jeroboam's surviving offspring are killed in a coup by Baasha who becomes king in his place.

However, the evil that Jeroboam started by establishing these centres of idol worship continued throughout the reigns of all the kings of Israel. Baasha led the people in the same way and his son Elah is killed in a military power struggle. Zimri, the commander of half the chariot force, seizes power only to be overthrown a week later by Omri – the chief of the army – who takes half the nation while Tibni takes the other half. After civil war within Israel for four years Omri gains overall power and establishes the fifth "house" in Israel in fifty years by proclaiming himself king.

What a mess! After all that David and Solomon had achieved in uniting the nation and putting the Lord at the centre the story of the divided kingdoms is a sorry disappointment.

Day 37
Elijah

The Early Years of Judah

While Israel is turning its back on God and plunging into civil unrest and political infighting what is happening in Judah? Alarmingly we find that Rehoboam is even more wicked than Jeroboam!

> Read 1 Kings 14:22–24

This sin, building on that which started during the reign of Solomon, lays them open to God's judgement and it comes very soon.

> Read 1 Kings 14:25–28

Judah is also constantly at war with Israel throughout Rehoboam's reign.

The speed of Judah's decline is breathtaking. Within five short years of Solomon's death the country is ruined by civil war and attack from its neighbours. Solomon's great temple, which was visibly filled with the glory of the Lord less than forty years earlier, is ransacked. Rehoboam's replacement of the gold shields with bronze ones is a pathetic attempt to hide the fact that the Lord's blessing has been removed from the nation.

It is Rehoboam's grandson, Asa, who is the first good king of Judah. (You may find it helpful to refer back to Timechart 7 on page 208 to see when the kings of Judah and Israel reigned.) He removed the evil of Rehoboam.

> Read 2 Chronicles 14:2–6

During his reign the Egyptians once again attacked Judah but Asa called on the Lord and he struck down their enemies before them. While Asa relied on God the nation was secure and many people from Israel moved to Judah to be part of a godly nation again.

Unfortunately, when Baasha, king of Israel, came to attack Judah late on in Asa's reign, Asa, rather than looking to God for help, used the treasure in the temple to buy support from the king of Aram (modern day Syria). This brought condemnation from the Lord through the prophet Hanani. Sadly Asa refused to listen to him – he even put him in prison – and, as a result of his sin, spent the last two years of his life with a severe disease in his feet. He is one of a number of kings who started well but failed to follow the Lord wholeheartedly as they got older. God is always eager to support those who are devoted – as Hanani said to Asa: *"For the eyes of the LORD range throughout the earth to strengthen those whose hearts are fully committed to him." (2 Chronicles 16:9)* – but we have to guard our hearts to avoid our devotion waning in later life.

Asa was succeeded by his son Jehoshaphat. Like Asa, Jehoshaphat also did right in his early years. He told the priests and Levites to go around the towns of Judah teaching the law and appointed god–fearing judges. Once more the life of God's nation was based on his laws. As a result the kingdom was wealthy and at peace during his reign. 2 Chronicles 20 gives an account of how Jehoshaphat dealt with an attack from Moab and Ammon. Despite having a large army his response is to seek the Lord and call the people to prayer and fasting. After a prophetic message telling him that God would defeat their enemies, Jehoshaphat went to meet them with the singers at the front of his army singing thanks to the Lord. As they went out in praise the enemy armies fell out with each other and were defeated before the men of Judah had to lift a sword.

The Wickedness of Ahab and Jezebel

While Judah was enjoying sixty years of godly rule under Asa and Jehoshaphat the situation in Israel was very different. During the reign of Asa Israel slid into political chaos, as we saw yesterday. Each king brought more wickedness than the previous one and Omri, who built a fortress on a hill of Samaria and made it the capital of Israel, was no exception. When he died, he was succeeded by his son Ahab who was a complete contrast to the godly Jehoshaphat. The scene is set for Ahab's reign in a few verses at the end of 1 Kings 16.

Read 1 Kings 16:29–34

Ahab, encouraged by his Sidonian wife Jezebel, added to the sins of Jeroboam (the worship of golden calves) by introducing vigorous worship of Baal and Asherah, the gods of the nations that were in the land before Israel took it from them. As we saw in the time of the Judges, for Israel to worship Baal and Asherah meant that they were completely forsaking their covenant with the Lord. They looked to them to provide rain for the land, children for the next generation and security from their enemies. Their "worship" involved sexual immorality and even, at times, child sacrifice.

The last verse, about the rebuilding of Jericho, shows us that all respect for the word of the Lord had long since vanished. Recorded in the book of Joshua was Joshua's solemn curse on anyone who attempted to rebuild the walls of Jericho: *"At the cost of his firstborn son will he lay its foundations; at the cost of his youngest will he set up its gates." (Joshua 6:26)*. In the time of Ahab these words were either forgotten or, more chillingly, were thought irrelevant and Hiel went ahead and suffered the consequences of the curse. It is into this situation that God sent the formidable prophet Elijah.

Elijah – The Greatest Prophet

Elijah is usually regarded as the greatest of the Old Testament prophets. When Jesus was on earth, there was an occasion when he went up a mountain and was transfigured – his face and clothes radiated light – and two men appeared and spoke with him about his coming death: Moses, the representative of the Law, and Elijah, the representative of the Prophets (see Matthew 17 and Mark 9). 1 & 2 Kings cover the 350 years from the end of Solomon's reign to the exile of Judah in 35 chapters. 15 of these are devoted to the ministries of Elijah and his successor Elisha. So, although there is no book called "Elijah" in the Old Testament, there is more written about him than about any of the minor prophets.

We know nothing of Elijah's background and he appears very suddenly on the national scene to confront the wicked Ahab.

> **Read 1 Kings 17:1–6**

Elijah's statement that there would be no rain is a direct challenge to Baal the god of fertility and the rain clouds. Why did Elijah say there would be no rain? Was this his idea or did it come directly from God? As with all the prophets, the origin of Elijah's words and actions come from God's law. He knew the curses that God promised would come on the land if the people did not obey God's laws and follow his laws and commands. Among them the Lord had said, *"The sky over your head will be bronze, the ground beneath you iron. The LORD will turn the rain of your country into dust and powder; it will come down from the skies until you are destroyed." (Deuteronomy 28:23–24)*. The Holy Spirit had brought these words to life for Elijah and given him the conviction that this was the time for this curse.

After the brook dried up the Lord directed Elijah to a widow in Sidon – the place that Jezebel came from – and miraculously provided them both with food. For three years Elijah remained in hiding while the country experienced devastating drought and famine waiting for the Lord to tell him what to do next. He faced a test of his faith when the widow's son died and he was used by the Lord to bring him back to life.

Despite extensive searches, Ahab fails to find Elijah until the Lord sends him back for a second meeting. This leads to Elijah's confrontation with the 400 prophets of Baal which is one of the most dramatic events of the Old Testament.

Read 1 Kings 18

No one who made the journey to Mount Carmel that day ever forgot it. Some were eager to see the worship of Baal removed from the land but were too afraid to speak up and kept their thoughts to themselves as Elijah challenged them to make a choice for the Lord or Baal and set up a contest between one man, himself, and 450 prophets of Baal. The atmosphere was electric as the prophets of Baal worked themselves into a frenzy to get Baal's attention. The people may have been amused when Elijah boldly ridiculed them from the sidelines (the expression in verse 27 which is translated "busy" in the New International Version of the Bible (NIV) is translated "gone aside" in the New American Standard Bible (NASB). Elijah seems to have been suggesting that Baal may have nipped out to the loo!) but they didn't dare laugh out loud while Ahab looked on. And then, in the silence that followed after the hours of chanting from the prophets of Baal, Elijah took time to build an altar, prepare a sacrifice and even manage to find twelve large jars of water at the top of a mountain after three years of drought! His simple prayer was answered by the incredible demonstration of the Lord's power as the fire fell on the sacrifice and consumed it along with the water and even the altar itself.

We read later that there were seven thousand in Israel who had remained faithful to God and, as news of this dramatic encounter reached them, they would have been greatly encouraged. Many others were unsure whether to follow Baal or the Lord but this event would

Day 37 – Elijah

have given them the courage to return to the Lord.

The Bible, as always, tells us the downs as well as the ups of its heroes. Elijah, who demonstrated incredible faith and courage on Mount Carmel is then frightened by the threats of one woman, the evil Jezebel. The Lord is very loving towards him and after revealing himself to Elijah gives him new tasks to do in appointing kings for Israel and Aram as well as a successor for himself.

We read of one more encounter between Elijah and Ahab and this is in connection with a vineyard belonging to a righteous man called Naboth. Ahab wants to buy it from him to extend his palace gardens in Samaria but Naboth refuses to sell it. Even in these godless times land in Israel is still seen as inheritance from the Lord and Ahab, the king, does not see himself as above the law. His wife Jezebel, however, does not have any such scruples. She comes from a pagan culture where the king can do as he pleases so she arranges for Naboth to be stoned for crimes he has not committed and sends Ahab to take possession of his new vineyard. Once again Ahab has the uncomfortable experience of meeting Elijah who brings him a word from the Lord that he and Jezebel will be killed and the kingdom taken away from his house. Surprisingly, Ahab listens to what he says and humbles himself before God and the punishment is put off until the days of his son.

Like Samuel, Elijah stood as the Lord's representative to the whole nation in his generation. His bold stand against the tide of wickedness which was engulfing the land is a demonstration of God's patience with his people and his enduring covenant love for them. However, the wickedness that Jezebel brought into Israel not only had an impact there but also spread into Judah too as we will see tomorrow.

Day 38
To the Brink

Elisha

One of the tasks the Lord gave Elijah after his encounter at Mount Carmel, was to anoint Elisha to be his successor as prophet.

> Read 1 Kings 19:19–21

Israel and Judah had a contrasting pair of kings in the time of Elijah: Ahab was the most evil of Israel's kings while Jehoshaphat was one of Judah's most godly. During their reigns Aram was gaining power and encroaching on Israel's territory. Ahab asked Jehoshaphat to go to war against Aram with him and Jehoshaphat unwisely agreed. They lost the battle and Ahab was killed. His first son died soon after taking the throne and his brother Joram became king of Israel. Timechart 8 on page 209 covers the period that we are looking at today.

During the reign of Joram, Elijah was taken into heaven and his servant Elisha took over his role as prophet. Elijah is one of two men who went to heaven without dying: the other was Enoch (see Genesis 5:24).

> Read 2 Kings 2

Elisha operated in the same amazing power as Elijah. During his lifetime he performed many miracles including healing a foreign army commander called Naaman from leprosy, producing cooking oil from thin air, making an iron axe head float and raising people from the dead. At the end of 2 Kings 4 he also fed a hundred men with a few loaves.

> Read 2 Kings 4:42–44

Such miracles have no equal in the Old Testament. The only man to perform such a range of miraculous signs was Jesus himself.

The attack on God's ultimate Promise

The evil influence that was brought into the nation of Israel through Jezebel was not ended by the death of Ahab. In fact it spread into neighbouring Judah where it even threatened to frustrate God's plans.

As we saw in 2 Samuel 7, the Lord made a promise to David that, *"Your house and your kingdom shall endure for ever before me; your throne shall be established for ever." (2 Samuel 7:16)*. This commitment meant that a descendant of David would sit on the throne of Israel forever. Initially this could only be fulfilled through his human descendants reigning over the Israelites from Jerusalem. Ultimately it pointed to the coming of Jesus, a descendant of David, who will reign over the world forever.

Satan is not unaware of God's plans and he sets out to try and wipe out David's line in order to frustrate them. The attack came in three stages.

Stage 1: Jehoram kills his brothers

The alliance between Ahab and Jehoshaphat was sealed by the marriage of Jehoshaphat's son Jehoram to Ahab's daughter Athalia. The influence of this woman, brought up in the godless court of Ahab, is seen when Jehoram became king. He follows the practice of pagan kings by murdering all his brothers and other potential rivals to the throne. He then went on to lead Judah into the evil that Jezebel had brought into Israel. God does not let his wickedness go unpunished and Elijah sent him a letter telling him that he will be very ill for a long time and then die in great pain. The end of 2 Chronicles 21 describes his end in gory detail and notes that his death was not marked by the usual signs of respect and honour and that *"he passed away, to no-one's regret" (2 Chronicles 21:20)*. There can be few worse epitaphs than that! He is succeeded as king by his son Ahaziah.

This first attack on David's family appears to leave Ahaziah as the only male descendant of David in Judah – see Figure 8 opposite. The bold arrows show the transfer of the throne in each nation. (This figure also indicates why this period is so confusing. Both kingdoms have a king called Ahaziah at a similar time and the names Joram and Jehoram can also be interchanged so having two of them close together does not help much either!)

Stage 2: Jehu wipes out most of Ahaziah's family

When Elijah fled from Jezebel after the confrontation with the prophets of Baal on Mount Carmel, the Lord commissioned him to anoint three men: Elisha to succeed him as prophet, Hazael as king of Aram, and Jehu as king of Israel. He himself only anointed Elisha and passed to him the task of anointing the other two.

Elisha went to Damascus to anoint Hazael as king of Aram and as he

Day 38 – To the Brink 219

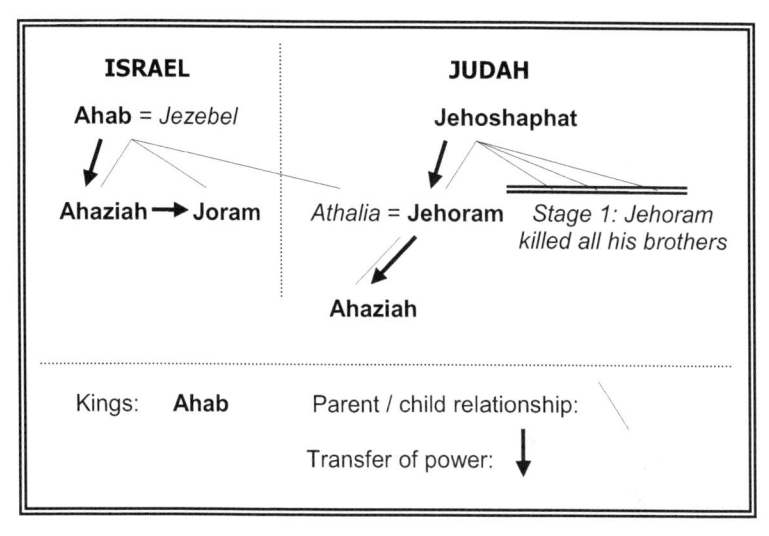

```
ISRAEL              │        JUDAH
Ahab = Jezebel      │    Jehoshaphat
   ↓                │       ↓
Ahaziah → Joram     │  Athalia = Jehoram    Stage 1: Jehoram
                    │        ↓               killed all his brothers
                    │     Ahaziah
─────────────────────────────────────────────
Kings:  Ahab         Parent / child relationship:
                     Transfer of power:  ↓
```

**Figure 8 – The Attack on David's Line:
Jehoram kills his brothers**

did, he wept because he knew that Hazael would wage terrible war against Israel. As in the time of the Judges, when God's people forsake him God raised up a strong enemy to punish his people and drive them back to him.

Israel and Judah continued their alliance against Aram and Ahaziah went to war against Hazael alongside Joram. Joram was injured in battle and, while he and Ahaziah were resting, Elisha sent an unnamed prophet to anoint Jehu to be king of Israel. This action led to major upheavals in both Israel and Judah.

Read 2 Kings 9

Jehu was clearly a man of action. He was not one to sit back and wait for prophecies to be fulfilled: he preferred to make sure they were fulfilled as soon as possible through his own efforts. And as for his driving – it was clearly the talk of the Israelite army. No one else was as mad as Jehu in a chariot!

Having taken control of the throne by killing Joram, Jehu goes on to wipe out the whole of Ahab's family. This is in fulfilment of a prophecy that Elijah had given to Ahab which Jehu had overheard. As part of this purge forty-two relatives of Ahaziah are also killed. He then tricks the prophets of Baal into a meeting where he has them all killed so destroying Baal worship in Israel. Because he did right in the Lord's eyes the Lord promises him that four generations of his would sit on the throne of Israel. This was a qualified blessing as Jehu did nothing to undo the sin of Jeroboam and let the people continue to worship the golden calves at Bethel and Dan.

Stage 3: Queen Athalia completes the job

While Jehu takes control of Israel his murder of Ahaziah leaves a power vacuum in Judah. As soon as the Queen Mother, Athalia, hears about her son's death she decides to take power herself and immediately has all the remaining descendants of David killed. The onslaughts of Jehu and Athalia appear to have completed the extermination of the royal line of David and broken God's promise to always have one of his descendants on the throne of David – see Figure 9.

For six years Athalia rules Judah. As far as she is concerned the dynasty of Omri, her grandfather, now rules Judah and the house of David is destroyed forever. If she had been right then not only would

Day 38 – To the Brink

ISRAEL

Ahab = *Jezebel*

Ahaziah → Joram

Jehu

Stage 2: Jehu wipes out the house of Ahab and kills Ahaziah along with 42 of the house of Judah

JUDAH

Jehoshaphat

Athalia = Jehoram *Stage 1: Jehoram killed all his brothers*

Ahaziah

Stage 3: Athalia wipes out the whole royal family

Kings: **Ahab**
Queen: ***Athalia***

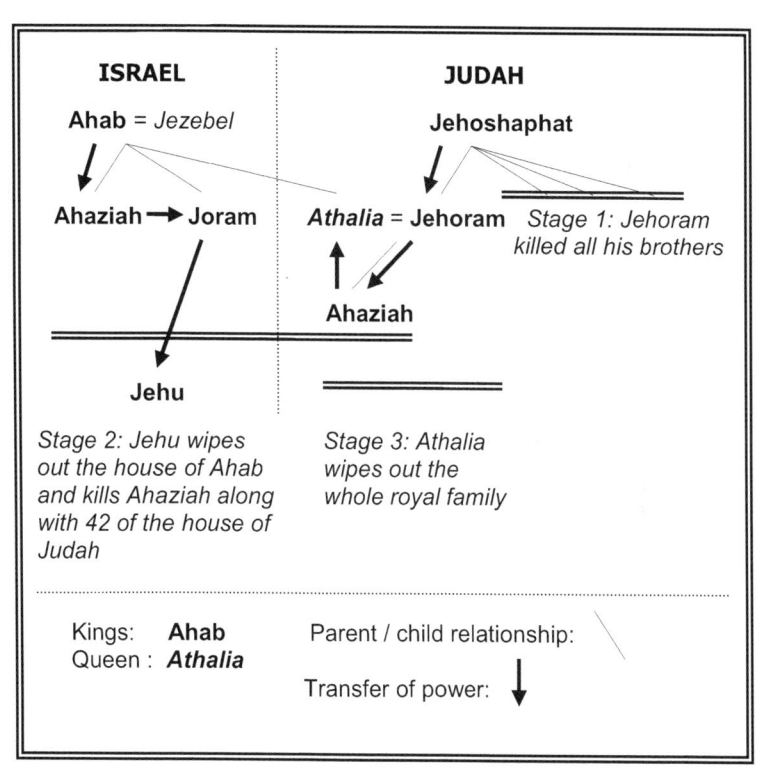

Parent / child relationship:

Transfer of power: ↓

**Figure 9 – The Attack on David's Line:
Jehu and Athalia wipe out Judah's Royal Family**

there have been no one to rule Judah in Jerusalem but God's whole plan of salvation would have been defeated.

God's Promise Remains

This promise, as with all of the Lord's promises, could not be broken and in 2 Kings 11 we read that in Athalia's purge of the royal family one of Jehoram's daughters, Jehosheba, manages to get her baby nephew Joash, the son of Ahaziah, away from the killing and hides him away in the temple. Her husband, Jehoida the priest, waits for his opportunity and then, when Joash is seven, he proclaims Joash as king with the support of the army commanders. Athalia is killed and Baal worship, which now has a temple, altars and a priest in Jerusalem, is destroyed.

So, we see that David's line continues through Joash – see Figure 10 – and with him, God's promise of a future king from the line of David who will reign forever. In the same way as Moses was rescued from death by Pharaoh's daughter, Satan's attack is thwarted by a woman protecting a baby.

Day 38 – To the Brink

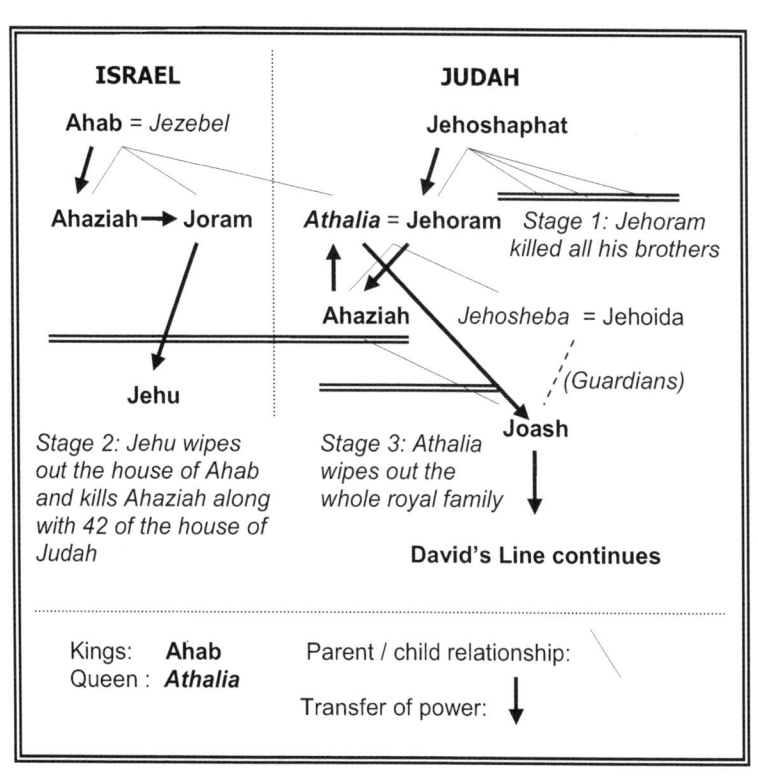

```
ISRAEL                          JUDAH
Ahab = Jezebel                  Jehoshaphat
   ↓                               ↓
Ahaziah → Joram     Athalia = Jehoram    Stage 1: Jehoram
                         ↑                killed all his brothers
                      Ahaziah    Jehosheba = Jehoida
                                         /
   ↓                                    / (Guardians)
  Jehu                              Joash
Stage 2: Jehu wipes    Stage 3: Athalia
out the house of Ahab  wipes out the
and kills Ahaziah along whole royal family
with 42 of the house of                 ↓
Judah                  David's Line continues

Kings:  Ahab         Parent / child relationship:
Queen : Athalia
                     Transfer of power:  ↓
```

Figure 10 – The Attack on David's Line: Joash Survives

Day 39
Israel into Exile

Decline

Following the upheavals in Israel and Judah both countries enter a period of stability. However, both are in decline politically and spiritually. Jehu is not careful to follow God and during his reign Israel loses power as Hazael, king of Aram, takes the territory east of the Jordan. Jehoahaz, his son, is evil and Israel is kept under Aramean power until they turn back to the Lord. Timechart 8 (see page 209) covers this period for Israel and Judah and the other nations involved in their story at this time.

In Judah, the nation is led well by Joash under the influence of his uncle Jehoida and Joash followed God wholeheartedly while Jehoida was alive. He restored the temple, which had fallen into disrepair during the reigns of Jehoram and Queen Athalia (she had even taken sacred objects for use in Baal worship), and re–established regular burnt offerings and worship. However, after the death of Jehoida, Joash abandoned God and even reintroduced worship of Baal and Asherah poles. Jehoida's son Zechariah brought a prophecy against Judah that the Lord had forsaken them and Joash, who must have known Zechariah since his early years as he grew up in Jehoida's family, rather than listening to him had him stoned to death. As a result of all this wickedness Judah is overrun by the Arameans and Joash is left wounded. His officials then assassinated him for murdering Zechariah and the writer of Chronicles notes that he *"was buried in the City of David, but not in the tombs of the kings." (2 Chronicles 24:25)*. A very sorry end for a king who started with such promise.

Joash's son Amaziah provoked a war with Jehoash, king of Israel, and was soundly defeated. Jehoash even broke down some of the wall of Jerusalem. The two countries regained territory under the kings Jeroboam II and Uzziah and both enjoyed a new golden age. During Jeroboam's forty–one year reign Israel even took control of the territory of Aram but once he died Israel was plunged into a period of great instability.

God had promised Jehu that four generations of his descendents would rule Israel and, as Israel continued to pursue wickedness, God acted swiftly once his promise was fulfilled. Jeroboam II's son, the fourth in Jehu's line, was assassinated after six months and this set the scene for a period of infighting for the throne. Over the next thirty years Israel had six kings, four of whom were assassinated.

The Exile Foretold

Seven hundred years earlier Moses had spoken to the people of Israel in the desert just before they entered the Promised Land. He restated the covenant the Lord had made with them and made it clear that if they obeyed him they would be blessed, but if they disobeyed then they would be cursed. This catalogue of blessings and curses can be found in Deuteronomy 28.

> **Read Deuteronomy 28**

The curses described in this chapter were to serve as a reminder to the Israelites to obey the Lord's commandments wholeheartedly. They progress from the bad to the awful to the horrific and, during its two hundred years as a nation, Israel experienced this progression. As we saw earlier, in the time of Ahab, Elijah remembered this passage and prophesied that there would be no rain for three years – see verses 23–24. At various times God allowed his people to be overrun by their enemies, particularly the Arameans – see verse 25. The description of life in a country overrun by its enemies in verses 53–57, when people were driven to eat their own children, was fulfilled during the reign of Ahab's son Joram when Samaria was put under siege by the Arameans (see 2 Kings 6:24–7:20). These awful acts were a fulfilment of God's promise in this passage.

But the worst fate is saved for the end of the chapter. If the people continued to ignore God's law and did not revere the name of their covenant Lord then ultimately they would lose the right to the land which they had been given. *"You will be uprooted from the land you are entering to possess. Then the LORD will scatter you among all nations, from one end of the earth to the other." (Deuteronomy 28:63–64).* The description that follows is of a people living as refugees in an alien, godless culture where they can find no peace and this was the ultimate fate that befell Israel.

The Assyrians

During Israel's last years as a sovereign nation the Middle East was dominated by the emergence of a military superpower – Assyria.

Assyria was to the northeast of Aram, within the present day country of Iraq. The reason that Israel regained territory from Aram during the reign of Jeroboam II was that the Assyrians came and subdued the Arameans.

During the reign of Israel's king Menahem the Assyrians attacked Israel and he had to tax the people to pay them off. This worked for about fifteen years before the Assyrians returned during the reign of Pekah and took control of territory in the north of Israel and deported some of its people. Israel then came under Assyrian control but the last king of Israel, Hoshea, turned to Egypt for help. This provoked the wrath of the Assyrians who came with all their army to crush the Israelites. Samaria was besieged for three years before it was captured and Hoshea was imprisoned by the Assyrians.

The Assyrians put a lot of effort and ingenuity into developing the art of warfare and it was this that enabled them to dominate the Near East. One nation after another fell before their efficient war machine. From their art we know that they used armoured horses and men, chariots and archers, as well as having battering rams to break down fortified cities and ladders to scale their walls. But the true horrors of warfare for the ordinary people caught up in it are brought out in this quotation:
"The Assyrian invasions of the eighth century BC were the most traumatic political events in the entire history of Israel. The brutal Assyrian style of warfare relied on massive armies, superbly equipped with the world's first great siege machines manipulated by an efficient corps of engineers. Psychological terror, however, was Assyria's most effective weapon. It was ruthlessly applied, with corpses impaled on stakes, severed heads stacked in heaps, and captives skinned alive."[H]
(NIV Study Bible).

Not only were the Assyrians accomplished at warfare but they also introduced government structures to support their conquests. The territory they captured was divided into provinces, each with its own governor. However, governing an occupied country is very difficult. Nations have no option but to submit to a superior military force but once the conquering army has moved on the people will look for ways to gain their freedom, as Hoshea demonstrated by looking to Egypt for help. So to ensure that this could never happen again, the Assyrians took all the nobles and rich people from the countries they conquered and moved them to other parts of their empire. Only the poorest people were left to look after the land. Those people who were taken out of the land suffered the ultimate curse in Deuteronomy – they were removed from the Promised Land. The prophetic writer of 2 Kings makes the reasons for this quite clear.

> **Read 2 Kings 17:1-24**

The Samaritans

Initially the people that the Assyrians brought in to the land from other parts of their empire added the rituals of worshipping the Lord to their worship of other gods. However, over the centuries that followed their descendants did become more committed to the Lord and the Law of Moses and rejected their other gods.

By the time of the New Testament, some seven hundred years later, their descendants were known as the Samaritans. Although the Jews refused to have any association with them the Samaritans did have some understanding of the truth despite their theological differences. Jesus spoke to a Samaritan woman at a well and many from her village believed in him (see John 4:4-42) and Samaria was the first area that churches were established after the Jewish areas of Judea and Galilee (see Acts 9:31).

Is the Exile consistent with God's Love?

Many people find it difficult to understand how a loving God could deal with his people in this way. How could he subject them to attack from such a brutal people as the Assyrians? The writer of 2 Kings makes it very clear that the Israelites were taken into captivity as a result of their persistent sin. Over hundreds of years they had continually broken their covenant with him. When looked at from that angle the real question is: How could God allow his people to blatantly reject him for so long? What is incredible is the Lord's patience.

When Moses was on Mount Sinai the Lord proclaimed his name to him as: *"The LORD, the LORD, the compassionate and gracious God, slow to anger, abounding in love and faithfulness, maintaining love to thousands, and forgiving wickedness, rebellion and sin. Yet he does not leave the guilty unpunished; he punishes the children and their children for the sin of the fathers to the third and fourth generation."* (Exodus 34:6-7). The overriding attributes of God are compassion, grace and love. That is why he is prepared to put up with his sinful people for so long. But that does not mean that he can ignore sin and leave the guilty unpunished forever. That would not be just.

When we look at the nation of Israel going into exile we should not be wondering about why God punishes his people but praising him for his grace and forgiveness. Tomorrow we will see how Judah reacted to seeing Israel taken into captivity.

References

[H] *The NIV Study Bible* Copyright © 1985 by the Zondervan Corporation. Used by permission of The Zondervan Corporation in North America and by permission of Hodder & Stoughton elsewhere. p. 538 "Assyrian Campaigns against Israel and Judah"

Day 40
Judah after Israel's Exile

Judah's Response

With Israel gone into exile how will Judah respond? Will it cause her to turn to God?

At the time Israel went into exile Judah was being ruled by Ahaz, one of the wickedest kings so far.

> Read 2 Kings 16:1–4

Ahaz turned to Assyria for help against his enemies and so Judah too became subject to the Assyrians. Not only did Ahaz take silver and gold from the temple to pay tribute to the Assyrians but he also installed a new altar, which was a copy of an Assyrian one, and moved the bronze altar of the Lord that had been in place since Solomon built the temple in order to please the Assyrians. Eventually he even shut up the temple and built altars on the street corners in Jerusalem.

The events of this period in Judah's history are shown on the next page in Timechart 9.

Revival

Although the warning from the fate of Israel was lost on Ahaz, his son Hezekiah got the message. When Hezekiah came to the throne he immediately set about turning the nation back to God. *"In the first month of the first year of his reign, he opened the doors of the temple of the LORD and repaired them." (2 Chronicles 29:3).* He then assembled the priests and Levites and set them to work to remove all the things relating to idol worship and had the temple purified. The work was completed in just over two weeks and the temple was reopened along with great celebrations.

Hezekiah then invited *"all Israel and Judah" (2 Chronicles 30:1)* to come and celebrate the Passover. With Israel no longer an independent nation the political barriers to the Israelites living in the north coming to the south were gone and, although Hezekiah's messengers were scorned in some parts of the land, many came to Jerusalem from Israel to join as one nation again in celebration.

The results of Hezekiah's call for the people to return to the Lord were

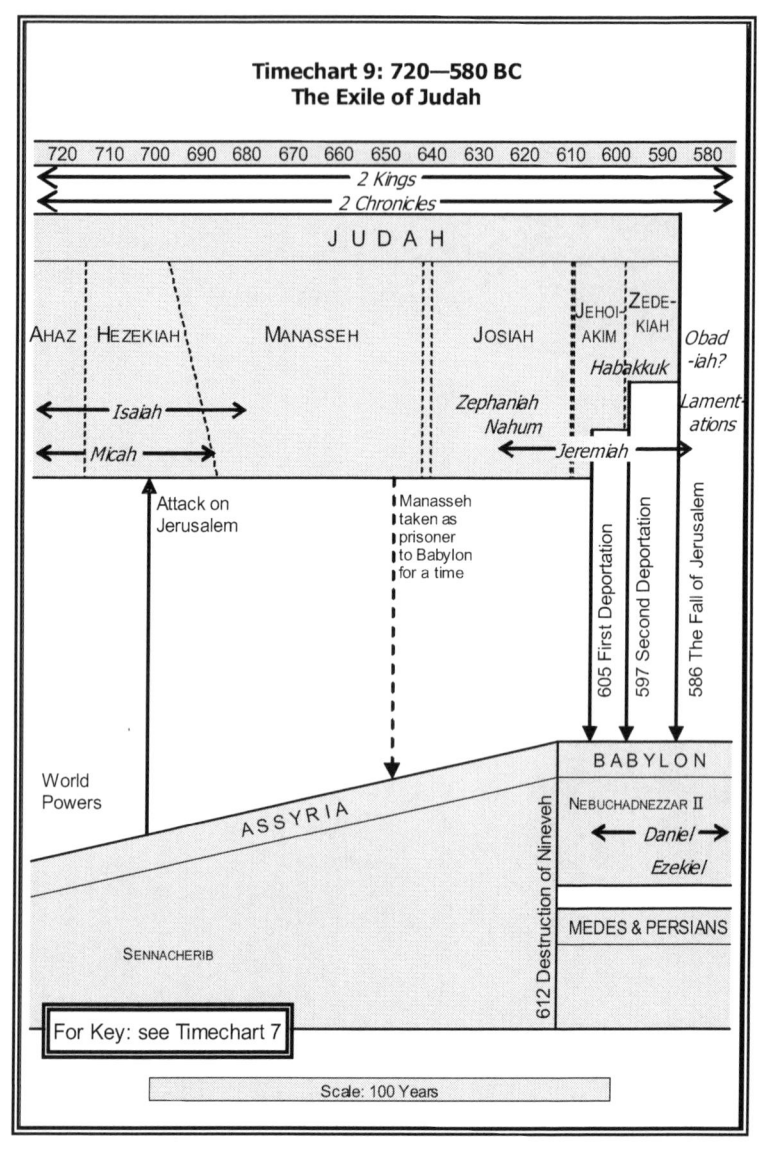

Timechart 9: 720–580 BC
The Exile of Judah

| 720 | 710 | 700 | 690 | 680 | 670 | 660 | 650 | 640 | 630 | 620 | 610 | 600 | 590 | 580 |

⟵ 2 Kings ⟶
⟵ 2 Chronicles ⟶

JUDAH

AHAZ | HEZEKIAH | MANASSEH | JOSIAH | JEHOIAKIM | ZEDEKIAH | Obad-iah?

Habakkuk

⟵ Isaiah ⟶

⟵ Micah ⟶

Zephaniah
Nahum

⟵ Jeremiah ⟶

Lamentations

Attack on Jerusalem

Manasseh taken as prisoner to Babylon for a time

605 First Deportation
597 Second Deportation
586 The Fall of Jerusalem

World Powers

ASSYRIA

SENNACHERIB

612 Destruction of Nineveh

BABYLON
NEBUCHADNEZZAR II
⟵ Daniel ⟶
Ezekiel

MEDES & PERSIANS

For Key: see Timechart 7

Scale: 100 Years

**Timechart 9 – 720–580 BC:
The Exile of Judah**

dramatic: *"in Judah the hand of God was on the people to give them unity of mind to carry out what the king and his officials had ordered, following the word of the LORD." (2 Chronicles 30:12).* Hezekiah's call started a revival which swept the whole land of Israel. As evidence of what God had done in their hearts the people destroyed the false altars in Jerusalem before the celebrations started. The priestly writer of 2 Chronicles notes that some of the people did not have time to purify themselves properly for the Passover but the Lord pardoned them in response to Hezekiah's prayer. In such times the detail of ritual was overlooked because of the right attitude of the people's hearts.

The week of celebration for the Passover was such a joyous occasion that the people decided to continue for a second week. This festival stands out as a spiritual high point in the three hundred years of the divided kingdoms. At the end: *"There was great joy in Jerusalem, for since the days of Solomon son of David king of Israel there had been nothing like this in Jerusalem. The priests and the Levites stood to bless the people, and God heard them, for their prayer reached heaven, his holy dwelling place." (2 Chronicles 30:26–27).* Once the celebrations were over the people set out to return home, but the change of heart that God had brought about in them was again demonstrated on the way: *"When all this had ended, the Israelites who were there went out to the towns of Judah, smashed the sacred stones and cut down the Asherah poles. They destroyed the high places and the altars throughout Judah and Benjamin and in Ephraim and Manasseh. After they had destroyed all of them, the Israelites returned to their own towns and to their own property." (2 Chronicles 31:1).*

How to Deal with Disaster

I am sure that those who returned to their homes after this celebration were confident that the Lord would now protect Judah. Having seen the disaster that came on Israel as a result of their sin they did not expect the same fate to come on them now they had repented and turned back to God. But fourteen years later the Assyrians attacked Judah, captured many of its cities, and besieged Jerusalem. All that Hezekiah has done in bringing the people back to God appears to have been in vain. Hezekiah stands firm in telling the people that the Lord will deliver them but their chances look increasingly slim.

And then Sennacherib, the king of Assyria, makes the mistake of challenging God. He sends a message to Hezekiah and the people of Jerusalem pointing out that the gods of the other nations have not saved them from his army so why should the Lord save Israel from him? It was not difficult for Hezekiah to say he trusted in God and arrange a Passover celebration. It was much more difficult for him to demonstrate his confidence when his nation was overrun and his capital city under siege. Hezekiah's response to disaster is to seek God. He goes to pray at the temple himself and sends his officials to consult with God's prophet, Isaiah.

> Read 2 Kings 19

The Lord's response, through Isaiah, to the arrogance of the king of Assyria shows that God is not disinterested in the affairs of this world. He plays an active part in history and can bring about seemingly impossible changes in situations overnight. In this case it was literally overnight as 185,000 Assyrian soldiers died on the field of battle without any human intervention – unfortunately not the last time that a large army has been destroyed through the arrogance of one man. The writer of 2 Kings highlights Hezekiah's confidence in God as an outstanding example among the kings of Judah: *"Hezekiah trusted in the LORD, the God of Israel. There was no one like him among all the kings of Judah, either before him or after him. He held fast to the LORD and did not cease to follow him; he kept the commands the LORD had given Moses." (2 Kings 18:5–6).*

Manasseh

Later Hezekiah becomes ill and Isaiah tells him that he is going to die but, after he prays, God gives him a further fifteen years. These years are not well spent. In an attempt to find allies against Assyria, he welcomes envoys from Babylon which, at that time, was a small power that had briefly escaped from Assyrian rule. Isaiah condemns his actions and prophesies that in the future Judah will go into exile in Babylon – a remarkable prophecy given the dominance of Assyria at this time.

Also in Hezekiah's last fifteen years his son Manasseh was born and he became the wickedest of all of Judah's kings. The contrast between Hezekiah's commitment to God and his son's commitment to evil could not be greater. Just as Hezekiah pursued godliness with great vigour so Manasseh led a revival of wickedness

> Read 2 Kings 21:1–6, 16

Day 40 – Judah after Israel's Exile

During Manasseh's reign the Lord sends prophets to tell the people of Judah that she, like Israel, will be destroyed as a nation and Jerusalem will be wiped out like Samaria. Manasseh's fifty–five year reign sealed the fate of the country. In his later life he was taken prisoner by the Assyrians who put a hook in his nose and took him to Babylon. He turned to God who listened to his pleas and brought him back to Jerusalem where he initiated some reforms but it was all too late.

Josiah

Manasseh's son Amon was assassinated after two years and Josiah came to the throne at the age of eight. When he was sixteen he started to seek God and, like his great–grandfather Hezekiah, set about bringing the nation back to God. Both Kings and Chronicles describe his reforms in detail.

> Read 2 Chronicles 34

The discovery of the Book of the Law in the temple shows how far the nation had strayed from God during the reign of Manasseh. Not even the priest had a copy! Josiah's response is to initiate reforms which are even more far reaching than Hezekiah's. Like Hezekiah, he leads a celebration of the Passover and goes on to clear the land of mediums, idols and other evil practices. The writer of Kings singles him out for the way he turned to the Lord: *"Neither before nor after Josiah was there a king like him who turned to the LORD as he did – with all his heart and with all his soul and with all his strength, in accordance with all the Law of Moses." (2 Kings 23:25).*

But despite Josiah's reforms it remains too late for the nation. The next verse goes on to say, *"Nevertheless, the LORD did not turn away from the heat of his fierce anger, which burned against Judah because of all that Manasseh had done to provoke him to anger. So the LORD said, "I will remove Judah also from my presence as I removed Israel, and I will reject Jerusalem, the city I chose, and this temple, about which I said, 'There shall my Name be.'" (2 Kings 23:26–27).* Josiah is promised that the nation will not be destroyed in his lifetime but the sentence has been passed for the sins of the people and it will be carried out.

The Kings of the Divided Kingdoms

The books of Kings and Chronicles tell a tragic story of God's people repeatedly forsaking their covenant Lord and eventually paying the ultimate price – being removed from the land he gave them and from his presence in the temple of Jerusalem. The honest accounts of their kings give us some encouraging stories of reforming kings – Jehoshaphat, Hezekiah, and Josiah – and some sobering stories of wicked kings and the punishments that came upon them. There are some serious warnings in the stories of kings who started out well but then deserted God in later life such as Uzziah, who was struck with leprosy for taking on the priestly role, and Joash, who started so well but ended up murdering the prophet who warned him that he was going astray. Leadership of God's people is a serious responsibility and is not to be undertaken lightly.

It would be great to think that a good king would pass on his commitment to the Lord to the next generation but this is not seen to be the case. Hezekiah fathered the evil Manasseh and Joash's sons too failed to follow the God of their father. However, the reverse of this is also true and good kings came from bad fathers. God's sovereignty is seen in that he will fulfil his purposes with men he chooses.

The books of Kings and Chronicles provide us with the historical background to the time of the divided Kingdoms but the heart of God for his people is expressed through his prophets. A number of the prophetic books in the Old Testament were written in this period and we shall now take a few days to look at them before returning to the story of Judah and how she too went into exile.

Day 41
The Prophets

Prophets – God's Spokesmen

When Moses was sent to tell Pharaoh to let God's people go he argued that he was not eloquent enough to do it. So God sent him with his brother Aaron and said: *"You shall speak to him and put words in his mouth; I will help both of you speak and will teach you what to do. He will speak to the people for you, and it will be as if he were your mouth and as if you were God to him." (Exodus 4:15–16)*. Aaron became Moses' spokesman. Later, the Lord spoke to Moses and said, *"See, I have made you like God to Pharaoh, and your brother Aaron will be your prophet." (Exodus 7:1)*. The word "prophet" was used here for a man who was speaking on behalf of another: "spokesman" and "prophet" are interchangeable.

Throughout history God has wanted to speak to people and he chooses to do so through spokesmen and women who are called prophets. In everyday use a prophet is thought of as foretelling the future, but in the Bible prophets are simply people who speak God's words. Sometimes they do foretell the future but mostly they speak to their generation on God's behalf.

The prophets speak from a deep understanding of God's law coupled with knowledge of what is going on in the world around them. They do not prophesy in a vacuum but seeing real situations and knowing God's law they denounce evil and call for repentance as God directs them. They are real men and their personal emotions come through in their writings. This passion provides a contrast to the law. In general terms the Law shows us the mind of God while the Prophets reveal his heart.

The Prophetic Books

The historical books in the Bible we have already looked at refer to a number of prophets – Abraham was the first to be called a prophet back in Genesis 20:7 – and the books themselves are prophetic, in the sense that they tell the history of God's people from God's perspective. But the Old Testament also contains 17 prophetic books, which contain the writings of God's spokesmen, most of whom lived in the time of the kings of Israel and Judah. Their words not only had relevance for their generation but have also spoken to God's people down through the centuries.

The prophetic books come at the end of the Old Testament: the first one is Isaiah, the last is Malachi. They are on the third shelf of the Bible Bookcase – see Figure 5 on page 36 – and from that you will see that the prophetic books make up about 30% of the Old Testament. In fact, altogether they are about the same size as the whole of the New Testament. You can also see that some of these books are very large and some are very small. Isaiah, Jeremiah (along with Lamentations which was also written by Jeremiah), Ezekiel and Daniel are known as "The Major Prophets" while the remaining twelve are called "The Minor Prophets". This refers to their size, rather than their importance. Isaiah and Jeremiah are the largest books in the Bible (Psalms is a collection of songs rather than a book), Ezekiel is also large and Daniel is a very significant book containing stories and some key foretelling of the future which is why it gets included in the Major Prophets. The twelve Minor Prophets were brought together by the Jewish scribes onto one scroll and became known as "The Book of the Twelve". They are roughly in the order they were written: the first six come from the time when Assyria was the world power and dominated Israel and Judah, the next three from the time immediately before the exile of Judah and the last three come from the time after the Israelites returned from the exile.

The prophetic books contain some of the parts of the Bible that are the hardest to understand. They are mostly made up of "oracles", "visions", and "words" in poetic form – there is very little narrative – and they can switch from one type to another without explanation. The writings go from being the words of the prophet to the words of God and back again and, unlike the neatly ordered history books, many are not in chronological order. You need to persevere with reading and studying the prophets in order to see their relevance and find encouragement.

Joel – A typical Prophetic Book

In order to try and understand the prophetic books we are going to start by looking at some of their typical features in one of the minor prophets, Joel. Then, tomorrow, we will look at the other eight minor prophets which were written during the time of the Kings before going on to look at the major prophets.

Some of the prophets indicate which king was reigning when they wrote but Joel gives us no indication of when he lived or prophesied and he is not mentioned in the books of the Kings. All we are told is that he is the son of Pethuel but as we don't know anything about him either that doesn't help us much! He is concerned about the fortunes of Judah and Jerusalem so it seems likely that he lived in Judah.

Outline of Joel	
1:1–2:17	Call to repentance in response to devastation of the land.
2:18–27	God's response to repentance..
2:28–32	How God will renew his people – a glimpse of the new Covenant
3:1–8	Judgement on the nations.
3:9–21	Final judgement on all nations and blessing on God's people – a glimpse of the "End Times".

A Call to Repentance

The first half of the book describes how the land and the economy has been devastated by plagues of locusts and severe drought. But this is not just a news report: Joel is interested in giving God's perspective on the situation. Joel interprets the disasters which have come on the land as a judgement by God. Note how he calls the invasion of locusts *"the day of the LORD"* (see 2:1–2, 11). This is a phrase that is often used in prophetic writings and means a time when God intervenes in judgement – firstly on his people, and then on their enemies.

Read Joel 1:1–2:17

Having proclaimed that the disasters the people are facing come from God, Joel calls them to repentance at the end of this passage. Note how in Joel 2:12–13 he calls the people to a genuine inner repentance, not just outward signs. He wants people to get their hearts right, not just to walk around with the outward signs of repentance. It is wrong to say that God is not interested in what we do in worship but getting our hearts right before him must be the priority. The prophets always emphasise heart attitudes. Note also how Joel refers to the Law. His description of God in verse 13 is a paraphrase of God's declaration to Moses when he gave him the law in Exodus 34:6–7. All the books of the Old Testament, and especially the prophets, build on the foundation of the Law.

Promises of Blessing

The second half of the book – from Joel 2:18 – describes the blessings God will bring to the people if they repent. It is very typical of prophetic writing in that it is not describing just one outcome, but a number which will be fulfilled at different times in the future. That makes it easier for us to interpret some of it now than it was when it was written!

Firstly, in Joel 2:18–27 we read that if the people repent they will have plenty to eat and victory over their enemies. This passage echoes the list of blessings promised in Deuteronomy 28 and interprets them into the current situation. The language used at the beginning of this passage emphasises the speed of God's response. Just like the way the father responds to the son who has gone away from home in Jesus' story of the prodigal son – *"while he was still a long way off ... he ran to his son" (Luke 15:20)* – so God is far more eager to forgive and restore than we are to turn to him.

> Read Joel 2:18–27

And afterwards...

Then in Joel 2:28 the scene changes abruptly to another period of time called "afterwards". God is now speaking through his spokesman about a time in the future when the Holy Spirit will be poured out on all his people. This was fulfilled on the day of Pentecost when the Holy Spirit was poured out on Jesus' disciples after he had returned to heaven. We know this because Peter quoted from this passage when he got up to explain why a group of uneducated Galileans were speaking about the wonders of God in many languages to the crowd who had gathered in amazement (see Acts 2:1–21) but those living in Joel's time, or reading his prophecy in the hundreds of years between him writing it and its fulfilment would not have been able to understand what he was talking about. Joel has jumped from a prophecy which could have been fulfilled in a matter of a few years to one which was to be fulfilled hundreds of years later.

> Read Joel 2:28–32

It is almost as if God gets carried away when he speaks through his prophets. His compassion for his people shines through as he is promising them that they will have plenty to eat but then he cannot but help jump forward to the blessings he wants to pour out on them in the future under the new covenant which has not even been announced.

And then he makes another jump. At the opening of chapter 3 he is talking about a time when Israel will be restored to her land and her enemies judged. According to the study Bible I have, verses 4–8 appear to be a passing statement about the cities of Tyre and Sidon which were fulfilled in the 4th century BC. This is where study aids come in useful! Then from verse 9 onwards the book slides into a description of the final judgement on the nations and everlasting peace and blessing for Judah and Jerusalem. This is a prophecy relating to the "End Times" which has yet to be fulfilled.

The Perspective of the Prophets

The way in which the prophets jump between times with phrases such as *"And afterwards"* and *"In those days"* make them hard to follow. It also raises the question, "Did the prophets know what they were writing about?" Clearly when they were describing the devastation of the land they were recording what they saw and when they interpreted it as God's judgement this was based on their understanding of God's law. But when they were talking about the future they could not have understood what they were writing. Peter throws some light on the way in which prophets worked in his New Testament letters: *"you must understand that no prophecy of Scripture came about by the prophet's own interpretation. For prophecy never had its origin in the will of man, but men spoke from God as they were carried along by the Holy Spirit."* (2 Peter 1:20–21). Even when they were describing events they had seen their words were inspired by God himself. Some of the prophets wanted to understand what they had written: *"Concerning this salvation, the prophets, who spoke of the grace that was to come to you, searched intently and with the greatest care, trying to find out the time and circumstances to which the Spirit of Christ in them was pointing when he predicted the sufferings of Christ and the glories that would follow. It was revealed to them that they were not serving themselves but you, when they spoke of the things that have now been told you by those who have preached the gospel to you by the Holy Spirit sent from heaven. Even angels long to look into these things."* (1 Peter 1:10–12). Joel did not understand what the pouring out of the Holy Spirit was about but his writings have provided explanation for all those who have experienced its fulfilment down through the centuries since Pentecost.

I remember my father comparing the prophets looking into the future with men looking at a mountain. It is easy to set out climbing a mountain only to discover half–way up that you have reached a summit and there is a large valley between you and the top of the peak that you thought you were climbing. What you thought was one mountain turns out to be two or even more. That is how the future looked to the prophets. They did not know which events would occur when and certainly could not see the valleys or how long they would be. Most of the prophets refer to the coming Messiah but the prophecies about Jesus' first and second comings are muddled up together. It is not obvious that there were at least two thousand years between their fulfilments. It is not surprising that many of Jesus' followers were confused, as we shall see later.

In addition to this a number of prophecies have double interpretations. Some of the events that Daniel foretold happened a few hundred years before Jesus came but Jesus quoted from them in prophesying about the future. The initial fulfilment foreshadowed a future one.

So What?

So what relevance has Joel got for us today? Just reading through it we gain insight into God's character. Some people see God as stern and aloof, others see him as easy going and indulgent. Joel makes it clear that neither are right. God will judge his people when they forsake him but he is full of mercy and sends troubles to turn his people back to him and his love. The passion of God's heart for his people shines through. He wants us to repent and turn to him so he can show us his grace and compassion.

As we read God's word the Holy Spirit will make some verses stand out for our situation or for the encouragement of others. Those who have spent many years wandering away from God, or come to him late in life will find encouragement in the words *"I will repay you for the years the locusts have eaten" (Joel 2:25)*. Evangelists preaching to crowds have used *"Multitudes, multitudes in the valley of decision! For the day of the LORD is near in the valley of decision." (Joel 3:14)* to challenge people to make a decision for Christ.

If you want to understand the prophets better then you will need to use a Bible study aid which will tell you who is speaking and about specific prophecies already fulfilled. But a lot of prophecy remains

Day 41 – The Prophets

unfulfilled and I think there are dangers in trying to pin down all the details of the prophetic writings too closely. Some like to try and interpret the "End Time" prophecies in light of current affairs and this often turns out to be wrong in the following years or decades. God has not given us prophecies to enable us to foretell the future but to be a comfort to us when it happens. In among the predictions of frightening events in chapter 3, Joel reminds us: *"But the LORD will be a refuge for his people, a stronghold for the people of Israel." (Joel 3:16).* Whatever situation we find ourselves in, the Lord will be there for us. The prophets bring us hope in a dark world.

Day 42
Hosea to Zephaniah –
Nine Minor Prophets

Prophets – God's Spokesmen

Having looked at Joel as a typical prophetic book yesterday, today we will look at the nine minor prophets who spoke to God's people during the reigns of the kings of Israel and Judah. Some of them make it very clear when they were writing – see for example the first verse of Hosea: *"The word of the LORD that came to Hosea son of Beeri during the reigns of Uzziah, Jotham, Ahaz and Hezekiah, kings of Judah, and during the reign of Jeroboam son of Jehoash king of Israel"* – while others, like Joel, give no indication of when they wrote.

Amos

Hosea and Amos both prophesied to Israel in her last years as a nation. Neither are mentioned elsewhere in the Old Testament. Amos was a shepherd who lived in Tekoa, a small town in Judah about 11 miles from Jerusalem, and prophesied around 760–750 BC during the reigns of Uzziah in Judah and Jeroboam II in Israel – see Timechart 8 on page 209.

Amos starts by speaking words from the Lord against a number of nations. Because they have not received God's law they are judged by the general moral law. Israel and Judah think they are safe because of God's promises but actually they are worse off because they have broken the covenant they made with the Lord. They still go through the outward signs of the covenant, but they live unrighteous lives the rest of the time. This is like the religions of the other nations where the way to please the gods is through performing rituals rather than by living holy lives.

Amos directs most of his words at Israel, God's covenant people. They were living in a time of prosperity and the nation had become corrupted by wealth. Amos is sickened by what he sees in the marketplace and denounces the traders who use dishonest measures to sell wheat at inflated prices (see Amos 8:5). He attacks the ruling classes who are living in luxury and who oppress the poor – they are even prepared to take the poor into slavery when they cannot afford to pay for their food! He also includes a condemnation of their wives who he calls "cows of Bashan" in Amos 4:1, an expression I remember finding very amusing when I discovered it as a child!

In among this corruption and wickedness some are looking forward to "the day of the Lord", expecting him to come and defeat their enemies but Amos warns that when it does come it will be a day of darkness for God's people, not light: *"Why do you long for the day of the LORD? That day will be darkness, not light." (Amos 5:18).*

In this passage we see the strength of the Lord's indignation at their behaviour (verse 7) and a declaration of the coming day of the Lord (from "In that day" in verse 9), a time when the people will no longer be able to find prophets who can declare the word of the Lord to them.

| Read Amos 8:4–12 |

Israel will go into exile away from her land and Amos describes the horrors that the Lord will bring on the nation but, as with so many of the prophetic writings about the exile, God cannot resist speaking about the time when he will restore his people after they have been punished and settle them in the land once again *"never again to be uprooted" (Amos 9:15).*

The main theme of the book is justice and it is summed up in the great statement in Amos 5:24: *"Let justice roll on like a river, righteousness like a never failing stream."*

Outline of Amos	
1:1–2:16	Judgements on the Nations.
3:1–5:17	Words against Israel and a call to repentance.
5:18–6:14	Announcement of the exile
7:1–9:10	Visions of God's judgement.
9:11–15	Promise of Restoration to the land.

Hosea

Hosea prophesied slightly later than Amos, from the time of Jeroboam II through to the exile of Israel (around 760–700BC) – see Timechart 8 on page 209. Although he has a similar message he has a different emphasis. Like Amos he speaks of the coming destruction of the nation but he emphasises God's love.

Hosea expresses God's tender love for Israel as a relationship between a husband and his wife. This has been pushed to the limit by their idolatrous practices, which he likens to adultery and prostitution. Israel is like a consistently unfaithful wife and so God is within his rights to destroy the nation (as an unfaithful wife may be stoned under the law) but his love for her is so great that he will only punish her in order to bring her to her senses and back to him. The exile is coming but, as in Amos, the book looks forward to the future restoration between God and his people.

The most incredible feature of Hosea is that Hosea is not only called to speak on God's behalf but, in order that he may really understand God's heart for his people, the Lord tells him to marry an unfaithful wife. He does this and she deserts him and becomes an adulteress but he goes after her, not to stone her, but to punish her and restore the relationship. Hosea is called to work out his message in his life. His experiences equip him to express God's deep love and emotion for his unfaithful people. God's aim is summed up in these two verses. (The word "betroth" is an old fashioned word meaning to make a commitment to marry.)

Read Hosea 2:19–20

Outline of Hosea	
1–3	Hosea is called to marry an unfaithful wife to illustrate God's relationship with Israel.
4–10	Israel's unfaithfulness and punishment.
11–14	The Lord's love.

Joel

The prophet Joel, whose book we looked at yesterday, is not mentioned elsewhere in the Old Testament. The date it was written is unclear as are no real clues in the book.

Obadiah

Obadiah is the shortest "book" in the Old Testament. It consists of just one chapter which is a denunciation of Edom (see Map 5 on page 205).

Day 42 – Hosea to Zephaniah – Nine Minor Prophets

Edom was the nation descended from Esau, the son of Isaac and the brother of Jacob who became the father of Israel and so the nation of Edom was the brother of Judah.

When Judah was attacked, Edom offered no support, gloated over their misfortune and even came and joined in the attack to share in the plunder. God is angry at their behaviour, here condemning them for their unwillingness to support their brother.

> **Read Obadiah 11–12**[6]

It is not acceptable to distance ourselves from the problems that other people face – especially those close to us – or worse, to be pleased that they have got what we think they deserve. Obadiah's message is that God will punish Edom and destroy it but Israel will be delivered. Obadiah is not mentioned elsewhere in the Old Testament and, like Joel, the date of his writing is unknown. In light of the events referred to it may have been written around 850 or 600 BC (he is shown at around 600 BC on Timechart 9 on page 230).

Jonah

2 Kings 14:25 tells us that Jonah, who came from the town of Gath Hepher in Israel, prophesied about the boundaries of Israel during the reign of Jeroboam II so he probably lived around 800–750 BC – see Timechart 8 on page 209. The book of Jonah is an account of an event in his life, which makes it unique among the prophetic books. All the rest are either all or mostly prophecies in poetic form but Jonah only contains eight words of prophecy (in the English translation) and these were a prediction which did not come true!

Jonah is called by God to go to Nineveh (see Map 6 on page 267), one of the greatest cities in the Assyrian empire, to call its people to repentance. God, the covenant Lord of Israel, is eager to show compassion to all nations, even Israel's enemies. But Jonah does not share God's compassion and is so displeased at the idea of going to Nineveh that he runs away from God and sets sail for Spain, a thousand miles in the opposite direction!

The account of what happened to him is one of the most famous Old Testament stories. God in his grace does not give up on his prophet but

---

[6] Obadiah is one of five books in the Bible that is too small to have chapters and is only divided into verses. The others are Philemon, 2 John, 3 John and Jude.

sends a storm to disrupt the ship's progress and then, when Jonah is thrown overboard by the sailors at his own request, sends a "great fish" to swallow him. (Many people seek to undermine the truth of scripture by claiming that such events could not possibly be true. However, there is an account of a man called James Bartley who, in 1891, fell from a whaling ship and was swallowed by a whale. Over 24 hours later he was found by the other whalers inside the whale's stomach as they cut it up. He had fainted through fear when he realised where he was. The only long term effect was that his skin was bleached white. Whether or not this is an accurate account it is hard to say but there is no doubt that whales can swallow large sea creatures whole and that there is air in a whale's stomach.)

Jonah stayed alive in the fish's stomach for three days and three nights and while he was there he made an interesting comparison between himself and the sailors up above:

> **Read Jonah 2:8–9**

Jonah has the remarkable insight, given his predicament, that he, who has disobeyed God, is, once again, experiencing God's grace by being saved by the fish while the sailors who appear to be much safer are missing out on it. Although he is running away from God, God does not give up on him. When he lands on the beach in a pile of fish vomit he is a living demonstration of the Lord's patient, saving grace!

Once Jonah is back on dry land the Lord tells him to go to Nineveh once more. This time Jonah goes and proclaims that God will destroy the city in 40 days. Remarkably, the 120,000 inhabitants turn to God and the king orders them to fast and pray and repent of their wickedness. God listens to their prayers and does not bring calamity on the city.

We then discover why Jonah was not keen to go to Nineveh in the first place. When he sees the people repenting and God letting them live he is very angry. He does not want God to show his compassion to Israel's enemies and is angry with him. God teaches him a lesson about his priorities but we are not told how Jonah responds as the book ends with Jonah sulking on his own outside the city and waiting for God to bring calamity on the people of Nineveh. The fact that this book was written suggests that he did learn the lesson and is a tribute to Jonah's humility. His honest account of his experience has a clear message for the Israelites that God is concerned with all men and not just his "chosen people". It also demonstrates the remarkable patience of the Lord in dealing with one of his people who at times, like us, runs away from him and is unhappy with the way he runs his world.

Outline of Jonah	
1	Jonah receives his message but runs away from God. God punishes him.
2	Jonah's prayer of thanks for deliverance.
3	Jonah goes to Nineveh and preaches. The people repent and God spares them.
4	Jonah's anger at the Lord's compassion for Nineveh.

Micah

Micah lived in Judah at the same time as Isaiah – see Timecharts 8 & 9 on pages 209 and 230 – and had a similar message: Israel and Judah will be destroyed and their people taken into exile but ultimately they will be restored. We know that Micah's warnings were heeded. A hundred years later when the people wanted to put Jeremiah to death for saying similar things as Micah, people remembered how Hezekiah, the king of Judah, had responded to Micah. His words are quoted in Jeremiah 26:18 where it is noted that after the people repented, God put off the disaster Micah had predicted.

Micah's messages of hope include a remarkable vision of *"the last days"* at the beginning of chapter 4, which is very similar to a passage we will look at tomorrow in Isaiah 2, and a prophecy that a ruler for Israel would come from Bethlehem (see Micah 5:2). Seven hundred years later the teachers of the law quoted from this when Herod asked them where the Messiah was to be born.

Micah's simple message for the Israelites is as relevant to us today as it was then:

"He has showed you, O man, what is good.
  And what does the LORD *require of you?*
To act justly and to love mercy
  and to walk humbly with your God." (Micah 6:8).

Outline of Micah	
1–3	Judgements against Israel and Judah.
4–5	Hope for God's people: Restoration and a shepherd from Bethlehem.
6	God's case against Israel.
7	Micah's lament at the state of his society and his hope in God.

Nahum

Nahum was from Judah and is not referred to elsewhere in the Old Testament. His short prophecy of only three chapters is against Nineveh, the capital city of Assyria, the brutally cruel empire which had destroyed many nations including Israel and threatened Judah (see Map 6 on page 267). Although the people of Nineveh had repented in response to the preaching of Jonah some 150 years earlier the city has returned to being a centre of wickedness. The Lord is *"slow to anger"* but he *"will not leave the guilty unpunished" (Nahum 1:3)*. Nahum prophesies the destruction of Nineveh and her empire as a judgement from God. This was fulfilled in 612 BC when the city was completely destroyed by the Babylonians. From events within the book his writings can be dated between 663 BC and 612 BC – see Timechart 9 on page 230.

Habakkuk

Habakkuk was written around 605 BC, shortly before Judah was exiled by the Babylonians in 597, probably during the reign of Jehoiakim – see Timechart 9 on page 230. His book is unique among the prophets as, rather than being a message for Israel or the nations, it is an account of a dialogue between a prophet and his God. Habakkuk has wrestled through some difficult questions with God and in writing the book is recording his own questions and God's answers for the benefit of other godly people in Judah who face the same issues. Sometimes his questions are referred to as "complaints". Like the writer of the Psalms, Habakkuk is not afraid to express his frustration with God's lack of action to God himself.

The book contains many remarkable statements given Habakkuk's situation. His almost throwaway comment that *"the righteous will live by his faith"* in 2:4 is frequently quoted in the New Testament to

	Outline of Habakkuk
1:1–11	Habakkuk's first question: "Why does Judah's evil remain unpunished?" God's answer: "The Babylonians will punish Judah."
1:12–2:20	Habakkuk's second question: "How can God use the wicked Babylonians?" God's answer: "They too will be punished, and faith will be rewarded."
3	Habakkuk's prayer of trust in God.

support the teaching that people are saved by faith, not works (see Galatians 3:11 for example). He demonstrates great faith in God (see 2:14 and 20) and ends with a determination to be joyful in all situations:

Read Habakkuk 3:17–18

Zephaniah

Zephaniah was a great–great–grandson of King Hezekiah and was evidently a person of considerable social standing in Judah. His words show that he was familiar with court circles and current political issues. He prophesied around 640–609 BC during the reign of King Josiah – see Timechart 9 on page 230 – and foretells the destruction of Judah and the surrounding nations, including Assyria. His theme is that the sin of Judah, which had become very wicked through Manasseh's fifty–five year reign, must be punished. It is possible that he was involved in initiating Josiah's reforms as he was from the royal family.

	Outline of Zephaniah
1:1–2:3	Warning of Judah's coming destruction.
2:4–15	Warning of destruction coming on other nations.
3:1–8	Prophecy against Jerusalem
3:9–20	The future of Jerusalem: Joy in the restored city.

Zephaniah, like some of the other prophets, ends with a positive note about the future of God's people. Jerusalem will be full of joy and the source of that joy is God himself. This passage contains a very well known verse.

> **Read Zephaniah 3:17**

The word translated "rejoice" literally means "to spin round under the influence of a violent emotion". God's joy over us, his restored people, is far beyond what we can imagine!

Day 43
Isaiah's Calling

Isaiah – The Man

Isaiah lived in Jerusalem and he prophesied around 740–680 BC. He had close connections with the royal family during the reign of four kings – see Timecharts 8 & 9 on pages 209 and 230. He started his writing in the year that king Uzziah died. Uzziah was a good king and we know from 2 Chronicles 26:22 that Isaiah wrote an account of his reign. Jotham, his son, was a reasonable king but he was followed by Ahaz, a wicked man who introduced all the idolatrous practices of other nations into Judah. It was during his reign that Assyria was gaining power and Israel was taken into exile. Isaiah had most influence during the reign of Ahaz's son Hezekiah. Hezekiah was a good king who reformed the nation and led them back to God. As we saw a few days ago it was in his time that Judah was attacked by Assyria and Hezekiah sent officials to Isaiah to find out what God had to say about the situation. Isaiah was given a word from the Lord that Jerusalem would be saved.

According to a Jewish tradition Isaiah was sawn in two during the reign of Hezekiah's wicked son Manasseh and it may be this that is referred to in Hebrews 11:37 where the writer lists heroes of the faith.

Isaiah – The Book

If you look at the Bible Bookcase (see Figure 5 on page 36) you will see that Isaiah is the first of the "major" prophets and takes up more shelf space than any other book in the Bible (other than Psalms which is a compilation of songs rather than a book). Although Jeremiah actually has more words than Isaiah, Isaiah is the largest book as it is mostly written in poetry. Isaiah is the greatest of the written prophetic books and it has the richest poetry in the Old Testament. Isaiah has a wider vocabulary than any other writer and uses many styles – oracles, songs, hymns and a wisdom poem.

Isaiah prophesied to Judah during traumatic times as she watched Israel falling to the Assyrians and her people being taken into exile. Judah thought she was safe but Isaiah prophesies that Judah will also be taken into exile for her sins. Although the Lord will rescue them from the threat of Assyria, Judah will be taken into exile by the Babylonians.

Like many of the other prophetic writings it is not always easy to understand what Isaiah is referring to in each chapter. The book does, however, fall naturally into two halves:

Outline of Isaiah
Isaiah 1–39   The Book of Judgement
Prophecies against Judah's wickedness and against other nations mixed in with promises of blessing later. Chapters 36–39 describe how the Lord saved Judah from the Assyrians during Hezekiah's reign and how Isaiah predicted that Judah would one day go into exile in Babylon.
Isaiah 40–66   The Book of Comfort
Isaiah writes as if he is in the future after the exile is complete and gives a number of prophecies mainly relating to when the people of Judah return to the land. He also speaks of the coming Messiah and of the end times.

The first 39 chapters have been called "The Book of Judgement" as it is mainly messages of judgement against Judah and the other surrounding nations. But it seems that God can never pass judgement on his people without his heart of love for them shining through and so these judgements contain calls to repentance and views of the future when God's people will return to him mixed in among them. This first section was probably written during the reigns of Jotham and Ahaz. At the end of this section, and in the middle of the whole book, there are four chapters (36–39) which give an account of the Assyrian attack on Judah and Jerusalem in 701BC. It is very similar to the account in 2 Kings 18:13–20:19 and describes how the Lord defeated the Assyrians and predicts Judah's future exile in Babylon. This historical interlude provides a bridge into the second half of the book.

Chapters 40–66 have been called "The Book of Comfort", because of its opening lines.

> **Read Isaiah 40:1–2**

In this section Isaiah writes as if he were living in the future – in the time after Judah has returned from exile. His writings contain promises about restoration for the Lord's people along with prophecies about the

Day 43 – Isaiah's Calling

coming Messiah and end times. The way he is projected into the future is similar to the way the apostle John is shown what will happen in the end times in the book of Revelation.

The distinct change in the middle of the book, and the fact that the second half is referring to a much later time has led scholars in recent times to suggest that the two halves were written by different authors. There are, however, strong arguments for the book being written by the one man. The language used is consistent throughout the book and some phrases not used elsewhere in the Old Testament are used in both halves. A good example is the expression "the Holy One of Israel" which is used 12 times in the first half and 14 in the second although it only appears 6 times elsewhere in the Old Testament. The historical account in the middle of the book both completes the prophecies of judgement and introduces the future exile in Babylon. The book of Isaiah is also widely quoted in the New Testament and all the gospel writers and Paul refer to Isaiah – the man – as the author when quoting from the second half of the book. John in his gospel uses two quotes from Isaiah to explain the unbelief of the Jews. The first is from Isaiah 53:1 which is in the second half of the book and the second from Isaiah 6:10 which is in the first half. John introduces the first quote as *"the word of Isaiah the prophet"* and the second with the words *"as Isaiah says elsewhere" (John 12:38 and 39)*, so ascribing both to the same man.

Isaiah's Calling

Isaiah's call to be a prophet to God's people is recorded in Isaiah 6.

Read Isaiah 6

The vision that Isaiah had of the Lord seated on a throne and surrounded by worshipping seraphs (some kind of angelic being which are not mentioned elsewhere in the Bible) is well known and his response to the Lord – *"Here am I. Send me!"* – is often quoted as a model response to God. But the purpose of his calling is not straightforward. Isaiah is called to challenge the people about their sins and tell them of coming judgement from God but the effect will not be that they turn back to the Lord but that their hearts will be hardened against him until his judgements have come to pass and the people are in exile.

Isaiah's Message of Judgement

Like Joel, the prophecies that Isaiah brought to the people relate to different periods of time and are all mixed up together. Having said that the book falls into two distinct halves, there are messages of hope in among the message of judgement in the first half of the book and in the second half there are calls for repentance.

Throughout the book (and throughout many of the other prophetic writings) the Lord speaks to his people as his child who has rebelled against him. Condemnation of their actions is mixed with calls to turn from their wicked ways. At times he is angry and almost seems to be shouting at them; at other times he pleads with them to turn from their wickedness. As you read through the message of judgement in the first chapter try and get a sense of the Lord's heart for his people: his sadness that his own children don't know him (v3), his frustration that they take their punishment without understanding that it could come to an end if they turned to him (v5), his anger at the way they go through religious rituals whilst ignoring justice (vv11–17), his appeal to reason from v18, and then back to jealous anger at their prostitution to wickedness (v21). And yet even in this passage there is a jump forward to the time after the exile too in verses 26 and 27.

> Read Isaiah 1

What God Requires of His People

When Moses addressed the people of Israel before he died he told them to *"Love the LORD your God with all your heart and with all your soul and with all your strength." (Deuteronomy 6:4)*. This love was to be expressed through keeping all of God's commandments. These included outward acts of worship and loving one another through the many social laws. One of the characteristics of God's people, both in Isaiah's day and at all other times in history, is that when their heart for God grows cold they continue to observe outward rituals of worship while ignoring the heart issue of love for God and for one another. Towards the end of Isaiah he launches a stinging attack on their observation of fasting and the Sabbath which has become a ritual without spiritual meaning. Note the contrast between the people's view of their fasting and the Lord's in verse 3: in the first half the people expect the Lord to be impressed by the fact that they have fasted, in the second half the Lord explains that going without food has no spiritual

Day 43 – Isaiah's Calling

value at all if people continue to live wicked lives. The Lord's idea of a fast is set out from verse 6: to deal with injustice, to feed the poor and to stop speaking ill of others. That is what will bring healing and favour from the Lord. This passage provides us with a timeless warning to keep the removal of injustice and feeding of the hungry at the top of our priority list if we want to please our God and enjoy his blessing.

Read Isaiah 58

Day 44
The Gospel in Isaiah

The Gospel?

As we will see when we start looking at the New Testament, the word "Gospel" comes from an Old English word meaning "Good News" and refers to the good news about Jesus coming to earth. Given that Isaiah lived 700 years before Jesus came to earth, how can the gospel be in Isaiah?

Let's jump forward those 700 years and look at an event that took place soon after Jesus lived and died. In the book of Acts there is an account of one of Jesus' followers, Philip, being sent to meet with an official from the Ethiopian government.

> Read Acts 8:26–39

It was customary in those days for people to read out loud and so Philip, while he was running to keep up with the government chariot, overheard the Ethiopian reading from Isaiah. The man is puzzled by what he is reading and cannot tell who Isaiah is referring to. Philip (once he has got into the chariot and got his breath back!) explains that Isaiah is referring to Jesus and, using Isaiah's prophecies, *"told him the good news about Jesus" (Acts 8:35)*. As a result the Ethiopian becomes a believer in Jesus and is baptised. He had never read the New Testament – it wasn't written then – but came to understand who Jesus was from reading the gospel – the good news – in Isaiah

The book of Isaiah contains a large number of significant prophecies about Jesus and, although Philip may well have referred to other Old Testament scriptures, he could easily have explained who Jesus was, how he lived his life and the purpose of his sufferings from the book of Isaiah. Our knowledge of Jesus would be much poorer without the gospel in Isaiah written 700 years before Jesus came. Let's look at what Isaiah has to teach us about Jesus.

A Remarkable Child will be Born

The New Testament opens with Matthew recording the ancestry of Jesus, making it clear that he was descended from Abraham and from David. He then goes on to describe *"how the birth of Jesus Christ came*

Day 44 – The Gospel in Isaiah

about" (Matthew 1:18) by explaining that Mary, the mother of Jesus, became pregnant by the Holy Spirit when she was still a virgin. This is a hard concept for anyone to get their mind round but Matthew has the advantage of writing for Jews who are familiar with the Old Testament and so he was able to write, *"All this took place to fulfil what the Lord had said through the prophet: "The virgin will be with child and will give birth to a son, and they will call him Immanuel" – which means, "God with us.""* *(Matthew 1:22–23)*. The concept of the "virgin birth" was one that had its roots in a prophecy from Isaiah. But although Matthew could look back on Isaiah's words and see that they were fulfilled in the birth of Jesus, what was Isaiah thinking about when he wrote *"The virgin will be with child" (Isaiah 7:14)*?

This prophecy was given early in the reign of king Ahaz when he was facing attack from Judah's old enemies, Aram and Israel. Isaiah is sent by the Lord to meet Ahaz and tell him that if he stands firm in his faith then Judah will be saved. The Lord then offers Ahaz a sign and, although Ahaz refuses to ask for one, is given a sign about a child.

Read Isaiah 7:10–16

The promise to king Ahaz is that a child is to be born to a woman who is currently a virgin and that before he is very old the lands of Aram and Israel will be laid waste by Assyria. This was fulfilled within a few years and so it seems likely that the virgin Isaiah is referring was his fiancée. At the beginning of the next chapter he describes the birth of their son and further prophecies that will be fulfilled early in the boy's life.

As with many Old Testament prophecies, Isaiah's words had two fulfilments, one very soon and the other further away. Isaiah thought he understood what he was saying but under the inspiration of the Holy Spirit he also foretold the coming of another child, born of a virgin, who would literally be Immanuel – "God with us".

Two chapters later Isaiah makes more statements about a remarkable child who is to be born.

Read Isaiah 9:1–7

Jesus started preaching and teaching in the Roman province of Galilee which was the same area as was assigned to the tribes of Zebulun and Naphtali. Matthew quotes from the beginning of these verses in

Matthew 4:12–16 to explain to his Jewish readers that Jesus fulfilled this prophecy in Isaiah.

"For to us a child is born" (Isaiah 9:6) is often quoted at Christmas time along with the incredible names given to him – *"Wonderful Counsellor, Mighty God, Everlasting Father, Prince of Peace"* – but these four names of God have much to teach us about who Jesus was and are worthy of meditation at all times of year, not just Christmas. Isaiah gives us a valuable insight into the character of Jesus.

The Way will be Prepared for His Coming

When Jesus started preaching in Galilee the people of his time had already been prepared for his message by John the Baptist. His birth was also miraculous (he was born to an older couple who had never been able to have children) and his role was to prepare the way for the coming of Jesus, the son of God. This role is explained in Isaiah 40:3–5 and all four gospel writers introduce John by quoting from all or part of this passage:

> Read Isaiah 40:3–5

He will be Anointed by the Holy Spirit for Purpose

In among his prophecies about the future of God's people Isaiah describes *"the year of the LORD'S favour"*.

> Read Isaiah 61

When Jesus was thirty years old he was baptised by John the Baptist and the Holy Spirit came on him to equip him for his ministry of preaching, teaching and healing. After spending forty days in the desert he returned to his home town and went to the synagogue (the Jewish place of worship) which he had attended since he was a child. The people there knew him well and had seen him grow up. He was a good man and well respected in the community but now he had to explain to them that he was about to start a ministry which would impact all the Jewish people and the whole world! To do this he quoted from the opening of Isaiah 61.

Isaiah had looked forward to the good news of freedom from captivity in Babylon but now Jesus announces the good news that the kingdom of heaven was at hand and that forgiveness of sins was available through a new covenant which would bring freedom for prisoners

Day 44 – The Gospel in Isaiah

everywhere, freedom for those held captive to sin. Jesus takes Isaiah's words and tells the people of his time that they are living in *"the year of the Lord's favour"*, not a calendar year but a period of time between the first and second comings of Christ that we still live in today when all men everywhere have an opportunity to enjoy the benefits of the new covenant.

It is interesting to note that Jesus stopped his quote mid-sentence and left out *"and the day of vengeance of our God"* as the time to proclaim that is yet to come. One day Jesus will return to earth and announce a short period of God's wrath but for now we are living in a period of God's favour which has already lasted for two thousand years.

Towards the end of Isaiah there are four songs which are sometimes referred to as the "servant songs". These passages refer to "my servant" or "his servant" and foreshadow the work of Jesus. The first of these is in Isaiah 42 and Matthew identifies this with Jesus in Matthew 12:15–21 where he quotes this passage almost in full.

Read Isaiah 42:1–4

The compassion of Jesus that he showed by healing ordinary people shines out in this passage. Jesus did not come looking for a big platform in the streets, he came to show God's love to those who are bruised and at the end of their own resources.

The second servant song, in Isaiah 49:1–7, makes reference to the fact that Jesus is not only coming for the Israelites but also for the rest of the world too. The Lord's heart is for all mankind and his purpose is to reach the world. The third servant song is Isaiah 50:4–9 and indicates that the coming servant will suffer but it is the fourth which deals with the suffering of the servant in most detail.

The Suffering Servant

The fourth of the servant songs is the Old Testament passage which is quoted more often than any other in the New Testament and is the part of Isaiah that the Ethiopian official was reading in his chariot when Philip met him. The song is an exquisitely crafted piece of poetry and the handiwork of the human author and the Holy Spirit are both evident in it.

There are few passages in the entire Bible which explain the gospel message so clearly and so comprehensively as it describes both the events of Jesus' last days on earth and their eternal significance. Note the references to the way Jesus kept silent at his trial (53:7), how he was disfigured by the flogging and crucifixion (52:14), how he was mocked (53:3), the nature of his burial (53:9) and his resurrection (53:11). But see also the way in which Isaiah makes it clear that this suffering was the Lord's will (53:10) and that its purpose was our forgiveness, and our healing (53:4–6, 12).

> **Read Isaiah 52:13–53:12**

Isaiah, the prophet who was called to bring a message to an unbelieving generation, has left a legacy for many future generations who have believed in Jesus, the despised son of God, who through his suffering brought us peace with God.

Day 45
Isaiah's Message of Hope

Isaiah Looks Forward to the Return from Exile

In the second half of his book, Isaiah speaks as if the exile of Judah into Babylon is already over. At times this is implied, at other times, he speaks of it in the past tense as in Isaiah 47:6 when God pronounces judgement on Babylon for the way they treated his people in the exile – *"I was angry with my people ..."*. These chapters are full of joy at what God has done in bringing his people back to the land.

The second half starts at chapter 40 and the first verse introduces the wonderful theme that Jerusalem's punishment for her sins is over. It then announces the coming of the Lord – note particularly the "good tidings" in verses 9–11 – and goes onto give a wonderful description of God's greatness and his power before ending with a promise to those who put their hope in the Lord.

> *Read Isaiah 40*

In Isaiah 52 the people of God are urged to wake up and prepare for the return to Jerusalem as the Lord announces that the time has come for his people to know him once again. Get a sense of the ecstatic joy that will accompany the news that the Lord is restoring his people to their rightful place and that God reigns among his people once again.

> *Read Isaiah 52:1–10*

Even though Isaiah has told the people that they will go into exile, they will go knowing that one day they will return with great joy:

"You will go out in joy
and be led forth in peace;
the mountains and hills
will burst into song before you,
and all the trees of the field
will clap their hands." (Isaiah 55:12)

What is the purpose of these writings that were written so many years before the exile, let alone the return from exile? The Lord explains this in Isaiah 48 where he tells the people: *"Therefore I told you these things long ago; before they happened I announced them to you so that you could not say, 'My idols did them; my wooden image and metal god ordained them.'" (Isaiah 48:5)*. God wants the people to know that he is in charge of international events. They look to images and idols for rain and fruitfulness but their true God has plans for them that stretch far into the future. Like Joel, Isaiah also prophesies about the new covenant, a time when the Lord says that *"I will pour out my Spirit on your offspring" (Isaiah 44:3)*.

Isaiah Looks forward to "The Last Days"

Some of Isaiah's prophecies look far further than the return from exile to a period of time we have still to reach and the fact that they sit alongside prophecies which were fulfilled hundreds of years after his time should give us confidence that these too will come to pass in God's time. The book lurches into *"the last days"* in its second chapter. In a passage which is also found in the prophecy of Micah, Isaiah looks forward to a time when the Lord will visibly rule on this earth:

> Read Isaiah 2:2–4

The last part of this passage was the inspiration for a sculpture in the United Nations garden at the UN Headquarters in New York called "Let us Beat Swords into Ploughshares". But Isaiah is not referring to a time when men will sit round a table and attempt to sort out their disputes through discussion, however preferable this is to war. He is looking forward to a time when God himself will rule the world and all men will look to him – the righteous judge – to settle their arguments. Isaiah continues with this theme in chapter 11 where he sees the coming of a man descended from David (Jesse, who is referred to in verse 1, was David' father) who will rule the world with great wisdom. Who would not want to live in the world described in the verses in Isaiah 11? Our natural response is in the next chapter.

> Read Isaiah 11:1–9 and Isaiah 12

Later Isaiah also refers to a time beyond the end of this world when the Lord says, *"Behold, I will create new heavens and a new earth. The former things will not be remembered, nor will they come to mind." (Isaiah 65:17)*. Isaiah is the only book in the Bible to refer to the new

Day 45 – Isaiah's Message of Hope

heavens (or heaven) and new earth before they are described in detail at the end of Revelation (chapters 21 and 22), apart from a reference back to Isaiah in 2 Peter 3:13..

The Legacy of Isaiah

Isaiah has left us a great legacy in his writings. We have looked at the major themes he covers but his book also contains many little treasures too, verses that jump off the page and deepen our knowledge of God. His language is rich and he paints many strong pictures.

If you doubt the strength of God's love for you then consider this question: *"Can a mother forget the baby at her breast and have no compassion on the child she has borne?"* Well of course she can't! But God's love is stronger than that: *"Though she may forget, I will not forget you! See, I have engraved you on the palms of my hands"* (Isaiah 49:15–16). Do you ever write notes for yourself on your hands? God has gone beyond that and had our names engraved so they cannot be removed!

Many think that Isaiah gives us insight into the character of Satan in his description of the king of Babylon in Isaiah 14:12–15. This proud man who has become like God in his own mind is a picture of Satan who also sought to become like God.

Perhaps one of the most amusing parts of Isaiah is his description of how people make idols in Isaiah 44:9–20. He really enjoys himself ridiculing those who use half a piece of wood to make an idol before putting the other half on the fire to cook a meal and keep themselves warm!

The Parable of the Vineyard

As we have already seen the prophetic writings are not always well ordered as they express the heart of a passionately loving God whose emotions are torn between the demands of his just nature to punish his people and his deep love that will last forever. In Isaiah 54 God's love for his people is expressed as a husband for a wife who has been abandoned:

""For a brief moment I abandoned you,
  but with deep compassion I will bring you back.
In a surge of anger
  I hid my face from you for a moment,
but with everlasting kindness

> *I will have compassion on you"*
>
> *says the LORD your Redeemer." (Isaiah 54:7–8).*

In Psalm 30:5 God's anger lasts for a moment and his favour for a lifetime – not a bad ratio – but here God's anger is a brief moment while his love lasts forever!

To end our brief tour of Isaiah we will look at a song expressing God's heart for his people, Judah at the beginning of Isaiah 5.

> *"I will sing for the one I love a song about his vineyard:*
>
> *My loved one had a vineyard on a fertile hillside.*
>
> *He dug it up and cleared it of stones and planted it with the choicest vines.*
>
> *He built a watchtower in it and cut out a winepress as well.*
>
> *Then he looked for a crop of good grapes, but it yielded only bad fruit."*

Isaiah uses a picture that his hearers would be familiar with to express what God has done for his people. They lived among vineyards and some worked on them so they knew the importance of choosing a good site and the work that went into preparing the ground, planting the vines and defending it against attack. Any man who put this much effort into creating a vineyard would expect good fruit.

> *"Now you dwellers in Jerusalem and men of Judah, judge between me and my vineyard.*
>
> *What more could have been done for my vineyard than I have done for it?*
>
> *When I looked for good grapes, why did it yield only bad?"*

Isaiah started his song talking about "his loved one" but it now changes to his loved one talking directly to the people. They cannot answer these questions as clearly the owner of the vineyard did his best to create the perfect environment for producing good fruit. But even before they have a chance to think about answering it becomes clear that this is no ordinary vineyard owner.

> *"Now I will tell you what I am going to do to my vineyard:*
>
> *I will take away its hedge, and it will be destroyed;*
>
> *I will break down its wall, and it will be trampled.*
>
> *I will make it a wasteland, neither pruned nor cultivated, and briers and thorns will grow there.*
>
> *I will command the clouds not to rain on it."*

Day 45 – Isaiah's Message of Hope

The failure of the vineyard was not the fault of the owner so it must be the fault of the vineyard itself. He has waited for the good fruit to come but as the bad fruit comes year after year the disappointment of the vineyard owner is so strong that he gives it over to destruction from outside and from within and even goes so far as to command no rain to fall on it. It has come to the point where it will no longer have the opportunity to bear good fruit even if it could.

This story would have captured the attention of Isaiah's audience. Maybe he sung it in the marketplace and people stopped to listen to this extraordinary tale. But once he had their attention he let them know the cry of God's heart.

"The vineyard of the LORD Almighty is the house of Israel,
and the men of Judah are the garden of his delight.
And he looked for justice, but saw bloodshed;
for righteousness, but heard cries of distress." (Isaiah 5:1–7)

God's heart was broken by his people and their continual disregard for him and his commands. God heard the cries of those who were downtrodden, wounded and killed and he was appalled at what was taking place among his people who had all the advantages of his laws and his covenant. When you read the prophets, don't try to work it all out. Look for God's heart. Love letters are not orderly documents!

Day 46
Jeremiah's Message

The Scene is Set

Before looking at the prophets we were looking at the history of Judah and had left them under the reign of the good king Josiah. He made a great attempt to bring the nation back to the Lord after the disastrous 55 year reign of Manasseh but, as we read in 2 Kings 23, it was too late: *"Neither before nor after Josiah was there a king like him who turned to the LORD as he did – with all his heart and with all his soul and with all his strength, in accordance with all the Law of Moses. Nevertheless, the LORD did not turn away from the heat of his fierce anger, which burned against Judah because of all that Manasseh had done to provoke him to anger. So the LORD said, "I will remove Judah also from my presence as I removed Israel, and I will reject Jerusalem, the city I chose, and this temple, about which I said, 'There shall my Name be.'"" (2 Kings 23:25–27).* The wickedness of Manasseh went so deep in the nation that a time of revival under Josiah only put off "the day of the Lord" when God would carry out his threat and remove them from the land.

The Babylonians

During the reign of Josiah (see Timechart 9 page 230) the world stage changed. Assyria reached the height of its power around 650 BC when Manasseh was taken prisoner for a while. At this time the Assyrian Empire extended from present day Egypt to Iran (see Map 6 on the next page) and, as with all empires, her resources became considerably overstretched. God had promised to punish Assyria for her wickedness through Isaiah and Nahum and he did this through an alliance of the Babylonians (who are also referred to as the Chaldeans in the Bible) from the south and the Medes and Persians from the North East. There was war between the superpowers which lasted for twenty years and finally Nineveh, the proud capital of Assyria, was destroyed in 612 BC fulfilling Nahum's prophecy.

The Babylonians and the Medes and Persians split the territory of the Assyrian Empire between them but for about seventy years the Babylonians were the major power in the region. However, this change of rule made very little difference to the surrounding nations as the

Day 46 – Jeremiah's Message 267

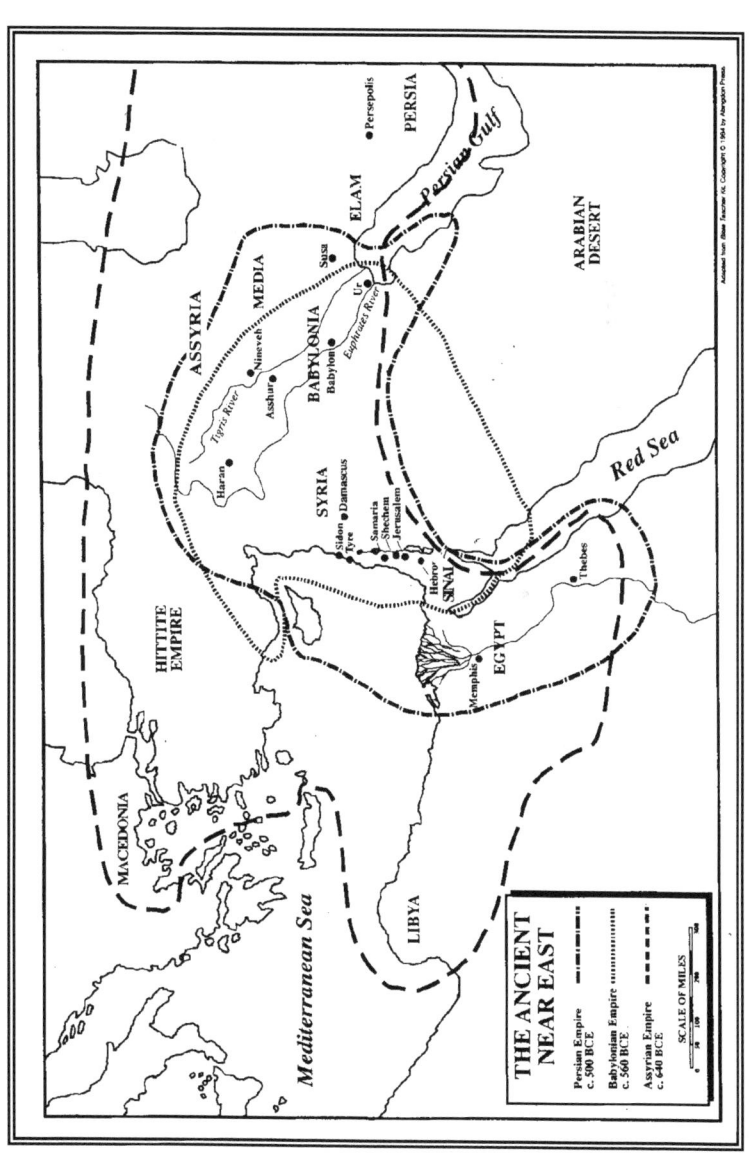

Map 6 – The Assyrian, Babylonian and Persian Empires

Babylonians followed the same brutal policies as Assyria in warfare and deportation of conquered nations. The main king of Babylon mentioned in the Bible was Nebuchadnezzar.

Because the Assyrian Empire was coming under pressure from the Babylonians during Josiah's reign, Judah was free from trouble. But when Assyria asked Egypt for help and the Egyptian army set out to march through Judah, Josiah unwisely got himself involved and went into battle against the Egyptians. 2 Chronicles gives us a full account and an assessment of the battle.

> **Read 2 Chronicles 35:20–27**

Josiah's heart for the Lord was the last thing holding back the judgement of God on the nation and once he died in 609 BC things moved rapidly. The twenty three years after his death were the worst the Israelites had ever known. Josiah had 3 sons who were alive when he was killed and in the twenty three years after his death all three ruled as well as one of his grandsons. Three of the four were taken into exile – one to Egypt where he died and the other two to Babylon. The writers of Kings and Chronicles sum up these years in a few short chapters but we are given insight into the situation in the land through the book of Jeremiah which provides a vivid account of the disasters that came on the nation and the Lord's perspective on his people.

Jeremiah – The Book

Jeremiah has the greatest number of words of any book in the Bible (Isaiah is slightly longer in most Bibles as more of it is in poetic form). The author was Jeremiah, a priest, and his prophecies spanned the reigns of the last five Kings of Judah – Josiah, Jehoahaz, Jehoiakim, Jehoiachin, and Zedekiah – from 626 to about 580 BC (see Timechart 9 page 230). As well as his prophecies it contains a fair bit of historical narrative that tells us the story of the final years of Judah.

The book is arranged more by subject than in chronological order.

Jeremiah – The Man and His Message

Jeremiah grew up during the reign of King Josiah and, as a young priest, he would have been alongside him as he went around the country destroying high places and idols and he would have performed ceremonial duties as the whole nation celebrated the Passover under the King's direction. He grew up alongside men who had a zeal for God and for his covenant. His love for Josiah is seen at the end of the

Day 46 – Jeremiah's Message

Outline of Jeremiah	
1	Jeremiah's call.
2–35	Warning to Judah.
36–38	Jeremiah's sufferings.
39–45	The fall of Jerusalem and what followed.
46–51	Judgements on the Nations.
52	Historical Appendix.
Looking at the events in Jeremiah chronologically they can be roughly assigned by the reigning King as follows:	
1–6	Prophecies probably written during the reign of good King **Josiah**. Jeremiah lamented his death (see 2 Chronicles 35:25).
7–20, 25–26, 35–36, 45–51	Prophecies and events relating to the reign of the wicked King **Jehoiakim** who was very hostile to Jeremiah (see especially Jeremiah 36).
21–24, 27–34, 37–38	Written during the reign of the weak King **Zedekiah** who both sought Jeremiah's advice and imprisoned him.
39–44, 52	The fall of Jerusalem and the subsequent events.

passage you've just read where it says that he composed laments for him after he died.

But it was while he was growing up in a country which was being led back towards God, that the Lord called him to be a prophet with an unpopular message. His call is recorded in the first chapter.

Read Jeremiah 1

Jeremiah's whole message is summarised in verse 10: *"to uproot and tear down, to destroy and overthrow, to build and to plant"* – one pair of positives but two pairs of negatives. Jeremiah's message is not good news for his nation. Their future is certain and it is to be one of disaster. Neither is this great news for him. He is part of the nation that is heading towards destruction and by proclaiming that the disaster is from the Lord because of the sin of the people he is going to make himself a very unpopular figure.

Day 47
Hope for the Future

The Beginning of the End

After Josiah died it was his second son, Jehoahaz, who was made king first. This may have been because he adopted an anti–Egyptian stance like his father as, after only three months, Pharaoh Neco came and took him prisoner to Egypt where he died. In his place Neco appointed Josiah's oldest son, Jehoiakim, to be king. Jehoiakim had to pay tribute to Neco but this did not last long as, three years into Jehoiakim's eleven year reign, Nebuchadnezzar, the fearsome king of the Babylonians, and his army invaded Judah on his way to defeat the Egyptians and so Jehoiakim became subject to them. Nebuchadnezzar ordered that some of the noble young men of Judah be taken to Babylon at that time and this group included the prophet Daniel. (See Timechart 9 on page 230. Note that the names of the kings like Jehoahaz who ruled for a very short time are omitted.)

Then, three years later, Jehoiakim decided to rebel against the Babylonians. This was not a wise move as Nebuchadnezzar responded by sending his army to Judah to defeat it. He laid siege to Jerusalem and finally captured it three months after Jehoiakim's death in 597 BC. Jehoiakim's 18 year old son Jehoiachin who had become king was taken prisoner to Babylon along with ten thousand of his subjects – the officials, the fighting men, and the craftsmen – who were taken into exile leaving only the poorest in the land. However, although Nebuchadnezzar plundered the temple treasury he left the walls of Jerusalem intact and Judah remained as a nation. Nebuchadnezzar appointed Josiah's youngest son, Zedekiah to be "king", although he was clearly under Babylonian control.

As you read the account in 2 Kings note how the writer once again sums up these kings as evil and how he links the destruction of the land to the sins of Manasseh.

> Read 2 Kings 24

Jeremiah continued to prophesy that the nation would be destroyed during the reign of Jehoiakim in the hope that the people would turn back to God. On one occasion he sent his friend Baruch to read his

Day 47 – Hope for the Future

words in the temple and the officials were alarmed by what they heard. Afraid for his safety they sent Baruch into hiding but brought his scroll to king Jehoiakim. Jehoiakim's reaction was a marked contrast to his father's. Josiah tore his clothes in repentance when he first heard the words of the Lord but his son Jehoiakim reacted differently:

> Read Jeremiah 36:21–25

This description of complete indifference to the word of the Lord sums up the attitude of the Lord's covenant people and explains why the Lord brought disaster on them.

The Message of Hope

However, despite the message of coming disaster that Jeremiah has to bring, his writings do contain hope. As we have just seen, during the reign of Zedekiah, many of the Israelites are already living in exile in a strange land. How are they to react to this situation? There are false prophets telling them that they will soon return to the land of Israel but Jeremiah writes to them with a different message.

> Read Jeremiah 29:1–23

The people should not expect to return for seventy years but this does not mean that the Lord has deserted them. In among his warnings of even more trouble to come for those left behind, the Lord tells the exiles that he has plans to prosper them and give them *"hope and a future"*. The promise of the return from exile is there – but only after the land has had its rest and the nation has been punished and turned back to God.

He goes on to give some amazing prophecies regarding the return from exile. As with many Old Testament prophecies they are a kaleidoscope of words relating to the return in seventy years time as well as words relating to events further away. As you read this chapter try and get a sense of the Lord's eagerness to "restore the fortunes" of his people.

> Read Jeremiah 30

The New Covenant is Announced

In among these messages of hope is one of the most significant prophecies of the Old Testament. Jeremiah 31:31 contains the only reference in the Old Testament to the new covenant. The old covenant

– the Law – which was given at Mount Sinai has failed. The Lord's people have not been able to keep it and so now the Lord promises a new one. Read this passage carefully as it contains details of the new covenant that we can enjoy today.

> **Read Jeremiah 31:31–34**

This new covenant has some remarkable differences from the old one. The law will now be in men's minds and hearts, not on tablets of stone. In the old covenant men only had access to the Lord through priests but in the new covenant everyone will have a personal relationship with the Lord for themselves. And forgiveness is freely given so doing away with the need for regular sacrifices.

Those of us who enjoy the benefits of the new covenant are in danger of taking it for granted but for Jeremiah, living in the shell of Jerusalem and awaiting its final destruction, it must have seemed an incredible dream. The Lord's grace is seen in the fact that Jeremiah, who had the hardest message for his own generation, is given the privilege of announcing the new covenant.

Day 48
The End of Judah

Judah's Last King

The last king of Judah, Zedekiah, reigned for eleven years but things do not improve under his leadership. Jeremiah continues to prophesy destruction for the nation, as well as writing to tell the exiles to settle in the lands they have been moved to, which makes him a traitor in the eyes of the people. Imagine how someone in Great Britain would have been viewed in World War II if they had said that Britain should surrender to the Nazis as they were God's instrument to bring punishment on the nation. This would not have made them popular!

Zedekiah was under Babylonian authority and had to pay tribute but, like his brother before him, he decided to rebel against Babylonian rule (perhaps because Egypt was gaining in strength again) and so Nebuchadnezzar decided that he had had enough. He came and besieged Jerusalem, determined to destroy its power once and for all. During the siege Zedekiah both sought Jeremiah's advice and punished him for giving it! Chapters 37 and 38 record the relationship between king and prophet. Note how Jeremiah summarises his entire message for Zedekiah in one sentence in 37:17 and how, despite being given clear advice to surrender in chapter 38, Zedekiah ignores Jeremiah's message.

> *Read Jeremiah 37–38*

The Fall of Jerusalem

The Israelites held out against the Babylonian siege for two and a half long years before they were defeated. Cut off from supplies of food and water conditions must have been dreadful although this particular siege is not described in the Bible. The awful, final act is described in three different places: 2 Kings 25, Jeremiah 39 and Jeremiah 52. Jeremiah 52 was added onto the book of Jeremiah by the person who compiled the book, possibly his friend Baruch, and it provides the fullest account. Note the fate of King Zedekiah who was promised safety for him and his family if he surrendered by Jeremiah at the end of chapter 38. See also how thorough the Babylonians were in their destruction of

Jerusalem – its walls, its buildings and the remainder of the temple furnishings were all destroyed. None of the previous invaders had ever bothered with the huge bronze altar before but now, almost four hundred years after Solomon had dedicated his temple, all the temple furnishings were systematically destroyed.

> **Read Jeremiah 52**

It is interesting to note that this was probably when the Ark of the Covenant was destroyed although it is not mentioned in the Biblical record. The Ark was the symbol of God's presence in the desert, it was brought to Jerusalem by David and then put in Solomon's temple in a ceremony during which the priests could not stand up to fulfil their duties due to the physical presence of the Lord. Then the Biblical record goes strangely quiet about it. The only reference to it after the time of Solomon is in the time of Josiah. Sometime before his reign, probably during the time of wicked Manasseh, the Ark was removed from the temple and Josiah tells the priest to return it to the temple (see 2 Chronicles 35:3). After that it is not mentioned again so it must have been destroyed during the destruction of the temple by the Babylonians. Jeremiah prophesies that after the exile it will be forgotten: *""In those days, when your numbers have increased greatly in the land," declares the LORD, "men will no longer say, 'The ark of the covenant of the LORD.' It will never enter their minds or be remembered; it will not be missed, nor will another one be made.""* (Jeremiah 3:16). It does reappear in heaven in Revelation 11:19 but it is never seen again on the earth.

Lamentations

Jeremiah was allowed to stay in Judah by king Nebuchadnezzar himself and so he lived to see the effects of the Babylonian devastation on Jerusalem. Even though he had predicted the fall of the nation for over forty years he was still horrified by seeing the city of David and the home of the Lord's temple in ruins and all her people taken to Babylon.

Jeremiah's heart for God is seen in the short book of Lamentations which follows his main book. It was almost certainly written by Jeremiah (we know that he wrote laments for Josiah following his death) and is a collection of five poems expressing the horror of the destruction of Jerusalem and the despair of the people left behind:

Day 48 – The End of Judah

> "How deserted lies the city,
>   once so full of people!
> How like a widow is she,
>   who once was great among the nations!
> She who was queen among the provinces
>   has now become a slave." (Lamentations 1:1).

The Hebrew name for the book is "How" (the initial word of the first, second and fourth poems) which expresses a mixture of shock and horror. Yet despite his horror Jeremiah used great care in constructing these poems. The first four are Hebrew acrostic poems like some of the Psalms which means that each verse starts with a different letter of the Hebrew alphabet. The 22 letters are reflected in each chapter having 22 verses (apart from the third which has 66, three times 22).

In the middle of Lamentations there is a statement of faith in God which is remarkable given that it was written in the ruins of the devastated city of Jerusalem.

Read Lamentations 3:21–26

After the End

Given the crushing blow inflicted on the nation by the Babylonians it is hard to imagine that things could get even worse. However, it did! The story of the people who remained in the land after the fall of Jerusalem is recorded in Jeremiah 40–44.

Having been defied by two kings of Judah, Nebuchadnezzar was not prepared to leave any descendant of David on the throne as he returned to Babylon. David and his descendants had ruled Israel and Judah for almost four hundred years but now Nebuchadnezzar appointed a governor, Gedaliah. Jeremiah stayed with him at his base in Mizpah, seven miles north of the ruins of Jerusalem.

Although most of the people were prepared to accept the rule of Gedaliah, there were some who were not happy with the imposition of a governor by Babylon. Within three months he was assassinated and the assassin forced to flee the country. The people remaining now had no ruler and were, understandably, frightened of what the Babylonians might do. Jeremiah 42 is an extraordinary account of how the leaders of the people came to Jeremiah to ask him to seek the Lord for direction. They promised to do whatever the Lord told them to do and were prepared to wait ten days for Jeremiah to hear the word of the Lord. The Lord's word to them is to stay in the land and he will build them up *"for I am grieved over the disaster I have inflicted on you" (Jeremiah 42:10)*. They are not to fear the king of Babylon; the Lord will save them from his hand. They are then warned not to go to Egypt as the sword, famine and plague – a common threesome in Jeremiah – will follow them there. Having waited ten days to hear what Jeremiah said you might expect the people to take the Lord's advice but they immediately reject it and the leaders take all the remaining people in the land, including Jeremiah, down to settle in Egypt.

Jeremiah, more than any other writer, was totally identified with the people he prophesied to. He prophesied disaster on the nation and, in his early sixties, saw it come horribly true as the city of Jerusalem was razed to the ground. His final words are in Jeremiah 44 where he brings a prophecy to the Israelites living in Egypt calling on them to turn away from the worship of "the Queen of Heaven" and to turn back to the Lord. He finished his life among his fellow countrymen who had turned their back on their Lord and were destined for disaster in the place they had fled for safety.

With the Promised Land now empty our focus now moves to follow the Lord's people in their captivity as seen through the eyes of the other two Major Prophets – Ezekiel and Daniel.

Day 49
Ezekiel, the Prophet in Exile

Life Outside the Promised Land

The first eleven chapters of Genesis describe the creation of man, how the flood wiped mankind from the face of the earth and the spread of people on the earth following the flood. Then in chapter 12 the account homes in on one man, Abraham, who God chose to become the father of a great nation, a nation that God would use to bless the whole world. But right from the start, the story of God's chosen people is closely tied up with the "Promised Land". In the opening line of Abraham's story God tells him to *"Leave your country, your people and your father's household and go to the land I will show you" (Genesis 12:1)* and later God made a covenant with Abraham to give the land to his descendants (see Genesis 15:18 and 24:7). At the end of Genesis Abraham's descendants move to Egypt but Exodus opens with the Lord preparing his people to leave Egypt and return to the Promised Land and settle in it as a nation. From then on the Bible provides an unbroken, 800 year account of God's people living in the land he promised them: from the conquest of the land under Joshua, through the time of the Judges, the establishment of a united kingdom under Saul, David and Solomon, the history of the divided kingdoms of Israel and Judah, and all the way to the time of the exile.

For the Israelites who lived at this time, going into exile was a traumatic event. This is, of course, a major understatement. What words can be used to describe the horror of a highly trained and ruthless army coming and destroying your town, killing many of your family and friends, and then brutally leading you on a four month route march to a land you have never seen and leaving you to establish a new life for yourself? But for the Israelites, the Lord's covenant people, the trauma went far deeper than this. It was a break with their history and with the land that was part of their covenant relationship with God. Reading the scriptures reminded them of their inheritance – the land. Reading about their kings reminded them of the Lord's promise to David to have one of his descendants on the throne of Israel forever – a promise that was no longer in operation. Reading about worship involved offering sacrifices at the temple, which was now a heap of rubble in the middle of Jerusalem – a city described as "desolate ruins" (see Jeremiah 44:6).

With the final crushing defeat by the Babylonian army, all the hopes of those who prophesied a quick return to the land were gone. Although there was still hope for a future return as prophesied by Isaiah and other prophets, they now have to accept the words of Jeremiah that there will be no return in their lifetime and they must now settle in the lands they find themselves in and build a life for themselves there.

The Old Testament gives us two major insights into life for the exiles in Babylon from completely different perspectives. Daniel, the last of the major prophets, rose to become prime minister of the Babylonian Empire and was used by God to have a direct influence on the most powerful man in the world, the tyrannical king Nebuchadnezzar. We will look at his story in a few days' time. At the other end of the social scale is Ezekiel, a priest who worked as a slave in central Babylon and we will look at his life and visions over the next two days.

Ezekiel – the Man and his Book

Ezekiel was a priest who was taken to the land of the Babylonians along with King Jehoiachin after the defeat of Judah in 597 BC (see Timechart 9 on page 230). He dates a number of his messages from the exile of King Jehoiachin – an indication of how great a traumatic personal event the exile was for Ezekiel and his contemporaries. Ezekiel lived among the ordinary Israelite people living in poor conditions in the desert. Unable to take up his priestly duties in Jerusalem he is called by the Lord to be a prophet.

His book has a similar structure to Isaiah and Jeremiah. The first part was written in Babylonia before the fall of Jerusalem in 587 BC and Ezekiel's prophecies are centred on the wickedness of the Lord's people and the final judgement still to come on the land. Other nations will not escape these judgements either and a section is devoted to them. After the exiles hear of the fall of Jerusalem, Ezekiel is then given prophecies about the future restoration of Israel. The theme of the book is God's sovereignty which is powerfully seen in the initial vision and is emphasised all the way to the last phrase of the last vision – "The Lord is there". Unlike Jeremiah, Ezekiel is mainly arranged in sequence which makes things easier to follow!

Day 49 – Ezekiel, the Prophet in Exile

Outline of Ezekiel	
1–24	Judgements against Israel: From 593 to 588 BC Ezekiel foretold the destruction of Jerusalem. He is told by God of the start of the siege in 588 in chapter 24.
25–32	Judgements against the Nations
33–48	Promises of Restoration for Israel. From 585 BC, when the first refugee arrived from the devastated Jerusalem, Ezekiel was given words of comfort for the exiles.

Ezekiel's Call

Ezekiel is called to be a prophet through a very dramatic vision – one of the most awesome visions of God in the whole Bible. The first three chapters describe the vision, the impact it had on Ezekiel, and his calling to be a watchman with responsibility to warn the other Israelites.

> **Read Ezekiel 1–3**

The last two verses of chapter 3 indicate that Ezekiel was struck dumb following his call. The only time he would be able to speak would be when he was given a message from God. To those who knew him this sudden affliction would increase their desire to understand what had happened to him.

The exiles, like those who remained in Jerusalem, believed that the exile was a short term, temporary event and that they would soon return to Israel. Although King Jehoiachin is in exile with them his brother, Zedekiah, is still ruling in Jerusalem and the city is intact. Ezekiel's message, like Jeremiah's, is to tell them that they will not return. Given that he cannot speak Ezekiel is called to use drama, or more accurately mime, to convey his message to the people. Immediately after his calling the Lord tells him to let the people know that Jerusalem will be destroyed by acting out the siege of Jerusalem which is to come. He is to do this by making a model of the city out of clay and then lying on his side by it for 15 months! As you read the account of this extraordinary scene try and imagine the impact that this man who had been struck dumb would have had on the Israelites living in exile as he lay there in the sand day after day! Ezekiel's message would have been heard far and wide even though he could not speak.

> *Read Ezekiel 4–5*

Day 50
Ezekiel's Message

Ezekiel Gets His Message Across

Following his calling Ezekiel gets his message across to the people in a number of ways despite being dumb. In chapters 8–11 he describes a vision he had when he was taken to the temple in Jerusalem to see the idolatry of the people even within the temple walls. Once again, he sees "the glory of the Lord" – the same image he saw in chapter 1 – and this time it is departing from the temple. Yet even this vision ends with a word of comfort about the return from exile that will come in the future. Like the other prophets, Ezekiel condemns Israel's wickedness and uses colourful language and powerful allegories to drive his message home. He also acts out the situation of those left in Jerusalem as he digs through a wall with his belongings packed to go into exile.

At the beginning of Ezekiel 24 the Lord reveals to him that on that day the Babylonian army has laid siege to Jerusalem. News travelled slowly in those days and he had to wait months for confirmation of the word of the Lord. This almost brings to an end Ezekiel's prophecies of destruction for the nation but before the end comes he is to face a personal tragedy. With the siege underway the Lord tells him that his wife – *"the delight of your eyes" (Ezekiel 24:16)* – will die very suddenly that day. His loss mirrors that of the people who are about to lose their home nation and remaining family and his message is that they are not to mourn or weep for their loss. They are to get on with their new lives in exile. Ezekiel's terrible loss is recorded in one verse: *"So I spoke to the people in the morning, and in the evening my wife died. The next morning I did as I had been commanded." (Ezekiel 24:18)*. His command was that he should show no outward sign of mourning and this is what he did. Like Hosea, his marriage is used to illustrate God's message in a bitterly painful way.

Confirmation of the fall of Jerusalem came from a man who had escaped from the destruction. The day before he arrived Ezekiel was able to speak again after being dumb for twelve years. His first words are for those remaining in the city and the devastated land and it is still not good news.

> Read Ezekiel 33:21–33

Note in verse 30 how Ezekiel, like Jeremiah, was recognised as a prophet of the Lord by the people of his own day. But like those who sought the word of the Lord through Jeremiah, those who listened to Ezekiel were not prepared to put them into practice.

Visions of Hope

In the second part of the book, written after the fall of Jerusalem, Ezekiel is given messages of hope for the people of Israel. As we have already seen Ezekiel saw some incredible visions and there are two in this section which are well known. In chapter 37 Ezekiel is taken in a vision to a valley of dry bones. He goes on to receive a prophecy concerning the restoration of one nation of Israel.

> Read Ezekiel 37

It is interesting to note that when the people returned after the exile there is no mention of the two kingdoms. Although the territory around Jerusalem is still referred to as Judah the people are called a variety of names including Judah and Israel interchangeably; for example those who are against them are called *"the enemies of Judah and Benjamin"* in Ezra 4:1, while the people are referred to as *"the families of Israel"* and *"the people of Judah"* in Ezra 4:3 and 4.

The book ends with a vision of a new temple which is described in Ezekiel chapters 40 to 48. This vision includes a detailed description of a new temple, the return of "the Glory of the Lord" (the vision Ezekiel saw in the first chapter) to the temple, regulations for priests and Levites, offerings and holy days, the division of the land around the temple and, very famously, a river which flows from the temple to the east and brings healing and life to all it touches. This river foresees the work that Jesus will start and which will continue in the work of the Holy Spirit through the church. The river appears again in the last chapter of the Bible where it flows from the throne of God in the New Jerusalem.

> Read Ezekiel 47:1–12

The New Covenant

Ezekiel contains wonderful promises of God's future love and the

Day 50 – Ezekiel's Message

return of the people to the land. The Lord likens himself to a shepherd in Ezekiel 34. Israel's earthly shepherds, their priests and kings, have failed so the Lord is looking to have a personal relationship with each person himself. In a passage that has echoes of the new covenant announced by Jeremiah, the Lord promises that he will take full responsibility for looking after his people directly: *"For this is what the Sovereign LORD says: I myself will search for my sheep and look after them. As a shepherd looks after his scattered flock when he is with them, so will I look after my sheep. I will rescue them from all the places where they were scattered on a day of clouds and darkness. I will bring them out from the nations and gather them from the countries, and I will bring them into their own land. I will pasture them on the mountains of Israel, in the ravines and in all the settlements in the land. I will tend them in a good pasture, and the mountain heights of Israel will be their grazing land. There they will lie down in good grazing land, and there they will feed in a rich pasture on the mountains of Israel. I myself will tend my sheep and have them lie down, declares the Sovereign LORD. I will search for the lost and bring back the strays. I will bind up the injured and strengthen the weak, but the sleek and the strong I will destroy. I will shepherd the flock with justice." (Ezekiel 34:11–16)*.

Ezekiel also preaches personal responsibility, another contribution to the new covenant. In the Ten Commandments, the old covenant, God promises judgement on children to the fourth generation if a man sins. Ezekiel now undoes this in Chapter 18 which spells out how a good man will not be punished for his father's wicked acts, nor will a wicked man live because he has a righteous father. This seems very obvious to us but notice in this chapter how the message is spelled out in painstaking detail and then how many times the objections are dealt with. This was revolutionary teaching for its day!

Read Ezekiel 18

Ezekiel's call for repentance sets the scene for personal salvation offered by Jesus. In Israel's darkest hour the two men who had the most unpopular messages for their nation, Jeremiah and Ezekiel, were also the ones who spoke about the new covenant which was to come.

Day 51
Daniel

Daniel – God's Man in High Places

The book of Daniel records some events from the life of another prophet who lived during the exile along with some of his prophecies. However, the contrast with his fellow countryman Ezekiel, could not have been much greater. While Ezekiel lived in poverty by the Kebar river, Daniel spent the exile living in a palace in Babylon. While Ezekiel was lying in the mud on his side acting out a word for the Israelites, Daniel was being used by God to speak to the great King Nebuchadnezzar himself.

Daniel was taken into exile with the first deportation during the reign of king Jehoiakim in 605 BC and so got to Babylon eight years before Ezekiel (see Timechart 9 on page 230). In the first chapter of Daniel we find that he was from a noble family and was one of a number of young Israelite men who were chosen to be trained for the civil service working for king Nebuchadnezzar who had come to the throne three years earlier. In Babylon, Daniel and his friends were receiving the best education on earth and were being prepared to administer the greatest empire the world had ever known.

However, Babylon was a pagan culture and one of the themes of Daniel's life is that he consistently put his commitment to God above his service to kings, a course that meant risking his life on a number of occasions. For Daniel and his three friends this clash of loyalties starts as soon as they are in Babylon. As elite students they are given royal food and wine to ensure that they develop well physically as well as mentally but this food had not been prepared according to God's law and was probably offered to idols, so Daniel and his friends boldly ask if they can eat vegetables and drink water instead. This was a risky thing to do as they might start looking less healthy than the other students but Daniel shows great wisdom and faith by asking the official in charge of them to give them a ten day trial and looking to God to ensure that they thrive. God not only honours their stand by giving them good health but also gives Daniel and his three friends such great wisdom and understanding that they came top of the class.

Daniel 2, which we will read part of in a few days time, tells how

Day 51 – Daniel

Daniel came to the attention of Nebuchadnezzar by being given the interpretation of a dream he had. As a result of giving him the interpretation he is made ruler over the entire province of Babylon, a position of responsibility second only to Nebuchadnezzar himself. There are striking similarities with the way Joseph came to the attention of Pharaoh in Egypt some 1200 years earlier. At Daniel's request, Nebuchadnezzar also appointed his three friends, Shadrach, Meshach and Abednego, as administrators to work with him. They are famous for the account of the fiery furnace that we will read in a few minutes.

Nebuchadnezzar Learns about the Most High God

From the first three chapters of Daniel we not only learn about the faithfulness of Daniel and his friends but we also learn about the most powerful man on earth of his time, Nebuchadnezzar. Nebuchadnezzar was the king of a powerful empire which he ruled as an unchallenged dictator in a brutal and ruthless way. He was the head of a highly trained and efficient army and through them could order the total destruction of cities and nations and the mass deportation of peoples, as he did with Judah and Jerusalem. Those closer to him were no safer. When his astrologers were unable to tell him what he had dreamt about the night before, his answer was swift and to the point: *"If you do not tell me what my dream was and interpret it, I will have you cut into pieces and your houses turned into piles of rubble."* (Daniel 2:5). Their very polite attempts to get more information from him infuriated him so much that, despite all the effort and money he had put into educating them, he ordered the execution of all the wise men of Babylon. They were only saved through the intervention of Daniel and his God. This was a man used to getting his own way!

Nebuchadnezzar built the huge city of Babylon as an expression of his power and glory (see Daniel 4:30). It was built on the river Euphrates and had strong walls which were so large that a four horse chariot could turn on the top of it. Inside the city was one of the wonders of the ancient world, the Hanging Gardens of Babylon, which Nebuchadnezzar had built for his wife. Nebuchadnezzar lived in luxury while his subjects lived in poverty.

One of the important messages of the Bible is that God is interested in every human being. In particular he has a passionate heart of love for the poor, the weak, and the underprivileged. From this emphasis we can conclude that God is not interested in those who are rich, strong or born with privilege, but nothing could be further from the truth. In Daniel chapters 3 and 4 we read a remarkable account of how God used Daniel and his three friends to challenge the most powerful and proud man in the world. No one had more to boast about from an earthly point of view but God brought him to the point where he acknowledged "the Most High God" as far greater than him.

The first challenge came as a result of Daniel's friends refusing to worship an idol of Nebuchadnezzar. Note the size of Nebuchadnezzar's ego expressed in the size of his image in verse 1 and, by contrast, the incredible expression of courage and faith in God from Shadrach, Meshach and Abednego in verses 17 and 18.

Read Daniel 3

Not surprisingly, God's deliverance of Shadrach, Meshach and Abednego from the fiery furnace has a big impact on Nebuchadnezzar. He not only offered praise to their God but also passed a blasphemy law in his characteristic, no nonsense style: *"I decree that the people of any nation or language who say anything against the God of Shadrach, Meshach and Abednego be cut into pieces and their houses be turned into piles of rubble" (Daniel 3:29)*! But although the fiery furnace got Nebuchadnezzar's attention for a while it did not change his heart and it is in Daniel 4 we see what lengths the Lord is prepared to go to in order to bring a man to his senses. This chapter describes how the Lord dealt with Nebuchadnezzar's pride by causing him to go mad for a period of seven years during which time he lived in the palace gardens like an animal! It is an awesome story and one that demonstrates the grace of God.

God gave Nebuchadnezzar a dream as a warning and had arranged for his man, Daniel, to be on hand to interpret it. Daniel not only interprets the dream but is also prepared to urge the king to repent of his wickedness in oppressing others. Not many men would have been prepared to suggest that to Nebuchadnezzar! Nebuchadnezzar is then given a full year to take Daniel's advice before the Lord moves to fulfil his word. The impact on Nebuchadnezzar is seen in two statements he makes – one before and one after his madness. Before God intervened in his life his pride is evident. Surveying his great city he proclaimed, *"Is not this the great Babylon I have built as the royal residence, by my mighty power and for the glory of my majesty?" (Daniel 4:30)*. But once he was restored to sanity he had a different perspective: *"Now I,*

Nebuchadnezzar, praise and exalt and glorify the King of heaven, because everything he does is right and all his ways are just. And those who walk in pride he is able to humble." (Daniel 4:37). When God decides to humble someone he will go to any lengths to do it!

The Book of Daniel

The book of Daniel is the last of the Major Prophets. Although it is much smaller than the first three it is still twice the size of the largest Minor Prophet, Hosea. The first half of the book (chapters 1–6) is a series of narratives which are concerned with God's dealings with world rulers. The second half (chapters 7–12) contains highly symbolic visions concerning events relating to world powers for the 500 years after Daniel's lifetime and on to the end times.

If you read the stories from Daniel's life quickly it sounds very action packed but it is remarkable to note that he lived through the entire exile and so they span nearly seventy years! Taken into captivity in Babylon in the first deportation in 605 BC he lived to see the overthrow of Babylon at the hands of Cyrus the Persian and Darius the Mede and the first exiles return to Jerusalem in 538 BC (see Timechart 10 on page 296). Daniel was appointed to high office by the Babylonian King Nebuchadnezzar and by the Medes and Persians under Darius and so he held senior government posts of one sort and another on and off for 66 years! The outline on the next page arranges the chapters of Daniel in time sequence and gives an indication of Daniel's age. I've assumed that he was 20 when he was taken to Babylon as Daniel 1:3 calls him a "young man" but it may be that he was a few years younger. At least it gives an idea of his age in the various accounts of his life.

Belshazzar's Feast and Daniel in the Lion's Den

The last two stories from Daniel's life took place around the time of the end of the Babylonian Empire. They are well known "Sunday school stories", as they are dramatic demonstrations of the power of God, but, like the rest of Daniel, we must remember that these are factual accounts of events which are firmly rooted in history. The Babylonians, like many great empires, lost their power through internal corruption and in chapter 5 we meet King Belshazzar throwing a huge party for a thousand of his nobles. He is complacent about the state of his empire and more interested in revelry and blasphemy than defending his city. God intervenes and ruins the party by writing on the wall. This sobers the king up very rapidly and, after his wise men are unable to interpret

Outline of Daniel

Chap-ters	Year (BC)	Daniel's Age (approx)	
1	605	20	Daniel and his friends are deported to Babylon and given high positions in government by King Nebuchadnezzar.
2	604	21	Daniel interprets Nebuchadnezzar's dream.
3	?		Shadrach, Meshach and Abednego refuse to bow to Nebuchadnezzar's image of gold and are thrown into the fiery furnace.
4	?	?	Nebuchadnezzar is humbled by God.
	562	*63*	*Nebuchadnezzar's death.*
7	553	72	Daniel's vision of four beasts.
8	551	74	Daniel's vision of a Ram and a Goat.
5	539	86	Belshazzar's feast. Babylon is overthrown by the Medes and the Persians
6	539/ 537?	86/88?	Daniel is appointed to the government of Darius the Mede. He is thrown into the Lion's den.
9	539	86	Daniel realises that the 70 years prophesied by Jeremiah are nearly complete.
	538	*87*	*The first exiles return to Jerusalem (see Ezra 1:1–4)*
10–12	536	91	Daniel's vision of Israel's future.

the words, Daniel is brought in to solve the mystery.

The message from God is that Belshazzar's days are nearly at an end and that his kingdom will be given over to the Medes and Persians. The word of the Lord is fulfilled that night as the city of Babylon is captured by Darius the Mede. It is said that the Medes diverted the river Euphrates into canals so that they could enter the city walls through the dried up riverbed.

Somehow Daniel comes to the attention of Darius and, even at his great age, is given one of the top three jobs in the new administration. Again, God uses Daniel's position to teach a powerful ruler who is king in the most famous of all stories from Daniel's life.

> **Read Daniel 6**

There are some great paintings of Daniel in the lion's den which show a strapping young man alongside the hungry looking animals but note that Daniel was well into his eighties when this took place! The account ends with Daniel once again prospering in high office working for a dictatorial ruler who has been forced to acknowledge the true God through his dealings with Daniel.

Daniel's Visions

The second half of Daniel contains his dreams and visions and they are among the most wide ranging prophecies of the Old Testament. They describe the rise and fall of kingdoms up to the time of Christ some 550 years later with great accuracy and we will look at them in some more detail in a few days time. Because of their accuracy, some scholars have suggested that Daniel was written a few centuries later but this does not take account of the fact that many of his words were not fulfilled until the time of Christ and the book of Daniel was part of the Old Testament some 200–300 years before that.

Daniel 7:13 is the only place in the Old Testament where the title *"son of man"* is used for the Messiah. Jesus used this title for himself many times in the gospels (for example see Mark 8:31) making it clear that he was the Messiah. Daniel also uses the expression *"everlasting life"* in 12:2, which is the first clear reference to a resurrection, another key element of the new covenant.

Daniel Prays for the Return from Exile.

When the Medes and Persians conquered Babylon, Daniel, from reading the prophecies of Jeremiah, realises that the exile is due to finish. It is interesting to note that he refers to Jeremiah's words as "the Scriptures": *"In the first year of Darius son of Xerxes (a Mede by descent), who was made ruler over the Babylonian kingdom – in the first year of his reign, I, Daniel, understood from the Scriptures, according to the word of the LORD given to Jeremiah the prophet, that the desolation of Jerusalem would last seventy years. So I turned to the Lord God and pleaded with him in prayer and petition, in fasting, and in sackcloth and ashes." (Daniel 9:1–3)*. Daniel pleads with the Lord to show mercy on his people for the sake of his name. The way in which he identifies with the sins of his forefathers in his prayer is amazing considering that he left the land 66 years earlier. He was rewarded by living to see the first exiles return to Jerusalem in the following year.

Daniel gives us a remarkable insight into the way in which God deals with kings and empires. We may not think that God takes any notice of the excesses of powerful dictators or gets involved in the affairs of governments, but Daniel shows us that God can put his men into positions of great influence and can intervene directly in the lives of any people as he did with the dictator Nebuchadnezzar. Daniel's prophecies also show that God is behind human history. He is not going to be caught out by the rise and fall of empires – he has already foreseen them and will work his purpose out.

Day 52
Return from Exile –
The Temple Rebuilt

A Different Cultural Context

There are six books in the Old Testament from the period after the people of Israel returned from exile: the last three of the history books and the last three minor prophets. Of the history books, Ezra and Nehemiah describe the return of the people and the rebuilding of the temple and the walls of Jerusalem while the last history book of the Old Testament, Esther, is an account of how God protected his people who remained in exile. Two of the minor prophets, Haggai and Zechariah, were used by God to encourage the returning exiles to rebuild the temple and finally Malachi, the last book to be written in the Old Testament, contains messages for God's people who have resettled the land.

When the people of Israel returned from exile things were not the same as when they left. Before the exile Judah was an independent nation – a sovereign state in today's terminology – and she had her own king, descended from King David, who could rule as he pleased. When they returned they were a territory of the Persian Empire and were ruled by governors appointed by the king of the empire. They paid taxes to the king and to his governor and their freedoms were limited by laws that they had no power to change.

As the people of Israel went into exile in Babylon, not only did they come under foreign rule but they also became influenced by the Babylonian culture and language. The Old Testament is almost all written in Hebrew, the language of the people of Israel. However, the language used in the Babylonian empire was Aramaic and some parts of the Bible were originally written in Aramaic. Daniel starts in Hebrew and then switches to Aramaic in the middle of a sentence in Daniel 2:4! The narrative then remains in Aramaic through to the end of chapter 7, as it relates to God's dealings with the leaders of the empires of Babylon and the Medes and Persians, before switching back into Hebrew for the last five chapters. The book of Ezra is also partly in Aramaic when it quotes from official documents.

Of course this distinction is not noticeable in our English translation of the Bible but the Babylonian influence is seen in a new word that appears in the Bible around the time of the fall of Jerusalem. Up until this time the Bible refers to the descendants of Jacob as "the people of Israel" or "the Israelites". After the kingdom divided the people of the southern kingdom were sometimes called "the people of Judah" and from this the other nations referred to them as "Jews".

The introduction of this word into the language of the Israelites can be dated to the time of the Babylonian siege of Jerusalem and the destruction of Jerusalem by studying the book of Jeremiah. He refers to the people as "the house of Israel", "the people of Israel" or just "Israel" many times but during the months leading up to the final destruction of Jerusalem he refers to them as "Jews" on a few occasions (Jeremiah 34:9 is the earliest use). Then, in describing the events after the fall of Jerusalem in Jeremiah 40–44, he only refers to the people as "the Jews" (or sometimes "the people of Judah") but never as the Israelites.

Ezra and Nehemiah use the word "Jew" and "Israelite" interchangeably – see for example Ezra 6:14–21 where "the elders of the Jews", "the people of Israel" and "the Israelites" are all used in one passage. Esther makes no mention of "Israel" or "the Israelites" and only uses the word "Jew" to describe God's people. By the time of the New Testament the word "Jew" was used to describe all Israelites and is more common than "the people of Israel".

The Book of Ezra

The books of Ezra and Nehemiah document the returns from exile. In

Outline of Ezra		
	Date (BC)	
1:1–4:5, 4:24	538–536	The first return of exiles and the start of work on rebuilding the temple.
5–6	520	Completion of the temple.
7–9	458	Ezra leads the second return from exile. He challenges the people about intermarriage with other nations and they repent.
4:6–4:23	445	Later opposition to the rebuilding of the wall of Jerusalem.

Day 52 – Return from Exile – The Temple Rebuilt

the Hebrew scripture they are one book, and the similarity of style leads some people to suggest that they were compiled by one man, probably Ezra, although if he did then he clearly used much material direct from Nehemiah himself. Ezra and Nehemiah are also very similar in style to 1 and 2 Chronicles which were possibly also compiled by Ezra. All these books contain lists of names and lots of details about the temple furnishings and rituals.

The First Return from Exile

When the Medes and the Persians defeated the Babylonians in 539 BC and took over their empire, King Cyrus of Persia immediately reversed the policies of the Assyrians and Babylonians and encouraged people in his empire to return to their countries of origin and re-establish the worship of their own gods. His motivation may have been to limit social unrest across his new empire but we know that he was being used by God to fulfil his own purposes as Isaiah had even prophesied about him by name nearly two hundred years earlier (see Isaiah 44:28 and 45:1).

The events in the first chapter of Ezra took place around 538 BC, sixty-seven years after the first deportation in 605 BC when Daniel was taken to Babylon. Eighty years later Ezra himself led a second return. Timechart 10 on the next page covers this period. In this introduction to the return from exile note how the Lord is seen to be working his purposes out by moving the heart of Cyrus (verse 1) and the hearts of the people who returned (verse 5).

Read Ezra 1

Each of the people who responded to Cyrus's proclamation and returned to the land to build the temple would have had their own picture of what the land was like. Some had lived through the whole exile and were returning to the land they remembered from their youth. They would remember it as a bustling city with its strong walls and impressive buildings, including Solomon's great temple. Some had been deported before the final destruction of Jerusalem so they would have left the city while it was still intact. But most had been born in captivity. Their only knowledge of the land would come from stories of life under the kings when Jerusalem was a bustling city with worship of the Lord at the temple being the focal point of national life. The reality now was very different. They returned to find a desolate land and the city of Jerusalem devastated – little more than a ruin.

Day 52 – Return from the Exile – The Temple Rebuilt

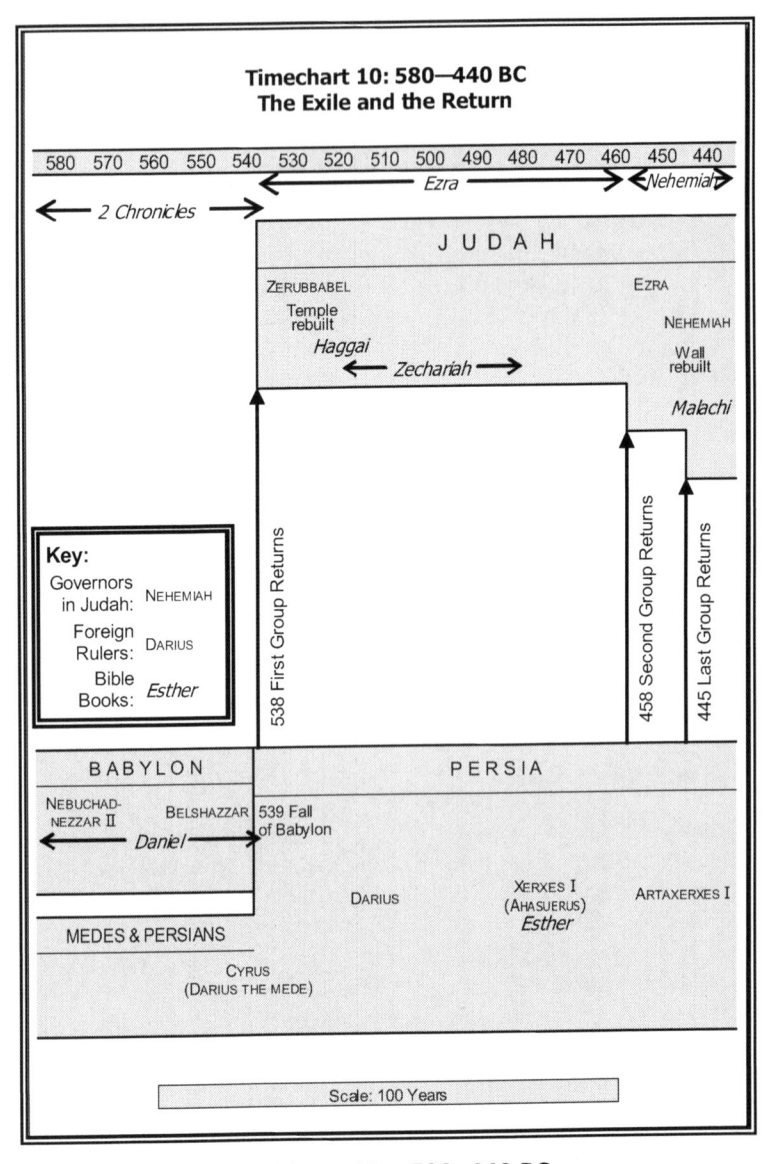

Timechart 10: 580—440 BC
The Exile and the Return

| 580 | 570 | 560 | 550 | 540 | 530 | 520 | 510 | 500 | 490 | 480 | 470 | 460 | 450 | 440 |

← Ezra → ← Nehemiah

← 2 Chronicles →

JUDAH

ZERUBBABEL — EZRA
Temple rebuilt — NEHEMIAH
Haggai — Wall rebuilt
← *Zechariah* →
Malachi

538 First Group Returns
458 Second Group Returns
445 Last Group Returns

Key:
Governors in Judah: NEHEMIAH
Foreign Rulers: DARIUS
Bible Books: *Esther*

BABYLON | **PERSIA**

NEBUCHADNEZZAR II | BELSHAZZAR | 539 Fall of Babylon
← *Daniel* →

DARIUS | XERXES I (AHASUERUS) *Esther* | ARTAXERXES I

MEDES & PERSIANS
CYRUS (DARIUS THE MEDE)

Scale: 100 Years

**Timechart 10 – 580–440 BC:
The Exile and the Return**

Day 52 – Return from Exile – The Temple Rebuilt

The people were led by two key men – Zerubbabel and Jeshua. Zerubbabel, whose name means "offspring of Babylon", was the grandson of King Jehoiachin who had been taken into captivity by Nebuchadnezzar and he was appointed as governor of the province. Jeshua was from the priestly line and was appointed High Priest.

The Rebuilding of the Temple

As soon as the people settle back in the land they set up an altar and sacrifice offerings to the Lord. Then, in the second year they start to rebuild the temple. This is a dramatic moment in the history of Israel. The act of starting to rebuild the temple, the symbol the Lord's presence among his people, resulted in a great outburst of emotion from the people. The exile was over and the Lord's covenant people were being restored to the Promised Land.

> **Read Ezra 3:10–13**

However, soon after starting the building work the Israelites meet opposition from the Samaritans – the people who had been settled in the northern half of Israel by the Assyrians – and other neighbouring groups who fear the potential of a thriving Jewish State. They hired men – called "counsellors" in Ezra 4 – with the specific aim of frustrating the building work and they successfully lobbied the government so that work on the temple was stopped for sixteen years throughout the reign of King Cyrus.

Then in 520 BC God raised up two prophets, Haggai and Zechariah, who encouraged the people to get back to rebuilding the temple. Haggai gives four messages promising blessing if the people are obedient in the building work. Zechariah has a series of eight visions (all in one night!) which encourage the people by indicating God's love for the people now they are restored. In particular he has special words for Jeshua, the high priest, and Zerubbabel, the governor. Zechariah has a vision of Jeshua (who is called Joshua in the book of Zechariah) with Satan at his side ready to accuse him. Jeshua, who is wearing filthy clothes, is given rich garments and told that if he walks in the ways of the Lord then he will govern the house of the Lord. Through another vision Zerubbabel is told that he will complete the rebuilding, *"'Not by might nor by power, but by my Spirit,' says the LORD Almighty" (Zechariah 4:6)*, a reminder that a man can only achieve something for the Lord through the power of his Spirit.

Day 52 – Return from Exile – The Temple Rebuilt

The surrounding nations are furious when the building work restarts and write to the new king, Darius, to get the work stopped, but their protests backfire as he not only upholds the right of the Jews to rebuild the temple but also provides material support to their efforts (along with the usual threat of punishment for those who opposed government decrees in those days in 6:11!). Ezra brings a new style of writing into the Bible in his record of events by quoting from official government memoranda! The work is completed in three and a half years and the people celebrate with great rejoicing.

> Read Ezra 5–6

The Second Return from Exile

The second return from exile was led by Ezra and is described in Ezra 7 and 8. The beginning of Ezra 7 also tells us about Ezra himself. He was descended from Aaron and, if he had been born before the exile, he would have served as a priest in Jerusalem. However, being brought up in exile, away from the temple and its rituals he had *"devoted himself to the study and observance of the Law of the LORD and to teaching its decrees and laws in Israel." (Ezra 7:10)*. It was in exile that the role of the priest as teacher – the word used in the Hebrew literally means "scribe" – became so important.

Ezra is sent to Jerusalem by King Artaxerxes himself with a letter telling him to find out how well the people of Israel were keeping the law of God and with money to ensure that regular sacrifices were made as the king wanted to ensure that the gods of his empire were favourable towards him. The king is so keen that the people obey God's laws that he finishes his letter by writing that, *"Whoever does not obey the law of your God and the law of the king must surely be punished by death, banishment, confiscation of property, or imprisonment." (Ezra 7:26)*. Ezra is in a strong position!

When he arrives he is horrified to discover that the people who settled from the first return have already intermarried with the surrounding nations and are starting to worship other gods as a result. Ezra challenges the people about this and the people respond by returning their wives! This brings that generation back to God but, as we will see tomorrow, the slide into wickedness that led the Israelites to finally be removed from the land by the Lord is now starting all over again with those who have returned and continues in later generations.

Day 53
Nehemiah Rebuilds the Walls of Jerusalem

The Book of Nehemiah

The book of Nehemiah is named after the man who rebuilt the wall of Jerusalem. Nehemiah was a Jew who grew up in exile and came to hold a position of great trust under King Artaxerxes of Persia. He was appointed Governor of Judah from 445 BC and the first 12 chapters of his book are set in that year while the last chapter records events from 433 BC – see Timechart 10 on page 296.

Outline of Nehemiah	
1–2	Nehemiah returns to Jerusalem in 445 BC.
3–6	The rebuilding of the wall of Jerusalem.
7	Lists of exiles
8–12	Reading of the Law by Ezra: spiritual revival and recommitment.
13	12 years later (433 BC): Nehemiah calls the people to repentance.

Nehemiah Returns to Jerusalem

Thirteen years after Ezra led the second batch of exiles to Jerusalem he was joined by Nehemiah. Nehemiah was a cupbearer to King Artaxerxes, which meant that he had to taste the king's wine before giving it to him to check that it was not poisoned. This was clearly a place of great trust (not to mention high risk!) and God uses his position with the king to further his purposes.

> Read Nehemiah 1–2

Throughout the book Nehemiah is seen to be a man of prayer. His first response to the news about Jerusalem is to pray and when he did get his opportunity to speak to the king Nehemiah prays what must be the shortest prayer in the Bible: *"The king said to me, "What is it you* want?" Then I prayed to the God of heaven, and I answered the king, "If it pleases the king ..."" (Nehemiah 2:4–5). I remember being taught as a child that this was an example of a "lightening prayer", a quick "Lord help me" when in a difficult situation. All of Nehemiah's prayers during the four months between hearing the news about Jerusalem and that moment were summed up in that rapid prayer. His prayers were answered and he was not only allowed to go to Jerusalem to rebuild the walls but was sent by the king as the governor of Judah (see Nehemiah 5:14).

The Rebuilding of the Walls

Nehemiah was not only a man of prayer but also a capable administrator, in a similar mould to Joseph and Daniel. Once he arrived he galvanised the people into action and brought about the rebuilding of the walls of Jerusalem in fifty two days[7]! This was a remarkable feat after a hundred and forty-one years of desolation. Despite being achieved in such a short timescale it was a very eventful period which is described in Nehemiah 3–6.

The way in which the walls of the city of God were rebuilt has much to teach us about how God wants to restore and build his church today. Nehemiah built a physical wall, but under the new covenant the focus is on bringing people into relationship with God and one another. Peter describes how Christians coming to Christ are *"like living stones, ... being built into a spiritual house"* (1 Peter 2:5) and so the wall, which was only effective when every stone was in place, provides a picture of how we must take our place in the local church in our day. Nehemiah 3 describes how different groups of people took responsibility for building each section of the wall. Everyone joined in: the priests, the temple servants, men from surrounding towns as well as the goldsmiths, the perfume-makers and the daughters of one of the rulers of Jerusalem – not people who were used to heavy manual labour! The only people who refused to co-operate were some of the nobles *who "would not put their shoulders to the work under their supervisors" (Nehemiah 3:5)*. In God's church the same commitment is required from all of God's people, to make the building of his church their top priority – not in terms of bricks and mortar but in terms of reaching out to people and incorporating them into God's church.

---

[7] As one of my reviewers dryly commented, "It takes us longer to get through your book than it took for the walls to be rebuilt"!

Day 53 – Nehemiah Rebuilds the Walls of Jerusalem 301

Like the building of the temple, the rebuilding of the walls brought opposition from the surrounding peoples. Chapter 4 paints a vivid picture of the intensity of the emotions during this time and shows how Nehemiah gave priority to prayer and used his gifting to lead the people through this difficult situation.

> **Read Nehemiah 4**

All this effort going in to the rebuilding programme put a strain on the economic situation and brought to a head problems which were being caused by some of the Jewish nobles and officials taking advantage of the poorer people by charging interest on loans made to them. Some of the poor people were even being forced to sell their sons and daughters into slavery to pay off their debts. Nehemiah challenged them to obey God's law, which forbade the charging of interest on debts to fellow Israelites, and the crisis was averted. At the end of Nehemiah 5 he also records that in the twelve years he was governor of Judah he did not tax the people to support himself despite having to provide for 150 officials and foreign visitors to the land each day.

Nehemiah then returned to the rebuilding work. Note a couple more short prayers from him in this passage.

> **Read Nehemiah 6:1–16**

The Joy of the Lord is Your Strength

A few weeks after the walls were complete the people gathered together to hear Ezra read the law to them. As we saw yesterday Ezra was a teacher, or "scribe" and it is clear from this passage that Ezra not only read the law but also taught from it as he, along with some of the Levites, *"read from the Book of the Law of God, making it clear and giving the meaning so that the people could understand what was being read."* *(Nehemiah 8:8)*. This event sparked a spiritual revival among the Israelites and they celebrated the Feast of Tabernacles with great joy.

> **Read Nehemiah 8**

Slipping Back into Old Ways

The last chapter of Nehemiah is the last recorded history in the Old Testament and it is a sad reflection on the state of God's covenant saved. The king is horrified that anyone should plan to kill his queen and demands to know who has devised such a plan. Haman, who was still deeply aggrieved at having had to honour Mordecai, is now suddenly terrified as he discovers that Esther is a Jew and his plot to kill the Jews includes killing the queen of the king he served! While the king angrily rampages round the garden considering his options Haman finally seals his fate by clinging onto Esther and pleading for his life. The king returned to the room to see Haman *"falling on the couch where Esther was reclining" (Esther 7:8)*. Needless to say the king is not pleased to see Haman molesting his Queen and immediately orders Haman's execution. One of his attendants helpfully points out that Haman has built a gallows for Mordecai and so the king ensures that it doesn't go to waste!

Following Haman's death Esther reveals her relationship to Mordecai and the king is delighted to give him the position that Haman held as second in the kingdom. As no laws passed by the Medes and Persians could be revoked Mordecai's first duty is to write a law allowing the Jews to protect themselves and attack any who seek to destroy them. When the day comes the Jews are saved from their enemies and Mordecai and Esther made sure that the event was remembered by laying down regulations for celebrating its anniversary which is known as "the feast of Purim".

The Coming Messiah – Hope for the Future

During the time of captivity Daniel had prophesied about an "Anointed One" who would come to rule the Lord's people. The Hebrew for "Anointed One" is "Messiah"; in Greek it is "Christ". At the end of the Old Testament the last two prophets, Zechariah and Malachi, contain a number of prophecies about the coming Messiah. As we have already seen, Israel is not a nation again, it is a province of the Persian Empire and the Lord now focuses their attention on the future, rather than letting them think that things would return to how they were.

Two days ago we saw that Zechariah, a priest, prophesied alongside Haggai encouraging the people to rebuild the temple. The first eight chapters of his book were written around that time (520–518 BC) and a further six chapters were written over forty years later and look to the future – see Timechart 10 on page 296.

Zechariah is full of references to the coming Messiah. In the first part of his book he has some remarkable prophecies for Joshua, the high priest. The Hebrew name Joshua means, "the Lord saves" and its Greek

Day 54 – A Story from Exile and the Promised Messiah

Outline of Zechariah	
Part 1 – Encouragement to Rebuild the Temple	
1:1–6	A call to repentance
1:7–6:8	Eight night visions.
6:9–8:23	Words to the people.
Part 2 – Concerning the Messiah	
9–11	The coming of the Messiah and his rejection.
12–14	"End Times" – the deliverance of Jerusalem and the reign of the Messiah.

form is Jesus and it seems that Joshua is a "type" of Christ – an Old Testament character who foreshadows the coming Messiah. At the end of Zechariah 6 the prophet is told to make a crown of silver and gold and put it on Joshua's head and deliver a remarkable prophecy: *"Here is the man whose name is the Branch, and he will branch out from his place and build the temple of the LORD. It is he who will build the temple of the LORD, and he will be clothed with majesty and will sit and rule on his throne. And he will be a priest on his throne. And there will be harmony between the two."* (Zechariah 6:12–13). The expression "the Branch" was used of the coming Messiah by Isaiah and Jeremiah and here is applied to Joshua. How it was fulfilled in Joshua's lifetime is not clear but its final fulfilment was in Jesus who is both our great high priest and our king.

In the second part of Zechariah there are many references to the coming Messiah, some of which were fulfilled by Jesus when he came to earth the first time, but many of which are yet to be fulfilled when he returns. It is not at all clear just from reading Zechariah's prophecy which parts refer to the first coming and which to the second. It is only because we have the New Testament that we can discern which is which. As you read Zechariah 9, note the reference to a gentle king riding into Jerusalem on a donkey in verse 9, which was fulfilled at Jesus' first coming, and the later reference to the Lord appearing with his arrow flashing like lightening and the sound of the trumpet, which seems to refer to his second coming (compare verse 14 with 1 Thessalonians 4:16).

Read Zechariah 9:9–17

There are further references to Jesus' first coming. In Zechariah 11:12–13 there is a reference to Zechariah being paid thirty pieces of silver which he threw to the potter, a prophecy identified by Matthew as referring to the price paid to Judas Iscariot for betraying Jesus. And Zechariah 13:7 says *"Strike the shepherd and the sheep will be scattered"* which Jesus quoted to his disciples just before they deserted him.

But the last chapter of Zechariah looks forward to a time when the Lord will come in person to defend Jerusalem. It talks about a time similar to that described in Isaiah 2 and Micah 4 when the Lord will rule the land of Israel and Jerusalem will have security from her enemies. This was not fulfilled in the first coming of Jesus and so must refer to a second coming.

Read Zechariah 14

The Coming Messiah – Who can Stand when He Appears?

Those reading Zechariah's words would have looked forward to the coming of the Lord with eager anticipation but this is balanced by the last Old Testament prophet, Malachi. Although nothing is known of Malachi from outside his short book it is thought that he was a contemporary of Nehemiah and prophesied around 430 BC – see **Timechart 10** on page 296. This was a similar time to when Nehemiah was berating the people for intermarrying once again. Despite the spiritual revival some fifteen years earlier when Ezra read the law it is clear from Malachi's prophecy that both the priests and the people had become unfaithful to God and become complacent about his laws.

Outline of Malachi	
1:1–2:16	The unfaithfulness of the priests and the people is rebuked.
2:17–4:6	The coming of the Lord is promised. He will come in judgement and, unless His people repent, the land will again be cursed.

After condemning the priests and the people for their sins Malachi promises the coming of the Lord who he calls *"the messenger of the covenant whom you desire" (Malachi 3:1)*. But although the people

Day 54 – A Story from Exile and the Promised Messiah

look forward to his coming they will receive a shock if they continue in their wicked ways. Malachi's description is of a Messiah coming in judgement on his people, not one who will save them from their enemies.

Read Malachi 3:2–5

Malachi goes on to call the people to repentance. Judgement is not inevitable if they honour their marriage commitments, give their tithes to God and get their hearts right towards him.

The last chapter of the Old Testament is very short but covers an interesting range of subjects. In six verses Malachi talks about the day of the Lord when evildoers will be destroyed while those who revere God's name receive their reward. But this is not imminent. After a call to the people to remember God's laws the Lord promises to send "the prophet Elijah" before judgement comes.

Read Malachi 4

These last two verses of the Old Testament refer to John the Baptist, who was sent to prepare the way for the coming Messiah over four hundred years later (see Luke 1:17). He prepared people's hearts for Jesus. As Malachi prophesied, some accepted him and saw healing in their family relationships while many rejected him and saw the land of Israel struck with a curse as the people of Israel were once again removed from the Promised Land.

The End of the Old Covenant

As the Old Testament closes both Nehemiah and Malachi present a picture of the Lord's covenant people slipping away from God. They have not learned the lesson of the exile and are once again being unfaithful to the Lord and his law. The old covenant is not working. The time is coming for the New Covenant to be introduced.

As the Old Testament draws to a close the Jews, thanks to Zechariah and the other prophets, are waiting for a Messiah who will come in power to establish his kingdom on earth – a second David to make them a great nation once again. What they don't realise is that they have a long wait. The Old Testament records over six hundred years of almost unbroken history from the time of Samuel to Nehemiah but the New Testament, which starts with the birth of the promised Messiah, starts after a gap of over four hundred years.

Day 55
Between the Old and New Testaments

A Different World

Tomorrow we are going to start looking at the New Testament which describes the coming of the Messiah, when God himself came to earth in human form. Jesus came not only to teach us about the New Covenant but also to make it possible by paying the price demanded for our sins by the old covenant through his own death. But when we start reading the accounts of the life of Jesus Christ, and of his followers who spread the good news about him, we find that it all takes place in a world which is very different from the one we left behind at the end of the Old Testament. Four hundred years have passed and much has changed in the world and in Israel during that time.

The political situation is different: we left Israel ruled by Jewish governors on behalf of a distant Persian king in the east but in the New Testament the focus has switched to the west and Israel is part of the Roman Empire. The language is different: the Old Testament was written in Hebrew, the language of the Israelites, but by the time of Jesus, the Jewish people spoke Aramaic, while the common language of the Roman Empire was Greek, which is the language that the New Testament was written in. And the religious scene in Israel is different: worship in the Old Testament centred around the temple and the priests and, although these still exist in the New Testament, the Jews meet to worship in places called synagogues and there are a number of religious groups such as the Pharisees and Sadducees.

In order to understand why things are so different we need to look at what happened to the Jews in the land of Israel over the four centuries between the Old and New Testaments.

Nebuchadnezzar's Dream

As we saw a few days ago, Daniel came to the attention of King Nebuchadnezzar of Babylon because God gave him the interpretation of the king's dream. We will read this now as the interpretation explained to Nebuchadnezzar what was going to happen over the next six hundred years which covers the period between the Old and New

Day 55 – Between the Old and New Testaments

Testaments.

Read Daniel 2:26-49

The kingdoms that Daniel talked about in his interpretation of the dream can be clearly identified as four major kingdoms that would rule the Middle East, and in particular Israel, over the next five to six hundred years. Later, Daniel himself was given a dream about four great beasts along with other prophetic visions and messages which describe the rise and fall of these empires in more details in the last six chapters of his book. You can follow the account of these empires on Timecharts 11 and 12 on the following pages.

In the statue the value of the metals decreases from the head to the toes representing the decreasing splendour of the empires, while the strength of the metals increases indicating a growing strength in the empires, each one of which lasted longer than the previous one. At the time that Nebuchadnezzar had the dream he ruled over the Middle East as a complete dictator. Daniel identified his empire, the Babylonian Empire, as the head of gold of the statue. The glory of this empire, with its hanging gardens, was not to be surpassed, but within seventy years it was defeated by the Medes and the Persians – the chest of silver in the statue – who conquered the Babylonians and took over control of the region. As we have already seen, during the time of the Persians, the Israelites returned to Judah and rebuilt the temple and the walls of Jerusalem. But they were not a nation. They were just one of the 127 provinces of the Persian Empire which stretched from India to Ethiopia.

Alexander the Great brings Greek Rule to Israel

The empire of the Medes and Persians survived about two hundred years before a man called Alexander the Great led the Greeks in the conquest of the entire Medo–Persian Empire in a very short space of time. Alexander's father, Philip of Macedon, had united the Greek nation and Alexander set out with his army to conquer the world. He swept east through Asia Minor (present day Turkey), south through Syria and Israel into Egypt and then came back and continued east across the heart of the Persian Empire through to India where his troops refused to go any further! This established the Greek Empire which is the thighs of bronze in Nebuchadnezzar's statue.

Alexander's desire was to see the Greek language and culture imposed

Timechart 11: 460—180 BC
The Time between the Testaments

| 460 | 440 | 420 | 400 | 380 | 360 | 340 | 320 | 300 | 280 | 260 | 240 | 220 | 200 | 180 |

JUDAH

| Under Persian Rule | Greek Rule | Under Egyptian Rule | Seleucid Rule |

↑ Alexander conquers the East
↑ Ptolemy I conquers Jerusalem

World Power:

| PERSIA | GREECE | EGYPT |

ALEXANDER THE GREAT

PTOLOMIES

SELEUCID (SYRIA)

Key: Rulers: PTOLOMIES

Scale: 100 Years

**Timechart 11 – 460–180BC:
The Time between the Testaments**

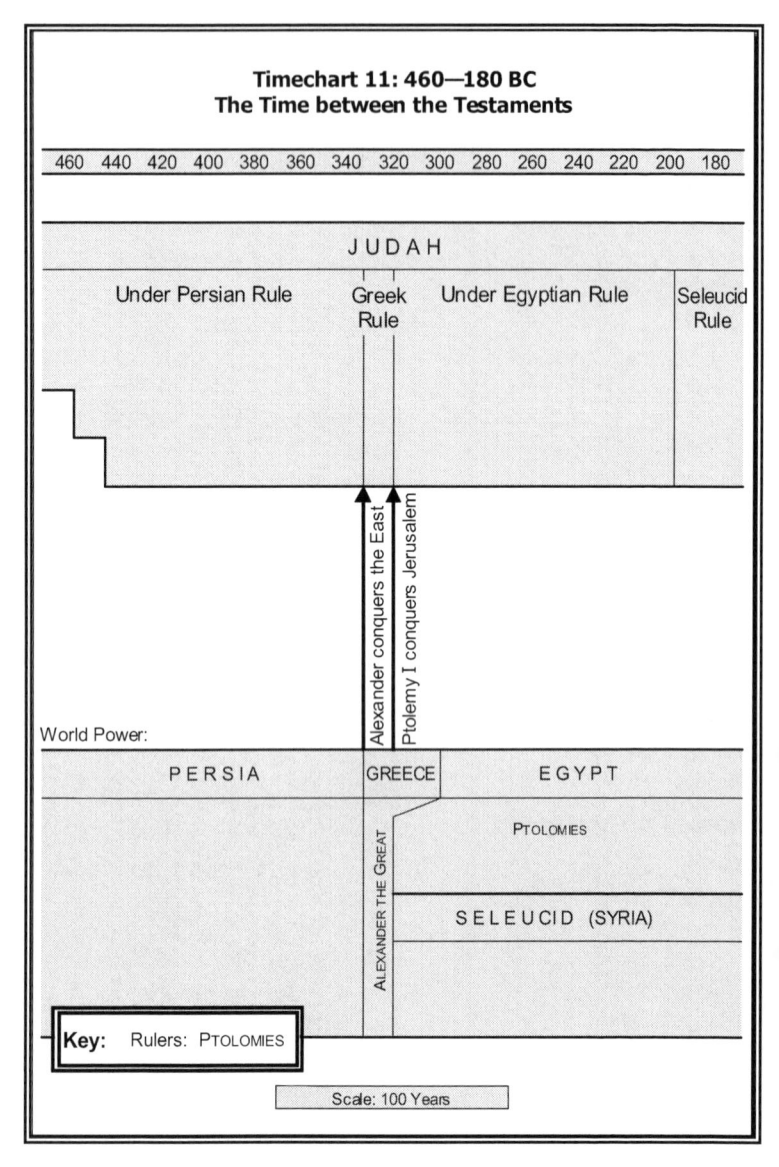

Day 55 – Between the Old and New Testaments 313

Timechart 12: 180 BC—100 AD
New Testament Times

| 180 | 160 | 140 | 120 | 100 | 80 | 60 | 40 | 20 | 0 | 20 | 40 | 60 | 80 | 100 |

← BC AD →

Gospels
Acts

JUDAH

Seleucid Rule	Independent Jewish State	Under Roman Rule
	JUDAS MACCABEUS	HEROD THE GREAT PILATE

Antiochus Epiphanes desecrates the temple

JESUS ✝

Temple built

AD 70 Destruction of Jerusalem. The Jews removed from the land.

Pompey captures Israel

← PETER →
← JOHN →
← PAUL →

New Testament Letters

EGYPT   **ROME**

CAESAR AUGUSTUS   TIBERIUS   NERO

SELEUCID

ANTIOCHUS EPIPHANES

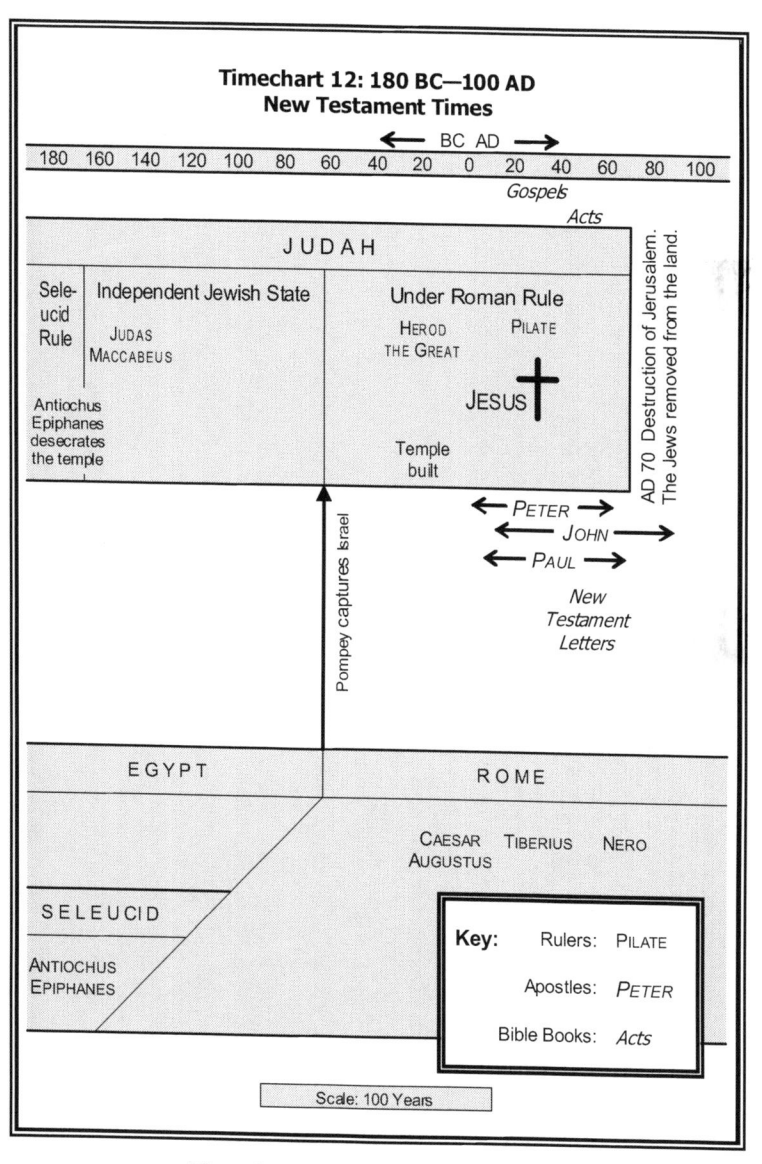

Key: Rulers: PILATE
           Apostles: PETER
           Bible Books: *Acts*

Scale: 100 Years

**Timechart 12 – 180 BC–AD 100:
New Testament Times**

on the world and, despite dying at the age of thirty–three, his wish was achieved – but not in his lifetime. After he died, the single Greek Empire that he had created split into four empires ruled by four of his generals but all of these adopted the Greek language and culture. Two of them founded dynasties which would rule Israel for the next century and beyond: the Ptolomies, based in Egypt, and the Seleucids based in Syria.

After a short period of direct Greek rule Israel came under the control of the first Ptolomy, Soter, who established a power base in Egypt. The Ptolomies, who ruled Israel for over one hundred years, allowed religious freedom and the Jews lived in relative peace. This was shattered in 198 BC when the Seleucids took control. They were not tolerant of other religions and King Antiochus IV took the title "Epiphanes", which means "God made manifest", and set out to eradicate Judaism. He stopped all worship of God at the temple and sent in his soldiers to destroy as many copies of the Law as could be found. Then he set up a statue to the Greek god Zeus in the temple and sacrificed a pig in the temple courts.

The pig is classified as an unclean animal in the Law of Moses so this act was a violation of the Jewish law deliberately intended to make the temple unclean or unholy. Three times in the latter part of Daniel there is reference to a king setting up *"an abomination that causes desolation" (Daniel 9:27, 11:31 and 12:11)* in the temple – a reference to this pagan altar. However, this is one of these prophecies that has more than one fulfilment as Jesus referred back to this prophecy (see Matthew 24:15 or Mark 13:14) as one still to be fulfilled at *"the end of the age" (Matthew 24:3)*.

The Greek Legacy – A Common Language

Although Alexander did not found an enduring empire, he did achieve his dream of spreading the Greek culture across the world and, in particular, Greek became the common language used throughout the Empires he left behind. This legacy survived beyond the fall of his empires to the Romans and, even though Latin was the official language of Rome, Greek was the common language used throughout the Roman Empire at the time of Jesus.

Sometime around 250 BC a start was made on translating the Old Testament into Greek. According to the Jewish historian Josephus, a translation of the Law was made by seventy–two Hebrew scholars at the request of the Egyptian king, Ptolemy Philadelphus, who was creating a great library in Alexandria. Whether or not this is true is disputed, but it is likely that the Law was translated around this time with the other books following. What is clear is that the whole Old Testament was available in Greek well before the time of the New Testament. The translation, which is known as the Septuagint, made the Jewish scriptures accessible to the many Jews who were scattered around the world, growing up in towns and cities where Greek was the main language for learning. The apostle Paul, who grew up outside the land of Israel, clearly knew the Septuagint translation as he quotes from it in his letters. The word "Septuagint" comes from the Latin word for seventy (which is rather odd given that it is a Greek translation of the Hebrew scriptures!) and is sometimes abbreviated to LXX, the Roman numerals for seventy, in Biblical reference books.

The fact that the use of Greek was so widespread meant that the gospel spread very rapidly. People across the Roman Empire heard the gospel in Greek, were able to study the Old Testament scriptures in Greek, and, later, could read accounts of the life of Jesus and receive letters from Christian leaders in Greek. Alexander the Great's ambitions were used by God for a purpose he never envisaged.

The Maccabees and the Apocrypha

The desecration of the temple by Antiochus Epiphanes outraged the Jews and, thirty years later in 166 BC, a man called Matthias led an uprising against the Seleucids. The war lasted for twenty-four years and finally led to the Jews becoming independent again. For a while the Jews were led by Matthias and his sons, the most well known of whom is Judas Maccabeus.

Some of our knowledge of these events comes from two books called 1 & 2 Maccabees which can be found in the "Apocrypha." This is a collection of books written in the time between the Old and New Testaments that the Jews eventually left out of their Hebrew scriptures saying that although they were valuable for private study and edification they were not part of the word of God. Jesus did not quote from any of these books and there is only one reference to any book from the Apocrypha in the New Testament (see Jude verses 14–15).

The debate over the status of the Apocrypha continued in the church until the 16th Century when twelve books were formally included in the Bible by the Roman Catholic Church but excluded by the Protestants. The Apocrypha contains some historical inaccuracies (which is not true of the Old Testament) and also some doctrines which are at odds with other parts of the Bible, such as praying for the dead in 2 Maccabees.

Roman Rule in Israel

The Jews enjoyed their independence for almost a hundred years until Israel fell to the fourth of the empires in Nebuchadnezzar's statue, the legs and feet of iron, which was the strong Roman Empire. In 63 BC General Pompey took Jerusalem after a three month siege. He massacred priests in the temple area and entered the Most Holy Place, so starting Roman rule in a way that the Jews never forgot or forgave.

The Jews gave their conquerors continual trouble and the Romans faced terrorist attacks on their soldiers and institutions. The Roman governors had a responsibility to Rome to keep order in their provinces and took brutal steps to keep the peace, as hinted at in the reference to the governor Pilate mixing the blood of some Galileans with the Jewish sacrifices in Luke 13:1. Although some of the Jewish political and religious establishment worked with the Romans there were various uprisings which finally culminated in a successful revolt in AD 66 when the Jews regained their freedom. This was very short lived, and the Romans returned with a vengeance in AD 70, destroyed Jerusalem and levelled the walls and the temple to the ground once again, so fulfilling Jesus' prediction that *"not one stone here will be left on another; every one will be thrown down." (Matthew 24:2)*. The Romans then took the Jews who had caused them so much trouble and scattered them all over the Roman Empire, and they remained scattered throughout the nations until they returned to the land of Israel in 1948 after the horrors of their persecution during the Second World War.

The Roman Influence on Israel

As a result of Roman rule there are new place names in the New Testament. The Romans divided their conquests into provinces. Map 7 on the next page shows how the land of Israel was divided in the time of Jesus. Judea in the south and Galilee in the north were provinces mainly occupied by Jews. In between them was the province of Samaria which was inhabited by the descendants of the people the Assyrians settled there following the deportation of Israel. They followed a corruption of the Jewish religion and worshipped at Bethel where Jeroboam had set up the golden calf. These three provinces are the setting for most of the gospel accounts.

The Romans were a military occupying force in Israel. They had a well

Day 55 – Between the Old and New Testaments   317

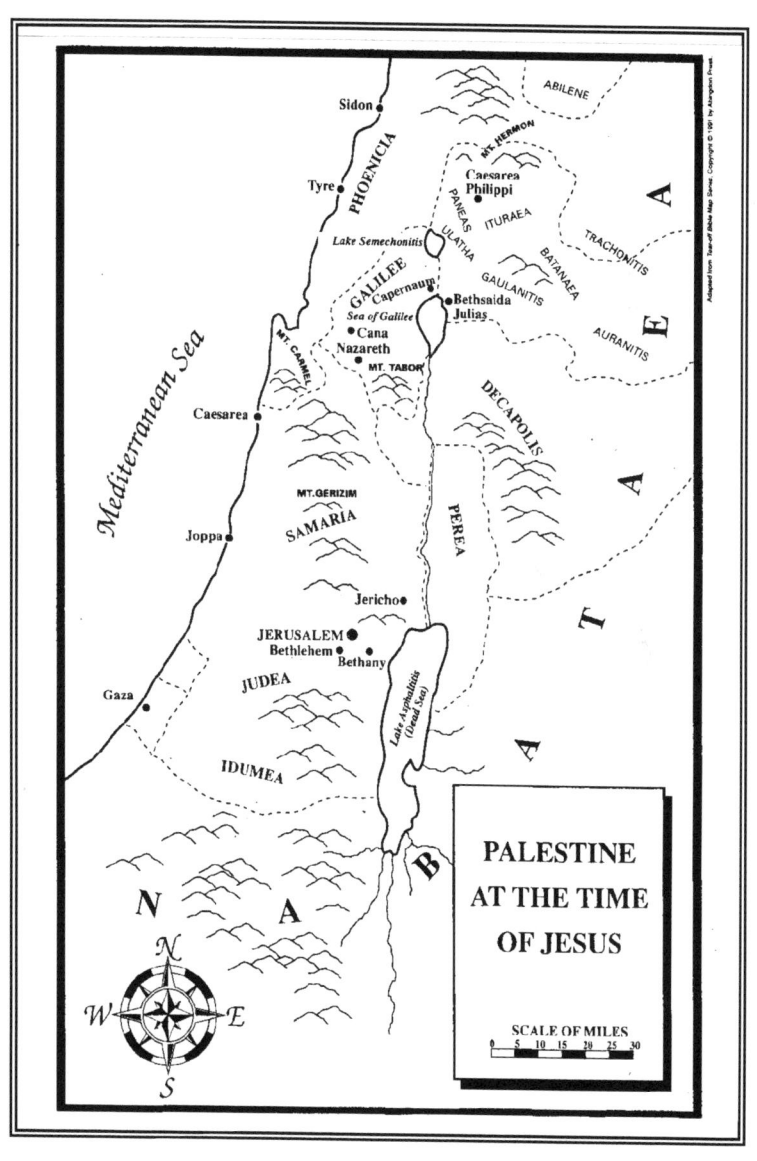

Map 7 – Israel at the Time of Jesus

trained and well equipped army organised into military units under centurions – officers in charge of a hundred men – and higher ranks and they used them to keep the peace and apply their legal system. As long as the Jews kept within the Roman law and paid their taxes the Romans allowed them to follow their own religion.

The Herods

In order to pacify the Jews the Romans allowed Israel to be ruled by various "kings" called "Herods". There are a number of these mentioned in the New Testament and their family tree is shown in Figure 11 (see opposite). The first of these was called "Herod the Great". He was from Jewish descent, and got himself into a favoured position in the eyes of the Romans who gave him the title "King of the Jews" in 37 BC. He wiped out the family of the Maccabees and, during his life, killed his wife and most of his own sons in order to stop them taking power before his death. Herod the Great is referred to in Matthew 2 where he met the wise men who came and asked him *"Where is the one who has been born king of the Jews?" (Matthew 2:2)*. Herod dealt with this potential challenge to his throne in the same brutal way he dealt with all the other challenges, in this case by massacring all the babies in Bethlehem. This action was not out of character.

All this, along with his pro–Roman policies, meant that the Jews hated him rather than being pleased to be ruled by one of their own people so, in order to try and win their favour, Herod set out to build a grand temple. Whether Zerubbabel's temple had actually survived for five hundred years is unclear but it was never that grand a structure and so Herod set out to create a much more impressive building. It was a long building programme that was still underway in Jesus' time many years after Herod's death – there is a reference to the building taking forty-six years in John 2:20 – and one which impressed Jesus' disciples (see Mark 13:1).

On Herod the Great's death in 4 BC the kingdom was split between his three remaining sons. The one who succeeded him in Judea, Achelaus, was so bad that the Romans deposed him and replaced him with a Roman Procurator, or Governor, directly appointed from Rome. Pilate was one of these. Another one of Herod the Great's sons, Herod Antipas, also known as Herod the Tetrarch, ruled in Galilee and was the one who beheaded John the Baptist and met Jesus before his death. Both the Herod Agrippas are mentioned in Acts.

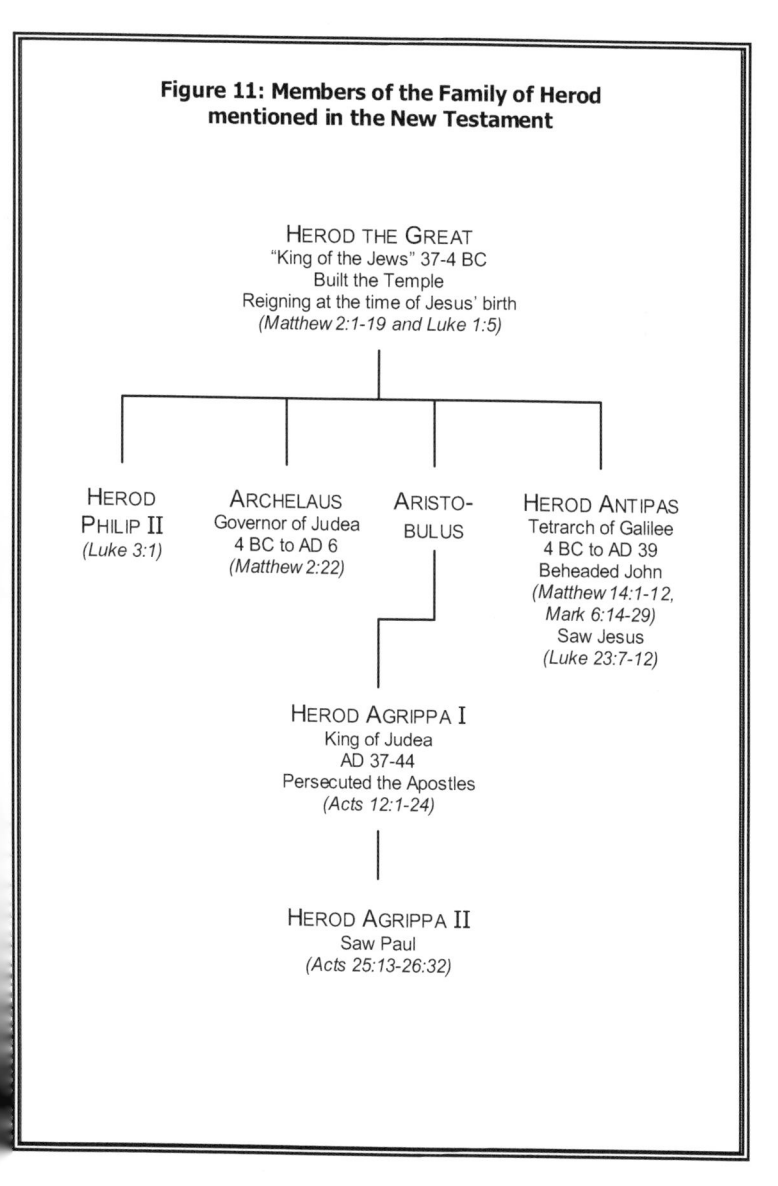

Figure 11: Members of the Family of Herod mentioned in the New Testament

HEROD THE GREAT
"King of the Jews" 37-4 BC
Built the Temple
Reigning at the time of Jesus' birth
(Matthew 2:1-19 and Luke 1:5)

- **HEROD PHILIP II**
  (Luke 3:1)

- **ARCHELAUS**
  Governor of Judea
  4 BC to AD 6
  (Matthew 2:22)

- **ARISTOBULUS**

- **HEROD ANTIPAS**
  Tetrarch of Galilee
  4 BC to AD 39
  Beheaded John
  (Matthew 14:1-12, Mark 6:14-29)
  Saw Jesus
  (Luke 23:7-12)

HEROD AGRIPPA I
King of Judea
AD 37-44
Persecuted the Apostles
(Acts 12:1-24)

HEROD AGRIPPA II
Saw Paul
(Acts 25:13-26:32)

Figure 11 – Members of the Family of Herod mentioned in the New Testament

The Roman Contribution to Spreading the Gospel

The fact that Jesus came to Israel during the time of Roman occupation was not an accident. Throughout the centuries before he came there were many wars but when Jesus came to earth there were none. Roman rule, although imposed by wars, led to a time of peace known as the "Pax Romana" – the peace of Rome. This time of peace allowed for the good news about Jesus to spread rapidly throughout the Roman Empire following Jesus' death. A quote from the 1971 Guinness Book of Records brought home to me how remarkable this situation was: *"It has been calculated that in the 3,467 years since 1496 BC there have been only 230 years of peace throughout the civilised world."*[1] *(The Eighteenth edition of the Guinness Book of Records pg 194).* Jesus came to one of these brief periods of peace.

Living, as we do, in the age when communication times between countries is measured in seconds and we can get to countries on the other side of the planet within twenty-four hours, it is hard to imagine life without efficient transport and communication systems. But before Roman times, travel was very difficult. The creation of a large empire led to the need for fast transportation of soldiers, officials and goods from province to province and so the Romans built straight roads all over their empire and bridged large rivers. Ports were created all around the Mediterranean and shipping moved freely between countries.

When you read in the book of Acts how the gospel spread into Asia, Africa and Europe it is easy to take the way the apostles moved around for granted. But without the combination of a common language from the Greeks and the development of efficient transport and postal systems by the Romans, Paul and others would not have been able to spread the gospel so widely in such a short space of time following Jesus' death. If Jesus had been born a hundred years earlier or a few hundred years later conditions would have made it much more difficult. Even today, with our mass communication systems, it would not be possible for a small group to spread the gospel around the Mediterranean so quickly given the many languages and the political barriers. The empires that Nebuchadnezzar learned about through his dream were all used to prepare the world to receive the Kingdom of God, *"a kingdom that will never be destroyed" (Daniel 2:44).*

References

[1] From the 18th edition of the *Guinness Book of Records,* 1971, p. 194. With thanks to Guinness World Records for permission to quote.

Day 56
The Four Gospels

Good News!

Today we are going to start to look at the New Testament by taking a bird's eye view of the first four books, the Gospels. There are four Gospels – Matthew, Mark, Luke and John – and they are accounts of the birth, life, death and resurrection of Jesus. The word "gospel" comes from the Old English "godspel" which means "good story" or "good news" and this is how Mark introduces his book: *"the gospel (good news) about Jesus Christ, the Son of God." (Mark 1:1)*.

We saw yesterday how God prepared the world for his coming through the rise and fall of empires during the four hundred years between the Old and New Testaments. Use of the Greek language was widespread so that the good news could be understood by a large number of people and the Romans had built roads and ships to speed the message into Europe, Africa and Asia. But as we start looking at the four gospels we also find that things have changed within the spiritual life of God's people. Although the priests continue to perform their sacrificial duties in the temple in Jerusalem and also teach the people the Law of Moses, we find that worship takes place in Synagogues and there are other religious leaders called Pharisees and Sadducees. How did this come about?

Synagogues, Pharisees and Sadducees

When the Israelites were scattered by the Assyrians and the Babylonians they found themselves in a foreign land, far away from the temple with its priests and sacrifices. To keep their faith alive they established meeting places called synagogues where they read the Law of Moses and the other Old Testament books and where they worshipped and prayed. "Synagogue" means "gathering" or "a bringing together" and can either refer to the people or to a building. (Note how similar this is to the word "church" which is used in the New Testament to describe a gathering of people but has, over the years, also come to be used for the building where people meet.) The emphasis in the synagogues was no longer on a corporate national religion but on personal holiness and piety and on a personal relationship with God. This form of faith and worship was a good

Day 56 – The Four Gospels

preparation for the introduction for Christianity.

In New Testament times the synagogues were run by the Pharisees. They were closely associated with the Scribes who copied and studied the scriptures and sat as judges to settle disputes. The Pharisees saw the exile as a punishment from God for not keeping the law and so they studied it carefully, made their own interpretations of it and added to it in order to provide a code by which the people might become holy. As the number of rules grew they became very pedantic and so, while Jesus supported the law, he condemned the Pharisees for placing intolerable burdens on the people and for their hypocrisy: *"Then Jesus said to the crowds and to his disciples: "The teachers of the law and the Pharisees sit in Moses' seat. So you must obey them and do everything they tell you. But do not do what they do, for they do not practice what they preach.""* (Matthew 23:1–3). However, the Pharisees were very popular with the Jews as they stood for holiness, the ideal they wanted, and they taught the people about the coming Messiah. Paul, who took the gospel to the Gentiles, was brought up as a Pharisee and was not ashamed of this fact after he became a Christian. The Pharisees were the forerunners of the Rabbis in modern day Judaism.

The other main group talked about in the New Testament is the Sadducees. They ran the temple and appointed the High Priest and they taught that Temple worship, not personal holiness, was central. They were a very political group who were interested in maintaining good relations with the Romans in order to preserve peace in the land. The Sadducees only accepted the five books of Moses and rejected doctrines such as the resurrection which are found outside it. Note that in Luke 20:27–38 Jesus quotes from Exodus to refute the Sadducees on this issue and wins praise from the teachers of the law!

The Pharisees and Sadducees sat together in a council called the Sanhedrin. This group had been formed during the period of Jewish independence to govern the country and be the highest court in the land. It survived into the time of the Roman occupation where it continued to rule Judea but its powers were limited by Rome. It was the Sanhedrin which ordered Jesus to be arrested and which tried him but it did not have the power to pass a death sentence on him which is why he was sent to Pilate, the Roman governor. Paul was brought before the Sanhedrin and used the fact that it was a mixture of Pharisees and Sadducees to his advantage by saying *"I stand on trial because of my hope in the resurrection of the dead."* (Acts 23:6) which resulted in the two groups getting into such a fierce argument that Paul had to be removed from the court for his own safety!

Jewish Expectations

Before we started reading through the Old Testament we saw how the two halves of the Bible complement one another:

"The New is in the Old Concealed;
The Old is in the New Revealed."

and as we have gone through the Old Testament we have seen how it points to the coming of Jesus. It is easy for us to do that because we have the benefit of having read the New Testament and so we can see the hidden meaning, but the people we meet in the New Testament did not have that advantage. The way in which the Jewish leaders and the ordinary people reacted to Jesus was conditioned by their understanding of the Old Testament and the teaching they had received.

The people's expectations were bound up in the Messiah. This is the Hebrew word for "God's Anointed one"; the Greek equivalent is "Christ". There are many references to the Messiah in the Old Testament and the teachers of the law knew them well and would have taught the people that he would be from the line of David, as David had been promised a son to sit on his throne forever (see 2 Samuel 7:16), and that he was to be born in Bethlehem (Micah 5:2). They taught that Elijah would come first (Malachi 4:5–6) and that the Messiah would bring in justice (Isaiah 42:1–4) and peace (Micah 4:1–5). He would come as a warrior (Zechariah 14:3–5) and establish an everlasting kingdom – so the people were looking forward to him throwing off Roman rule (Daniel 2:44–45).

Roman rule was oppressive and this teaching kept the people's hopes alive. Various "Messiahs" appeared and attracted followings (see a reference to some in Acts 5:36–37). Some were peaceful while others, such as the Zealots, waged terrorist campaigns against the Romans, killing their soldiers, in order to try and get them to leave the country.

These were the expectations that the people around Jesus had of a Messiah. He fulfilled some of the prophecies but left others unfulfilled. This disappointed the people and that disappointment, ultimately, contributed to his death.

The Four Gospel Writers

We have four gospels from four different authors. Two were eye

Day 56 – The Four Gospels

witnesses to Jesus' life. **Matthew** and **John** were two of the twelve disciples, or apostles, chosen by Jesus *"to be with him" (Mark 3:14).* This meant that they went everywhere with him during his three years of preaching, teaching and healing the sick. They saw Jesus in operation with the crowds and they had the privilege of talking with him one to one as they travelled from place to place. Matthew (who is known by his other name, Levi, in Mark and Luke) was a tax collector for the Romans (which made him even less popular than tax collectors are today!) before he was called by Jesus. John was a fisherman and one of the inner band of Jesus' closest three friends along with Peter and James (John's brother). John also wrote three letters – 1, 2, & 3 John – and the book of Revelation.

According to the traditions of the early church, **Mark** was a close associate of Peter and his gospel was a compilation of Peter's preaching. Although Mark was not with Jesus for three years like Matthew and John, it is likely that he also was an eye witness to part of Jesus' life and it is thought that the "young man" mentioned in Mark 14:51 is a reference to Mark himself. From the book of Acts we know that he also accompanied Paul and Barnabas (Mark's cousin) on missionary journeys – see Acts 13:5,13; 15:36–39 and 2 Tim 4:11. (Just to confuse matters he is sometimes referred to as John in some of these references – Act 12:12 links the two names.)

Luke was a doctor who also wrote the book of Acts. He was a travelling companion of Paul (see the reference to "we" in Acts 16:11–12 for example) and his close friend (see Colossians 4:14). Like Paul, Luke never met Jesus.

Written with Purpose

Jesus lived from around 6 BC to AD 30[8] (see Timechart 12 on page 313). For the next twenty years his followers were concentrated mainly in Israel and there were many of his followers alive to tell the good news to others. But as churches became established throughout the Roman Empire and the number of eyewitnesses decreased, Jesus' followers began to write down accounts of his life. The gospels were written as complete accounts so that new converts throughout the world

---

[8] The calendar we use is based on the date of Jesus' birth. The years before his birth are called BC, which stands for "Before Christ", and the years after his birth are called AD, which stands for "Anno Domini" – a Latin expression meaning "In the Year of our Lord". Due to an error in working out the calendar the actual date of Jesus' birth was sometime between 11 and 5 BC.

and in future generations might know the truth.

It is thought that Matthew, Mark and Luke were probably written between AD 50 and 70 while, traditionally, John is thought to have been written later, around AD 85, to supplement them. Looking at the gospels we see that the four authors wrote for different audiences and for different purposes. They also reflect the personality of the writers.

Matthew

Matthew's account of Jesus' birth, life and death is written primarily for Jews. His prime purpose is to prove to them that Jesus is the Messiah and he refers to Jesus as the "Son of David" which was a popular Jewish title for the Messiah. The opening to his gospel – the selective list of forty–two generations from Abraham to Jesus – demonstrates that Jesus had the right ancestry to be the Messiah. Maybe it also shows us something of his character as only an accountant could start such an exciting story with a list! He goes on to show how Jesus fulfilled Old Testament prophecies with many quotations. One of the characteristics of his gospel is the use of the word *"fulfilled"* which appears thirty–eight times, for example: *"And so was fulfilled what the Lord had said through the prophet ..."* and *"Then what was said through the prophet Jeremiah was fulfilled ..."* (Matthew 2:15 and 2:17).

Matthew records what Jesus said in five discourses, or sermons – see chapters 5–7, 10, 13, 18 and 24–25 – the most well known of which are the Sermon on the Mount (Matthew 5–7) and the Parables of the Kingdom (Matthew 13).

Mark

Mark's account of Jesus' ministry is written primarily for Romans, possibly for the church in Rome originally. We know that Peter eventually spent time with the church in Rome and Mark may have written his gospel for them. He explains Jewish customs, as in Mark 7:2–4 where he explains what it means for the disciples to have "unclean" hands, and translates Aramaic words for his readers (see for example in Mark 5:41), asides that Matthew did not need to include for his Jewish audience. Mark starts his gospel with an account of John the Baptist's ministry. This would have been well known to Romans as we know from Luke 3:14 that Roman soldiers went out into the desert to see John. There are many references to suffering and discipleship in the gospel and it may be that Mark wrote to prepare the church for a time of persecution.

The main characteristic of Mark's gospel is that it is very fast moving. It is the shortest gospel and jumps around from one event to another. A Greek word which can be translated "immediately", "at once", "quickly" or "just then" appears forty–seven times! As you read through the first chapter of Mark the speed of action is breathtaking: *"At once the Spirit sent him out into the desert ... At once they left their nets and followed him ... Without delay he called them ... Just then a man in their synagogue cried out" (Mark 1:12,18,20,23).* It is like some films where the camera work is all jerky and jumps from scene to scene without warning! To me this is strong evidence for Peter's involvement in the writing of Mark's gospel as Peter was always the first of the disciples to open his mouth or jump into situations without thinking about the consequences. I can imagine him dictating and before Mark has the chance to write down one event, Peter is rushing on to the next with "and don't forget about... Oh! ... and then Jesus did...".

Luke

Luke's gospel is a complete contrast to the rapid, quick–fire account from Mark. If Mark is a cameraman giving us snapshots then Luke is the artist. His account of Jesus' life was written for Greeks. The Greek culture encouraged people to think for themselves and question things so Luke's gospel is for those who like to think things through. Luke has an outstanding command of the Greek language and the book has a range of styles, sometimes close to that of classical Greek literature.

Luke sets out his purpose in writing his gospel in the first four verses which are addressed to a man called Theophilus, who may have requested Luke to write the account and sponsored its copying and distribution: *"Many have undertaken to draw up an account of the things that have been fulfilled among us, just as they were handed down to us by those who from the first were eyewitnesses and servants of the word. Therefore, since I myself have carefully investigated everything from the beginning, it seemed good also to me to write an orderly account for you, most excellent Theophilus, so that you may know the certainty of the things you have been taught." (Luke 1:1–4).* As the early church developed people began to question what they had heard and the accounts became corrupted. Luke took great care to ensure the accuracy of his book so that people could be certain about the facts. He records dates very carefully to help his readers put the events into context, as in one of the most famous passages from the Christmas story: *"In those days Caesar Augustus issued a decree that a census should be taken of the entire Roman world. (This was the first census that took place while Quirinius was governor of Syria.)" (Luke 2:1–2)*. This stops you getting confused by the second census that happened more recently! The reference to Quirinius also helps you pinpoint the time, although unfortunately no one now seems to know when he governed Syria! My mental picture of Luke is that of the traditional family doctor, thorough and unhurried, carefully checking all the symptoms before coming to any conclusions.

The opening of Luke's gospel presents us with an insight into how the Bible – the inspired word of God – was written. Luke is careful to check his facts, investigate events and spend time putting them in order and the end result is a document that fully reflects his personality. But it is also totally inspired by the Holy Spirit. The Holy Spirit speaks through our individual characters.

Luke shows us the human side of Jesus. While Matthew traces Jesus' ancestry back to Abraham, the father of the Jews, Luke traces it back to Adam, the father of all humanity, and also traces it through the ancestry of Mary, Jesus' mother, which was an unusual approach for the time. He gives us a number of details about Mary and in general highlights stories about women.

The first three gospels contain a lot of common material. Over 90% of the events in Mark are also in Matthew and 50% are in Luke. Very little of Mark is unique and only about half of each of Matthew and Luke. As a result Matthew, Mark and Luke are sometimes referred to as the "Synoptic" Gospels, from the Greek word meaning "seeing together". However, as with any eye–witness accounts they record the same events in different ways. This causes some people to question the accuracy of the accounts but we have to remember that most of the dialogue took place in Aramaic but was then written in Greek, and of course we are now reading it in English! The writers also seek to bring out different aspects of the same story so where one writer refers to one man and another to two there is not necessarily any contradiction: if there were two men then there was also one man!

John

John wrote his gospel much later than the other three and it contains mainly new material to supplement the three accounts already in circulation which he almost certainly knew about. His book is written for all people everywhere and he is clear as to its purpose: it is *"written that you may believe that Jesus is the Christ, the Son of God, and that by believing you may have life in his name" (John 20:31)*.

At the opening of his gospel John refers to Jesus as "the Word": *"In the beginning was the Word, and the Word was with God, and the Word was God. He was with God in the beginning." (John 1:1–2)*. This would have been understood as a reference to God by both Greeks and Jews, and traces Jesus back to eternity. The notes in the NIV Study Bible explain that *"Greeks used this term not only of the spoken word but also of the unspoken word, the word still in the mind—the reason. When they applied it to the universe, they meant the rational principle that governs all things. Jews, on the other hand, used it as a way of referring to God. Thus John used a term that was meaningful to both Jews and Gentiles."*[1]. However, John is very careful to make it clear that Jesus – "the Word" – is not some sort of concept but he *"became flesh" (John 1:14)* and John, who walked the earth with him for three years, is a witness to this.

John records far fewer parables and miracles than the other three writers but devotes more space to lengthy discourses and dialogues. Within these he includes seven *"I am"* statements made by Jesus, for example *"I am the bread of life"*, *"I am the light of the world" (John 6:35 and 8:12 – see also, 10:7, 10:11, 11:25, 14:6 and 15:1)*. The word used for *"I am"* echoes the name of God given to Moses in Exodus 3:14 – *"I am who I am"* – a point not lost on the Pharisees who recognised his claim to be God.

The early church fathers decided that these four gospels were the only accurate accounts of the life of Jesus. They are all we know of his life although there is much more that could have been written as John comments at the end of his gospel: *"Jesus did many other things as well. If every one of them were written down, I suppose that even the whole world would not have room for the books that would be written." (John 21:25)*.

The Contents of the Gospels

The table on the next page outlines the main events described by the gospels. Only Matthew and Luke give details about the birth of Jesus. All three of the synoptic gospels describe when Jesus was baptised by John the Baptist, which was the start of Jesus' public ministry – the three years he spent teaching, preaching, healing the sick and casting out demons. To start with it seems that he spent most of his time in

Outline of the Four Gospels			
	Matthew	**Mark**	**Luke**	**John**
In the beginning				1:1–18
Jesus' birth and early years	1–2		1–2	1:19–51
John the Baptist and the beginning of Jesus' ministry	3:1–4:11	1:1–13	3:1–4:13	
Jesus in Galilee	4:12–14:12	1:14–6:29	4:14–9:9	
Times away from Galilee	14:13–17:21	6:30–9:32	9:10–50	
In Galilee	17:22–18:35	9:33–50		
In Judea and Perea	19–20	10	9:51–19:27	
Other incidents – mainly in Judea				2–11
The week leading up to Jesus' death – Passion week	21–25	11:1–14:11	19:28–21:18	12–17
The Last Supper; Jesus' trial and crucifixion	26–27	14:12–15:47	22–23	18–19
The Resurrection and Jesus' appearances to his disciples (see also 1 Corinthians 15:3–7)	28	16	24:1–49 & Acts 1:3–8	20–21
Jesus' return to heaven (The Ascension)			24:50–53 & Acts 1:9–11	
Amount of Unique Material	*42%*	*7%*	*59%*	*92%*

Day 56 – The Four Gospels

Galilee where his popularity grew rapidly. He then withdrew to other areas to get away from the crowds and be with his disciples, sometimes with little success as the crowds followed him relentlessly. Jesus also spent time in Judea and Jerusalem. The synoptic gospels write about this at the end of his ministry, John fills in other times, which were probably earlier on, when he also visited Judea.

All four gospels cover the events of the last week of Jesus' life, which was spent in and around Jerusalem. This is high drama and the tension is palpable. The crowds love his teaching but the religious establishment are desperate to find a way to get rid of Jesus, partly out of envy for his popularity, partly from conviction that he was a blasphemer, and partly through fear of what the Romans would do if events got completely out of hand. Jesus, in the centre of all this excitement, demonstrates great wisdom in dealing with those who try to catch him out, gives details of events to come in the future and continues to show his compassion to those in need. At the end of the week all four gospels describe how he ate his last supper with his disciples, was arrested, tried and then executed by crucifixion – one of the cruellest forms of capital punishment ever invented.

However, the story does not end there. All four gospels describe the resurrection of Jesus and his subsequent appearances to his disciples. Luke completes the story with his account of his ascension into heaven which he records at the end of Luke and the beginning of his second book, Acts.

The whole of the Old Testament points forward to the coming of God in human form and the rest of the New Testament builds on the person and life of Jesus Christ. The accounts of his life, death and resurrection are central to our faith. We will spend the next nine days reading through the gospels, starting tomorrow with Christmas!

References

[J] *The NIV Study Bible* Copyright © 1985 by the Zondervan Corporation. Used by permission of The Zondervan Corporation in North America and by permission of Hodder & Stoughton elsewhere. p. 1561 Notes on John 1:1.

Day 57
The Birth of Jesus

Today we will start to read through the gospels looking at the life of Jesus. Two of them, Matthew and Luke, give an account of his birth but from very different perspectives.

Joseph's Perspective

Matthew, writing for Jews, starts his gospel with a family tree which links Jesus back to the Old Testament covenants with Abraham and David. Abraham was told that *"all peoples on earth will be blessed through you" (Genesis 12:3)* and David was promised that *"your throne will be established forever" (2 Samuel 7:16)* and Jesus is the fulfilment of both promises. This family tree is for Joseph, the man who became Jesus' legal father and brought Jesus up as his own son. Although Matthew makes it very clear that Mary became pregnant through the power of the Holy Spirit, he emphasises the part that Joseph played in Jesus' birth and upbringing.

Through Matthew's account Joseph is seen to be a godly man who was prepared to take difficult decisions for God. As you read these verses put yourself in Joseph's position. Here he is looking forward to marrying Mary and then she comes and tells him that she is *"with child through the Holy Spirit" (Matthew 1:18)*. That takes quite a lot of believing and even after Joseph is convinced that she is telling the truth by an angel he cannot expect the rest of the village to believe such a story! By marrying Mary he will be seen to be guilty of fathering the child and his reputation in his community will be damaged.

> **Read Matthew 1**

Matthew misses out Joseph and Mary's journey to Bethlehem and the birth of Jesus and instead records the visit of the Magi, which he uses to point out to his Jewish readers that Jesus being born in Bethlehem fulfilled the words of the prophet Micah. The Magi who visited Jesus were probably astrologers from Persia. They are sometimes referred to as "the wise men", which would reflect their learning, or "the three kings" which is inaccurate as they were not kings and we are not told that there were three, simply that there were three types of gift. Their visit is likely to have taken place a year or more after Jesus was born as they went to the house where Jesus was, not a stable, and Herod ordered all the boys under two to be killed. As we saw a couple of days ago, Herod's action was in keeping with his character. It is interesting to note that Jesus did some of his early growing up in Egypt before Joseph and Mary were able to return to Nazareth, their home town.

> **Read Matthew 2**

Mary's Perspective

Luke records the birth of Jesus from Mary's perspective. He records her concern at the words of the angel and her questions. He includes her song of praise, which is like that of Hannah the mother of Samuel, and says how she treasured things up in her heart – typical of a mother! In general, Luke takes time to record stories about women in his gospel and his medical training shows through in the way he records family and medical details. Note in this passage how he gives us information about Elizabeth's condition and mentions the baby jumping in the womb.

Although all four gospel writers record the work of John the Baptist, Luke is the only one to give us details about his birth. From this passage we see that he too had a miraculous birth, which has a number of similarities with that of Samson in the Old Testament.

> **Read Luke 1:1–66**

Luke's account of Jesus' birth is far more comprehensive that Matthew's. We have already learned about Gabriel appearing to Mary and in the next passage we will read about the census, the trip to Bethlehem, the fact that there was *"no room for them in the inn"* and the visit of the shepherds. Christmas would be a lot poorer without Luke!

> **Read Luke 2:1–20**

Luke also gives us the only snippet from Jesus' childhood – his visit to the temple at age twelve. Clearly Jesus already understood who he was and had some idea of his calling by this age yet he is prepared to go home to Nazareth and work as a carpenter for another eighteen years.

> **Read Luke 2:41–52**

The two accounts of Jesus' birth tell us that even before Jesus started his public work he had already fulfilled Old Testament prophecies. Some people have argued that Jesus could have fulfilled the prophecies about the Messiah by reading them himself and then acting them out. While this could be true of some it is clearly not true about all those concerning his ancestry, his place of birth and the fact that he was born to a virgin. God was at work in those circumstances and the preparations were now underway for Jesus' life and death. Those living in Israel at the time had no idea what was about to happen until, almost thirty years later, John, the miracle baby, emerges onto the national scene from the desert proclaiming his uncompromising message.

Day 58
Jesus Hits the Headlines

Back to Eternity

While Matthew and Luke go back to the birth of Jesus, John in his gospel goes back to eternity. Jesus is called "the Word" who was with God in the beginning and who played an essential role in creation. The first 18 verses of John's gospel sum up the mind–blowing message, that *"The Word became flesh and made his dwelling among us." (John 1:14)*.

> Read John 1:1–18

John the Baptist

The John referred to in the passage you've just read is John the Baptist whose birth we read about yesterday in Luke 1. While Jesus was still an unknown carpenter, he burst onto the scene in Israel by preaching a message of repentance and baptising those who came to him as a sign that they were turning away from their sins. John, the gospel writer, is thought to have been one of the disciples referred to in verse 35 who was pointed towards Jesus by John the Baptist.

> Read John 1:19–51

The importance of John the Baptist in preparing the way for the coming of Jesus cannot be overstated. He was sent by God in fulfilment of the prophecy through Malachi over four hundred years earlier to prepare people for Jesus' message. As the angel Gabriel said to his father Zechariah: *"Many of the people of Israel will he bring back to the Lord their God. And he will go on before the Lord, in the spirit and power of Elijah, to turn the hearts of the fathers to their children and the disobedient to the wisdom of the righteous – to make ready a people prepared for the Lord." (Luke 1:16–17)*. When he started preaching and baptising by the river Jordan Matthew tells us that, *"People went out to him from Jerusalem and all Judea and the whole region of the Jordan" (Matthew 3:5)*, while Mark says that *"The whole Judean countryside and <u>all the people of Jerusalem</u> went out to him." (Mark 1:5)*. Luke tells us that tax collectors and soldiers were among the crowds asking what they should do in response to John's message. We are not told how many he baptised but it is clear that the number ran into thousands if not tens of thousands. He had his own disciples who followed him including Andrew and probably John who later became Jesus' disciples.

John the Baptist's message to the people was for them to turn from their sins. He baptised them as a sign of their forgiveness and gave them instructions on how to live rightly before God. The importance of his preaching is explained in a little comment that Luke inserts after describing what Jesus said about John: *"All the people, even the tax collectors, when they heard Jesus' words, acknowledged that God's way was right,"* – why? – *"because they had been baptised by John. But the Pharisees and experts in the law rejected God's purpose for themselves,"* – why? – *"because they had not been baptised by John."* (Luke 7:29–30). What Luke is saying is that the way in which the people responded to Jesus was *directly related* to the way in which they responded to John! The Pharisees hardened their hearts to John's words and so were even less prepared to respond to Jesus. The people had listened to John, turned from their sins and were ready to hear more about the grace of God from Jesus. John's preparation was vital to Jesus' "success" in preaching to the crowds.

Later in the New Testament we discover that John's impact went far beyond his own country and time. At the beginning of Acts 19 Paul, on his third missionary journey, visited Ephesus and met twelve men who are described as "disciples" but seem to have a limited understanding of what Jesus has done for them. This is because they have received John's baptism and are not aware of Jesus' teaching. Paul baptises them in the name of Jesus and they receive the Holy Spirit. Given that this event took place some 25–30 years after John was baptising in the Jordan and over 500 miles away we can see that John's message had a huge impact across the Roman world.

Great Popularity

Mark starts his gospel with the dramatic arrival of John the Baptist on the Jewish scene and then, after a short account of Jesus' baptism and his temptations in the desert, plunges headlong into an account of Jesus' early ministry – his teaching in the synagogues, the call of the first disciples, the driving out of evil spirits and many healings. Following on from John's preaching the arrival of Jesus has such a huge impact on the people of Galilee and his popularity grows so

Day 58 – Jesus Hits the Headlines

quickly that by the end of Mark 1 he is unable to enter towns freely because of the crowds. Mark moves along at an incredible pace – it is a bit like a fast roller coaster ride so please make sure you have your seat belt securely fastened before you start reading this!

Read Mark 1

Jesus' popularity did not go unnoticed by the religious leaders of his day and from early on Mark records the Pharisees' opposition to Jesus – for forgiving sins and for eating corn on the Sabbath. Then in Mark 3 Jesus heals on the Sabbath and the Pharisees, who are waiting for an opportunity to catch him out, start plotting with the Herodians to kill Jesus. The Pharisees were angry at Jesus' claims and at the way he flouted their regulations. The Herodians were a political pro–Roman group who feared civil unrest. Jesus is angry at their silent stubbornness. These leaders, who should have recognised their Messiah, were so blinded by their petty regulations that they would rather see a man stay maimed than see him healed on the Sabbath!

But despite the opposition from their leaders the people were eager to see this man that everyone was talking about, receive healing and hear his teaching. They flocked to the countryside in hot pursuit. Jesus had hit the headlines.

Read Mark 2:1–3:12

Day 59
Apostles, Parables and Miracles

Jesus' Closest Friends

As Jesus' popularity grew so he gathered together a band of disciples who followed him around the Galilean countryside. Because they were with him more than the folk who just heard him in their own towns, these disciples learnt more from Jesus than others and he equipped them to do the works that he did. In Luke 10 we read that Jesus sent out seventy–two in pairs to go and heal people and preach the gospel. But Matthew, Mark and Luke also record that Jesus chose twelve of these followers in particular. Note how Mark describes their purpose:

> *Read Mark 3:13–19*

These twelve men were called apostles, from a Greek word meaning messenger or "one who is sent", and the primary reason they were chosen was *to be with Jesus*. Later he sent them out to preach and drive out demons, like the seventy–two. It is not easy for us to understand the fact that Jesus was fully God and yet fully human. Because Jesus was God we recoil from the idea that he had some friends who were closer than others as we know that God loves all of us equally. But when Jesus was in human form he was restricted by time and space in the same way we are so he, like us, had people he spent more time with than others – his close friends. This doesn't mean that he liked them any more than the others – from Luke we learn that he spent the night in prayer before choosing them so the choice was God's not his – but it does mean that he spent a lot more time with them, explained his teaching to them in special ways and equipped them to spread the gospel effectively. In the way Jesus operated we see a principle for us in sharing what we know of God: most of us will never have the opportunity to preach to large crowds but we can befriend people and pass on what God has taught us to those closest to us.

The twelve apostles are listed in Matthew, Mark and Luke as well as the first chapter of Acts (omitting Judas Iscariot). In each the order is slightly different but they seem to fall naturally into three groups of four which make them easier to remember.

Day 59 – Apostles, Parables and Miracles

The Inner Four

A lot is written about the first four, Peter, Andrew, James and John, two pairs of brothers who were called to follow Jesus when they were fishermen as we saw in Mark 1 yesterday. Jesus often took just three of these, Peter, James and John with him into situations, see for example the raising of Jairus's daughter (Mark 6:37), the Transfiguration (Matthew 17:1), and when Jesus prayed before his arrest in the garden of Gethsemane (Matthew 26:37).

Simon Peter was a fisherman brought to Jesus by his brother Andrew. Never short of something to say he is often quoted in the gospels and became the leader of the twelve. He is the leading character in the first twelve chapters of Acts and wrote the letters 1 and 2 Peter. It is thought that he was also a major influence in the writing of Mark's gospel.

Andrew was Peter's brother and from John 1:35–42 we know that he was a disciple of John the Baptist before following Jesus. After he brought Peter to Jesus not much is written about him as he is overshadowed by his brother. He is included in a private meeting with Jesus and the other three in Mark 13:3.

James the son of Zebedee is always referred to along with his brother John and nearly always listed first. They had a pushy mother (see Matthew 20:20) and a hot temper (see Luke 9:54) which earned them the nickname "Sons of Thunder" from Jesus! He was the first of the twelve apostles to die for his faith when he was killed by Herod (see Acts 12:2). (The James who is referred to from Acts 12:17 onwards is one of Jesus' brothers who led the Jerusalem church.)

John, the brother of James, is rarely referred to apart from his brother in Matthew, Mark and Luke. John wrote the fourth gospel and in that he never refers to himself by name but always as the "disciple" (see for example John 18:15–16) or "the disciple whom Jesus loved" (see for example John 13:23 and 20:2). Some see this phrase as expressing John's wonder that Jesus loved him, others see it as showing that John was Jesus' closest friend. This second explanation seems likely as, when Jesus was on the cross, he committed the care of his mother Mary to John who looked after her in his home (see John 19:26–27). He is closely associated with Peter in Acts 3–4 and was the last of the twelve apostles to die. In addition to his gospel John wrote three letters – 1, 2 and 3 John – and Revelation in his old age.

The Middle Four

We have very limited information about the middle four apostles with only one or a few incidents about each being recorded in the gospels. We are particularly indebted to John who provides the only information about three of them. Just to confuse us two have alternative names!

Philip is only mentioned in the lists in Matthew, Mark and Luke. He is mentioned in four stories in John (1:43–48, 6:5–7, 12:21–22, 14:8–9), in two of which he is bringing people to Jesus. (The Philip in Acts 8 is a different man.)

Bartholomew (or ***Nathanael***) is only mentioned in the lists in Matthew, Mark and Luke. John refers to him as Nathanael and tells us how he came to Jesus through his friend Philip in John 1:45–51.

Matthew (or ***Levi***) was a tax collector and his call to follow Jesus is recorded in Matthew 9, Mark 2 and Luke 5. Mark and Luke call him Levi; he is not mentioned in John. Matthew was the author of the first gospel.

Thomas is only mentioned in the lists in Matthew, Mark and Luke. John mentions him in four places (11:16, 14:5, 20:24–29, 21:2), most famously for doubting Jesus' resurrection although he did subsequently demonstrate such great faith in his Lord that John puts him second only to Peter in the list of apostles in John 21. His nickname was Didymus, the Greek word for "twin" (Thomas comes from the Hebrew word for twin).

The Last Four

The last four apostles include three about whom we know almost nothing and Judas Iscariot, the man who betrayed Jesus.

James son of Alphaeus is only mentioned in the lists in Matthew, Mark and Luke.

Thaddaeus or ***Judas son of James*** is called Thaddaeus in the lists in Matthew and Mark and Judas in the list in Luke. The only other reference to him is to a question he asked at the Last Supper in John 14:22 when he is called *"Judas (not Judas Iscariot)"*.

Simon the Zealot is also only mentioned in the lists in Matthew, Mark and Luke. Presumably Simon was an ex–member of the Zealots, a terrorist group who refused to pay taxes to the Romans or speak Greek.

Judas Iscariot is *always* referred to as the betrayer or traitor when he is mentioned in the gospels apart from during the account of his betrayal. "Iscariot" probably refers to the town he came from in Judea. Apart from his betrayal of Jesus the only other thing we know about Judas is that he was entrusted with looking after the money for Jesus and the disciples but he was a thief (John 12:4–6). His betrayal of Jesus is described in all four gospels. Matthew tells us that afterwards Judas was seized with remorse and, after returning the money he was given to the priests, he went and hanged himself (see Matthew 27:3–10). The priests who had been happy to pay Judas to betray Jesus were too pious to accept the "blood money" back into the temple treasury so bought a field and Luke tells us that Judas' body was thrown there in Acts 1:18.

Parables

When Jesus taught the people he told stories called parables. The word "parable" comes from a Greek word meaning "a placing beside" as they are comparisons or illustrations. Parables are similar to the Proverbs found in the Old Testament and some of the songs or poetry written by some of prophets. Jesus told these stories from nature and ordinary life to illustrate spiritual truths. There are forty parables recorded in the synoptic gospels with some recorded in more than one gospel. Matthew contains 23, Mark 9 and Luke 28. John contains none. Mark 4 contains four parables.

Read Mark 4:1–34

As Mark says in the last verse you just read, Jesus did not teach any crowd without using parables. Why did he use parables? Was it to make it easier for people to understand his teaching or to make it harder? After Jesus told the parable of the sower and the seed, the twelve asked for an explanation. Even Jesus' closest followers did not see the meaning in the stories he told! Jesus quoted from Isaiah's calling where the prophet was told to speak God's words to the people but warned in advance that they would not understand what he told them. For many people, far from making things clear, the parables obscured the truth and exposed their hard–heartedness. For others, the stories stimulated their interest and for those who searched for meaning and were given insight by God these parables revealed truth in a memorable way.

Three of the most well known parables – the lost sheep, the lost silver and the lost (or prodigal) son – are in Luke 15. The first two illustrate the joy there is in heaven at the repentance of one sinner; the last presents the love of God the Father – and the resentment of the Pharisees.

> Read Luke 15

Miracles

Although the people were astonished at his teaching it was Jesus' healings and miracles that demonstrated that he was from God. At this stage in his ministry even his closest disciples did not realise who Jesus was. Note their reaction to his extraordinary miracles at the end of Mark 4 and 5.

> Read Mark 4:35–5:43

There can be no greater miracles than calming a storm and raising someone from the dead. After his initial widespread popularity Jesus is now gathering a close group of friends together to teach them about the power he has and to equip them to go and do the works he is doing.

Day 60
The Sermon on the Mount

Jesus' Topsy–Turvy Teaching

We have seen the action in Mark. Now we are going to see a complete contrast in Matthew. Matthew gives us some summaries of Jesus' teaching and the best known of these is "the Sermon on the Mount" in Matthew 5–7. It may have been one sermon that Jesus preached at one time or it may be a compilation of his teaching. Luke records some similar teaching in "the Sermon on the Plain" in Luke 6:17–49 as well as in other places.

Jesus starts with a series of statements about people who are "blessed". These are sometimes known as the "Beatitudes" from the Latin word for blessed. To be "blessed" in the Bible does not just mean to be happy in the sense of a passing emotional state but to be those who are sharing in God's goodness. People who only see things from man's perspective cannot see how being meek will lead to inheriting the earth. Jokes such as "Blessed are the meek, for they will inherit the earth – if that's all right with the rest of you" demonstrate a lack of understanding about God's ways of working as well as about what being meek means. Mary understood the topsy–turvy ways of the Lord when she sang *"He has brought down rulers from their thrones but has lifted up the humble. He has filled the hungry with good things but has sent the rich away empty." (Luke 1:52–53)*. The statements Jesus makes at the beginning of his sermon help us to see things from God's perspective which encourages us to take note of the instructions to change our behaviour to be more like Jesus. Even those who are persecuted are told to *"Rejoice and be glad"* as they focus on the future reward they will receive from God rather than their immediate circumstances.

Jesus then takes the Law of Moses to new heights. The law condemns murder; Jesus condemns anger. The law prohibits adultery; but Jesus warns against lust. His teaching is in contrast to that of the Pharisees who stressed outward cleanness. There can be no law against anger or lust as they cannot be judged externally. Jesus stresses inner purity. However, while Jesus upholds the Law of Moses he also challenges the "extras" that the Pharisees have added. In Matthew 5:43–44 it sounds as if Jesus is contradicting the law when he says *"You have heard that it was said, 'Love your neighbour and hate your enemy.' But I tell you: Love your enemies and pray for those who persecute you ..."*, but in fact, while *"Love your neighbour"* comes from Leviticus 19:18, *"hate your enemy"* is not in the Law at all. It is a later addition which Jesus overturns.

> **Read Matthew 5**

Prayer and Rewards in Heaven

Jesus continues the theme that what is in your heart is more important than outward show. He talks about giving in secret, praying in secret and hiding the fact that you are fasting. This is in contrast to the 'hypocrites' who do these things as publicly as possible in order to win praise from men. Jesus says that they receive their reward on earth whereas we should look to store up treasures in heaven. Note also that Jesus says "when you give", "when you pray" and "when you fast" – he assumes that his followers will do these things regularly.

Jesus' teaching on prayer includes a prayer which appears in a similar form in Luke 11 where Jesus taught it to his disciples in response to the request *"Lord, teach us to pray." (Luke 11:1)*. This prayer, known as "The Lord's Prayer", is regularly prayed in churches throughout the world today but there is a danger that when we simply say it as part of a congregation we can rush through it without appreciating its meaning. In the context in Matthew 6 it is intended to be used for private, personal prayer and there is great value in praying through it line by line and using our own words to expand on each phrase. So, start your time in prayer thinking about God being your Father, that intimate, close relationship, and then move on to think about what it means for him to be in heaven, majestic and surrounded by unapproachable light, his name is so holy that no-one could dare to come close to him without having their sins dealt with by Jesus. It is only after we get our perspective on God right that we can bring our requests to him.

Chapter 6 ends with very practical advice about not worrying. This is not just issued as a command but Jesus gives reasons in a style similar to that found in the early chapters of Proverbs.

> **Read Matthew 6**

Day 60 – The Sermon on the Mount

Absurd Pictures and the Importance of Fundamentals

Jesus' teaching is never boring. We looked yesterday at some of his stories, or parables, that he used to make a point. The Sermon on the Mount is full of pictures, some of which are deliberately absurd. There is a man walking around with a plank of wood in his eye, a father giving his son a live snake to eat, and wolves dressing up as sheep – these sound more like scenes from children's cartoons than illustrations from one of the most sublime sections of teaching in the Bible! But the people who heard his teaching on the mountainside didn't forget the pictures or the message behind them

Jesus finishes with another absurd picture – of a man building his house on sand. This story, usually called the parable of the wise and foolish builders, emphasizes the paramount importance of getting the fundamentals right in your life. The Sermon on the Mount is not advanced teaching for people who have been Christians for years, it is fundamental teaching for beginners and old–timers alike on how we should conduct our lives on a day to day basis. As Allan Johnson said when he was asked if he was a fundamentalist, "It is better to be fundamentally right than fundamentally wrong!"[9] We need to apply Jesus' teaching in the Sermon on the Mount to our lives in order to have strong foundations.

Read Matthew 7

---

[9] Allan Johnson is the Lead Elder of Cowfold Christian Fellowship. This response was made to a question in a youth group meeting and neatly avoided answering the direct question as either a "Yes" or "No" could easily have been misinterpreted!

Day 61
Miracles and Revelation

Grief and Miracles

We have already seen how John the Baptist made a huge impact on the people of Israel with his lifestyle, his preaching and his baptising. John had a clear message to proclaim – *"Repent for the kingdom of heaven is near" (Matthew 3:2)* – and he was ready to apply that to the individual circumstance of anyone who would listen to him, including tax collectors and soldiers. John was never afraid of upsetting his audience with his message and at some point he was faced with the ruler of the area, the ruthless Herod Antipas. John's message to him was simple and totally politically incorrect! Herod had persuaded Herodias, his brother's wife, to leave her husband and marry him instead and John told him quite clearly that this was "unlawful". While it may have been acceptable in the eyes of Rome it was a clear violation of God's law. The shabby way in which this led to John's death is recorded in Matthew and Mark.

Jesus knew that he, like John, would die soon but hearing of John's death must have brought home to him what he was on earth to do. With Mary and Elizabeth being related it is quite probable that Jesus and John knew each other as children and would have talked about their understanding of God and their missions as they grew up. Now John was dead, and Jesus would have felt more isolated as he faced his own death.

The way in which Jesus reacts to the news of John's death shows us that he experienced the depth of human emotions. He needs time alone in order to deal with his grief at John's death but we see that he is, once again, faced with a large crowd. His compassion leads him to heal and teach them as well as providing food for them. The feeding of the five thousand is the only miracle recorded in all four gospels. In John's account he notes that Jesus withdrew to a mountain to avoid the people making him king by force. There were a number of occasions when Jesus had to leave Galilee in order to escape the crowds.

> *Read Matthew 14*

The miracle of the feeding of the five thousand is followed by one of

Day 61 – Miracles and Revelation

the most remarkable miracles that Jesus ever performed. The expression "he walks on water" is sometimes used today to indicate that someone is perfect, or at least thinks they are! But the description of this event indicates that this was not Jesus demonstrating his perfection but his faith. When Peter started sinking Jesus didn't tell him to be good but to have more faith.

The Pharisees and others often asked Jesus for a "miraculous sign" as proof that he was from God but, as we will see later at the beginning of Matthew 16, Jesus condemned them for asking and refused to give them any sign other than "the sign of Jonah", which Matthew explained earlier was that Jesus would be raised from the dead after three days in the earth (see Matthew 12:40). This was because Jesus knew that even then they would not believe. It was only to his closest disciples who were already committed to him that Jesus was prepared to give a sign in order to strengthen their faith.

Challenging Traditions

As a further reminder of Jesus' mission there are more and more references to the Pharisees and their open challenges to Jesus and his disciples. In Matthew 15 we read how the Pharisees challenged Jesus over the way his disciples broke the "traditions of the elders". These traditions, which started during the Babylonian exile, were extensions of the Law of Moses laid down in meticulous detail, and designed to make people holy. The Pharisees were careful to follow these and quick to point out when others did not. Jesus knows about their ways and points out that their "traditions" break God's commands. Not content with simply pointing out their faulty logic he also denounces them as hypocrites, unclean and blind guides! Later in Matthew there is a complete chapter (23) recording the most vehement of Jesus' attacks on the Pharisees. The disciples grew up in the Jewish culture honouring the Pharisees and teachers of the law – as children they would have learnt the scriptures at their feet – so they are seriously worried by what Jesus said to the Pharisees. Note the alarm in the disciples voices in Matthew 15:12 when they say to Jesus *"Do you know that the Pharisees were offended when they heard this?"* Clearly Jesus cannot have missed the fact that his words were offensive. What bothered the disciples was that he did not seem to care!

Although Jesus' teaching in this passage about "cleanness" coming from within rather than from external rituals seems obvious to us, it was radical teaching to the ears of his disciples. They find it very hard to break with the traditions they have been brought up with and Peter still follows them much later on. The Lord has to challenge him on this in Acts 10 in order to prepare him to preach to the Gentiles (non–Jews) and later still Paul tells him off for going back to following these traditions and forcing Gentile Christians to follow them too (see Galatians 2:11–14). Jesus continually warns them about the teaching of the Pharisees as we see in both Matthew 15 and 16.

> **Read Matthew 15**

We do not know how long it was between the feeding of the five thousand and the feeding of the four thousand but both Mark and Matthew put them fairly close together and both record the way in which Jesus presented the problem of feeding the people to his disciples. In this second incident the disciples, once again, look at the problem from a completely human perspective. They do not appear to have any faith for a repeat of the earlier miracle. It is easy for us to wonder at their lack of faith but how often do we look at things from a human perspective despite what the Lord has done in our lives in the past?

The other interesting thing to note about the feeding of the four thousand is that the account is very similar to that of the feeding of the five thousand apart from the numbers of people, loaves, fishes and baskets. If this was only recorded in Matthew and the feeding of the five thousand only in, say, Luke then people might conclude that one of them had got the numbers wrong. But because both are recorded in Matthew and in Mark (and Jesus refers to both in Matthew 16:9–10) it is clear that these were two separate incidents. There are a number of other stories in the gospels which appear similar to each other but differ in details and some people are quick to point these out as examples of errors in the gospel accounts. The two accounts of feeding thousands demonstrate that other similar stories in different gospels may simply be records of different incidents.

Revelation

In Matthew 16 Jesus asks the disciples who people think he is. There are a number of views, but all realise that he is a prophet from God. Then Jesus asks them who they think he is. They have already acknowledged him as the Son of God after he walked on the water but Peter, always the impetuous one, is the first to blurt out the truth: he is the Messiah, the Christ, the Son of the living God. Jesus tells his

Day 61 – Miracles and Revelation

disciples not to tell people who he is as he knows that the Jews expect a warrior Messiah who will throw off Roman rule. He wants people to know him through revelation from God.

As soon as the disciples realise who Jesus is he starts to explain to them that he must die and this becomes the focus of the rest of his time on earth. It is all in the scriptures, in passages such as Isaiah 53 and Psalm 22, but the disciples do not understand. They have the popular view of a warrior Messiah, at least in part. The three closest disciples are then privileged to see Jesus as he is in heaven ("transfigured" means changed in form or appearance) talking with Moses, the man who gave Israel the law, and Elijah, the greatest of the prophets. Luke tells us that Jesus discussed his coming death with them, his death that would fulfil the Law and the Prophets. All this talk of coming death alarms the disciples and as he continues to teach them about it they are filled with grief.

Read Matthew 16:1–17:23

Day 62
Compassion and Confrontation

Passing Conversations

John's gospel is very different in its style from the other three gospels and, in many ways, is written at a deeper level. It does not include any parables but does record a number of conversations that Jesus had as well as long talks that he gave to his followers and some prayers he prayed.

I recently had the privilege of hearing David Bracewell[10] speak about John and he compared it to detective novels that operate on different levels. You can just read them and enjoy the narrative or you can spend time looking for the deeper meaning by studying the clues. John's gospel also works on two levels. You can read it and enjoy the narrative, as we shall for the next two days, or you can spend time studying the depth of meaning in the little passing comments that John puts in throughout his narrative. One of the early church fathers commented on John's gospel that "It is shallow enough for a child to play in, but deep enough for an elephant to drown in." Two conversations in John 3 and 4 illustrate the point perfectly. Both can be read as simple narrative but both contain profound statements from Jesus which have great significance for us all.

Jesus was willing to speak to people from all levels of society and dealt with each person as an individual and the conversations that John records give us an insight into Jesus' compassion and love for people. Neither of the encounters that we are going to read was planned by Jesus, and yet in both he took the time to explain deep truths at the same time as challenging them at a personal level. In John 3 Jesus is approached by Nicodemus, a leading Pharisee. Jesus had reason to be on his guard against such a man, as we saw yesterday, but Jesus engages him in a conversation which introduces the concept of being "born again" as well as including probably the most famous verse in the Bible – John 3:16.

> *Read John 3:1–21*

---

[10] David Bracewell is the Rector of St Saviour's church in Guildford.

Day 62 – Compassion and Confrontation 351

The other conversation is with someone at the opposite end of the social spectrum from Nicodemus. One of the Pharisees' main complaints about Jesus was that he mixed with the outcasts of society – 'sinners' and tax collectors – even being prepared to eat with them and in John 4 we find Jesus initiating a conversation that would have confirmed the Pharisees worst fears about him. Jesus speaks to a woman, which is something that the Jewish teachers would not consider worth doing (note the disciples' surprise in verse 27). She is also a Samaritan, and there is great hostility between the Jews and the Samaritans such that normally they would not associate with one another (see verse 9). But on top of all that, she has a background which makes her the sort of woman that the Pharisees would definitely not expect any self respecting individual to associate with – and especially not a teacher! In his conversation with the Samaritan woman Jesus shows her great regard simply through being prepared to speak to her and answer her questions, but he goes much further and demonstrates his deep compassion in the gentle way in which he brought truth into her life. None of us are beyond the compassion of Jesus.

Read John 4:4–42

Direct Conflict

Yesterday we saw how the opposition to Jesus increased. John also records some of the head-on confrontations between Jesus and the authorities. In John 7 Jesus goes to the feast of Tabernacles in Jerusalem. He is away from Galilee where the large crowds follow him and goes secretly to avoid publicity. But then in the middle of the feast he starts teaching in the temple courts and soon attracts capacity crowds. John gives a very detailed account of people's reactions to him in this chapter. The Pharisees are plotting to kill him and send the temple guards to arrest him but they are so amazed at his teaching that they return empty handed. Many people believe in him as they cannot see how the Christ could be any better than this but others are confused as Jesus is from Galilee and they know that the Christ must come from Bethlehem. See how vividly John records the tensions between Jesus and these different groups as you read this chapter.

Read John 7

It is interesting to note that, once again, one of Jesus' most important statements is made in the middle of this volatile situation. He chooses a moment of great significance and great tension to stand up and make the greatest offer available to mankind: *"If anyone is thirsty, let him come to me and drink. Whoever believes in me, as the Scripture has said, streams of living water will flow from within him." (John 7:37–38)*. The prophecies relating to the coming of the Spirit were now being fulfilled and yet those who knew these prophecies inside out failed to recognise it.

A Trap

In the next chapter the teachers of the law and the Pharisees try to trap Jesus by bringing him a woman caught in the act of adultery. They want to stone her as the law of Moses required but they cannot carry out this punishment without the permission from the Romans. They were quite happy to let the man escape and just humiliate the woman as their reason for bringing her to Jesus was simply to provide an opportunity to present him with an impossible choice. If he upheld the law of Moses then he would be in conflict with the Romans; if he didn't he would be seen to undermine God's law. The way in which Jesus responds totally disarms them. He upholds the law but exposes their total hypocrisy. Note how he then shows compassion for the woman without excusing her sin.

> Read John 8:1–11

Day 63
The Scene is Set

The Man Born Blind

In John 8 Jesus has a verbal confrontation with the Pharisees that ends with him almost being stoned. Then in chapter 9 he heads into further conflict with the authorities by once again healing on the Sabbath.

The account of the healing of the man who was blind from birth is brilliantly written and brings out the characters so clearly that you can imagine being there and seeing it all happen: the Pharisees searching for any possible alternative explanation for this miracle in order to avoid facing up to the truth; the parents of the man, terrified at the hostile questioning of their leaders but still sharp enough to avoid saying the wrong thing; and the wonderful sarcasm of the man who eventually loses patience with the Pharisees and points out to them the inescapable logic that Jesus is from God. It is a highly entertaining story! But the cruel way in which the Pharisees treat the blind beggar is in sharp contrast to the compassion that Jesus shows him and demonstrates that it is them who are blind to what God is doing.

> Read John 9

Jesus' Friends

In John's account of Jesus' life we see the variety of ways in which people responded to Jesus. There were always crowds following him. They loved his teaching and miracles. Some believed that he was the Christ but many were not sure. They knew he was a great prophet but could not be sure that he was the promised Messiah. The Pharisees, the teachers of the law and the Jerusalem religious establishment – often referred to as "the Jews" in John – did not believe that Jesus was the Christ because his teaching ran counter to their dogmatic traditions and they opposed Jesus all along the way.

But in addition to the nameless crowds and the Pharisees we also learn that Jesus had some close friends and they played a significant role in the weeks leading up to his death. When Jesus went to Jerusalem he and his disciples stayed in the house of a woman called Martha who had a sister called Mary and a brother called Lazarus. They lived in

Bethany, a town two miles east of Jerusalem and their house provided a haven of peace for Jesus and his disciples when they were in that area. Luke records a well known incident about Mary and Martha.

> **Read Luke 10:38–42**

C J Mahaney[11] in his preaching has commented that food was one of the disciples' top preoccupations (note how Jesus was by himself at the well in Samaria when he spoke to the woman in John 4 as it took all twelve of them to go and buy food!) and the arrival of at least thirteen hungry men in her house would have provided much for Martha to be distracted about. This is a challenge to us to make spending time with Jesus a top priority however busy we are. The only other incidents we know about this family are in John 11 and 12.

One Man Must Die for the People

Jesus has been telling his disciples for some time that he must die in Jerusalem and the time for this to be fulfilled is now fast approaching. With tensions high between him, the crowds and the religious leaders, events are unexpectedly brought to a head by the death of Lazarus. All the main characters involved in the week leading to Jesus' death are involved in this story. As you read it note Martha's faith and the way in which Jesus shows his humanity through his grief at death, even though he knew what was about to happen.

> **Read John 11:1–12:11**

The Jews believed that the spirit stayed close to the body for three days so when Jesus brought Lazarus back from death after four days it had a huge impact on all those involved with Jesus. Many of the crowds put their faith in him while others, perhaps unsure what to think, went to the Pharisees to get their views (see 11:45–46). For the first time the Pharisees called a meeting of the Sanhedrin to discuss the "Jesus issue". They need to get the support of the whole religious establishment behind them and they succeed. Caiaphas, the high priest, wants one man to die rather than face the danger of a public uprising and the inevitable Roman backlash. If Jesus attracts a large crowd who decide that it is time to throw off Roman rule then the consequences for the Jews are unthinkable. There is no doubt that the Romans will act to

---

[11] A typical insight from CJ Mahaney – see footnote on page 91

Day 63 – The Scene is Set

defend their power and no doubt that they would win any confrontation. Many Jews would die. At the meeting an official plan to kill Jesus is agreed. Later this plot is extended to include Lazarus as he is becoming an attraction in his own right and causing many to believe in Jesus through his own story.

We are not told of the reaction of the disciples to Lazarus being raised from the dead but it seems that Mary is the only one who understands that Jesus will die soon and she anoints him for burial on the day before Jesus enters Jerusalem on the start of the greatest week in history.

Jesus Enters Jerusalem

With the whole of Jerusalem in turmoil and the people believing that Jesus was about to proclaim himself king (see Luke 19:11), Jesus rode into Jerusalem on a young donkey. We will return to Luke for this event, which is sometimes known as "Palm Sunday".

> **Read Luke 19:28–48**

This act is a direct fulfilment of Zechariah's prophecy:

"Rejoice greatly, O Daughter of Zion!
Shout, Daughter of Jerusalem!
See, your king comes to you,
righteous and having salvation,
gentle and riding on a donkey,
on a colt, the foal of a donkey." (Zechariah 9:9).

The people are excited. They know this verse and, what is more, many of them will be familiar with the next:

"I will take away the chariots from Ephraim
and the war-horses from Jerusalem,
and the battle bow will be broken.
He will proclaim peace to the nations.
His rule will extend from sea to sea
and from the River to the ends of the earth." (Zechariah 9:10).

This is what the people were waiting for. The king had come to Jerusalem and was about to drive out the Romans and establish his kingdom. The people could not see the gaps of time that lay between the prophecies but Jesus knew that it was not yet time to fulfil the second prophecy and to throw out the Romans. In fact it would be the

Jews, who rejected their Messiah, who would be driven from the city in AD 70 when the Romans finally lost patience with their rebellions. Jesus wept as he foresaw the awful destruction of the city and its inhabitants.

Day 64
Jesus' Last Week on Earth

Verbal Challenges

Despite the careful plotting of the religious leaders, Jesus followed up his dramatic entry into the city by openly teaching in the temple courtyard. The people love his teaching and the crowds form a protection against the chief priests who wish to kill him. Frustrated in their attempts to arrest Jesus they decide to catch him out with some clever questions.

They start with a direct attack. Who gives him his authority? Jesus turns the tables on them with a question about John the Baptist's authority. They are too hard hearted to admit that he was from God and yet too scared to deny it in front of the crowd. Jesus follows up with a parable which sums up the Jewish response to God's prophets and, now, to God's own son.

Then the chief priests retreat and send other men to Jesus who *"pretended to be honest."* These brave but foolish men stand before the all powerful Son of God and try to trick him by asking him a question about taxes! His answer astonished them and left them silent. The Sadducees follow up with a very contrived question which Jesus deals with so skilfully and with such authority that no one dares to question him again. This is one of the most dramatic dialogues in the whole of the Bible.

> **Read Luke 20**

Signs of the End Times

All three of the synoptic gospels record the teaching Jesus gave to his disciples about the end times. The disciples are having a discussion about the beauty of the temple building when Jesus tells them that it will be completely destroyed. This leads into him talking about the destruction of Jerusalem, which took place within 40 years in AD 70, and his return to earth in power and glory which is yet to be fulfilled. Note how this future prophecy, just like many Old Testament prophecies, interweaves events which will take place at least two thousand years apart: some of it relates to the destruction of Jerusalem in AD 70, some relates to Jesus' return which is yet to come and some probably relates to both.

> Read Luke 21

The Last Supper and Jesus' Arrest

At the end of the Passover week Jesus celebrated the Passover. The meal looks back to the liberation from Egypt and involved the death of a sacrificial lamb. Jesus indicated during the meal that he is about to be the new Passover lamb and took the symbols of the Passover – the bread and wine – and turned them into the symbols of the New Covenant saying "do this in remembrance of me". Most Christian churches today eat bread and drink wine together to remember Jesus in a celebration which is called various things including, "the Lord's Supper", "communion", "breaking of bread" or "the Eucharist" (meaning "thanksgiving"). Jesus looked forward to this meal with his disciples. He wanted to be with them as he faced death. However, not only is one of them a betrayer, but the rest return to their favourite subject, which of them is the greatest (see Luke 22:24). Despite being with Jesus for three years they are still insensitive to his feelings.

John, who records what Jesus said to his disciples that night at some length, tells us that before the meal Jesus washed the disciples' feet. This was the job of a servant but with no servant present none of the disciples were prepared to offer to do it. Jesus set an example in humility by being prepared to take on this dirty, menial job. As a contrast to their desire to be the greatest he calls on them to do the same for one another. Some have interpreted this literally and still wash one another's feet to this day; others see Jesus' example of service as applying more generally – we are to be prepared to offer menial service to one another in whatever way is appropriate in the situation.

Washing the disciples' feet meant that Jesus washed the feet of Judas Iscariot. Judas was one of the twelve apostles chosen by Jesus and, like the others, he went out preaching the good news, healing people and casting out demons. Despite this, Judas failed to comprehend the spiritual values that Jesus taught. He was the one who was quick to condemn Mary's actions in anointing Jesus with perfume and he is disappointed that Jesus does not fulfil his view of what the Messiah should be. This disappointment is used by Satan himself who is eager to see the Son of God killed, not understanding the devastating consequences for his own future. It is ironic that the chief priests need a betrayer not because Jesus is hard to find but because they must find him alone in order not to be mobbed by the crowds who hang on his every word.

> Read Luke 22:1–62

Peter's Betrayal and his Lesson in Forgiveness

All four gospels record Peter's betrayal of Jesus. Peter, the impetuous one who is the first to speak up in front of the other disciples and pledge his support for his beloved master and the one prepared to follow Jesus after his arrest, discovers that he is not even strong enough to speak out his allegiance to Jesus to a servant girl. With Jesus now going to trial and then to his death Peter is left devastated that he has let down the man he has loved so dearly for three years. He did not understand that Jesus would rise from the dead and faces the prospect of never being able to put right the wrong he has done to Jesus.

Peter went through three days of tormenting himself for what he had done but once the news came that Jesus had risen from the dead Peter was still eager to see his master. But would Jesus be prepared to see him? We know from Luke 24:34 and 1 Corinthians 15:5 that Jesus was not only prepared to see him but that he appeared to Peter before he appeared to all the disciples. We are not told what took place in that one to one meeting but we know that Jesus forgave Peter and he was able to lead the disciples after Jesus returned to heaven. But Peter learned some valuable lessons through this experience. He was the one who asked Jesus *"Lord, how many times shall I forgive my brother when he sins against me? Up to seven times?" (Matthew 18:21)*, but in his letter many years later he writes *"Above all, love each other deeply, because love covers over a multitude of sins." (1 Peter 4:8)*. Peter learned the lesson of forgiveness. If he could be forgiven for betraying his Lord then what right did he have to hold anything against someone else?

Day 65
Jesus' Death and Resurrection

A Travesty of Justice

All four gospels record Jesus' arrest, trial, crucifixion and burial. It is the central event in the life of Jesus and the reason he came to earth. In fact it is the central event in the whole Bible. As we have seen, the Old Testament contains many prophecies relating to the death of God's son from Genesis 3:15 through the law, the Psalms and the prophets.

Jesus' trial was a travesty of justice. After being arrested in the garden called Gethsemane he was taken to the High Priest's house where the Sanhedrin was hurriedly assembled to try him. Matthew tells us that they looked for false evidence to use to sentence him to death but even though false witnesses came forward they could not make a story hang together. Without any just cause they then mocked him and beat him before bringing him before the whole Sanhedrin.

At this assembly the High Priest questions Jesus but Jesus refuses to answer him. Finally the High Priest asks him outright if he is the promised Messiah, the Son of God. Jesus answers very clearly that he is. This leaves his listeners with only two options: either he is the Son of God or he is guilty of blasphemy. If they accept his claim then their whole lives would be turned upside down. Despite all the miracles Jesus had performed and his incredible teaching they cannot see that he could be the Messiah so to them this is an act of blasphemy. Matthew and Mark tell us that the High Priest is so horrified by this claim that he tore his clothes. No witnesses are required any more. The punishment for blasphemy is very clear in the law: *"anyone who blasphemes the name of the LORD must be put to death."* (Leviticus 24:16).

This leaves the Jewish leaders with a problem. They cannot carry out a death sentence without Roman consent so they take Jesus to Pilate, the Roman governor. Pilate is clearly not interested in the case. He sees it as a matter of religious jealousy and is not impressed by their false accusations. Somewhere in among all their accusations Pilate picks up on the fact that Jesus is a Galilean and uses that as an excuse to send him to Herod. This is the man who had beheaded John the Baptist. He has had his opportunity to listen to the gospel and ignored the words of John so he gets absolutely nothing out of Jesus. Frustrated by this man who so clearly defies his authority he has him ridiculed by his soldiers – something that would have gone far beyond mere words – and sends him back to Pilate.

Pilate finds Jesus very alarming. For much of the time Jesus is silent and when he does answer, Pilate cannot understand his claims. John records a conversation between them about Jesus' claims and the nature of truth while Matthew tells us that Pilate's wife had a dream warning him to have nothing to do with Jesus. The blame for Jesus' death rests primarily with the Sanhedrin and the crowd who, whipped into a frenzy by the priests, willingly take the blame on themselves and their children as Pilate washes his hands of the case (see Matthew 27:24–25), but Pilate has the ultimate responsibility for signing the death warrant.

> Read Luke 22:63–23:25

A Cruel Death

Jesus is then crucified, the Roman punishment for serious crimes committed by slaves and other criminals who were not Roman citizens. None of the gospel writers go into great detail about crucifixion as it was well known to their contemporaries but we know from other sources that it was a barbaric and extremely painful death. Large iron nails were driven through the victim's wrists and ankles onto a rough wooden cross which was then stood upright. The victim then died slowly and in great pain, often over a period of some days, through a combination of blood loss and suffocation as the legs became too weak for the sufferer to push himself up to breathe. Most pictures of Jesus on the cross show him wearing a loincloth but victims of crucifixion would have been naked and so become objects of vulgar insults. Crucifixion was a disgrace and a humiliation as well as a lingering, painful death.

Matthew and Mark tell us that the chief priests were among the rulers who openly mocked Jesus and called on him to prove that he was the Messiah by coming down from the cross. Then they would believe him! John tells us that they protested to Pilate about the sign he put over Jesus' head but Pilate brushed their complaint aside.

> Read Luke 23:26–49

Each gospel's account records slightly different details and John tells us that Jesus cried *"It is finished" (John 19:30)* as he finally gave up his spirit. He had completed the work he came to do as his blood and broken body became the perfect sacrifice meeting the requirements of the Law of Moses and expressing the heart of God as written in the prophets. Matthew and Mark record that the curtain in the temple, which hid the inner part of the temple, the Most Holy Place, from human view, was split from top to bottom as God himself demonstrated to the horrified priests on duty that the way into his presence was now open.

Into the Grave

Jesus was then buried by Joseph of Arimathea, a member of the Sanhedrin who was probably absent from the meeting which condemned Jesus to death. John tells us that he was accompanied by Nicodemus who had come to talk to Jesus at night as we read in John 3.

> **Read Luke 23:50–56**

Jesus was hastily buried on the Friday before sunset when the Jewish Sabbath began. There was no time to give him a proper burial and the men and women who had followed Jesus went home to spend the Sabbath day resting. Less than a week earlier, on the previous Sunday, they had accompanied Jesus as he rode into Jerusalem surrounded by a joyful crowd singing his praises. Now they were celebrating the Sabbath with heavy hearts and weeping eyes, their hopes dashed.

The Resurrection – Jesus is Alive!

The women spent the Sabbath at rest and then the next night went to give Jesus a proper burial by anointing him with spices and perfumes. We will take up the account of what happened early on the Sunday morning in John's gospel as John was one of the first to see the empty tomb. The "other disciple" referred to from verse 2 is John.

> **Read John 20:1–18**

Despite all that Jesus had said, none of his friends and disciples expected him to rise from the dead. As we read the account of the resurrection we find that when Jesus appears to the disciples they are terrified, not thrilled! Jesus made a number of appearances after his resurrection. Some are mentioned in the gospels, and Paul provides a list in 1 Corinthians 15:3–8 where he gives an account of the

Day 65 – Jesus' Death and Resurrection

resurrection to ensure that Corinthian church are acquainted with the facts.

Before Jesus met with the other apostles, Jesus appeared to Peter, as we saw yesterday, and to two disciples not mentioned elsewhere in the gospels. Luke tells their story.

> Read Luke 24:13–35

It is interesting to note that in both Jesus' appearance to Mary and to these two disciples his new body is not instantly recognisable to his friends. The two friends heard an entire sermon from Jesus explaining the reasons why he had to suffer from the Old Testament (it is a shame we don't have the tape!) without realising it was him. He only became recognisable by the way he said or did certain things.

As we have just read, the two from Emmaus hurry back to Jerusalem to tell the apostles and while they are talking Jesus appears to them. Luke's account includes the little detail about Jesus asking for some food to prove to them that he is not a ghost.

> Read Luke 24:36–49

John tells us that Thomas was absent from this meeting and could not believe that Jesus had risen from the dead even though all ten of his fellow apostles insisted that *"We have seen the Lord!" (John 20:25)*. He tells them that he refuses to believe unless he sees and touches the marks of the nails in Jesus' hands. A week later Jesus appeared again and this time Thomas was there. Jesus showed him the wounds on his hands and side and Thomas believed.

Jesus appeared to his followers over a period of forty days. The apostles returned to Galilee and Jesus met them by the lakeside. He also spoke on the mountains of that region, at one time to more than five hundred people! When Paul wrote his account of the resurrection to the Corinthians it is clear that he has met many of these people as he records the fact that most are still alive at the time of his writing – over twenty years later – although some had died (see 1 Corinthians 15:6). It is possible that this was the occasion when Jesus gave his followers what has become known as "the Great Commission" which ends Matthew's gospel.

> Read Matthew 28:18–20

The Ascension

Jesus final appearance was to a number of his followers near Bethany. Mary, Martha and Lazarus may have been there. To indicate that they will not see him again he went up into heaven – an event known as "the Ascension".

> Read Luke 24:50–53

The gospels tell the story of the most wonderful man that ever lived. But what was the purpose of Jesus' life on earth? There are many prophecies relating to Jesus in the Old Testament. He fulfilled the law of Moses by offering his perfect life as a sacrifice for our sin and there is no longer any need for the Old Testament sacrifices as *"we have been made holy through the sacrifice of the body of Jesus Christ once for all." (Hebrews 10:10)*. Jesus was the son of David who fulfilled God's promise to David that he would always have a son reigning on the throne. And he brought in the New Covenant spoken of by Jeremiah and the other prophets, a covenant of forgiveness and of an open relationship with God himself.

Jesus also left behind a wealth of teaching and a demonstration of God's love for individuals. This is recorded in the gospels and in the letters. But, although Jesus made reconciliation with God possible, he returned to heaven leaving only a small group of frightened disciples behind. If all we had were the gospels we would be left wondering what happened to them and how the good news about Jesus would be spread to the rest of the world. Fortunately for us, Luke takes up the story of the birth of the church in his second volume, Acts, which we start looking at tomorrow.

Day 66
The Church is Born

A Line in History

In the early afternoon of 31st December 1999 I switched on the television to watch huge crowds celebrate the dawn of a new millennium in Sydney Australia. Fireworks lit up Sydney harbour as people partied the night away. Half a day later it was our opportunity to celebrate as we listened to Big Ben chime in the new millennium here in the UK. Later those in the Americas and then in small Pacific islands held their festivities. All around the world people were celebrating the arrival of the year 2000. But few paid any attention to the reason why that time in particular was chosen to be 2000.

The full name for the year is AD 2000 and AD is an abbreviation for "Anno Domini", the Latin for "In the year of our Lord". The coming of Jesus was seen as so important that a sixth century Scythian scholar called Dionysius Exiguus devised a new calendar starting from the year of Jesus' birth. He actually got it wrong by a few years but the adoption of his calendar all around the globe has made the life of Jesus a dividing line in history. The years since the birth of Christ are called "Anno Domini" or AD; the years before his birth are called "Before Christ" or BC. The New Testament documents the events surrounding this point in history. The four gospels describe the events of Jesus' life death and resurrection, as God himself came to earth in human form, while the rest of the New Testament describes the start of a radical change in the dealings of God with man.

The Old Testament is primarily the account of God's covenant relationship with his chosen people, the Israelites. We have already seen how the world changed politically and culturally in the four hundred years after the end of the Old Testament but after Jesus returned to heaven a much more significant change took place. The New Covenant, promised by Jeremiah, came into operation and a new way of relating to the Lord became available not only to the Israelites but to all mankind. God's promise to Abraham that *"all peoples on earth will be blessed through you" (Genesis 12:3)* became a reality as the Holy Spirit came and the church was born.

The Acts of the Apostles

The book that describes the early years of the church is called either "The Acts of the Apostles" or "The Acts of the Holy Spirit" but it is usually abbreviated to just "Acts". It is a vital book sitting in the middle of the New Testament and providing a bridge between the gospels and the letters which make up the rest of the New Testament. It was written by Luke as a sequel to his gospel and gives the background to the people and places relevant to many of the letters.

Luke starts Acts with a recap of the gospel, which he refers to as *"all that Jesus <u>began</u> to do and to teach until the day he was taken up to heaven" (Acts 1:1–2)*. Having documented Jesus' life, death, resurrection and ascension to heaven, his account of the spread of the church is, by implication, an account of what Jesus <u>continued</u> to do and teach – not in his physical body but through his church. Acts spans a period of around thirty years after Jesus' death during which time the gospel spread from Jerusalem to Rome. The book deals with the spread of the gospel in distinct phases and to two distinct groups of people. Up to chapter 12 the gospel is preached in Israel to the Jews and Peter, the leader of the twelve apostles, is the leading man in this. Then there is a huge push to take the gospel to the Gentiles, the non–Jews, and this work is mainly led by Paul. Acts was probably written around AD 63 when Paul was under house arrest in Rome which is referred to at the end of the book.

Contents of Acts	
1–2	The coming of the Holy Spirit at Pentecost.
3–7	The spread of the gospel in Jerusalem.
8–9	The spread of the gospel throughout Judea, Galilee and Samaria.
10–12	The spread of the gospel as far as Phoenicia, Cyprus and Antioch – and to the Gentiles.
13:1–15:35	Paul's first missionary journey and report to Jerusalem.
15:36–18:22	Paul's second missionary journey.
18:23–21:16	Paul's third missionary journey.
21:17–28:31	Paul's arrest, imprisonment and transfer to Rome.

Day 66 – The Church is Born

Wait!

Luke's gospel ends with Jesus' Resurrection and Ascension (his return to heaven) and he starts Acts with the same events. From the opening verses of Acts we can see that Jesus appeared to his disciples on a number of occasions and continued to teach them. Luke says that he *"spoke about the kingdom of God" (Acts 1:3)* and this puzzles the disciples. Although Jesus came and fulfilled many of the Old Testament prophecies he did not fulfil them all and they are still waiting for him to establish an earthly kingdom as described in Zechariah 14. But Jesus tells them to wait in Jerusalem for the baptism in the Holy Spirit when they will receive power to be witnesses to what they have experienced. The instructions are very precise as they are told that they will be witnesses *"in Jerusalem, and in all Judea and Samaria, and to the ends of the earth" (Acts 1:8)*. Luke uses these three geographical areas to structure his book with the first seven chapters focused around Jerusalem, chapters 8–12 describing some of the move into Judea and Samaria and the account of Paul's missionary journeys from chapter 13 taking the gospel all over the Roman Empire.

Read Acts 1

Apostles

During their ten day wait for the Holy Spirit to come on them the eleven apostles appointed a replacement for Judas Iscariot to make their number back up to twelve. Matthias, the one who was chosen is not mentioned in the gospels and is never heard of again in the New Testament but the word "apostle" does occur many times. Both Barnabas and Paul are referred to as apostles later in Acts and a number of others are given this title in the New Testament letters. What is an apostle?

The Greek word "apostle" means messenger or "one who is sent" and given that we are all called to take the message of the gospel to those we meet we are, in some sense, all apostles. But in the New Testament the role of an apostle is described as key to the establishment of the church. Apostles play the same role as the priests in the Old Testament in being the guardians of true doctrine. The supreme example for all apostles is Jesus himself who is described as an apostle in Hebrews 3:1. He was sent to earth and is the greatest king, prophet, shepherd, evangelist and apostle, and is the model for all others who have these roles. He is also the one who appoints them and gives them authority.

Jesus appointed twelve apostles (see Mark 3:14–19) to be with him, to send them out to preach and to have authority to drive out demons. But we know that others followed him during his time on earth and, as we have just read, after Judas betrayed Jesus and committed suicide, Judas was replaced by one of these. From the qualification that Peter laid down for a replacement in Acts 1:21–22 we learn that these twelve stand as the key witnesses on earth to what Jesus did on earth: his ministry from start to end and, in particular, that he rose from the dead. In Revelation 21:14 we find that their names are on the foundations of the New Jerusalem below the names of the twelve tribes.

However, there were other divinely appointed apostles after the twelve. Paul is the greatest of these in the New Testament but others are also called apostles: Barnabas (Acts 14:14), James the brother of Jesus (Paul refers to him as an apostle in Gal 1:19), Andronicus and Junias in Rome (Romans 16:7). Then in 1 Corinthians 12:27–28 and Ephesians 4:11–13 Paul lists the role of an apostle along with a number of roles that God gives or appoints in the church – including prophets, evangelists, pastors, teachers and those able to help others – which indicates that the function of an apostle is one that continues on in the life of the church. Their key role, as Paul showed by example, is planting churches (i.e. creating them from nothing), establishing local leadership, teaching, and counteracting error.

The Church is born

Acts 2 describes how, on the day of Pentecost, the Holy Spirit was sent from heaven to empower the group of people Jesus left behind. The disciples, who forty days earlier were cowering in fear of the Jewish authorities, became bold and preached on the streets of Jerusalem where three thousand people became Christians. This event marks the birth of the church and is one of the most important events in world history. On that day the gospel was preached to people from all over the Roman Empire and the people who heard Peter's message went to their own countries and spread the good news to others. Acts describes how this one event gave rise to the growth of the church throughout the Roman Empire. Two thousand years later, according to the Guinness World of Records 2001, *"Christianity is the world's predominant religion, with some two billion adherents in 1999, or 33% of the world population."*[K] Whether this is a measure of those living in so–called "Christian countries" or a measure of true believers is, of course

Day 66 – The Church is Born

debatable – the Guinness World of Records does go on to say, *"However, religious statistics are necessarily only tentative, as the test of adherence to religion varies widely in rigour"* – but, whatever the true figure is, the impact of the events of Acts 2 cannot be underestimated.

> **Read Acts 2**

Peter's address to the crowd is one of eleven messages that Luke provides a summary of in Acts – four from Peter, one from Stephen, and six from Paul. They sum up the message of the apostles for us and this one is typical in the format they used. They start from the events that people are seeing or the questions they have and provide an explanation, they tell them the facts of the gospel in a nutshell – Jesus' life, death and resurrection – and they end with a challenge to the people to repent and be baptised.

The end of Acts 2 gives us an insight into the life of the early church. Whatever our views on how church should operate today we must be challenged by the devotion and enthusiasm of the people and yearn for God to move in power so that we too are filled with awe and enjoy the favour of all the people as these early disciples did. We have much to learn from them.

Rapid Growth

You may be tempted to think that with three thousand new converts there would be a period of consolidation in the early church but what we read about is continued, rapid growth. The last verse of Acts 2 tells us that the Lord added to the number daily and in Acts 3 we find that a healing sparks another growth in the number of believers.

On the way to the temple, Peter and John are asked for money by a man who had been crippled from birth. His family had been putting this man here for years and Jesus must have passed near him on many occasions without healing him but we do not need to look too far to see a good reason why he was not healed earlier. On this day Peter, prompted by the Holy Spirit, told him to get up and walk and his legs instantly became so strong that *"he went with them into the temple courts, walking and jumping and praising God" (Acts 3:8)*. The sight of this well known, crippled beggar jumping around while he was hanging on to Peter and John quickly drew a large crowd of astonished people and Peter took the opportunity to preach to the people with the result that many more believed in Jesus and the church grew once again – up to five thousand men alone as recorded by Luke in Acts 4:4. The church was never meant to be small or to stop growing!

References

[K] From "The Guinness World of Records", 2001. With thanks to Guinness World Records for permission to quote.

Day 67
Early Days

Baffled!

The healing of the crippled beggar and Peter preaching about Jesus to a large crowd did not go unnoticed by the Jewish religious authorities as these events took place in the temple courts. It was only a few months since Jesus caused similar "trouble" and they thought that they had dealt with him and his teaching by putting him to death. Now his followers are boldly proclaiming that he has risen from the dead so they arrest them and bring them before the Sanhedrin, the same body that tried Jesus. The Jewish leaders are totally baffled. They cannot deny that the cripple had been healed but they cannot accept that Jesus has risen from the dead – the Sadducees do not believe in any form of resurrection at all – and are amazed at the courage of these two *"unschooled, ordinary men" (Acts 4:13)*. Here are two uneducated, working class men discussing theology with the Jewish intellectual elite and leaving them speechless! Luke records that the Sanhedrin *"took note that these men had been with Jesus" (Acts 4:13)*. The transformation brought about by the coming of the Holy Spirit is demonstrated in Peter who, the last time he came near the Sanhedrin stood outside in the courtyard and denied any connection with Jesus, but this time stood before them and boldly proclaimed that Jesus had been raised from the dead.

> Read Acts 4

Holiness in the Church

The end of Acts 4 provides another small insight into the life of the early church where no one was in need as the believers shared their possessions. Barnabas, who features later in the book of Acts, was one of a number who was motivated by the Holy Spirit to sell land and give the proceeds to the apostles for distribution to the poor. However, in Acts 5 we read about a couple whose motivation was different. Although those like Barnabas who gave their possessions to the poor were motivated by the Holy Spirit, they would also have received appreciation and respect from the other believers. It is only natural for us to be impressed by good acts done by fellow Christians but we must be careful to glorify God, the one who has motivated them, rather than to glorify the people themselves. Ananias and Sapphira provide us with a stark warning about what can happen if we let the approval of others become our motivation.

> **Read Acts 5:1–14**

Before moving on there are a number of points to note about this event. Firstly, Ananias and Sapphira were struck dead because they lied, not because they didn't give all the proceeds of their property sale to the apostles. Peter made it clear to Ananias that he could have done what he wanted with the money he received. His sin was to declare that he was bringing the full amount to the apostles, presumably to gain the recognition of men. He was more interested in hearing people comment on his generosity than being honest. Secondly, Peter makes it clear than in lying to the church he was lying to God. In the same way as David recognised his sin with Bathsheba by saying *"I have sinned against the LORD" (2 Samuel 12:13),* so lying to other people is lying to the Lord. Thirdly, an interesting point that someone made in a sermon once which had never crossed my mind is that Ananias and Sapphira were believers and through death went to be with the Lord. As believers one day we will meet them in heaven. They were punished for their sin as we all can be but they did not lose their salvation.

Fourthly, we have to note that the Lord killed this couple. It was not a judgement carried out by the church, the Lord intervened. In the same way that the Lord killed Uzzah for touching the ark so the Lord killed this couple to indicate his high standards for holiness in the church. The result was a healthy fear of God which meant that no–one dared to "join" the disciples although men and women continued to be "added" to their number (as we just saw in Acts 5:13 & 14). Becoming a disciple of Jesus was not a casual thing. You can join a club or a political party and not change your lifestyle but you cannot treat the church in the same way. It requires a belief in the Lord and an acceptance that he has the right to do whatever he will with your life: every part of your life is impacted.

And finally we have to thank God that he does not continue to work in this way on a regular basis! We often ask God to move in his church now as he did in the early church but what would you do if two people were struck dead in one of your church meetings? Explaining it to the police might prove difficult!

Day 67 – Early Days 373

Before the Sanhedrin Again

The rest of Acts 5 deals with the second appearance of the apostles before the Sanhedrin. This time their lives are saved by a leading teacher called Gamaliel, who we later discover trained the apostle Paul when he was a Pharisee (see Acts 22:3).

> Read Acts 5:15–42

The Problems of Growth

When an organisation grows rapidly the demands placed on its leaders will grow even faster and new structures will be required to deal with emerging issues. This was true of the early church where, initially, the leadership team of the twelve apostles were not only in great demand as teachers and pastors but also became increasingly bogged down in the administration required to operate any large organisation. At the beginning of Acts 6 seven men are chosen to be responsible for distributing food to the poor. We saw in the Old Testament how the law evolved in response to different situations, here the church is evolving a structure to cater for the situation it is facing.

> Read Acts 6:1–7

The Impact of Stephen and Philip

Despite being called to "wait on tables" these seven men – who were chosen by the people not the apostles – were not selected for their "natural" gifts but because they were full of the Spirit. Again there is a parallel from the early times of the Old Covenant when Bezalel was chosen to make the Ark of the Covenant firstly because he was filled with the Spirit of God and secondly because of his skill as a craftsman (see Exodus 31:2–5). The stature of these men is demonstrated by accounts of two of them in Acts – Stephen and Philip – who emerge as great preachers and miracle workers.

The rest of Acts 6 records the impact that Stephen had in Jerusalem. His wisdom in argument and demonstration of God's power in the signs he performed brought him great opposition from the Jews and he, like the apostles before him was brought before the Sanhedrin. Acts 7 is his defence before the Sanhedrin which ends with Stephen denouncing them as the murderers of Jesus, who he calls "the Righteous One", a clear reference to the name given to God in Isaiah and elsewhere in the Old Testament. The Sanhedrin are so infuriated that they dragged Stephen out of the city where they stoned him to death. As he, the first Christian martyr, is dying he echoed the words of Jesus by praying that the Lord would not hold this sin against them.

This act unleashes a great evil as a wave of persecution breaks out against the church. Saul, a young Pharisee who is eager to see the Jewish law upheld, sets out with others to destroy the church. However, we know from the later writings of Saul, who became the apostle Paul, that *"in all things God works for the good of those who love him, who have been called according to his purpose" (Romans 8:28)* and this persecution is no exception.

To Judea and Samaria

Read Acts 8:1–8

As we saw at the beginning of Acts, just before Jesus returned to heaven he told his disciples that after they had received the Holy Spirit they would be his witnesses *"in Jerusalem, and in all Judea and Samaria, and to the ends of the earth" (Acts 1:8)*. Luke includes a number of checkpoints throughout Acts where he updates us on the overall situation of the church and in Acts 6:7 he tells us that the church *in Jerusalem* is continuing to grow rapidly. The apostles do not appear to have a plan to reach out to the surrounding area as there was no end to the good work that needed doing in Jerusalem, both in reaching out to those who had not yet heard the gospel, in teaching the new converts and ensuring that the poor were being looked after. But that was not fulfilling the commission that Jesus had given to the church. It was the persecution that followed the death of Stephen which led to phase two of the church's expansion. The church in Jerusalem was devastated in numbers as its members were scattered but the result was that the good news about Jesus was proclaimed throughout Judea and Samaria. Only the apostles stayed in Jerusalem supporting those who were being persecuted.

Philip, another one of the seven, provides an example of the way in which the gospel spread. He went to Samaria where he carried on in the same way as the apostles did in Jerusalem. The result was that many believed in Samaria. Peter and John visited later and preached throughout the villages of Samaria on their way back to Jerusalem. Maybe they visited the town where Jesus had spoken with the woman by the well and updated those who believed in Jesus then with what

Day 67 – Early Days

had happened to him after he had left their town.

Philip was also led by the Lord to stand by the roadside south of Jerusalem where he led an Ethiopian official to salvation through his reading of Isaiah. We looked at this when considering "The Gospel in Isaiah". We know very little about how the gospel spread into Africa, but here is a link to Egypt and Ethiopia. Similarly we have no knowledge from Acts of the spread of the gospel east but we know that people were present at Pentecost from eastern countries and cities and legend has it that the apostle Thomas went to India to spread the gospel.

Although phase two of Jesus' commission was now underway the gospel continues to be only for the Jews. Up until this phase in the church's development the church is made up of those who had either grown up as Jews or, like Nicolas, one of the seven, had converted to Judaism before becoming Christians. The church was Jewish in its outlook and that meant that they continued not to mix with Gentiles. Once again, God's intervention was required to make the church reach out to new people groups with the gospel.

Day 68
The Gospel for the Gentiles

The Road to Damascus

As we saw yesterday, the persecution in Jerusalem was led by a Pharisee named Saul. In his zeal for God he decides to take his persecution to Damascus but on the way Jesus meets with him and he instantly becomes a follower of Jesus rather than one who persecutes him. The account of his conversion is dramatic and "a road to Damascus experience" is still used as a common phrase for an occasion when someone suddenly "sees the light" and completely changes their point of view. Note too the courage and obedience of the "disciple named Ananias" who almost certainly never knew how significant the man he went to see in fear and trembling would be in the spread of the gospel.

> Read Acts 9:1–31

Saul was a Pharisee from Tarsus who had been brought up to know the law and all the rules that the Pharisees had added and he had done his best to observe them. When he was persecuting the Christians he did it because he was eager to stand up for what he believed was right. To us he might not seem the obvious choice to become a Christian, let alone be given the responsibility to take the message about salvation through Jesus to the Gentiles. The Jews did not even mix with non–Jews in order to avoid being polluted by them and Saul would have grown up observing this rule carefully. But God is far greater than all that. He humbles Saul on the road to Damascus and then uses Paul's thorough grounding in the Old Testament scriptures to quickly convince him that Jesus was the promised Messiah. Within a few days he is preaching that Jesus is the Son of God to the Jews in Damascus much to the astonishment of his hearers! Paul's understanding of the scriptures, combined with the conviction of the Holy Spirit, is a powerful weapon in God's hand. From Saul's later writings (as the apostle Paul) we know that the "many days" of Acts 9:23 included three years away in Arabia (see Galatians 1:17–18) when he presumably studied the scriptures again in the light of his new understanding of who Jesus was. At the end of the passage we just read is another one of Luke's summary statements. Following Saul's conversion the persecution diminished and the church throughout the land of Israel *"enjoyed a time of peace" (Acts 9:31)*. We saw in Acts 8 that persecution led to growth in the church and I have heard people say that we in the western world need to see persecution in order to see growth. But Acts 9:31 provides a comforting response to this in that the church grew in a time of peace. The lesson from the early chapters of Acts is that the church can grow in persecution or in peace. Nothing can stop its growth!

Peter's Thinking is Transformed

Saul, the Pharisee, needed to completely change his way of thinking before he could preach that Jesus was the Son of God. The twelve apostles required no convincing about Jesus but they too needed to undergo a transformation in their thinking in order to be able to fulfil the task that Jesus had given them. Up until this point everyone in the church seemed to assume that the good news about Jesus was for the Jews. They all came from a Jewish background and kept to the regulations of the law. Despite the fact that God had promised that *"all peoples on earth" (Genesis 12:3)* would be blessed through Abraham's descendants, the regulations that the Israelites had developed kept them separate from other peoples. In Acts 10 the Lord uses Peter to spearhead a change of thinking among the apostles and the church. He was brought up as a Jew to follow the law and was still thoroughly committed to it but he is about to learn that the New Covenant is all about grace, not about keeping rules and regulations.

> **Read Acts 10:1–11:18**

Although Peter's vision is strange to us it was very important in changing Peter's thinking as it prepared him to preach to a Gentile. Jews were not even able to visit Gentiles (as Peter comments in 10:28) and even Jesus had kept away from Gentiles in the main during his time on earth as he was sent to God's people, Israel. In his encounter with Cornelius, Peter learns as much as Cornelius does! If God is prepared to send the Holy Spirit to Gentiles then who is Peter to refuse them baptism into the faith? With Peter's thinking blown to pieces he returns to a storm of protest from the church in Jerusalem. After he explained what happened we read that they understood that God's purposes included the Gentiles. This is the first time that the church in Jerusalem realised this and it is very good news for all of us who are not Jewish that they did!

Day 68 – The Gospel for the Gentiles

The Word is Out!

As we read on in Acts 11 we discover that the timing of Peter's encounter with Cornelius was critical. Peter was not the only disciple spreading the good news about Jesus to the Gentiles. Unnamed Christians who had fled the persecution in Jerusalem travelled well beyond the boundaries of Israel and some started talking to Greeks about Jesus in Antioch where the first mixed church – including Jews and Gentiles – was established. If news of this had reached Jerusalem before Peter had his revelation then the church may have found this difficult to deal with. God could have sent an unknown disciple to speak to Cornelius too but the fact that it was Peter who turned up in Jerusalem with the account of Gentiles receiving the Holy Spirit gave it a credibility which it would not have had if some unnamed disciple had reported it.

> **Read Acts 11:19-30**

Antioch, which is in present day Turkey, just north of the border with Syria, was the third city of the Roman Empire after Rome and Alexandria and the church there became the key base for the next phase of God's work. Jerusalem provided the base for the gospel to reach Judea, Samaria, Syria and Cyprus; Antioch provided the base for a push into Asia (incorporating a number of Roman provinces in modern day Turkey), Macedonia, and Achaia (Greece) (see Map 8 on page 383). The name "Christian", meaning "belonging to Christ", also came from this church, although whether it was first used by those in the church or as a term of abuse from those outside is not recorded. It is more likely to be the latter as the word only appears three times in the New Testament and in one of the other references it is used by someone hostile to the faith (see Acts 26:28) and in the other in the context of suffering persecution at the hands of others (see 1 Peter 4:16). Throughout the gospels and Acts those who followed Christ are referred to as "disciples" nearly three hundred times.

The Fruit of Encouragement

Luke introduces us to Barnabas at the end of Acts 4. His real name was Joseph but he was such an encouragement to everyone he met that the apostles nicknamed him Barnabas, which means "Son of Encouragement". He was clearly a man who saw the best in everyone and it was he who first arranged for Saul to meet the apostles, a meeting they must have been very nervous about given his background. Sending Barnabas to Antioch had far reaching consequences as he not only encourages the church there but also gets Saul involved and it was Saul, who is also called Paul, who was to spearhead the spread of the gospel throughout the Roman Empire. Paul provides us with the greatest insight into how to establish churches both through Luke's account of his journeys, which take up most of the rest of Acts, and through his thirteen letters which form a third of the New Testament. Maybe if we all followed the example of Barnabas in encouraging one another there would be more people like Paul in the church today!

Day 69
Paul's First Missionary Journey

Paul provides a model for Evangelism

Historical narrative provides the backbone of the Bible. The Law is not given to us as a dry set of regulations but is framed by the early history of Israel, God's covenant people. The stories of Israel's kings provide the background to the books of wisdom and the prophets and the gospels interweave the teachings of Jesus with an account of his life so we can see love in action as well in words. So it is with Acts and, in particular, the account of Paul's journeys. Luke's careful recording of Paul's journeys is central to our understanding of how the good news about Jesus spread in the early days. Paul provides a model for those reaching out to regions where the gospel has not been preached before and highlights the importance of the church which is at the centre of God's will and purpose in evangelism. His letters contain much of the New Testament's teachings but our understanding of them would be poorer without our knowledge of his life.

In Acts we have a record of Paul making three journeys – often referred to as his missionary journeys – spreading the gospel to the Gentiles, followed by an account of his journey to Rome which includes a dramatic shipwreck. Acts finishes abruptly with Paul in prison in Rome and it is thought that he may have made other journeys after that before returning to prison in Rome where he was martyred. Paul is not the only one who took the gospel to new regions. On the day of Pentecost many people from around the Empire heard the apostles preaching and took the message back to their own lands. Paul himself wrote to the church in Rome, which was established well before he went there, and churches in areas not visited by Paul are mentioned in other letters. But Paul's activities are recorded to show us a pattern for evangelism and church planting.

Although the leaders in Jerusalem acknowledged that the Lord was reaching out to Gentiles as well as Jews the real push to reach out to the Gentiles came from the church at Antioch, the church that was established as a mixed church – Jewish and Gentile – from the beginning. During a time of worship and fasting the Holy Spirit called the church to send out Barnabas and Saul, two of its top five men, to take the gospel to other places. This was a big sacrifice for the church but their loss was to be for the gain of many others. During the account of the first missionary journey note that Saul's name is changed to Paul, and that during the journey the expression "Barnabas and Saul" is replaced by "Paul and Barnabas" as Paul takes the lead. You can follow this journey around Cyprus and Galatia on Map 8 (see opposite). It probably took place around 15 years after Jesus died.

> **Read Acts 13–14**

In this first missionary journey we see a pattern for Paul's work which is repeated on his later journeys. He always preached first to the Jews (see Acts 13:46). With their background knowledge of the Law and the Prophets they could quickly understand who Jesus was. Some accepted the message; some did not. Then they went to the Gentiles. Again some accepted; some did not. The Jews who refused to accept that Jesus was the Messiah were often the ones to lead the opposition to Paul's preaching.

In addition to preaching, Paul performed miracles and healings. As we saw in Lystra, this caused some people to worship them, but in general the demonstration of God's power caught people's attention and confirmed the truth of Paul's preaching. As he wrote to the church in Corinth: *"My message and my preaching were not with wise and persuasive words, but with a demonstration of the Spirit's power, so that your faith might not rest on men's wisdom, but on God's power."* (1 Corinthians 2:4–5).

Then, after leaving a period of time for the church to become established, Paul and Barnabas appointed elders to be responsible for the churches in each town. It is not clear from the word used whether Paul and Barnabas chose these men themselves or whether it was done by election or consultation but however it was done, this was a serious responsibility. There were no telephones or emails at this time and, although communications were good in the Roman Empire, if trouble arose then the elders had to deal with it without immediate help from the apostles. Their appointment was accompanied with prayer and fasting as Paul and Barnabas asked the Lord to give them strength for the task of looking after the new church.

The Council in Jerusalem

One of the most instructive aspects of the Bible narratives is that they

Day 69 – Paul's First Missionary Journey 383

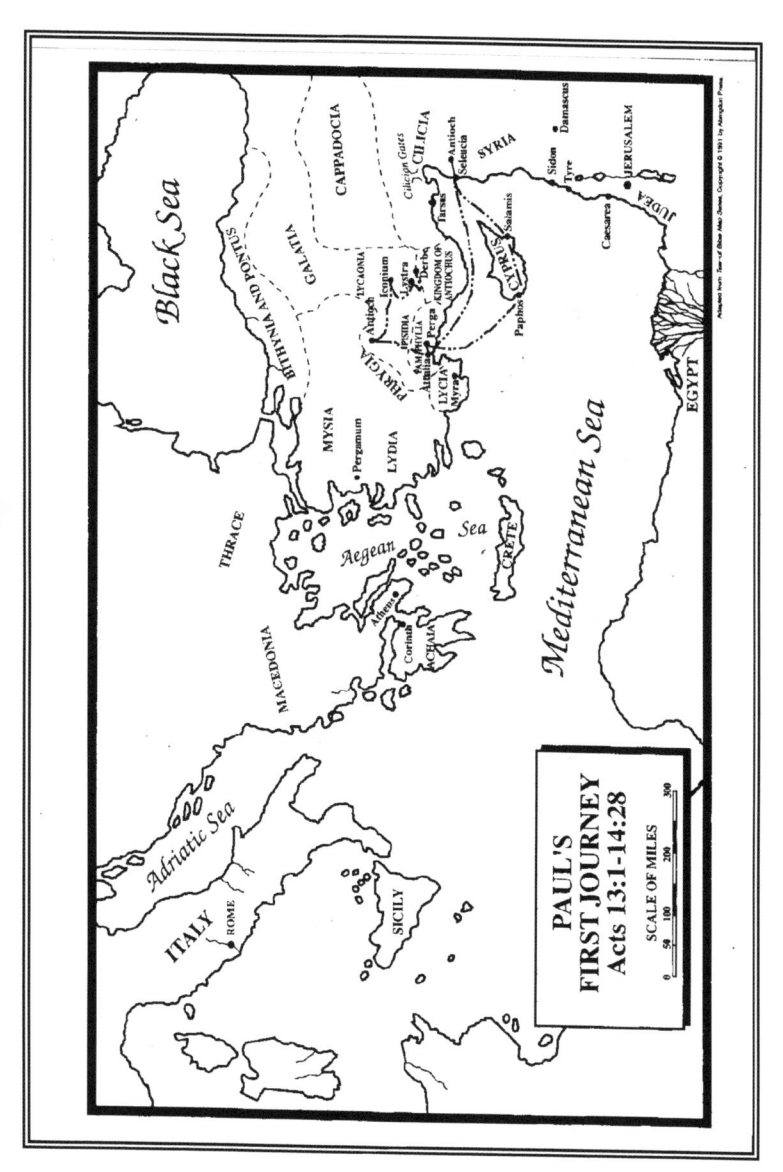

Map 8 – Paul's First Missionary Journey

include the problems as well as the triumphs of those who seek to follow the Lord. Acts 14 ends on a high point as the church in Antioch enjoys both the benefit of having Paul and Barnabas back with them and hearing about the new churches they had founded while they were away but at the start of Acts 15 we read of a problem in the Antioch church.

It all started in the Jerusalem church. Back in Acts 6:7 Luke tells us that a large number of priests had become Christians and here in Acts 15 we find that a number of Pharisees have also been added to the Jerusalem church. These Pharisees, who had been brought up to revere the Law of Moses, wanted all believers to share in the riches of the Old Testament and taught that Christians should observe all the regulations of Moses. When they came to Antioch, which was mainly a Gentile church, and started teaching that the Gentile believers had to be circumcised according to the law before they were saved, it caused serious confusion among the church members. Even though Paul and Barnabas opposed them people were still unsure of the truth. These men were from Jerusalem where the original twelve apostles were based! How could they be wrong? In order to settle the dispute, Paul and Barnabas were sent to consult with the apostles in Jerusalem. This meeting is referred to as the Council in Jerusalem. James, who takes the lead in this meeting, is the brother of Jesus, not the apostle, who became the first martyr among the twelve when he was executed by Herod Agrippa I (see Acts 12:2)

Read Acts 15:1–35

This decision taken by the apostles in Jerusalem was very important for the church in Antioch, for the churches of that time and for all of those of us who are Christians today. If they had decided that it was necessary for the Gentiles to follow the law of Moses then we would all be subject to the law and unable to enjoy the freedom of God's grace which is at the heart of the New Covenant. Thankfully they heard the Holy Spirit and, through the letter they sent, brought freedom to the churches of their time and, through Luke including it in his history, brought freedom to us too.

The Antioch church was encouraged by the letter and by the two prophets sent from Jerusalem, Judas and Silas. Although verse 33 says that they returned to Jerusalem we will discover tomorrow that Silas returned and became Paul's travelling companion on his second missionary journey.

Day 70
The Rest of Paul's Journeys

Paul's Second Missionary Journey

After their trip to Jerusalem, Paul and Barnabas spent some time in Antioch before Paul suggests returning to the churches they had visited on their first journey to see how they were getting on. Barnabas, true to his nature as an encourager is keen to give John Mark, who deserted them on their first trip, a second chance but Paul is not prepared to take the risk. Luke provides an honest record of the disagreement between these two church leaders and we see that God brings good from their falling out as they set off independently in different directions to encourage the churches! Thanks to Paul's letters we also learn that this disagreement did not lead to a lasting hostility between him and Barnabas and we also learn that he later worked with Mark, as he recommends him to the church in Colossae (see Colossians 4:10) and sends greeting from him to Philemon referring to him as a "fellow worker". We know that in Paul's eyes Mark more than made up for his earlier desertion over the years that followed as, in his last letter before he died, Paul asks Timothy to bring Mark to him *"because he is helpful to me in my ministry" (2 Timothy 4:11).*

Paul makes his second journey with Silas and they start by visiting the churches that he founded on his first journey with Barnabas. As they travel they are joined by Timothy in Lystra and by Luke, the writer of Acts, in Troas (note the change from *"they"* in Acts 16:8 to *"we"* in Acts 16:10). From there they sail to Macedonia and Achaia – both Roman provinces which are in modern day Greece – where they establish churches in Philippi, Thessalonica, Berea, Athens and Corinth. Their experiences in each town are very different showing us that there is no set way to reach a town for Jesus. The Lord opened up different opportunities for Paul in each situation and his team had to be flexible to respond to what they found. Paul was able to reason from the scriptures in the Jewish synagogues as well as quote from Greek poets when he is debating with the philosophers in Athens. He was welcomed with eagerness in Berea but met hostility and physical suffering in a number of towns. We will read most of this journey up until Paul's time in Athens. You can follow the route on Map 9.

Day 70 – The Rest of Paul's Journeys   387

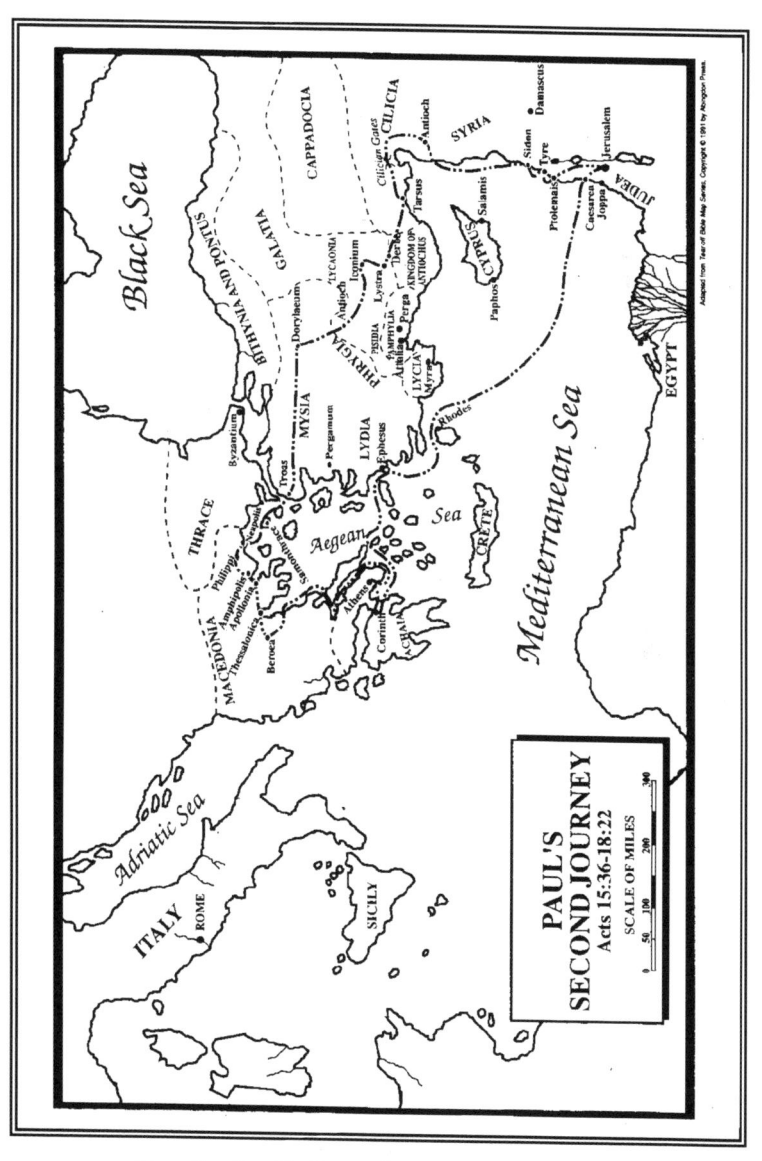

Map 9 – Paul's Second Missionary Journey

Day 70 – The Rest of Paul's Journeys

> Read Acts 15:36–17:34

At the beginning of Acts 18 Paul moved on to Corinth where he stayed for eighteen months and founded the church that 1 & 2 Corinthians are addressed to.

Paul's Third Missionary Journey

Luke tells us that Paul spent "some time" in Antioch after returning from his second journey but gives no details. Instead he goes straight into an account of Paul's third journey. At the end of his second journey Paul visited Ephesus but, despite an invitation from the local Jews to stay, he only stayed briefly on his way back to Antioch. It obviously made an impression on him though and, after visiting the churches he founded on his first journey, he headed for this influential city in the west of Asia (present day Turkey). Using a public lecture hall as his base he spoke with the people of the region daily so that the whole province heard about Jesus. It is likely that the church in Colossae was founded during Paul's time here along with the other churches referred to in the opening chapters of Revelation. See Map 10 opposite for details of his route.

Paul's stay in Ephesus was brought to an end by a riot. Try and imagine the scene as you read Luke's brilliant account of Paul's time at Ephesus during his third journey.

> Read Acts 19

After he left Ephesus Paul visited the churches in Macedonia and Achaia and then headed for Jerusalem.

Paul's Journey to Rome

Paul clearly feels that God is leading him to Jerusalem as, despite being warned by a prophet that he will be imprisoned there and his friends pleading with him, he sets his face to go. When he is there he is recognised by Jews from Asia who stir up the Jewish crowds against this man who is leading the Jews astray with talk of Jesus. There is such an uproar that the Roman authorities are forced to intervene and arrest Paul to stop him being killed. Luke then gives a full account of Paul's defence before the Jewish crowd, to the centurion who arrested him, before the Sanhedrin (which he splits down the middle by mentioning the resurrection which the Pharisees believed in and the Sadducees didn't!), before the Roman governors Felix and Festus and

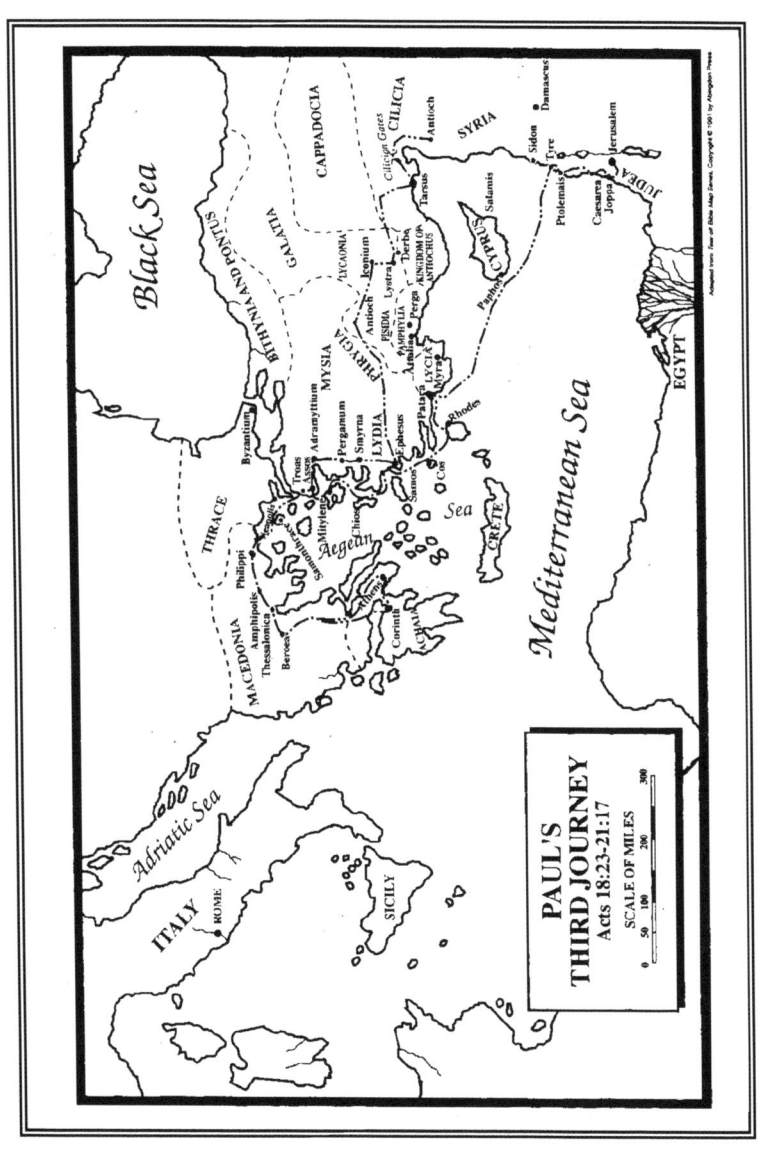

Map 10 – Paul's Third Missionary Journey

to the Jewish King Herod Agrippa II in Acts 22–26. During this lengthy legal process of over two years Paul made use of his right as a Roman citizen to appeal for his case to be heard by Caesar. So, although the Roman governor is not really sure of the charges being brought against Paul he grants him his right and sends him to Rome.

The last two chapters of Acts describe Paul's journey to Rome including a dramatic account of a storm at sea and a shipwreck on the island of Malta – Map 11 on the next page shows his route. Having devoted five chapters to Paul's defences in the lower courts we might expect an account of his trial before Caesar but Acts ends abruptly with Paul still awaiting trial in Rome after two years. He is not in prison but is allowed to preach and teach freely in his own rented house where he met with the Jews and the Christians in Rome. From his letters it seems likely that he was later released and journeyed again. According to tradition he was executed in Rome by Caesar Nero.

The account of Paul's life and work among the churches gives us a valuable insight into the work of an apostle. In the thirty years following the coming of the Holy Spirit at Pentecost and the birth of the church the good news about Jesus had spread throughout the Roman world. But most of our understanding of how we are to live as Christians comes from the letters that Paul and the other apostles wrote and tomorrow we will start to look at them.

Day 70 – The Rest of Paul's Journeys

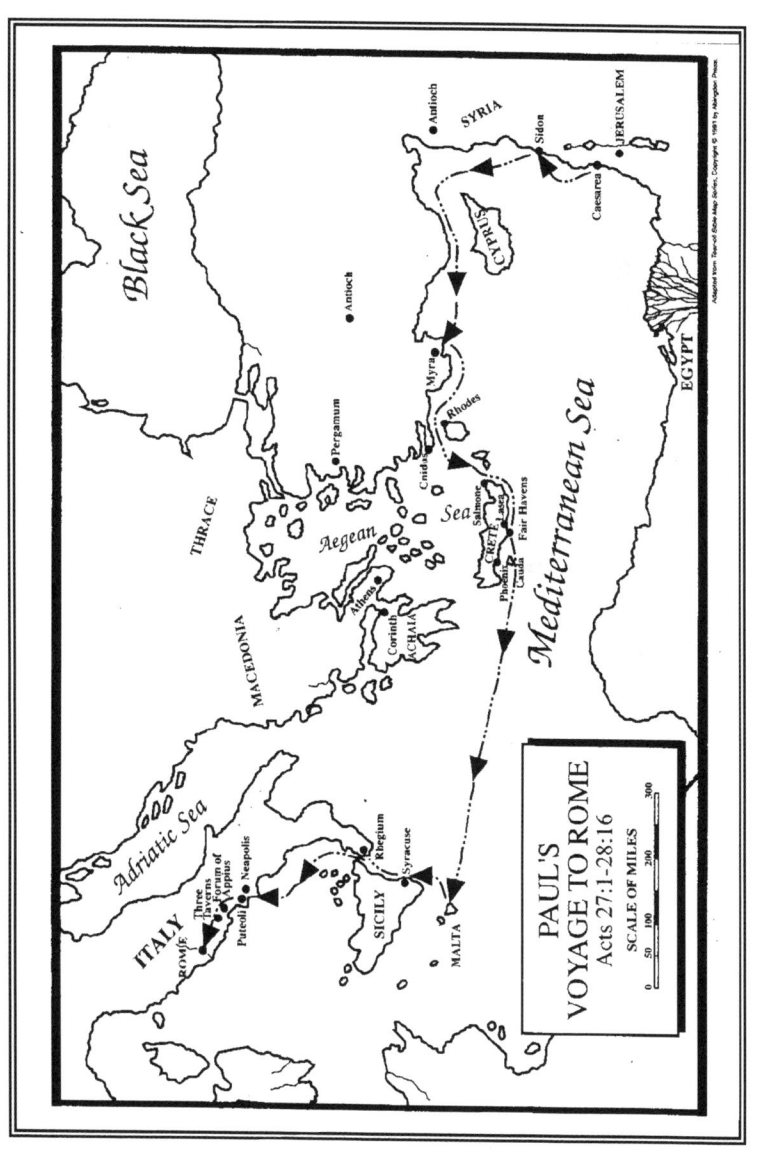

Map 11 – Paul's Journey to Rome

Day 71
Paul's Letters

Bringing the New Testament Together

Before we start looking at the New Testament letters we will take a few moments to consider how we have come to have the New Testament in the form it is now. It is important that we can be sure that the books of the Bible are not just interesting ancient documents but that they are the word of God, his revelation to us through the writings of these men.

As we saw in Day 55, the Old Testament was brought together in its current form in the centuries before the time of Jesus. This was not a process of sifting through documents to decide if they were inspired by God or not but more a bringing together of books that were in regular use by the Jews. They were known to be from God at the time they were written. The first five books of the Old Testament, written by Moses, are referred to as "the Book of the Law" shortly after Moses died in Joshua 1:8 when the Lord told Joshua to be careful to obey all that was in it. It was not that a group of people sat down hundreds of years later and discussed what they thought of Genesis, or decided that there should be ten commandments rather than twelve, the people living in the time it was written knew that this was the word of God. Similarly the prophets were recognised to be speaking for the Lord in their own lifetimes as we saw when Daniel referred to the words of Jeremiah as "the Scriptures" in Daniel 9:2.

It was the same with the New Testament. The books and letters were recognised as being inspired by God shortly after they were written by those who knew the writers. When Paul wanted to support a point he was making in 1 Timothy 5:18 he wrote, *"for the scripture says"* and went on to quote from Deuteronomy and Luke. He had already put the writings of his friend Luke on the same level as that of Moses, recognising his well researched account of the life and words of Jesus as having the same God–given authority. Similarly Peter refers to the writings of Paul as *"Scriptures"* in 2 Peter 3:16. He knew that they were the word of God even during Paul's lifetime.

All the writings of the New Testament took place within the sixty years following the death of Jesus. Initially the good news about him spread from the apostles by word of mouth but, as time went on and the church spread, the apostles saw that they would die before Jesus returned so they or their close associates documented the life of Jesus and wrote letters to churches setting out the truths of the new faith. These documents circulated in the early church along with others and it was not until late in the second century AD that the church leaders of the time made decisions about which books should be considered as inspired by God and which should not. Their motivation was to safeguard the truths that had been handed down from the original apostles as some leaders were teaching different ideas. Three factors were used to assess the New Testament books. Firstly whether they were written by the apostles, or at least by those close to them as in the case of the gospels of Mark and Luke. Secondly, they considered how widely the books were in use in the church of that time, and, thirdly, whether their teaching was in line with the rest of the apostles' teachings. By the end of the second century most of the books we currently have in the New Testament were accepted (there was some uncertainty about the inclusion of the letter to the Hebrews as it was not known who wrote it although it satisfied the other criteria) and by the end of the fourth century the books we currently have were agreed. Entire copies of the New Testament exist from the fourth century AD.

The Writings of Paul

Acts provides information about Paul's life but we learn most about him through his letters. Paul wrote thirteen letters to various churches and individuals – more "books" than any other writer. His 87 chapters mean that he contributed more to the Bible than any other writer apart from Moses – more than any of the major prophets.

Paul's letters provide an insight into his life, his character, his role as an apostle, his feelings and into church life in the early years. He explains the gospel, with many references back to the Old Testament which he knew so well, gives practical teaching about how to live the Christian life and new teaching on church structure and the second coming of Jesus.

As with the Old Testament law and prophets all this material is mixed in together. Paul's letters jump around and he has a habit of being long–winded and frequently digresses. As if to prove the point, when I copied one of Paul's sentences into this document the grammar checker on my word processor highlighted it with the message "Long sentence – no suggestion". It is a shame Paul didn't have a PC! But as with the law and prophets the message comes across with the heart of the writer rather than as a dull rulebook. The best commentary on Paul's letters comes from Peter who wrote, *"He (Paul) writes the same way in all his letters, speaking in them of these matters. His letters contain some things that are hard to understand, which ignorant and unstable people distort, as they do the other Scriptures, to their own destruction." (2 Peter 3:16).* This is very comforting for the rest of us who also find his writings hard to follow!

Paul's Letters

In the Bible Bookcase (see Figure 5 on page 36) you will find Paul's letters sandwiched between Acts and Hebrews. There are nine letters to churches: Romans, 1 & 2 Corinthians, Galatians, Ephesians, Philippians, Colossians and 1 & 2 Thessalonians. The next three, 1 & 2 Timothy and Titus, are to disciples of his who were leading churches and contain instructions for pastors. The last, Philemon, is to a member of the church in Colossae.

It is possible to deduce when some of Paul's letters were written by their contents and by reference to Acts. Figure 12, on the next page, indicates roughly when they *may* have been written. Map 9 on page 387 shows where the churches were (apart from Colossae which was about 100 miles east of Ephesus).

As Figure 12 shows, most of the letters that Paul wrote were to churches that he was instrumental in founding so a major emphasis is in dealing with errors which have crept in since he left. (The church in Colossae was not founded by Paul personally but by one of his converts during the time he was in nearby Ephesus.) Romans is the main exception to this as we will see later. The main themes of Paul's letters are listed in Figure 13 – see overleaf.

Paul's Life and Letters		
Year (approx)	Main Events in Paul's Life	When the Letters were written
28	*Crucifixion and Resurrection of Jesus*	
35	Martyrdom of Stephen	
35	Conversion of Saul	
43–45	In Antioch	
46–48	First missionary journey – planting churches in **Galatia**	
50–52	Second missionary journey – revisited the Galatian churches and is joined by **Timothy**. Went on to establish churches in **Philippi**, **Thessalonica**, Berea, Athens and **Corinth**.	*1 & 2 Thessalonians* written in Corinth **Galatians**?
53–57	Third missionary journey – spent two years in **Ephesus** (during which the church in Colossae was probably established) as well as revisiting the churches founded earlier.	*1 Corinthians* sent from Ephesus *2 Corinthians* sent from Macedonia *Romans* sent from Corinth?
59	Journey to Rome	
59–??	Imprisoned in Rome	*Ephesians*, *Colossians*, *Philemon* and *Philippians* written in Rome
??	Later journeys	*1 Timothy* and *Titus*
67–68	Imprisoned in Rome	*2 Timothy* written in prison in Rome
68	Executed in Rome	

Figure 12 – Paul's Life and Letters

The Themes of Paul's Letters

Letters to Churches	Main Theme	Other Topics
Romans	God's plan of salvation	The relationship of Jews and Gentiles
1 Corinthians	Church problems: divisions, immorality, food, public worship, the use of spiritual gifts	Love. The Resurrection
2 Corinthians	Paul's ministry as an apostle – a personal defence	A collection for other churches
Galatians	Justification by faith, not by works or by keeping regulations	The Fruit of the Spirit
Ephesians	God's eternal purpose	Practical teaching on relationships; Spiritual warfare
Philippians	Joy	Humility
Colossians	That Christ is completely adequate for our salvation	Warning against false teaching
1 Thessalonians	Teaching on End Times and the second coming of Christ	
2 Thessalonians	Teaching on End Times and the second coming of Christ	Warning against idleness
Letters to Individuals		
1 Timothy	Instructions for overseeing a church: false teachers, worship, church leaders	
2 Timothy	Encouragement to a church leader	
Titus	A recipe for building the church	
Philemon	The return of a slave	

Figure 13 – The Themes of Paul's Letters

The Structure of Letters

In a letter it is quite acceptable to move from one subject to another. They don't have to be related to each other or have an overall theme any more than a conversation has to be structured in a specific way. If you were writing a letter to a close friend who you had not seen for a while then you might tell them about your concerns for them and that you have been thinking about them and praying for them, you might share some truth that has come clear to you in recent weeks, tell them about some recent events in your life and send greetings from a friend who was with you. If you knew them really well and had heard things about them that concerned you then you might offer some advice. This is how Paul's letters come across; they are written from a man to a group of close friends.

Paul's letters contain a variety of material and in order to try and understand them better we will consider six elements which occur throughout them all:

- ***Prayer*** – Paul's prayer for the church.
- ***Doctrine*** – Fundamental teaching, particularly about who Christ is.
- *Apostles* – Insight into the life of an apostle.
- *Correction* – Correction of error in the church.
- *Instructions* – How to live a godly life.
- *Greetings* – From fellow workers and to individuals.

All these subjects appear in Paul's letter to the Colossians and so we will look at that letter in detail – covering three of these elements today and three tomorrow – before moving on to spend three days looking at Paul's other letters.

A Typical Letter – Colossians

Colossians, like a number of Paul's letters, was written from prison. The church in Colossae was founded by a man called Epaphras during Paul's three–year stay in Ephesus (see Colossians 1:7–8 and Acts 19:10). It is now about five years later: Paul is in prison in Rome and Epaphras has come to him to report on the church. As we will see when we look at the detail of the letter, the main reason for Paul writing to the Colossians was to combat the Greek heresy (heresy means teaching which contradicts or undermines true teaching about Christ and our salvation) which taught that salvation came through secret knowledge or wisdom, not through faith in Christ. Paul refutes this by showing how Christ is completely adequate for salvation and the Christian life. It is very relevant today in distinguishing orthodox Christianity – which has no secrets and requires no additional revelation – from sects who offer secret knowledge to those who join them and add to the gospel.

Outline of Colossians	
1:1–14	Paul's prayer for the church
1:15–23	Doctrine: The supremacy of Christ
1:24–2:5	Paul's life as an apostle
2:6–23	A denunciation of heresies
3:1–4:6	Rules for life
4:7–18	Greetings

Let's look in detail at the first three sections of this letter.

Paul's Prayer for the Church

Paul often starts his letters with a prayer of thanks for the church he is writing to and he is always encouraging. Imagine how you would feel to hear that someone is praying for you in this way.

Read Colossians 1:1–14

Paul is often aware of some awful situations in some of the churches he is writing to but that doesn't stop him finding good things to thank God for about them. Rather than concentrate on the negative things at the beginning he indicates that he is praying that they will grow in their knowledge of God and grow to be more like him. Paul only got occasional news from the churches by letter or from a fellow worker who travelled to see him so he gets before God on a daily basis to thank him for the progress they are making and to seek him for strength for the churches. He does not have the opportunity to pick up the phone and intervene himself!

Doctrine – Fundamental Teaching

The original teaching in the early churches was all spread by word of mouth. The apostles and others who had lived alongside Jesus repeated his teaching but, as people received the gospel third or fourth hand, things became distorted and heresy crept in. When writing to Timothy, a church leader, Paul tells him to *"Watch your life and doctrine closely." (1 Timothy 4:16)*. To Titus he says, *"You must teach what is in accord with sound doctrine." (Titus 2:1)*. Doctrine means a body of teaching and Paul is concerned in his letters to make sure that his churches are aware of the truth about Jesus. He had grown up as a Jew and been taught the Old Testament as a Pharisee and so he knew how fundamentally important it was to know and understand the scriptures.

The Lord Jesus Christ is absolutely central to Paul's teaching – who he was, what he has done for us, and the future hope we have in him. His teaching draws on the Old Testament and his research into what Jesus said and did. The church in Colossae had particular need to understand who Jesus was and Paul packs an incredible amount of truth about him into the few verses starting in chapter 1 verse 15. Read this passage slowly and carefully to appreciate what Paul is saying about who Jesus is.

Read Colossians 1:15–23

Each letter has a different emphasis in its teaching, which we will look at in more detail over the next few days.

Insight into the Life of an Apostle

Paul goes on to talk about his physical, mental and spiritual struggle with and for his churches as he proclaims the gospel, teaches them and corrects error. He is not boastful about what he has done but wants them to know his heart for them and to learn the truth from him as he is always eager to see them growing to maturity. The early church had many teachers including a number who preached error very eloquently and Paul is very concerned that they do not get led astray. Although he is not physically present with them he wants them to know that he is "present in spirit" – an expression he also used to the Corinthian church – and act as though he is there in person.

Read Colossians 1:24–2:5

Paul clearly saw the churches that he had founded as *his* churches. While he welcomes those who build on what he has done he is not afraid to speak to them very strongly and urge them not to follow those who will lead them astray. He holds himself up as an example to follow: *"Follow my example, as I follow the example of Christ." (1 Corinthians 11:1)*. Being an apostle carries with it great responsibilities.

Paul also suffered much for the gospel and as a result of his calling to be an apostle. Some of this is described in Acts where he was imprisoned, stoned and beaten but we learn that he suffered even more than that from passages in his letters, particularly in 2 Corinthians 11. But through all suffering he rejoices to see the churches growing. *"I ... delight to see how orderly you are and how firm your faith in Christ is." (Colossians 2:5).*

Philemon

A further insight into Paul's situation at this time comes from the little letter of Philemon. Although it comes at the end of Paul's letters in our Bibles it was written at the same time as Colossians and sent with it to a man called Philemon in the church in Colossae. The letter is about Philemon's slave, Onesimus, who had deserted him. While he was on the run, Onesimus had been converted through contact with Paul and become his helper but Paul is now sending him back to his master with this plea for him to be received as a brother in Christ rather than punished for his actions. Paul does not command Philemon but makes a very personal appeal as *"an old man" (Philemon 9)* who is now a prisoner and in chains – his situation while he was writing the letter to the church in Colossae.

Tomorrow we will see the other three elements in Paul's letters as we look at the rest of Colossians.

Day 72
Correcting Wrong Ideas

There are six elements which can be found in most of Paul's letters. Yesterday we looked at three: prayer, doctrine, and insight into the life of an apostle. Today we will look at the other three: correction of error, instructions on how to live a godly life and greetings from fellow workers.

Correction of Error

As we saw yesterday, the original teaching in the early churches was all spread by word of mouth and so it is not surprising that Christians incorporated ideas from their own background and from the culture they lived in into their beliefs and the way in which they practiced their faith. As time progressed a number of distinct heresies, or false teachings, developed.

Each church was subject to different heresy and it appears that a number of the letters were written to combat specific errors. It is not always stated what these were in the letters but it can be deduced from the contents and from knowledge of the early church from other sources. Each church was subject to its own influences which we will look at in more detail tomorrow. Paul not only warns against false teaching but, particularly when he is talking to church leaders, he also warns against false teachers.

There are two main errors which the early church fell into and, despite the cultural differences, both are still very relevant today.

> Read Colossians 2:6–23

The Jewish Heresy – Legalism

The church started out as 100% Jewish and the Jews had been brought up to follow the regulations in the Old Testament. This included rules about what they should eat, who they should associate with, and that they should be circumcised. When Gentiles (non–Jews) were converted they had a completely different background.

From Acts 10 we saw the struggle it was for Peter to go and preach the gospel in the house of a Gentile and his surprise that God should pour out the Holy Spirit on them too. Even having gone to the house of a

Day 72 – Correcting Wrong Ideas

Gentile brought Peter into criticism: *"So when Peter went up to Jerusalem, the circumcised believers criticized him and said, "You went into the house of uncircumcised men and ate with them.""" (Acts 11:2–3)*. Only after Peter had explained himself were they happy to accept that the gospel was for the Gentiles too.

But as the gospel spreads among the Gentiles, more and more churches grew up which were mainly Gentile. The church in Antioch was one of these and Jews who came to it were unhappy to find that people had become Christians without first keeping the Old Testament law. *"Some men came down from Judea to Antioch and were teaching the brothers: "Unless you are circumcised, according to the custom taught by Moses, you cannot be saved."" (Acts 15:1)*. This led to a sharp dispute and Paul and Barnabas were sent to Jerusalem to get a ruling from the apostles. During a long debate Peter points out that the Jews have been unable to keep the law so asking the Gentiles to do so is futile anyway. *"We believe it is through the grace of our Lord Jesus that we are saved, just as they are" (Acts 15:11)* is Peter's conclusion and the meeting agreed that it was not necessary for new believers to be circumcised or asked to attempt to keep the Old Testament law.

Despite this ruling the Jewish element persisted throughout the early church. Although Paul was brought up as a Pharisee he became totally convinced that people become Christians through grace, a totally free gift from God, not through keeping regulations and his letters are full of teaching on grace. He also makes some direct attacks on the Jewish heresy in his letters. The Colossian church had a Jewish element and Paul tells the whole church *"In him you were also circumcised, in the putting off of the sinful nature, not with a circumcision done by the hands of men but with the circumcision done by Christ" (Colossians 2:11)*. Later he tells them *"Here there is no Greek or Jew, circumcised or uncircumcised, barbarian, Scythian, slave or free, but Christ is all, and is in all." (Colossians 3:11)*. This undermined any attempt by the Jews to insist that the Greeks were circumcised before they could become Christians.

While the Jewish element of many present day churches is very small or non–existent, Christians throughout the centuries have often reduced Christianity to a series of rules and regulations. Despite the wonderful message of grace, salvation has been made dependent on doing this or not doing that. Some sects actually preach this but even in mainstream churches who clearly preach grace people still look down on those who do not keep the rules. This attitude is sometimes called legalism.

This does not only affect those in the church but is the message that is projected outside too. Today many people believe that they will get to heaven because they have lived a good life. They are offended to be told that they, like the rest of us, are sinners in need of a free gift from God.

The Greek Heresy

Philosophy was at the centre of Greek culture and between 600 and 200 BC, as the Greek civilisation flowered, men such as Pythagoras, Socrates and Plato debated ideas and developed explanations of the material world and what lay beyond it. The Greeks who became Christians came from this philosophical background and some of them added ideas from their culture to their new faith. By the second century AD an entire system of belief known as Gnosticism was developed. This took ideas from Greek philosophy, Eastern religion, magic and astrology and added them to Christianity. The word Gnostic is a Greek word meaning "knowledge" and one of the key features of the Gnostic teachers was that the teaching of the apostles had to be supplemented with the "higher knowledge" that they (the Gnostics) claimed to possess.

The Gnostic teaching was not a coherent set of beliefs but included a whole range of ideas. One part of the teaching of Gnosticism was that the spirit is entirely good and matter is entirely evil. From this flowed the idea that salvation could only be obtained by escape from the body which was achieved not by faith in Christ but by special knowledge. The body, since it was evil, had to be treated harshly in order to subdue it but, on the other hand, men could do what they liked with their bodies since they were evil anyway. The idea that God could take on a material body which they saw as intrinsically evil was unthinkable and so Christ's true humanity was denied.

In addition to all this Gnostic teachers devised systems of angels between men and God and these could be learned about and worshipped in order to get closer to God.

The letters of Colossians and 1 John are most direct in their attacks on the Gnostic ideas. Paul's teaching on who Christ is in Colossians 1:15–20 deals with wrong ideas about who Jesus is and in Colossians 2:3 he refers to Christ *"in whom are hidden all the treasures of wisdom and knowledge."* There is no secret knowledge outside Christ for them to find. In Colossians 2:8 Paul directly warns them *"See to it that no one takes you captive through hollow and deceptive philosophy, which*

Day 72 – Correcting Wrong Ideas

depends on human tradition and the basic principles of this world rather than on Christ" and at the end of chapter 2 he denounces the keeping of regulations as of no value in *"restraining sensual indulgence."*

Although Gnosticism in the form it was taught in the early Christian years is no longer taken that seriously (although recent TV documentaries in the UK have sought to elevate early Gnostic writings to the same level as the Bible), the heresy has a very contemporary ring about it. Today the mixing of Christianity with other faiths and ideas is commonplace both outside the church and, sadly, within it. Outside the church there are many pseudo–religious organisations such as Freemasonry which offer "secret" knowledge. Eastern religions have gained popularity in the West and, with their all encompassing nature, have been happy to incorporate Christianity by saying that Jesus was one of many gurus or enlightened ones. When people become Christians today they need clear teaching on who Jesus is as they are quite likely to already have ideas about him which are unbiblical.

The church in its attempt to keep up with the changes in society has reached out to other faiths and, instead of preaching the message of the gospel, has sought to compromise it and look for common ground. Paul's teaching about Jesus is just as important for the church today as it was to those who first received the letter.

Instructions on How to Live a Godly Life

When Paul teaches doctrine it is not just so that his audience will gain knowledge: he is always concerned that they should apply it to their daily living. In all of his letters to churches Paul brings practical instruction on how to live as a Christian.

Paul clearly teaches that salvation comes as a free gift of God's grace and cannot be earned by keeping rules and regulations. We are not called to live godly lives in order to win God's favour but as a response to what he has done for us. The practical teaching he gives in Colossians 3:1–4:6 is firmly embedded in teaching on who we are in Christ. The reason why we should put to death the desires of our sinful nature is not to earn our salvation or make us more godly but because we have died with Christ and been raised with him. In Paul's mind there is a direct link between our understanding of who Jesus is and who we are as a result of his sacrifice for us and how we should live our lives. Note how Colossians 3 starts with the word "since" and the use of the word "therefore" in verses 5 and 12.

> **Read Colossians 3:1–4:6**

Paul's teaching is not only concerned with what we should put to death in our lives but he also provides positive teaching on loving one another and letting Christ bring peace. This teaching too is based on what God has done for us. Why should we be compassionate to others? Because we are loved by God. Why should we forgive others? Because the Lord has forgiven us (see 3:12–13). As well as teaching for everyone Paul included specific teaching for wives and husbands, children and fathers, slaves and masters. These are down to earth practical words that are to be worked out on a daily basis in the home and the workplace. Paul's teaching is thoroughly consistent with the Old Testament moral law and with Jesus' teaching. He encourages his church members to take personal responsibility for their lives. When Paul is writing to church leaders (Timothy and Titus) he also gives instructions on church leadership, worship, and what they should teach.

Greetings from Fellow Workers

Paul always ends his letters with greetings from fellow workers and to individuals in the church he is writing to. From Colossians 4:7 he talks about his fellow workers: Tychicus and Onesimus who will carry the letter to them, Aristarchus who is a fellow prisoner, and Doctor Luke the author of the gospel and of Acts. Although these verses are not directly relevant to us today we gain an insight into how Paul worked. He relied on strong relationships and worked alongside men and women he could trust to help him in the task of looking after the churches. He took young men under his wing and trained them.

> **Read Colossians 4:7–18**

Paul is also concerned about individuals in the church he is writing to. To appreciate this I'd like you to imagine that you were there on the day when the church in Colossae received this letter.

News had gone around the town that at their meeting on the coming Sunday there was going to be a reading of a letter sent from Paul so there was a real buzz in the meeting that morning and everybody was there. The lecture hall in Colossae where they met was packed out – standing room only at the back. As the reader stood to read there was an expectant hush.

Day 72 – Correcting Wrong Ideas

As he reads about Paul's prayer for them they are so encouraged. Paul not only finds time to mention them in prayer but he gives thanks for them! His prayer for them to grow to maturity is met with murmurs of approval around the hall. Then they hear *"He is the image of the invisible God, the firstborn over all creation ..."* and their minds reel with the concepts that are coming at them. One of the leaders cuts in at this point to say that there is so much teaching in these few lines that they will spend the next few weeks looking at what Paul has written. Then they hear about Paul's life and how he is struggling for them and their hearts go out to him as they try and take on board what he is doing for them.

Up to this point they are united but as the reader continues things change. The church in Colossae was like most churches and had factions within it – groups with different ideas who looked down on the others – and the next few verses were hard to hear as different groups couldn't conceal their delight!

"See to it then that no–one takes you captive through hollow and deceptive philosophy ..." The Jews love this. They are all sitting together and can hardly keep to their seats as they look over at the Greeks with very self–satisfied looks and jeers. "We told you Greeks about all your philosophy..." they say, and now they have the backing of Paul himself. That will put them in their place! But suddenly the tables are turned as the letter continues. *"...not with a circumcision done by men ..."*. This gets the Greeks up out of their seats as Paul clearly sides with them against the Jews who want people to follow Old Testament regulations. Imagine the uproar as each group applies Paul's words to the others in the meeting!

Then there is all the practical teaching and people go quiet as they all feel convicted about something in the list. And then the uproar returns.

"Wives, submit to your husbands..." Yes! The husbands cannot conceal their delight at hearing Paul saying exactly what they wanted him to say. But their delight is short lived as they hear *"Husbands, love your wives and do not be harsh with them"* and the men are quickly silenced as the wives swap big smiles with their friends and make a note to mention that when they get home. *"Children, obey your parents..."* brings groans from the front where all the children are sitting on the floor. But these turn to cheers as they hear *"Fathers do not embitter your children ..."* which instantly becomes the only bit

they remember! Slaves and Masters all find something for them in this section too.

Then the noise subsides as they hear about Paul's fellow workers and they sense the letter is coming to an end. They note that the church in Laodicea has also received a letter and there is an appeal for anyone travelling to Laodicea in the coming week to pick up a copy.

And then, imagine that you are Archippus, a member of the church in Colossae, sitting among that congregation. The reader has been reading for quite a time and you are expecting him to read Paul's final words when suddenly you hear *"Tell Archippus: "See to it that you complete the work you have received in the Lord.""(Colossians 4:17)*. Wow! As he went home his head was reeling. Paul, with all the churches he is concerned about has not forgotten him, an ordinary man in one of Paul's many churches. Paul is not only concerned with the big picture but also has time to think about the individuals too.

Day 73
Romans

Romans is different from Paul's other letters in that it was not written to a church that he founded himself. As a result it does not contain much in the way of personal details, nor does he spend time correcting error or answering questions from them. Instead, we have a systematic explanation of the gospel, complete with answers to potential issues that can arise.

As we saw, Peter said that Paul's letters *"contain some things that are hard to understand"* and this is true of Romans where there has been a variety of opinions as to how to interpret some of the middle chapters over the centuries. For many though, the mysteries of the book have been best explained through the teachings of Dr Martyn Lloyd–Jones, a man who trained as a medical doctor but gave up a brilliant medical career to become a Presbyterian minister. In 1938 he moved to Westminster Chapel in the heart of London where he was the minister for thirty years and in October 1955 he began a series of Friday night Bible studies on Romans that continued through until February 1968 covering Romans 1:1–14:17 in an incredible 372 sessions! These sermons are now available in book form[12] and, although their length appears daunting at first sight, they are well worth reading if you want to gain a deeper understanding of the gospel.

I am not ashamed of the Gospel!

After his introduction and prayer for the church Paul announces his theme at the beginning of the letter: *"I am not ashamed of the gospel, because it is the power of God for the salvation of everyone who believes: first for the Jew, then for the Gentile. For in the gospel a righteousness from God is revealed, a righteousness that is by faith from first to last, just as it is written: 'The righteous will live by faith.'"* (Romans 1:16–17). These two verses sum up his whole message which he then expounds in more detail from verse 18 onwards.

Paul has good news – that is what "gospel" means – for everyone. This good news is about salvation, a word used throughout the Bible to

---

[12] The full set of fourteen books of Dr Martyn Lloyd–Jones sermons has been published by "The Banner of Truth Trust". They all have a title beginning "Romans".

describe being saved from something and for something. As Christians we are delivered from the guilt of sin we have committed and from the punishment we deserve for it (see Romans 1:18–3:31), from the power that sin has over us (see Romans 5:12–8:39) and from the corruption of our nature by sin (mentioned in Romans 7). But we have also been saved into a secure, intimate relationship with God which we enjoy through the power of the Holy Spirit living within us (Romans 8). Through this salvation we can be assured of eternal life, the promise of spending eternity in the presence of God. This is very good news and

Outline of Romans	
1:1–15	Introduction
1:16–17	Summary of Paul's message – the Gospel
1:18–3:20	Man's condition without God – Everyone is a sinner
3:21–4:25	God's offer: A Righteousness from God – Justification by Faith
5–8	The Security of the Christian:
5:1–10	– Secure because God has done it all
5:11–21	– Secure because we are united with Christ
6	Objection! Such teaching will encourage people to go on sinning
7	Objection! This ignores God's law
8:1–27	– Secure because the Holy Spirit is within us
8:28–39	– Summary of our Security
9–11	God's Purpose in Salvation
9	– Salvation is entirely God's doing
10	– Salvation, which can only be obtained by faith, is for both Jew and Gentile
11	– Has God rejected the Israelites? No!
12–13	Putting it into practice in the church and in the world
14:1–15:13	Being considerate towards weaker Christians
15:14–33	Conclusion
16	Personal greetings

certainly not something we need to be ashamed of!

Now most members of the church in Rome were Gentiles but, like all the major cities of that time, there was also a large Jewish community and some of them were part of the church. Some Jews found it hard to accept that they needed this salvation as they already had the law of God, while others found it hard to accept that God could also save Gentile 'sinners' and believed that salvation was only for the Jews. Paul makes it plain that God's good news of salvation is for everyone, both Jew and Gentile (see Romans 9–11).

After he has completed his exposition of the gospel Paul works out its practical application from Romans 12 onwards before ending with personal greetings.

The state of Man without God

Why do we need "a righteousness from God"? The answer is in the next verse: *"The wrath of God is being revealed from heaven against all the godlessness and wickedness of men who suppress the truth by their wickedness..." (Romans 1:18).* The natural state of mankind is to act without reference to God and to be wicked, which means to break God's righteous laws, and God hates wickedness with a passion. Wrath is a strong word meaning "anger" or "indignation" and the message is that God will punish sin.

The Jews have had God's laws and so have no excuse for their wickedness and as for the Gentiles, Paul says that they have no excuse either as creation demonstrates *"God's invisible qualities – his eternal power and divine nature" (Romans 1:20).* The rest of Romans 1 describes the level of sin that the Gentiles sink to, which ends not only with them doing things that they know in their hearts to be wrong but also approving of others who do them – a stern warning for those who argue that because certain immoral acts have always gone on in private so we should make them acceptable or even promote them as being good.

It is easy to read this passage and feel that because I don't behave like that I must be all right. But in Romans 2 and 3 Paul attacks this comfortable feeling and makes it clear that all are sinners and so under the wrath of God. His conclusion, supported by a long list of Old Testament references is that *"Jews and Gentiles alike are all under sin." (Romans 3:9).*

Justification by Faith

Having argued the case that all men are sinners, Paul now starts to describe the salvation that is on offer in more detail.

> Read Romans 3:21–28

Paul is saying that as sinners we can never become righteous through our own efforts but God has now made righteousness – the ability to stand perfect before him – available to us. How do we receive this? It is through faith in Jesus Christ, there is no other route. Who is this offer available to? Everyone! But does this mean that God has ignored our sin? No, his justice demands that sin be punished and Jesus has taken that punishment.

The central message of the gospel is that we can be "justified by faith". This principle was lost to most of the church for hundreds of years. Over the centuries the church fell into the heresies we looked at yesterday, particularly legalism, and it laid down rules and regulations for living and told people that they could only obtain salvation through keeping rules and through making up for their sins through penance (fasting or punishing themselves). Then, in the early sixteenth century, Martin Luther, a young German monk, realised through reading Romans that, despite all his efforts to discipline himself and follow all the monastery rules, he could never obtain salvation through his own efforts but that God had made a way open for him to be fully justified before God through faith! His understanding of this truth led to the start of the Reformation, a movement that gave birth to the Protestant church and swept across Europe and the world as people realised that they too could be justified – made fully right with God – by faith.

Paul goes on in Romans 4 to point out that this is a teaching fully supported by the Old Testament. Abraham, the man the Jews looked back to as the father of their nation, was also counted as righteous before God because of his faith, not through any merit of his own.

What an Amazing Salvation!

Having established the principle of "justification by faith" Paul starts to draw conclusions from it. Note the use of the word "Therefore" at the beginning which indicates that it logically follows from what has already been said.

> Read Romans 5:1–11

Romans 5:6–8 makes it crystal clear that your salvation is not dependent in any way, shape or form, on your effort! Two words are to describe my condition without God: powerless and ungodly. I am not naturally inclined towards God, in fact I would prefer to live my life without reference to him, and even if I was, I can no more make myself right with God through my efforts than flap my arms and fly to the moon! Someone had to die for my sins to bring about reconciliation with a holy God.

Now throughout history we can find some rare examples of men being prepared to die in the place of another. But these heroic acts are usually done for great men, maybe for men that people think of as good, or for close family. But to die for someone who is an ungodly sinner is an act that could only come out of an extraordinary love. The fact that Christ died for us demonstrates the depth of God's love.

So when you start to think that maybe God does not love you anymore because you have done something wrong, or not done enough good, just remember that he first loved you when you were a powerless, ungodly sinner. God's love is not dependent on what you do! We have a secure hope that we will see God in his glory and will be saved from God's wrath – for God to achieve that is easy compared to dying in our place. What an amazing salvation this is! What good news!

Objection!

In fact, when you think about it, this is fantastic news! If, as Paul teaches, I have been justified by faith and I can be 100% confident that I will be saved from God's wrath and will live with him in his glory forever *whatever I do*, then that means that I can live my life exactly how I want to, doesn't it? If God's grace is so great that he is willing to forgive my sin why don't I continue sinning to give him opportunity to demonstrate even more grace? Paul addresses this question head on in Romans 6: *"What shall we say, then? Shall we go on sinning so that grace may increase? By no means! We died to sin; how can we live in it any longer?" (Romans 6:1–2)*.

At first sight it may appear ridiculous for a Christian to be suggesting that he should continue sinning but Dr Lloyd–Jones makes an interesting comment about this objection. *"The true preaching of the gospel of salvation by grace alone always leads to the possibility of this charge being brought against it... If my preaching and presentation of the gospel of salvation does not expose it to that misunderstanding, then it is not the gospel."*[L]. If you believe, as many both inside and outside the church do, that we can earn our salvation through not sinning and trying to be good then this is not an issue. It is only when someone understands that they can be justified by faith alone that there is the danger that they will abuse the gift of God and continue to sin.

So what is the answer to this objection? Paul makes it clear that we must not continue to sin because *"we died to sin" (Romans 6:2)* when we became Christians. The problem is that we don't realise this fact and often continue as if sin still had power over us so Paul tells us to *"count yourselves dead to sin but alive to God in Christ Jesus." (Romans 6:11)*. There is no need to die again, but we need to live in the good of what Christ has done for us in his amazing salvation.

The Work of the Holy Spirit

In Romans 8 Paul returns to the main thread of his argument and talks about the security that comes from the work of the Holy Spirit in our lives. It starts with another "Therefore", echoing the start of chapter 5, linking his argument back to justification by faith. As you read this well known passage see how Paul contrasts life lived under the power of sin with life lived "according to the Spirit."

> **Read Romans 8:1–17**

Note how the Holy Spirit controls our mind, will raise us from the dead, will help us to put sin to death in our lives and gives us assurance that we are God's children. In the following verses we read how he includes us in God's great purposes for the universe and helps us to pray. The Holy Spirit is central to living the Christian life.

Absolute Security

Having discussed the security of the Christian Paul now sums up his argument so far in some very well known verses at the end of Romans 8.

> **Read Romans 8:28–39**

These are very remarkable verses! We, as Christians, have been *"called according to his purpose"* and for us, God works for our good *"in all things"*! Paul is not saying that being a Christian is an easy life but it is one where we can be totally secure that God, who has already sacrificed his own son in order to justify us, will bring us safely to his glorious presence. In life it is easy to feel separated from God's love but these verses spell out the fact that there is nothing in this life that can do that. And when I had the privilege of reading these verses at my uncle's funeral, his family and friends were comforted by the assurance that we are not separated from God's love in death either.

God's Eternal Purpose

The doctrine of justification by faith raises many important issues and in Romans 9–11 Paul continues to argue the case for it and to show how the gospel is a continuation of what God has been saying in the Old Testament. As part of this great argument he also deals with two particular issues: predestination and the position of the Jews.

The issue of predestination, which Paul refers to in Romans 8:29, is one that many have puzzled over down the centuries. The idea that God "foreknew" and "predestined" people to become Christians leaves him open to accusations of injustice as there is the clear implication that he has not predestined others. How can it be right that God elects or predestines some to salvation but not others? Paul defends God's right to do as he will in this passage. He also makes it clear that those who refuse to accept God will be held fully responsible for their actions, and so their punishment will be just and fair, while those who admit their need of God and put their faith in him will know that God is fully responsible for their salvation, and will give all the credit to him.

Paul also speaks as a Jew about the position of the Israelites in God's plan. Although they as a nation rejected God, his offer of salvation to all men does not mean that they no longer have a special place in his heart. Paul looks forward to a day when *"all Israel will be saved" (Romans 11:26)* on the same basis as everyone else, through faith in Jesus Christ.

Living Sacrifices

For Paul the gospel is not a dry set of doctrines, it has application for daily living. So, after ending his exposition of the gospel with an outburst of praise at the end of Romans 11 he draws practical conclusions. Again he starts with the word "Therefore" indicating the direct link between theory and practice.

> **Read Romans 12**

Paul goes on to give instructions for dealing with civil authorities, paying taxes, and being considerate to those in the church who see things differently from you. There is nothing "other worldly" about the gospel. It has very practical down–to–earth relevance.

The Gospel in a Nutshell

Romans contains the clearest explanation of the gospel of any book in the Bible and whether you are thinking about becoming a Christian, or have recently become one, or have been a Christian for many years, time spent studying Romans will give you a better understanding of the amazing gospel – *"the power of God for the salvation of everyone who believes."*

References

[L] *The New Man*, D M Lloyd–Jones, chap 6, p. 8. ISBN 0851511589, Banner of Truth, Edinburgh. www.banneroftruth.co.uk

Day 74
The Fruit and Gifts of the Spirit

Having looked at Colossians and Romans we will now look at the rest of Paul's letters in less detail over the next two days. We will look at them in the order they were probably written so today we will look at 1 & 2 Thessalonians, Galatians and 1 & 2 Corinthians.

1 & 2 Thessalonians

Paul and Silas founded the church in Thessalonica (see Map 9 on page 387) during Paul's second missionary journey (see Acts 17:1–10). They aroused hostility from the Jews and were soon forced to leave. Paul moved on to Athens and then Corinth and, as he was unable to return to Thessalonica himself, he sent Timothy back to help the young church (see 1 Thessalonians 2:17–3:3). When Timothy rejoined Paul (see 1 Thessalonians 3:6), Paul wrote to encourage them and give them teaching.

\	Outline of 1 Thessalonians
1	Thanks for the Thessalonians.
2	Paul's ministry to them.
3	Timothy's ministry with them and his report.
4:1–12	Instructions for life.
4:13–5:11	Teaching on the second coming of Christ.
5:12–28	Further instructions.

2 Thessalonians was probably written very soon after 1 Thessalonians.

\	Outline of 2 Thessalonians
1	Paul's prayer for the church
2	Teaching on the end times
3	Warning against idleness

The Coming of the Lord

There is a very strong emphasis on "End Times" running through both the letters to the Thessalonian church. Jesus taught that he would return to earth and many in the early church thought that the end would come soon. Some at Thessalonica seemed to think that it had already happened (see 2 Thessalonians 2:1–2). What they had missed was that Jesus talked about things which must come before the end. Paul corrects their thinking by talking about what will happen both before and when Jesus returns.

Paul reassures the church that those among them who have already died ("fallen asleep") will be participants in the return of Christ along with those Christians who are alive at that time. There is great encouragement for us as Christians in this passage as after death we will live with the Lord for ever and so, although we mourn when those close to us die, we do not *"grieve like the rest of men, who have no hope." (1 Thessalonians 4:13)*. What an incredible faith we have!

> **Read 1 Thessalonians 4:13–5:11**

Paul is very clear that we cannot know when Jesus will return. It will be unexpected but that does not mean that we should not be ready. We are called to live our lives each day with Christ, as we will after his return. Maybe as a result of too great an emphasis on Jesus returning soon there was an issue with idleness in Thessalonica. Paul has no time for this and his teaching is summed up in the phrase *"If a man will not work, he shall not eat" (2 Thessalonians 3:10)*.

Galatians

Galatians is a circular letter to churches in the Roman province of Galatia (see Map 8 on page 383). Paul planted churches in the towns of Antioch, Iconium, Lystra and Derbe during his first missionary journey (see Acts 13–14).

The letter is almost entirely aimed at correcting the Jewish heresy. It seems that the churches in Galatia have come under the influence of Jewish Christians who taught that Christians had to observe a number of the Old Testament regulations, including circumcision, in order to be saved. This influence was widespread in the early church and even Peter succumbed to it (see 2:11–14). The heart of Paul's message is that we are justified before God by faith alone, a point he makes abundantly clear, at one point stating three times in one verse that we:

"know that a man is not justified by observing the law, but by faith in Jesus Christ. So we, too, have put our faith in Christ Jesus that we may be justified by faith in Christ and not by observing the law, because by observing the law no one will be justified." (Galatians 2:16). The letter makes this one point and the argument is followed through without digressions.

Outline of Galatians	
1–2	Paul's defence of his teaching from his experience and dealings with other apostles.
3–4	Arguments from the Old Testament that the Law is inadequate and that *"The righteous will live by faith"* (3:11).
5–6	Call to live in freedom and by the Spirit.

The relevance of Galatians is not limited to the first century church. As we saw yesterday, the principle of "justification by faith" was lost to the church for many centuries until Martin Luther rediscovered it. He then often used Galatians as the basis for his arguments.

The Fruit of the Spirit

As in Romans, Paul emphasizes the importance of living the Christian life "by the Spirit". We are not called to be good by our own efforts but through walking day by day in step with the Holy Spirit. In Galatians 5 Paul talks about the fruit of the Spirit: *"The fruit of the Spirit is love, joy, peace, patience, kindness, goodness, faithfulness, gentleness and self–control." (Galatians 5:22–23)*. Fruit does not suddenly appear but grows slowly over time and the fruit of the Spirit are the characteristics of a mature Christian who has walked with the Spirit over many years. Later today we will see how Paul encourages us to desire the gifts of the Spirit in 1 Corinthians but how in that passage he stresses the importance of using our gifts with love, self–control and the rest of the fruit of the Spirit.

Returning to his theme that no–one is justified by keeping the law, Paul comments on the fruit of the Spirit that *"Against such things there is no law." (Galatians 5:23)*. We can use rules and regulations to stop wrong behaviours but the law is totally inadequate at bringing about a positive change in our hearts. That comes through us staying close to God on a daily basis.

Letters to Corinth

The two letters to the Corinthian church are each almost as big as the letter to the Romans and between them they provide the biggest insight into Paul's relationship with a church. Paul founded the church in Corinth during his second missionary journey (see Acts 18). On his third journey he spent two years in Ephesus where he hears disturbing reports from the church in Corinth and receives a letter asking for advice. 1 Corinthians is the response to that letter (see 1 Corinthians 7:1) and contains a wealth of material.

Outline of 1 Corinthians	
1:1–9	Introduction and prayerful thanks for the church
1:10–17	Divisions in the church
1:18–2:16	The foolishness of man's wisdom
3–4	Divisions in the church
5–6	Immorality and Legal Disputes
7	Marriage
8–10	Food offered to idols – exercising love over our rights
11	Behaviour in public worship, The Lord's Supper
12–4	The use of Spiritual Gifts, Love.
15	The Resurrection of Christ and of the Dead
16	Conclusion: Practical and Personal Matters.

After writing 1 Corinthians Paul made a visit to the church to deal with the issues he had written about. This visit was painful and he then wrote a second letter in preparation for a third visit (see 2 Corinthians 2:1 and 13:1). It appears that the Corinthian church has been infiltrated by false apostles and Paul writes to denounce them and their teaching and to make clear his own authority over them. 2 Corinthians is written in a very different style from 1 Corinthians. Paul writes very spontaneously and there is not a clear structure. His heart for the church shines through this very personal letter.

Day 74 – The Fruit and Gifts of the Spirit

Outline of 2 Corinthians	
1–7	Paul explains the reason for his change of plan and explains his ministry as an apostle to them.
8–9	Teaching on Giving. Encouraging the Corinthians to complete their collection for the church in Jerusalem.
10–13	Paul defends his apostolic authority and denounces the false apostles who have deceived the Corinthians

The City of Corinth

Corinth was a very large commercial city in the heart of Greece which in Paul's time was the capital of the Roman province of Achaia (see Map 9 on page 387). It was situated on the small strip of land linking north and south Achaia and had two harbours, one to the east and one to the west, which made it a very significant crossroads for land and seagoing trade. Much of the trade between Rome and the eastern Mediterranean passed through Corinth.

The influence of Greek philosophy was strong and the Corinthians placed a high value on wisdom. Paul makes a strong attack on human wisdom starting at the beginning of 1 Corinthians (see 1:17–2:16) and contrasts worldly wisdom with God's grace early in 2 Corinthians (see 1:12). What Corinth was most famous for, however, was its immorality. Corinth, like its close neighbour Athens (see Acts 17:16) contained many temples including one to Aphrodite, the goddess of love. Worship of Aphrodite involved immoral practices and a thousand 'sacred prostitutes' served her temple. Even among the corruption of the Roman Empire Corinth managed to gain a reputation for wickedness and "to live like a Corinthian" meant to live a life of immorality and debauchery.

Sexual Morality

Given the nature of the city it is not surprising that the church Paul had founded some three years earlier faced some serious moral issues. 1 Corinthians 5 and 6 deal with issues of sexual morality and Paul takes the same line as Jesus in making it quite clear that sexual activity outside marriage, whether it be adultery, sex outside marriage, or homosexuality, is not acceptable behaviour for a Christian. Paul's arguments are summarised at the end of 1 Corinthians 6.

> **Read 1 Corinthians 6:18–20**

Some people think that the Bible's stance on sexual morality is old fashioned as it was written in a very different culture from our own. But the fact that these words were written to the church in Corinth gives it very direct relevance to today's society which not only tolerates but actively promotes immorality through all the media that people "worship" today such as TV, films, music and advertising.

Paul's love for his church is incredible considering his background. He had been brought up as a devout Jew and trained as a Pharisee. This would have trained him to avoid "sinners" and yet here we find him pouring out his love for a church which included those who had been adulterers, male prostitutes, homosexuals, thieves and drunkards (see 1 Corinthians 6:9–11).

How to Exercise Your Spiritual Gifts

The latter part of 1 Corinthians contains some very well known passages which deal with some fundamental issues. Chapter 11 includes some instructions on how to celebrate the Lord's Supper and some serious warnings about approaching it with the right attitude. Paul says that some of the people in the church in Corinth were sick and some had even died through eating and drinking the bread and wine in an unworthy manner. In chapter 15 Paul includes a detailed look at the resurrection. He lists some of Christ's appearances and explains that we too will rise from the dead with new "imperishable" bodies – what a wonderful thought!

In between these two passages there are three chapters where Paul deals with another issue that the church in Corinth is struggling with: how to use the gifts that God has given you. Paul starts by providing a simple test to see if a gift is from God and then lists some of the different kinds of gifts that God gives to individuals, similar to the list we read yesterday in Romans 12. The problem in the church at Corinth was very similar to a problem found in most churches today. There were people who thought that their gift was the most important and that everyone should have it. They did not appreciate that God gives a diversity of gifts for the benefit of the whole church. Paul makes this point by comparing the church to a body. In a series of amusing imaginary conversations between different parts of the body Paul makes the point that the strength of the body is in the diversity of its parts. So it is in the church.

> *Read 1 Corinthians 12*

In chapter 14 Paul continues to give instructions on the use of spiritual gifts, particularly the gifts of tongues and prophecy, in public meetings. Building on the picture of the body where all the parts contribute to the whole, Paul provides simple direction for meetings: *"When you come together, everyone has a hymn, or a word of instruction, a revelation, a tongue or an interpretation. All of these must be done for the strengthening of the church." (1 Corinthians 14:26)*. He goes on to limit the number of tongues or prophecies that are brought and makes it clear that those who exercise such gifts retain self-control. Paul would not agree with those who insist that they cannot help speaking out. Spiritual gifts are to be exercised in an orderly fashion.

The Primary Importance of Love

It is in the context of the use of spiritual gifts that Paul talks about love, which is not a gift but the first fruit of the Spirit. 1 Corinthians 13 is probably the best known chapter in the Bible, although few appreciate its context. Although Paul starts by stressing the importance of exercising spiritual gifts in love he gets carried away and almost inadvertently provides us with one of the greatest descriptions of love ever written. It is no surprise to find it read at wedding services as all marriages would be strengthened if husbands and wives regularly meditated on the characteristics of love listed in verses 4–7.

> *Read 1 Corinthians 13*

Day 75
Practical Teaching for Churches and Leaders

Today we will complete our quick review of Paul's letters by looking at those written after the end of Acts.

Ephesians

Paul made Ephesus (see Map 10 on page 389) a base for evangelism for over two years at the start of his third missionary journey (see Acts 19). By the end of his time the whole of the province of Asia had heard the gospel and a strong church was founded in Ephesus. The letter to the Ephesians was written from prison (see the references to prison in Ephesians 3:1, 4:1 and 6:20), probably in Rome.

Ephesians follows the pattern of most of Paul's letters by falling into two halves – a section of doctrine and a section of practical teaching. It does not appear to be aimed at any particular error in the church in Ephesus but contains all the major doctrines. As a result it is an excellent sermon for new Christians, although it contains such depths that Christians of all ages can continue to learn from it.

Outline of Ephesians	
1–3	Paul shows how man's salvation is part of God's eternal purposes to bring all things under Christ's control.
4:1–6:9	Practical teaching on unity, living in the light, and relationships in the family and at work.
6:10–24	Victorious Christian living and Spiritual Warfare using the Armour of God.

The Big Picture

The opening of Ephesians contains an incredible catalogue of all the blessings that God has given to us as Christians. But Paul is not preaching a "me centred" faith. He superimposes the personal blessings on the backcloth of God's purpose for the entire universe from before creation to beyond the end of the world! Paul's ability to pull these

Day 75 – Practical Teaching for Churches and Leaders

concepts together is breathtaking and all the more amazing when you learn that verses 3–14 are one sentence in the original Greek!

> **Read Ephesians 1:1–14**

Just in that one sentence Paul describes how God chose us before the creation of the world, made us part of his family through adoption, has redeemed and forgiven us, and has "lavished us" with wisdom and insight so we can understand his purposes, which are to bring healing and harmony to the whole universe as God brings all things under the loving control of Christ. When we see the purpose of our own salvation and the purpose of the church in that light it will change the way in which we live our lives. Paul's teaching on unity in the church, righteous living, loving and submissive relationships and spiritual warfare in chapters 4–6 can only be understood and worked out in the light of understanding this background.

Paul makes it very clear that all three members of the trinity are actively involved in working out God's purposes for our lives and for the universe: all our blessings come from God the Father by his grace and for his glory and they come through what Christ has done – the phrase "in Christ" appears eleven times – and by the Spirit who is the guarantor of our faith.

Practical Teaching for Everyday Life

After expanding our vision and understanding of God's purposes for the universe and for our lives Paul provides some very down to earth teaching. In Paul's mind, if you really grasp the truth of what God has done for you, it will affect your daily living at a very practical level. Christianity is not something that we practice on Sunday but will affect our behaviour seven days a week in terms of our personal morality, the conversations we participate in, and our family and business relationships. Note that although I have talked of Ephesians being in two neat halves, with doctrine in one half and practical teaching in the other, this is only a very general distinction. Paul continues to bring doctrine into his teaching.

> **Read Ephesians 5:1–6:9**

There are some people who consider Paul's teaching about women to be harsh. In this passage wives are called on to submit to their husbands, immediately after a call for all of us to submit, or yield our rights, to one another. But this does not mean that Paul is siding with husbands as he calls on them to love their wives *"just as Christ loved the church and gave himself up for her" (Ephesians 5:25)*. In the same way that Jesus taught his disciples to wash one another's feet rather than lording it over them, so husbands are called on to serve their wives and put their needs ahead of their own. Husbands and wives who follow Paul's teaching will have a relationship full of mutual love and respect, not one where the woman is a second class citizen.

Spiritual Warfare

Ephesians ends with a well known passage about the armour of God. As Christians we are involved in a battle, not against people, but against spiritual forces. It would be great to think that as Christians who are part of God's eternal plan we no longer face any dangers but the truth is that the devil continues to have power in this world he is working to destroy our faith and frustrate the purposes of God.

There are two mistakes we can make about the devil. We can underestimate his power or we can overestimate it. At one extreme there are those who don't believe that the devil even exists and see evil as something that is just in human beings. Others talk of the devil as having no power over them as Christians. The Bible takes a different view. We saw how the Lord allowed Satan to afflict Job. God limited his power but Satan still had a devastating impact on his life. Is this an isolated account from the Old Testament? No. At the Last Supper, Jesus told Simon Peter that Satan had asked to "sift him like wheat". I think if I was Peter I would have liked to hear Jesus reassure me that he had told Satan not to touch me but Jesus said *"I have prayed for you, Simon, that your faith may not fail" (Luke 22:32)*. After that Peter's faith was severely tested when he denied Jesus and many years later he wrote, *"Be self-controlled and alert. Your enemy the devil prowls around like a roaring lion looking for someone to devour." (1 Peter 5:8)*. The devil poses a real threat to us as Christians.

However, it is equally wrong to overestimate the power of the devil. He is a created being, not equal to God, and his power is strictly limited by God. James wrote, *"Submit yourselves, then, to God. Resist the devil, and he will flee from you." (James 4:7)*. As we come close to God and submit our lives to him by purifying our hearts so the devil has to retreat. He cannot touch our ultimate security in God.

Paul gives very practical advice for dealing with the devil and his evil forces. He uses the picture of the Roman soldier and six pieces of

Day 75 – Practical Teaching for Churches and Leaders

armour that he has to protect himself and fight – often called "the Armour of God". The first three are to do with standing our ground through proclaiming truth and the righteousness that we have in Christ and the last three are about advancing through faith, remembering our salvation and through using God's word – the sword of the Spirit.

> **Read Ephesians 6:10–18**

Philippians

Paul founded the church at Philippi (see Map 9 on 387) on his second missionary journey and revisited it on his third (see Acts 16:11–40 and 20:1–6). He is now in prison in Rome (see 1:13–14), has received a gift from them and writes to thank them for their concern (4:10–19). He also reports on his situation, encourages them to live in humility and warns them against heresies, particularly the Jewish heresy in chapter 3. The word for joy occurs 16 times in its various forms in the letter and Philippians 4:4 sums up the theme when Paul writes *"Rejoice in the Lord always. I will say it again: Rejoice!"* There are no references to the Old Testament as Philippi was a thoroughly Roman city and there were few Jews.

Outline of Philippians	
1:1–11	Introduction and prayer for the church
1:12–30	Paul's situation
2:1–18	Christ's humility – an example to us
3:1–4:1	Warnings against heresies
4:2–4:9	Practical instructions – rejoice, pray and get your thinking right
4:10–23	Thanks for their gift and final greetings.

In Philippians 2 there is an amazing poem about Jesus and his humility (see verses 6–11). This is one of a number of examples of Paul using poetry and it is thought that it may be a hymn that was sung in the early church.

> **Read Philippians 2:1–11**

Letters to Leaders

The three letters 1 & 2 Timothy and Titus were written to men who were pastors of churches. After the end of Acts it seems likely that Paul travelled widely again. He found various problems in the church at Ephesus and left Timothy there to sort them out. He also evangelised Crete with Titus and left him there to establish churches.

The content of these letters is different from those written to the churches. Warnings against false teaching and false teachers is a main theme in all three letters, but Paul also includes instructions about public worship, the qualifications for leaders, and what to teach different groups in the church. There is very little doctrine, as Timothy and Titus already know it, and Paul often gets carried away in worship.

Timothy the Man

Timothy was brought up in Lystra, a town in Galatia (see Map 8 on page 383), where Paul founded a church on his first missionary journey. He had a devout Jewish Christian mother who brought him up to know the Old Testament scriptures (see 2 Tim 1:5, 3:15). When Paul returned to Lystra on his second journey Timothy joined him (see Acts 16:1–3) and became his close companion throughout his second and third missionary journeys and his journey to Rome where Timothy stayed with Paul while he was imprisoned (see Philippians 1:1). It appears that Paul was released from his imprisonment in Rome and travelled again with Timothy before leaving him to deal with problems in the church in Ephesus (see 1 Tim 1:3).

Timothy was Paul's closest companion and he viewed him as a son. In Philippians he wrote, *"I have no one else like him, who takes a genuine interest in your welfare. For everyone looks out for his own interests, not those of Jesus Christ. But you know that Timothy has proved himself, because as a son with his father he has served with me in the work of the gospel." (Philippians 2:20–22)*. Timothy is never referred to as an apostle but operated with Paul's authority. Timothy had spent so much time with Paul that he knew what Paul would say and do in a situation. This gave Paul such confidence in him that when he sent Timothy to the Corinthian church he wrote, *"I am sending to you Timothy, my son whom I love, who is faithful in the Lord. He will remind you of my way of life in Christ Jesus, which agrees with what I teach everywhere in every church." (1 Corinthians 4:17)*

1 Timothy

In his first letter to Timothy Paul gives him instructions on how he should oversee the church in Ephesus. A number of heresies have come into the church and Timothy is told to oppose them, both the men and the message. Paul opens the letter, *"As I urged you when I went into Macedonia, stay there in Ephesus so that you may command certain men not to teach false doctrines any longer" (1 Timothy 1:3)* and he returns to that theme a number of times. The oversight of a church involves keeping it safe from such men and their message.

Paul urges Timothy to keep true to the faith. 1 Timothy 1:18–20 is sobering reading as Paul makes it clear that anyone can go astray. Even Timothy who has worked alongside Paul for many years is not immune from such dangers. In 1 Timothy 4:13–16 Paul tells him to read the scriptures, preach and teach, to use his gift and, above all, *"Watch your life and doctrine closely. Persevere in them, because if you do, you will save both yourself and your hearers." (1 Timothy 4:16)*. He returns to this theme in 2 Timothy 4:1–2 where he uses very strong words to urge Timothy to stay true to his calling.

\multicolumn{2}{c}{Outline of 1 Timothy}	
1	Warning against false teachers. The Lord's grace to Paul.
2	Instructions on Public Worship
3	Qualifications required for Leadership. They must be "above reproach".
4	Dealing with false teaching
5:1–6:2	Dealing with groups in the church.
6:3–21	Various other instructions.

1 Timothy is more personal than the letters to the churches. However, although it includes special reference to Timothy, it is clear that Paul meant parts of it for a wider circulation.

Titus

Titus, who was a convert of Paul, is not referred to in Acts but is mentioned in some of Paul's other letters as a fellow worker (see 2 Corinthians 7:6–7). After Paul was released from house arrest in Rome he travelled to Crete with Titus and preached the gospel in many towns. He then left Titus there to complete the establishment of churches in the towns where there were converts (see Titus 1:5).

The Cretans were renowned for being liars and lazy. Paul quotes a well-known Cretan poet in Titus 1:12 who wrote, *"Cretans are always liars, evil brutes, lazy gluttons"* – not a quote that was used by the local government when trying to win inward investment! Paul emphasises self-control and doing what is good.

The letter to Titus is a very compact recipe for building the church in 46 verses.

Outline of Titus	
1	Rules regarding Elders. Dealing with false teachers
2	Teaching for different groups in the church.
3	Teaching for the whole church.

2 Timothy

2 Timothy is the last of Paul's letters. It was written from his final imprisonment in Rome when he knows that he is near death. The church is facing persecution under the emperor Nero and Paul urges Timothy to endure.

Outline of 2 Timothy	
1:1–2:13	Paul's encouragement to Timothy to endure.
2:14–3:9	Instructions regarding false teaching
3:10–4:5	Paul's charge to Timothy.
4:6–22	Paul's personal situation

The last few verses contain a mixture of great spiritual statements, as Paul reviews his life and looks forward to his crown of righteousness, of very human comments about his friends, both those who have stood by him and those who have deserted him, and touching practical touches as he asks Timothy to bring his favourite cloak. As you read Paul's final words thank God for what he has left behind in his 13 letters which have contributed so much to our understanding of Jesus

Day 75 – Practical Teaching for Churches and Leaders

Christ and his church.

Read 2 Timothy 4:6–18

Day 76
Letters from Leaders

The first letter that was not written by Paul in our New Testament is the long letter called Hebrews. This is then followed by seven shorter letters written by some of the early church leaders: Peter and John, two of the twelve apostles, and James and Jude, brothers of Jesus. None of these eight letters are addressed to specific churches. The size of Hebrews is very helpful as it makes a good landmark in the New Testament dividing up Paul's letters from the rest. If you are looking for one of Paul's letters then look before Hebrews: if you are looking for a letter by another writer look after it! The main themes of the letters are summarised in Figure 14 below.

\multicolumn{3}{c}{The Themes of Letters from Leaders}		
Letters	Main Themes	Other Topics
Hebrews	Jesus, the supreme mediator between us and God.	Faith
James	Patience in trials and suffering; the tongue; faith and deeds	Humbling yourself. Prayer for healing
1 Peter	Be holy; be submissive; live in harmony; rejoice in suffering	Teaching for elders
2 Peter	Warning against false teachers	The Day of the Lord – coming judgement
1 John	Love: God's love, our love for God, our love for one another.	Warning against antichrists – those who deny that Jesus is God.
2 John	Warning against antichrists	Love
3 John	Encouragement to an individual	
Jude	Warning against false teachers	

Figure 14 – The Themes of Letters from Leaders

We will look at each letter in turn.

Hebrews

Hebrews is primarily addressed to Jewish, or Hebrew, Christians. Its purpose is to demonstrate from the Old Testament – the Hebrew Scriptures – that Jesus is the only one who can mediate between us and God. Like Romans it has one main argument which is followed through from the beginning to nearly the end of the letter.

Outline of Hebrews	
1–2	Christ is superior to angels.
3:1–4:13	Christ is superior to Moses.
4:14–7:28	Christ is superior to Aaron the priest.
8:1–10:18	God has given us a better covenant, a better holy place and a better sacrifice.
10:19–39	A call to keep to the faith.
11	Examples of faith from the Old Testament
12	Encouragement to keep to the faith.
13	Instructions and Conclusions.

As we have already noted, there is no indication as to who the author is but it is clear that whoever he was he had a thorough knowledge of the Old Testament and was associated with Timothy (see 13:23). Suggestions have included Apollos (see Acts 18:21) and Barnabas (see Acts 4:36). The letter was written before the destruction of the temple in AD 70 as the author talks about the temple system continuing (see for example Hebrews 9:25).

The opening verses of Hebrews summarises its message that Jesus is the Son of God who has fully paid the price for our sins. The writer then goes on to use a series of Old Testament quotations to support his argument.

Read Hebrews 1

In addition to its main purpose this chapter also provides a valuable insight into worship. The whole idea of giving praise and worship to a king is fairly alien to our culture these days and we tend to see people bowing down before a king as something that happened in history or only in despotic regimes. So when we are asked to praise God it is easy to get a picture of a sombre God who takes a cold satisfaction from seeing his subjects bow down dutifully before him.

But what we see in Hebrews 1 is that God the Father loves to praise the Son. As you read from verse 8 you can imagine him getting carried away and singing – he is so pleased with the way in which his Son has behaved! Then in Hebrews 2 there are quotations where Jesus sings his praise to the Father for us to hear (see Hebrews 2:12). Worship is something that goes on between the members of the trinity and when we are asked to worship God we are being invited to join in! Being part of God's family means becoming part of a loving, praising relationship that had always gone on between God the Father, Son and Holy Spirit and will continue forever.

In Hebrews 4 there is a verse that describes the power of the word of God: *"For the word of God is living and active. Sharper than any double–edged sword, it penetrates even to dividing soul and spirit, joints and marrow; it judges the thoughts and attitudes of the heart." (Hebrews 4:12)*. We may have thought that the sword of the Spirit that Paul referred to in Ephesians 6:17 was to be used against others, but it also has a purpose in our own lives. As we read our Bibles so we will find that our innermost motivations are exposed to the glare of the powerful spotlight of the word of God that can convict us of hidden sin.

Another very well known verse in Hebrews is at the beginning of chapter 11 where we have a definition of faith: *"Now faith is being sure of what we hope for and certain of what we do not see" (Hebrews 11:1)*. The writer then goes on to list heroes of faith from the Old Testament before issuing us with a challenge. All the people who have gone before did not see the promise of God fulfilled through the coming of Jesus in their lifetime but they lived by faith. We now have the knowledge of what Jesus has done for us so, in the light of the example of those who have lived by faith before us, we too must persevere in our faith despite opposition.

> Read Hebrews 11:39–12:3

James

The author of this letter is James the brother of Jesus. He was probably Jesus' eldest brother as he is first in the list in Matthew 13:55. Initially he, along with other members of Jesus' family, did not believe in Jesus and tried to stop him preaching (see Mark 3:20–21,31) but after Jesus' death and resurrection James believed in him and later became a leading figure in the church in Jerusalem (see Galatians 1:18–19 and Acts 15:13). James does not make any mention of his special earthly relationship to Jesus but introduces himself as *"James, a servant of God and of the Lord Jesus Christ" (James 1:1)*. It is his current spiritual relationship to Jesus that is important, not his historical human one.

The letter is addressed to *"The twelve tribes scattered among the nations" (James 1:1)*. Jewish Christians were scattered by persecution early in the life of the church (see Acts 8:1 and 11:19) and went throughout the Roman Empire spreading the gospel to fellow Jews. James wrote to instruct and encourage the scattered flock. The fact that James was written when the church was still mainly Jewish makes it possibly the earliest of the New Testament writings, written maybe around AD 50.

James does not contain much in the way of doctrine but consists of practical teaching which is similar in style and content to Jesus' teachings in the Sermon on the Mount in Matthew 5–7. This is not surprising as James lived in the same home as Jesus for many years and must have heard him speak on a number of occasions, even if he did not believe in him at the time.

	Outline of James
	Main subjects:
1, 5	Patience in trials and suffering.
1, 3	The tongue
2	Faith and Deeds.
4	Humbling yourself.
5	Prayer for healing

Faith and Deeds

The part of James that has been most misunderstood is at the end of chapter 2 when he deals with the subject of the importance of faith being demonstrated through deeds. He makes the statement *"You see that a person is justified by what he does and not by faith alone" (James 2:24)* which, at first sight, appears to contradict Paul's teaching in Romans and Galatians that justification comes through faith alone. However, they both use the same quotation from Genesis in their argument – *"Abraham believed God, and it was credited to him as righteousness"* – indicating that salvation, or righteousness before God, comes through faith. The point James is making is that an intellectual faith which simply says "I believe in God" but does not recognise the claim that God makes on our life will not result in a change of behaviour. When we truly put our faith in God then his lordship over our life will result in a change that is evident through our deeds.

> **Read James 2:14–26**

Some have tried to see a difference between James and Paul on this subject but Paul himself recognised the importance of true faith producing action. In Galatians, which is his strongest defence of justification by faith, Paul writes that *"The only thing that counts is faith expressing itself through love." (Galatians 5:6)*. Both Paul and James expected to see evidence of faith in people's lives through their deeds.

1 Peter

1 Peter was written by the apostle Peter with the help of Silas (see 1 Peter 5:12). It is addressed to Christians in the northern provinces of Asia Minor (present day Turkey). We know from other sources that Peter travelled and he may have visited or even founded some of these churches. Peter's purpose is to encourage his readers and to clarify the truth (see 1 Peter 5:12). The letter covers a number of subjects.

Outline of 1 Peter	
The letter is full of strong commands including those to:	
1	Be holy.
2, 5	Be submissive to God and the authorities
3	Live in harmony.
4	Rejoice in suffering.
Chapter 5 also includes teaching for elders.	

We have already referred to a number of well known verses in 1 Peter and his letter contains some well known, practical down–to–earth advice. Peter, who had promised to stand by Jesus even if all the others deserted him, had learnt about how God deals with the self-confident the hard way and he encourages us to take the initiative in developing a right attitude towards ourselves in relation to God: *"Humble yourselves, therefore, under God's mighty hand, that he may lift you up in due time." (1 Peter 5:6).*

Over the years Peter also learnt to follow Jesus' advice not to worry through regularly praying to him and tells us to: *Cast all your anxiety on him because he cares for you." (1 Peter 5:6–7).* What a wonderful verse! God is interested in our day to day concerns and wants to hear about them because he cares for us!

2 Peter

Peter's second letter was written shortly before he was martyred in Rome. His purpose is clear.

Read 2 Peter 1:13–15

Peter, as an eye witness, has spoken to many about Jesus, his teaching, his life, death, resurrection and promised return, but as he now faces death he is determined to put some of that teaching into writing for future generations.

The churches Peter is writing to have been influenced by false teachers and one of his main purposes in writing is to warn the church against them. The language Peter uses is very similar to that found in Jude.

Outline of 2 Peter	
1:1–11	Encouragement to press on towards godliness.
1:12–21	Peter's reason for writing
2	False teachers.
3	The Day of the Lord – coming judgement.

Peter also writes about "the day of the Lord", referring to the time when Jesus will return. The early Christians believed that Jesus would return very soon but as time went on people realised that it may not happen in their lifetime. Peter warns against thinking that because he has not yet returned he may never return – *"Where is this coming he promised?" (2 Peter 3:4).* As long as we remain on this earth, God, in his patience, is continuing to give people an opportunity to repent.

1, 2 & 3 John

John was probably the youngest of the twelve apostles. Although his brother James was the first of the twelve to die John outlived the others and late in life wrote five books which are in the New Testament. His gospel was written to provide supplementary material to the three already in circulation. He then wrote his three letters and, finally, Revelation. The letters were, therefore, probably written between AD 85 and 95.

It is thought that John was based in Ephesus during his later years (see Map 10 on page 389) and 1 John may be a circular to churches in the surrounding area. From the contents of the letter it appears that the churches were under the influence of false teaching that John is aiming to correct. 1 John has three themes that are interwoven.

The first theme is **love**, both God's love for us and our love for one another. The word "love" appears 43 times in the letter. The main section on this theme is 1 John 4:7–5:2 which includes the famous statement *"God is love"* and talks of our love for God and for one another. Like James, John sees a clear link between words and deeds. God demonstrated his love for us through sending Jesus: we demonstrate our love for God and for others through active obedience to God's commands.

> Read 1 John 4:7–5:2

John's second theme is **warnings against false teaching**, particularly aimed at the Greek Heresy, or Gnosticism, that Paul wrote about to the Colossians. The Gnostics believed that matter, and therefore man's physical body, was evil. This led them to say that Jesus, as the Son of God, could not have had a physical body. Either it was some sort of illusion or he just took over the body of a man. John challenges such ideas head on from the start of his letter: *"That which was from the beginning, which we have heard, which we have seen with our eyes, which we have looked at and our hands have touched – this we proclaim concerning the Word of life."* (1 John 1:1). John's testimony is indisputable. He had lived alongside the Son of God for three years and knew his humanity.

John's third theme is **walking in the light** as children of God. *"God is light; in him there is no darkness at all"* (1 John 1:5). As Christians we must live open lives before God and before one another. If we sin and try and ignore it we are not being true to ourselves and put a barrier between ourselves and God. The solution is both simple and glorious: *"If we confess our sins, he is faithful and just and will forgive us our sins and purify us from all unrighteousness." (1 John 1:9)*. Many churches have "confession" as part of their regular worship and it is helpful to be reminded that we are sinners who need God's forgiveness. Applying this simple truth to our lives enables us to live in fellowship with God and one another.

2 & 3 John are very short letters to individuals – the chosen lady and Gaius – which supplement John's warnings against heresy in his first letter. 3 John is the shortest "book" in the Bible with 219 Greek words. 2 John has the fewest verses. 2 John is a warning not to support false teachers by offering them hospitality and 3 John is written to commend Gaius for supporting missionaries who preached the truth while the leader of the local church is putting people out of the church for listening to their message. In both letters we get an insight into what gives John the greatest pleasure in his old age: *"I have no greater joy than to hear that my children are walking in the truth." (3 John 4)*.

Jude

Jude was another brother of Jesus (see Matthew 13:55 where he is called Judas). Although Jesus' brothers did not understand his message during his lifetime, at least some joined with the apostles after his resurrection (see Acts 1:14). Jude introduces himself as *"Jude, a servant of Jesus Christ and a brother of James."* Rather than claim any special privilege from his human relationship with Jesus he links himself to his older brother James who, as a leader of the church in Jerusalem, would have been well known to his readers.

Jude is keen to write about the salvation he shares with his readers but, because of false teachers who have come into the churches preaching that God's grace gave them a licence to be immoral, he writes to warn them against such men and to urge them to keep to the true faith. He uses very colourful language (see especially verses 12–13) which is similar in parts to 2 Peter 2.

In his closing verses Jude appeals to us to persevere. In verse 20 he calls on us to work at our faith and to avoid the danger of being led astray by those who want to deceive us. But he suddenly cuts short his practical advice as he breaks into an outburst of praise to God for the absolute security that we have in him. Yes, we must persevere, but at the same time we must not be in any doubt that the security of our salvation is not dependent on our efforts but on the ability of our amazing God.

> **Read Jude 24–25**

Day 77
Getting to Grips with the Bible

Yesterday we finished looking at the letters in the New Testament and there is only one book left for us to look at in the Bible! But before we look at Revelation, I want to encourage you to continue getting to grips with the Bible after you have completed your eighty day journey.

Once you have finished "Through the Bible in 80 Days" then it does not matter if you never read it again, or if you put it in the bin. However, when it comes to the Bible itself it is vital for your development as a Christian that you continue to explore it for the rest of your life. I'm not saying that to condemn you – you won't get zapped if you fail to read it for a day, or a week! – but to encourage you to continue the journey you have started. The Bible is your spiritual food and can influence all you do for good.

Today we will look at five tools that you can use to get to grips with the Bible, as illustrated in the picture of the hand in Figure 15 on the next page. (Thanks to my son Toby for the loan of his hand!). Throughout today there are a number of references to Psalm 119 – the longest chapter in the Bible – which is a wisdom poem all about the word of God that provides a wealth of material for study and meditation on the value of the Bible.

Read

"Read" is on the thumb of the hand as reading the Bible is the most important thing to do with it. There is no substitute for reading the Bible for yourself. This may sound obvious but it is easy to only ever hear the Bible read in church or use Bible Study notes which contain one verse and then a page of thoughts from someone else. I'm not saying that there is anything wrong with hearing preaching or reading Study notes – far from it – but these must not become a substitute for reading the Bible for ourselves. Alternatively you can have it read to you, either by a friend or by listening to a tape.

The Bible itself contains many examples of the importance of reading the Bible. After the people of Israel entered the Promised Land Joshua assembled the entire nation together to offer sacrifices to the Lord and then to read them the books of the Law (see Joshua 8:34–35). He was very keen that they should not forget all that God had said to them.

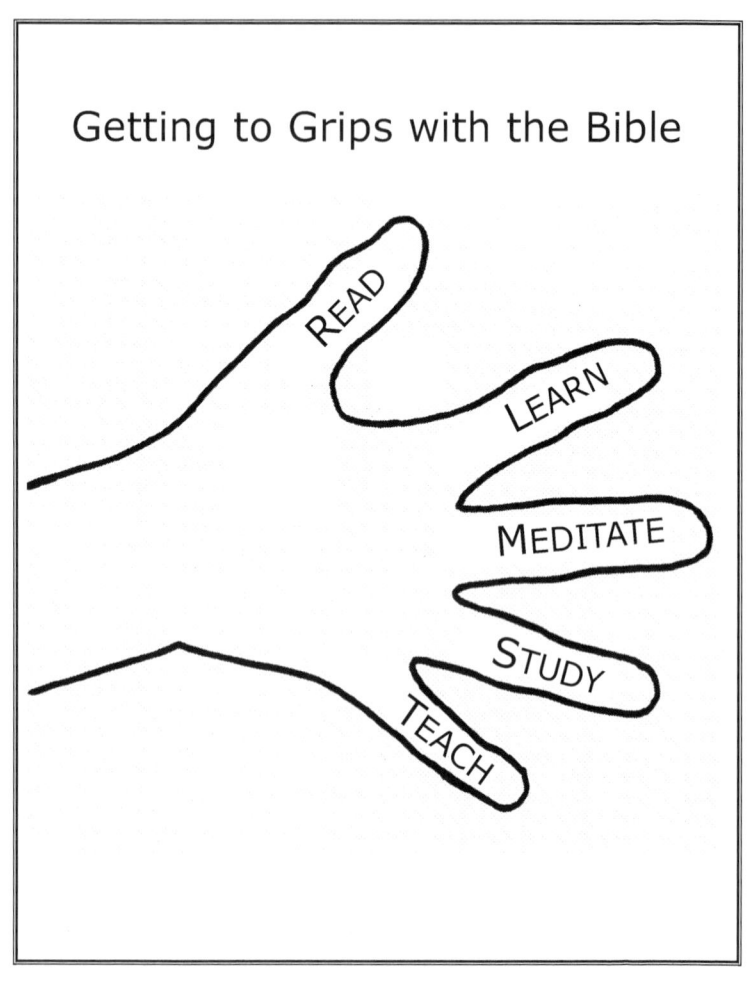

Figure 15 – Getting to Grips with the Bible

Day 77 – Getting to Grips with the Bible

Hundreds of years later when King Josiah came to the throne the word of God was not only forgotten but it had been lost altogether! When the priests discovered a copy of the book of the law it had such an impact on the king and the people that they swept away the evil in the land and put off the judgement of God for a whole generation (see the account in 2 Kings 22–23). Years later, when the people returned to Jerusalem, Ezra read the word of God to the people for seven days (is this an early mention of a "Bible week"?!) and the people joyfully carried out the Lord's commands (see Nehemiah 8). In the New Testament when Paul sent Timothy a letter telling him how to run a church he told him to *"Devote yourself to the public reading of scripture." (1 Timothy 4:13).* It is important that we hear the word of God frequently.

How should we go about reading the Bible for ourselves? Do we just dip into our favourite bits each day as we feel like it? Or do we start at the beginning and simply read all the way through?

Reading the whole Bible on a regular basis is a good thing to do. We need to be reminded of the whole sweep of what God has written for us. If we only ever read the gospels or the Psalms we will miss out on aspects of God's character and his provision for our lives. Although we may find some parts of the Bible difficult to understand that does not mean that we can ignore them. God has written it all for us. It is not up to us to pick and choose the easy bits. When Joshua read to the people it was reported that *"There was not a word of all that Moses had commanded that Joshua did not read to the whole assembly." (Joshua 8:35)* However, we have not been left to understand it all by ourselves as we have the Holy Spirit to help us, so when you come to read the Bible ask him to help you understand it: *"May my cry come before you, O LORD; give me understanding according to your word." (Psalm 119:169).*

So how do we go about reading the whole Bible regularly? There are many Bible reading notes or schemes available to us today which take you through the Bible over a period of time. If you use these I would encourage you to use one that asks you to read a passage each day, not just a verse, so that you do get to read the word yourself. When I was at university Denis Clarke came to speak to the Christian Union and recommended that we read the whole Bible by reading ten chapters of the Old Testament and three of the New each day. By doing this you can read the whole Bible in about 13 weeks. This is an excellent thing to do and I would particularly encourage you to do it when you are young and have time. It is not so easy to find the time when you have a full time job and young children who don't sleep! Alternatively you can use the annual reading plan in Appendix B (see page 483) which takes you through the Bible in a year.

When you read the whole Bible on a regular basis you will find that you come across passages that you have completely forgotten! It may be discouraging to find how much – or how little! – of it stays in our memory but I was encouraged by a story told by Allan Johnston[13] about an old bishop and his gardener. There was an old bishop who was sitting in the summer sun reading his Bible while the gardener was tidying up the garden. After a while the gardener stopped, came up to the bishop and said, "What are you reading that old book for? You can't even remember what you had for tea yesterday. Everything goes in one ear and out the other. What's the point of reading that?" The bishop smiled kindly at him and replied, "You see that old sieve over there? Go and fill it up from the pond." The gardener thought "he's gone completely mad now," but he picked up the sieve and headed to the pond to "fill it up" with water. When he returned he said to the bishop, "There you are. It's completely empty." "Go and fill it up again," said the bishop, so the gardener did. "Completely empty again," he said. "Yes, but it's much cleaner now, isn't it?" said the bishop.

If you read the Bible regularly you will not remember it all, but it will have a powerful effect on your life.

Learn

The second finger on the hand is "Learn". In addition to reading the Bible it is important to learn verses or passages from scripture. The writer of Psalm 119 said: *"I have hidden your word in my heart that I might not sin against you"* and *"Though the wicked bind me with ropes, I will not forget your law." (Psalm 119:11, 61).*

The first quote indicates an important reason for learning Bible verses. Knowledge of God's word will equip us to identify and resist temptation. Jesus provided us with a great example of this. When he was tempted in the desert by the devil, Jesus quoted scripture to resist him. Three times he responded to the devil with *"It is written"* and a quotation – he did not use some special, supernatural powers (see Luke 4:1–13). We too need to learn Bible verses so that we can do the same. Interestingly, all three quotes that Jesus used came from Deuteronomy chapters 6–8. Does this indicate that he was reading through

---

[13] See footnote on page 345

Deuteronomy at this time? There are other references in the Old Testament that convey the same meaning but maybe this shows us that Jesus was reading and learning verses in a systematic way.

Which verses should you learn? There are some key verses which it is helpful for all Christians to know, such as John 3:16 which summarises the gospel in a nutshell. But if you are reading your Bible regularly then you will not need to search for verses to learn. Often when you are reading a passage, one particular verse will jump out of the page with meaning that you did not see before. Write it out on a small card with its reference and carry it around with you through the day. As you get free time – walking, waiting at photocopiers, or whatever! – say the verse over to yourself and use the card to check how well you have learned it. For most of us there are enough dead moments in the day to make this an effective way to remember it. Many of our songs are taken from scripture and this is probably the easiest way to learn Bible verses. Encourage songwriters to set passages to music so you can learn them. Another way to impress verses which have meant a lot to you on your memory is to write them out and put them in a place where you will see them often – over the sink, on your desk, or even on the back of the toilet door! Moses put it more politely than that when he told the children of Israel to: *"Write them [the LORD'S commandments] on the doorframes of your houses and on your gates." (Deuteronomy 6:9)*!

Learning passages by heart is not encouraged by our modern, western education system but it can be done. According to the Guinness Book of Records[M], Mehmed Ali Halaci of Ankara Turkey recited 6,666 verses of the Koran from memory in 6 hours on 14th Oct. 1967! Not many of us could match that but we would benefit from learning to "hide the word of God in our hearts" on a regular basis.

Meditate

The book of Psalms opens with David writing *"Blessed is the man who does not walk in the counsel of the wicked ... but his delight is in the law of the LORD, and on his law he meditates day and night." (Psalm 1:1–2)*. Meditation is another important tool in the Christian's toolbox for life.

In recent years "meditation" has become associated in our minds with Eastern religions. Eastern meditation, which can be known as Transcendental or New Age meditation, involves blanking out the mind and opening it up to whatever comes from within. This is a dangerous exercise as it opens us up to negative influences both from within us and from outside. Even if "nice peaceful thoughts" emerge, the process only serves to suggest that we can find what we need to improve out lives from within which is pride, a form of idolatry. The Bible is clear about the state of our heart: *"The heart is deceitful above all things and beyond cure. Who can understand it?" (Jeremiah 17:9)* so we should not be deceived into thinking that we will find answers to the issues of everyday living from within our own heart.

Christian meditation involves filling our minds with God's word and mulling it over. As a friend of mine once described it, it is like worrying about something, but positively. If you have a concern about a relationship or a problem to solve then you will naturally go over and over it in your mind. If you can stop yourself going into a negative spiral of worry and instead remind yourself the truth of God's word and start thinking about how to apply that to the situation you face then you will be meditating. Obviously it helps if you have learned some scriptures but you don't need to be able to quote verses in order to bring God's truth into a situation. If you have financial worries why don't you think about what the Bible has to say about making giving to God a first priority? If you have fallen out with someone then it is easy to let yourself think about all the things they should have done differently, but try seeing how you could apply Ephesians 4:32 to the situation: *"Be kind and compassionate to one another, forgiving each other, just as in Christ God forgave you."* If you are having trouble loving someone then go through 1 Corinthians 13 line by line and think of practical ways to apply it to yourself in that relationship. There is no shortage of work to be done in applying God's word to our lives!

Study

Psalm 119:34 says: *"Give me understanding and I will keep your law."* The truths of the Bible are like precious metals and jewels. They do not lie on the surface for the casual passer by to pick up but they require us to dig in and work hard to find them. Jesus said *"seek and you will find" (Matthew 7:7)* and the word "seek" has the meaning of persistent seeking, not a quick look. As you will hopefully have learnt from this book it is important to understand the background to some passages if you are to appreciate them fully. Many people take Bible verses out of context and use them to their own ends. An extreme example of that came from the communist USSR which taught in its schools that the Bible says, *"There is no God"*. This is true, it does! However, if you

Day 77 – Getting to Grips with the Bible

make a short study of the whole of the first verse of Psalm 14 you will see that it is saying something different from the message in that short quote. Studying the Bible systematically is a good way to make sure that you really understand what it is saying and are better able to judge what you hear.

We are fortunate in having many ways of studying the Bible. In my late teens I used a study guide called "Search the Scriptures[14]", a three year course which takes you through the Bible giving some background information and asking questions to make you think about what the passage is saying. I think it took me seven years to complete it, but the value was in being made to think about what every part of the Bible meant. For the last sixteen years I have used the NIV Study Bible[15], which contains some very helpful explanatory notes about passages and books. Simply reading a passage or a book along with the notes gives you better insight into the meaning. There are other similar Bibles available with studies of characters and themes to help us apply what is being said to our lives.

If you want to find out what the Bible says about a subject then a concordance is a very useful study aid. This lists the places in the Bible that a word occurs and some Bibles, like the NIV Study Bible, have short concordances in the back. If you want to be sure of finding all the references for a word then you will need an "Exhaustive Concordance". I have a very old and very large one of these and I used to think that "Exhaustive" referred to how you felt after carrying it, but what it actually means is that it will give you a complete list of all the references where a word occurs. Concordances are available for a number of the versions of the Bible and it is worth getting one for the version you are most familiar with. If you have a PC then you can get the Bible on a CD and this usually includes the ability to search for words or phrases – an on–line concordance. A number of web sites also provide this facility, with many versions of the Bible available.

There are so many study books that I cannot list them all here. If you want to make a study of a Bible book or subject then go to your local Christian bookshop or ask someone you know who does a lot of Bible study and see what they can recommend.

---

[14] Search the Scriptures is edited by Alan Stibbs and published by IVP (Inter–Varsity Press)

[15] The NIV Study Bible is published by Hodder & Stoughton in the UK and Zondervan in the US.

Teach

The final finger on our hand is labelled "teach" and you may already be thinking that this does not apply to you. If that's true then maybe you have got the wrong idea about teaching. Moses said to the children of Israel, *"These commandments that I give you today are to be upon your hearts. Impress them on your children. Talk about them when you sit at home and when you walk along the road, when you lie down and when you get up." (Deuteronomy 6:6–7).* Teaching the scriptures to those closest to you, particularly your children, and talking about the scriptures in your own home is so important. I don't mean that you need to sit the other members of your family behind desks and stand in front of a blackboard, but simply encouraging questions and being prepared to have discussions about the Bible is healthy for children and adults alike.

Teaching something to someone else has a benefit for both the person being taught and the teacher. It is very easy to think you understand something when you've heard it but you really find out what you've understood when you try and explain it to someone else. Answering your children's questions is a great challenge and if you accept it you will find that you will learn too. Small children ask very silly questions, or at least questions that appear silly until you try and answer them! My oldest son, Ben, once said, "I don't think jealousy is wrong. I'm jealous of how my friend plays football." Explaining that is not entirely straightforward! Trying to use words that a small child can understand is not easy either. The best illustration for me also came from Ben after we got home from a baptism. I think he was about two or three and I remember him lying on a sofa with his feet in the air – like small children do – and asking me what "baptism" meant. I did my best to give a simple explanation and then, after a pause he said, "Dad…" I waited for a follow up question which would demonstrate how much he had understood. When his statement came it left me in no doubt as to how brilliant my explanation had been. "Dad, there's a fly on the window." Clearly I had missed the mark! But we must *"always be prepared to give an answer to everyone who asks you to give the reason for the hope that you have." (1 Peter 3:15)* and there is no better place to start than at home. And if you don't know the answer then go away and study it for yourself. Seeing you studying the Bible to find answers yourself will be the most valuable lesson you will ever give to your children.

Day 77 – Getting to Grips with the Bible

Apart from discussing issues in your own home, if you want to develop your understanding of God's word quickly then find opportunities to teach. Without knowing anything about your local church I could almost guarantee that you could get yourself an opportunity to teach very easily. "Oh, our pastor would never let me preach on a Sunday morning" you say, and I expect you would be right, but if you went to the person in charge of your children's work and offered to help teach one of the age groups it is very likely that they would welcome you with open arms! Most churches have a shortage of children's workers and this provides a golden opportunity for you to learn more through teaching than you will through listening. It is also an opportunity to teach truths to people who may never have heard them before which is a great privilege. Most children's teaching groups use some form of lesson plans that give you all the material you need so it is not as difficult as you might think. What you will find, though, is that you are forced to explain Bible stories and Biblical truths in simple terms and doing that will benefit you. If the thought of this frightens you then ask if you can watch someone else in action first or say you'll do a few weeks and see what you think after that.

Other opportunities for "teaching" are available in most churches. If you are part of a house group then you could offer to run a session there. The golden rule in this setting is to keep it short and to the point and get people involved by asking them questions. If you have the opportunity to take a friend on an Alpha course then you will get asked some very interesting questions which will really make you think about what you believe and what the Bible says. Not all of us are called to be "teachers", in the sense of standing up in front of a large group of people, but teaching is about passing on what we know to others and all of us have something to share so take some of these "teaching opportunities" that I have listed and they will challenge you and help you get to grips with the Bible.

And Finally ...

I hope that today has given you some useful ideas about how to move forward in your exploration of the Bible after you have finished your journey "Through the Bible in 80 days". It is not my intention to make you feel that you need to spend three hours a day reading, studying and learning in a frenzied attempt to know the Bible better. You will not keep it up and will end up disappointed or, worse, feeling guilty. Please take some time to pray about what you should do next and set yourself some achievable goals. Do not try and take on too much!

This whole chapter, and in fact this whole book, has been about getting to know the Bible, but there is no point in doing that if we do not seek to put it into practice. The writer of Psalm 119 wrote, *"Your statutes are my delight; they are my counsellors." (Psalm 119:24)*. What do good counsellors do? They give us wise advice for living. Is that any use to us? Not unless we take their advice! You need to strengthen the fingers on your own spiritual hand so you can use it. *"How can a young man keep his way pure? By living according to your word." (Psalm 119:9)*. Reading, learning, meditating, studying and teaching God's word will have no impact on our lives unless we put it into practice. It is better to read a little, take notice of what it says and let it change your heart and life than that you spend hours in academic study. That way, according to Psalm 119, you will very quickly get to know the Bible better than your church leaders! *"I have more understanding than the elders, for I obey your precepts." (Psalm 119:100)*. God will not judge us by a Bible knowledge quiz but on how our actions measure up to what we have understood.

References

[M] From the 18th Edition of "The Guinness Book of Records", 1971. With thanks to Guinness World Records for permission to quote.

Day 78
Revelation – Letters to Churches

The Book of the Apocalypse

We have reached the last book of the Bible – I don't expect that you ever thought you would get this far when you started this book! – and as we read it we will discover prophecies that relate to our own times as well as details of events which have yet to take place. Up until this point the New Testament consists of accounts of the life of Jesus and his followers and of straightforward teaching, but this last book is completely different in style, more like some of the stranger Old Testament prophetic books. The title of the last book of the Bible is taken from its first word in the Greek, "Apocalypse", which means "unveiling", "disclosure" or, as we know the book today, "Revelation". It was written by the apostle John (who also wrote the gospel of John and the three letters 1, 2 and 3 John) near the end of his life, probably around AD 95 when John was in his eighties. If you have read it before and been puzzled by it then please note that it is perhaps the most misunderstood book of the Bible and has puzzled many generations of Christians so, although we are about to spend three days looking at it, please do not expect to go away with all your questions answered (or even any of them!). Many people have tried to link the prophecies in it to specific world leaders or events throughout history and have often been proved wrong. This does not mean that we should not try to understand it but we do need to be careful not to put too much confidence in such specific predictions.

John was exiled on the island of Patmos off the west coast of Asia Minor and the church was facing persecution as the Roman authorities were enforcing worship of the emperor. This letter was written to encourage the churches, particularly the seven in Asia mentioned in chapters 2 and 3, to stand firm, even to the point of death. Although there will be a major confrontation between God and Satan, God's people will be saved, and ultimately will enjoy a wonderful new home with God forever.

The contents of Revelation are open to many interpretations. Some view its events as having taken place in the first century, some see it as a description of events starting then and going on to the end of history, some expect to see it fulfilled in the end times, while others see it as symbolic of the struggle between good and evil throughout history. While it is unwise to become obsessed with interpreting the details of Revelation in the light of world events, the book is very important for today's church living in the end times and facing persecution. There are some clear underlying messages in the book which are relevant for all times, and especially for the times we live in now.

Throughout history God's people have faced opposition and Revelation teaches that God's people must stand firm and hold to the truth in the face of persecution and deception. Despite what we see about us, the vision that John was given assures us that God is in control of world events. Many of the troubles we see in the world today are actually sent by God himself both to judge the peoples of the earth for their wickedness and to turn people to him. At the end of Revelation we are given a vision that should bring us great hope at all times: God will finally triumph, Satan will be banished and God's people will enjoy their Lord forever in a new heaven and a new earth.

The Book of Revelation

In the first three chapters of Revelation John is given a vision of Jesus who dictates seven letters to him addressed to seven churches in Asia. We will look at these today. After that John is given a vision of heaven and of events which are to come in the future. The last two chapters describe our future hope, living forever in a new heaven and new earth.

Outline of Revelation	
1	Introduction. John sees a vision of Jesus.
2–3	Letters of warning to the seven churches.
4–5	A vision of heaven.
6–11	The seven seals and the seven trumpets bring various troubles on the earth.
12–14	Various events in heaven and on earth.
15–16	The seven bowls – plagues on the earth.
17–19	Babylon (symbolic of the world system) and its fall; the return of Christ.
20	The final judgement.
21–22	The new heaven, the new earth, and the new Jerusalem.

Day 78 – Revelation – Letters to Churches

"I was in the Spirit"

As we saw when we looked at 1 John, there were those in the early church who denied that Jesus Christ really existed in human form, preferring to believe that God could only exist as a Spirit. John, who was one of the twelve apostles who lived alongside Jesus during the last three years of his earthly life, was an important eyewitness to the fact that Jesus was not a spirit – he was a human being, as well as being the Son of God. At the beginning of his gospel, John wrote about Jesus as "the Word" and said of him: *"the Word became flesh and made his dwelling among us." (John 1:14)*. When he wrote his first letter he opened it by talking about his own personal experience of Jesus as a man: *"That which was from the beginning, which we have heard, which we have seen with our eyes, which we have looked at and our hands have touched – this we proclaim concerning the Word of life." (1 John 1:1)*. John had lived with Jesus for three years and knew him as a man. Even after his resurrection, when many of Jesus' closest friends failed to recognise him, it was John who realised that the man by the side of the lake was Jesus when he appeared to them in Galilee (see John 21:7).

But at the beginning of Revelation John receives a vision of Jesus, not as an ordinary man, but as a figure so awesome, so powerful, so overpowering that he falls at his feet in terror. He cannot even find words to describe the Jesus he now sees. All we get is a series of 'like' statements – *"like a son of man"*, *"like wool"*, *"like blazing fire"* – as John struggles to describe him. It is fitting that John, who is a witness to the fact that Jesus was 100% human, also becomes witness to the fact that he is fully God, expressed in the images that we read in Revelation. This is not an alternative Jesus or a return to a different Old Testament God, this is the same Jesus who was from the beginning, is now, and will be the same forever.

Read Revelation 1

Seven Letter to Seven Churches

As we saw at the end of Revelation 1, Jesus appears to John in order to reveal to him *"what will take place later"* but before that, John is given seven short, specific letters for seven churches. These are churches in the west of the Roman province of Asia that were founded as a result of the two years that Paul spent in Ephesus (see Acts 19:10) some forty years before John received his vision. The churches are still there and, in many ways are thriving, but false teachings have been accepted and sinful practices and attitudes have come into each church. It is likely that John knew some, if not all, of these churches well as there is evidence that John lived in Ephesus in his later life. In his messages to these churches Jesus commends them for their strengths, rebukes them for their sins and encourages them to follow him wholeheartedly. It is clear that the churches are facing, or are about to face, persecution and in each church a promise is given to *"he who overcomes"*. Rewards are there for those who stay true to the faith to the end.

There are a couple of references to the Nicolaitans, probably followers of a man who taught the Greek Heresy, or Gnosticism, that John wrote about in his first letter and Paul wrote about to another Asian church, Colossae. This heresy taught that our physical body was completely separate from our spiritual being and so allowed people to practice physical immorality and idolatry, while maintaining spiritual purity. The reference to the Old Testament characters Balaam and Jezebel, who both led Israel into these practices, refers to the same false teaching, which is strongly condemned. Another passing reference is made to the Gnostic teaching that salvation is achieved through secret knowledge in the ironic reference to *"Satan's so-called deep secrets"* (Revelation 2:24). The churches were facing a particular issue with idolatry at this time as the Romans were enforcing emperor worship which made life difficult for Christians who would only offer worship to God. The city of Pergamum was the official centre of emperor worship in the province of Asia which is why it is called the city *"where Satan lives"* (Revelation 2:13).

Read Revelation 2–3

Some people have seen in these seven churches a picture of seven ages of the church throughout history with us now in the "Laodicean Age", an age where Christians are lukewarm. This may be a good description of the church in the west but does not describe the church in many parts of the world today. Jesus' message to the church in Laodicea includes the well known verse: *"Here I am! I stand at the door and knock. If anyone hears my voice and opens the door, I will come in and eat with him, and he with me." (Revelation 3:20)*. This was the inspiration for a very well known painting called "The Light of the World", by Holman Hunt, which shows Christ with a lantern standing at a door and

Day 78 – Revelation – Letters to Churches

knocking[16]. When it was first finished, one of Hunt's friends pointed out that he had forgotten to paint a handle on the door. Hunt replied that this was a picture of the door of a human heart and the handle was on the inside. Jesus will not force his way into our lives. This verse and picture are often applied to those who are not Christians but it is interesting to note that it is part of a letter to a church and it applies just as much to those of us who have been Christians for some time as we too can close our hearts to our Lord.

Others see the faults of these churches as typical of the faults of individual churches down through the ages. What is clear is that Jesus has a strong passion for the purity of his church, which means that he has a keen interest in your local church and mine. The church is his representative on earth and if a local church does not measure up to his standards then he will not hesitate to remove it from the face of the earth as he threatens the church in Ephesus: *"I will come to you and remove your lampstand from its place" (Revelation 2:5)*. It would seem logical to think that a church would close down if Jesus lost interest in it but the truth is that some churches may close down directly because he does take an interest in them! At some point in history all seven of these churches ceased to exist and all churches which fail to properly represent the head of the church, Jesus Christ, will eventually close. We need to take the warnings against losing our first love, against tolerating idolatry or immorality, and against being lukewarm very seriously.

---

[16] The original painting was painted in 1854 and is in Keble College Oxford. Hunt painted a second version in 1904 which can be seen in St Paul's Cathedral, London.

Day 79
What must take place

After this ...

Immediately following the letters to the seven churches Revelation abruptly changes gear with the words *"After this"* at the beginning of chapter 4. We came across similar links in the book of Joel in the Old Testament where he wrote, *"And afterwards"* and *"In those days"*. These statements transport us into a different time and place and this is certainly true of Revelation where what we read in the rest of the book will puzzle, amaze and astound us. We are about to discover prophecies that relate to our own times as well as details of events that have yet to take place.

The book of Revelation is written in a style which was familiar to the people of its day but which will seem strange and puzzling to us. John sees a lot of pictures and images that are symbols which represent other things or ideas. Sometimes the symbols are explained – we have already seen how the seven lampstands represent seven churches – but sometimes they are not and this leaves us with many pictures where we cannot be sure about what they represent. Some of these refer back to passages in the Old Testament, particularly in Daniel and Ezekiel, but often the meaning is unclear there too. Another feature is the use of the number seven – it appears over fifty times in the book – which represents completeness.

Because of the nature of the book we need to be very careful in how we interpret it and even more careful not to fall out with other Christians who take a different view! Many people have tried to explain the fine detail of Revelation. Some take parts of it literally while others come up with interpretations of the pictures. The important thing is to try and understand what its message is for you today. An explanation linking a specific army to Russia or China may be interesting but does it have any impact on the way we live our lives? For those who want to study the end times more I would thoroughly recommend "The End Times" by John Hosier[17] as a good place to start. He provides a very balanced

---

[17] "The End Times" is part of the "Thinking Clearly Series" published by Monarch Books. John Hosier is an elder of Church of Christ the King in Brighton and is a respected Bible teacher within New Frontiers.

description of the various interpretations of End Time prophecies, including his own views for interest but majoring on the important lessons. My advice with Revelation is to read it through quickly, preferably in one or two sittings, and get the overall messages into your heart that there will be great troubles and tribulations in this world but God is in control! All of us hear about the troubles in the world and many of us experience them to a greater or lesser extent and so it is important that we get a deep conviction in our hearts that God is in control.

A Vision of God in Heaven

The vision starts with John being taken up into heaven to see *"what must take place after this" (Revelation 4:1)* but before he is shown the future he is taken to the throne of God. It is not easy to understand what will take place "after this" unless you accept the sovereignty of God over all creation. As you read his description of what he saw there you will get the sense that, once again, he finds it hard to find adequate words to describe what he saw. The four living creatures around the throne of God are similar to those seen in visions by Isaiah (see Isaiah 6:2–3) and Ezekiel (see Ezekiel 1:4–9).

> **Read Revelation 4**

After this majestic opening scene full of praise to God the next chapter opens with a puzzle. There is a scroll, sealed with seven seals that no one is worthy to open – apart from Jesus. In chapter 1 John was confronted by a vision of him in great power, but in this vision he appears as a lamb bearing the marks of having been killed. He is worthy to open this scroll not because of his power and strength, but because he offered himself freely as a sacrifice for mankind. The judgements that come on the people of earth as a result of the seals being opened are not the acts of a vengeful, vindictive God but of a loving God who offered himself for their sins and made the way to God open to them through his own sacrifice.

> **Read Revelation 5**

At the beginning of Revelation 8 John records that there was silence in heaven for about half an hour, a noteworthy event as heaven is a noisy place, full of praise to God. Revelation contains a number of songs of praise to God and for his acts, many of which are familiar as they are used as songs today. However, the context in which they appear is not so familiar.

Many Troubles on the Earth

In Revelation 6 the first six of the seven seals are opened and each one causes great troubles to come on the earth and its people – war, famine, drought, plague, and a great earthquake. Then at the beginning of chapter 8 the seventh seal is opened and this leads to seven angels blowing seven trumpets which bring even worse disasters on the earth. A third of the earth is burned up, a third of the sea is turned to blood, a third of the waters turned bitter, and a third of the daylight disappears. The following chapters describe great wars and tribulations, evil forces being unleashed on the earth and the prophets that God sends to turn people to him destroyed. We will just get a flavour of this from reading Revelation 6.

> **Read Revelation 6**

Exactly how all this will be fulfilled is not clear but a key message here is that the disasters that come on this earth do not catch God unawares. His plans are not thrown into confusion by wars, famines and earthquakes. What we have to try and understand is that they actually are part of his plan! God loves this world so much that he will do anything to get men to turn to him. Awful though these things seem to us, they are but momentary afflictions in God's eternal plan.

In Revelation 7:14 there is a reference to "the Great Tribulation", a time of unprecedented suffering for God's people, and many Christians have sought to discover whether or not they are the ones who will endure it. Most generations have come to the conclusion that they were, given what was going on in the world around them. However, when Jesus spoke about returning he talked of wars, famines and earthquakes as *"the beginning of birth–pains" (Matthew 24:8)* and made it clear that these would continue throughout the period before he returned. From our perspective two thousand years later we see that this is entirely in keeping with history. In fact, it seems that those who have lived in peace and security are the minority when we consider the scale of disasters that previous generations have experienced. 75 million people were killed by the Black Death which wiped out around a quarter of the population of Europe in the four years 1347–1351. The health scares we face today pale into insignificance alongside this! Just looking back at recent times' Jesus words about wars, famines and earthquakes still ring true. Over 56 million people died in World War II. A famine in China between 1959 and 1961 caused the deaths of about 40 million people. Fifteen years later, on 28 July 1976, an earthquake in eastern China killed around 750,000 people. Many people have lived through great suffering in each generation.

But what about God's people? Will they suffer more than the rest? Jesus promised his followers that they would be persecuted and put to death until the gospel had been preached in the whole world (see Matthew 24:9–14) and today it is estimated that around 250 million Christians are persecuted with 160,000 being killed each year. As Christians we are not promised an easy life here on earth but we are called to stay true to Jesus in whatever circumstances we find ourselves. Our strength comes from knowing that Jesus is in charge of this world. He said: *"In this world you will have trouble. But take heart! I have overcome the world." (John 16:33)* and in Revelation his authority over the world is made clear throughout.

The Antichrist

After the disasters on the earth caused by the seven trumpets the scene changes in Revelation 12. First John sees a woman who gives birth to a son and then he sees a dragon, representing Satan, who tries to kill the son. There is war in heaven between the archangel Michael and his angels and the dragon and his angels, and Satan loses his place in heaven and is thrown down to earth along with his angels. He then wages war against *"those who obey God's commandments and hold true to the testimony of Jesus." (Revelation 12:17)*. This period of intense persecution is described in the next chapter when someone called "the beast" rules the whole earth with the authority of Satan. This man is referred to by John in his letters as "the antichrist" and by Paul in 2 Thessalonians as "the man of lawlessness." Throughout history people have tried to identify the antichrist: from Caesar Nero in Roman times, through Muhammad and various popes in the Middle Ages, to military leaders such as Napoleon Bonaparte, Stalin and Hitler in more recent times. Both John and Paul indicate that a number of antichrists will come before the final one – John says that *"Many deceivers, who do not acknowledge Jesus Christ as coming in the flesh, have gone out into the world. Any such person is the deceiver and the antichrist" (2 John 7)* while Paul says that *"the secret power of lawlessness is already at work" (2 Thessalonians 2:7)*.

There are a few points to notice in this description of the worldwide rule of the beast. We learned from the book of Job that Satan's powers are limited by God himself and Revelation teaches us the same. It is God, not Satan, who has final authority over this world and he limits Satan's power and the time that he has to exercise it. Similarly, John emphasizes that the power of the beast is limited by repeating a number of times that his authority is given him by Satan, whose powers are already limited by God. The beast also receives worship, a clear sign that he is not from God. The word "antichrist" does not mean against Christ, but rather "instead of Christ". His main danger to those who do not believe in Jesus is not the words he speaks against Christ but the fact that he will take the place of Christ in their hearts by becoming someone they worship. His powers, which include the ability to perform great signs, will help him deceive people and we as Christians need to be on our guard against thinking that those who exercise spiritual powers must be right. Their words must be measured against the Bible.

As you read this chapter remember that it was written so that we might be ready to endure and stay faithful to the end, not to make us fearful. The temptation to give up may come our way but *"God is faithful; he will not let you be tempted beyond what you can bear. But when you are tempted, he will also provide a way out so that you can stand up under it."* (1 Corinthians 10:13).

Read Revelation 13

At the end of this chapter the beast takes control of all trade in the world by forcing people to have his mark on them. Control of the world's financial system is a key element of his power and authority but, as we will see tomorrow, this system is not beyond the judgement of God.

Day 80
The End of All things – and Beyond!

The God of Love and Justice

Why does God allow wicked men to prosper? Why are cruel leaders allowed to pursue policies that result in the deaths of millions of people? Why does God allow evil men and women to abuse, maim and kill innocent children? These questions are a puzzle to those who don't know God and to Christians too. Why does God not take action to deal with those who are wicked? The good news from Revelation is that God will not let wickedness go unpunished forever: one day he will bring punishments on the earth. Yesterday we read about the disasters that resulted from the opening of the seven seals and the blowing of the seven trumpets but, as if they were not enough, they are followed in Revelation 15 and 16 by seven angels pouring *"the seven bowls of God's wrath on the earth." (Revelation 16:1)*. These result in dreadful disease, total pollution of the sea and of water supplies, intense heat from the sun, darkness, earthquakes, hailstorms and preparations for war. Like the Egyptians, who had a taste of these 'plagues' in the time of Moses, people will refuse to repent and turn to God but instead will curse him.

Of course when people ask why God does not punish wickedness they have other people in mind. These sorts of punishments should be reserved for the big villains, like Hitler and Stalin, not poured out indiscriminately upon the world. How can God's actions here be reconciled with God being a God of love? Even as Christians we can be so focused on the love of God that we forget that he is also a God of justice. What the Bible teaches us is that God is slow to anger and the fact that men are still on this earth with breath in their lungs and the option of turning to him is a demonstration of the patient love of God who wants everyone to have the opportunity to turn to him. We must not worship a God who is sentimental and puts up with wickedness like an indulgent uncle. No, we must learn to sing with David, *"I will sing of your love and justice" (Psalm 101:1)*.

The Fall of Babylon

In Revelation 14 there is a reference to the fall of "Babylon". An angel says, *"Fallen! Fallen is Babylon the Great, which made all the nations drink the maddening wine of her adulteries." (Revelation 14:8).* Babylon the Great is mentioned again at the end of Revelation 16 before John is shown a vision of a woman sitting on a beast in Revelation 17. Her name is *"MYSTERY, BABYLON THE GREAT, THE MOTHER OF PROSTITUTES AND OF THE ABOMINATIONS OF THE EARTH." (Revelation 17:5)* and she is drunk with the blood of the saints. Who is this woman and what does Babylon represent?

The first mention of Babylon is early in Genesis and the closer we get to the end of Revelation, the last book in the Bible, the more references we find to the beginning of Genesis, the first book. Genesis 11 describes how men built a city that included a tower, probably used for religious ceremonies, which acted as a centre for commerce and government and *"so that we may make a name for ourselves" (Genesis 11:4)*. It represented all that man could do himself and the Lord put a stop to their plans by introducing different languages, which meant that they could no longer work together easily. As a result of that it became known as "Babel", meaning confusion, the same Hebrew word which is translated "Babylon". Later Babylon became the capital city of the Babylonian Empire which took the nation of Judah into captivity. Daniel lived in Babylon and became Prime Minister to the proud king Nebuchadnezzar who, you will remember, was humbled by God when God sent him mad for a time. Immediately before his period of madness he said *"Is not this the great Babylon I have built as the royal residence by my mighty power and for the glory of my majesty." (Daniel 4:30)*. Babylon, once again, had become a powerful centre of commerce, religion and military power built for the glory of man. So, in Revelation it is reasonable to assume that Babylon represents the man made world system – the political system with its glory and its military power, the commercial and financial systems, and the man made religions.

Revelation 18 describes the fall of Babylon. God's people are called to come out of her so that they will not share in the judgement that is coming upon her. Her destruction is mourned by world leaders, who enjoyed the glory, riches and pleasure she brought them, and by merchants and sea captains who made their money through trade. This leads into praise in heaven for the destruction of the system which has led to the death of many of the Lord's servants.

The Second Coming

After the destruction of Babylon we see Jesus returning in power. His

Day 80 – The End of All things – and Beyond!

"Second Coming", is foretold over three hundred times in the New Testament, over eight times as many times as the number of references to his first coming in the Old Testament. The first time he came as a weak, helpless baby, born to a poor family in a stable, but when he returns it could not be more different. He comes in might and with power to wage war on the forces of evil and rule the nations. For those who love him and are waiting for his return this will be a joyful occasion: *"Let us rejoice and be glad and give him glory! For the wedding of the Lamb has come, and his bride has made herself ready"* (Revelation 19:7). Jesus is coming for his bride, the church, and he is so eager to be with her that Paul tells us that *"we who are still alive and are left will be caught up together with them [those who have already died] in the clouds to meet the Lord in the air." (1 Thessalonians 4:17)*. This is great news! All the trials and tribulations of life on this earth will finally be over for God's people.

But for those who do not know him the news is very different. His coming will not go unnoticed by them as John has already told us: *"Look, he is coming with the clouds, and every eye will see him, even those who pierced him; and all the peoples of the earth will mourn because of him."* And for those who are sceptical of this message, John adds, *"So shall it be! Amen." (Revelation 1:7)*. Because we live in a world that has rejected the Biblical view of the world it is hard for us to really take on board the fact that one day soon, Jesus will return to this earth. We are taught that the world is billions of years old and that it will be billions of years before the sun expands to a point where life on this planet is no longer viable. The idea that God will intervene in history and put an end to it is a fundamental Biblical message and one that we need to get deep into our heart and mind so it affects our thinking.

Many people have predicted the date when Jesus will return to earth but this is a pointless exercise as Jesus himself made it very clear to his disciples that *"No–one knows about that day or hour, not even the angels in heaven, nor the Son, but only the Father." (Matthew 24:36)*. When Jesus returns it will be *"like a thief in the night" (1 Thessalonians 5:2)* – sudden and unexpected. The line from the Negro spiritual, *"This world is not my home, I'm just a–passin' through"* is a true statement for the Christian and we need to live our lives every day in such a way that we would not be embarrassed or ashamed at any moment to welcome the return of our Saviour.

The Millennium

However, before the world is finally destroyed, Revelation talks about Christ ruling on earth for a thousand years (a millennium) along with those who had been martyred during the time of the beast. The prophecies of Isaiah 2 and Micah 4 about God's people living in peace and prosperity probably relate to this period. We have already seen that Revelation is a book full of symbolism so whether this reference to a thousand years should be taken literally or whether it just indicates a long period of time is open to question. Over the years a lot of time has been spent trying to reconcile all the Biblical references to the end times and "the Millennium" – Christ's reign on earth for a thousand years – have been used to define the different views people have taken. There are three basic views – premillennialism, postmillennialism, and amillennialism – which I have no intention of trying to explain here! Suffice it to say that if you compare each of the views with all the Biblical references relating to the end times then each has verses that support it and each has verses which challenge it. If you do investigate this further at a later date and come to a conclusion yourself then it is important to remember that many great Christians have looked into this whole area over the years without agreeing so do not fall out with those that take a different view! A friend of mine[18] once told me that he was a "panmillennialist", a view I had never heard of before. When I asked what he meant he said that he believed that "it will all pan out all right in the end!" I am sure this would not satisfy those who study this subject in detail but it does sum up the overall message of Revelation very well!

> Read Revelation 20

Judgement

The account of the judgement at the end of chapter 20 is very sobering. Every person who has lived on the earth, whether they were a king or a poor beggar, a well-known celebrity or not known by anyone, will stand alongside one another as Christ reviews what they have done. You will be there and will be asked to give an account of what you have done in this life as recorded in the books in heaven. Despite the huge number of people that will be judged Jesus will not be rushed, he will take his time and you can be confident that he will make a totally

---

[18] Allan Johnson again – a remarkable man! See footnote on page 345.

impartial assessment of your actions – both good and bad – and fully understand your motivations, knowledge that is hidden from an earthly court. For all of us this will be an uncomfortable process and living with the knowledge that it will happen should encourage us to avoid wrong behaviour now. The good news for Christians is not that they will escape this judgement – the Bible is clear that all men will be judged – but that those whose names are found in the book of life will escape the punishment for their sins in the lake of fire. This is not because they were found to be without sin in what they had done, but because their sins had been dealt with by the sacrifice of the judge himself.

A New Heaven and a New Earth!

The Bible opens with a picture of absolute perfection. The first two chapters of Genesis describe how the world that God created was good in every respect. Then Satan appears in the third chapter and sin is introduced into God's world to spoil it. As we have just seen, three chapters from the end of the Bible, in Revelation 20, Satan is finally dealt with and his influence over mankind is removed. Sin is dealt with at the last judgement and the final two chapters of the Bible describe a perfect earth, which will be the home of God's people forever. The symmetry is remarkable: two chapters of sinless perfection at the beginning and two at the end of the Bible, and between them, 1,085 chapters detailing man's rebellion against God and the love of God for man. As you read about the amazing home that God is preparing for those who love him, it is easy to read through the words without taking in their meaning. As John tries to describe the new heaven, the new earth and the new Jerusalem he returns to using the word 'like' at times as there is nothing equivalent to them in this world. What will life without tears, without death and without pain be like? It is beyond our comprehension.

> Read Revelation 21–22

The Message of Revelation

As we have seen, there is a lot in Revelation which is hard to understand. It is not wise to try and interpret all the details or try to read more into it – we are warned against this in Revelation 22:18. A lot of prophecy in the Bible is given so that we will recognise its fulfilment when it happens and take appropriate action. There are many troubles in the world today and maybe many of these are God's judgements on mankind. Whether they are or not we can be assured that he is working his purposes out. Take heart! God is looking for those who overcome. Jesus is the only hope for this world and he will return one day for his bride. We need to ask him to come soon but until he does we also need to pray for others and work with the Holy Spirit to say "Come!" to those who are thirsty.

What are you going to do now?

Eighty days ago you may never have thought you would get through this book but here you are at the end! Along the way we have looked at every book on the Bible Bookcase opposite and the important question for you is: "What are you going to do with the Bible now?" The Bible is your guide for life, God's love letter to you. It is not just for reading in church on Sundays but it is to be read and studied throughout your life. Be like the people of Berea who are described as having a more noble character than the Thessalonians, *"for they received the message with great eagerness and examined the Scriptures every day to see if what Paul said was true." (Acts 17:11)*. Look back at Day 77 where we looked at "Getting to grips with the Bible" and prayerfully set yourself some goals for the coming months so that you can become surer of your faith over the coming years.

I hope that you have enjoyed this journey "Through the Bible in 80 days" and have gained a better understanding of the landscape of this incredible book, have made some friends along the way who you will revisit over the coming months and years and, above all, that you have developed a love for its author, God himself. May you continue to enjoy God's word until that day when we live in that city where we *"will see his face" (Revelation 22:4)* for ever and ever.

Day 80 – The End of All things – and Beyond! 467

The Bible Bookcase

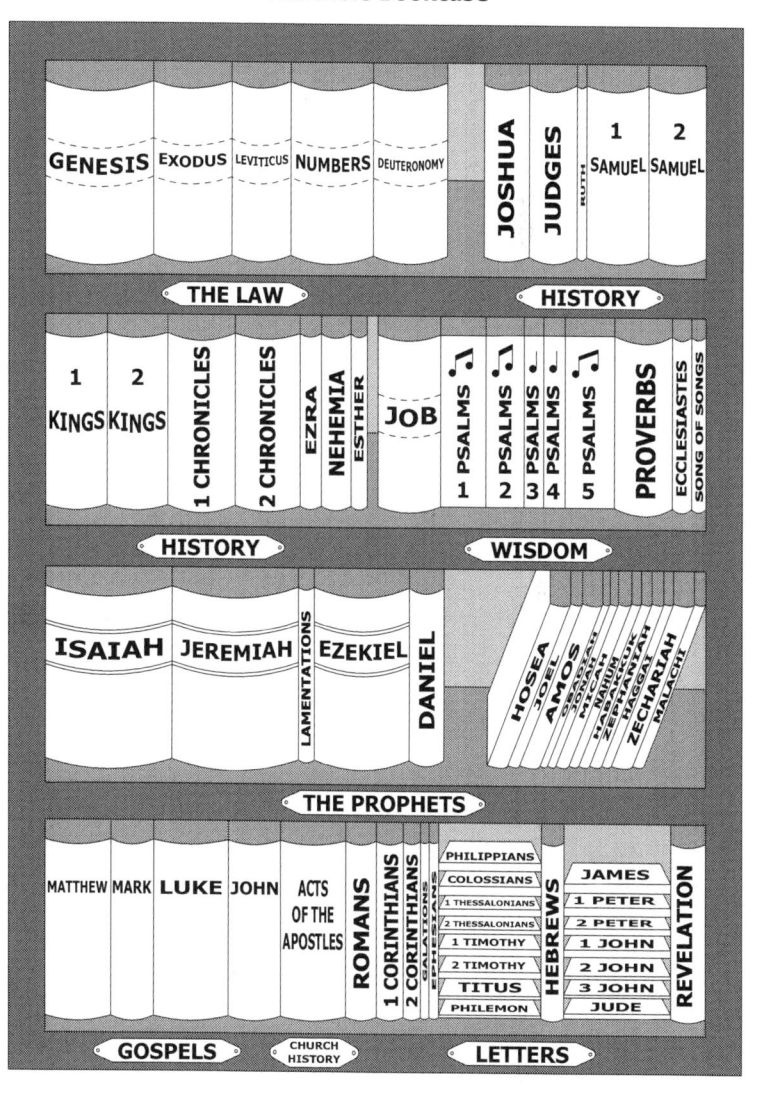

Appendix A
Timecharts of the Bible

The Timecharts in this appendix are included in the body of the book for ease of use but are brought together here to show the complete sweep of Biblical history.

Timecharts 1–4 cover the whole Bible at a high level, showing some key people, the history of Israel and the world powers that had an impact on the Biblical account.

Timecharts 5–12 show key events and approximately when leaders, kings, prophets and other Biblical characters lived from the time of the Exodus through to the New Testament.

The structure of these more detailed charts, working from the top, is:

- Title
- Dateline (BC apart from the end of Timechart 12)
- The books of the Bible that tell the history of that period.
- A grey block showing the history of Israel. This splits into the two nations of Judah and Israel for Timecharts 7 and 8. Only Judah is shown from Timechart 9 onwards.
- Leaders, judges, prophets and kings are shown within the history of Israel and Judah.
- Lines separate the reigns of the kings. Dashed lines indicate that the next king is a son (or sometimes another relative) of the previous king; solid lines indicate the start of a new dynasty, i.e. a king from a new family. Slanting lines indicate an overlap between the reigns of kings. The names of kings who ruled for a very short periods are left out.
- The grey blocks at the bottom of the Timecharts (apart from 6 and 7) indicate the other nations and world powers that invaded or ruled the land of Israel. The names of some kings are included, usually where they are mentioned in the Bible.
- Arrows up and down indicate attacks on Israel, Israelites going into exile and their return from exile.
- Wisdom and Prophetic books of the Bible are shown at the time they were written.

Note that there is uncertainly over dates before 1000 BC.

Appendix A – Timecharts of the Bible

Timechart 1	– Creation–1800 BC:	Events in Genesis 470
Timechart 2	– 1600–1000 BC:	Israel from Egypt to a United Nation ... 471
Timechart 3	– 1000–400 BC:	The Kingdoms of Judah and Israel 472
Timechart 4	– 400 BC–AD 200:	The Time around the New Testament .. 473
Timechart 5	– 1450–1240 BC:	The Exodus, Conquest of Canaan and early Judges 474
Timechart 6	– 1210–1000 BC:	The time of the Judges and King Saul .. 475
Timechart 7	– 1000–860 BC:	David, Solomon and the Divided Kingdom 476
Timechart 8	– 860–720 BC:	Judah and Israel to the Exile of Israel ... 477
Timechart 9	– 720–580 BC:	The Exile of Judah 478
Timechart 10	– 580–440 BC:	The Exile and the Return 479
Timechart 11	– 460–180 BC:	The Time between the Testaments 480
Timechart 12	– 180 BC–AD 100:	New Testament Times 481

470　　　　　　　　　*Appendix A – Timecharts of the Bible*

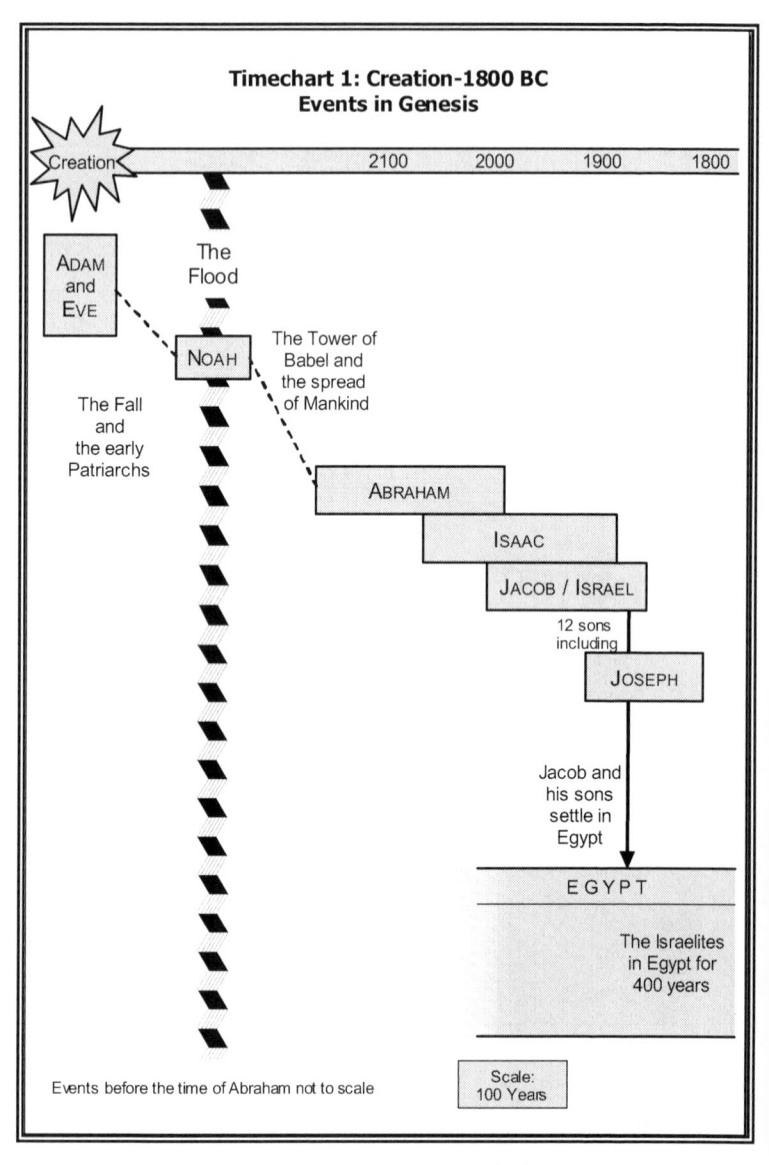

Timechart 1: Creation–1800 BC
Events in Genesis

Creation　　　　　　　2100　　2000　　1900　　1800

ADAM and EVE

The Flood

NOAH

The Tower of Babel and the spread of Mankind

The Fall and the early Patriarchs

ABRAHAM

ISAAC

JACOB / ISRAEL

12 sons including

JOSEPH

Jacob and his sons settle in Egypt

EGYPT

The Israelites in Egypt for 400 years

Events before the time of Abraham not to scale

Scale: 100 Years

**Timechart 1 – Creation–1800 BC:
Events in Genesis**

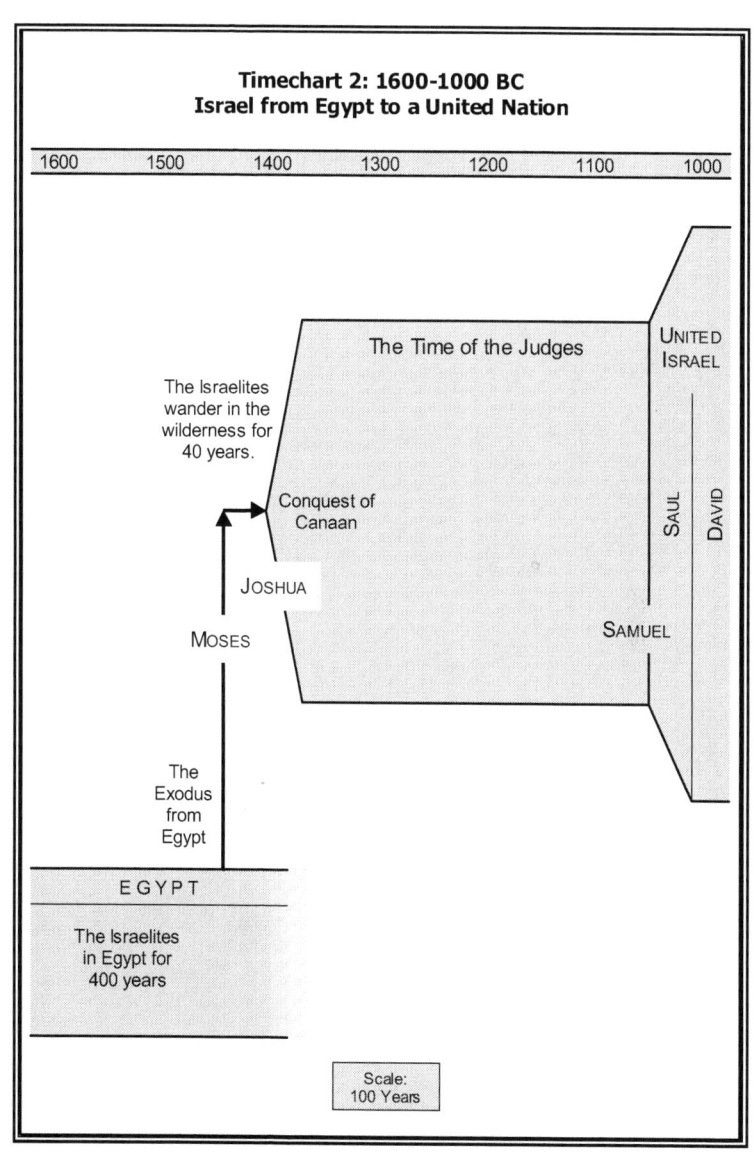

Appendix A – Timecharts of the Bible 471

Timechart 2: 1600-1000 BC
Israel from Egypt to a United Nation

| 1600 | 1500 | 1400 | 1300 | 1200 | 1100 | 1000 |

The Time of the Judges

UNITED ISRAEL

The Israelites wander in the wilderness for 40 years.

Conquest of Canaan

JOSHUA

SAUL

DAVID

MOSES

SAMUEL

The Exodus from Egypt

EGYPT

The Israelites in Egypt for 400 years

Scale: 100 Years

**Timechart 2 – 1600–1000 BC:
Israel from Egypt to a United Nation**

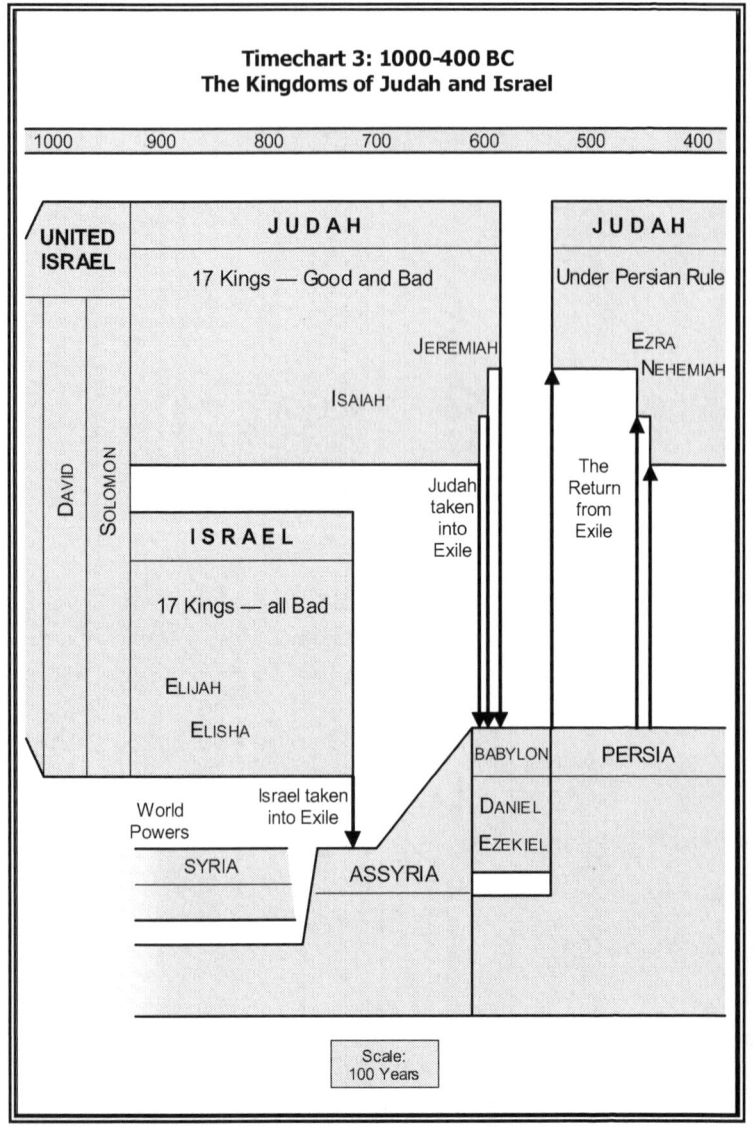

Appendix A – Timecharts of the Bible

Timechart 3: 1000-400 BC
The Kingdoms of Judah and Israel

| 1000 | 900 | 800 | 700 | 600 | 500 | 400 |

UNITED ISRAEL
DAVID
SOLOMON

JUDAH
17 Kings — Good and Bad
JEREMIAH
ISAIAH
Judah taken into Exile

JUDAH
Under Persian Rule
EZRA
NEHEMIAH
The Return from Exile

ISRAEL
17 Kings — all Bad
ELIJAH
ELISHA
Israel taken into Exile

World Powers
SYRIA
ASSYRIA
BABYLON
DANIEL
EZEKIEL
PERSIA

Scale: 100 Years

**Timechart 3 – 1000–400 BC:
The Kingdoms of Judah and Israel**

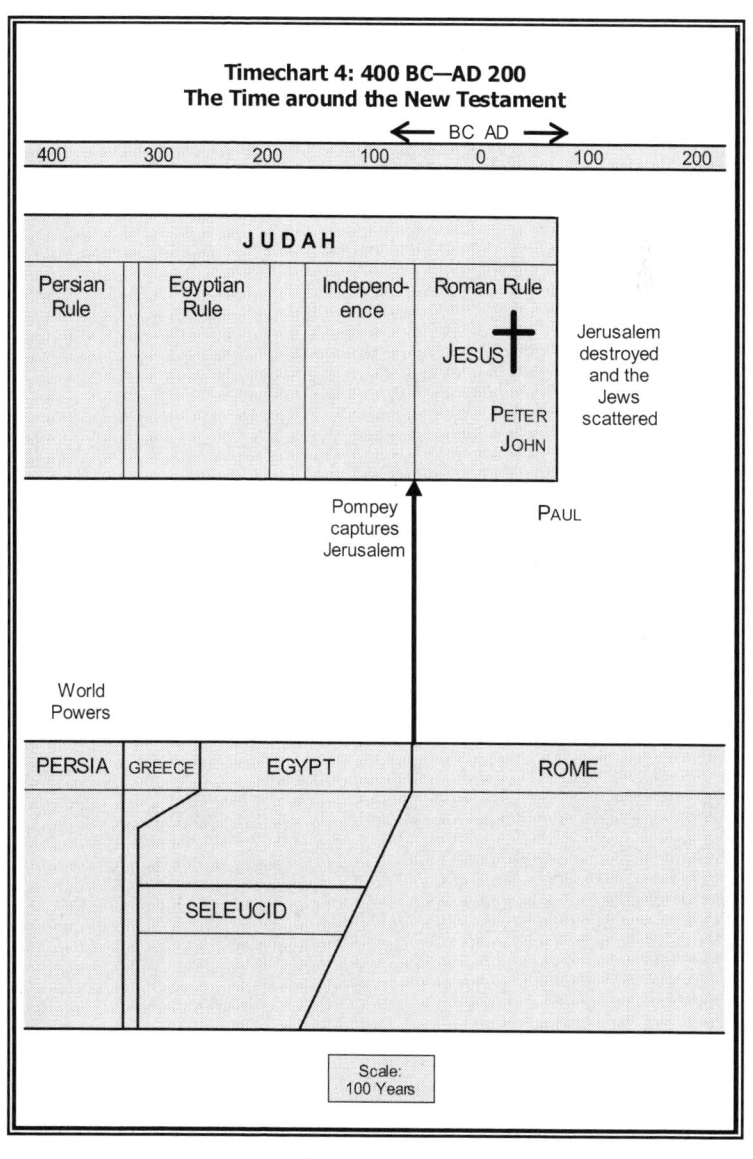

Appendix A – Timecharts of the Bible 473

Timechart 4: 400 BC—AD 200
The Time around the New Testament

← BC   AD →

| 400 | 300 | 200 | 100 | 0 | 100 | 200 |

JUDAH

| Persian Rule | Egyptian Rule | Independence | Roman Rule | Jerusalem destroyed and the Jews scattered |

JESUS ✝

PETER
JOHN

Pompey captures Jerusalem

PAUL

World Powers

| PERSIA | GREECE | EGYPT | ROME |

SELEUCID

Scale: 100 Years

**Timechart 4 – 400 BC–AD 200:
The Time around the New Testament**

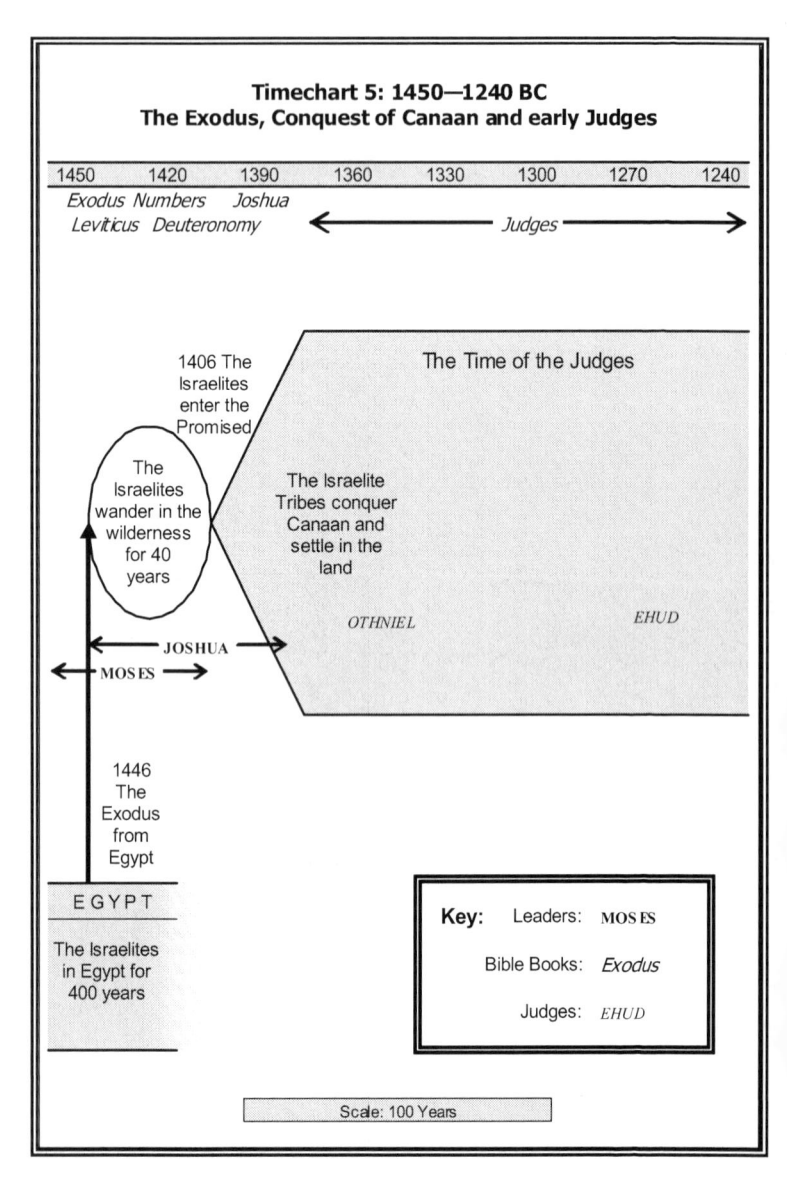

474   *Appendix A – Timecharts of the Bible*

Timechart 5: 1450—1240 BC
The Exodus, Conquest of Canaan and early Judges

| 1450 | 1420 | 1390 | 1360 | 1330 | 1300 | 1270 | 1240 |

Exodus   Numbers   Joshua
Leviticus   Deuteronomy   ⟵———— Judges ————⟶

1406 The Israelites enter the Promised

The Israelites wander in the wilderness for 40 years

The Time of the Judges

The Israelite Tribes conquer Canaan and settle in the land

OTHNIEL   *EHUD*

⟵ JOSHUA ⟶
⟵ MOSES ⟶

1446 The Exodus from Egypt

EGYPT

The Israelites in Egypt for 400 years

Key: Leaders: MOSES
Bible Books: *Exodus*
Judges: *EHUD*

Scale: 100 Years

Timechart 5 – 1450–1240 BC:
The Exodus, Conquest of Canaan and early Judges

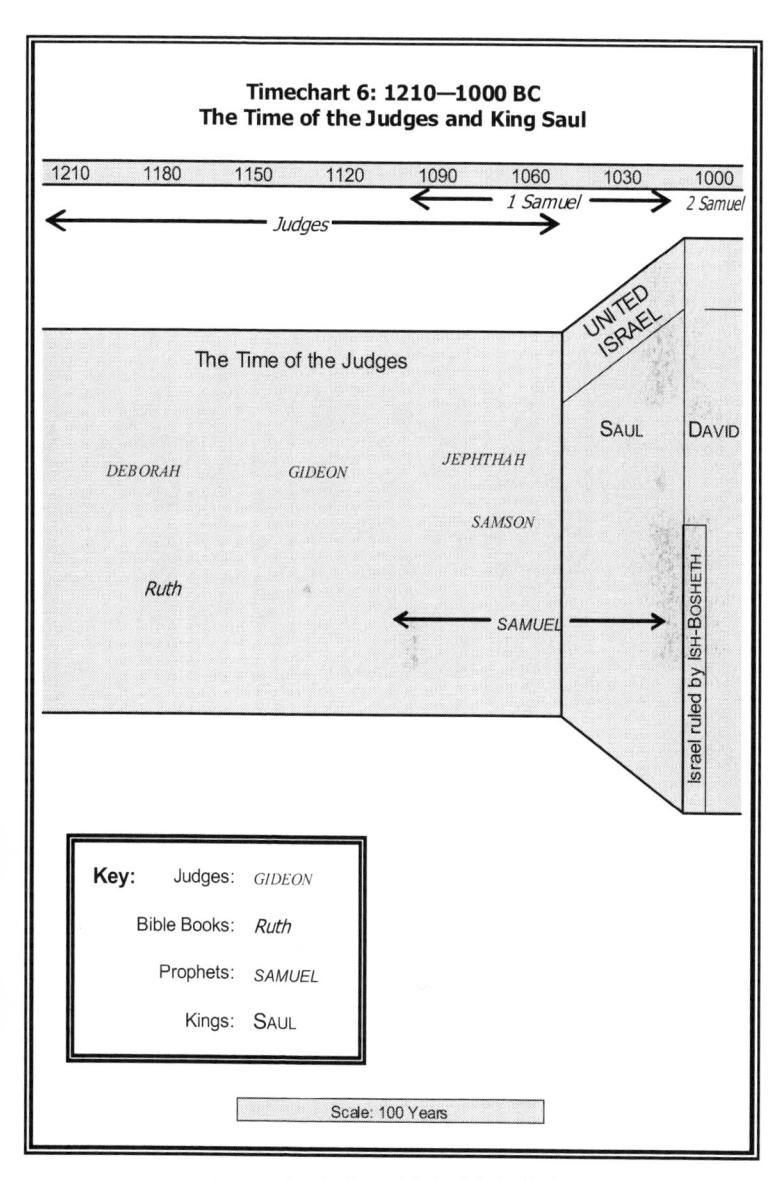

Appendix A – Timecharts of the Bible 475

Timechart 6: 1210—1000 BC
The Time of the Judges and King Saul

| 1210 | 1180 | 1150 | 1120 | 1090 | 1060 | 1030 | 1000 |

← 1 Samuel → 2 Samuel

← Judges →

The Time of the Judges

UNITED ISRAEL

SAUL   DAVID

DEBORAH   GIDEON   JEPHTHAH

SAMSON

Ruth

← SAMUEL →

Israel ruled by ISH-BOSHETH

Key:
- Judges: *GIDEON*
- Bible Books: *Ruth*
- Prophets: SAMUEL
- Kings: SAUL

Scale: 100 Years

**Timechart 6 — 1210–1000 BC:
The time of the Judges and King Saul**

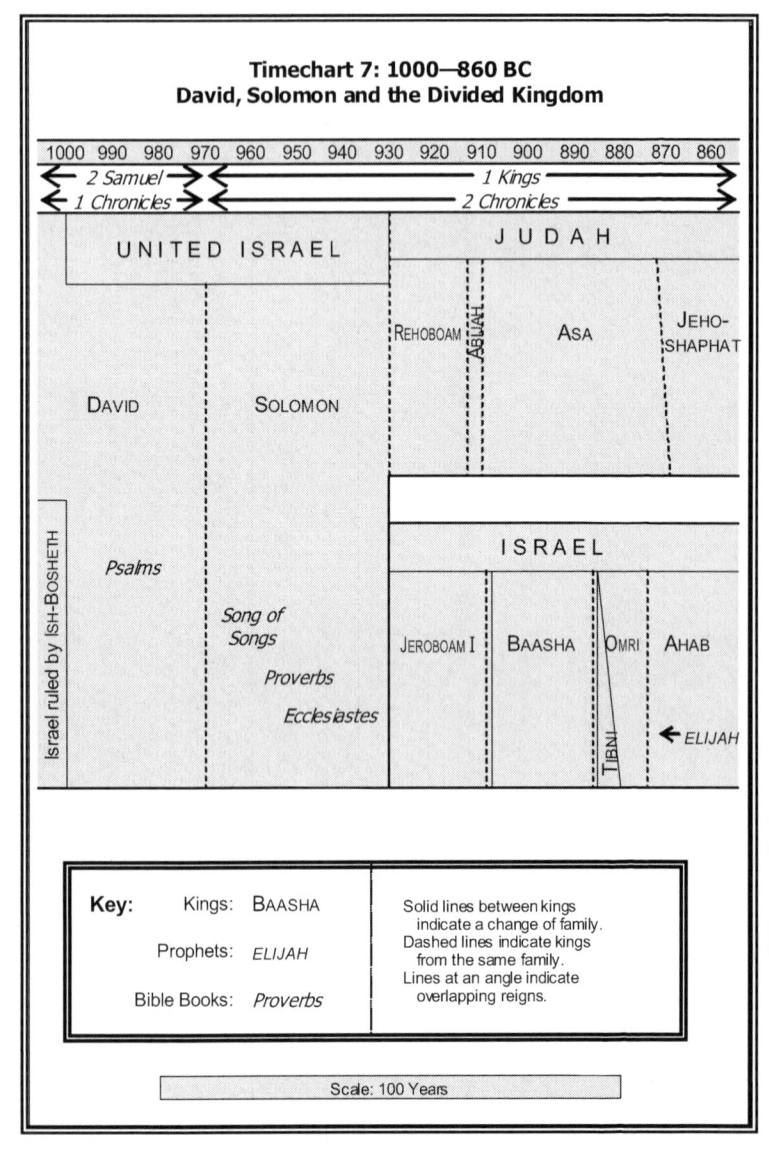

Appendix A – Timecharts of the Bible

Timechart 7: 1000—860 BC
David, Solomon and the Divided Kingdom

| 1000 | 990 | 980 | 970 | 960 | 950 | 940 | 930 | 920 | 910 | 900 | 890 | 880 | 870 | 860 |

← 2 Samuel →　　←——————— 1 Kings ———————→
← 1 Chronicles →　←——————— 2 Chronicles ———————→

UNITED ISRAEL | **JUDAH**

REHOBOAM | ABIJAH | ASA | JEHO-SHAPHAT

DAVID | SOLOMON

Israel ruled by ISH-BOSHETH

Psalms

Song of Songs

Proverbs

Ecclesiastes

ISRAEL

JEROBOAM I | BAASHA | OMRI | AHAB

TIBNI

← ELIJAH

Key:
- Kings: **BAASHA**
- Prophets: *ELIJAH*
- Bible Books: *Proverbs*

Solid lines between kings indicate a change of family.
Dashed lines indicate kings from the same family.
Lines at an angle indicate overlapping reigns.

Scale: 100 Years

**Timechart 7 – 1000—860 BC:
David, Solomon and the Divided Kingdom**

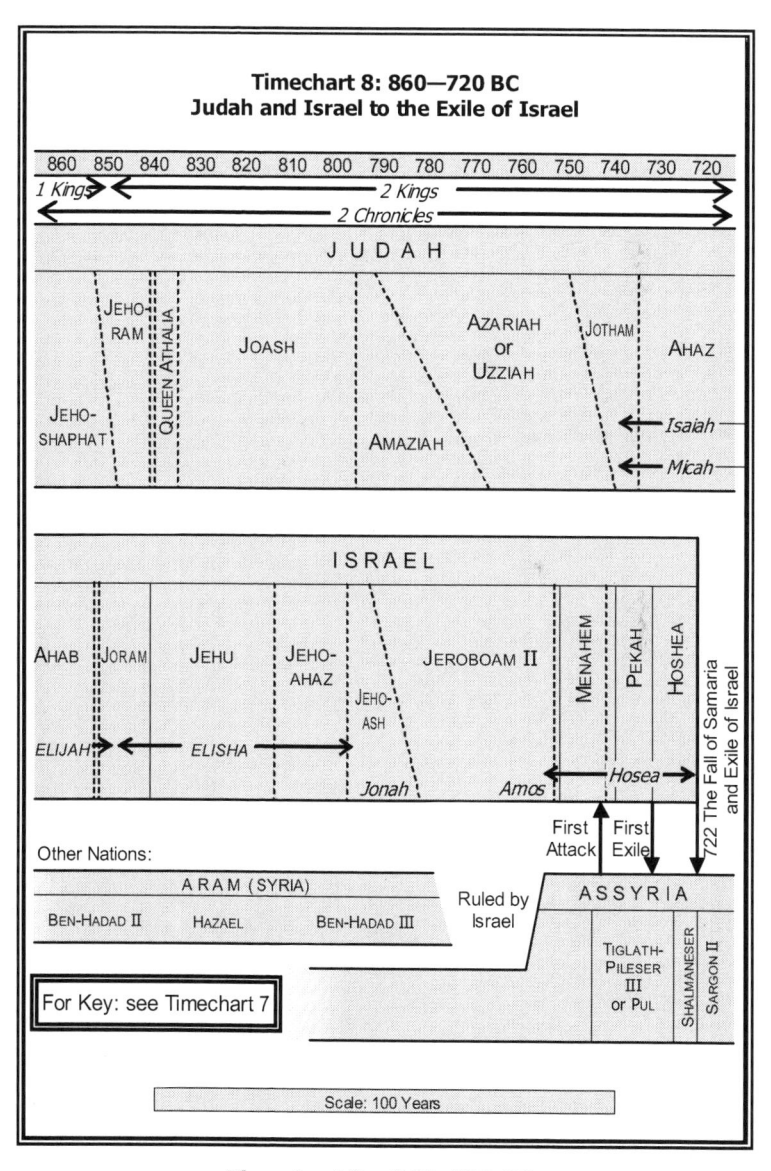

Appendix A – Timecharts of the Bible

Timechart 8: 860—720 BC
Judah and Israel to the Exile of Israel

| 860 | 850 | 840 | 830 | 820 | 810 | 800 | 790 | 780 | 770 | 760 | 750 | 740 | 730 | 720 |

1 Kings ⇐ ————— 2 Kings ————— ⇒
⇐ ————— 2 Chronicles ————— ⇒

JUDAH

JEHO-SHAPHAT | JEHO-RAM | QUEEN ATHALIA | JOASH | AMAZIAH | AZARIAH or UZZIAH | JOTHAM | AHAZ

← Isaiah
← Micah

ISRAEL

AHAB | JORAM | JEHU | JEHO-AHAZ | JEHO-ASH | JEROBOAM II | MENAHEM | PEKAH | HOSHEA

ELIJAH ⇐ ELISHA ⇒
Jonah | Amos | ← Hosea →

722 The Fall of Samaria and Exile of Israel

First Attack | First Exile

Other Nations:

ARAM (SYRIA) | Ruled by Israel | ASSYRIA

BEN-HADAD II | HAZAEL | BEN-HADAD III

TIGLATH-PILESER III or PUL | SHALMANESER | SARGON II

For Key: see Timechart 7

Scale: 100 Years

**Timechart 8 – 860–720 BC:
Judah and Israel to the Exile of Israel**

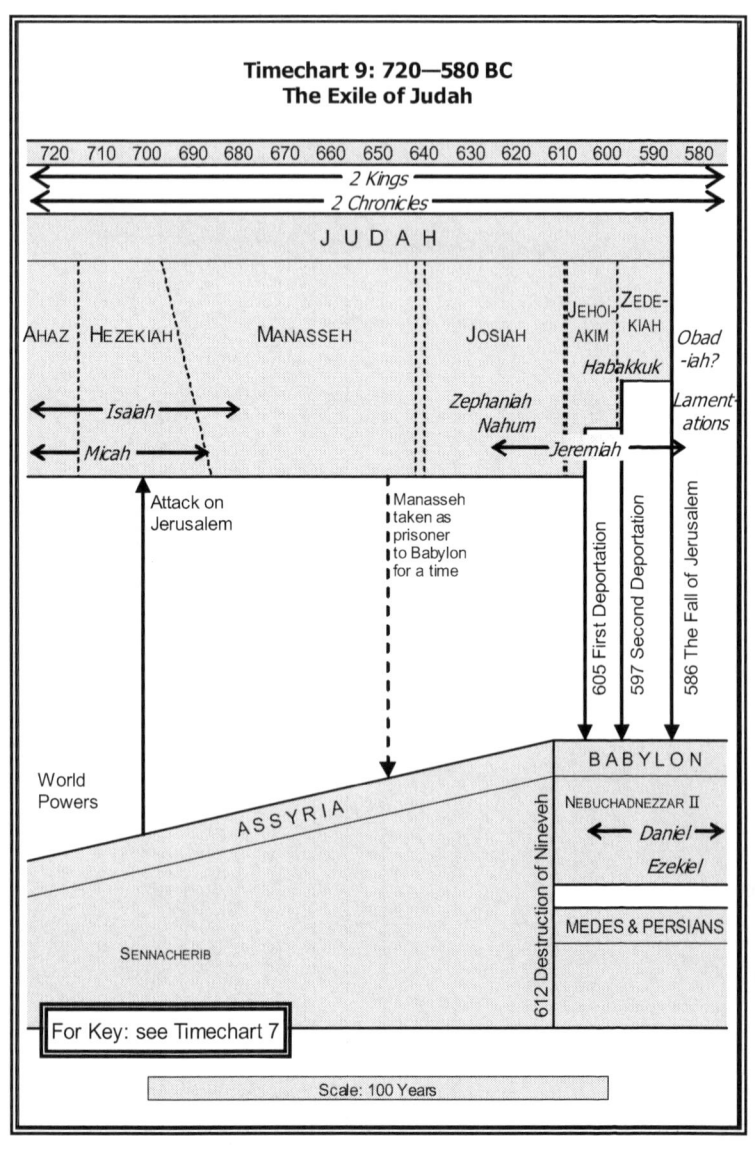

Appendix A – Timecharts of the Bible

Timechart 9: 720—580 BC
The Exile of Judah

| 720 | 710 | 700 | 690 | 680 | 670 | 660 | 650 | 640 | 630 | 620 | 610 | 600 | 590 | 580 |

⟵—————— 2 Kings ——————⟶
⟵—————— 2 Chronicles ——————⟶

JUDAH

AHAZ | HEZEKIAH | MANASSEH | JOSIAH | JEHOIAKIM | ZEDEKIAH | Obadiah?

Habakkuk

⟵ Isaiah ⟶

⟵ Micah ⟶

Zephaniah
Nahum

⟵ Jeremiah ⟶

Lamentations

Attack on Jerusalem

Manasseh taken as prisoner to Babylon for a time

605 First Deportation
597 Second Deportation
586 The Fall of Jerusalem

World Powers

ASSYRIA

SENNACHERIB

612 Destruction of Nineveh

BABYLON

NEBUCHADNEZZAR II

⟵ Daniel ⟶

Ezekiel

MEDES & PERSIANS

For Key: see Timechart 7

Scale: 100 Years

**Timechart 9 – 720–580 BC:
The Exile of Judah**

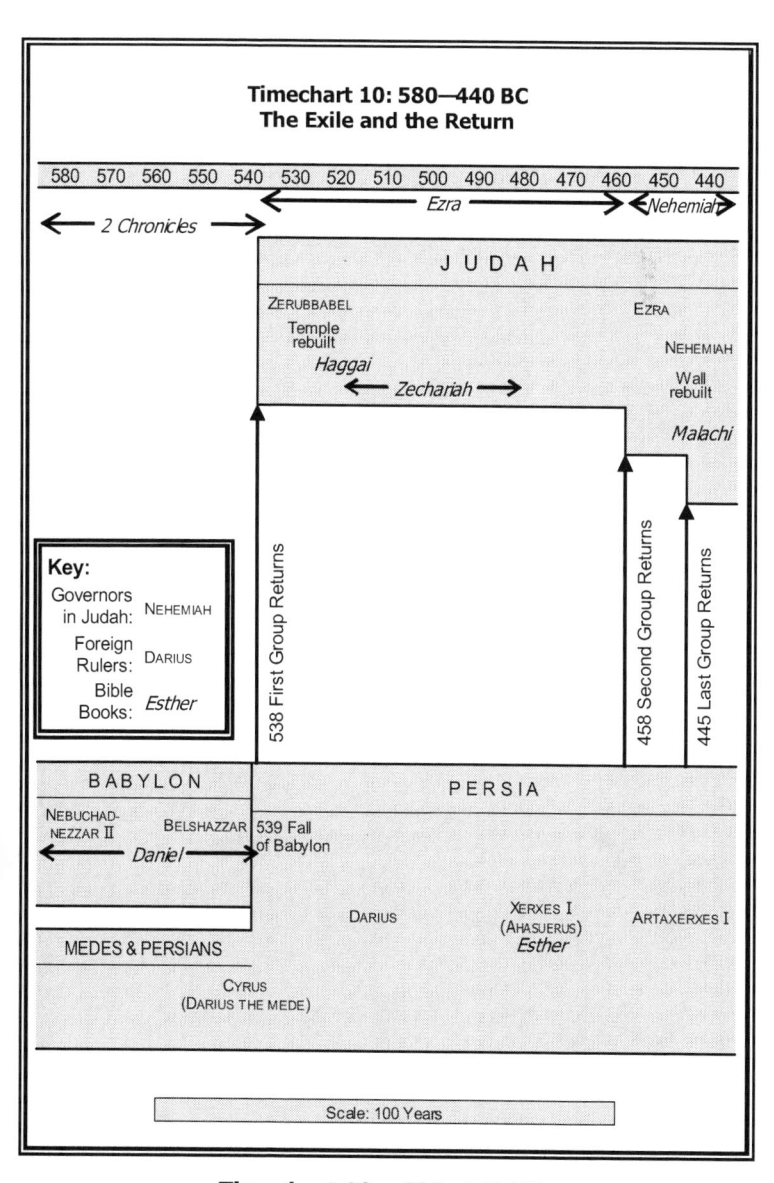

Appendix A – Timecharts of the Bible 479

Timechart 10: 580—440 BC
The Exile and the Return

| 580 | 570 | 560 | 550 | 540 | 530 | 520 | 510 | 500 | 490 | 480 | 470 | 460 | 450 | 440 |

←——— Ezra ———→ ←Nehemiah→

←— 2 Chronicles —→

JUDAH

ZERUBBABEL — EZRA

Temple rebuilt — NEHEMIAH

Haggai — Wall rebuilt

←— *Zechariah* —→

Malachi

Key:
- Governors in Judah: NEHEMIAH
- Foreign Rulers: DARIUS
- Bible Books: *Esther*

538 First Group Returns
458 Second Group Returns
445 Last Group Returns

BABYLON | **PERSIA**

NEBUCHADNEZZAR II | BELSHAZZAR | 539 Fall of Babylon

←— *Daniel* —→

DARIUS | XERXES I (AHASUERUS) *Esther* | ARTAXERXES I

MEDES & PERSIANS

CYRUS (DARIUS THE MEDE)

Scale: 100 Years

**Timechart 10 – 580–440 BC:
The Exile and the Return**

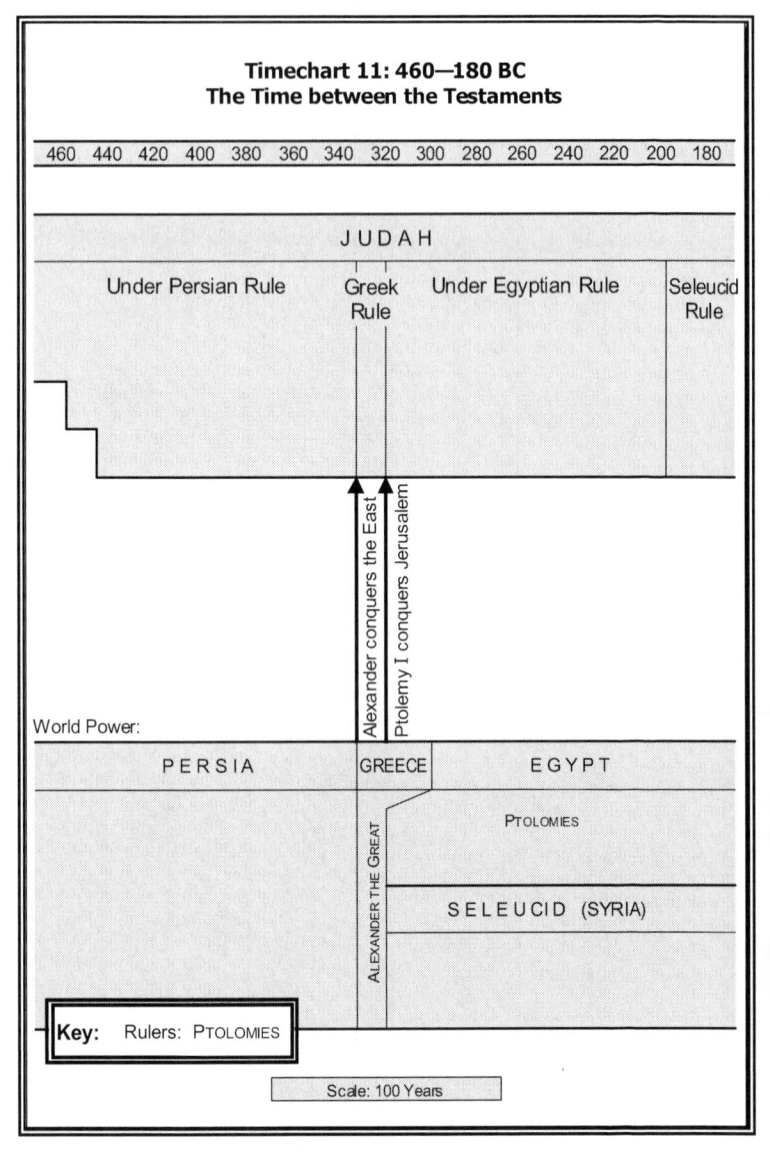

Timechart 11: 460—180 BC
The Time between the Testaments

| 460 | 440 | 420 | 400 | 380 | 360 | 340 | 320 | 300 | 280 | 260 | 240 | 220 | 200 | 180 |

JUDAH

Under Persian Rule | Greek Rule | Under Egyptian Rule | Seleucid Rule

Alexander conquers the East
Ptolemy I conquers Jerusalem

World Power:

PERSIA | GREECE | EGYPT

ALEXANDER THE GREAT

PTOLOMIES

SELEUCID (SYRIA)

Key: Rulers: PTOLOMIES

Scale: 100 Years

**Timechart 11 – 460–180BC:
The Time between the Testaments**

Appendix A – Timecharts of the Bible 481

Timechart 12: 180 BC—100 AD
New Testament Times

← BC AD →

180 160 140 120 100 80 60 40 20 0 20 40 60 80 100

Gospels
Acts

JUDAH

Seleucid Rule	Independent Jewish State	Under Roman Rule
Antiochus Epiphanes desecrates the temple	JUDAS MACCABEUS	HEROD THE GREAT / PILATE — JESUS † — Temple built

AD 70 Destruction of Jerusalem. The Jews removed from the land.

Pompey captures Israel

← PETER →
← JOHN →
← PAUL →

New Testament Letters

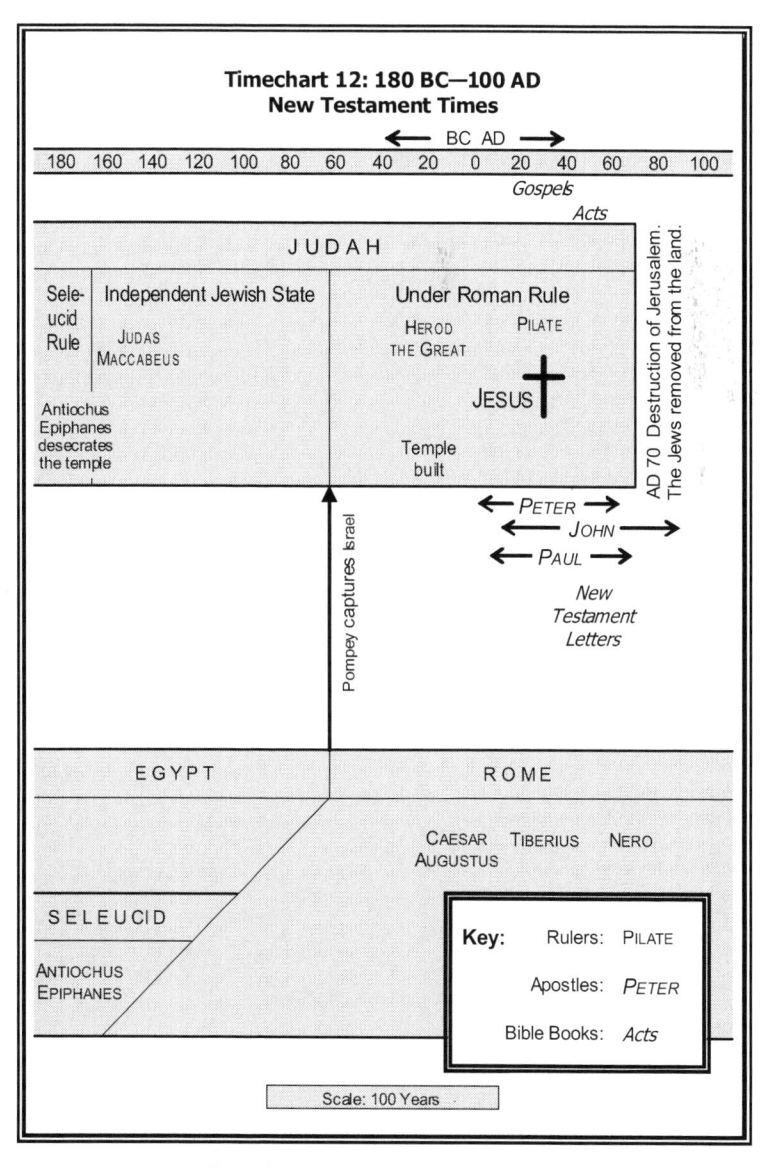

EGYPT

ROME

CAESAR AUGUSTUS   TIBERIUS   NERO

SELEUCID

ANTIOCHUS EPIPHANES

Key: Rulers: PILATE
Apostles: *PETER*
Bible Books: *Acts*

Scale: 100 Years

**Timechart 12 – 180 BC–AD 100:
New Testament Times**

Appendix B
Reading through the Bible in a Year

The plan on the following pages, which was devised by my father, takes you through the entire Bible in a year by setting readings from the Old and New Testaments for each day. Where possible, it attempts to put the Old Testament readings into the order the events took place. This means that there is quite a lot of jumping around during the time of the kings and prophets so I have separated out the historical books from the wisdom and prophetic books using two columns.

Use of Bible References

If you are unfamiliar with finding your way around in the Bible then here is a short explanation of how parts of the Bible are referred to.

Chapters are the first number after the name of the book. A dash is used to indicate a sequence of chapters, a comma to indicate a list, so:

> ***Genesis 24*** means the 24th chapter of Genesis,
>
> ***Genesis 1–3*** means the first three chapters of Genesis,
>
> ***Psalm 34, 56*** means the 34th and 56th Psalms.

Verses are shown by two numbers, the chapter, followed by the number of the verse and separated by a colon:

> ***John 3:16*** is the sixteenth verse in the third chapter of John

To indicate a passage with a number of verses a dash is used. If the passage is all within one chapter then only the verse is shown after the dash. Where the passage includes parts of more than one chapter then the new chapter is shown:

> ***Matthew 5:1–16*** is the first sixteen verses of the fifth chapter of Matthew
>
> ***Proverbs 22:17–24:34*** is the passage starting at the 17th verse of Proverbs 22 and continuing right through chapter 23 and on to the 34th verse of chapter 24.

In a couple of cases in the readings below one day's reading stops in the middle of a verse and this is indicated by use of 'a' and 'b'. The passage 1 Chronicles 28:1–29:22a stops in the middle of 1 Chronicles 29:22 while the next passage, 1 Chronicles 29:22b–30, starts with the second half of the verse. It will make sense when you get there!

I have also abbreviated a few book names to make it easier to follow.

Appendix B– Reading through the Bible in a Year

Day	Old Testament History	Wisdom & Prophets	New Testament
Jan 1	Genesis 1–3		Matthew 1
Jan 2	Genesis 4–7		Matthew 2
Jan 3	Genesis 8:1–11:26		Matthew 3
Jan 4	Genesis 11:27–15:21		Matthew 4
Jan 5	Genesis 16–18		Matthew 5:1–16
Jan 6	Genesis 19–20		Matthew 5:17–48
Jan 7	Genesis 21–23		Matthew 6
Jan 8	Genesis 24		Matthew 7
Jan 9	Genesis 25–26		Matthew 8:1–22
Jan 10	Genesis 27–28		Matthew 8:23–9:17
Jan 11	Genesis 29–30		Matthew 9:18–34
Jan 12	Genesis 31–32		Matthew 9:35–10:42
Jan 13	Genesis 33–35		Matthew 11
Jan 14	Genesis 36–38		Matthew 12:1–21
Jan 15	Genesis 39–40		Matthew 12:22–37
Jan 16	Genesis 41–42		Matthew 12:38–50
Jan 17	Genesis 43–44		Matthew 13:1–23
Jan 18	Genesis 45–46		Matthew 13:24–43
Jan 19	Genesis 47–48		Matthew 13:44–58
Jan 20	Genesis 49–50		Matthew 14:1–21
Jan 21		Job 1–3	Matthew 14:22–36
Jan 22		Job 4–7	Matthew 15:1–20
Jan 23		Job 8–10	Matthew 15:21–31
Jan 24		Job 11–14	Matthew 15:32–16:12
Jan 25		Job 15–17	Matthew 16:13–38
Jan 26		Job 18–19	Matthew 17:1–21
Jan 27		Job 20–21	Matthew 17:22–18:14
Jan 28		Job 22–24	Matthew 18:15–35
Jan 29		Job 25–28	Matthew 19:1–15
Jan 30		Job 29–31	Matthew 19:16–20:16
Jan 31		Job 32–34	Matthew 20:17–21:11
Feb 1		Job 35–37	Matthew 21:12–22
Feb 2		Job 38–39	Matthew 21:23–46
Feb 3		Job 40–42	Matthew 22:1–14
Feb 4	Exodus 1–2		Matthew 22:15–46
Feb 5	Exodus 3–5		Matthew 23:1–22
Feb 6	Exodus 6–8		Matthew 23:23–39
Feb 7	Exodus 9–10		Matthew 24:1–28
Feb 8	Exodus 11:1–13:16		Matthew 24:29–51
Feb 9	Exodus 13:17–15:21		Matthew 25:1–13

Appendix B– Reading through the Bible in a Year 485

Day	Old Testament History	Wisdom & Prophets	New Testament
Feb 10	Exodus 15:22–17:16		Matthew 25:14–30
Feb 11	Exodus 18–20		Matthew 25:31–46
Feb 12	Exodus 21–22		Matthew 26:1–16
Feb 13	Exodus 23–24		Matthew 26:17–35
Feb 14	Exodus 25–26		Matthew 26:36–56
Feb 15	Exodus 27–28		Matthew 26:57–75
Feb 16	Exodus 29–30		Matthew 27:1–26
Feb 17	Exodus 31–33		Matthew 27:27–54
Feb 18	Exodus 34:1–36:7		Matthew 27:55–28:10
Feb 19	Exodus 36:8–38:31		Matthew 28:11–20
Feb 20	Exodus 39–40		Hebrews 1
Feb 21	Leviticus 1–3		Hebrews 2
Feb 22	Leviticus 4:1–6:7		Hebrews 3
Feb 23	Leviticus 6:8–7:38		Hebrews 4:1–13
Feb 24	Leviticus 8:1–10:7		Hebrews 4:14–5:14
Feb 25	Leviticus 10:8–12:8		Hebrews 6
Feb 26	Leviticus 13		Hebrews 7
Feb 27	Leviticus 14–15		Hebrews 8
Feb 28	Leviticus 16–17		Hebrews 9
Mar 1	Leviticus 18–19		Hebrews 10:1–18
Mar 2	Leviticus 20–21		Hebrews 10:19–39
Mar 3	Leviticus 22–23		Hebrews 11:1–19
Mar 4	Leviticus 24–25		Hebrews 11:20–40
Mar 5	Leviticus 26–27		Hebrews 12
Mar 6	Numbers 1–2		Hebrews 13
Mar 7	Numbers 3–4		Mark 1:1–20
Mar 8	Numbers 5–6		Mark 1:21–45
Mar 9	Numbers 7		Mark 2:1–22
Mar 10	Numbers 8:1–10:10		Mark 2:23–3:19
Mar 11	Numbers 10:11–12:16		Mark 3:20–35
Mar 12	Numbers 13–14		Mark 4:1–20
Mar 13	Numbers 15		Mark 4:21–41
Mar 14	Numbers 16–17		Mark 5:1–20
Mar 15	Numbers 18–19		Mark 5:21–43
Mar 16	Numbers 20–21		Mark 6:1–29
Mar 17	Numbers 22:1–23:12		Mark 6:30–56
Mar 18	Numbers 23:13–25:18		Mark 7:1–23
Mar 19	Numbers 26:1–27:11		Mark 7:24–37
Mar 20	Numbers 27:12–29:40		Mark 8:1–26
Mar 21	Numbers 30–31		Mark 8:27–9:13

Appendix B– Reading through the Bible in a Year

Day	Old Testament History	Wisdom & Prophets	New Testament
Mar 22	Numbers 32–33		Mark 9:14–29
Mar 23	Numbers 34–36		Mark 9:30–50
Mar 24	Deuteronomy 1–2		Mark 10:1–27
Mar 25	Deut 3:1–4:43		Mark 10:28–52
Mar 26	Deut 4:44–6:25		Mark 11:1–26
Mar 27	Deut 7–8		Mark 11:27–12:17
Mar 28	Deut 9–11		Mark 12:18–44
Mar 29	Deut 12–13		Mark 13:1–13
Mar 30	Deut 14:1–16:17		Mark 13:14–37
Mar 31	Deut 16:18–19:21		Mark 14:1–21
Apr 1	Deut 20–21		Mark 14:22–52
Apr 2	Deut 22–23		Mark 14:53–72
Apr 3	Deut 24–26		Mark 15:1–23
Apr 4	Deut 27:1–28:35		Mark 15:24–47
Apr 5	Deut 28:36–29:29		Mark 16
Apr 6	Deut 30–31:29		James 1
Apr 7	Deut 31:30–32:52		James 2
Apr 8	Deut 33–34	Psalm 90	James 3
Apr 9	Joshua 1–3		James 4
Apr 10	Joshua 4–6		James 5
Apr 11	Joshua 7–8		1 Peter 1:1–21
Apr 12	Joshua 9–10		1 Peter 1:22–2:10
Apr 13	Joshua 11–13		1 Peter 2:11–25
Apr 14	Joshua 14–16		1 Peter 3:1–12
Apr 15	Joshua 17–19		1 Peter 3:13–4:6
Apr 16	Joshua 20–21		1 Peter 4:7–5:14
Apr 17	Joshua 22		2 Peter 1
Apr 18	Joshua 23–24		2 Peter 2
Apr 19	Judges 1:1–2:9		2 Peter 3
Apr 20	Judges 2:10–3:31		Jude
Apr 21	Judges 4–5		Luke 1:1–25
Apr 22	Judges 6		Luke 1:26–55
Apr 23	Judges 7–8		Luke 1:56–80
Apr 24	Judges 9:1–10:5		Luke 2:1–20
Apr 25	Judges 10:6–12:15		Luke 2:21–39
Apr 26	Judges 13:1–15:8		Luke 2:40–52
Apr 27	Judges 15:9–16:31		Luke 3
Apr 28	Judges 17–18		Luke 4:1–30
Apr 29	Judges 19		Luke 4:31–44
Apr 30	Judges 20–21		Luke 5:1–16

Appendix B– Reading through the Bible in a Year

Day	Old Testament History	Wisdom & Prophets	New Testament
May 1	Ruth 1–2		Luke 5:17–39
May 2	Ruth 3–4		Luke 6:1–19
May 3	1 Samuel 1–2		Luke 6:20–49
May 4	1 Samuel 3–5		Luke 7:1–17
May 5	1 Samuel 6–8		Luke 7:18–35
May 6	1 Samuel 9–10		Luke 7:36–50
May 7	1 Samuel 11–13		Luke 8:1–21
May 8	1 Samuel 14		Luke 8:22–39
May 9	1 Samuel 15–16		Luke 8:40–56
May 10	1 Samuel 17	Psalm 7	Luke 9:1–17
May 11		Psalm 9, 10, 109	Luke 9:18–45
May 12	1 Samuel 18–19	Psalm 59	Luke 9:46–62
May 13	1 Samuel 20		Luke 10:1–24
May 14	1 Samuel 21	Psalm 34, 56	Luke 10:25–42
May 15	1 Samuel 22	Psalm 57, 142, 52	Luke 11:1–28
May 16		Psalm 64, 140, 143, 17, 26	Luke 11:29–54
May 17	1 Samuel 23	Psalm 54, 41, 58	Luke 12:1–21
May 18	1 Samuel 24–25		Luke 12:22–48
May 19	1 Samuel 26	Psalm 35, 11, 141	Luke 12:49–13:9
May 20	1 Samuel 27–29	Psalm 55	Luke 13:10–35
May 21	1 Samuel 30–31 1 Chronicles 10	Psalm 131, 22	Luke 14:1–24
May 22	2 Samuel 1–2		Luke 14:25–15:10
May 23	2 Samuel 3:1–5:5 1 Chronicles 11:1–3	Psalm 30	Luke 15:11–32
May 24	2 Samuel 5:17–25 1 Chronicles 14:8–17 2 Samuel 23:13–17 1 Chronicles 11:15–19 2 Samuel 5:6–10 1 Chronicles 11:4–9	Psalm 110, 122	Luke 16:1–13
May 25	2 Samuel 23:8–12 1 Chronicles 11:10–14 2 Samuel 23:18–39 1 Chronicles 11:20–47 1 Chronicles 12	Psalm 116	Luke 16:14–17:4
May 26	2 Samuel 22	Psalm 18, 95	Luke 17:5–37
May 27	1 Chronicles 1:1–4:23	Psalm 88, 89	Luke 18:1–34
May 28	1 Chronicles 4:24–6:38	Psalm 42, 43, 84	Luke 18:35–19:10

Appendix B– Reading through the Bible in a Year

Day	Old Testament History	Wisdom & Prophets	New Testament
May 29		Psalm 44, 45, 85, 87	Luke 19:11–27
May 30	1 Chronicles 6:39–81	Psalm 77, 73	Luke 19:28–48
May 31	1 Chronicles 7–8	Psalm 78	Luke 20:1–18
Jun 1	1 Chronicles 9	Psalm 81, 82	Luke 20:19–21:4
Jun 2	2 Samuel 5:11–16 1 Chronicles 14:1–7 2 Samuel 6:1–11 1 Chronicles 13	Psalm 68	Luke 21:5–36
Jun 3	1 Chronicles 15:1–24 2 Samuel 6:12–19 1 Chronicles 15:25–16:3	Psalm 24, 118	Luke 21:37–22:23
Jun 4	1 Chronicles 16:4–22	Psalm 105	Luke 22:24–54
Jun 5	1 Chronicles 16:23–43	Psalm 96, 106, 93, 99	Luke 22:55–71
Jun 6	2 Samuel 6:20–7:29 1 Chronicles 17	Psalm 132	Luke 23:1–25
Jun 7	2 Samuel 8 1 Chronicles 18	Psalm 60, 108	Luke 23:26–56
Jun 8		Psalm 16, 20, 21	Luke 24:1–35
Jun 9	2 Samuel 9	Psalm 8, 19, 23	Luke 24:36–53
Jun 10	2 Samuel 10 1 Chronicles 19	Psalm 6, 12, 27, 28, 29	Acts 1:1–14
Jun 11	2 Samuel 11:1–12:23 1 Chronicles 20:1	Psalm 51	Acts 1:15–26
Jun 12	2 Samuel 12:24–31 1 Chronicles 20:2–3	Psalm 32, 38, 39	Acts 2:1–13
Jun 13		Psalm 33, 103, 104	Acts 2:14–47
Jun 14	2 Samuel 13	Psalm 13, 14, 53, 15, 25	Acts 3
Jun 15	2 Samuel 14	Psalm 36, 37	Acts 4:1–31
Jun 16	2 Samuel 15	Psalm 3, 61, 62, 124	Acts 4:32–5:16
Jun 17	2 Samuel 16	Psalm 4, 5	Acts 5:17–42
Jun 18	2 Samuel 17	Psalm 63, 70, 40	Acts 6
Jun 19		Psalm 71, 31	Acts 7:1–16
Jun 20	2 Samuel 18	Psalm 144, 69	Acts 7:17–43
Jun 21	2 Samuel 19–20		Acts 7:44–60

Appendix B– Reading through the Bible in a Year

Day	Old Testament History	Wisdom & Prophets	New Testament
Jun 22	2 Samuel 21 1 Chronicles 20:4–8	Psalm 101, 102	Acts 8:1–25
Jun 23	2 Samuel 23:1–7 2 Samuel 24 1 Chronicles 21:1–27		Acts 8:26–40
Jun 24	1 Chronicles 21:28–22:19	Psalm 138, 139	Acts 9:1–31
Jun 25	1 Kings 1		Acts 9:32–10:23
Jun 26	1 Chronicles 23–25		Acts 10:24–45
Jun 27	1 Chronicles 26–27		Acts 11:1–18
Jun 28	1 Chronicles 28:1–29:22a	Psalm 91	Acts 11:19–30
Jun 29	2 Kings 2:1–11 1 Chronicles 29:22b–30	Psalm 145	Acts 12
Jun 30		Song of Songs 1–4	Acts 13:1–12
Jul 1		Song of Songs 5–8	Acts 13:13–41
Jul 2	1 Kings 2:12–3:15 2 Chronicles 1:1–13		Acts 13:42–14:7
Jul 3	1 Kings 3:16–4:34 2 Chronicles 1:14–17	Psalm 127	Acts 14:8–28
Jul 4	1 Kings 5 2 Chronicles 2	Psalm 128	Acts 15:1–35
Jul 5	1 Kings 6:1–7:22 2 Chronicles 3		Acts 15:36–16:8
Jul 6	1 Kings 7:23–51 2 Chronicles 4:1–5:1		Acts 16:9–34
Jul 7	1 Kings 8:1–21 2 Chronicles 5:2–6:11	Psalm 72	Acts 16:35–17:15
Jul 8	1 Kings 8:22–53 2 Chronicles 6:12–42		Acts 17:16–34
Jul 9	1 Kings 8:54–9:9 2 Chronicles 7	Psalm 97, 98, 100	Acts 18:1–17
Jul 10	1 Kings 9:10–28 2 Chronicles 8	Psalm 135, 136	Acts 18:18–28
Jul 11	1 Kings 10 2 Chronicles 9:1–28	Psalm 49	Acts 19:1–20
Jul 12		Proverbs 1–3	Acts 19:21–41
Jul 13		Proverbs 4–6	Acts 20:1–15

Appendix B– Reading through the Bible in a Year

Day	Old Testament History	Wisdom & Prophets	New Testament
Jul 14		Proverbs 7–9	Acts 20:16–38
Jul 15		Proverbs 10–12	Acts 21:1–16
Jul 16		Proverbs 13–15	Acts 21:17–36
Jul 17		Proverbs 16–18	Acts 21:37–22:29
Jul 18		Prov 19:1–22:16	Acts 22:30–23:22
Jul 19		Prov 22:17–24:34	Acts 23:23–24:9
Jul 20		Proverbs 25–27	Acts 24:10–26
Jul 21		Proverbs 28–30	Acts 24:27–25:27
Jul 22	1 Kings 11 2 Chronicles 9:29–31	Proverbs 31	Acts 26
Jul 23		Ecclesiastes 1–4	Acts 27:1–19
Jul 24		Ecclesiastes 5–8	Acts 27:20–44
Jul 25		Ecclesiastes 9–12	Acts 28:1–15
Jul 26	1 Kings 12:1–24 2 Chronicles 10:1–11:4		Acts 28:16–31
Jul 27	1 Kings 12:25–14:20		Romans 1:1–17
Jul 28	1 Kings 14:21–31 2 Chronicles 11:5–12:16		Romans 1:18–32
Jul 29	1 Kings 15:1–12 2 Chronicles 13–14		Romans 2:1–24
Jul 30	1 Kings 15:13–24 2 Chronicles 15–16		Romans 2:25–3:20
Jul 31	1 Kings 15:25–17:24		Romans 3:21–4:8
Aug 1	1 Kings 18–19		Romans 4:9–25
Aug 2	1 Kings 20–21		Romans 5
Aug 3	1 Kings 22:1–28 2 Chronicles 17:1–18:27		Romans 6:1–7:6
Aug 4	1 Kings 22:29–40 2 Chronicles 18:28–20:30		Romans 7:7–8:11
Aug 5	1 Kings 22:41–22:53 2 Kings 1–2 2 Chronicles 20:31–37		Romans 8:12–39
Aug 6	2 Kings 3–4		Romans 9:1–29
Aug 7	2 Kings 5:1–6:23		Romans 9:30–10:21
Aug 8	2 Kings 6:24–8:15		Romans 11

Appendix B– Reading through the Bible in a Year 491

Day	Old Testament History	Wisdom & Prophets	New Testament
Aug 9	2 Kings 8:16–29 2 Chronicles 21:1–22:6		Romans 12
Aug 10	2 Kings 9–10 2 Chronicles 22:7–9		Romans 13
Aug 11	2 Kings 11 2 Chronicles 22:10–23:21		Romans 14:1–15:13
Aug 12	2 Kings 12 2 Chronicles 24		Romans 15:14–33
Aug 13		Joel 1:1–2:17	Romans 16
Aug 14		Joel 2:18–3:21	1 Corinthians 1:1–2:5
Aug 15	2 Kings 13–14 2 Chronicles 25:1–26:2		1 Corinthians 2:6–3:9
Aug 16		Jonah	1 Corinthians 3:10–4:5
Aug 17		Amos 1–3	1 Corinthians 4:6–21
Aug 18		Amos 4–6	1 Corinthians 5–6
Aug 19		Amos 7–9	1 Corinthians 7:1–24
Aug 20		Hosea 1–3	1 Corinthians 7:25–40
Aug 21		Hosea 4–7	1 Corinthians 8
Aug 22		Hosea 8–10	1 Corinthians 9
Aug 23		Hosea 11–14	1 Corinthians 10:1–11:1
Aug 24	2 Kings 15:1–7 2 Chronicles 26:3–15	Isaiah 1	1 Corinthians 11:2–34
Aug 25		Isaiah 2:1–4:1	1 Corinthians 12:1–30
Aug 26		Isaiah 4:2–5:30	1 Corinthians 12:31–13:13
Aug 27	2 Kings 15:8–31 2 Chronicles 26:16–23	Isaiah 6	1 Corinthians 14:1–25
Aug 28	2 Kings 15:32–16:9 2 Chronicles 27:1–28:21		1 Corinthians 14:26–40
Aug 29	2 Kings 16:10–18 2 Chronicles 28:22–25	Isaiah 7	1 Corinthians 15:1–28
Aug 30		Isaiah 8:1–10:4	1 Corinthians 15:29–58
Aug 31		Isaiah 10:5–12:6	1 Corinthians 16
Sep 1		Isaiah 13:1–14:27	2 Corinthians 1:1–11
Sep 2	2 Kings 16:19–20 2 Chronicles 28:26–27	Isaiah 14:28–16:14	2 Corinthians 1:12–2:11

Appendix B– Reading through the Bible in a Year

Day	Old Testament History	Wisdom & Prophets	New Testament
Sep 3		Isaiah 17:1–19:25	2 Corinthians 2:12–3:18
Sep 4	2 Kings 17		2 Corinthians 4
Sep 5		Micah 1–3	2 Corinthians 5
Sep 6		Micah 4–5	2 Corinthians 6–7
Sep 7		Micah 6–7	2 Corinthians 8–9
Sep 8	2 Kings 18:1–3 2 Chronicles 29	Psalm 50	2 Corinthians 10
Sep 9	2 Chronicles 30	Psalm 80, 133	2 Corinthians 11:1–15
Sep 10	2 Kings 18:4–12 2 Chronicles 31	Psalm 134	2 Corinthians 11:16–12:10
Sep 11		Isaiah 20–23	2 Corinthians 12:11–13:14
Sep 12		Isaiah 24–26	Galatians 1
Sep 13		Isaiah 27–28	Galatians 2
Sep 14		Isaiah 29–30	Galatians 3
Sep 15		Isaiah 31–33	Galatians 4:1–5:1
Sep 16		Isaiah 34–35	Galatians 5:2–26
Sep 17	2 Kings 18:13–37 2 Chronicles 32:1–19	Isaiah 36 Psalm 121, 123, 129	Galatians 6
Sep 18	2 Kings 19 2 Chronicles 32:20–23	Isaiah 37 Psalm 125, 126	Ephesians 1
Sep 19		Psalm 46, 47, 48, 75, 76	Ephesians 2
Sep 20	2 Kings 20:1–11 2 Chronicles 32:24	Isaiah 38 Psalm 120, 130	Ephesians 3
Sep 21	2 Kings 20:12–21 2 Chronicles 32:25–33	Isaiah 39 Psalm 65, 66	Ephesians 4:1–16
Sep 22		Isaiah 40:1–41:16	Ephesians 4:17–32
Sep 23		Isaiah 41:17–43:13	Ephesians 5:1–21
Sep 24		Isaiah 43:14–44:23	Ephesians 5:22–6:24
Sep 25		Isaiah 44:24–46:13	Philippians 1:1–26
Sep 26		Isaiah 47–48	Philippians 1:27–2:11
Sep 27		Isaiah 49–50	Philippians 2:12–30
Sep 28		Isaiah 51:1–52:12	Philippians 3:1–4:1
Sep 29		Isaiah 52:13–54:17	Philippians 4:2–20

Appendix B– Reading through the Bible in a Year 493

Day	Old Testament History	Wisdom & Prophets	New Testament
Sep 30		Isaiah 55–57	Colossians 1:1–23
Oct 1		Isaiah 58–60	Colossians 1:24–2:5
Oct 2		Isaiah 61:1–63:6	Colossians 2:6–3:4
Oct 3		Isaiah 63:7–65:12	Colossians 3:5–4:1
Oct 4		Isaiah 65:13–66:24	Colossians 4:2–18
Oct 5	2 Kings 21 2 Chronicles 33		1 Thessalonians 1
Oct 6	2 Kings 22:1–2 2 Kings 23:4–20 2 Chronicles 34:1–7	Zephaniah 1:1–2:3	1 Thessalonians 2
Oct 7		Zephaniah 2:4–3:20	1 Thessalonians 3
Oct 8		Nahum Psalm 83	1 Thessalonians 4
Oct 9		Jeremiah 1–2	1 Thessalonians 5
Oct 10		Jeremiah 3–4	2 Thessalonians 1
Oct 11		Jeremiah 5	2 Thessalonians 2
Oct 12		Jeremiah 6	2 Thessalonians 3
Oct 13	2 Kings 22:3–23:3 2 Chronicles 34:8–33		1 Timothy 1
Oct 14	2 Kings 23:21–24:7 2 Chronicles 35:1–36:8		1 Timothy 2
Oct 15		Habakkuk	1 Timothy 3
Oct 16		Jeremiah 26	1 Timothy 4
Oct 17		Jeremiah 7–8	1 Timothy 5:1–6:2
Oct 18		Jeremiah 9–10	1 Timothy 6:3–21
Oct 19		Jeremiah 11–12	2 Timothy 1
Oct 20		Jeremiah 25 Daniel 1	2 Timothy 2
Oct 21		Jeremiah 46–47	2 Timothy 3
Oct 22		Jeremiah 48	2 Timothy 4
Oct 23		Jeremiah 49:1–33	Titus 1
Oct 24		Jeremiah 36:1–8 Jeremiah 45 Jeremiah 36:9–32	Titus 2
Oct 25		Daniel 2	Titus 3
Oct 26		Daniel 3	Philemon
Oct 27		Jeremiah 14–15	John 1:1–18
Oct 28		Jeremiah 16–17	John 1:19–34
Oct 29		Jeremiah 18–20	John 1:35–51

Appendix B– Reading through the Bible in a Year

Day	Old Testament History	Wisdom & Prophets	New Testament
Oct 30		Jeremiah 35, 22	John 2:1–22
Oct 31		Jeremiah 23, 13	John 2:23–3:21
Nov 1	2 Kings 24:8–20a 2 Chronicles 36:9–11	Jeremiah 24, 29, 27	John 3:22–36
Nov 2		Jeremiah 28 Jeremiah 49:34–50:46	John 4:1–42
Nov 3		Jeremiah 51:1–23	John 4:43–54
Nov 4		Jeremiah 51:24–64	John 5:1–23
Nov 5		Ezekiel 1–3	John 5:24–47
Nov 6		Ezekiel 4–7	John 6:1–21
Nov 7		Ezekiel 8–11	John 6:22–71
Nov 8		Ezekiel 12–14	John 7:1–31
Nov 9		Ezekiel 15–16	John 7:32–53
Nov 10		Ezekiel 17–19	John 8:1–30
Nov 11		Ezekiel 20	John 8:31–59
Nov 12		Ezekiel 21–22	John 9:1–23
Nov 13		Ezekiel 23–24	John 9:24–41
Nov 14		Jeremiah 21, 34	John 10:1–21
Nov 15		Jeremiah 37–38	John 10:22–42
Nov 16		Jeremiah 30	John 11:1–37
Nov 17		Jeremiah 31	John 11:38–57
Nov 18		Jeremiah 32–33 Psalm 86	John 12:1–19
Nov 19		Ezekiel 25, 29, 30:1–19	John 12:20–50
Nov 20		Ezekiel 26	John 13:1–17
Nov 21		Ezekiel 27–28	John 13:18–38
Nov 22		Ezekiel 30:20–32:32	John 14:1–14
Nov 23	2 Kings 24:20b–25:21 2 Chronicles 36:12–21	Jeremiah 39, 52:1–30	John 14:15–31
Nov 24		Lamentations 1	John 15:1–17
Nov 25		Lamentations 2	John 15:18–16:15
Nov 26		Lamentations 3	John 16:16–33
Nov 27		Lamentations 4–5	John 17
Nov 28		Obadiah Psalm 79, 74	John 18:1–27
Nov 29	2 Kings 25:22–26	Jeremiah 40–43	John 18:28–19:16
Nov 30		Daniel 4	John 19:17–42

Appendix B– Reading through the Bible in a Year 495

Day	Old Testament History	Wisdom & Prophets	New Testament
Dec 1	2 Kings 25:27–30	Jeremiah 44, 52:31–34 Psalm 94, 137	John 20:1–18
Dec 2		Ezekiel 33–34	John 20:19–31
Dec 3		Ezekiel 35–37	John 21
Dec 4		Ezekiel 38–39	1 John 1:1–2:11
Dec 5		Ezekiel 40–41	1 John 2:12–29
Dec 6		Ezekiel 42–43	1 John 3:1–4:6
Dec 7		Ezekiel 44:1–46:15	1 John 4:7–21
Dec 8		Ezekiel 46:16–48:35	1 John 5
Dec 9		Daniel 7–8	2 John
Dec 10		Daniel 5, 9	3 John
Dec 11		Daniel 6	Revelation 1
Dec 12	2 Chronicles 36:22–23 Ezra 1–2	Psalm 107, 114, 115, 117	Revelation 2
Dec 13	Ezra 3–4		Revelation 3
Dec 14		Daniel 10–12	Revelation 4
Dec 15		Haggai Psalm 67, 92, 146, 147	Revelation 5
Dec 16		Zechariah 1–6	Revelation 6
Dec 17		Zechariah 7–10	Revelation 7
Dec 18		Zechariah 11–14	Revelation 8:1–9:12
Dec 19	Ezra 5–6	Psalm 148, 149, 150	Revelation 9:13–10:11
Dec 20	Esther 1–3		Revelation 11
Dec 21	Esther 4–7		Revelation 12
Dec 22	Esther 8–10		Revelation 13
Dec 23	Ezra 7–8		Revelation 14
Dec 24	Ezra 9–10		Revelation 15
Dec 25	Nehemiah 1–4		Revelation 16
Dec 26	Nehemiah 5–7		Revelation 17
Dec 27	Nehemiah 8–10	Psalm 1, 2	Revelation 18
Dec 28		Psalm 119:1–88	Revelation 19
Dec 29		Ps 119:89–176	Revelation 20
Dec 30	Nehemiah 11–13		Revelation 21:1–21
Dec 31		Psalm 111–113 Malachi	Revelation 21:22–22:21

Index of Bible Readings and Quotations

This is a complete index of all the Bible passages referred to in "Through the Bible in 80 Days". Those marked (R) are readings, the rest are quotes.

Genesis 1–2 (R) 40	Genesis 41:12 74
Genesis 2:17 47	Genesis 42:13 76
Genesis 2:24 111	Genesis 43:1–45:15 (R) 77
Genesis 3 (R) 47	Genesis 45:25–46:4 (R) 78
Genesis 3:15 49	Genesis 49: 1 78
Genesis 4 (R) 49	Genesis 49: 7 79
Genesis 5 (R) 50	Genesis 49:10 78
Genesis 6:9 39	Genesis 50:20 81
Genesis 6–8 (R) 51	Exodus 1 (R) 94
Genesis 9 (R) 57	Exodus 2:1–10 (R) 94
Genesis 11:10–32 (R) 58	Exodus 3 (R) 95
Genesis 11:4 462	Exodus 3: 6 95
Genesis 12 (R) 60	Exodus 3:14–15 96
Genesis 12:1 279	Exodus 3:15 71
Genesis 12:3 .... 332, 365, 378	Exodus 4:15–16 235
Genesis 15 (R) 62	Exodus 5:1–6:12 (R) 97
Genesis 15: 6 63	Exodus 6:6 102
Genesis 15:13 103	Exodus 7:1 235
Genesis 15:14 103	Exodus 7:8–9:35 and
Genesis 15:16 139	10:21–11:10 (R) 99
Genesis 16:16–17:1 63	Exodus 12:1–42 (R) 102
Genesis 17: 1 95	Exodus 13:17–14:31 (R) 103
Genesis 17: 7 110	Exodus 14:12 .... 104, 106
Genesis 17:23 64	Exodus 14:31 105
Genesis 18:17 65	Exodus 16 (R) 106
Genesis 22 (R) 64	Exodus 18 (R) 109
Genesis 26:25 67	Exodus 19 (R) 109
Genesis 27:1–40 (R) 68	Exodus 19:3–6 11
Genesis 27:41–28:22 (R) 69	Exodus 19:5 112
Genesis 29:20 69	Exodus 19:5–6 110
Genesis 32:24 70	Exodus 20: 1–21 (R) 112
Genesis 37:2 40	Exodus 20:11 45
Genesis 39:1–41:40 (R) 73	Exodus 20:14 195
Genesis 39:9 74	Exodus 24:3 113

Index of Bible Readings and Quotations

Exodus 32: 4 113	Joshua 24:31 147
Exodus 32:14 114	Judges 2:10–13 (R) 149
Exodus 32:32 114	Judges 6: 1 152
Exodus 34: 5–7 96	Judges 6: 1–6 (R) 152
Exodus 34: 6 22	Judges 6: 6 152
Exodus 34: 6–7 .... 114, 139, 227	Judges 6:11–40 (R) 152
Exodus 34:14 139	Judges 7 (R) 153
Exodus 40:34–35 115	Judges 8:28–35 (R) 154
Leviticus 11:45 116	Judges 8:33 154
Leviticus 19:18 120	Judges 17:13 154
Leviticus 24:16 360	Judges 21:25 .... 149, 155
Numbers 11:5 106	Ruth 1:16 156
Numbers 12:3 123	1 Samuel 1 (R) 158
Numbers 13–14 (R) 123	1 Samuel 1:8 158
Numbers 27:18 133	1 Samuel 2:11–26 (R) 159
Numbers 32:23 77	1 Samuel 2:30 160
Deuteronomy 1:28 123	1 Samuel 3 (R) 160
Deuteronomy 6:4 254	1 Samuel 3:19–20 160
Deuteronomy 6:4–9 (R) 130	1 Samuel 4:3 161
Deuteronomy 6:6–7 448	1 Samuel 7:15–17 (R) 162
Deuteronomy 6:9 445	1 Samuel 8 (R) 162
Deuteronomy 7:9 95	1 Samuel 9–10 (R) 163
Deuteronomy 8:15 106	1 Samuel 11 (R) 163
Deuteronomy 17:17 203	1 Samuel 12:14–15 (R) 163
Deuteronomy 17:18–20 184	1 Samuel 13:14 164
Deuteronomy 18:18–19 184	1 Samuel 15 (R) 164
Deuteronomy 20:16–18 139	1 Samuel 16 (R) 166
Deuteronomy 28 (R) 225	1 Samuel 16: 7 166
Deuteronomy 28:23–24 214	1 Samuel 16:14 168
Deuteronomy 28:63–64 .... 22, 225	1 Samuel 17 (R) 167
Deuteronomy 30 (R) 130	1 Samuel 18 (R) 168
Deuteronomy 32:46–47 130	1 Samuel 22:1–5 (R) 169
Deuteronomy 34 (R) 131	1 Samuel 23:17 168
Joshua 1–4 (R) 133	1 Samuel 23–24 (R) 169
Joshua 4:14 134	1 Samuel 24:6 169
Joshua 5:1 134	2 Samuel 1:11–12:25 (R) 185
Joshua 5:13–6:27 (R) 136	2 Samuel 1:19 172
Joshua 6:26 213	2 Samuel 5 (R) 172
Joshua 7 (R) 142	2 Samuel 6–7 (R) 173
Joshua 8:1–29 (R) 142	2 Samuel 7:16 .... 218, 332
Joshua 8:35 443	2 Samuel 12:13 372
Joshua 9:19 143	2 Samuel 21:17 187
Joshua 10:14 144	1 Kings 3 (R) 189
Joshua 11:18–20 144	1 Kings 4:29 192
Joshua 22:33 146	1 Kings 4:29–34 190

Index of Bible Readings and Quotations

1 Kings 10 (R) 191
1 Kings 11:1–13 (R) 203
1 Kings 11:26–40 (R) 204
1 Kings 12:1–24 (R) 204
1 Kings 12:25–13:6 (R) 210
1 Kings 14:22–24 (R) 211
1 Kings 14:25–28 (R) 211
1 Kings 15:1–3 and 9–11 (R) . 207
1 Kings 15:3,5 187
1 Kings 16:29–34 (R) 212
1 Kings 17:1–6 (R) 213
1 Kings 18 (R) 214
1 Kings 19:19–21 (R) 217
2 Kings 2 (R) 217
2 Kings 4:42–44 (R) 217
2 Kings 9 (R) 220
2 Kings 14:3 187
2 Kings 16:1–4 (R) 229
2 Kings 16:2 187
2 Kings 17:1–24 (R) 227
2 Kings 18:3 187
2 Kings 18:5–6 232
2 Kings 19 (R) 232
2 Kings 21:1–6, 16 (R) 232
2 Kings 23:25 233
2 Kings 23:25–27 266
2 Kings 23:26–27 233
2 Kings 24 (R) 272
1 Chronicles 16:4-6, 37-38 (R)176
2 Chronicles 5 (R) 190
2 Chronicles 7 (R) 190
2 Chronicles 11:16.................. 206
2 Chronicles 14:2–6 (R) 211
2 Chronicles 16:9.................... 212
2 Chronicles 20:7.................... 65
2 Chronicles 21:20.................. 218
2 Chronicles 24:25.................. 224
2 Chronicles 29:3.................... 229
2 Chronicles 30:1.................... 229
2 Chronicles 30:12.................. 231
2 Chronicles 30:26–27............ 231
2 Chronicles 31:1.................... 231
2 Chronicles 34 (R) 233
2 Chronicles 35:20–27 (R) 268
Ezra 1 (R) 295

Ezra 3:10–13 (R) 297
Ezra 4:1 284
Ezra 4:3–4................................ 284
Ezra 5–6 (R) 298
Ezra 7:10 298
Ezra 7:26 298
Nehemiah 1–2 (R) 299
Nehemiah 2:4–5...................... 300
Nehemiah 3:5 300
Nehemiah 4 (R) 301
Nehemiah 6:1–16 (R) 301
Nehemiah 8 (R) 301
Nehemiah 8:8 301
Nehemiah 13:25...................... 302
Esther 3:8–9............................. 303
Esther 4:13–14......................... 305
Esther 4:16............................... 305
Esther 6:9................................. 305
Esther 7:8................................. 306
Job 1: 8 85
Job 1:20 85
Job 1–2 (R) 85
Job 12:2–3 (R) 88
Job 2:13 86
Job 3:1–6 and 3:25–26 (R) 87
Job 4:1-9 (R)............................ 87
Job 4:8 70
Job 6:24 and 6:28–30 (R) 88
Job 10:10 84
Job 11:1–4 and 11:13–15 (R) ... 88
Job 15:1–6 (R) 88
Job 19:1–4 (R) 88
Job 19:25–26 (R) 88
Job 22:5–6 89
Job 23:1–7 (R) 89
Job 27:5–6 (R) 89
Job 28:28 89
Job 29:2 89
Job 30:1 89
Job 31:35 89
Job 32:6,8 90
Job 36:5–12 (R) 90
Job 38:1–7 (R) 90
Job 42:1–6 (R) 91
Job 42:7–17 (R) 91

Index of Bible Readings and Quotations

Reference	Page
Psalm 1 (R)	178
Psalm 1:1–2	178, 445
Psalm 13 (R)	181
Psalm 14:1	194
Psalm 22:14	41
Psalm 23 (R)	182
Psalm 25 (R)	179
Psalm 25:1–2	179
Psalm 29 (R)	178
Psalm 29:1–4	178
Psalm 32:3–5	186
Psalm 46:1	181
Psalm 48:1	181
Psalm 51 (R)	186
Psalm 85:1	70
Psalm 100 (R)	179
Psalm 100:1–2	179
Psalm 101:1	461
Psalm 103:1 AV	181
Psalm 119: 9	450
Psalm 119: 11	444
Psalm 119: 24	450
Psalm 119: 34	446
Psalm 119: 61	444
Psalm 119:100	450
Psalm 119:143	178
Psalm 119:169	443
Psalm 122 (R)	181
Psalm 131 (R)	181
Proverbs 1:7	194
Proverbs 1–2 (R)	193
Proverbs 3: 5–6	195
Proverbs 3: 9–10	195
Proverbs 3:14–15	195
Proverbs 4:23–27	195
Proverbs 5:3	196
Proverbs 5:4	196
Proverbs 5–6 (R)	195
Proverbs 6:32	196
Proverbs 10 (R)	197
Proverbs 10: 1	197
Proverbs 10: 4	197
Proverbs 10:20	197
Proverbs 11:22	198
Proverbs 14:15	194
Proverbs 16:18	305
Proverbs 18:17	197
Proverbs 20 (R)	197
Proverbs 20:13	198
Proverbs 20:14	197
Proverbs 20:19	198
Proverbs 25:11	198
Proverbs 26:17	198
Proverbs 27:14	198
Proverbs 27:15	198
Ecclesiastes 1 (R)	200
Ecclesiastes 1:1	199
Ecclesiastes 1:2	200
Ecclesiastes 4:9,12	200
Ecclesiastes 7:10	200
Ecclesiastes 7:14	200
Ecclesiastes 9:9	200
Ecclesiastes 12:13–14	201
Song of Songs 2:4	202
Song of Songs 2:7	202
Song of Songs 8:6–7 (R)	202
Isaiah 1 (R)	254
Isaiah 2:2–4 (R)	262
Isaiah 5:1–7	265
Isaiah 6 (R)	253
Isaiah 7:10–16 (R)	257
Isaiah 7:14	257
Isaiah 9:1–7 (R)	257
Isaiah 9:6	258
Isaiah 9:8	70
Isaiah 11:1–9 and Isaiah 12 (R)	262
Isaiah 40 (R)	261
Isaiah 40:1–2 (R)	252
Isaiah 40:3–5 (R)	258
Isaiah 41:8	65
Isaiah 42:1–4 (R)	259
Isaiah 44:3	262
Isaiah 47:6	261
Isaiah 49:15–16	263
Isaiah 52:1–10 (R)	261
Isaiah 52:13–53:12 (R)	260
Isaiah 54:7–8	264
Isaiah 55:12	261
Isaiah 58 (R)	255

Index of Bible Readings and Quotations

Isaiah 61 (R) 258
Isaiah 61:2 139
Isaiah 65:17 262
Jeremiah 1 (R) 269
Jeremiah 1:18 270
Jeremiah 2:1–13 (R) 270
Jeremiah 3:16 276
Jeremiah 6:1–15 (R) 270
Jeremiah 17:9 446
Jeremiah 18:1–12 (R) 270
Jeremiah 20:7–18 (R) 271
Jeremiah 29:1–23 (R) 273
Jeremiah 29:5–7 303
Jeremiah 30 (R) 273
Jeremiah 31:31–34 28
Jeremiah 31:31–34 (R) 274
Jeremiah 36:21–25 (R) 273
Jeremiah 37–38 (R) 275
Jeremiah 42:10 278
Jeremiah 52 (R) 276
Lamentations 1:1 277
Lamentations 3:21–26 (R) 277
Ezekiel 1–3 (R) 281
Ezekiel 4–5 (R) 282
Ezekiel 18 (R) 285
Ezekiel 24:16 283
Ezekiel 24:18 283
Ezekiel 33:21–33 (R) 284
Ezekiel 34:11–16 285
Ezekiel 37 (R) 284
Ezekiel 47:1–12 (R) 284
Daniel 2: 5 287
Daniel 2:26–49 (R) 311
Daniel 2:44 320
Daniel 3 (R) 288
Daniel 3:29 288
Daniel 4:30 .... 288, 462
Daniel 4:37 289
Daniel 6 (R) 291
Daniel 9:1–3 292
Daniel 9:27, 11:31 and 12:11 . 314
Hosea 1:1 242
Hosea 2:19–20 (R) 244
Joel 1:1–2:17 (R) 237
Joel 2:18–27 (R) 238

Joel 2:25 240
Joel 2:28–32 (R) 238
Joel 3:14 240
Joel 3:16 241
Amos 5:12 3
Amos 5:18 243
Amos 5:24 243
Amos 8:4–12 (R) 243
Amos 9:15 243
Obadiah 11–12 (R) 245
Jonah 2:8–9 (R) 246
Micah 6:8 247
Nahum 1:3 248
Habakkuk 2:4 248
Habakkuk 3:17–18 (R) 249
Zephaniah 3:17 (R) 250
Zechariah 4:6 297
Zechariah 6:12–13 307
Zechariah 9: 9 355
Zechariah 9:10 355
Zechariah 13:7 308
Zechariah 14 (R) 308
Zechariah 9:9–17 (R) 307
Malachi 3:1 308
Malachi 3:2–5 (R) 309
Malachi 4 (R) 309
Matthew 1 (R) 332
Matthew 1:1 175
Matthew 1:18 .... 257, 332
Matthew 1:22–23 257
Matthew 2 (R) 333
Matthew 2: 2 318
Matthew 2:15 and 2:17 326
Matthew 3:2 346
Matthew 3:5 335
Matthew 5 (R) 344
Matthew 5:43–44 343
Matthew 6 (R) 344
Matthew 7 (R) 345
Matthew 7:7 446
Matthew 14 (R) 346
Matthew 15 (R) 348
Matthew 15:11 120
Matthew 15:12 347
Matthew 16:1–17:23 (R) 349

Index of Bible Readings and Quotations 501

Matthew 18:21	359
Matthew 19:6	45
Matthew 19:8	111
Matthew 23:1–3	323
Matthew 24: 2	35, 316
Matthew 24: 3	314
Matthew 24: 8	458
Matthew 24:36	463
Matthew 28:18–20 (R)	363
Mark 1 (R)	337
Mark 1: 1	322
Mark 1: 5	335
Mark 1:12,18,20,23	327
Mark 2:1–3:12 (R)	337
Mark 3:13–19 (R)	338
Mark 3:14	325
Mark 4:1–34 (R)	341
Mark 4:35–5:43 (R)	342
Luke 1: 1–4	327
Luke 1: 3	4
Luke 1:16–17	335
Luke 1:1–66 (R)	333
Luke 1:52–53	343
Luke 2:1–2	328
Luke 2:1–20 (R)	333
Luke 2:41–52 (R)	334
Luke 7:29–30	336
Luke 10:30	41
Luke 10:38–42 (R)	354
Luke 11:1	344
Luke 15 (R)	342
Luke 15:20	238
Luke 19:28–48 (R)	355
Luke 20 (R)	357
Luke 21 (R)	358
Luke 22:1–62 (R)	359
Luke 22:32	426
Luke 22:63–23:25 (R)	361
Luke 23:26–49 (R)	361
Luke 23:50–56 (R)	362
Luke 24:13–35 (R)	363
Luke 24:36–49 (R)	363
Luke 24:50–53 (R)	364
John 1:1–18 (R)	335
John 1:1–2	329
John 1:14	329, 335, 453
John 1:19–51 (R)	335
John 3:1–21 (R)	350
John 4:4–42 (R)	351
John 6:35 and 8:12	329
John 7 (R)	351
John 7:37–38	352
John 7:38	270
John 8:1–11 (R)	352
John 8:58	97
John 9 (R)	353
John 9:2	83
John 11:1–12:11 (R)	354
John 12:38 and 39	253
John 14:16–17	33
John 16:33	91, 459
John 19:30	362
John 20:31	329
John 21:25	32, 329
Acts 1 (R)	367
Acts 1:1–2	33, 366
Acts 1:3	367
Acts 1:5	33
Acts 1:8	367, 374
Acts 2 (R)	369
Acts 3:8	369
Acts 4 (R)	371
Acts 4:13	371
Acts 5:1–14 (R)	372
Acts 5:15–42 (R)	373
Acts 6:1–7 (R)	373
Acts 8:1–8 (R)	374
Acts 8:26–39 (R)	256
Acts 8:35	256
Acts 9:1–31 (R)	377
Acts 9:31	378
Acts 10:1–11:18 (R)	378
Acts 11:19–30 (R)	379
Acts 11:2–3	403
Acts 13:36	188
Acts 13–14 (R)	382
Acts 15: 1	403
Acts 15: 1–35 (R)	384
Acts 15:11	403
Acts 15:36–17:34 (R)	388

Index of Bible Readings and Quotations

Reference	Page
Acts 17:11	466
Acts 19 (R)	388
Acts 23:6	323
Romans 1:16–17	409
Romans 1:17	116
Romans 1:18	411
Romans 1:20	44, 411
Romans 3:21–28 (R)	412
Romans 3:9	411
Romans 5:1–11 (R)	412
Romans 6: 1–2	413
Romans 6: 2	414
Romans 6:11	414
Romans 6:23	118
Romans 8:1–17 (R)	414
Romans 8:20–21	48
Romans 8:28	81, 374
Romans 8:28–39 (R)	414
Romans 11:26	415
Romans 12 (R)	415
Romans 12:15	92
1 Corinthians 2:4–5	382
1 Corinthians 4:17	428
1 Corinthians 6:18–20 (R)	422
1 Corinthians 10:11	104
1 Corinthians 10:13	460
1 Corinthians 11:1	400
1 Corinthians 12 (R)	423
1 Corinthians 13 (R)	423
1 Corinthians 14:26	423
2 Corinthians 1:3	96
2 Corinthians 10:3–5	140
Galatians 2:16	419
Galatians 3:6–9	66
Galatians 5: 6	436
Galatians 5:22–23	419
Galatians 5:23	419
Ephesians 1:1–14 (R)	425
Ephesians 2:20	184
Ephesians 4:32	446
Ephesians 5:1–6:9 (R)	425
Ephesians 5:25	426
Ephesians 6:10–18 (R)	427
Ephesians 6:12–13	141
Philippians 2:1–11 (R)	427
Philippians 2:20–22	428
Philippians 4:4	427
Colossians 1:1–14 (R)	399
Colossians 1:15–23 (R)	400
Colossians 1:24–2:5 (R)	400
Colossians 2: 3	404
Colossians 2: 5	401
Colossians 2: 6–23 (R)	402
Colossians 2: 8	404
Colossians 2:11	403
Colossians 3: 1–4:6 (R)	406
Colossians 3:11	403
Colossians 4: 7–18 (R)	406
Colossians 4:17	408
1 Thessalonians 4:13	418
1 Thessalonians 4:13–5:11 (R)	418
1 Thessalonians 4:17	463
2 Thessalonians 2:7	459
2 Thessalonians 3:10	418
1 Timothy 1:3	429
1 Timothy 4:13	443
1 Timothy 4:16	400, 429
2 Timothy 3:16	6
2 Timothy 4: 6–18 (R)	431
2 Timothy 4:11	386
Titus 1:12	430
Titus 2:1	400
Philemon 9	401
Hebrews 1 (R)	433
Hebrews 4:12	434
Hebrews 7:27	118
Hebrews 10:10	364
Hebrews 10:18	118
Hebrews 11:1	434
Hebrews 11:39–12:3 (R)	434
Hebrews 12:1–3	166
James 1:1	435
James 1:2–4	74
James 2:14–26 (R)	436
James 2:24	435
James 4:7	426
1 Peter 1:10–12	239
1 Peter 2:5	300
1 Peter 2:9	119
1 Peter 3:15	448

Index of Bible Readings and Quotations

1 Peter 3:18 33
1 Peter 4:8 359
1 Peter 5:6 437
1 Peter 5:6–7 437
1 Peter 5:8 426
2 Peter 1:13–15 (R) 437
2 Peter 1:20–21 .... 3, 239
2 Peter 3: 4 .... 55, 437
2 Peter 3: 5–6 56
2 Peter 3:16 395
1 John 1:1 .... 438, 453
1 John 1:9 439
1 John 4:7–5:2 (R) 438
2 John 7 459
3 John 4 439
Jude 24–25 (R) 440
Revelation 1 (R) 453
Revelation 1:7 463
Revelation 2: 5 455
Revelation 2:13 454
Revelation 2:24 454
Revelation 2–3 (R) 454
Revelation 3:20 454
Revelation 4 (R) 457
Revelation 5 (R) 457
Revelation 6 (R) 458
Revelation 12:17 459
Revelation 13 (R) 460
Revelation 14:8 462
Revelation 16:1 461
Revelation 17:5 462
Revelation 19: 7 463
Revelation 19:11–12, 15–16 ... 138
Revelation 19:16 96
Revelation 20 (R) 464
Revelation 21–22 (R) 465
Revelation 22:4 466

General Index

This is a general subject index. Its main aim is to help people who have read the book to find a passage or subject again.

There are two other indexes to help find references to parts of the Bible. The outlines of each Bible book are listed at the front on page iv and all the passages quoted are indexed starting on page 496.

A

Aaron 97, 113, 119, 123, 126
Abel 49
Abijah, king of Judah 187
Abner 172
Abraham, also known as Abram
   ancestor of Jesus 256
   called a prophet 235
   father of Ishmael 63
   justified by faith 412
   man of faith 66
   moves to Canaan 60
   name changed 63
   promised the land of Canaan 62
Absalom 186
Achan 142
Achelaus, son of Herod the Great
    318
Acrostic poems 179, 277
Acts 366
Acts of the Apostles 366
AD, meaning 325, 365
Adam 46
Adonijah, son of David 189
Adultery 195
Ahab, king of Israel 212
Ahaz, king of Judah . 187, 229, 251
Ahaziah, king of Judah 220
Ai, the town 142
Alexander the Great 311
Amalekites 133

Amaziah, king of Judah .. 187, 224
Ammonites 163
Amorites 126, 139
Amos 242
Anakites 146
Ananias and Sapphira 372
Ananias who anointed Paul 377
Andrew, the apostle 336, 339
Angels 46, 64, 253, 458
Anno Domini, see AD 325, 365
Antichrist 459
Antioch, the church 379, 381
Antiochus Epiphanes 314
Apocalypse, an alternative name
   for Revelation 451
Apocrypha 315
Apostles
   Jesus called one 367
   the Twelve 338, 367
   their role in the church 185, 367
Arab nations, their origin 63
Aramaic language ... 293, 310, 326
Archippus 408
Ark of the Covenant
   brought to Jerusalem 173
   captured by the Philistines .. 161
   destroyed 276
   in Shiloh 146
   made in the desert 115
   placed in the temple 190
Ark, Noah's 51
Armour of God 427

General Index

Artaxerxes, king of Persia 299
Asa, king of Judah 211
Asaph, the musician 180
Ascension 364
Asher, son of Jacob 80
Asherah pole 149
Ashtoreths 149
Assyrians 225, 231
Athalia, queen of Judah .. 218, 224
Atonement 117

B

Baal 127, 134, 149, 212
Baasha, king of Israel *210*
Babylon 287, 461
Babylonian Empire 311
Babylonians 266, 272, 275
Balaam 127, 139, 454
Balak 127
Barnabas 367, 371, 379
Bartholomew, the apostle, also
  known as Nathanael 340
Baruch 272, 275
Bashan, land of 126
Bathsheba 60, 185
BC, meaning 325, 365
Beast, alternative name for the
  Antichrist 459
Beatitudes 343
Beersheba 78, 160
Before Christ, see BC 325, 365
Belshazzar, king of Babylon ... 289
Benjamin
  son of Jacob 71, 73, 76, 80
  tribe of Israel 155, 162, 206
Bethel 70, 142, 210
Bethlehem 156, 169, 247, 332
Bible
  contents 1
  purpose 5
  structure 2
Bildad, Job's friend 87
Bilhah, wife of Jacob 80
Birthright 68

Boaz 156
Branch, prophetic name for the
  Messiah 307
Bread and wine, symbols of the
  New Covenant 358
Breaking of bread, see the Lord's
  Supper 103, 358
Bride of Christ 202, 463

C

Caiaphas, the high priest 354
Cain 49
Caleb 123, 146, 148
Canaan, the land
  conquered by Israelites 143
  divided between the tribes .. 144
  in the time of Joshua 138
  promised to Abraham 60
  promised to Abraham 62
  the Israelites enter it 134
  the view of the spies 123
Canaanites 72, 149
Carbon dating 52
Chaldeans, alternative name for
  the Babylonians 266
Christ, a title for Jesus
  died for us 413
  meaning 306, 324
  who he is 404
  who we are in him 405
Christian, origin of the term 379
Chronicles, 1 & 2 175
Church
  a theocracy 184
  how to build it 300
  its birth 368
  Jesus' passion for it 455
  oversight 429
  reasons for growth 378
Circumcision 64
Colossians 398
Communion, see the Lord's
  Supper 103, 358
Concordance 447

Confession 439
Corinthians, 1st letter 420
Corinthians, 2nd letter.............. 420
Cornelius 378
Covenant
 importance of honouring 143
 meaning of the word 2
 New Covenant 26, 273, 284, 358, 364
 of circumcision 64, 135, 167
 Old Covenant 11, 102, 109, 112, 129
 with Abraham 62, 136
 with David 173
 with Isaac 67
 with Israel 147
 with Noah 57
Creation 40, 55, 57
Crucifixion 361
Cyrus, king of Persia 289, 295

D

Dagon 161
Damascus road experience 377
Dan
 city in Israel 160, 210
 son of Jacob 80
Daniel
 the book 289
 the prophet 272, 286
Darius the Mede 289
David
 ancestor of Jesus 326
 anointed as king 166
 author of Psalms 177
 before he was king 168
 established as king 172
 God's covenant with him ... 173
 his ancestry 78, 137, 156
 his death 189
 his sin with Bathsheba 185
 prophecy concerning him ... 127
 Star of David 166
 the lamp of Israel 187
 when he lived 165
Day of Atonement 120
Day of the Lord 237, 243, 309, 437
Death
 destroyed 465
 introduced to the world 48
 not final for Christians 418
 the price of sin 117
Deborah, the judge 148
Delilah 153
Democracy 183
Deuteronomy 129
Devil, another name for Satan .. 47
Divorce 45, 111
Doctrine 399
Dome of the Rock, the Mosque 65
Dreams, gift of interpreting 73, 287

E

Ecclesiastes 192, 199
Edom 126, 244
Egypt 99
Ehud, the judge 148
Elah, king of Israel *210*
Elders, their role 184, 382, 436
Eleazar 147
Eli, the priest 159, 161
Elihu, Job's friend 89
Elijah 207, 213, 217, 349
Eliphaz, Job's friend 87
Elisha 207, 213, 217
Elizabeth, mother of John the Baptist 333
Elkanah, father of Samuel 158
End Time Prophecies 241, 307, 357, 418, 456
Enoch 50, 58
Epaphras 398
Ephesians 424
Ephraim
 son of Joseph 78, 80
 tribe of Israel 146, 153
Esau 67, 126, 245

Esther
- the book 304
- the woman 60, 304

Eucharist, see the Lord's Supper
.... 358

Eve 46

Evolution, the Theory of 42, 52, 55, 57

Exile
- of Israel 22, 224
- of Judah .23, 175, 232, 252, 272
- return from ...25, 252, 261, 291, 293
- time during 25, 280, 286, 303

Exodus
- the book 93, 109
- the departure from Egypt 93, 103

Ezekiel
- the book 280
- the prophet 280, 283

Ezra
- the book 294
- the priest 175, 298, 301

F

Faith
- defined 434
- demonstrated through deeds 435

Fall of man 46
Fear of the Lord 194
Firstfruits, the feast of 120
Flood, Noah's 51, 138
Fool, definition 194
Fossils 54
Fruit of the Spirit 419

G

Gabriel, the angel 333

Gad
- son of Jacob 80
- tribe of Israel 128, 146, 153

Galatians 418
Galilee, Roman Province 316
Gamaliel 373
Garden of Eden 46
Genesis 38, 45, 59
Geneva Convention 137
Gentile, meaning 3
Geology 53
Gibeonites 143
Gideon, the judge 148, 152
Gifts of the Spirit 422
Gnosticism 404, 438, 454

God
- a jealous God 139
- author of the Bible 3
- creator 40
- God of Abraham 71, 95
- God of Isaac 71, 95
- God of Israel 70
- God of Jacob 71, 95
- his grace 138
- his justice 461
- his love 263, 461
- his response to prayer . 114, 124
- I am, name of God 96, 114, 329
- is light 438
- is love 438
- judge of the earth 51, 64, 138
- our redeemer 51, 425
- the Father 46
- the Holy Spirit 46
- the Son 46
- three persons 45

Golden Calf
- in the time of Moses 113

Golden Calves
- set up by Jeroboam I 210

Goliath 167
Gomorrah 64
Gospel writers 324
Gospel, meaning 256, 322
Gospels (Matthew, Mark, Luke and John) 2, 322
Government, alternative methods
.... 183
Great Commission 363
Great Tribulation 458

General Index

Greek civilisation 404
Greek culture 327
Greek Empire 311
Greek heresy 404, 438, 454
Greek language 58, 314

H

Habakkuk 248
Hagar, mother of Ishmael 63
Haggai 297
Hallelujah, meaning 177
Ham, son of Noah 57
Haman 303
Hanani, the prophet 212
Handel's Messiah 88
Hanging gardens of Babylon .. 287
Hannah, mother of Samuel 158, 170
Hazael, king of Aram 218
Hazor 144
Heaven 457, 465
Hebrew language 177, 293, 315
Hebrews
    a name for the Israelites 94
    the letter 433
Hebron 123, 172
Heresy
    Greek (Gnosticism) 404
    Jewish (Legalism) 402, 418, 427
    meaning 398
Herod
    Agrippa I 318, 384
    Agrippa II 318, 390
    Antipas, or 'the Tetrarch' .. 318, 346, 360
    the Great 318, 333
Herodians 337
Hezekiah, king of Judah 187, 207, 229, 247, 251
High Priest
    role in New Testament 323
    role on Day of Atonement .. 120
Hiram, king of Lebanon 190

History Books (Joshua to Esther) 1
Holiness 116, 119, 371
Holy Place 115, 190
Holy Spirit
    author of the Bible 3
    baptism in 367
    fruit of 419
    gifts of 422
    his role in creation 46
    his role in the birth of the church 368
    poured out on Gentiles 378
    role in the birth of Jesus 257, 332
    role in the Christian life 414, 443
    role in the Old Testament ... 153
Hosea
    the book 243
    the prophet 207, 243
Hoshea, king of Israel 226
Humility
    of Jesus 358, 427
    of Moses 123
Hymns in the New Testament. 427

I

I am, name of God 329
Isaac 64, 67
Isaiah
    the book 251, 256, 261
    the prophet ..207, 232, 251, 261
Ishmael, son of Abraham 63
Israel the land
    divided among the tribes 144
    promised to Abraham 60, 62
Israel the nation
    before having a king 148
    established by David 173
    given a king 162
    God's chosen people .. 110, 116
    history 14
    under Solomon 191

General Index

Israel the northern kingdom
   history 19
   in the time of David 172
   into exile 226
   separates from Judah 204
   the early years 210
   the latter years 224
   under Ahab 212
Israel, the man also known as
   Jacob 69
Israel, the twelve tribes 79, 80
Israelites
   cross the Red Sea 105
   enter the land of Canaan 134
   in Egypt 94, 108
   leave Egypt 103
   made into a nation 119
Issachar, son of Jacob 80

J

Jacob, also known as Israel 67, 70, 78, 80
James
   the apostle, son of Alphaeus 340
   the apostle, son of Zebedee 339
   the brother of Jesus ... 368, 384, 434
   the letter 434
Japheth, son of Noah 57
Jehoash, king of Israel 224
Jehoiachin, king of Judah 280
Jehoiakim, king of Judah 272, 286
Jehoram, king of Judah 218
Jehoshaphat, king of Judah 207, 212
Jehovah, from the Hebrew for "I am", the name of God 96
Jehu, king of Israel 207, 218
Jephthah, the judge 148
Jeremiah
   the book 268
   the prophet ..207, 268, 272, 275
Jericho
   battle of 135
   rebuilt 213
Jeroboam I, king of Israel 203, 210
Jeroboam II, king of Israel 224, 242, 243, 245
Jerusalem
   capital of Judah 204
   captured by David 172
   destroyed by the Babylonians
      .... 269, 275, 283
   destroyed by the Romans .. 316, 357
   rebuilt by Nehemiah 300
   the New Jerusalem 368, 465
Jeshua, the high priest (also called Joshua) 297, 306
Jesse, father of David 166
Jesus
   his ancestry 137, 156, 175
   his ascension into heaven ... 364
   his baptism 336
   his betrayal and arrest 358
   his birth 257, 332
   his burial 362
   his childhood 333
   his compassion 351
   his conversations 350
   his crucifixion 361
   his early popularity 336
   his entry into Jerusalem 355
   his last week on earth 357
   his miracles 342, 346
   his parables 341
   his resurrection 362
   his role in creation 46
   his second coming 307, 418, 437, 462
   his suffering 259
   his teaching 343
   his transfiguration 213, 349
   his trial 360
   identified as God 97, 360
   John's vision of him in
      Revelation 453
   judge of the nations 138
   lamb of God 102, 457

Old Testament appearances. 64, 70
Old Testament prophecies about him ...49, 78, 127, 256, 307, 334, 364
son of man, name for Jesus 291
the Messiah 348
who he is 400
Jethro, father-in-law of Moses 109
Jew, origin of the word 294
Jewish heresy 402, 418, 427
Jezebel, wife of Ahab king of Israel 212, 217, 454
Joash, king of Judah 222, 224
Job
the book 82, 87, 192
the man 82, 87
Joel
the book 236, 244
the prophet 244
John
1st letter 438
2nd letter 439
3rd letter 439
alternative name for Mark .. 325
the apostle ...325, 339, 438, 451
the gospel 328, 335, 350
John the Baptist 258, 309, 326, 333, 335, 346
Jonah 245
Jonathan, son of Saul 168, 172
Joram, king of Israel 220
Joseph of Arimathea 362
Joseph, legal father of Jesus ... 332
Joseph, son of Jacob 71, 72, 76, 80, 103, 147
Josephus, Jewish historian 314
Joshua
in Zechariah – see Jeshua ... 306
the book 132
the man 123, 128, 132, 135, 142, 147
Josiah, king of Judah 207, 233, 249, 266

Jubilee, Year of 120
Judah
son of Jacob 77, 80
the southern kingdom .. 19, 172, 204, 211, 229
tribe of Israel 149, 172
Judas Iscariot, the apostle 340, 358, 368
Judas Maccabeus 315
Judas son of James, alternative name for Thaddaeus, the apostle 340
Judas, alternative name for Jude, the brother of Jesus 439
Jude
the brother of Jesus 439
the letter 439
Judea, Roman province 316
Judgement 464
Judges
the book 148
their role 162
Justification by faith 412, 419, 436

K

Kadesh 124
Kings
1 & 2, the books 175, 206
their role 162, 183

L

Laban 69
Lamb
as a sin offering 117
Jesus, lamb of God 102, 457
Passover lamb 102, 358
Lamech 49
Lamentations 276
Languages, their origin 57
Last days 262
Last Supper 358
Latin 314

General Index

Law
  contrasted with the Prophets 235
  contrasted with wisdom...... 195
  given to Moses 112
  The Law (the books Genesis to Deuteronomy)....... 1, 38, 111
Law and the Prophets, name for the Old Testament 131
Lazarus, brother of Martha 353, 364
Leah, wife of Jacob 80
Learning Bible verses 444
Legalism........................ 402, 412
Letters
  their structure 398
  to churches in Revelation ... 453
Letters (Romans to Revelation). 2, 34
Levi
  alternative name for Matthew, the apostle 325, 340
  son of Jacob 80, 130
  tribe of Israel 116, 130
Levites
  allocated towns in Israel.... 128, 146
  role as teachers of the law . 212, 301
  the priests 116, 154, 206
Leviticus................... 109, 116, 119
LORD, The LORD, a name of God 96
Lord's Prayer......................... 344
Lord's Supper 103, 358, 422
Lot, nephew of Abraham .. 60, 126
Love
  God's love for us.413, 438, 466
  its primary importance 423
  love one another 438
  wisdom's view 202
Luke
  the gospel 327, 333
  the man................325, 366, 386

Luther, Martin 412, 419
LXX – see Septuagint............... 315

M

Magi 332
Magicians, of Pharaoh 100
Major Prophets (Isaiah to Daniel) 2, 23, 236
Malachi................................... 308
Man of lawlessness, alternative name for the Antichrist....... 459
Manasseh
  king of Judah..... 207, 232, 251, 266, 272
  son of Joseph................. 78, 80
  tribe of Israel 128, 146, 153
Manna........................... 108, 135
Mark
  the gospel 326, 336
  the man...................... 325, 386
Marriage
  a covenant 143
  in the law............................ 111
  instituted by God................. 45
  New Testament teaching.... 426
  the impact of adultery.......... 196
  three strands 200
Martha 353, 364
Mary
  Magdalene......................... 363
  mother of Jesus.... 78, 159, 257, 333, 339
  sister of Martha 353, 364
Matthew
  the apostle, also known as Levi 325, 340
  the gospel 326, 332
Matthias Maccabeus 315
Matthias, the apostle chosen to replace Judas 367
Medes 266
Medes and Persians 290, 311
Meditating on the Bible 445
Menahem, king of Israel......... 226

General Index

Messiah
   expectations 324
   foretold............................... 306
   meaning.............................. 306
Methuselah 50, 58
Micah..................................... 247
Michael, the archangel............ 459
Michal, wife of David............. 169
Midian 95, 152
Midianites.............................. 152
Millennium, Christ's reign on earth for 1000 years............ 464
Minor Prophets (Hosea to Malachi)................... 2, 23, 236
Miracles
   of Elisha 217
   of Jesus....................... 342, 346
Miriam, Moses' sister.... 105, 123, 126
Moab 126, 156
Moabites.......................... 139, 156
Mordecai, Esther's uncle......... 304
Moses
   author of a Psalm 177
   author of the Books of the Law 38
   called to lead the Israelites ... 95
   his birth 94
   his death 130
   his humility 123
   led the Israelites out of Egypt 103
   man of faith........................ 101
   New Testament appearance 213, 349
   receives the Ten Commandments............. 112
   restates the Law.................. 129
Most Holy Place 115, 120, 190, 362
Mount Horeb, alternative name for Mount Sinai 106
Mount Moriah 65
Mount Sinai 106, 113

N

Naboth 215
Nadab, king of Israel *210*
Nahum 248
Naomi 156
Naphtali
   son of Jacob.......................... 80
   tribe of Israel...................... 257
Nathan, the prophet 173, 185, 189
Nathanael, alternative name for Bartholomew, the apostle ... 340
Nazareth 333
Nebuchadnezzar 272, 275, 287
Nehemiah
   governor of Judah............... 299
   the book....................... 294, 299
New earth 262, 465
New heaven 262, 465
New Testament..... 2, 29, 393, 432
Nicodemus...................... 350, 362
Nile, the river........................... 99
Nineveh 245, 248, 266
Noah 49, 51, 55, 57
Numbers 109, 121, 127

O

Obadiah 244
Offerings to God..................... 117
Og, king of Bashan 126
Old Testament ..2, 8, 18, 110, 112, 393
Omri, king of Israel 207, *210*, 212
Onesimus............................... 401
Othniel, the judge 148
Overseers, see pastors............. 184

P

Palm Sunday.......................... 355
Parable................................... 193
Parables of Jesus.................... 341
Passover
   celebrated by Hezekiah 229
   celebrated by Jesus............. 358
   celebrated by Josiah 233

General Index

celebrated in Canaan 135
regulations 112
the first one 102
the second one 122
Pastors, their role in the church
.... 184, 428
Paul
at the stoning of Stephen 374
called an apostle 367
his arrest and journey to Rome
.... 388
his conversion 377
his first journey 382
his letters 394, 417, 424
his second journey 386
his sufferings 401
his third journey 388
main events of his life 396
Pax Romana 320
Pekah, king of Israel 226
Peninnah 158
Pentateuch 111
Pentecost
the day the church was born 368
the feast of 120
Persians 266
Peter the apostle
also known as Simon 339
author of 1 & 2 Peter 436
his betrayal of Jesus 359
influence on Mark's gospel 325
leader of the twelve 366
preached at Pentecost 368
takes the gospel to the Gentiles
.... 378
Peter, 1st letter 436
Peter, 2nd letter 437
Pharaoh
in the time of Joseph 75
in the time of Moses 94, 99, 168
Pharisees
their opposition to Jesus 337, 347, 351, 353
their origin 323
their response to John the
Baptist 336
Philemon 401
Philip
one of the seven chosen in Acts
6 .... 256, 373
the apostle 340
Philippians 427
Philistines 153, 161, 170
Phinehas, the priest 146
Pilate, Roman Governor 360
Pillar of Cloud 104
Plagues of Egypt 99
Poetry
not to be taken literally 84
structure of Hebrew poetry. 177
Polygamy 45, 49
Pompey, Roman General 316
Potiphar's wife 74
Predestination 415
Priests
all priests under the new
covenant 119
initial regulations 119
responsible for teaching the law
.... 130, 210, 298, 301
their role as judges in Israel 129
their role as musicians 176
their role in a theocracy 183
Promised Land 9, 103, 126, 132, 135, 144, 279, 309
Prophetic book, meaning 38
Prophets
in the time of Samuel 170
the books Isaiah to Malachi 235
their role 21, 235
their role in a theocracy 184
their role in the church 185
Proverbs 182, 190, 192, 197
Psalms 177
Ptolomies, rulers of Egypt 314
Purim, the feast of 306

Q

Quail 123

Queen of Sheba 191

R

Rachel, wife of Jacob ... 69, 73, 80
Rahab............................. 134, 136
Rainbow 57
Reading the Bible 441
Rebekah, wife of Isaac 67
Red Sea, the Israelites cross it 105
Redeem, meaning 102
Redemption from Egypt 102
Reformation............................ 412
Rehoboam, king of Judah 204, 211
Resurrection 291, 362, 422
Reuben
   son of Jacob 73, 76, 80
   tribe of Israel.............. 128, 146
Revelation....................... 452, 465
Roman Empire........................ 316
Romans, the letter................... 409
Ruth 156

S

Sacrifice
   of animals for sin 118
   of Jesus........ 118, 362, 433, 457
Sadducees, their origin 323
Salvation.................. 409, 425, 439
Samaria
   capital of Israel.... 204, 212, 226
   Roman province 316
Samaritan woman 351
Samaritans
   their opposition to the returning Jews 297
   their origin.......................... 227
Samson, the judge........... 148, 153
Samuel, 1 & 2, the books 157, 175
Samuel, the prophet
   anoints David as king......... 166
   anoints Saul as king............ 163
   his birth 158
   his death 170
   his early life 159
   his role as a judge............... 162
   possible author of Judges ... 149
   possibly compiled Joshua... 132
   when he lived 165
Sanhedrin
   its origin 323, 371
   tried Jesus........................... 360
   tried Paul 388
   tried the apostles................. 371
Sarah, or Sarai, wife of Abraham
   .... 60, 62, 67
Satan
   finally banished.................. 465
   his character 263
   his power is limited 426, 460
   origin and meaning............... 47
   the accuser........................... 85
   working against God's plan. 94, 218, 358, 459
Saul, first king of Israel . 158, 162, 164, 168, 170
Saul, original name for Paul ... 382
Scapegoat............................... 120
Science and the Bible 41, 55
Scribe, teacher of the Law 298, 323
Seat of Atonement 120
Second Coming of Jesus......... 463
Seleucids, rulers of Syria 314
Septuagint, Greek translation of the Old Testament 315
Sermon on the Mount 343, 435
Sermon on the Plain................ 343
Serpent...................................... 47
Sexual morality....................... 421
Shadrach, Meshach and Abednego
   287
Shem, son of Noah 57
Shema 129
Shemaiah, the prophet 204
Shiloh 146, 158
Sihon, king of the Amorites.... 126
Silas, travelling companion of Paul 384, 386, 436

General Index

Simeon
   son of Jacob 76, 80, 130
   tribe of Israel.......130, 172, 204
Simon the Zealot, the apostle . 340
Simon, alternative name for Peter, the apostle 339
Sinai
   desert................................... 106
   mountain, see Mount Sinai. 121
Sodom 64
Solomon
   author of Proverbs 192, 197
   author of Song of Songs..... 201
   author of two Psalms.......... 177
   becomes king 189
   his folly 203
   his reign as king 191
   his wisdom 189
   probable author of Ecclesiastes 199
Son of David, a name for Jesus 326
Song of Songs......................... 201
Sons of Korah 180
Spies, the twelve spies.... 123, 133
Spiritual Gifts 422
Spiritual Warfare 140, 426
Stephen, one of the seven chosen in Acts 6 373
Studying the Bible 446
Suffering
   its origins........................ 83, 92
   of God's people 458
   of Jesus............................... 259
   of Paul 401
Sword of the Spirit 427, 434
Synagogue, meaning............... 322
Synoptic Gospels, meaning 328

T

Tabernacle 115
Tabernacles, the feast of. 301, 351
Teaching the Bible.................. 448

Temple
   1st (Solomon's).. 176, 190, 211, 224, 229, 276
   2nd (Zerubbabel's) 181, 297, 318
   3rd (Herod's)............... 318, 357
   at Shiloh 158
   in Ezekiel's vision 284
   site of................................... 65
Ten Commandments.. 11, 45, 112, 129, 185
Thaddaeus, the apostle, also known as Judas son of James 340
Theocracy............................... 183
Theophany, also see Jesus, Old Testament appearances......... 64
Theophilus.............................. 327
Thessalonians, 1st & 2nd letters 417
Thomas, the apostle 340, 363
Three Kings – see Magi.......... 332
Tibni, king of Israel *210*
Timothy
   1st letter............................... 429
   2nd letter.............................. 430
   the man....................... 386, 428
Tithing 117
Titus.. 429
Tower of Babel................. 57, 462
Traditions of the elders 347
Transfiguration 349
Tree of Life............................... 48
Trinity 46, 425, 434

U

Uriah....................................... 187
Uzzah...................................... 185
Uzziah, king of Judah 224, 242, 251

V

Virgin birth 257, 332

W

War
- between Israel and Judah .. 172, 210, 211
- justification for war against Canaan 137

Wisdom
- defined 194
- given to Solomon 189, 192

Wisdom Books (Job to Song of Songs) 1, 82, 192, 199

Wise men – see Magi 332

Worship
- at the Tabernacle 115
- between God the Father and Son 433
- established in Jerusalem by David 176, 210
- first mention in the Bible...... 65
- instructions for the church.. 428
- through offerings 117

Wrath of God 411

X

Xerxes, king of Persia 304

Y

Yahweh, Hebrew for "I am", the name of God 96
Year of Jubilee 120
Yom Kippur, see Day of Atonement 120

Z

Zadok the priest 189
Zebulun
- son of Jacob 80
- tribe of Israel 257

Zechariah
- son of Jehoida 224
- the book 306
- the prophet 297, 306

Zedekiah, king of Judah .. 272, 275
Zelophehad's daughters 128
Zephaniah 249
Zerubbabel, governor of Judah 297
Zilpah, wife of Jacob 80
Zimri, king of Israel *210*
Zophar, Job's friend 87

Made in the USA
Charleston, SC
19 November 2013